THE COMPLETE GUIDE TO

Professional Wedding Photography

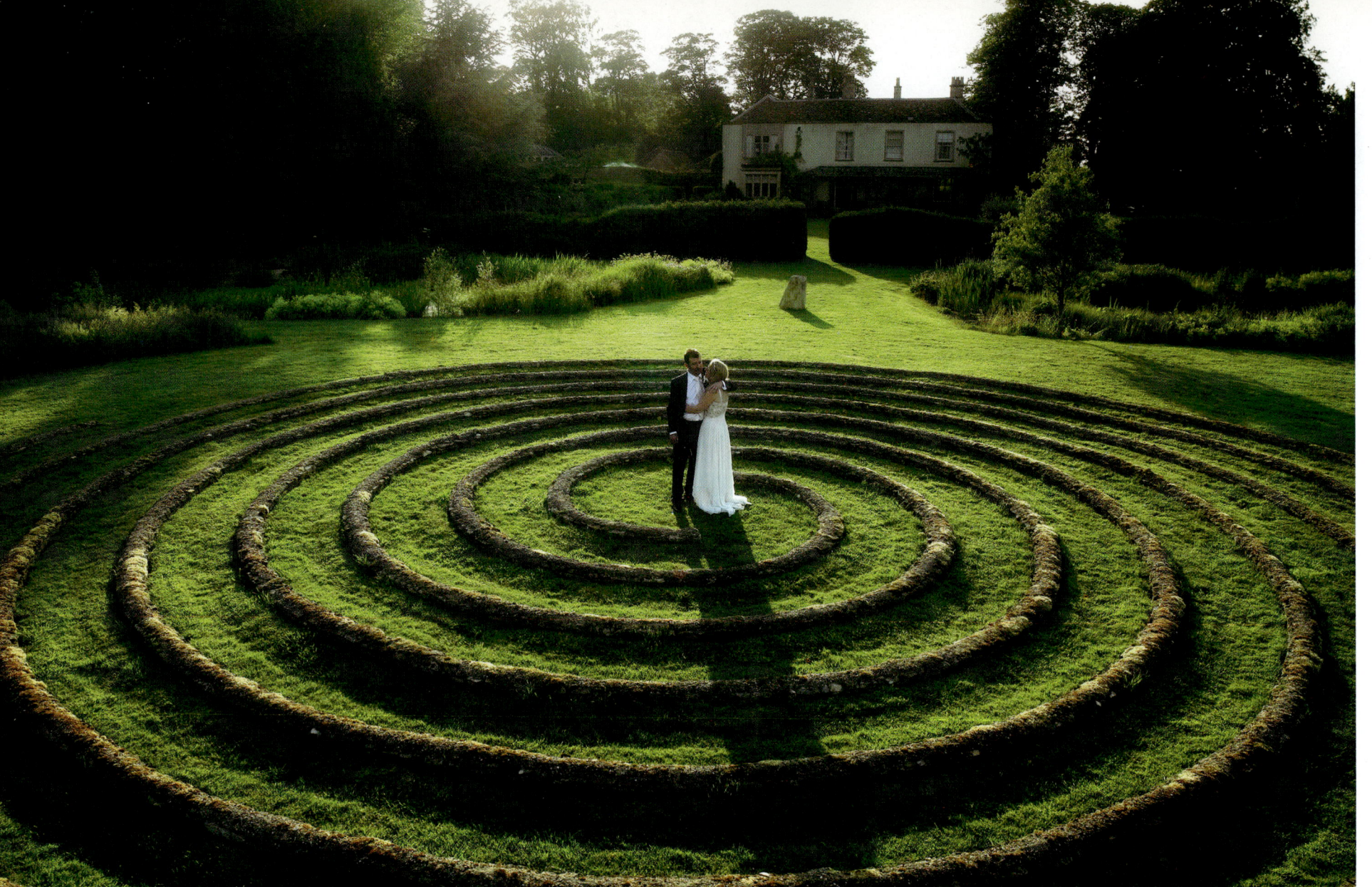

ISO 400 f/9.5 at 1/200th

Late evening sunshine casts the couples shadow like the hand of a clock on this spiral feature at the Matara in Gloucestershire. I achieved the high viewpoint by using the camera's self-timer while it was hoisted high above my head on the end of a monopod. With $30,000 of Hasselblad, lens, and Phase One digital back balanced high on a pole you need nerves of steel.

THE COMPLETE GUIDE TO

Professional Wedding Photography

Creating a more profitable and fulfilling business

DAMIEN LOVEGROVE

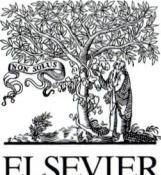

Amsterdam • Boston • Heidelberg • London
New York • Oxford • Paris • San Diego
San Francisco • Singapore • Sydney • Tokyo
Focal Press is an imprint of Elsevier

ELSEVIER

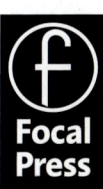

Acquisitions Editor:	Diane Heppner
Assistant Editor:	Stephanie Barrett
Publishing Services Manager:	George Morrison
Senior Project Manager:	Brandy Lilly
Marketing Manager:	Joanna Smith
Cover Design:	Alisa Andreola
Interior Design:	Alisa Andreola
Technical Editor:	Michael
Damien's Sub Editor:	Christopher Wordsworth

Focal Press is an imprint of Elsevier
30 Corporate Drive, Suite 400, Burlington, MA 01803, USA
Linacre House, Jordan Hill, Oxford OX2 8DP, UK

Recognizing the importance of preserving what has been written, Elsevier prints its books on acid-free paper whenever possible.

Library of Congress Cataloging-in-Publication Data
Lovegrove, Damien.
 The complete guide to professional wedding photography : creating a more profitable and fulfilling business / by Damien Lovegrove.
   p. cm.
 Includes bibliographical references and index.
 ISBN-13: 978-0-240-80890-1 (casebound : alk. paper) 1. Wedding photography—Handbooks, manuals, etc. 2. Photography--Business methods. I. Title.
 TR819.L68 2007
 778.9'93925—dc22

                                                            2007014049

British Library Cataloguing-in-Publication Data
A catalogue record for this book is available from the British Library.

ISBN: 978-0-240-80890-1

For information on all Focal Press publications visit our website at www.books.elsevier.com

08 09 10 11 5 4 3 2

Printed in China

Table of Contents

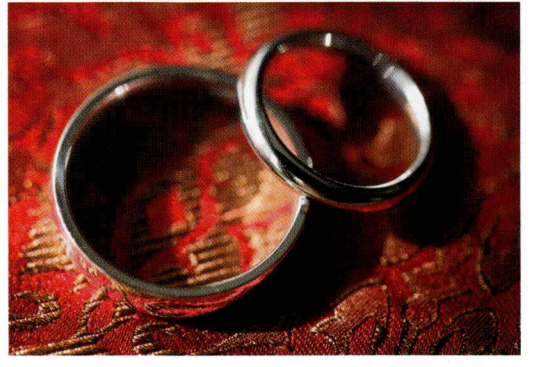
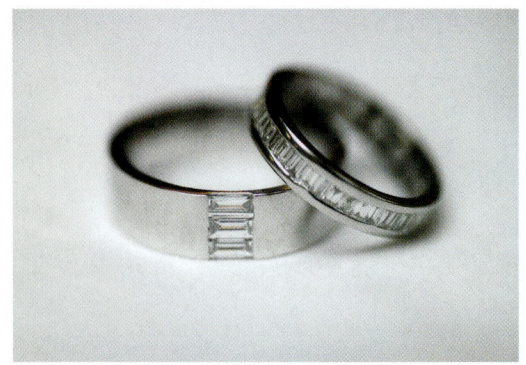
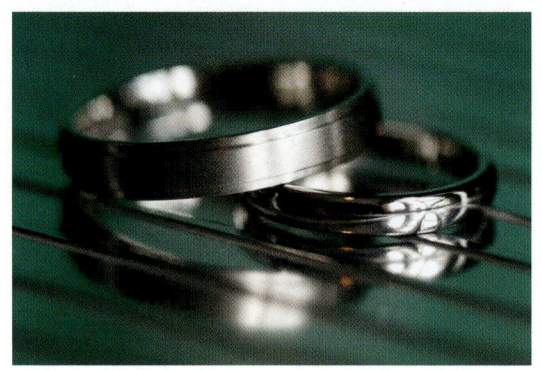
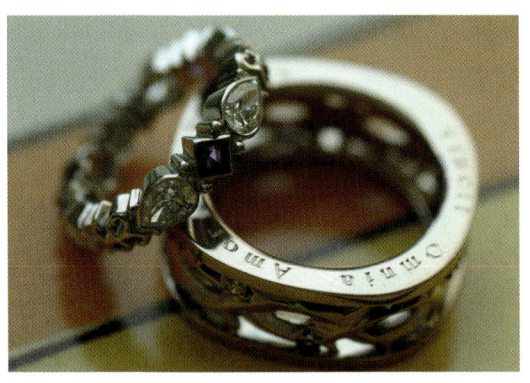
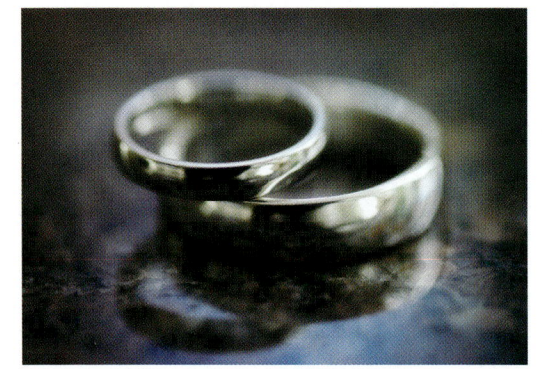
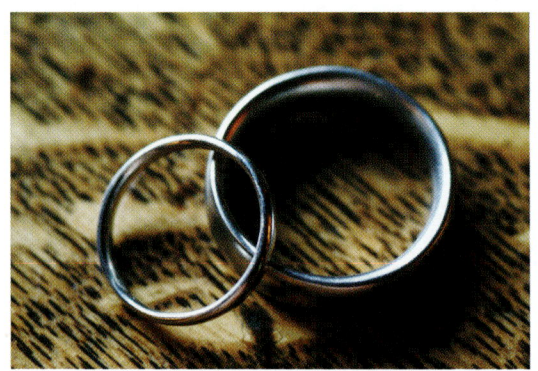
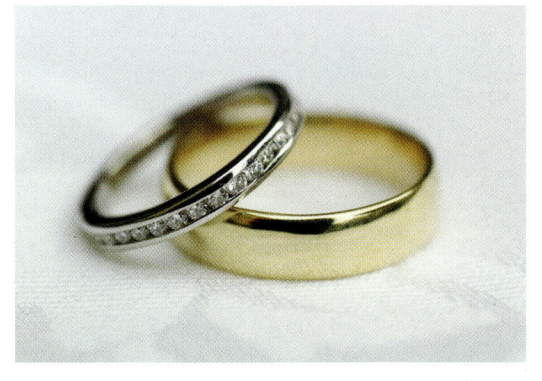
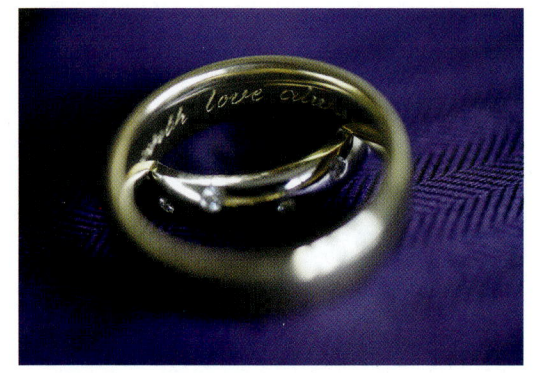
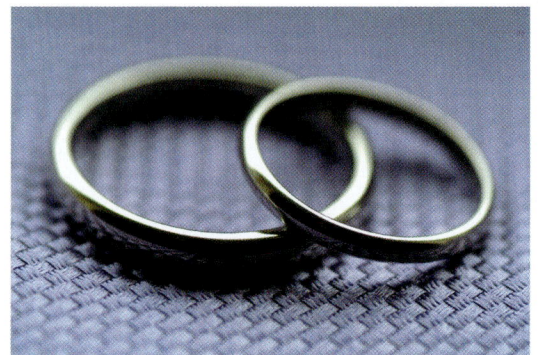

Preface

It's no secret that I make a good living from wedding photography. But it wasn't always like that. When I left the BBC after a successful career as a lighting cameraman, I imagined the transition to professional stills photography would be a piece of cake. It wasn't. I managed to get work but my photography was dull and uninspiring. I suppose I just hadn't grasped that 'decisive moment' stuff which is the difference between movies and stills.

When it came to weddings I was floundering. I'd walk into a hotel and struggle to find anywhere to shoot. There was always a reason why a shot would not work – too much clutter, too dark, too busy, too boring, and so on. In fact, my results were so disappointing that I once told my wife Julie, 'Never let me shoot another wedding.' And I meant it.

Fortunately I persisted, proved myself wrong, and 200 bookings later, I love every wedding! So what happened? Basically I saw the light – literally. Knowing how to use that light is what makes shooting a wedding fun. I also obtained 'the knowledge.' That meant looking at other people's wedding pictures, going on courses, having my own work assessed, and reading books like this one. As a result, I now have the confidence to create images in any situation using just about any light source I come across. But although light is what creates our pictures and makes them look good, something extra is required to guarantee a sale.

opposite

Fig. 1

Keep your style evolving and try not to repeat shots from wedding to wedding. This is a good way to stay creative. I always look for a new way to shoot a subject, even the rings.

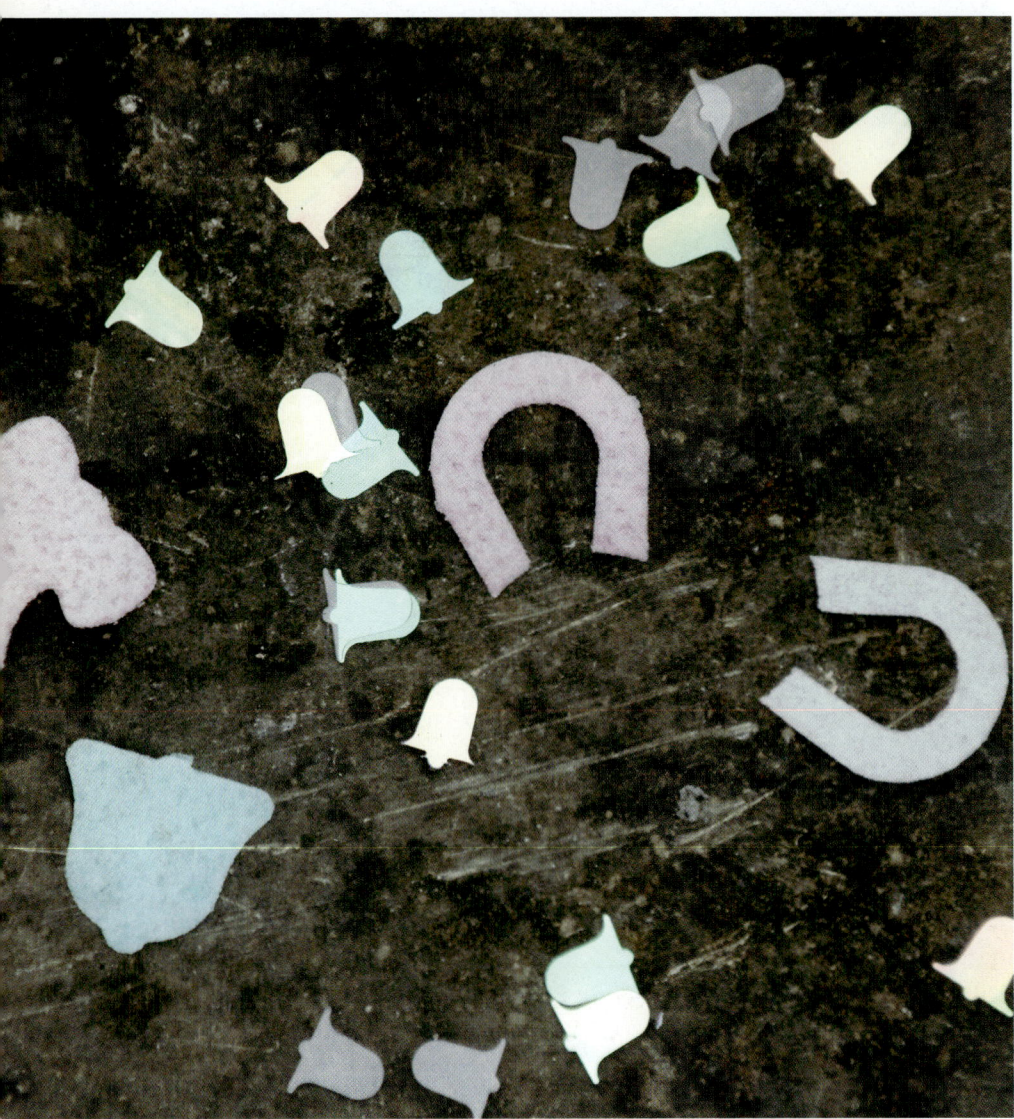

FIG. 2   ISO 400 f/4 at 1/1000th

An album picture may come from the most unusual places. The random scatter of confetti on this stone pavement caught my eye at a recent wedding.

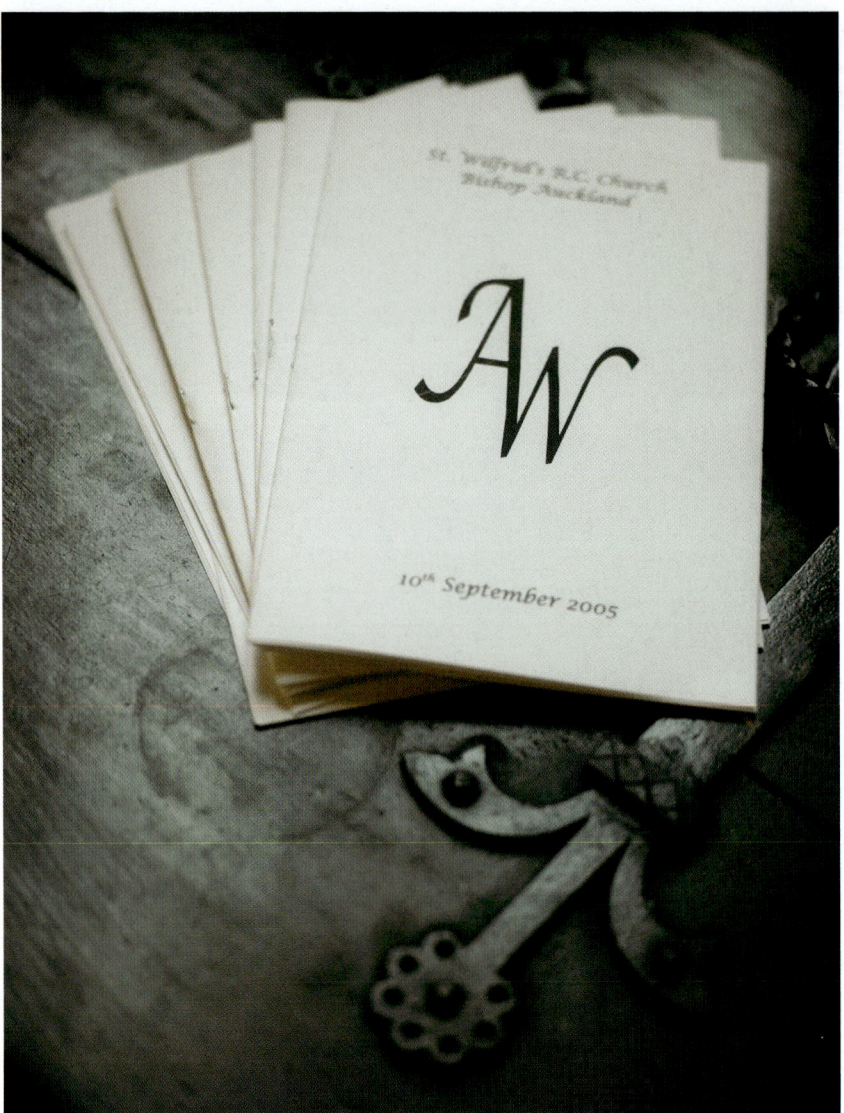

FIG. 3   ISO 400 f/3.2 at 1/90th

I laid these orders of service booklets out on an old chest at the back of the church. A vignette was added in post-production to create the illusion of a pool of light.

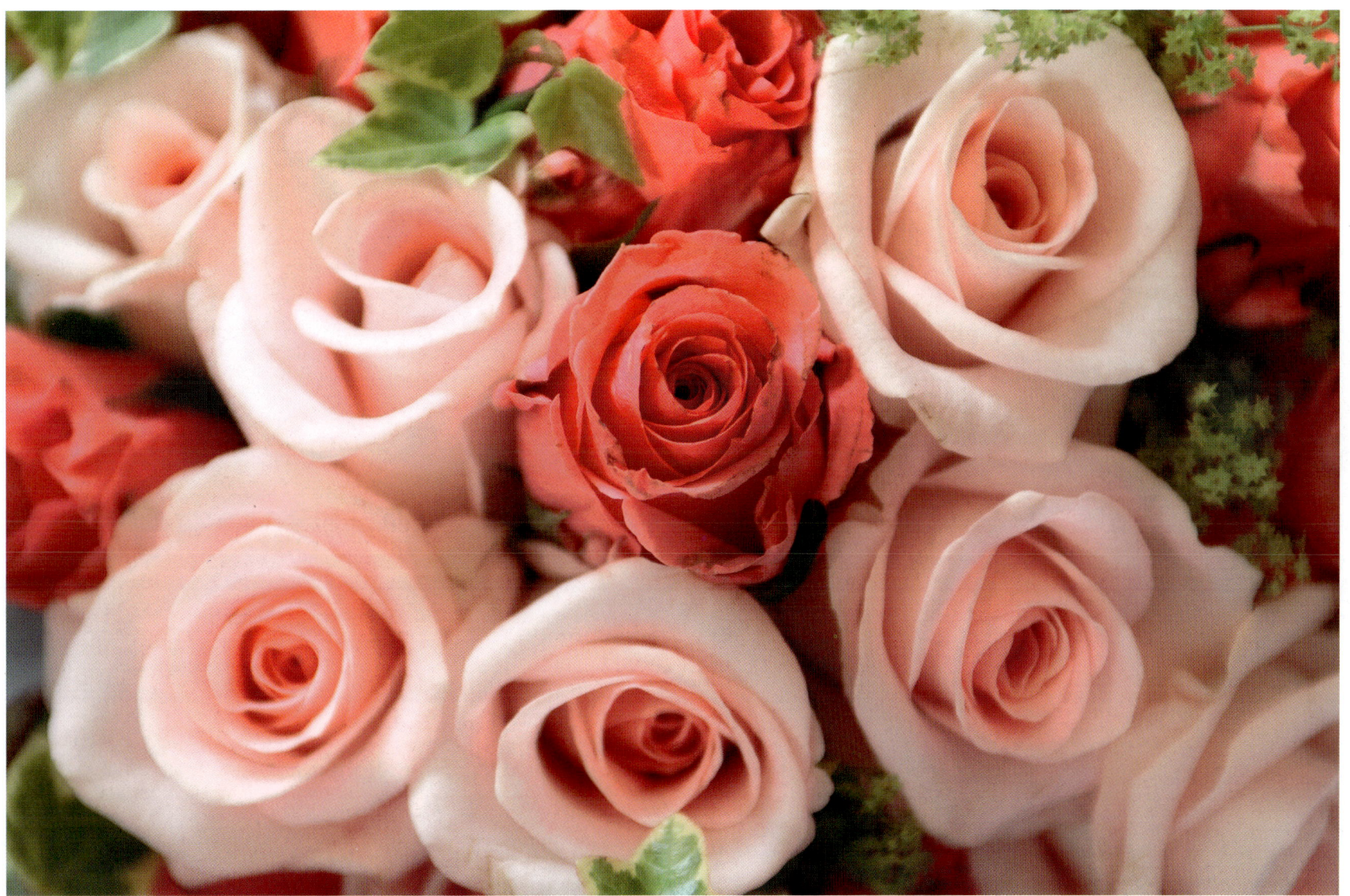

Fig. 4 ISO 400 f4 at 1/125th

Julie's full detail shot of these roses excluded all extraneous clutter. Going in tight solves many problems at times.

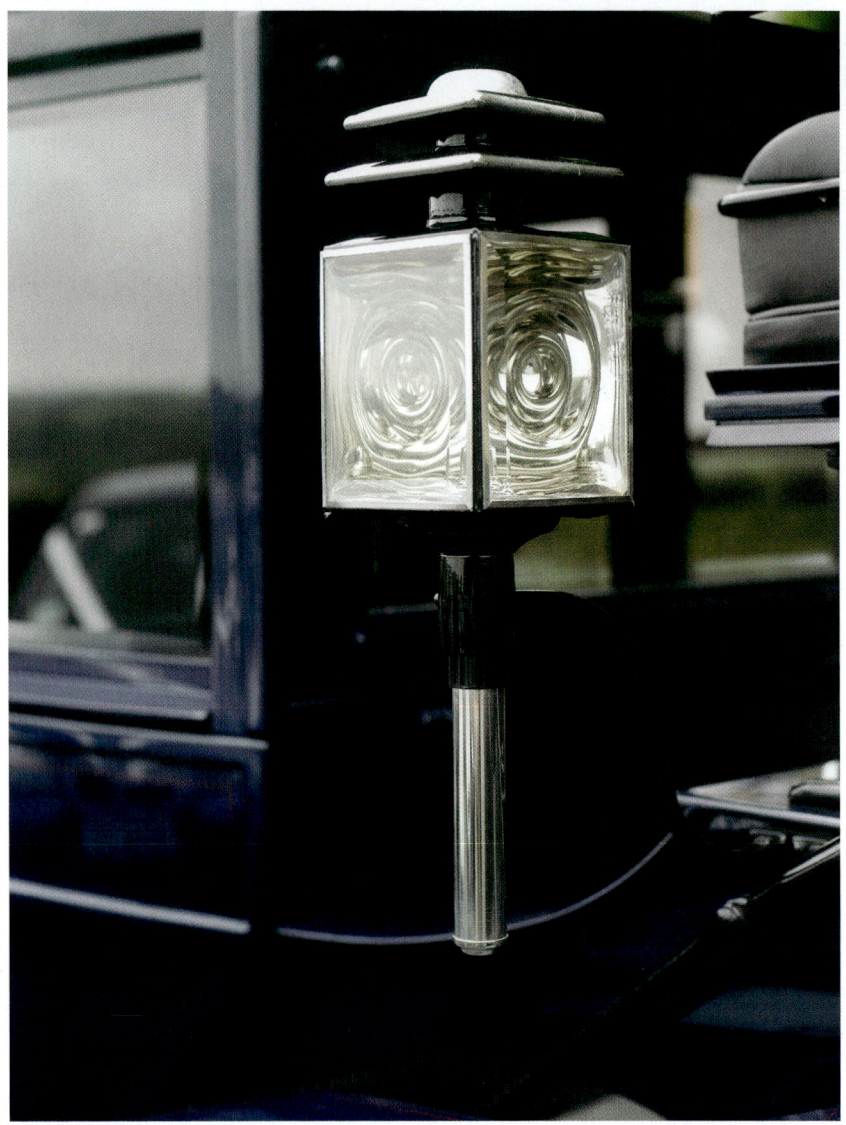

FIG. 5   ISO 400 f/4 at 1/100th

Vehicle details have always been a good subject to shoot. You will have to do them well if you want a client to buy them though.

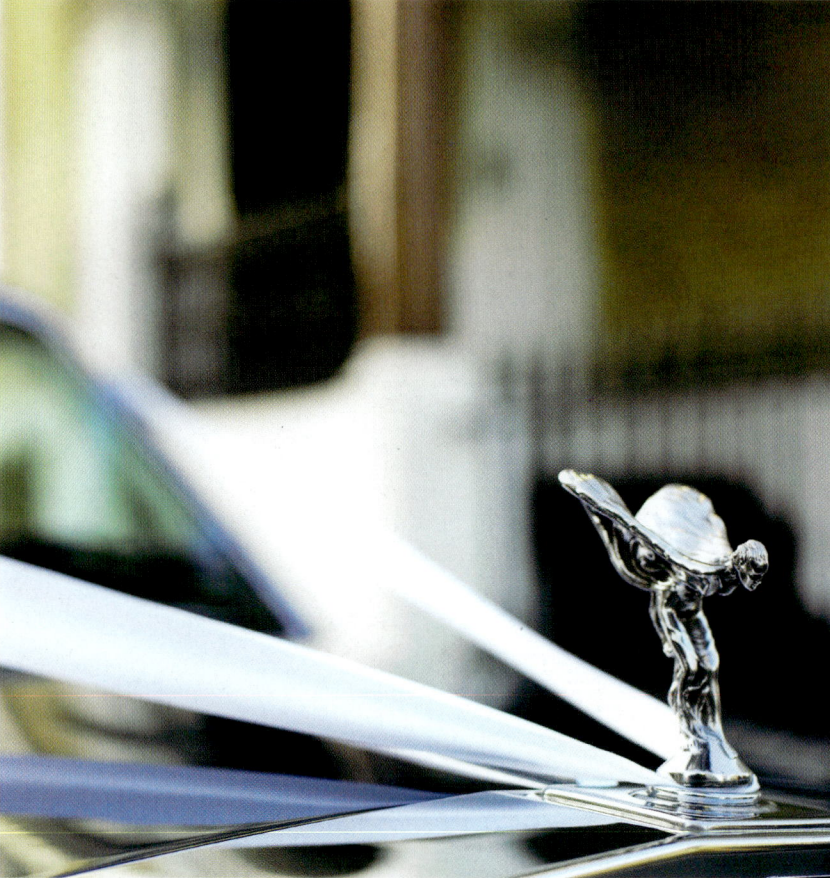

FIG. 6   ISO 400 f/4.5 at 1/180th

The out of focus part of this image is as important as the in focus bit. I often compose pictures using the out of focus background. I chose the Hasselblad H1 camera system because of the excellent bokeh of the lenses. Bokeh is the name given to the characteristic of the out of focus part of an image as created by a particular lens. I used my 210 mm lens on my H1 with its Phase One P25 digital back to get this look.

FIG. 7   ISO 400 f/3.5 at 1/125th

Pictures like these make great visual punctuation marks in wedding album design.

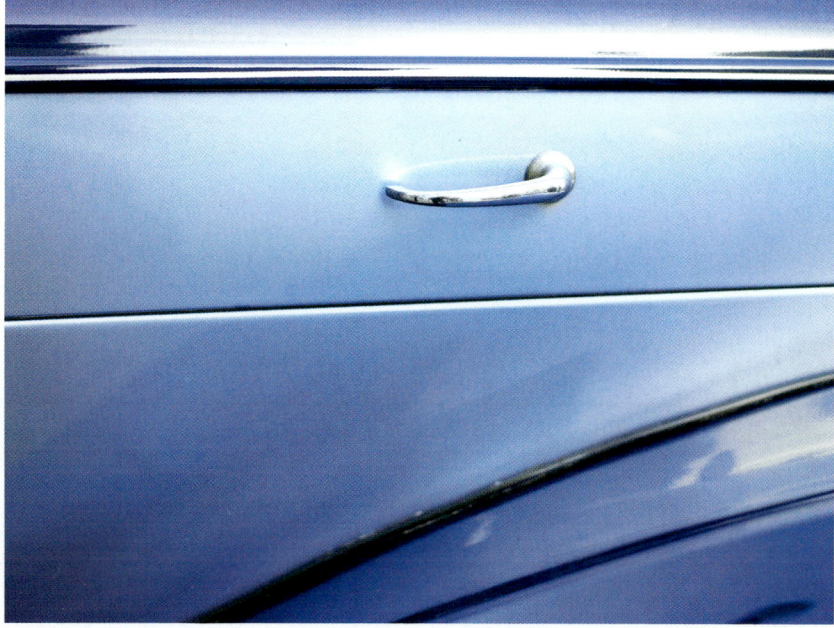

What's needed is the ability to capture emotion. It's here that I'm grateful to Julie who has always been the best critic of my work. In the early days, before she had even picked up a camera, she instinctively knew which of my shots the clients would want. Unlike many photographers, Julie wasn't bogged down by the technicalities of photography, she just saw clearly which shots worked and which didn't. Later, as a photographer, that made her a natural.

Together, we embarked on a journey. Yes, we wanted commercial success. But we wanted to achieve it through excellence. We would do this by creating a first-class brand. In short, we wanted to present to our clients with the best possible wedding coverage – precious memories that would help them to relive the joy, the love, the humor, the excitement, and the fulfillment of their special day.

Our journey has not always been smooth – in fact it's been a roller-coaster ride. But it's always been exhilarating and we've never stopped learning. In this book, we'd like to share with you our experiences, our passion, and the lessons we have learned. It's such a gift to be able to take pictures that make people happy!

Damien Lovegrove

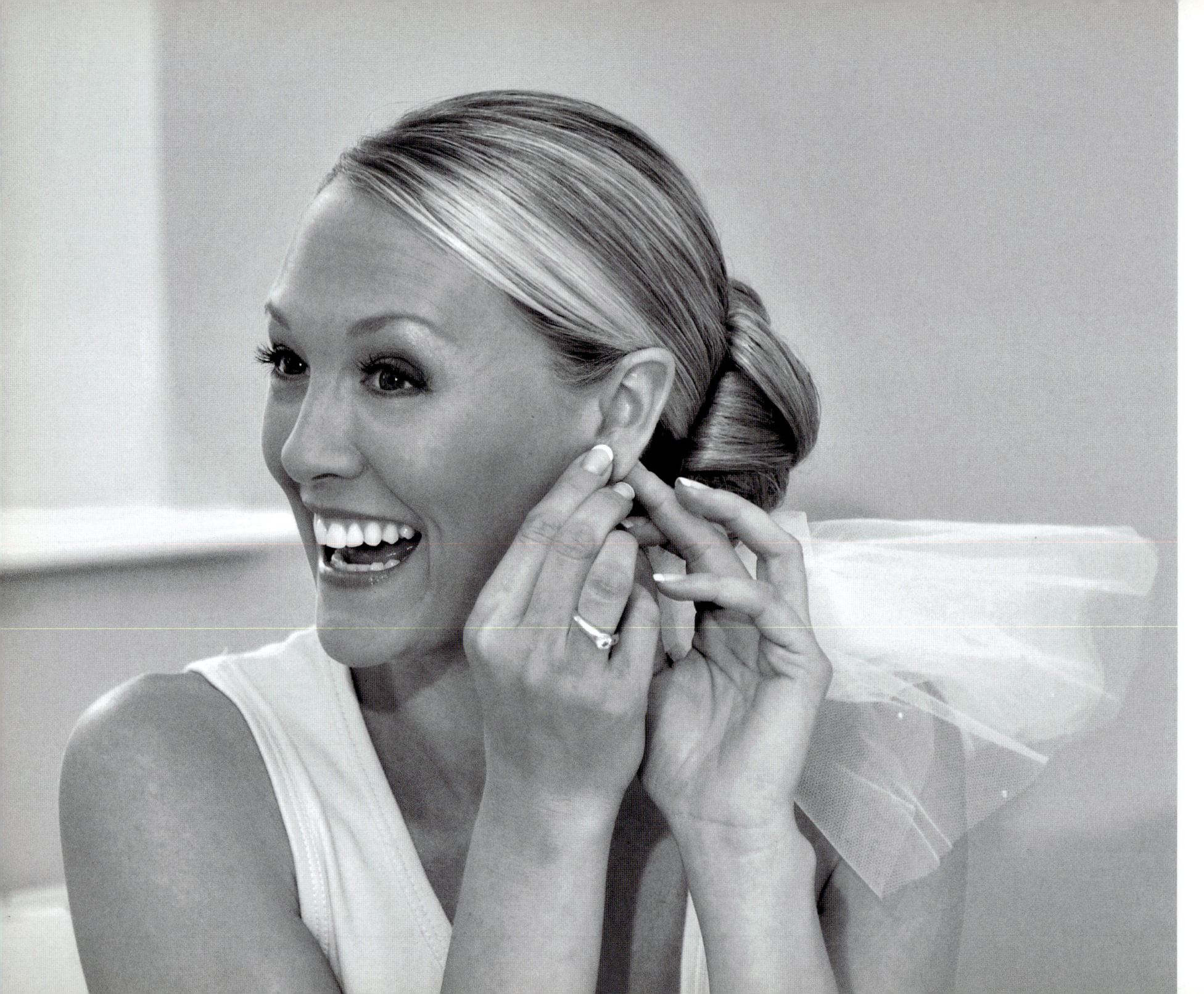

Foreword

When Damien Lovegrove asked me to help edit this book, I didn't know quite what to expect. Of course I was aware of the powerful reputation that he and Julie have built up in a very short time. I'd also been impressed with their work and working practices when I interviewed Damien recently for a photo magazine. But despite all this, did we really need another book on professional wedding photography?

I needn't have worried. Editing a book in progress can be an exciting process. As Damien emailed me the words and pictures, chapter by chapter, the project began to take shape. The more I read, the more I realized that this isn't just another professional guide, it's a blueprint for success. What separates it from other wedding books is a coherent message that pulls together in a frank and honest way every aspect of the business – planning, photographic style and techniques, lighting, people skills, selling, marketing, business strategy, post-production, presentation, even how to prepare a business plan for investors.

Becoming a wedding photographer is the easy part. Amateurs start up every week. All you need is to buy a camera, find a few clients who don't want to pay much and muddle on through. What's difficult is joining the élite, the top wedding photographers who earn big money. Even then it's not enough to be a good photographer. You've got to be good at everything else too.

That's where this book comes in. Every chapter derives from the hard-won experience, attention to detail, and determination that took the Lovegroves from deep in the red to massive success as one of UK's top-earning wedding studios in just 5 years.

Twenty-five years as a photographic journalist have taught me a lot. In the course of editing several professional magazines

opposite

FIG. 1   ISO 160 f/4 at 1/60th

A splash of off-camera flash coupled with an increase of exposure using in-camera compensation gives this picture the bright high key look Julie was after. The ingredients good timing and a great expression, bring this shot to life.

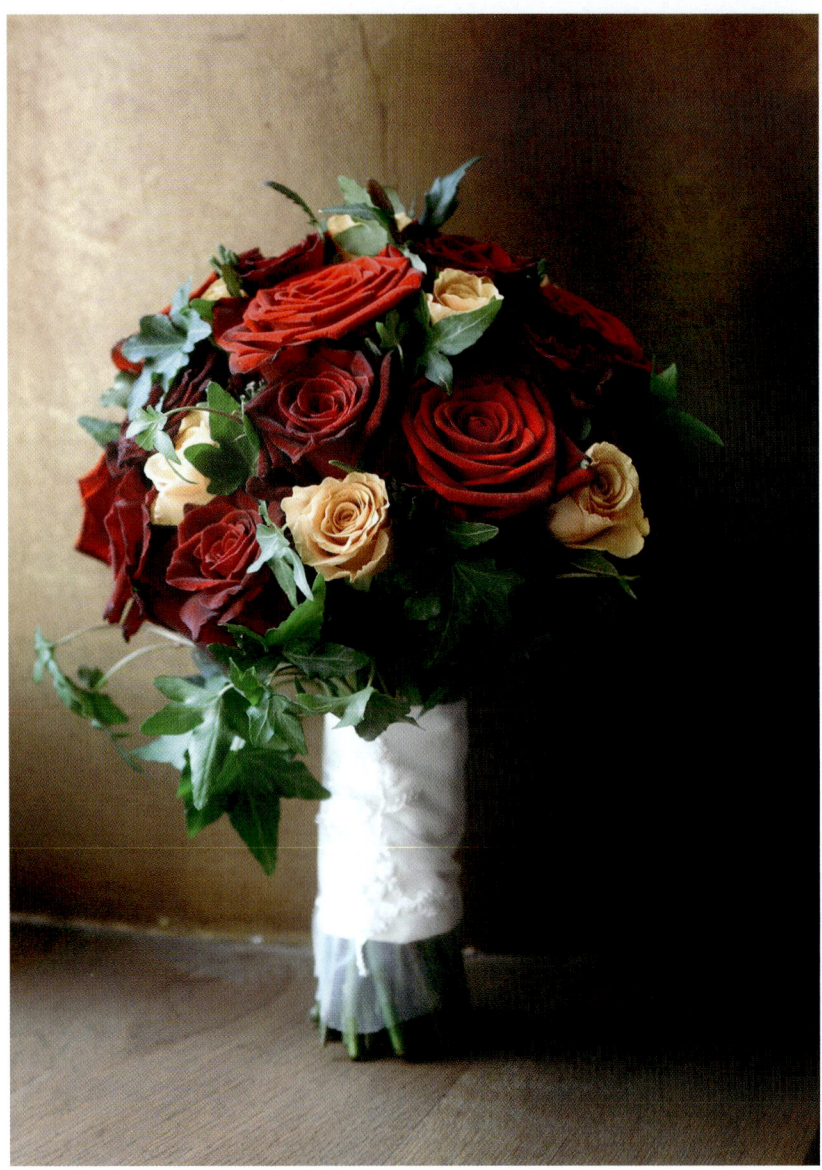

Fig. 2 ISO 400 f/4 at 1/60th

When simple elements come together magic often happens.

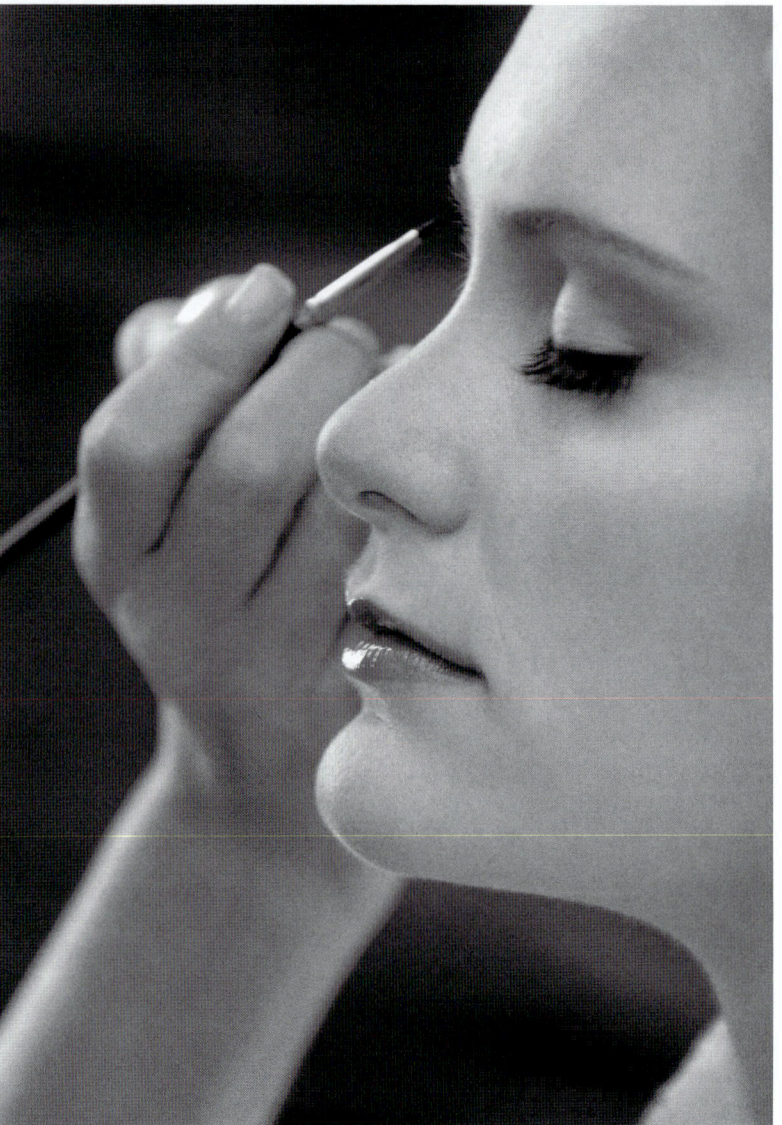

Fig. 3 ISO 200 f/4 at 1/60th

Tight composition, a strong diagonal structure, and the rim light created by a nearby window make this shot of Julie's a favorite of mine.

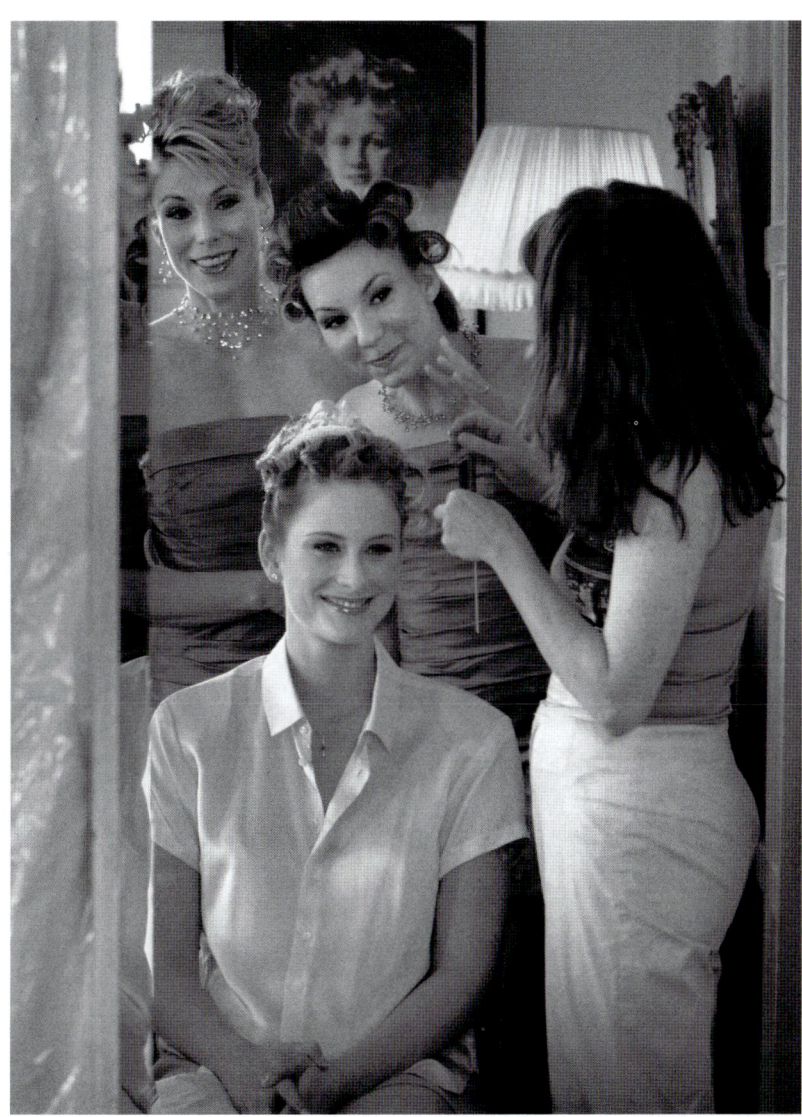

FIG. 4   ISO 800 f/4 at 1/125th

This clever mirror shot brought together a recession of faces including the portrait on the wall at the world famous Cliveden House in Royal Berkshire. Julie used ambient light for the picture.

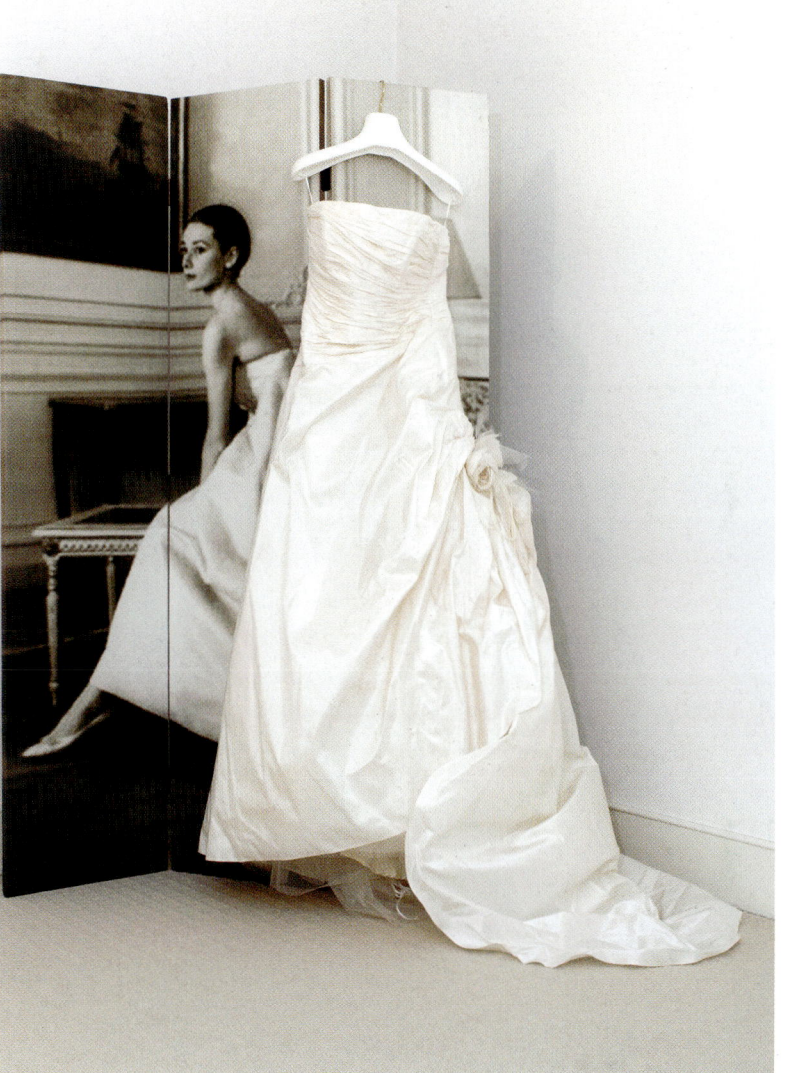

FIG. 5   ISO 800 f/5 at 1/60th

This screen depicting a classic wedding scene was already at the bride's parents' home. All Julie needed was a dress to hang on it to create a simple shot for the album.

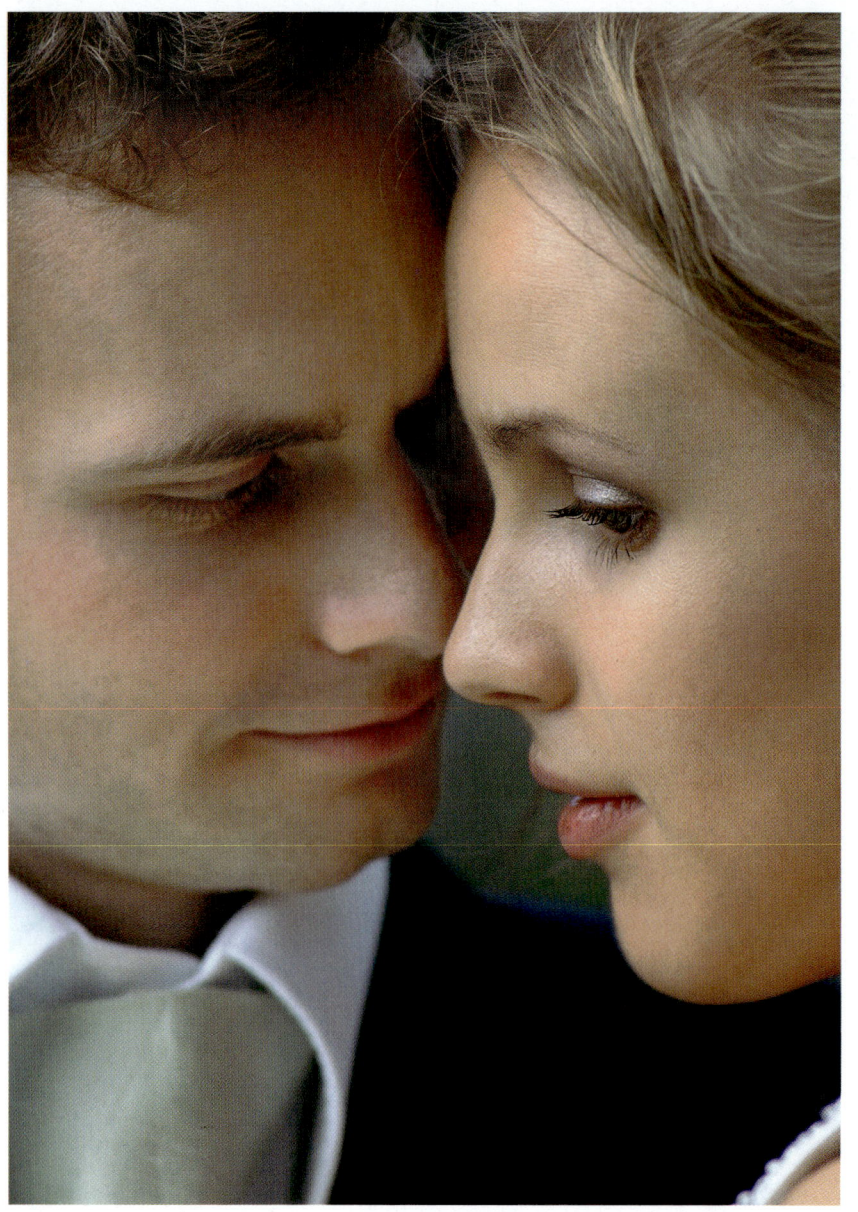

Fig. 6 ISO 400 f/4 at 1/400th

Intimacy without eye contact or passion is very powerful when shot in close up. Julie won many top awards with this picture.

and writing books on wedding and portrait photography, I've interviewed most of the top wedding practitioners about their photographic styles, business techniques, and what makes them successful. That's how I know that this book is the real thing.

So find out for yourself how you can transform your business and dramatically increase your earnings. I won't promise that the journey will be easy. Just like the Lovegroves you'll need lots of drive, persistence, and hard work. But you'll have fun too and this book will give you all the guidance, wisdom, and inspiration you'll need along the way.

Bon voyage
Christopher Wordsworth
Consultant Editor

This book is dedicated to Yvonne & Ivor – Julie's parents, without whom photographing weddings would not have been possible. Thank you for taking such an active part in Francesca's upbringing and giving us the freedom to pursue our careers.

Acknowledgement

I'd like to thank Catherine Connor and Gregory Haddock for their ongoing life and career guidance.

Thanks go to our clients for making our job on your wedding days so easy and a truly pleasurable experience. Thank you also for the wonderful pictures.

Thank you Gemma for collating the pictures from over 700 DVDs and thank you Marko for your wonderful picture editing.

Thank you Francesca for your big smiles when we get home.

Thank you Julie for your loyalty, love, fun, and friendship.

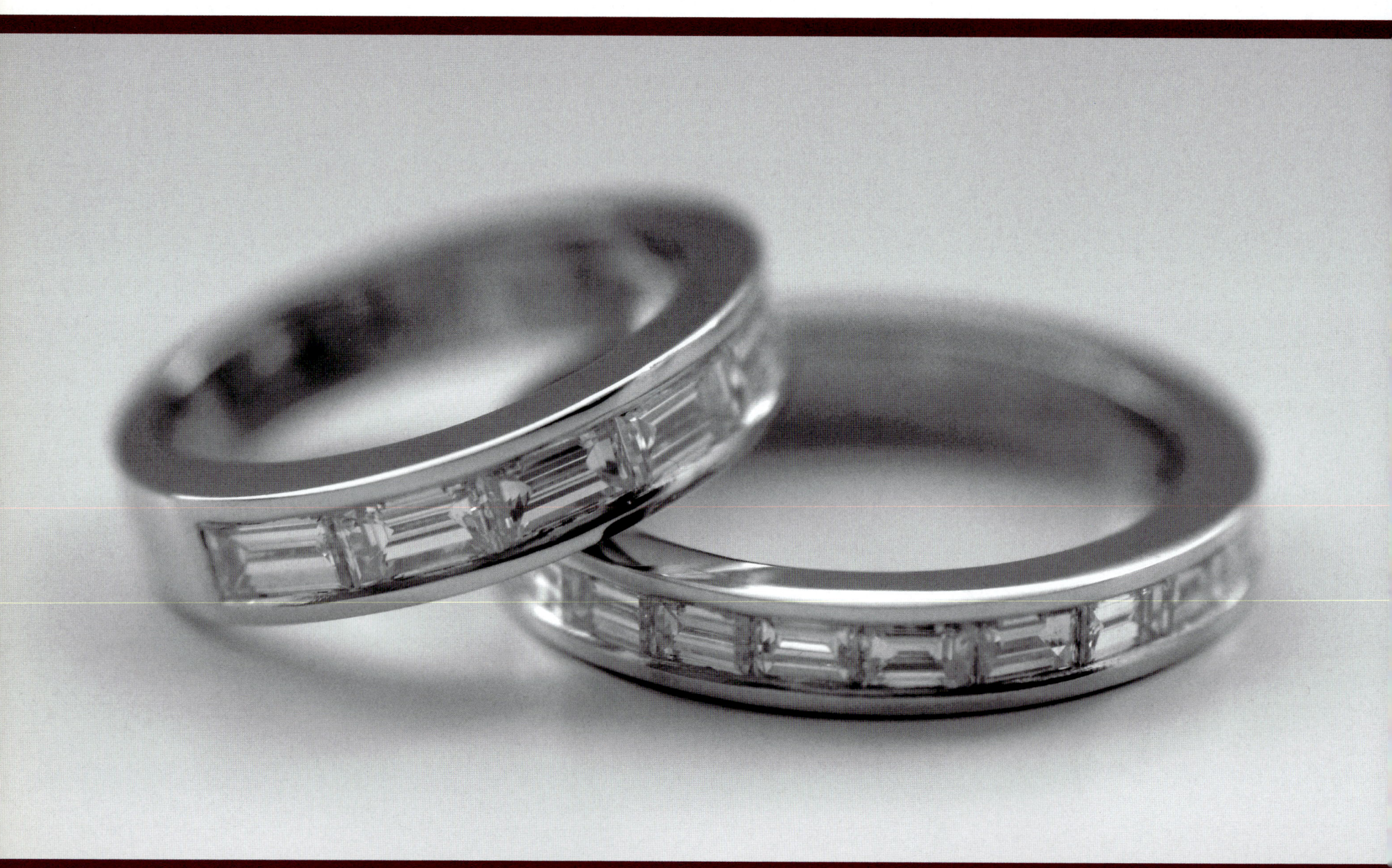

OVERVIEW OF
Wedding Photography

Over the next few pages, I'll be sharing with you a series of pictures that Julie and I shot for an American bride at the famous Hempel Hotel in London. As the hotel is known for its stark, minimalist décor, we all agreed it might be fun to reflect this in the pictures. As a result, most of the images are strong, simple, uncluttered compositions in black and white with a few color shots for contrast. The hard, directional lighting we chose to use also brings out the angularity of the hotel's interior design. Above all, our aim was to make these images elegant and stylish – just like the bride and groom.

What does wedding photography really mean? When a bride-to-be follows up a recommendation, calls a wedding studio, or clicks the address of a wedding website, what can she expect? There are a wide variety of 'styles,' ancient and modern, around

today – with some photographers 'mixing and matching.' Here's a mini guide:

Traditional wedding photography is a record of the occasion: recording the guests, what they look like, what they are wearing, and what is happening on the day. The customers are given a set of formulaic prints that document their marriage. Just like my first attempts, traditional images are well crafted but often lack soul.

Storybook wedding photography is where record photography goes one stage further. All the details and moments of the day are captured, telling the story of the day often through 'rose

opposite

FIG. 1   ISO 800 f/4 at 1/500th

A photograph of these eternity rings was important to the couple. It always pays to include special details like this.

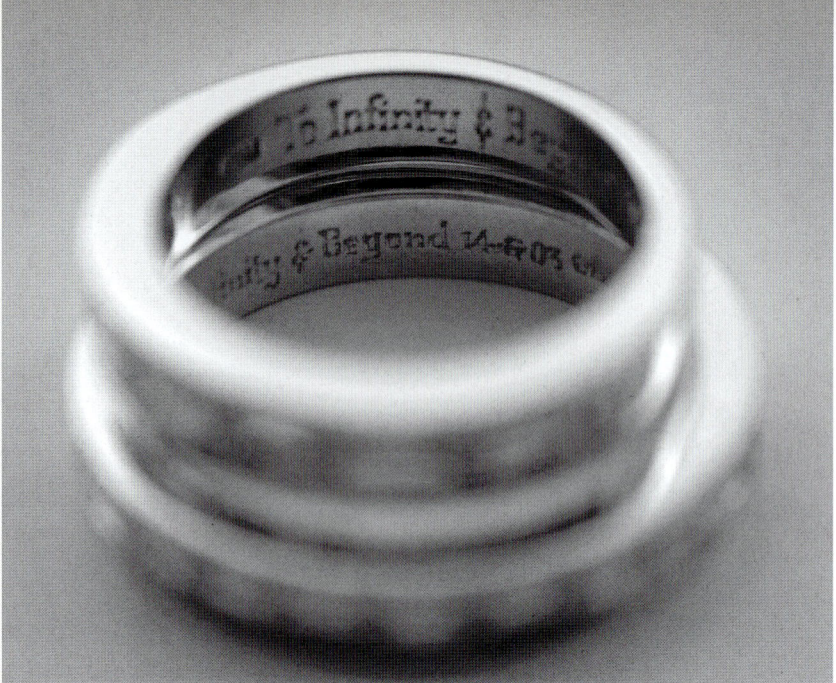

Fig. 2   ISO 800 f/4 at 1/500th

It didn't make it any easier that the inscription was on the inside of the rings! So I used a shallow depth of field to emphasize the message.

tinted glasses.' Even the bride's shoes get their own shot! This is still essentially record photography, but usually the 'people pictures' take on a less formal style with only a few of the people showing eye contact with the camera.

Reportage comes next and out goes the rose tinted glasses! The reportage style is meant to show it as it is. Reportage is the purest form of record photography. It is all too easy to do reportage badly, shooting all day to produce nothing of real substance. The great reportage photographers are just that, great craftsmen and women of the highest caliber. They have the uncanny ability to always be in the right place at the right time with the right lens and get the shot in difficult light without being noticed.

Brand or personal style is a departure from record photography. There is a whole gamut of genres labeled with a particular brand or a personal style ranging from mainstream fashion to simple minimalism. This work is the product of a directed photo shoot, an extreme degree of photographer intervention. This is where photographers take control and implement their own unique style. The directed shoot is often made to look natural and as if it really happened without intervention. The key to this kind of work is in the subject itself. Even though a photograph has been totally set up it can have immense value. This style has been the key to our success over the past 5 years. The Lovegrove style is very much in demand and often copied.

THE BOTTOM LINE

It's easy to photograph the bride and groom, but it's much more difficult to capture the love that exists between them. It's the

Fig. 3   ISO 400 f/4 at 1/60th

The bride was obviously proud of her hair style so Julie made a feature of it with this shot. A blip of flash high above the camera acts as a 'hair light' while the pensive expression reflects the gravity of the occasion.

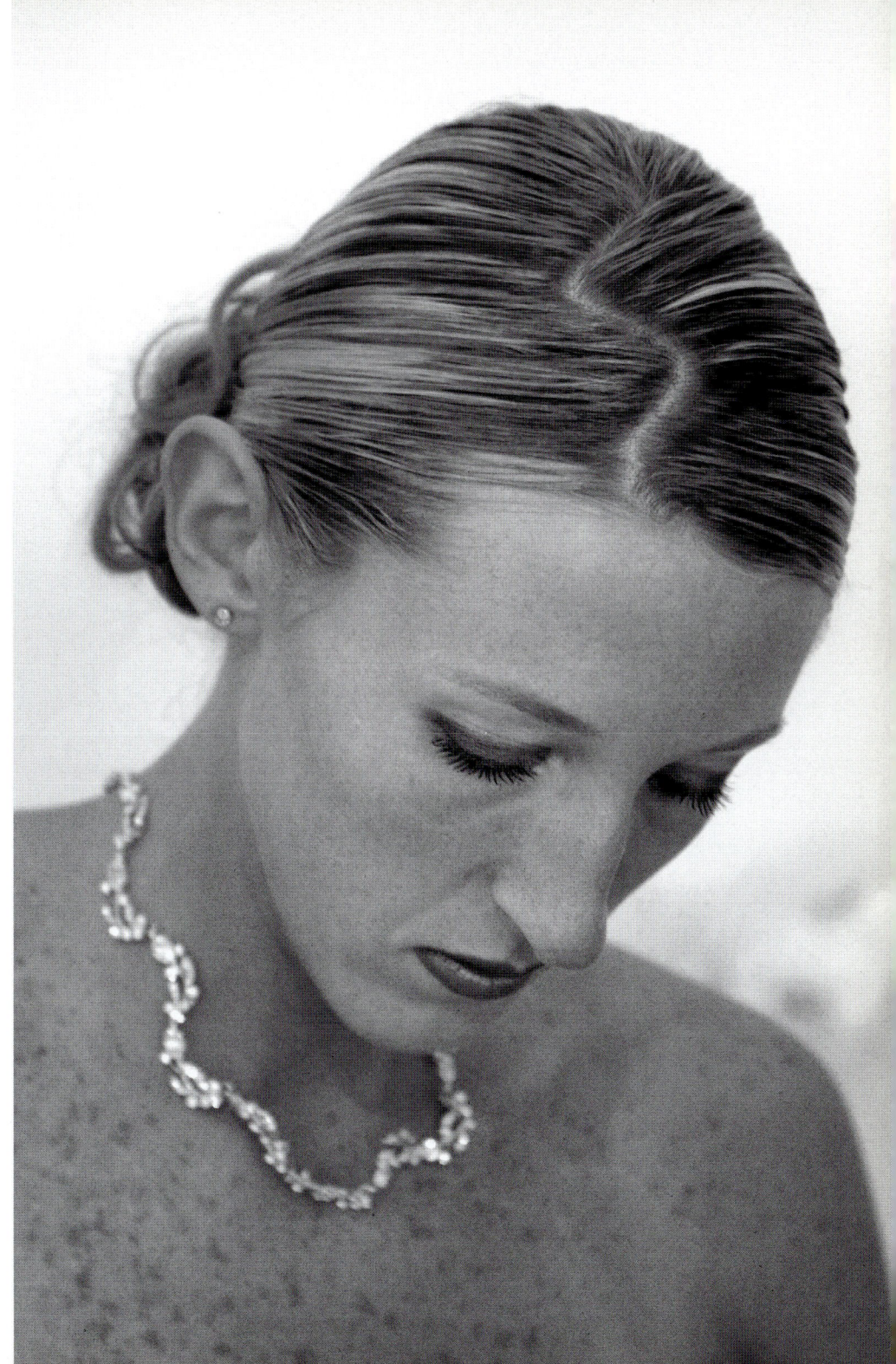

ability to shoot love, fun, tenderness, and beauty that makes the work of the great wedding photographers stand head and shoulders above the rest.

The digital revolution, or should I say evolution?, is here. Some 15 years since the world of music embraced digital capture and delivery to the retail buyer, photography has followed suit. Through the ages, photography has reinvented itself several times. With each new phase came a new set of craft skills and opportunities.

In the early days before color, a photographer regarded exposure as only a small part of the process. All photographers processed their own negatives and printed their own images under the enlarger.

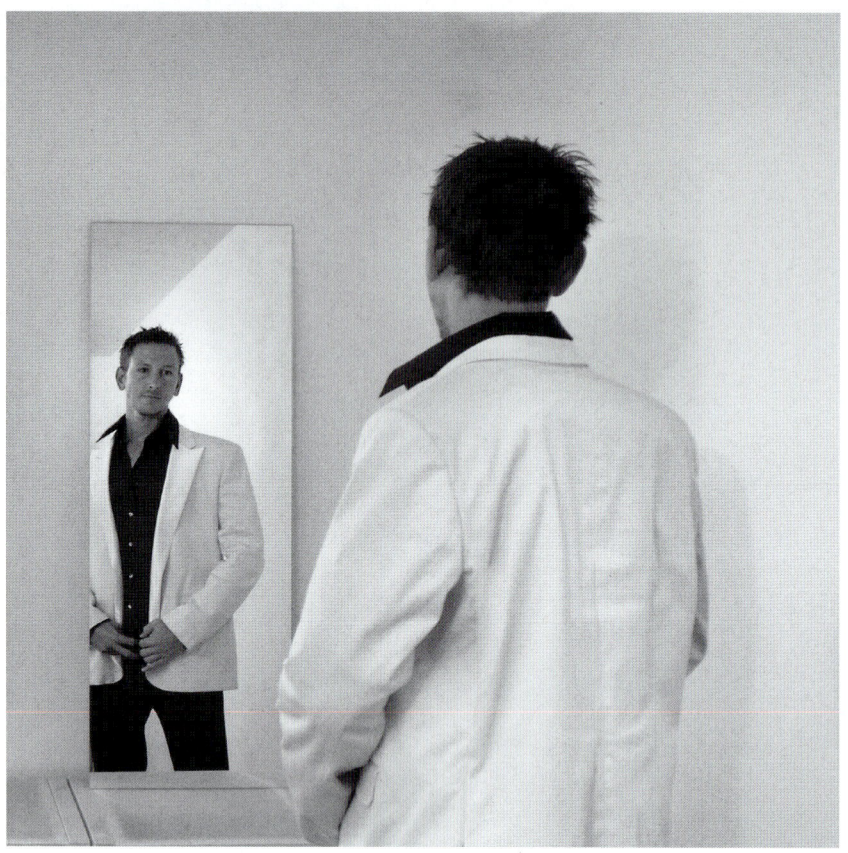

Fig. 4 ISO 400 f/4 at 1/125th

An interestingly complex portrait: mirrors are great for adding extra depth – and a touch of mystery – to a composition. Here I bounced the flash off the wall behind me: this increases the apparent depth and draws the viewer toward the bright highlight behind the mirror image of the groom.

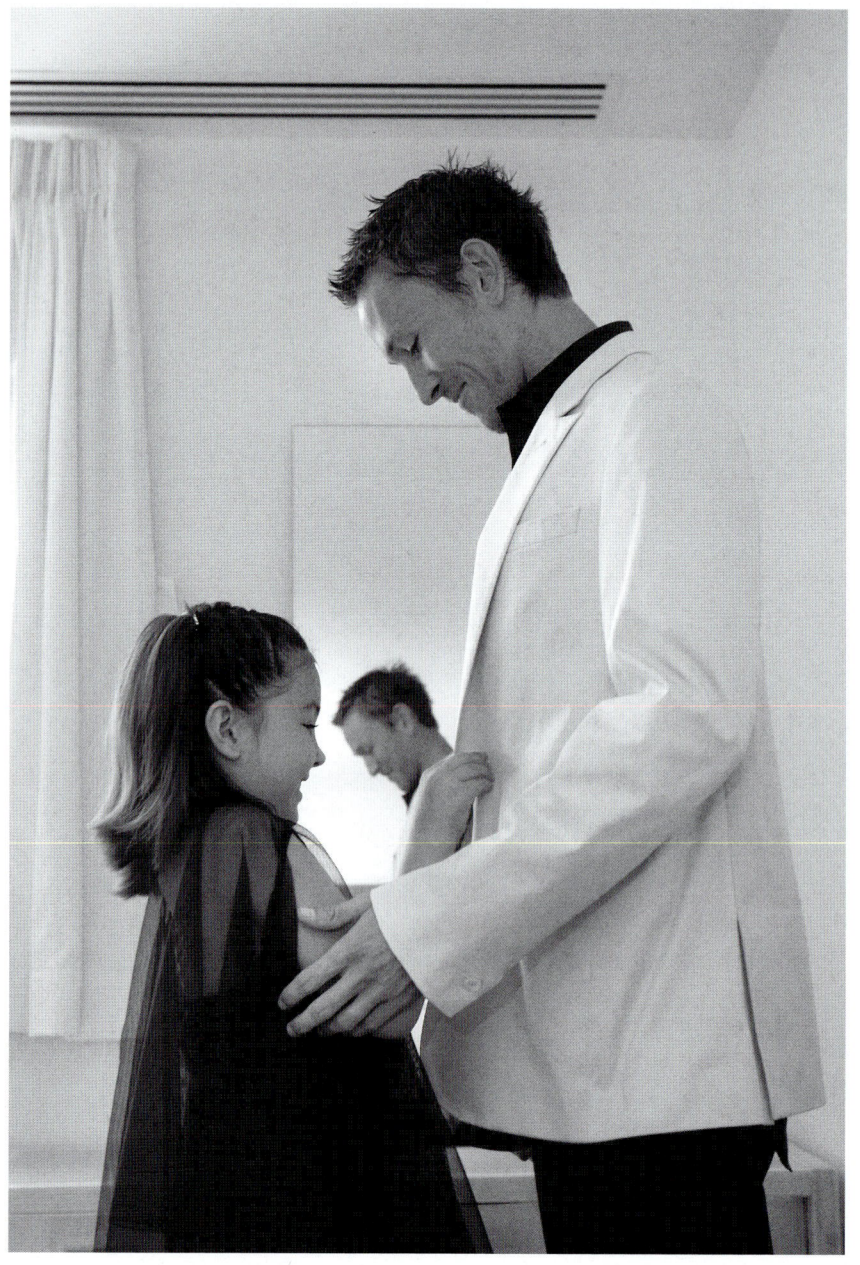

Fig. 5   ISO 400 f/4 at 1/90th

Excitement and tenderness: you can't beat expressions like this. Shooting from below the little girl's eye line allowed me to frame the faces on the same horizontal plane.

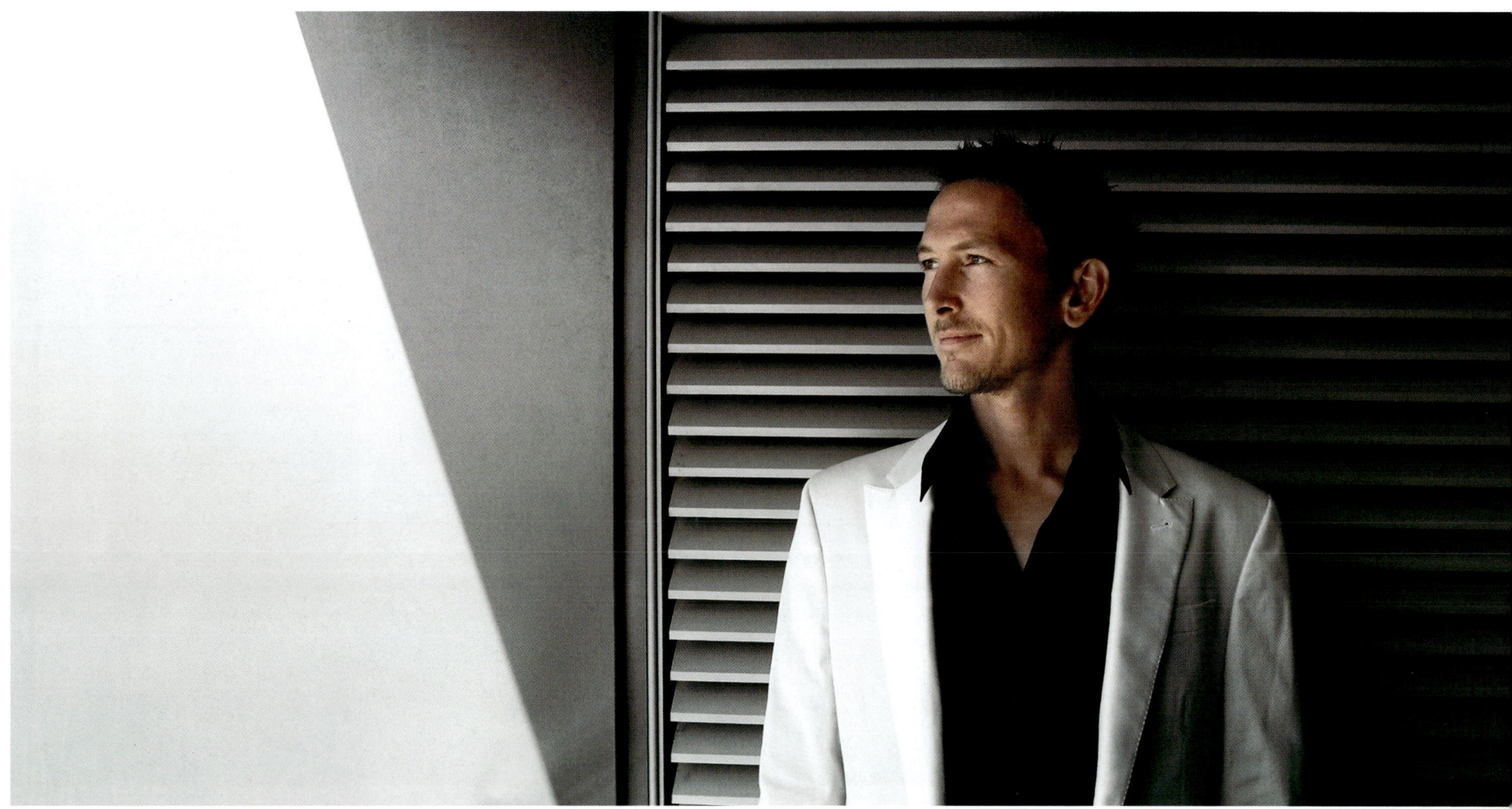

FIG. 6   ISO 200 f/4 at 1/500th

Everything came together for this pleasing portrait: lovely directional light, strong shapes, and a wonderful expression. It all began with that slatted ventilation duct that was just crying out to be used in a picture!

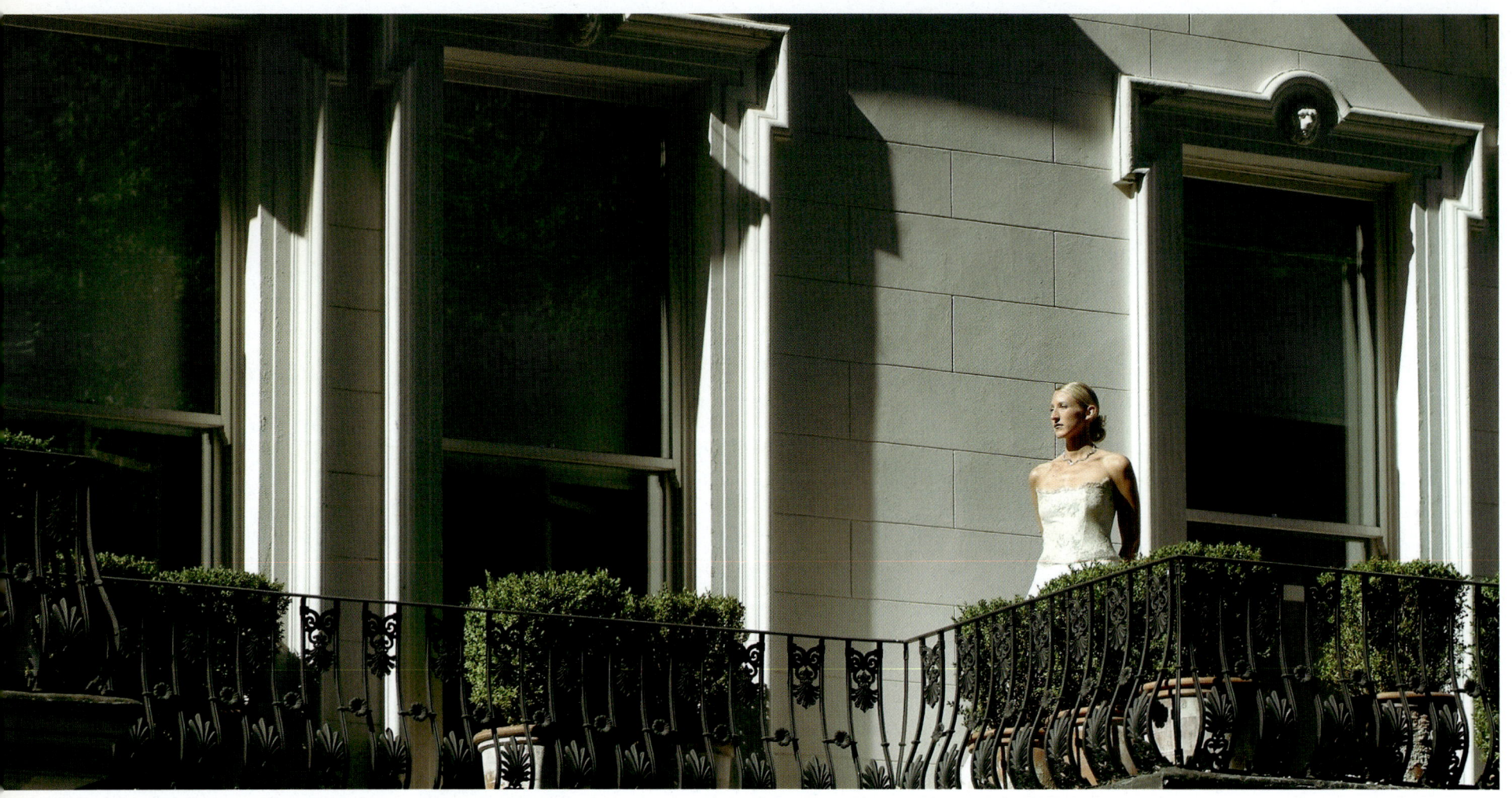

Sunlight on the balcony picks out the bride. Another color shot in pastel shades –
strong saturated colors don't really go with minimalism!

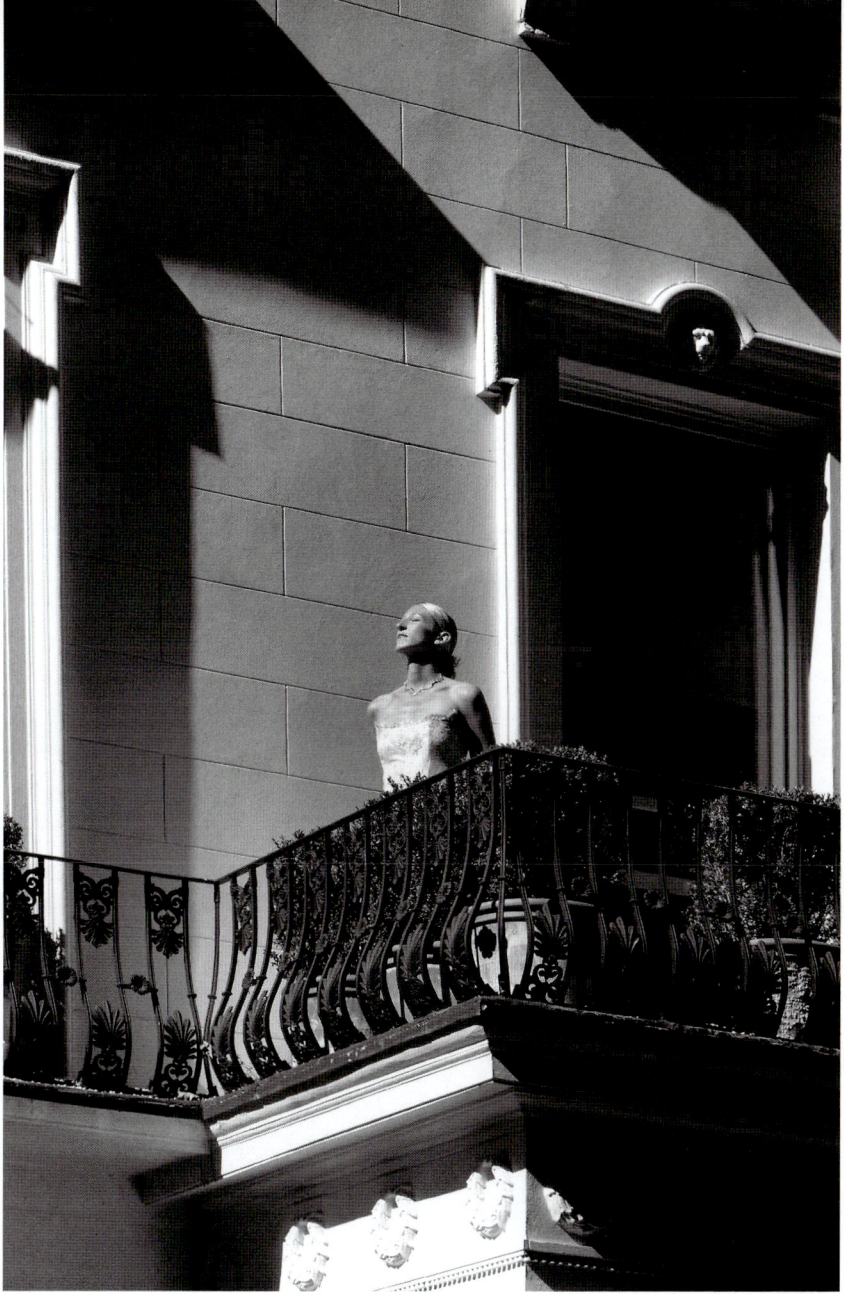

FIG. 8

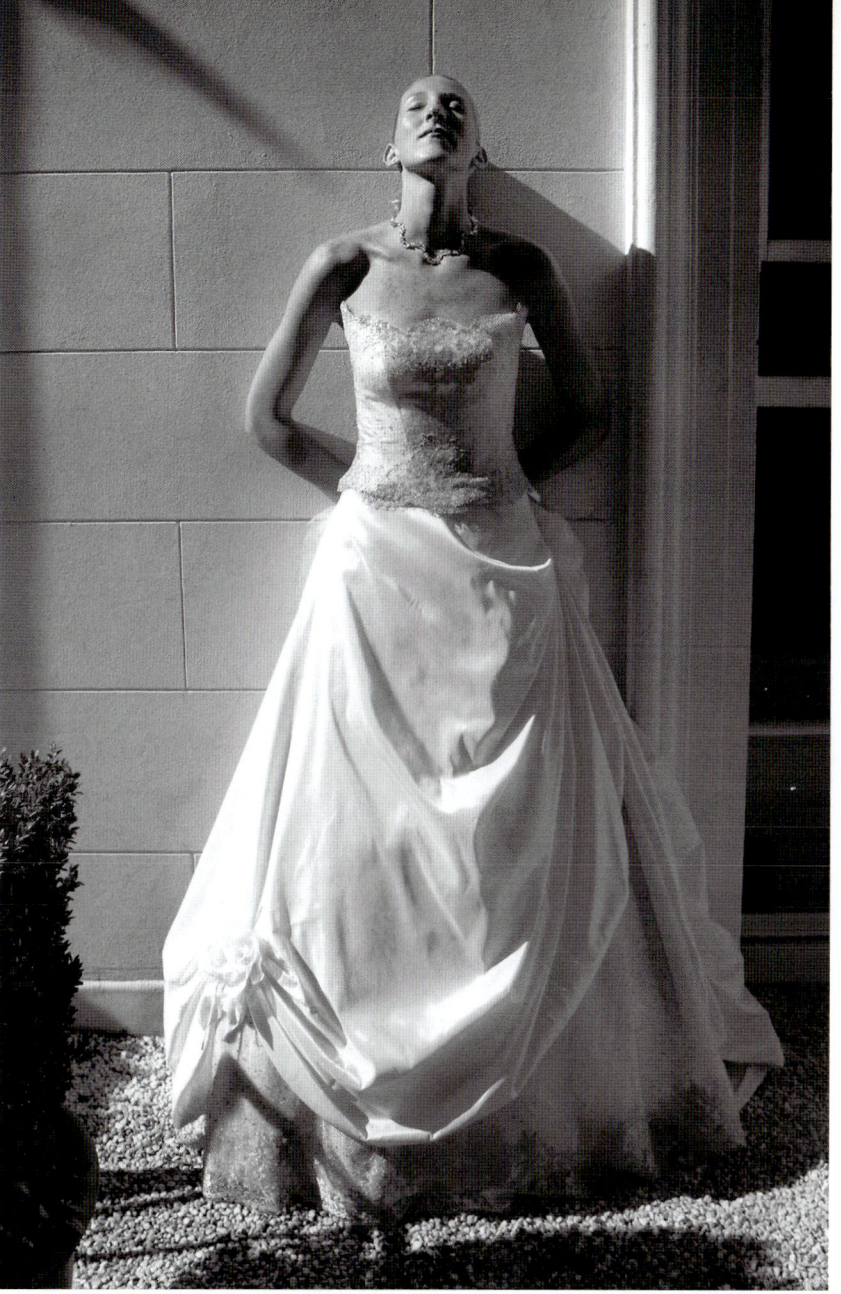

Fig. 9   ISO 400 f/4 at 1/4000th

This is another bold composition in which Julie used the sunlight to create an almost sculptural effect.

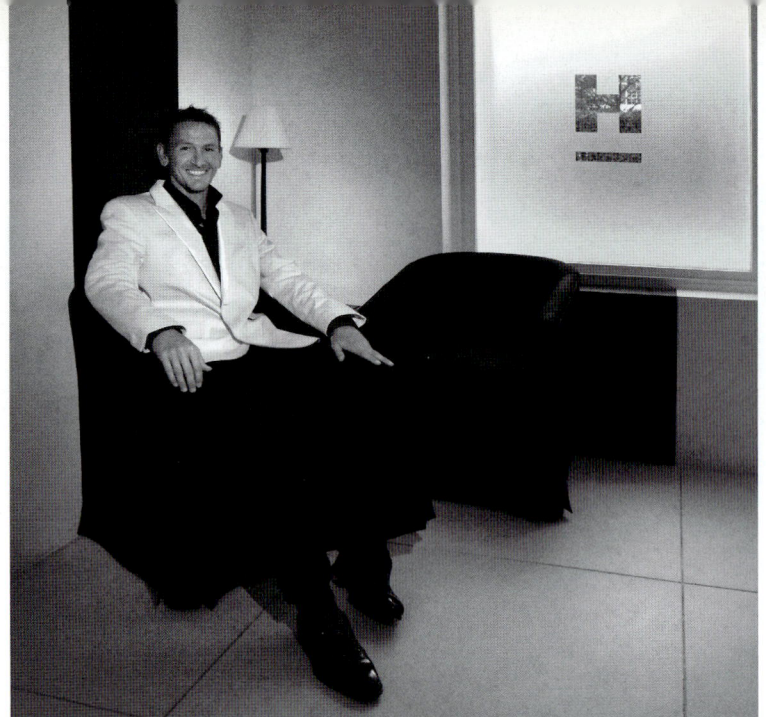

FIG. 10   ISO 800 f/4 at 1/60th

While Julie is doing her stuff on the balcony, I'm having fun too. Here I have added a spot of light from a 300 Watt tungsten lamp with the barn doors cropped in tight to attenuate the light. It's easy to get too serious when trying to create cool compositions – raising a spontaneous smile like this can be priceless.

FIG. 11   ISO 800 f/4 at 1/60th with hand held off camera flash.

This is one of those shots you couldn't set up even if you tried: the moment when the bride enters the ceremony room. Julie's timing was crucial. The expressions, body language, and design are all spot on.

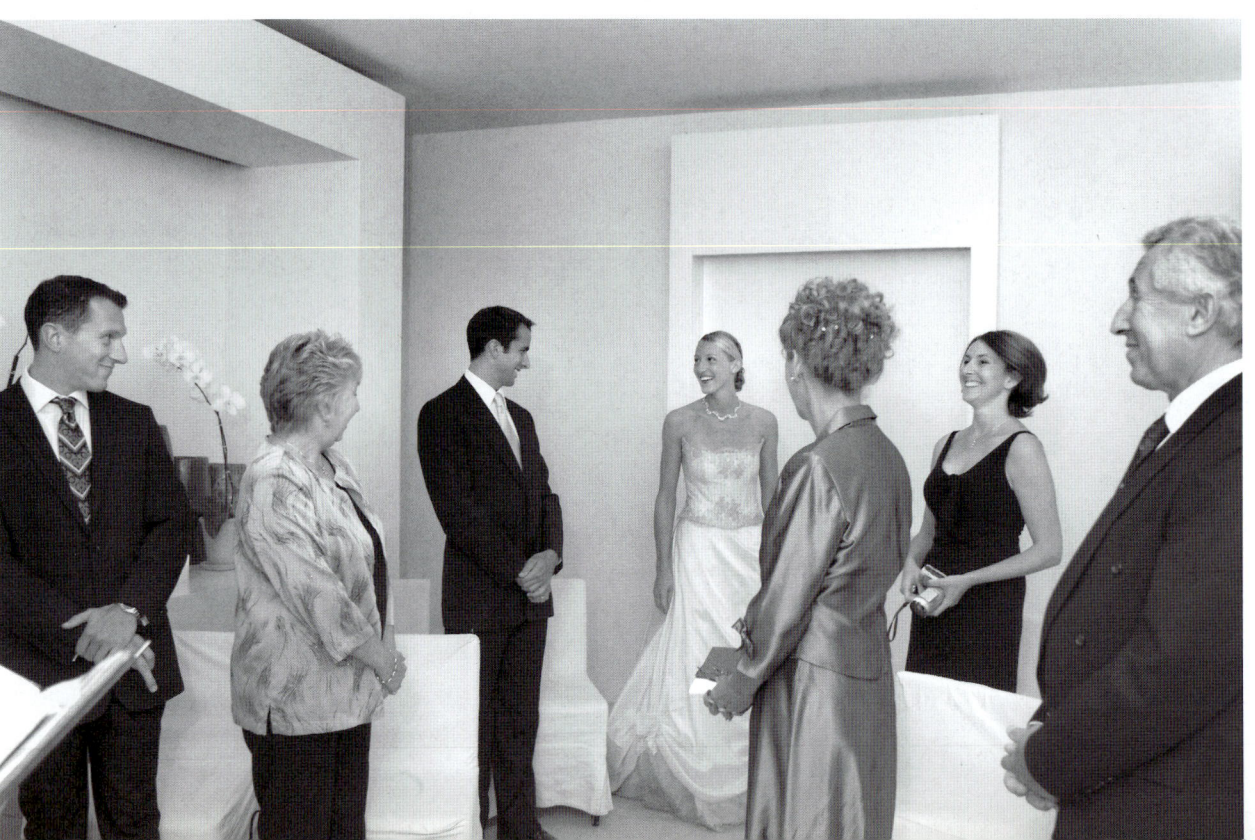

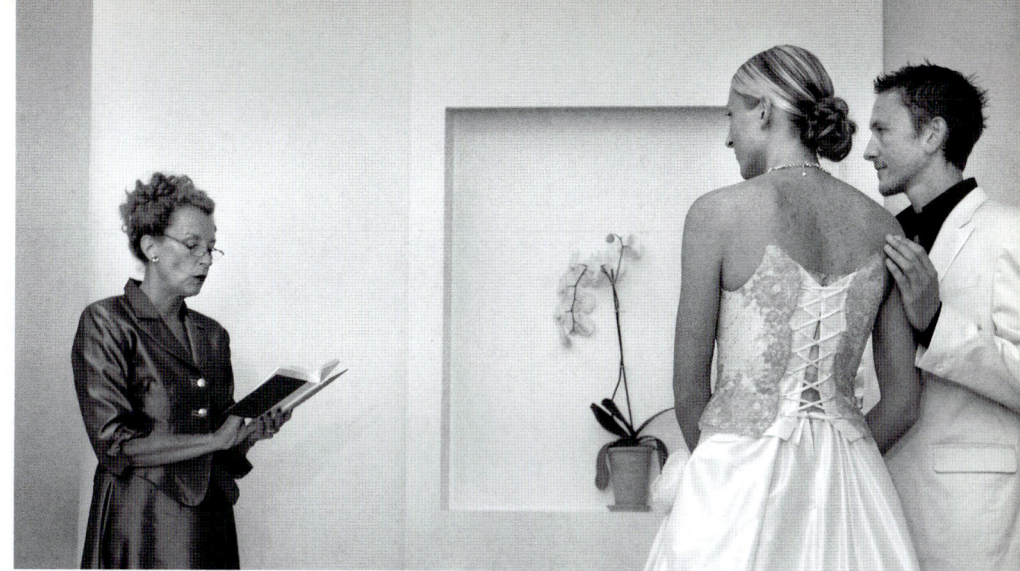

Fig. 12   ISO 800 f/4 at 1/60th

Another fine composition with a touch of tenderness against the cool, geometric background.

bottom

Fig. 13   ISO 800 f/4 at 1/60th

As the happy couple come toward me, I'm walking backwards holding a TTL flash in my left hand above the camera. One way or another, it's a moment of fun and spontaneity {AQ5} which the couple's expressions reflect.

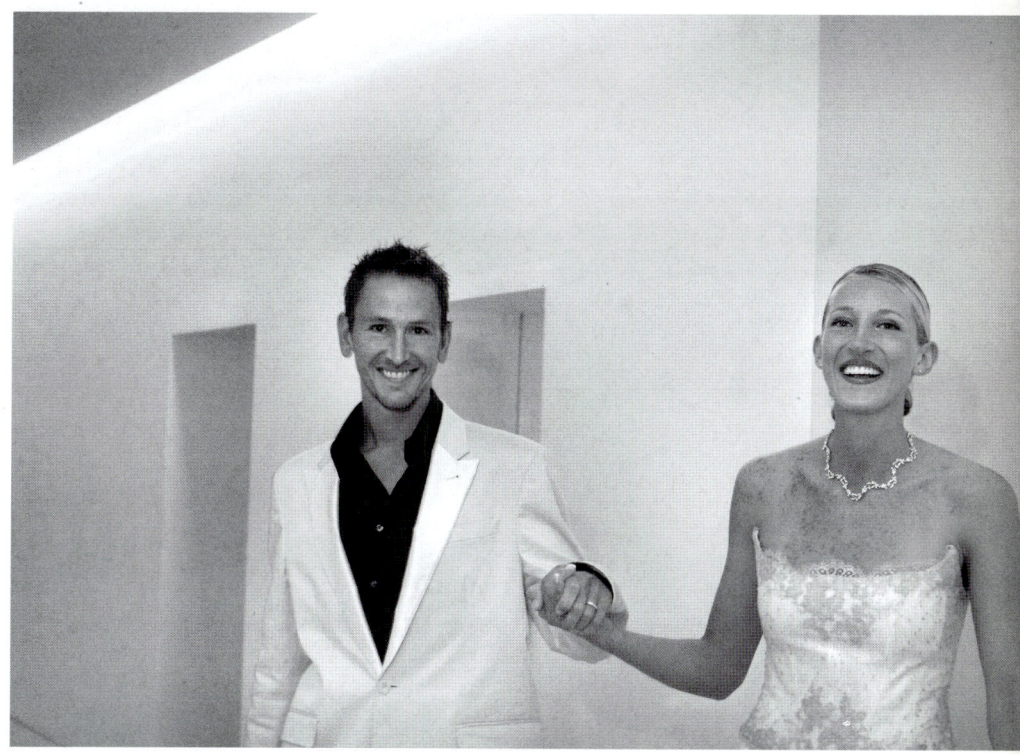

With the arrival of the color film the professional lab emerged with automated processing and printing. This meant that the printer's art was lost by a whole generation of photographers who handed their films into the lab on a Monday and picked up their prints a few days later. The color and density grading was done on-screen by a machine operator. The exposure latitude of film allowed photographers to rely on the camera's inbuilt meter.

With the arrival of digital capture, the roles are once again being reversed with the photographer taking back the control and relearning the printer's art. It is for this reason a large part of this book explores good working practice and core craft skills. No longer can you leave your camera on auto and leave the rest to the lab! Whether you choose to have a Joint Photographic Experts Group (jpeg) or RAW workflow, some tone grading

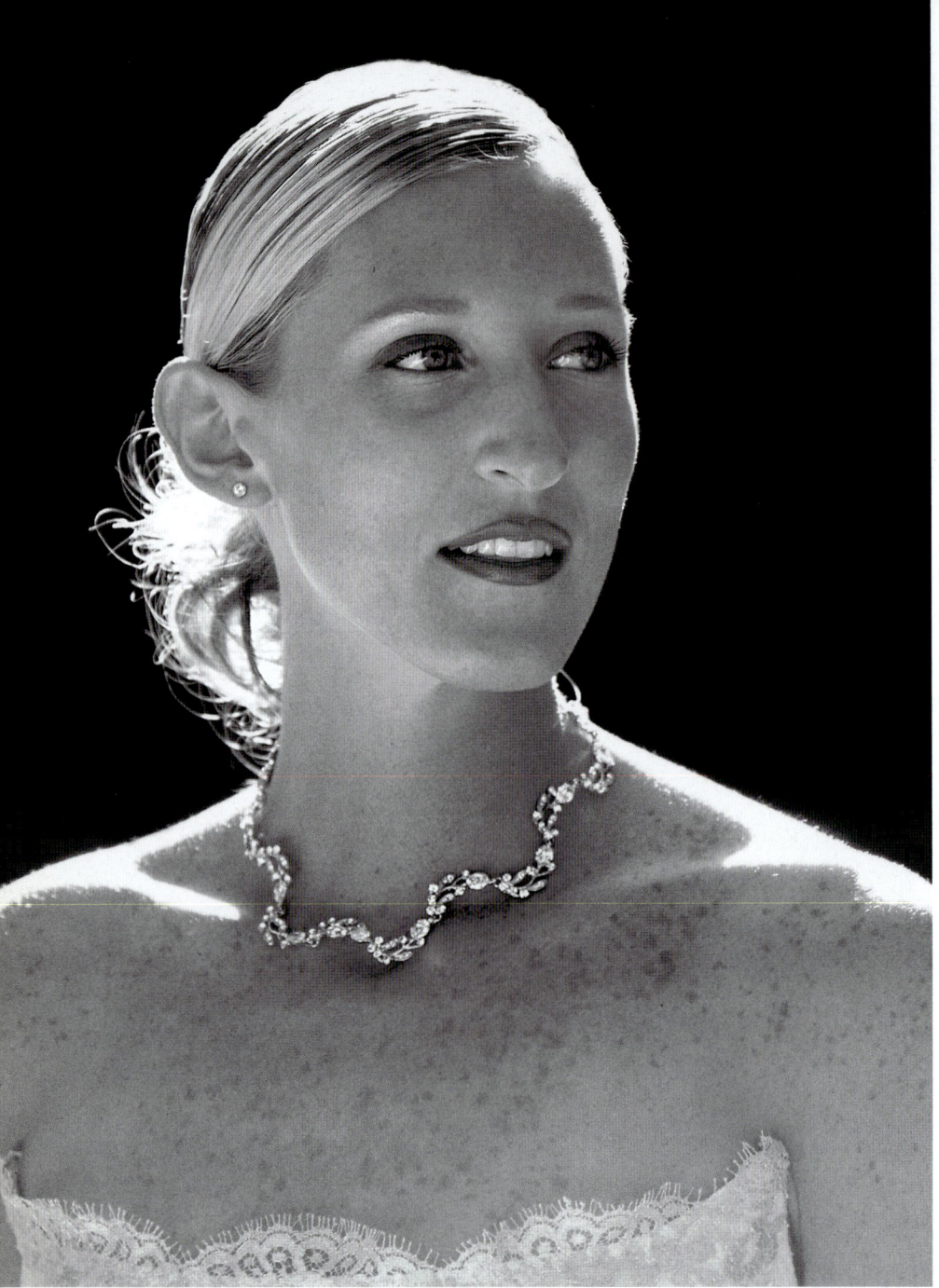

FIG. 14   ISO 800 f/4 at 1/700th

A stunning image: the bride was lit beautifully by the late sun shining through some distant trees. We always use Photoshop when an image demands it – in this case the dark bushes behind the bride were rendered to black.

and color correction will still be necessary by the photographer. This raises a new set of problems of its own. Photographers with some degree of color blindness may not find the switch to digital easy.

The difference between good amateur photographs taken at a wedding by 'Uncle Henry' and those by an official professional photographer is to a large part down to exposure and printing skills. Digital photography is now there for all, and no longer the prerogative of wealthy hobbyists and professionals. Once again we find the craft of photography is back. Professional work is being pushed to new, higher standards to keep the edge over mainstream amateur work.

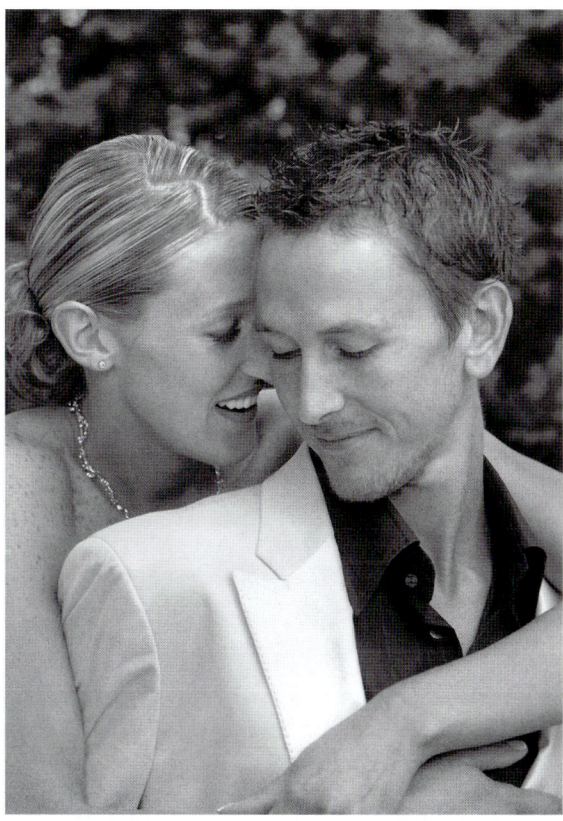

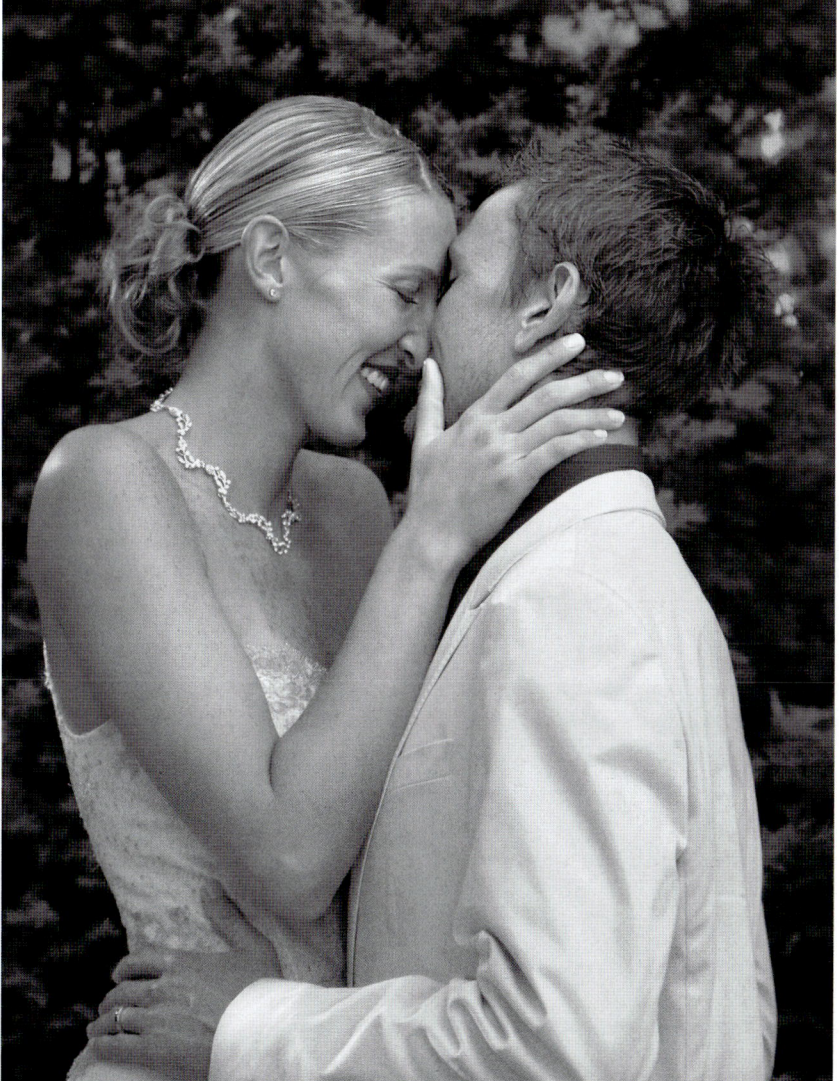

It can be fun to shoot a wedding in homage to the minimalist style that developed in the 1950s where 'less is more.' It does however take a surprising amount of effort to achieve a convincing look. Throughout this chapter, I share with you a set of wedding images in the minimalist style that Julie and I took for an American bride at the world famous Hempel Hotel in London.

FIGS 15 & 16   ISO 800 f/4 at 1/180th

Stepping back out of the sunlight of the previous picture and just using the bushes as a backdrop, these intimate moments were set up and then captured spontaneously. Sometimes couples make their own magic!

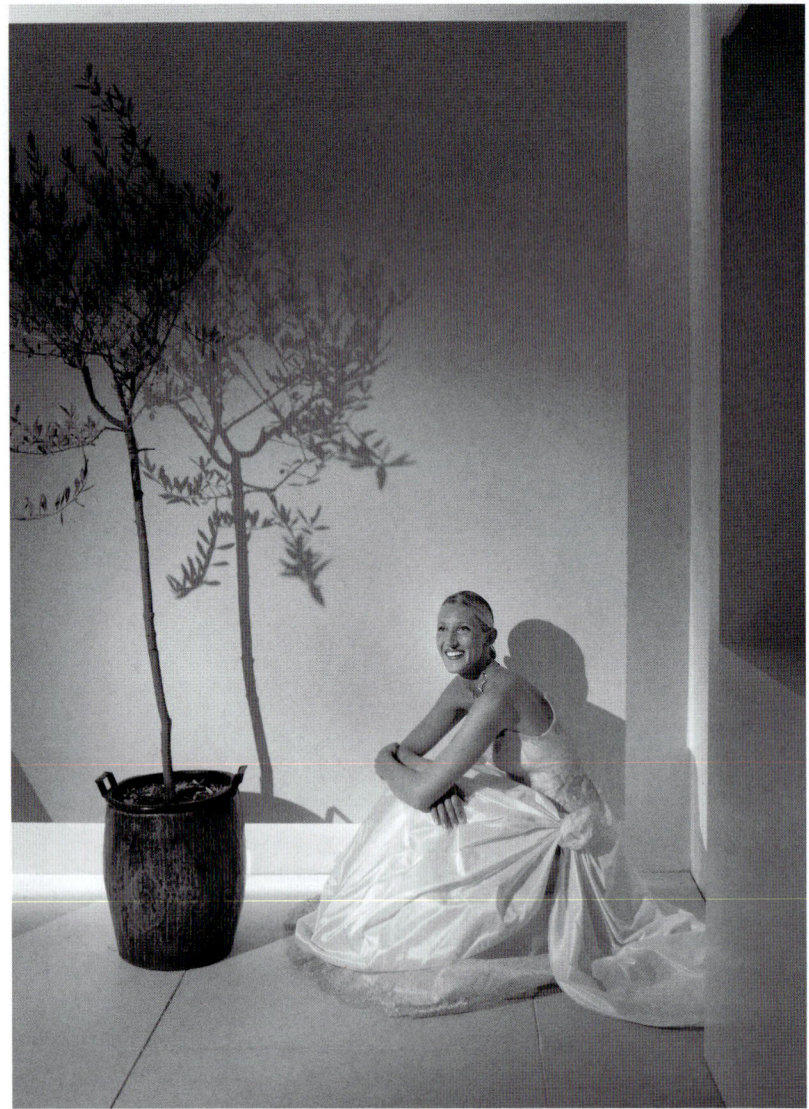

FIG. 17   ISO 400 f/4 at 1/30th

It pays to prepare. After setting up my small 300 Watt tungsten spotlight (with barn doors for greater control) on a stand, and planning a trio of shots with Julie, we called in the bride and groom. Panning the light between pictures allowed its stand to stay in the same place while we shot the pre-rehearsed images in quick succession.

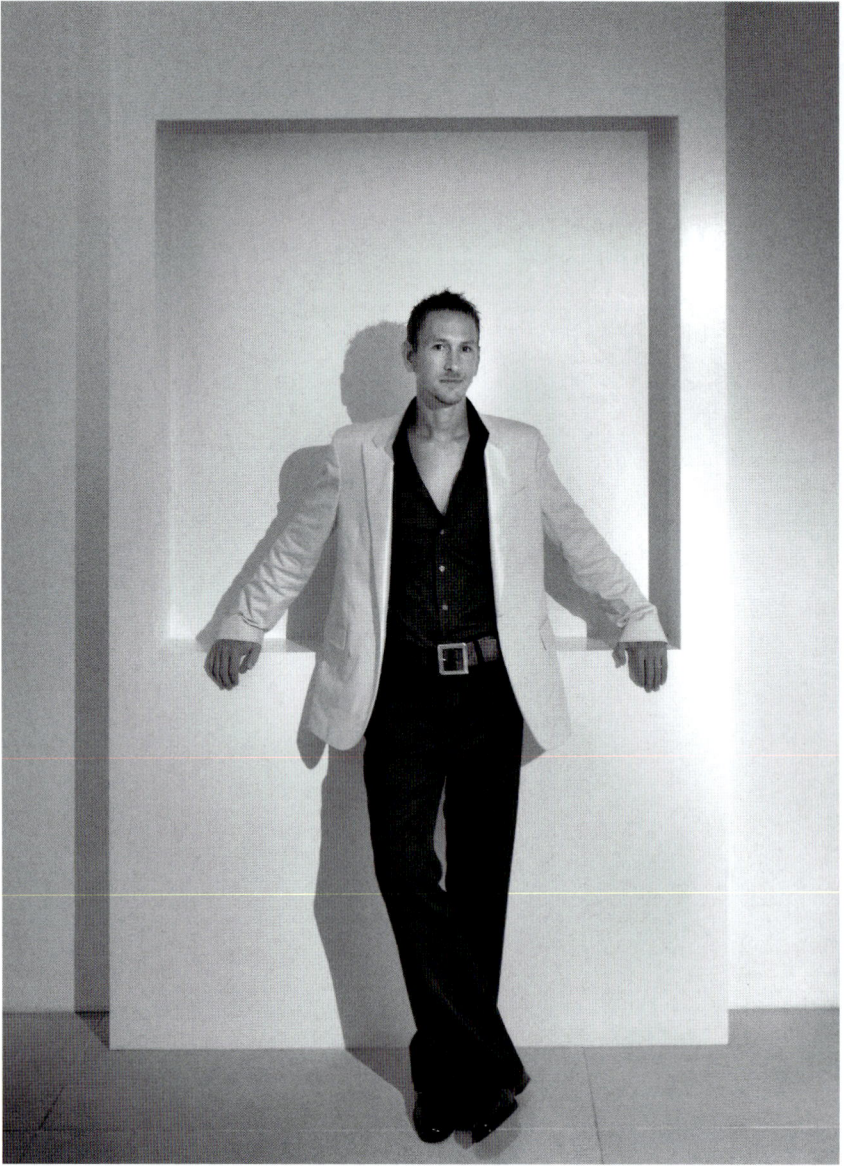

FIG. 18   ISO 400 f/4 at 1/11th

Here I created a pool of light for the groom to stand in and placed him right in the middle of the frame just breaking the symmetry with his crossed legs. I always use a monopod to hold the camera steady in these situations.

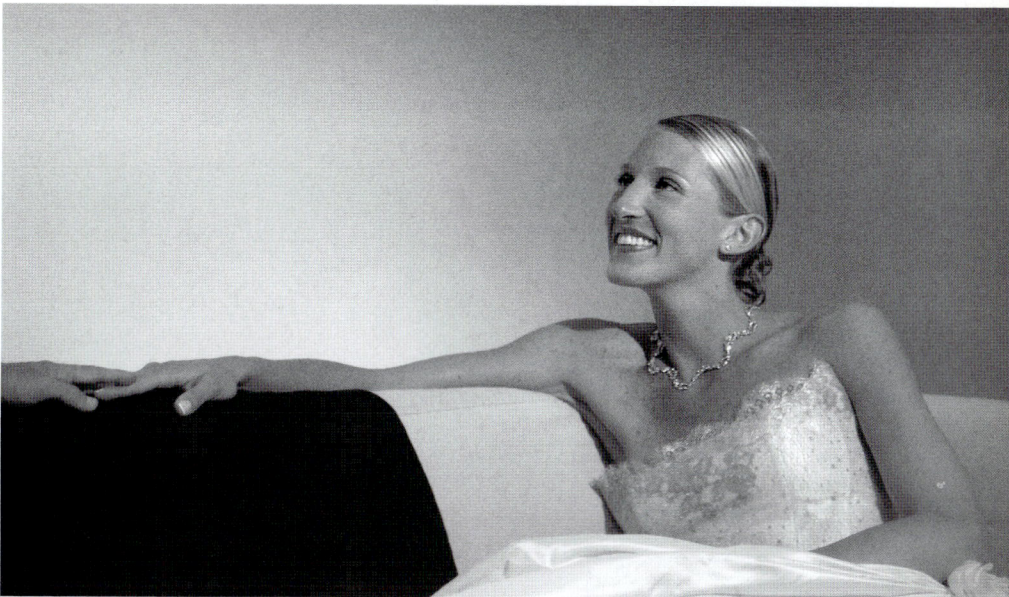

FIG. 19   ISO 800 f/4 at 1/125th

The touch of the hands and the look of love make this image work for me. The light position should have been to the left of the camera but because the barn doors kept the spill from creeping up the wall behind the bride, I got away with it.

bottom

FIG. 20   ISO 400 f/4 at 1/45th

Having re-rigged my spotlight in the hotel foyer, we set about having fun with shapes and shadows – carefully controlling just one light with the barn doors. The items in the hotel nearly cluttered the shot but in black and white it's much less distracting than it might have been in color.

BRINGING IT ALL TOGETHER

An understanding of the changing role that photography has played in the recording of weddings together with knowledge of the equipment, techniques, and systems of the past help us to understand the current market and predict future trends. Products change too. Albums of prints are always likely to be a key product in some market sectors but increasingly slideshows on DVD and CD-ROM are emerging as the new high value products. Changing attitudes toward artistic copyright throughout the world may well force photographers to offer pictures supplied at high resolution on disk as part of a package dictated by demand.

The pace of change is fast and the way people use digital imagery is changing too. The business strategies of the top wedding photographers will stay positive in such a volatile

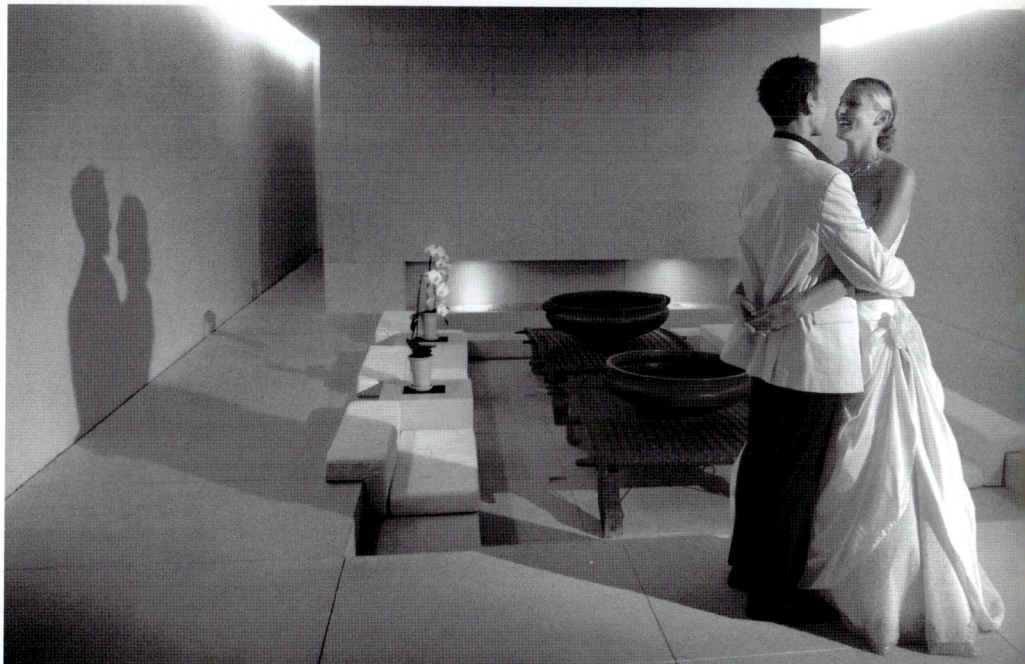

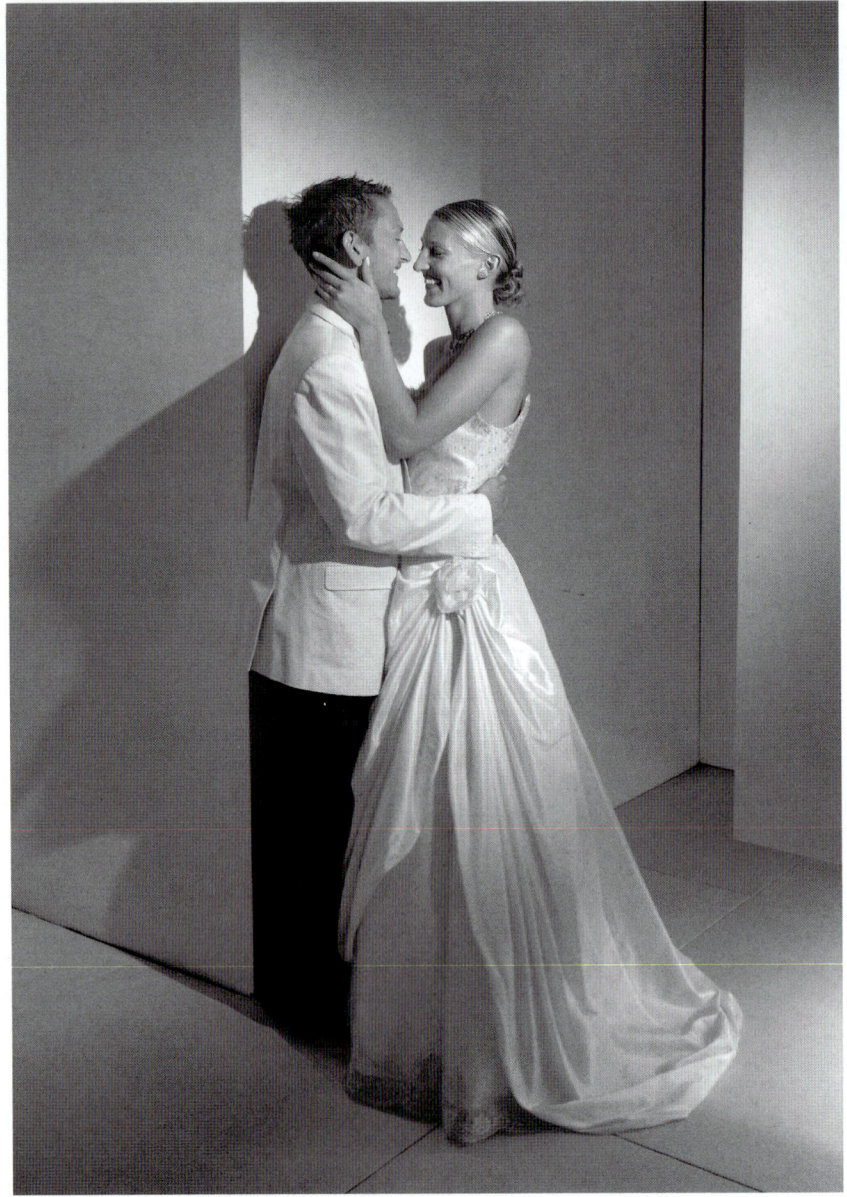

FIG. 21   ISO 400 f/4 at 1/60th

These images remind me of a love scene from a classic movie – planes of continuous tone cut with slashes of light. As usual I shoot the wide angles while Julie goes in for the closeups. Create the moment once and capture it twice on different lenses from different angles.

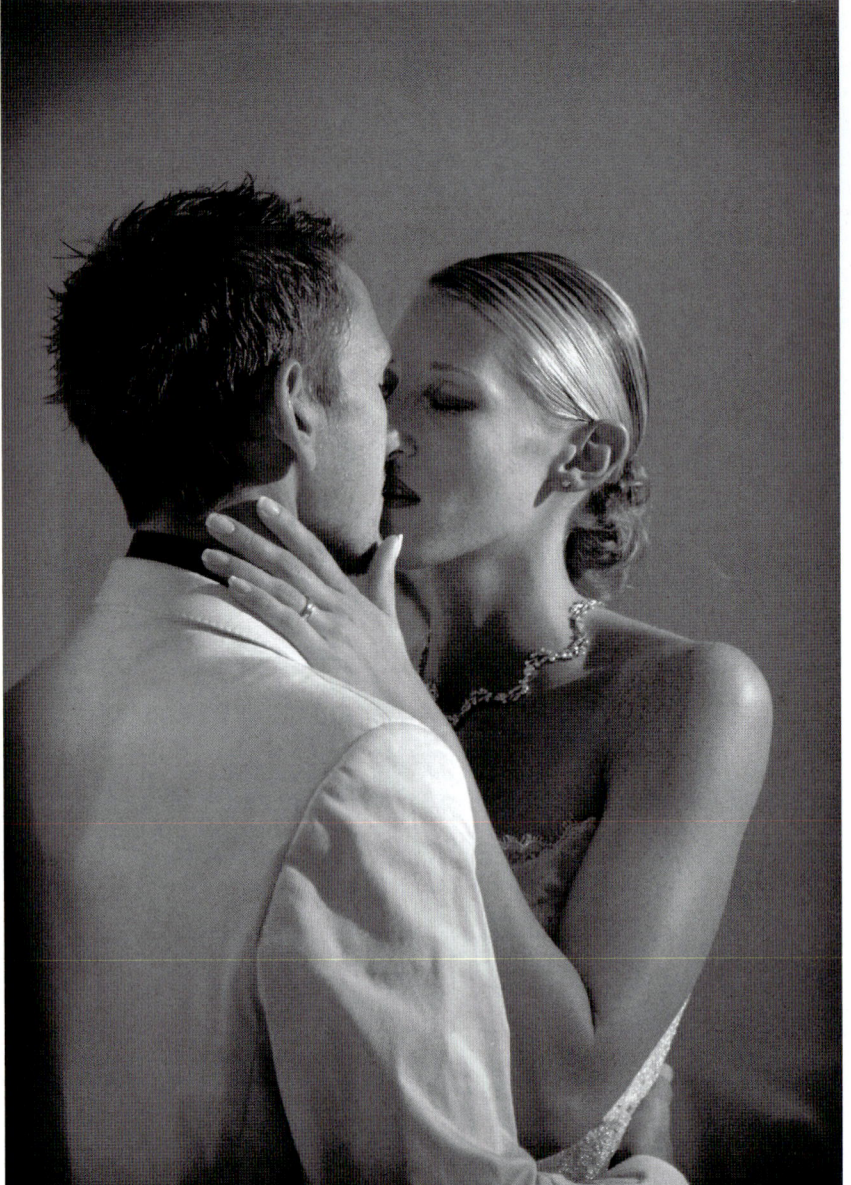

FIG. 22   ISO 800 f/4 at 1/125th

Julie's closeup of tenderness and beauty ends the hotel lobby shoot. Images like this have a very high value to the client, not just for the present but for generations to come. Their children and grandchildren will hold this image in high regard as it shows true passion.

FIG. 23   ISO 400 f/4 at 1/60th

I shot this image of the bride using a splash of flash as the groom entered the room. The moment when their eyes met was the one not to miss.

bottom

FIG. 24   ISO 800 f/4 at 1/8th

I wanted to use only available light for this shot but I had to hold my breath! I use only a monopod to keep my camera steady, so I've needed a lot of practice to be able to get useable shots at this shutter speed. No additional light was needed, just a balanced, symmetrical composition.

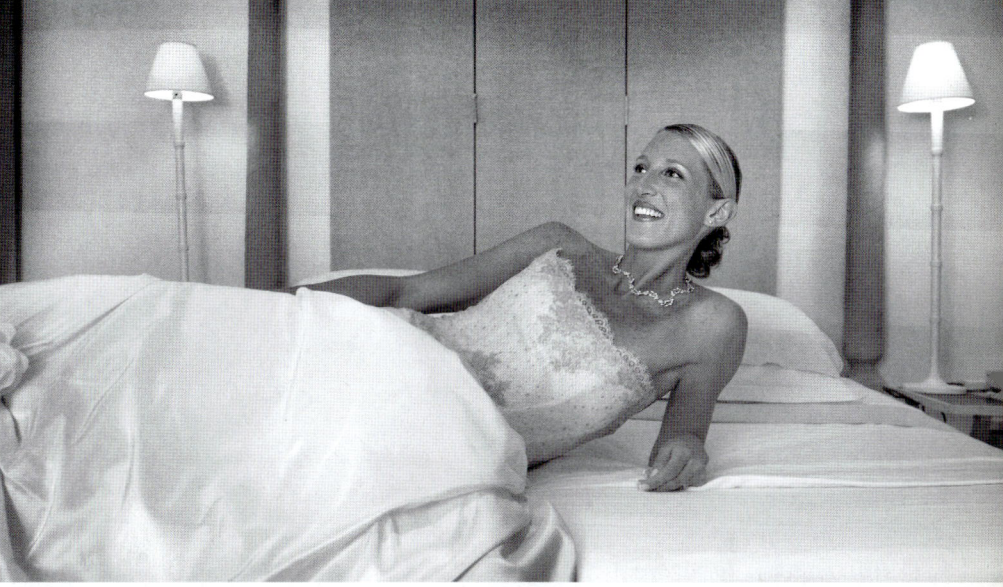

and changing marketplace. Some photographers will be strong advocates of a classic wedding album aiming to get the investment of the more traditional clients. Other photographers will offer the latest products and gadgets to attract the trendy market. These will include slideshows for mobile phones, digital photo frames, prints on textiles, and multimedia presentations. The weak photographers will resist change with a negative attitude or go with the flow undirected.

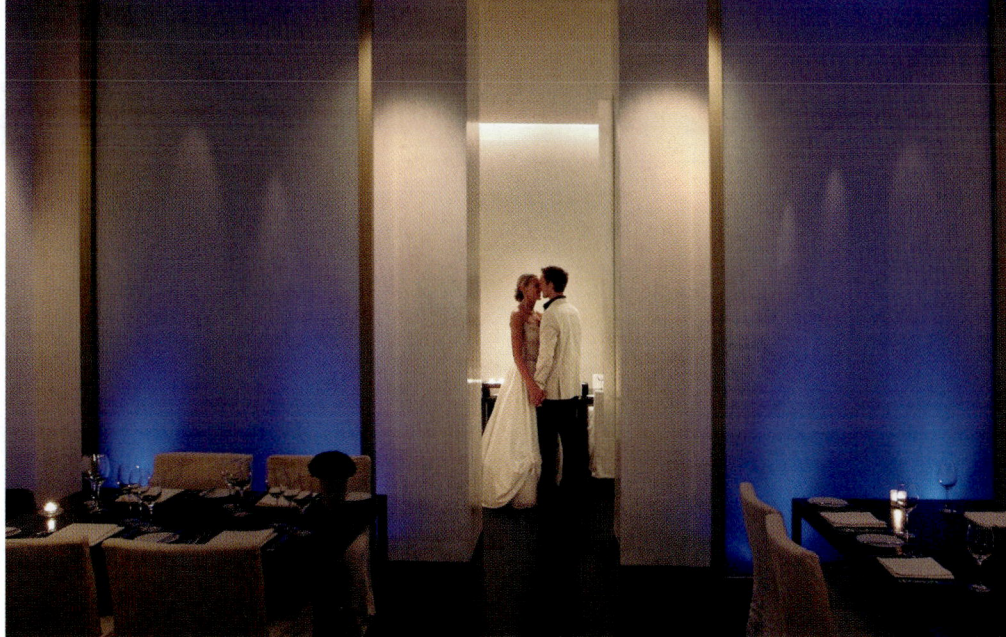

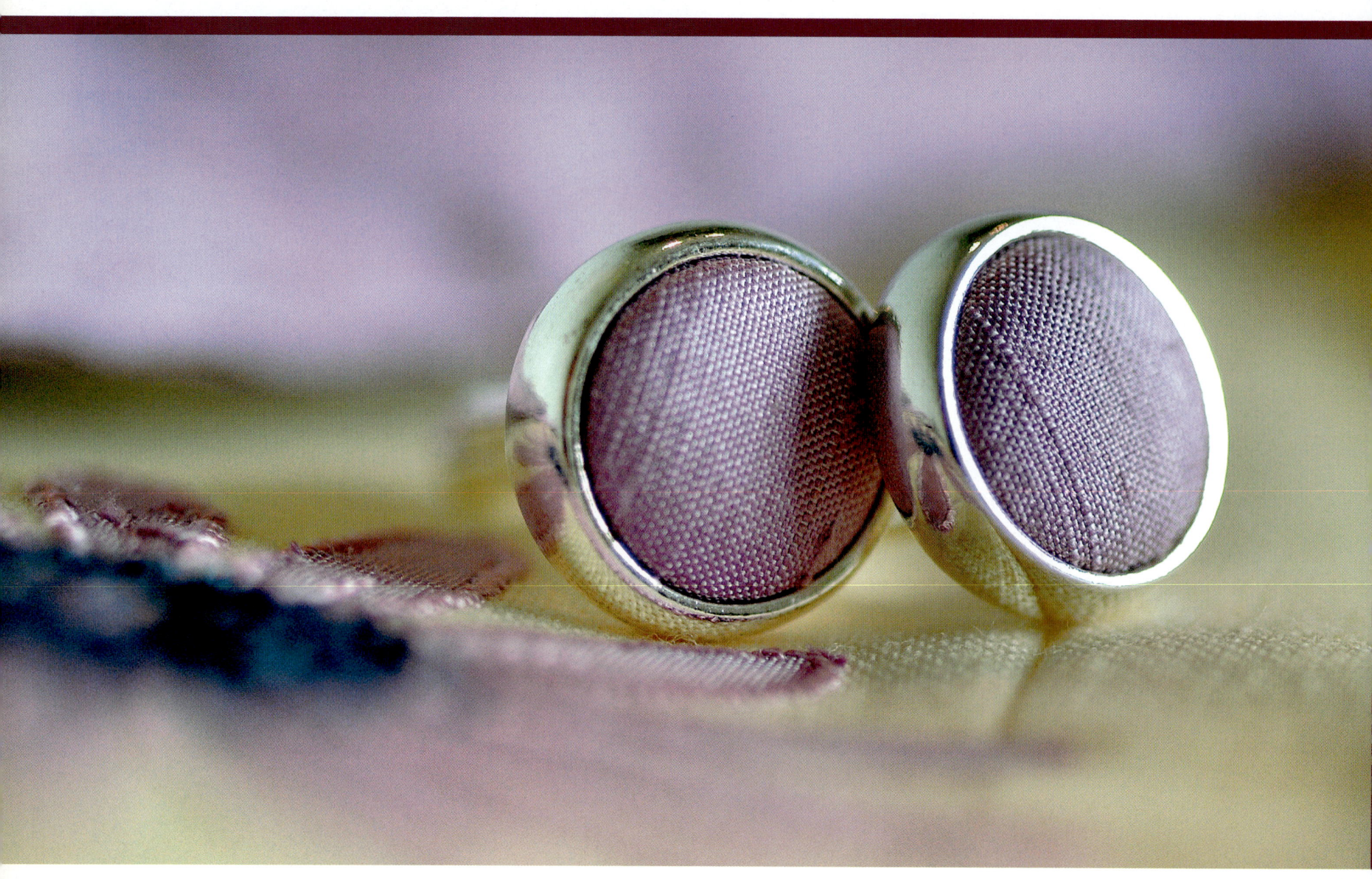

2
Developing a Style

Why should you need a distinct and coherent style? Because your work and the way it is presented needs to be recognizable – it needs to stand out from the work of other photographers. That's the key to generating continuing demand for your work.

Magnum photographer Martin Parr once told me 'an album of pictures should be a complete body of work that is eloquent and self-supporting.' He's right of course, and the best work will also stand the test of time. In fact, this longevity is vital to wedding photography. So my advice is to avoid gimmicks like spot color, pictures taken on angles, extreme color, cross-processing, or excessive diffusion. In a few years' time these will look very dated and will ruin what might have been a great album.

Let me give you an actual example. Back in the 1970s, it became fashionable to heavily vignette prints and even superimpose the bride and groom in a wineglass. Those collections of prints have low value and integrity today. Compare them with good photo journalistic photography of the 1970s and you will see that work that is less gimmicky has vastly increased in value. A bride and groom invest in wedding photography not just for the present but also to share with their children and grandchildren for many years to come. So stick to good photographic principles, present your pictures well, and your work will be worth investing in.

opposite

Fig. 1   ISO 400 f2.8 at 1/60th

This closeup study of cufflinks was shot wide open at an aperture of f/2.8 on a 105-mm macro lens. Food photographers had set this trend of shallow depth of field in the late 1990s and this was my take on their style.

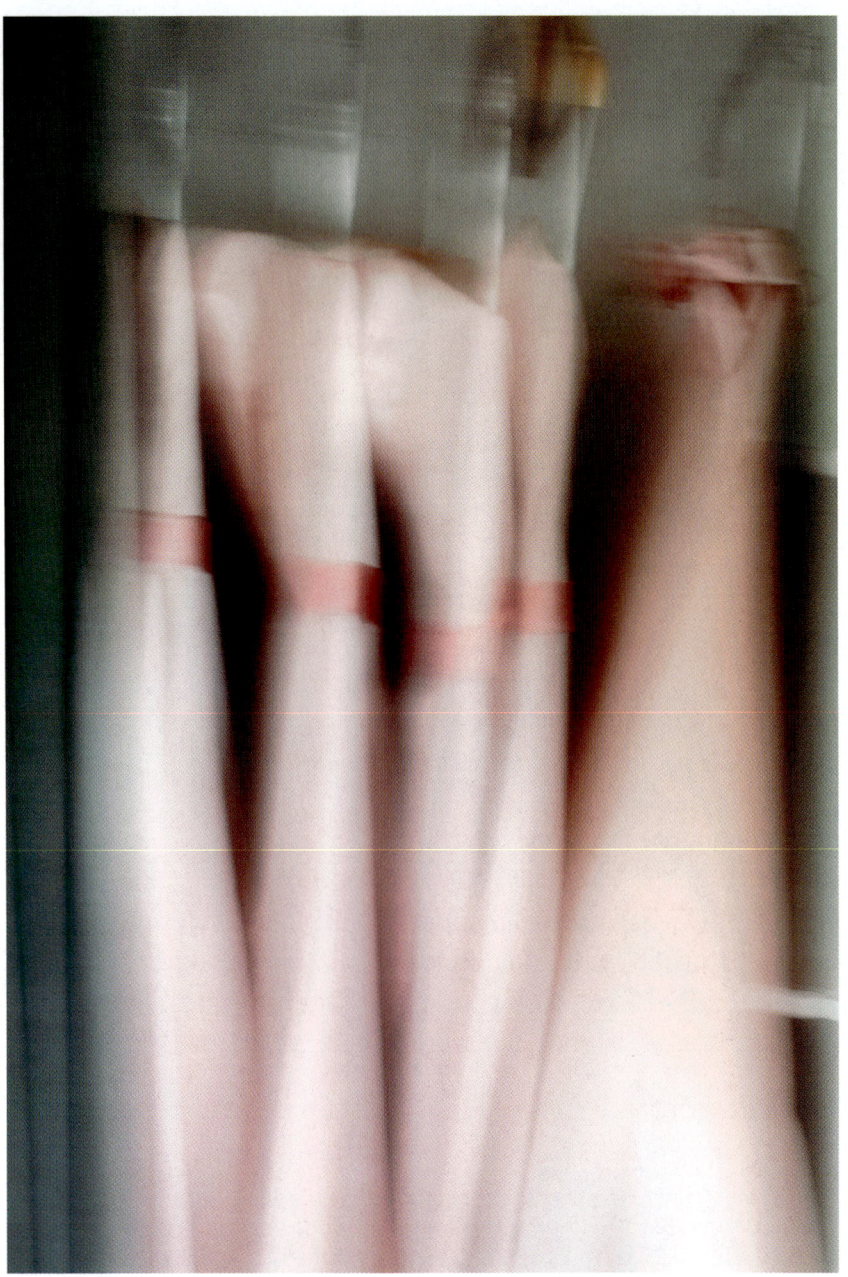

Fig. 2   ISO 100 f/4 at 1/8th

Deliberate panning of the camera while using a slow shutter speed can make a great shot from humble beginnings.

I was told some years ago that the best photographers *steal ideas* and adapt them while the worst photographers simply *copy* the work of others. By all means be inspired by the work of other photographers but the sooner you develop your own 'look' the sooner you will command high enough fees to make a decent living. I regularly study photographs and paintings to find out how they work – what makes an image great. I have learnt to read a picture and to break it down into its core elements. This deconstruction helps me to develop my craft skills and helps me to see potentially great images unfolding in front of me. I get my inspiration from the main fashion-based women's magazines, the editorial photography in the weekend color supplements, good fashion catalogues, old books on photography from the 1930s to the 1970s, and the great master painters.

When Julie and I started photographing weddings we used shooting techniques that I had been taught in my previous

FIG. 3   ISO 200 f/5.6 at 1/10th

I used a slow shutter speed to get some movement into this picture of bridesmaids entering a church.

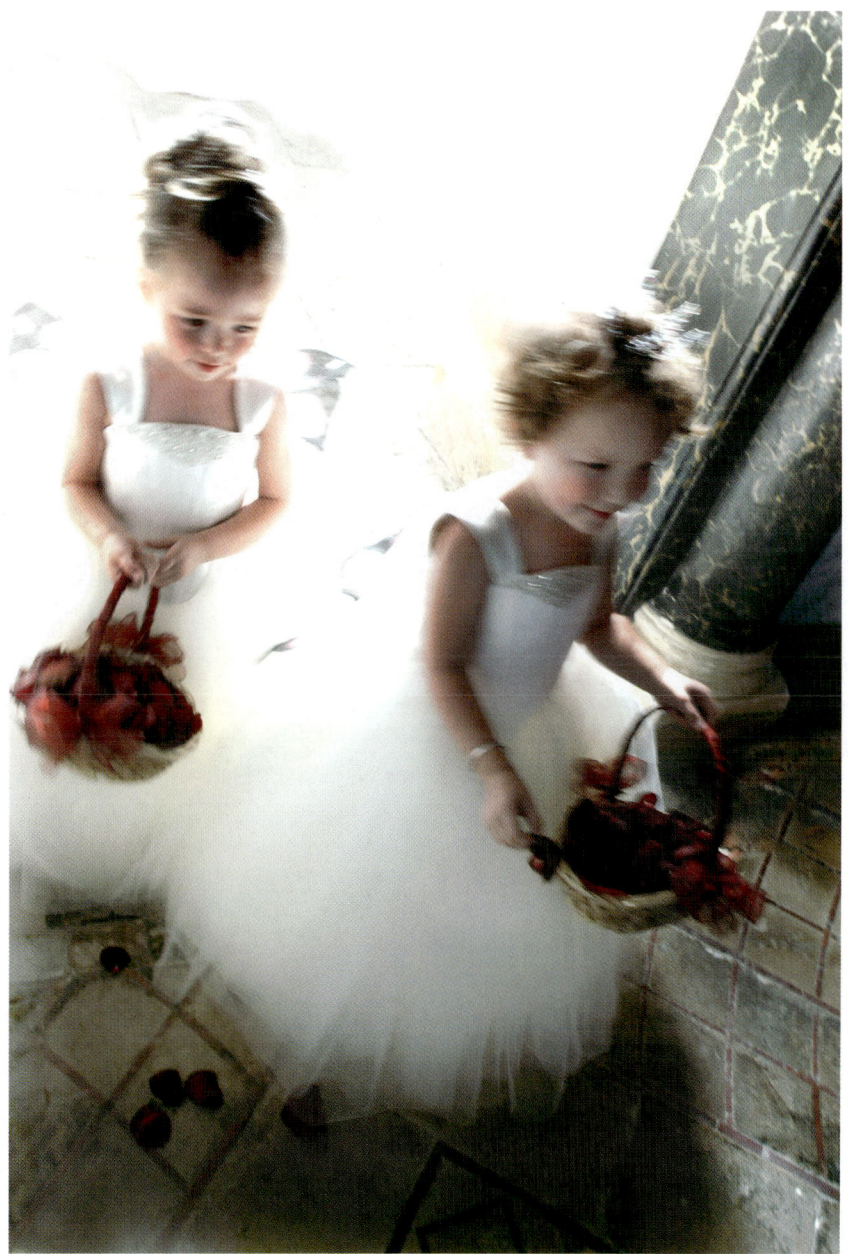

career at the BBC. When shooting our first 200 or so weddings we left our cameras set at f/4 and shot continuously at that aperture. This was how I shot dramas for television. Over a period of 10 days or so (the time it takes to shoot a 50-minute episode), we would shoot every frame at the same aperture. This gave the finished edited show a continuity of look. It also helped to isolate the principal points of interest in each shot using differential focus. Treating our weddings the same way allows our wedding albums to show a consistent approach and style throughout. In other words, the pictures taken at the beginning of the day are in harmony with those taken at the end of the day and so on.

Shooting every frame at f/4 was just the start. We also endeavored never to include the sky unless it was dramatic; this also gave our albums a different look. To further restrict and focus our style, I decided to have just two lenses in my kit, a 17

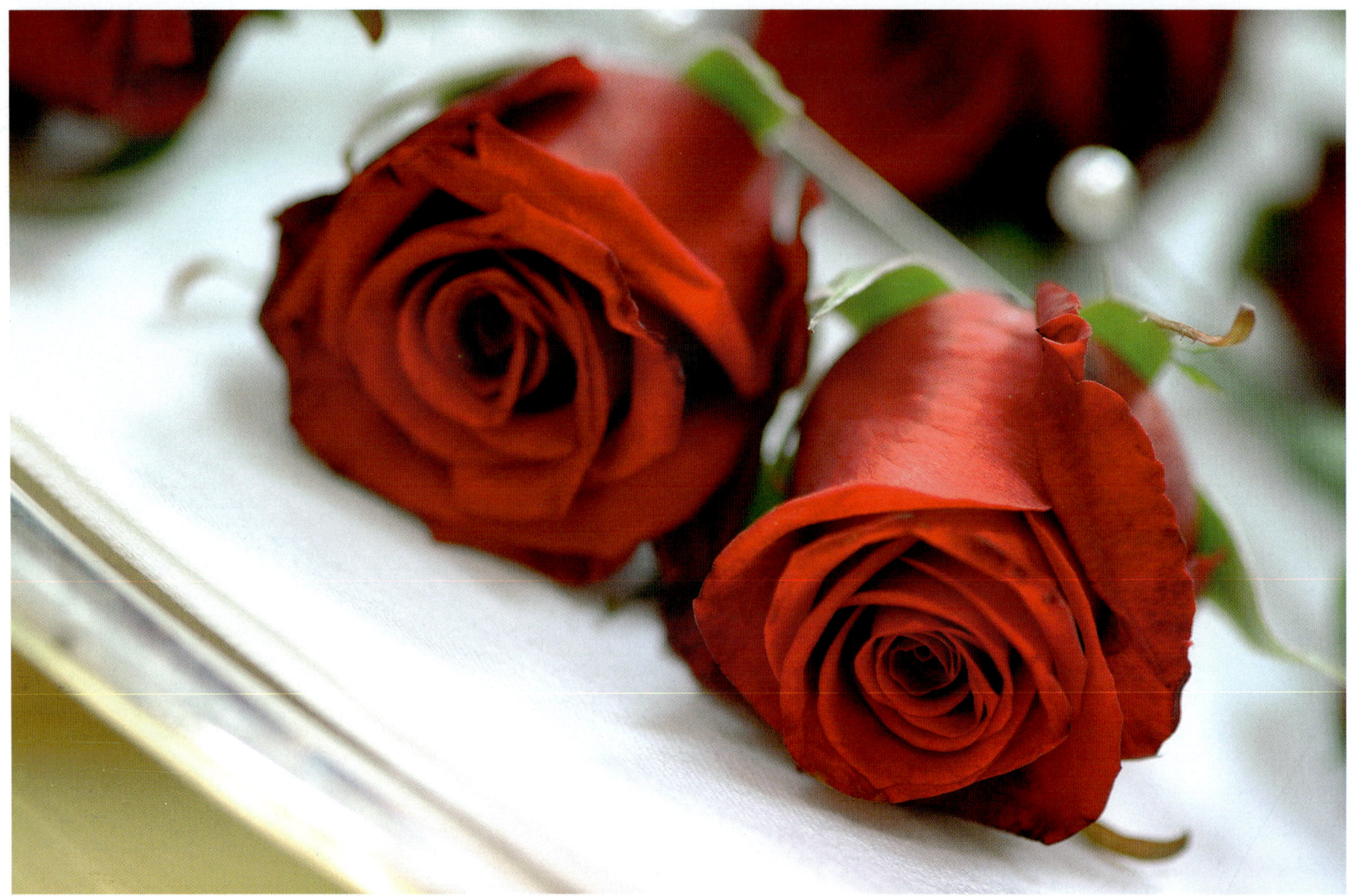

FIG. 4   ISO 400 f/2.8 at 1/100th

By 2001, fashion photographers and some editorial photographers had begun tilting shots to add an extra dynamic quality. This style soon became overused and we had dropped all tilted shots by 2002. This picture combines a shallow depth of field with a tilt.

Backlit flowers became a look we championed from the early days of digital imaging. Using the camera screen as an exposure guide Julie was able to accurately judge the amount of exposure increase that was necessary to record the white lilies, white feathers, and the Venetian blind in this picture.

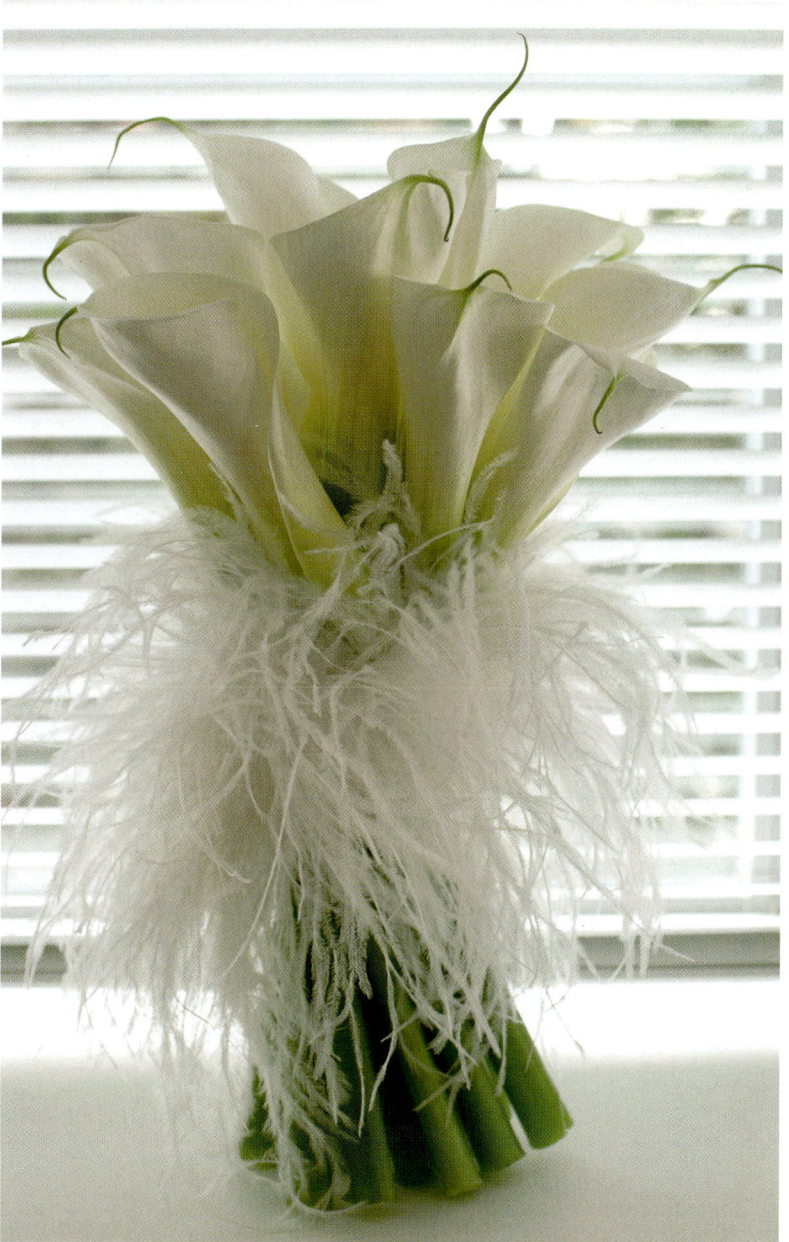

to 35 and an 80 to 200 mm f/2.8. As I used no lenses *between* 35 and 80 mm, I was forced to shoot either tight or wide. These top-shelf professional lenses designed for use at wide open apertures produce phenomenal sharpness at just one stop down at f/4. Amateur series lenses that start at f/4 or f/5.6 don't reach their optimum performance until f/8 or so and by then focus subject distinction is lost.

Here's another storytelling trick I learned at the BBC. Establish the location in a wide shot, then go in tight for the closeups and details. Shoot each scene in wide and tight shots from forward and reverse angles. Scene setting and storytelling were always shot with the wide lens whereas beauty and emotion were shot in closeup on the tight lens. This made putting albums together a delight, just like editing a movie.

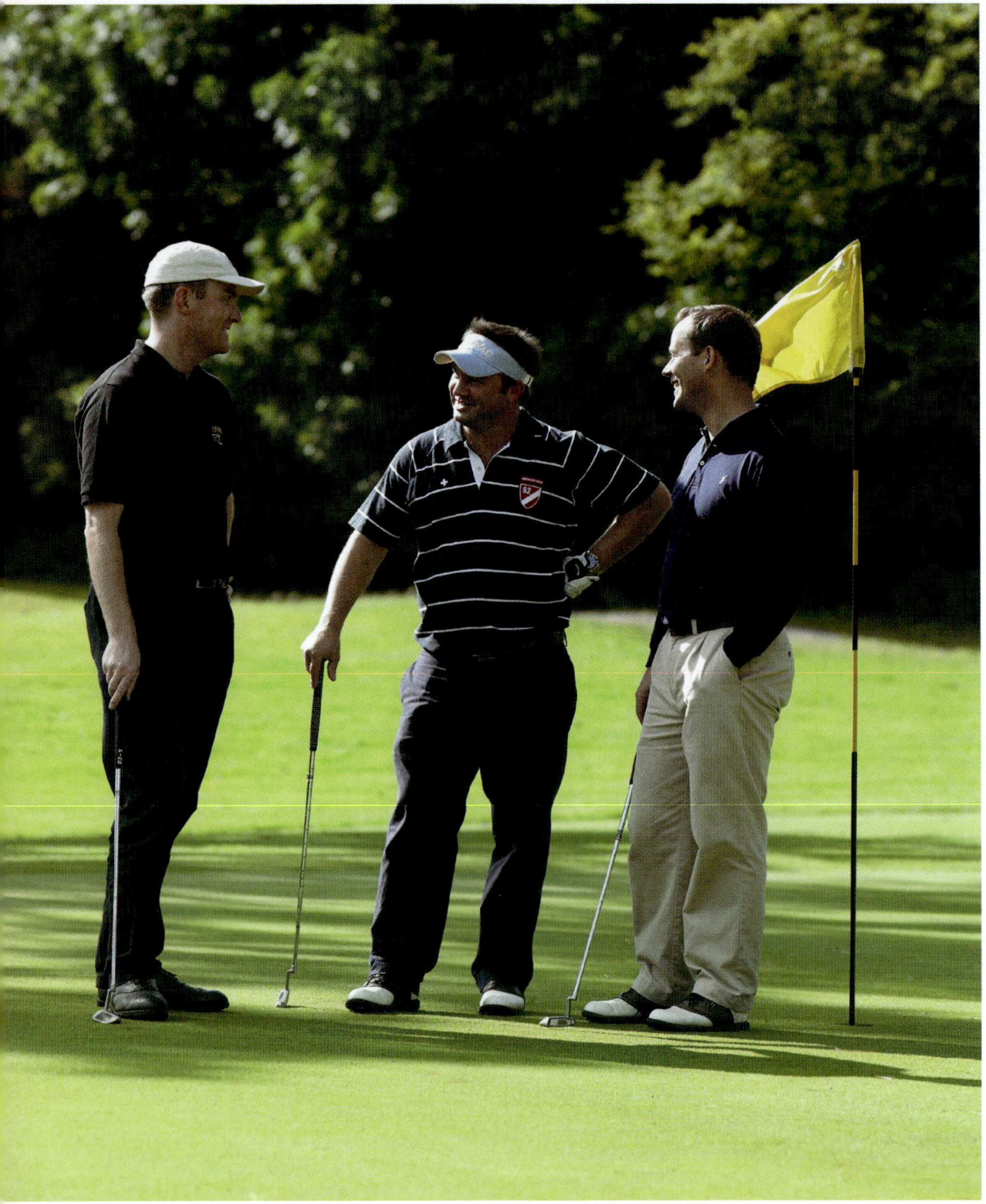

These two pictures of the same golfers taken just a few minutes apart on a wedding morning show how much latitude there is to develop a style.

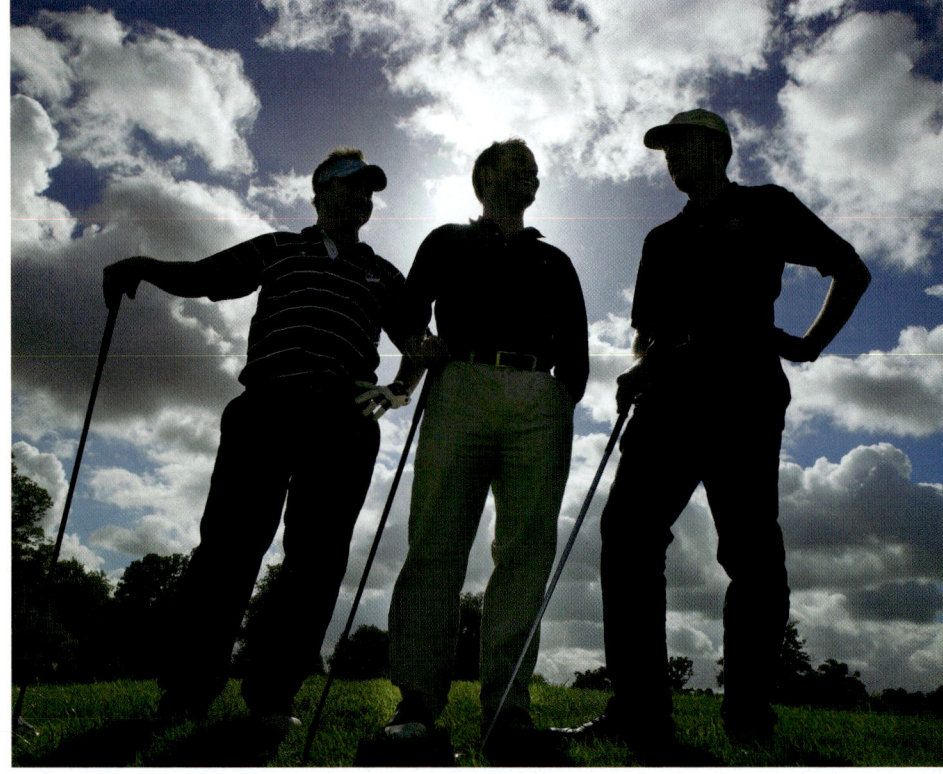

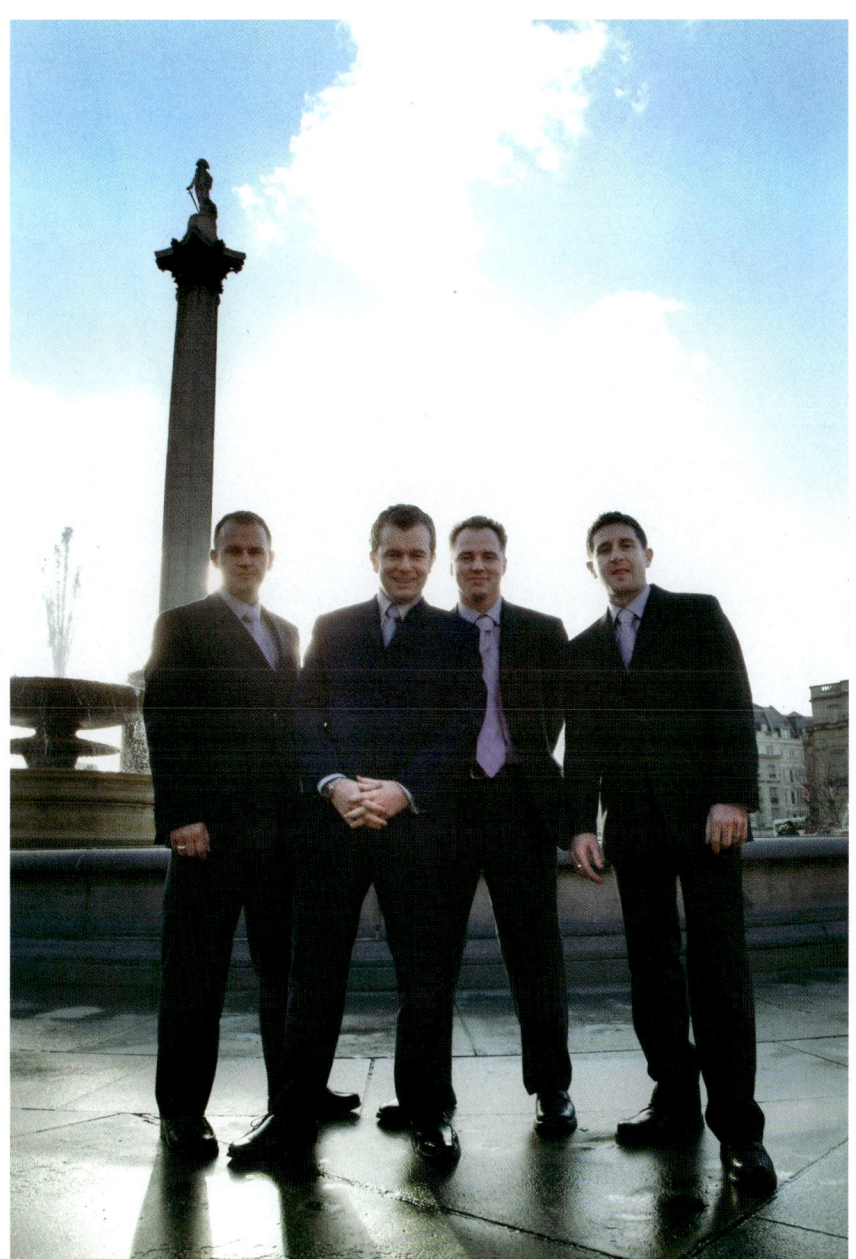

These two pictures include massive monuments in the background and were shot into the sun. By 2001, we had started to exclude the sky from our pictures unless there was a good reason to include it.

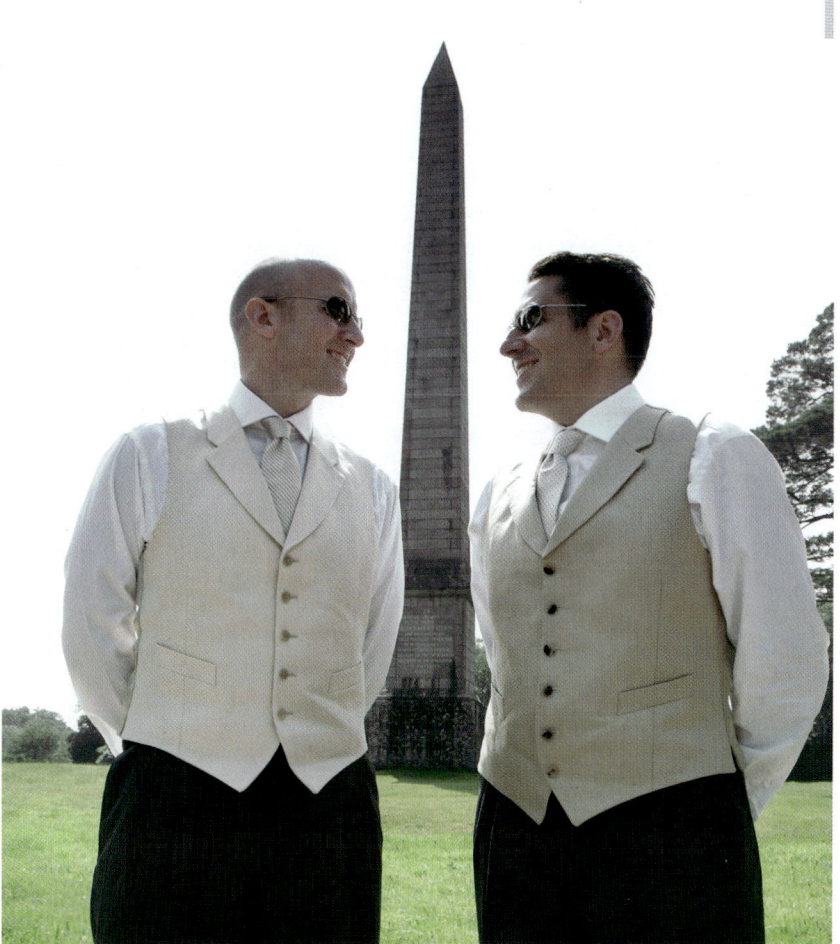

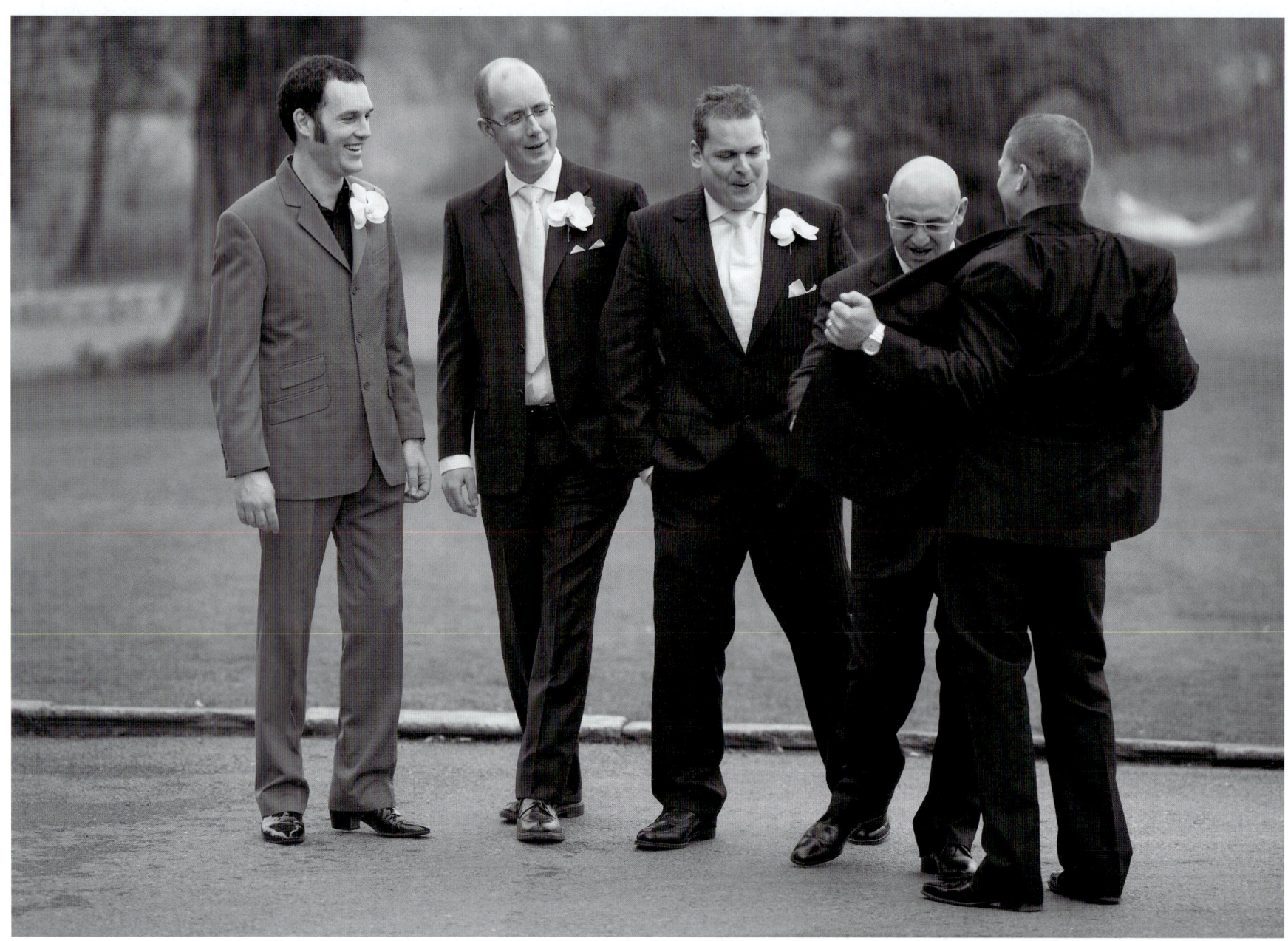

opposite

Fɪɢ. 10   ISO 400 f/4 at 1/250th

I asked the usher on the right to go up to join the other guys and give them a flash of his purple suit lining. I was ready to capture the reaction with my 210-mm lens. Distant shots like this on a long lens create a very different look to the more obvious wide angle coverage from close in.

TIP: BE ADVENTUROUS – Allow your picture shooting style to evolve continually and keep looking for new ways to develop it. Occasionally you will find that the emergence of a new technology enables you to create a new look that you can call your own – for a while. Digital shooting with instant feedback enabled Julie and I to shoot using extremes of exposure compensation up to − or + five stops. We started to shoot in risky light without fear. On film it might be considered foolhardy to attempt such dramatic looks on a client's wedding day without the time for a Polaroid test.

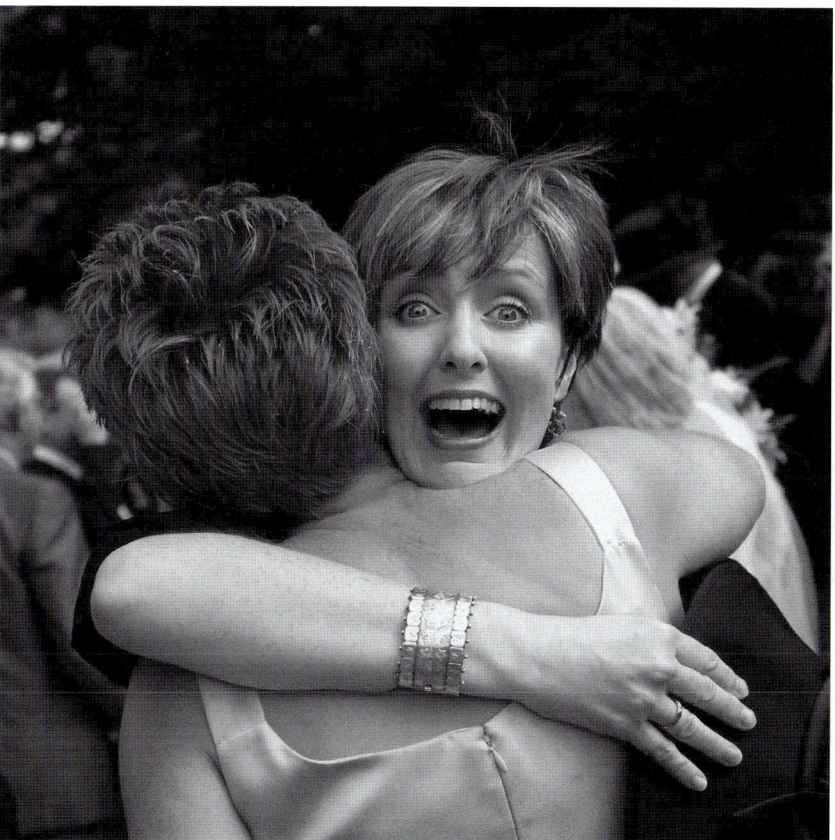

Fɪɢ. 11   ISO 200 f/4 at 1/750th

Moments like this happen all the time at weddings. The trick to capturing these situations is to be in the right place at the right time with the right lens and the right exposure set on your camera. Photojournalists stay prepared and watch situations like this develop. I had made my presence known here already and the reaction on the girl's face was aimed at the camera.

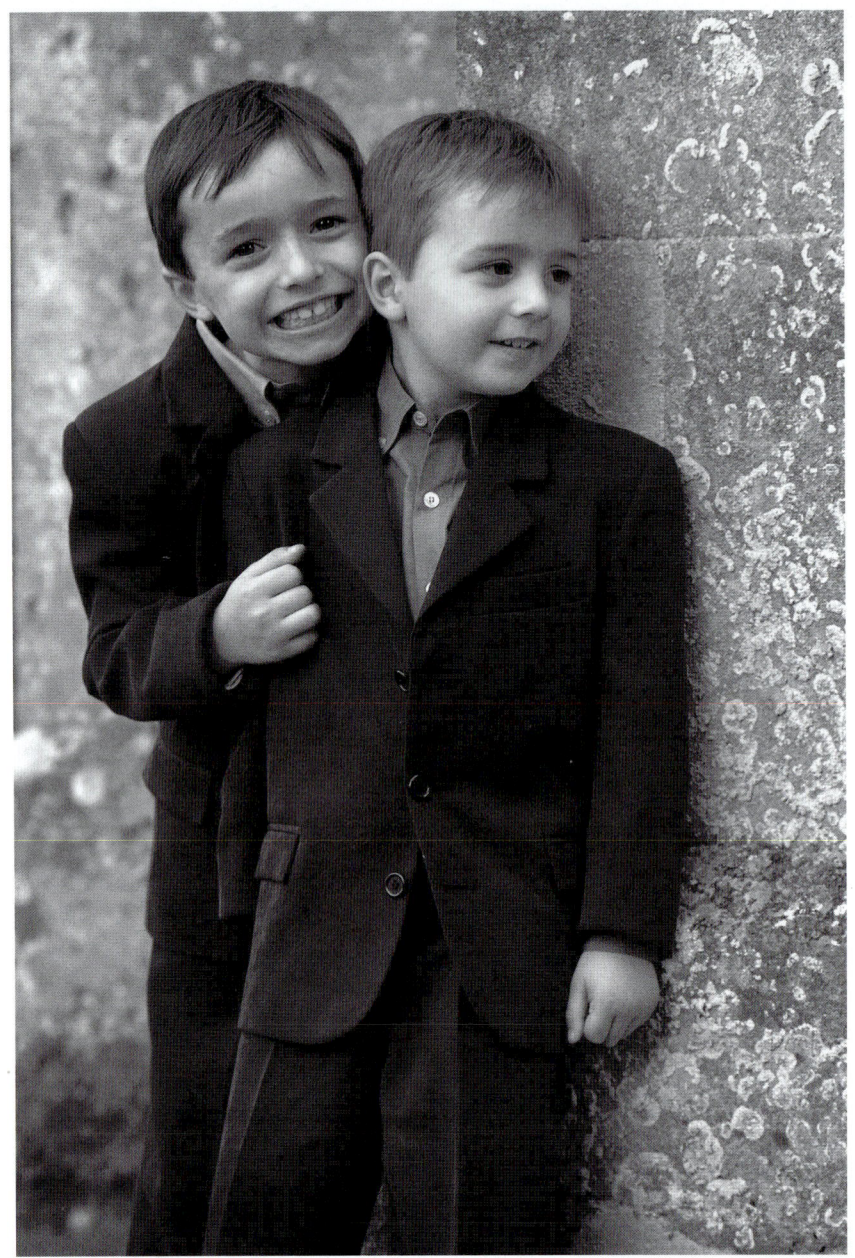
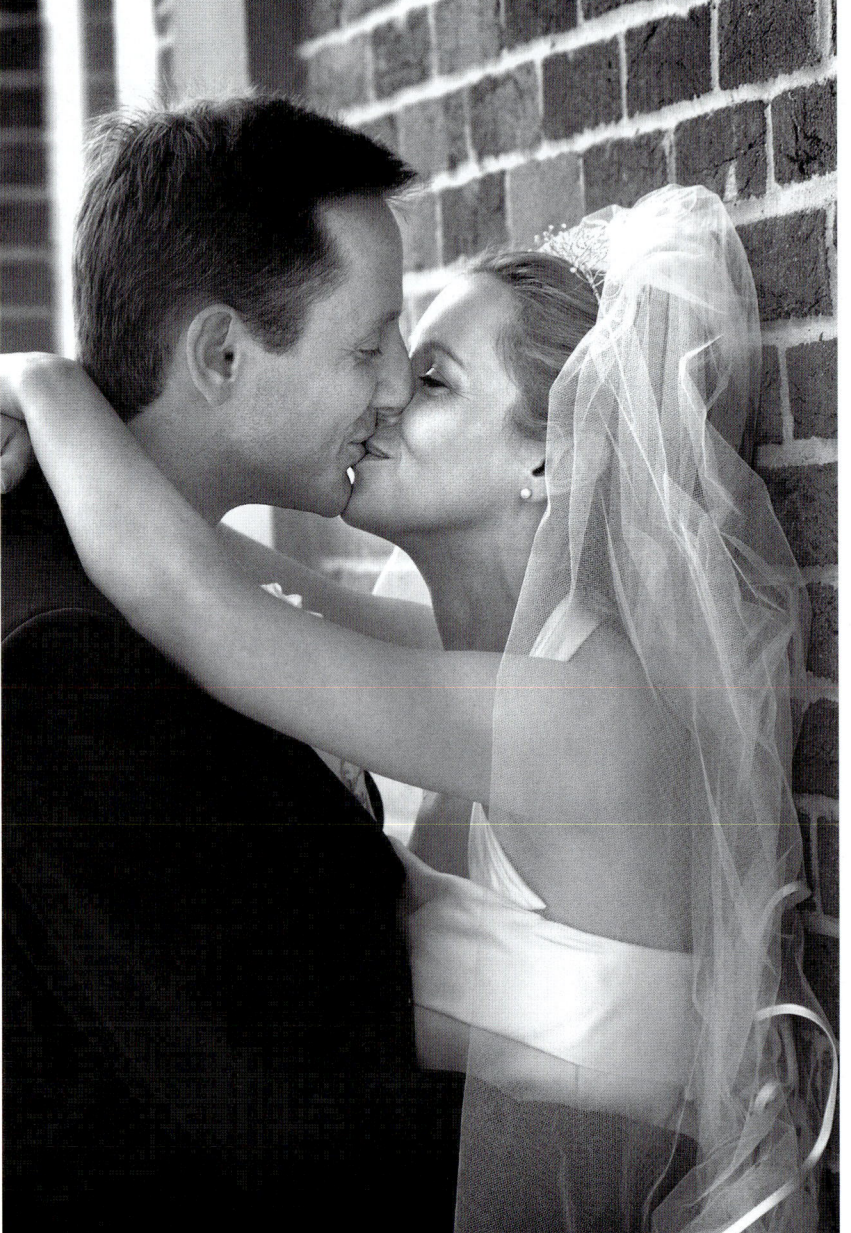

Chapter Two: Developing a Style

FIGS 12 & 13   ISO 400 f/4 at 1/300th and ISO 400 f/4 at 1/800th

Think in sequences and bring elements of humor into your work. Storytelling becomes more fun when you can think on your feet and put together frames like these.

BASIC EQUIPMENT

When choosing (and using) your equipment, keep in mind three things:

- the photographer sees the picture
- the lens makes the image
- the camera records it.

The style of the images you want to create will determine the equipment you need to do the job properly. Don't let the kit you already own dictate your style. In most places, you can rent the camera bodies or lenses you need for a particular job. This is especially useful if you are starting out.

Always remember that the greatest differentiation between a good photographer and a poor one is not his or her equipment, it's the ability to see a picture. No amount of equipment will make this process easier, though in my case, I have learnt to cheat a bit. My constant use of prime lenses (wide or tight) has trained me to 'see' a scene in a more specific way. I don't mean when I'm looking through the camera, I mean when looking directly at the scene. It's like having horse blinkers on (though I'm also aware of peripheral vision). Film directors use their hands at arm's length to 'frame' the scene they have in front of them. As a photographer I can 'see' the world through my Hasselblad 35 mm lens or my 210 mm quite clearly without having the camera to hand. My digital medium format kit also gives me thinking time between frames. I use this to fine-tune my composition.

The lens that produces the image is the one bit of kit that can separate the professional photographer from the amateur. Amateurs will never justify the vastly increased price of faster

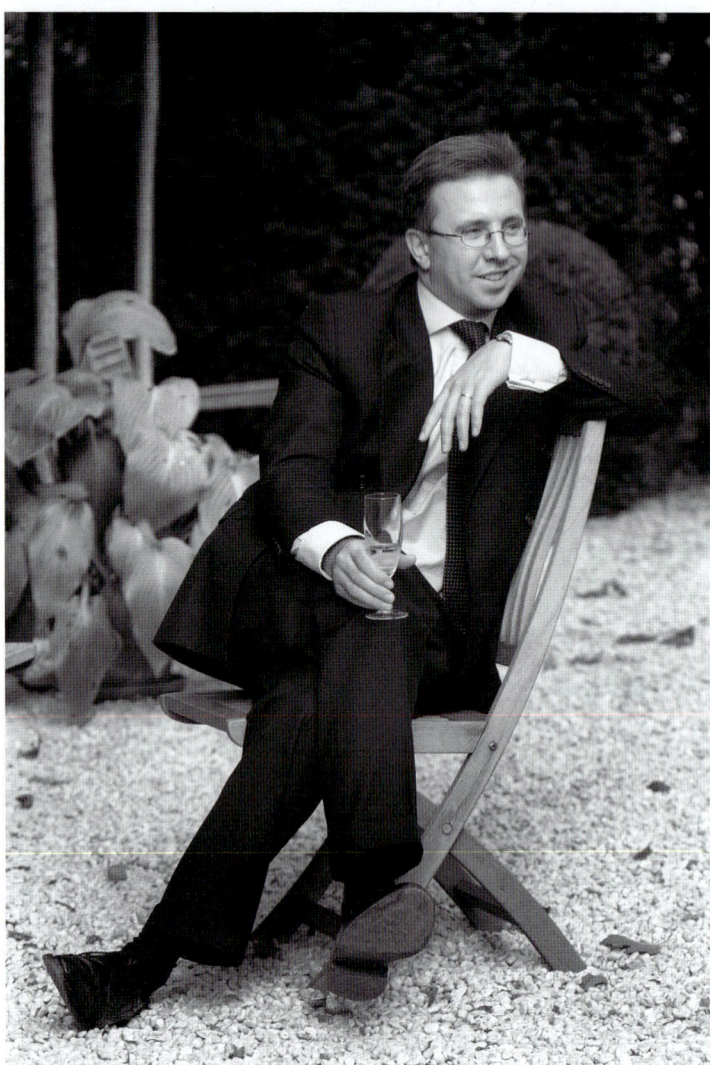

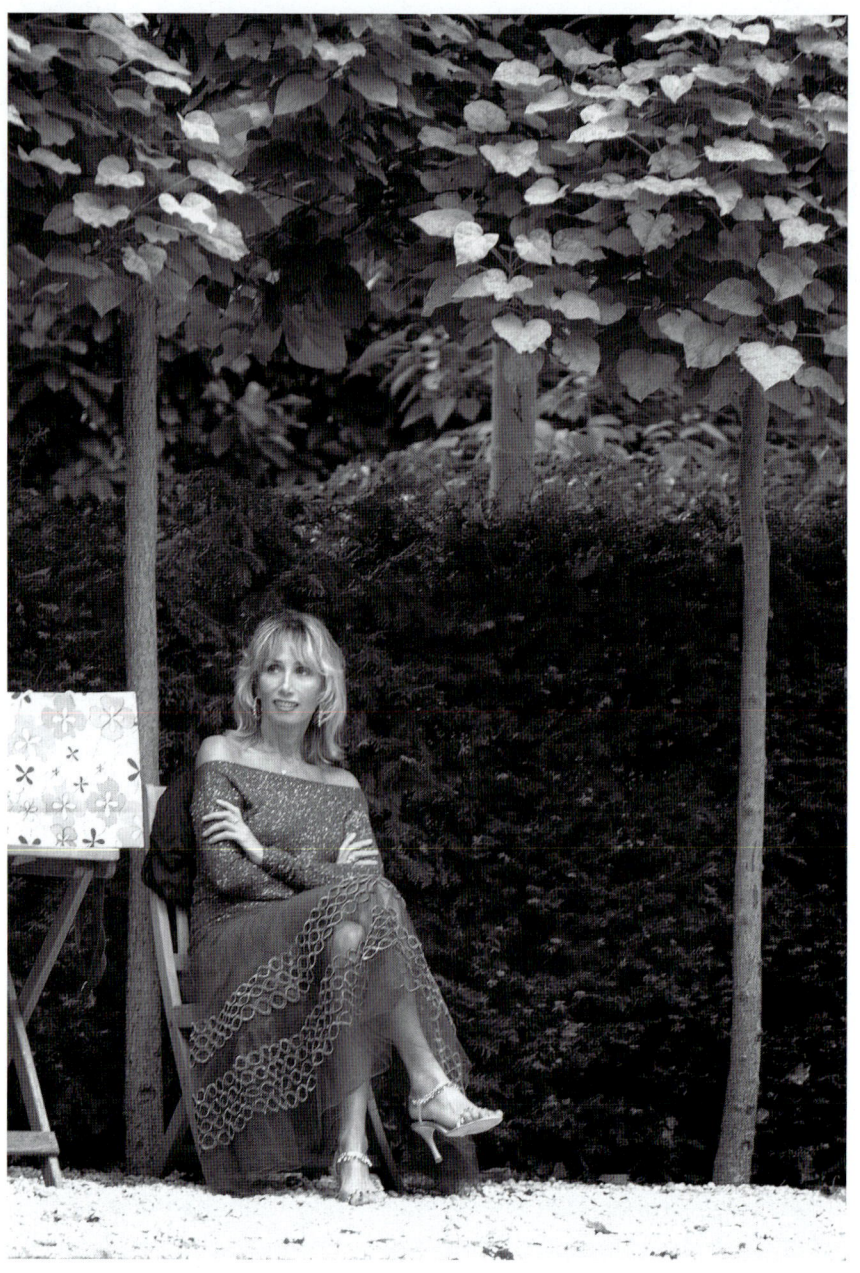

Figs 14 & 15 ISO 320 f/4 at 1/200th and ISO 320 f/4 at 1/70th

Watch the guests at a wedding and look for echoes in behavior. I could have improved this pairing by using a longer lens and being further away when I took the picture of the man. I had plenty of time to retake the shot, as he doesn't look as though he was going anywhere. The composition of the picture of the girl is far stronger.

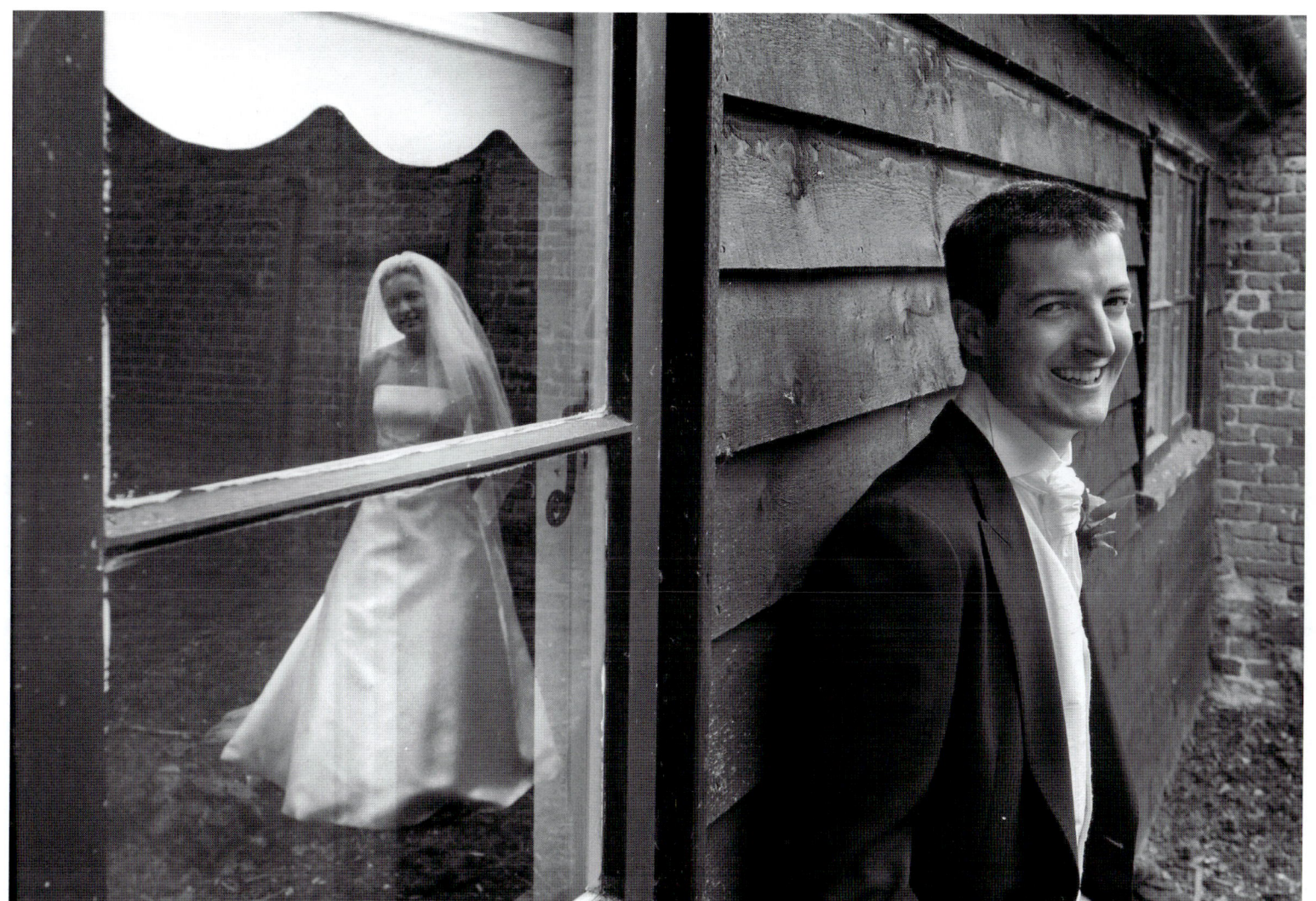

FIG. 16   ISO 200 f/5.6 at 1/125th

I like to be a bit clever with my work at times. Creating reflection shots like this is a fun part of the photo shoot. In this instance, I am the focus of attention and I asked the bride to look at my reflection in the window. Pictures like these rarely get set up and taken by guests on the wedding day.

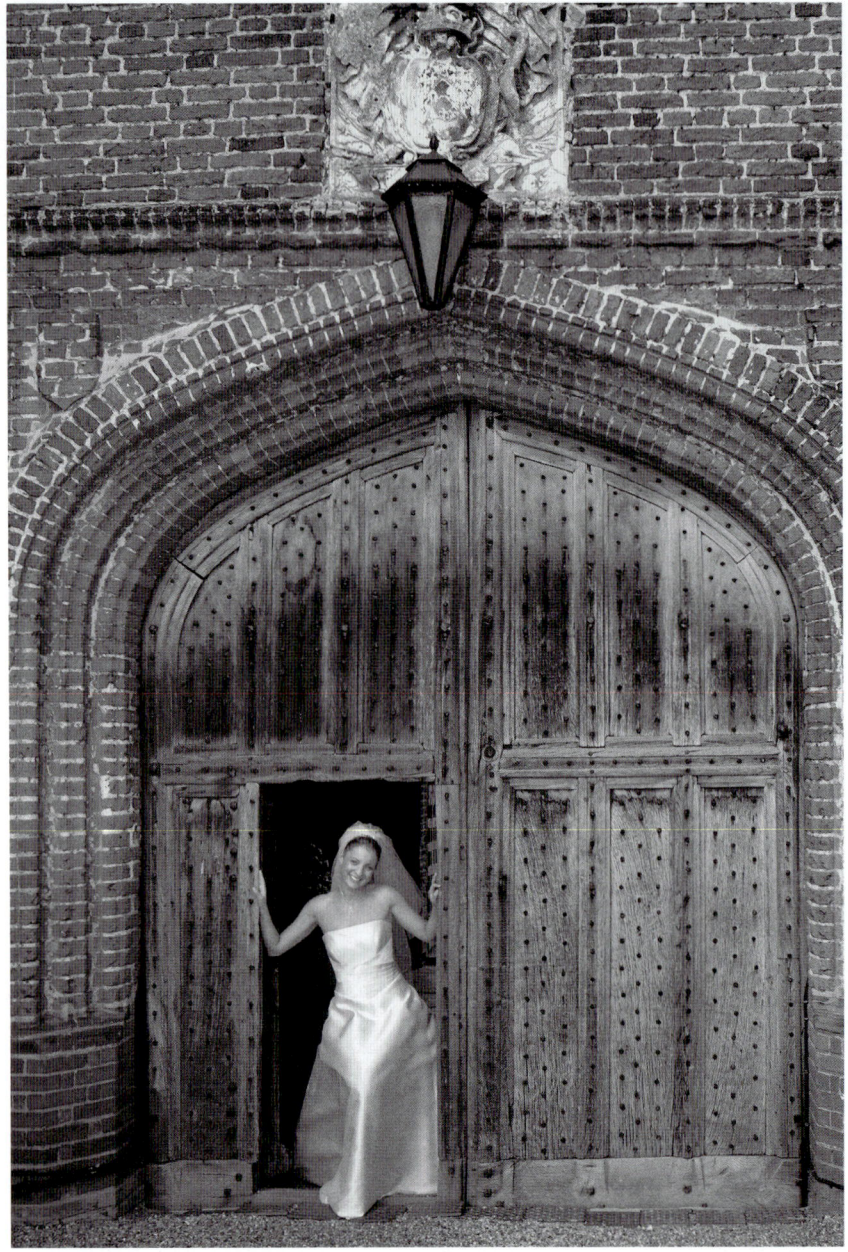

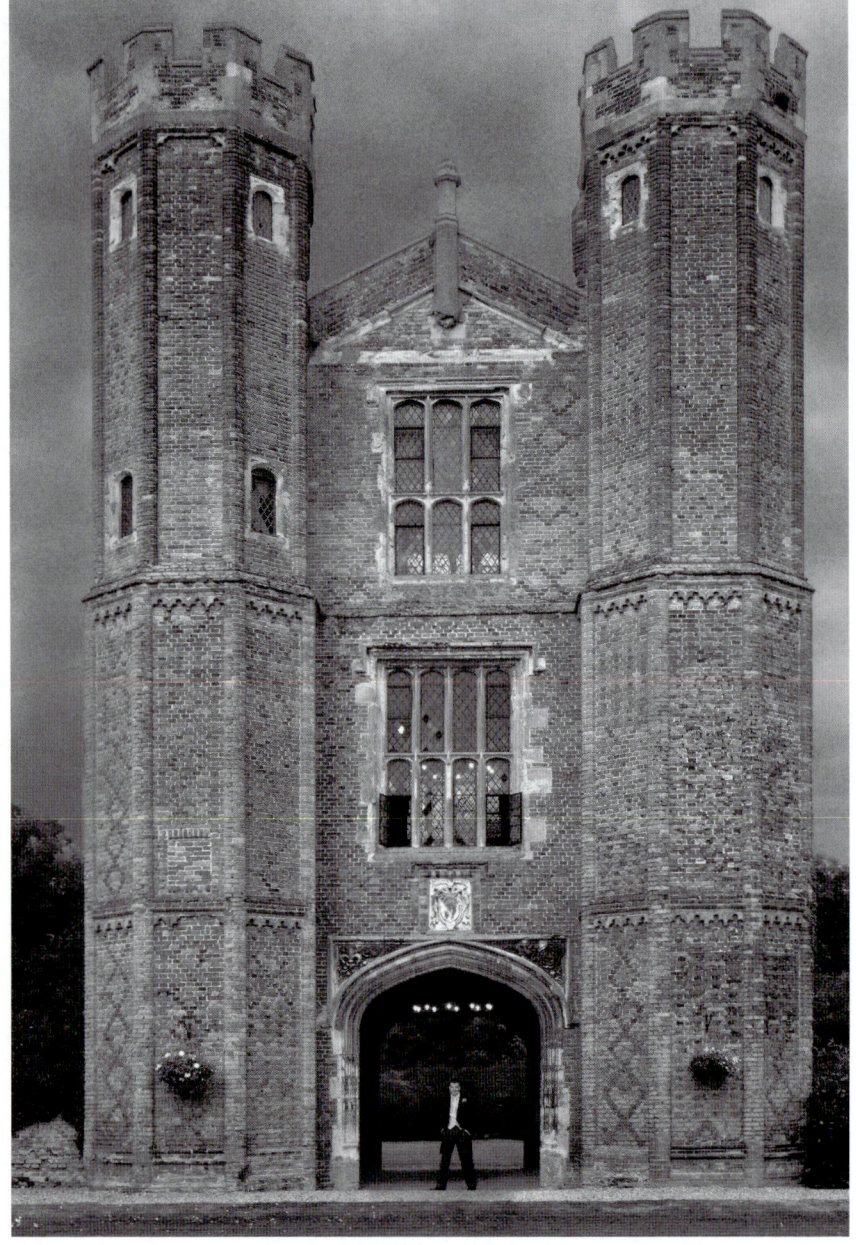

Chapter Two: Developing a Style

Figures in landscape pictures work well if you get the framing right. Both these pictures were shot square on to the buildings and have symmetry in the architecture.

lenses. I think 'f' numbers are one mystery in photography that will inadvertently help to keep the Pro–Am divide. 'Why pay more money for less f' I hear the amateurs cry.

So here's my advice: always buy the best glass there is. Great lenses stay great lenses for a very long time; so don't think twice about buying the best. Price and build quality are good indicators of performance.

What about camera bodies? There is now far less to choose between 'amateur' and 'professional' single-lens reflex (SLR) cameras. In fact, the digital revolution has brought a multitude

TIP: HOW LOW CAN YOU GO? If you want to be able to shoot in low light without having to illuminate the scene, then two key factors come into play: the maximum aperture of your lens and the slowest shutter speed that will allow you to produce acceptably sharp images. Vibration reduction (sometimes called 'image stabilization') systems in modern lenses allow the use of slower shutter speeds (up to three stops of advantage). But don't be fooled into thinking you can now shoot a ceremony in a church at 1/15th and get great images. Vibration reduction does not stop subject movement. In this instance, fast lenses rule. Many a top wedding photographer uses a 50 mm f/1.4 or even f/1.2 prime lens in a dark church.

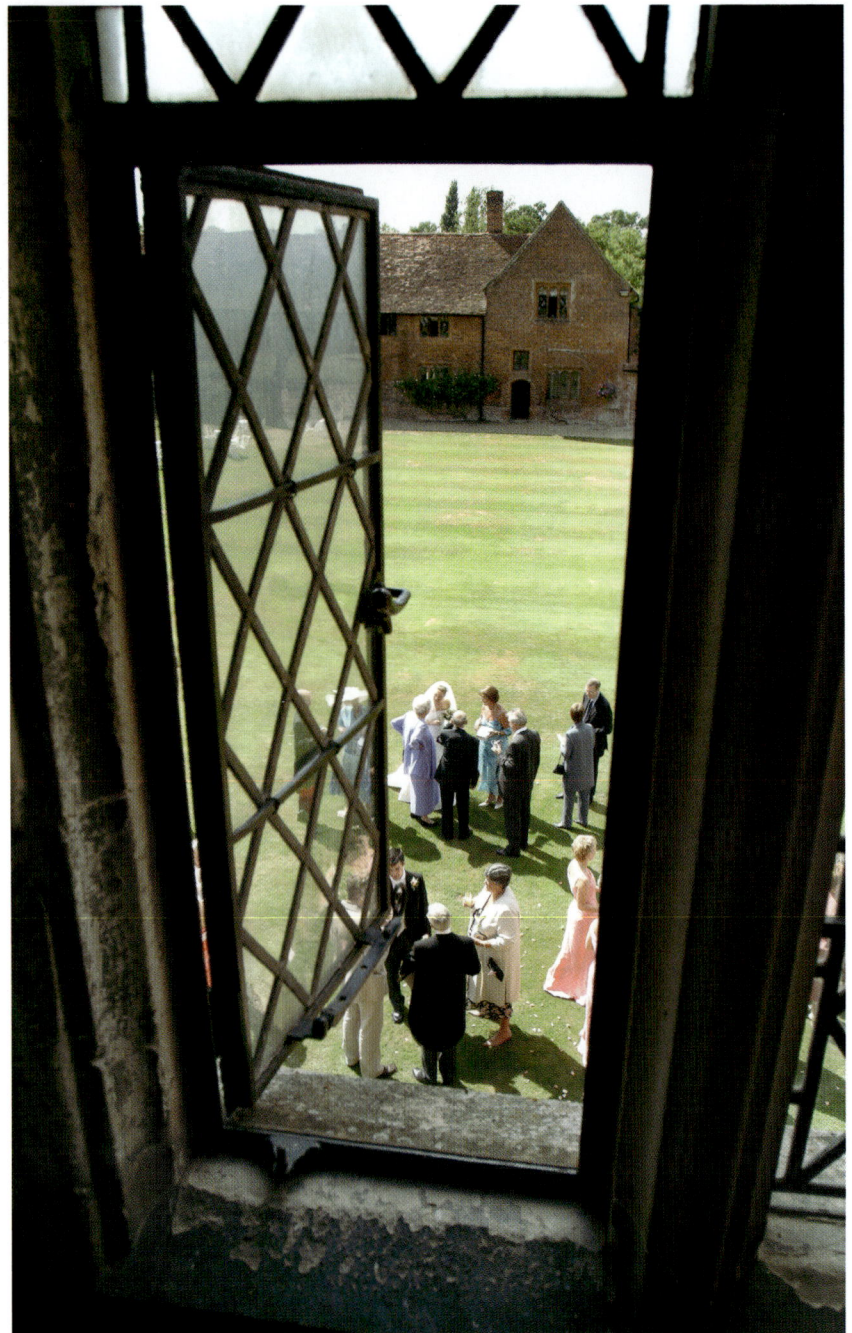

FIG. 19   ISO 200 f/6.7 at 1/180th

Shooting through a window tells more about the venue than just photographing the scene from the window. I carefully placed the distant building in the top of the window opening.

of decent SLRs to amateurs and professionals alike. It seems that all the current crop of digital SLRs have excellent handling and sensors. In fact, if you believe the equipment reviews, it is now seemingly impossible to buy a bad digital SLR from the main manufacturers! You can choose from across the range of cameras and as long as you have a good eye for a shot, good shooting technique, and of course, fine lenses, almost any camera will do. That's not to say that all cameras are equal, but Julie chose her last camera from the amateur range because it's nearly half the weight of the top spec body. It has the same sensor, the same screen, great metering, and accepts the same lenses. So, why do most professionals pay the extra for 'pro' camera bodies? Mostly because of build quality: pro cameras are made with more robust materials and

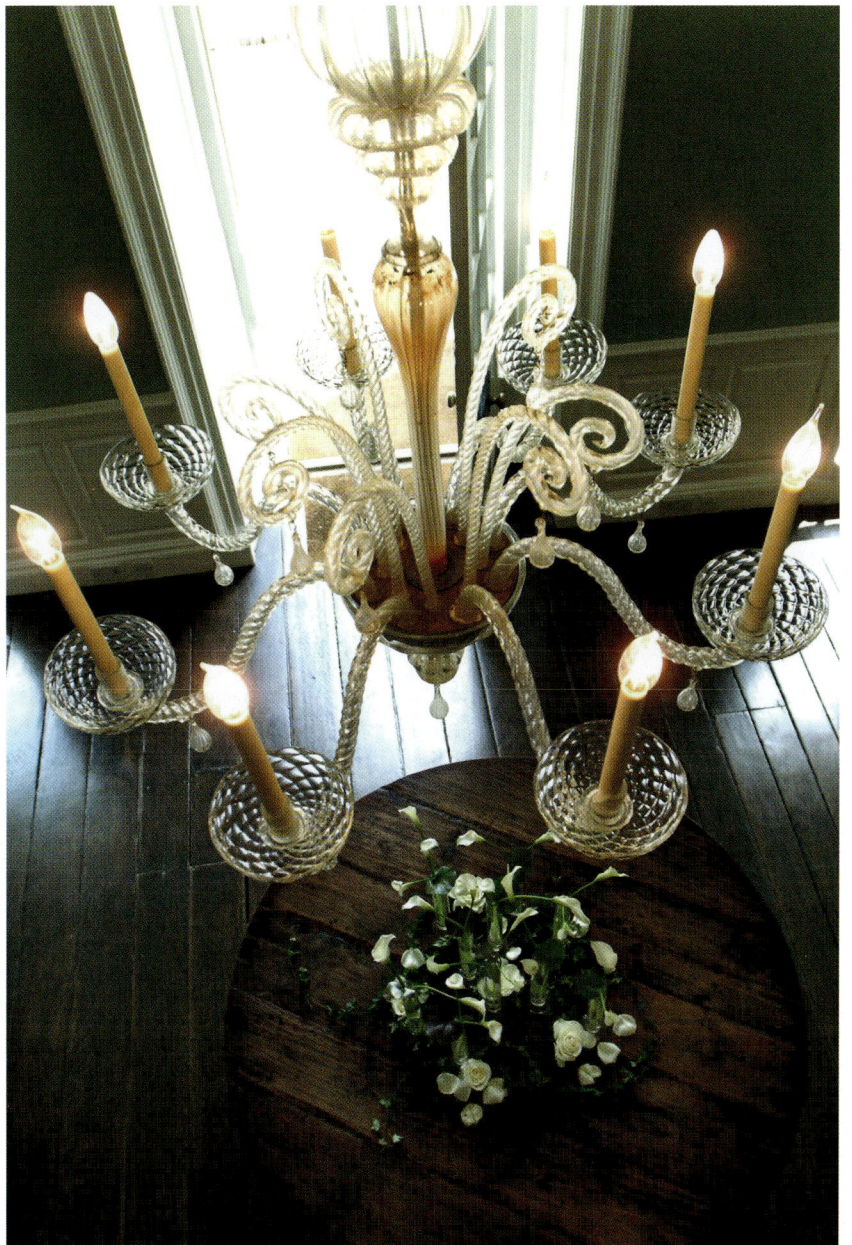

Fig. 20   ISO 800 f/4 at 1/180th

This is another high viewpoint picture. I took this picture with the camera on the ceiling held in place using my monopod. The camera was triggered using the self-timer set at 10 seconds.

therefore last longer and can take the rough and tumble of professional life.

Developing a style is the best way to concentrate your mind on the wedding day shoot. Reportage photographers have to learn how to react to what's going on and predict what will happen next. Non-reportage photographers have to make the best use of light and people. Wedding photography has many current shooting styles and products that sell well. Almost anything goes as long as it's good. The shooting style that Julie and I have developed is a combination of reactive and proactive shooting. But I strongly urge you to resist labeling yourself. If you call yourself a pure photojournalist and this style of work ceases to become fashionable or command high prices it may be difficult to reinvent yourself. Keep an open mind about style and accept evolution to some extent.

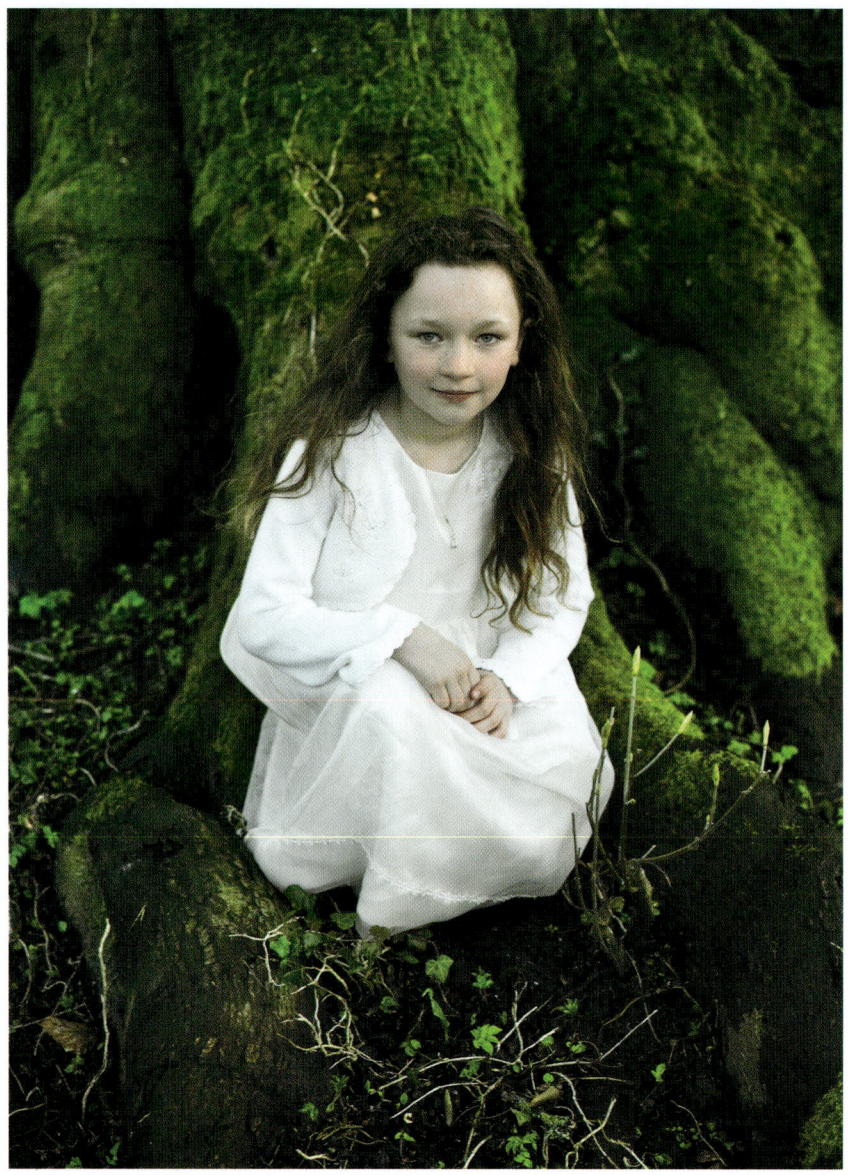

Fig. 21   ISO 400 f/4 at 1/180th

The big old tree provided the perfect setting for this bridesmaid picture. A high viewpoint makes the girl seem vulnerable and the image might have been better if I had knelt down. Explore your viewpoint and its effect on the resulting images at the taking stage. Then question your shooting decisions when you review your images after the wedding.

Let's take my own career path as an example. I've been many a 'specialist' in my lifetime and I'll probably morph into a few more careers as time goes by. Back in 1984, I started as a TV cameraman; then came spells as a lighting cameraman, a lighting director, a news cameraman, and all this time I was shooting stills for a stock library in my time off. I then spent some time as a commercial photographer before deciding that people are more fun to shoot than products. I became a portrait photographer and eventually a full-time wedding photographer back in 2000. The thing is, my image-making style has evolved along with my job title. Maintaining openness to external influence and inspiration from other photographers has given me a special outlook on the image-making process.

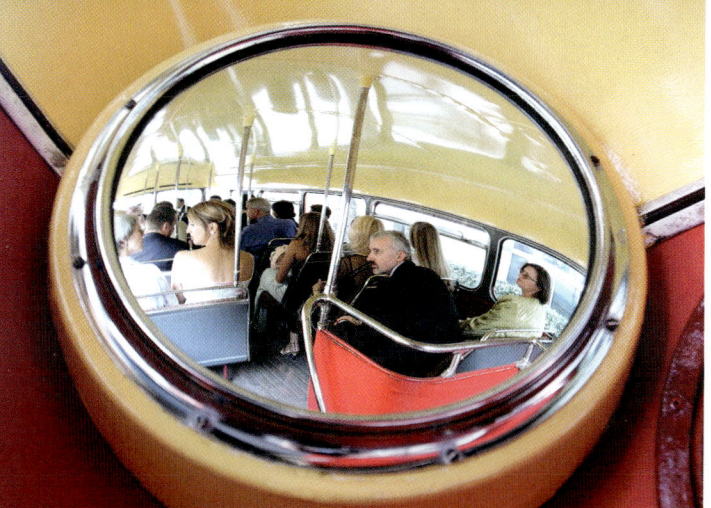

FIGS 22–24   ISO 400 f/4 at 1/860th and ISO 400 f/4 at 1/45th
and ISO 800 f/4 at 1/45th

It's too obvious at times to shoot a big wide shot of a bus like this. That is just what the amateur photographers at the wedding were doing. I set my work apart and took a more creative approach by shooting a close sequence of details.

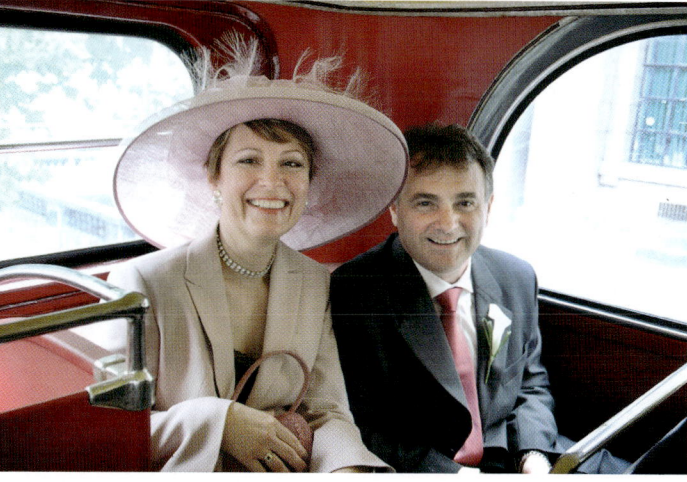

MY PERSONAL STYLE TIPS:

1. Shoot emotion   Create a relaxed ambience and use it to make pictures. Make opportunities for fun, whoop it up a bit, and shoot. Feel and be involved, not just an observer. Have fun with the wedding guests and bridal party then capture it in camera. Forget jokes and one-liners.
   Take FUN PICTURES!

2. Think first then shoot   This is the way Julie and I work. Occasionally, having a 'shoot first' approach to capture the reality of the situation can be an advantage. But this only works well if you are prepared. So when you walk into a room, automatically set your camera to a suitable exposure so that you can react instantly and effectively.

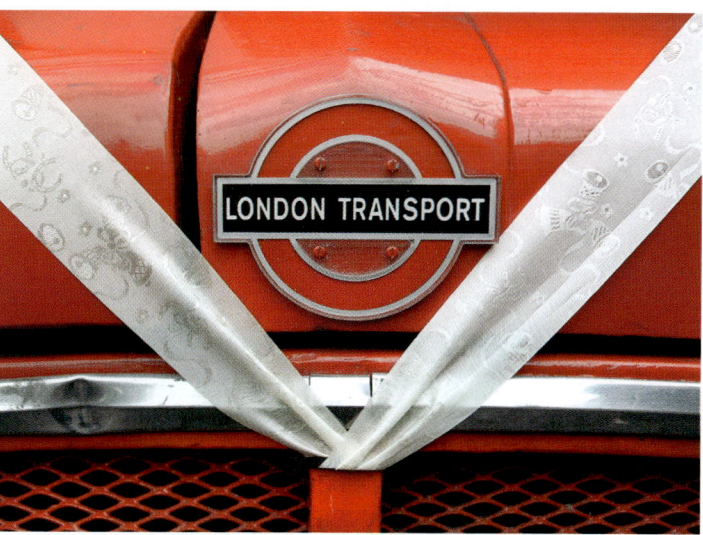

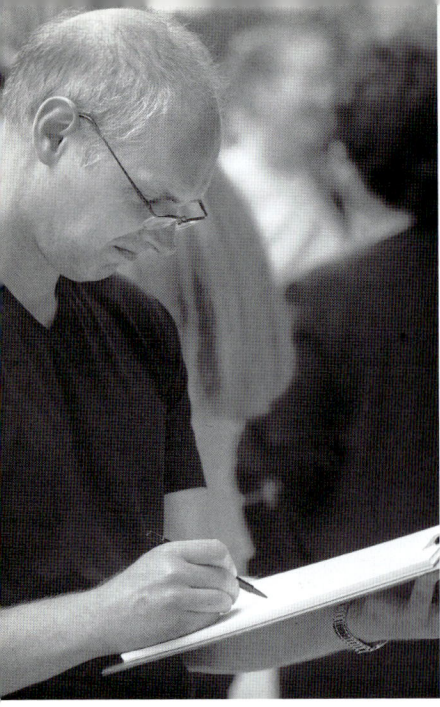 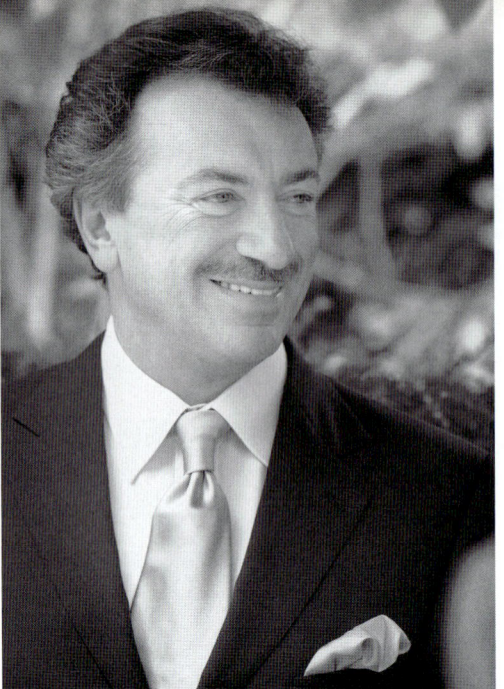 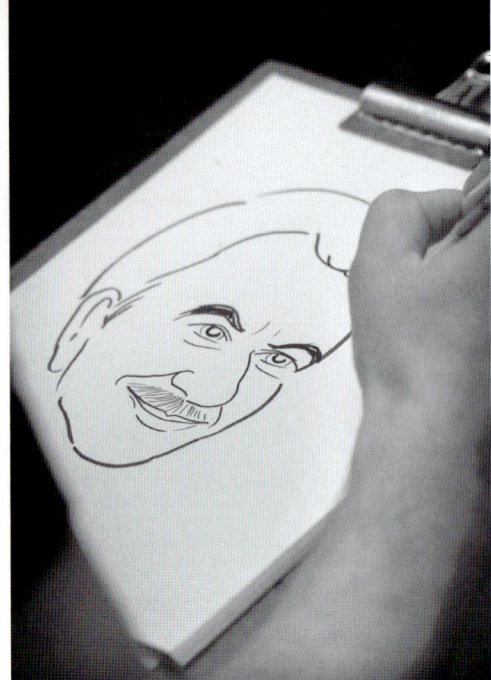 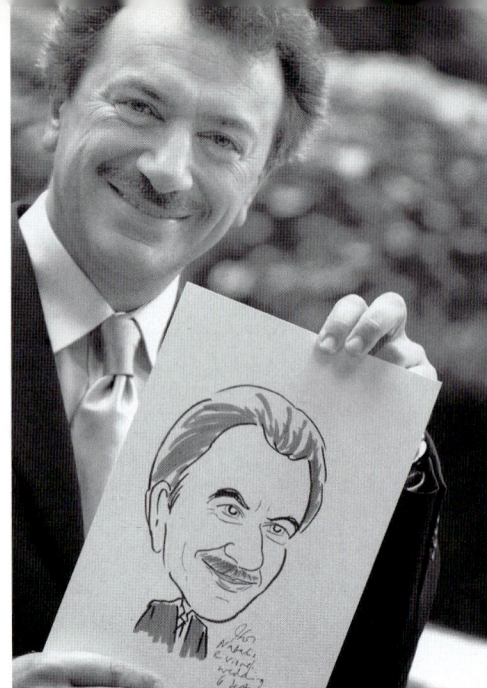

FIGS 25–28 ISO 320 f/4 at 1/125th

I chose to shoot this sequence of an artist at work using a 80 to 200 mm lens. The long lens together with the tight crops ensures a continuity of style for all the pictures. From a business point of view it makes obvious sense to shoot and sell four images rather than a single wide shot that tells the whole story by itself.

3. *Move don't zoom* Create pictures in three dimensions. Using the zoom to compose images is like cropping a two-dimensional image. Try to create depth. Moving helps align the foregro und, midground, and background elements of an image. If you feel lazy and want a bit of work to do, use prime lenses. Your composition will get worse before it gets better, but it will eventually be worth the effort.

4. *Tell the story* To achieve this, use a 'less is more' technique. Single out key elements. This style works well if you keep the edges of the frame clear of distracting detail.

5. *Shoot sequences* This makes it easier to create dynamic layouts. Why take one shot where three or four will do the job better?

6. *What's hot and what's not?* Out goes spot color and pictures on angles. In comes an increase of saturation and pictures that seem to glow. Look to advertising to see what's current. Don't go crazy, just a hint of a look is fine. Remember that advertisers usually have only one image to get the effect or look-over to the buying public. You have hundreds right throughout the album, so go easy on it. Don't mix and match. Make your black and whites and your color style consistent.

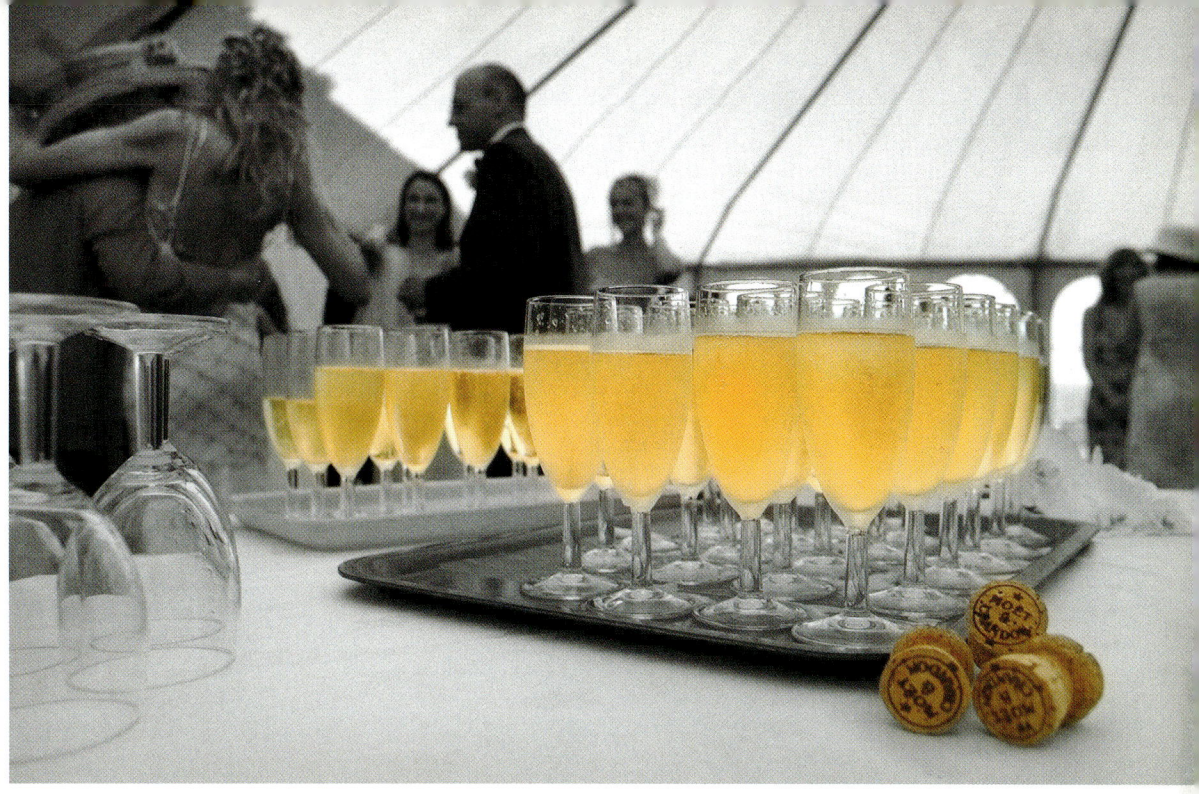

FIG. 29   ISO 320 f/4 at 1/60th

In 2001, I used spot color for the first time. It soon became widespread and by 2003 we had stopped post-processing in this way. This one picture of spot color champagne was the most requested by our clients at the time. I am now far less inclined to go with fashion at the expense of longevity.

Think long term and ask yourself... In 20 years time will this look naff or good?

7. *Take control* Controlling your surroundings, your subjects, and the light is the first and most obvious way to develop a style. Beyond the physical control is the emotional control. This is where a photographer creates a moment of fun or reflection and captures it. This ability to create and capture emotions leads to fantastic wedding photography. Like film making, telling a story with pictures often relies on a good *director*.

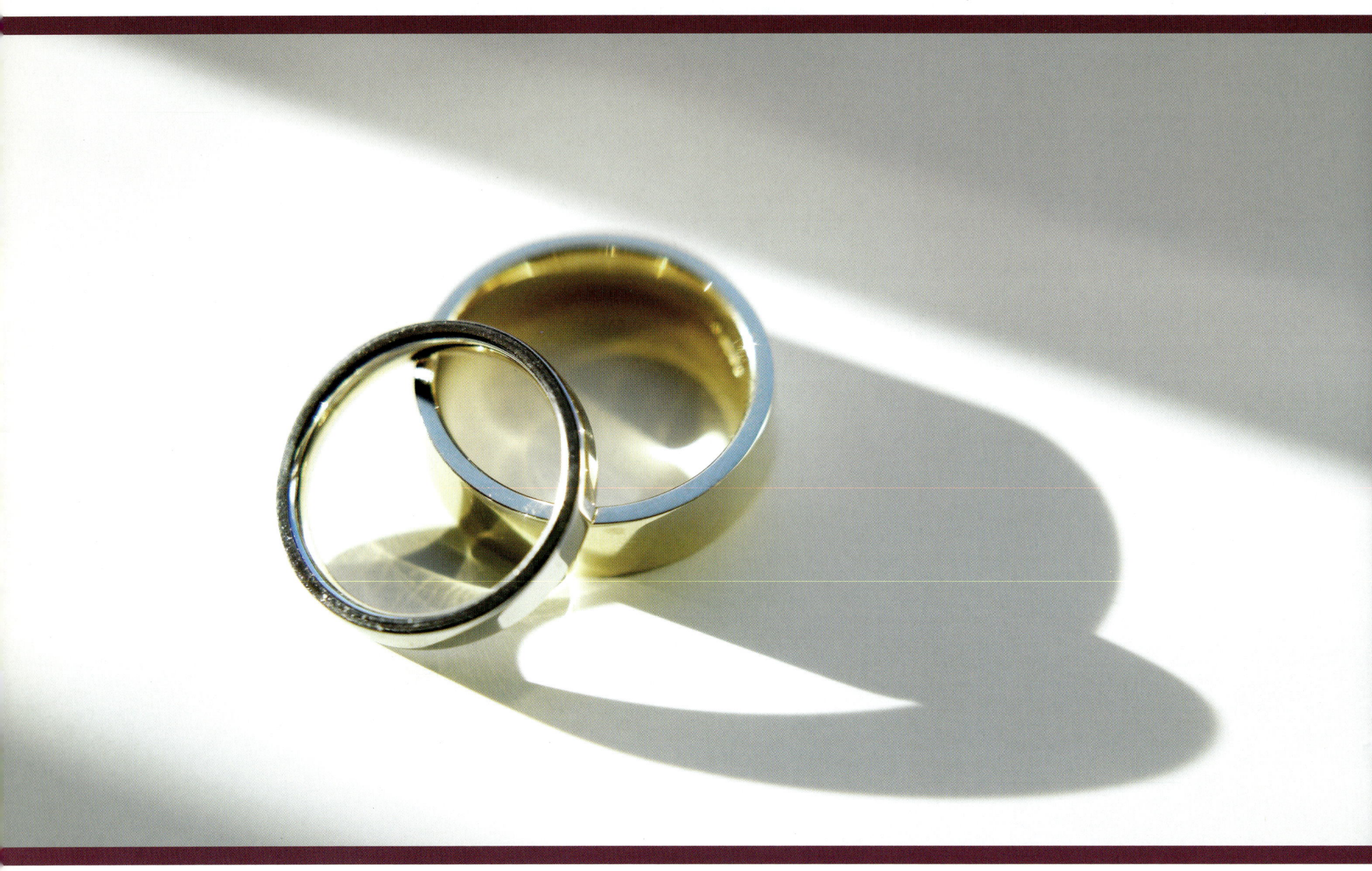

Chapter Three: Light Matters

3
Light Matters

It is common knowledge that photography (literally 'light-writing') depends for its existence on light. Yet, how many of us *really* understand the way light behaves, how it can be controlled, and the impact it has on our images?

When I came into social photography from the once 'glamorous' world of television, I was surprised to find that in the United Kingdom at least there was no obvious established training route for core camera and lighting skills designed specifically for wedding photographers. The extensive knowledge I had gained from my formal training seemed to have no equal in the 'still' photography world. I'm talking about 6 weeks' full-time studying lighting and a further 6 months on attachment as a lighting director in the studios of London. I can see now that this was worth more, far more than I gave credit for at the time. I believe

there is no substitute for a thorough understanding of light and its application when creating images, whether still or moving. In this chapter, I want to touch on some of the most common lighting decisions Julie and I take when shooting weddings. It's also worth noting that the majority of techniques we use on the wedding day are equally applicable to portraiture.

Whatever the situation, the first step is to assess the light around you. When we enter a room or anywhere that we are going to be taking photographs, we immediately consider the *direction* and *quantity* of light. We then look at the suitability of

opposite

Fig. 1   ISO 400 f/5.6 at 1/250th

The rings in this shot were placed on a bit of white paper on a windowsill in direct sunlight. A simple but effective composition with shadows.

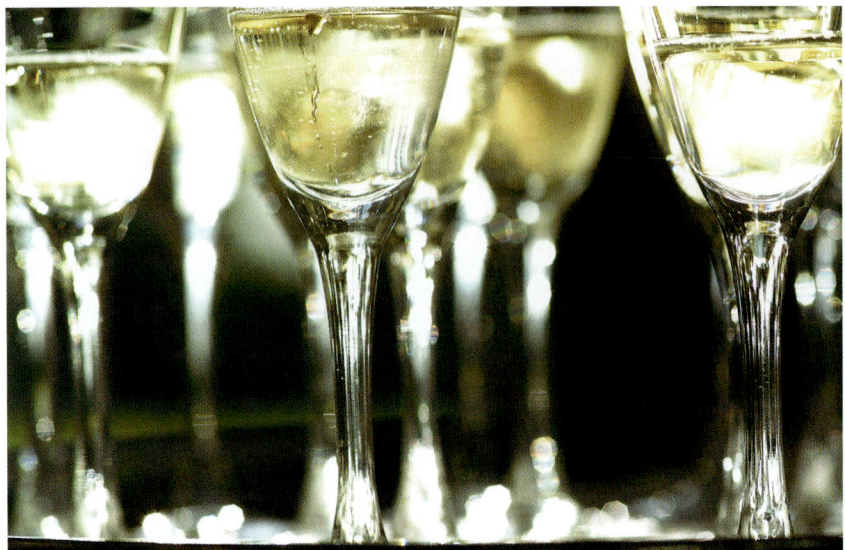

FIG. 2   ISO 800 f/4 at 1/2000th

Dramatic backlight from the sun attracted me to these glasses. The background is a hedge out of focus and in shadow.

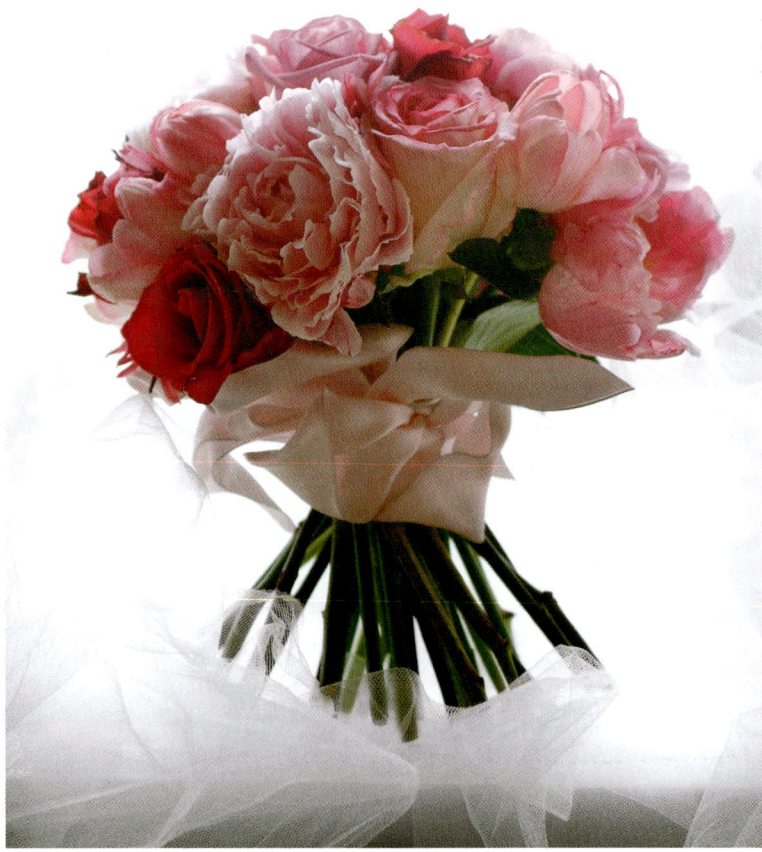

the background. For example, when Julie photographs the bride getting ready, it's quite normal for her to rearrange the position of the people and some furniture in the room so that the bride is well lit against an uncluttered background.

Both the *uncluttered* and *well-lit* factors are trademarks of our style. We take a proactive approach to getting this type of image. We certainly like to set up and simplify the environment we shoot in. We also set up all of our still life images: this is how we get our 'look.' Having established the 'ideal' environment for our shots, Julie and I can let the action take place without intervention, knowing all the pictures will be clean.

During hectic wedding preparations, it sometimes happens that the only available clutter-free background in a bedroom is the window. That's fine – shooting into a window has many

FIG. 3   ISO 400 f/4 at 1/180th

These backlit flowers needed plus two stops of exposure compensation to get the look that Julie was after. The flowers were placed on a spare piece of veil Julie keeps in her camera bag.

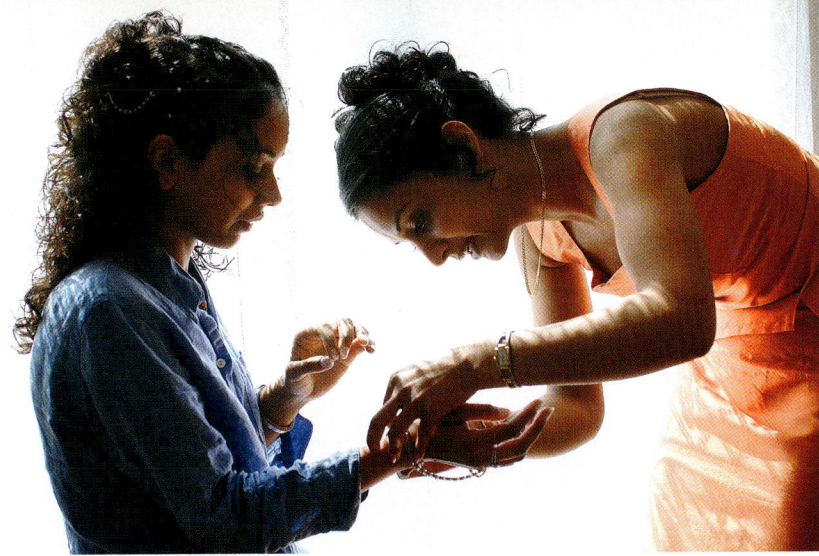

Fig. 4   ISO 320 f/4 at 1/500th

For this wonderful shot of the girls getting ready Julie deliberately shot into the sunlit window. An exposure increase of plus three stops was dialed in to avoid the obvious silhouette that the camera's meter alone would have delivered. For this kind of shot to work top lenses are needed, as flare can soon become a problem when using extreme exposure increases.

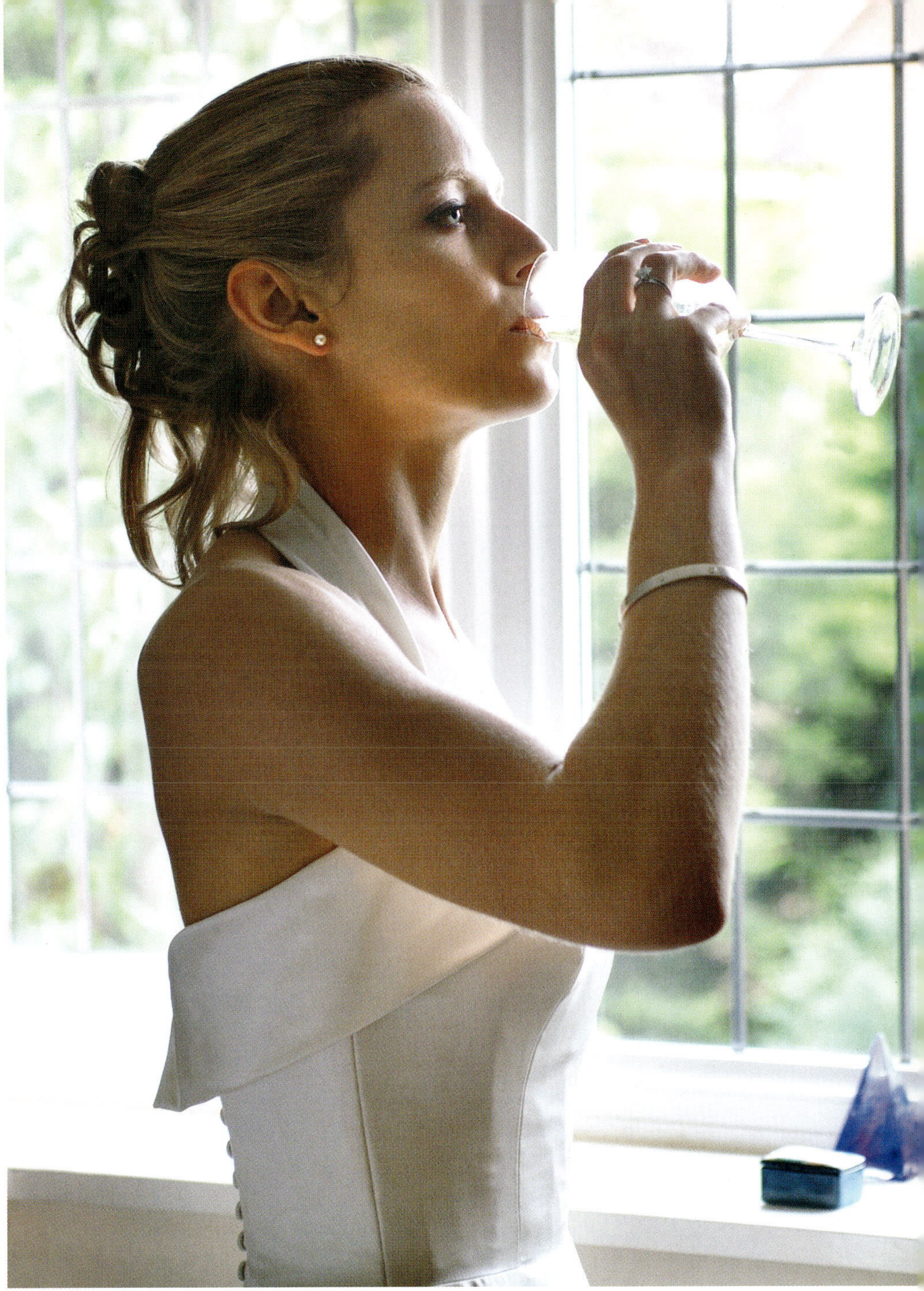

Fig. 5   ISO 400 at f/4 1/100th

For this shot into the window Julie again used exposure compensation. A setting of plus two stops was necessary on this occasion. This technique works well even if it is raining outside. It produces brightly lit pictures that look 'sunny.'

benefits. Windows provide strong graphic background shapes of bright, high-key tone. They can also add depth and sometimes emphasize the illusion of three dimensions in the resulting prints. Window-backed images can be made with a simple exposure increase or are remarkably easy to light with through the lens (TTL) handheld flash. Even if it's gloomy or raining outside the pictures, we shoot into windows to give a bright vibrant look to the wedding album.

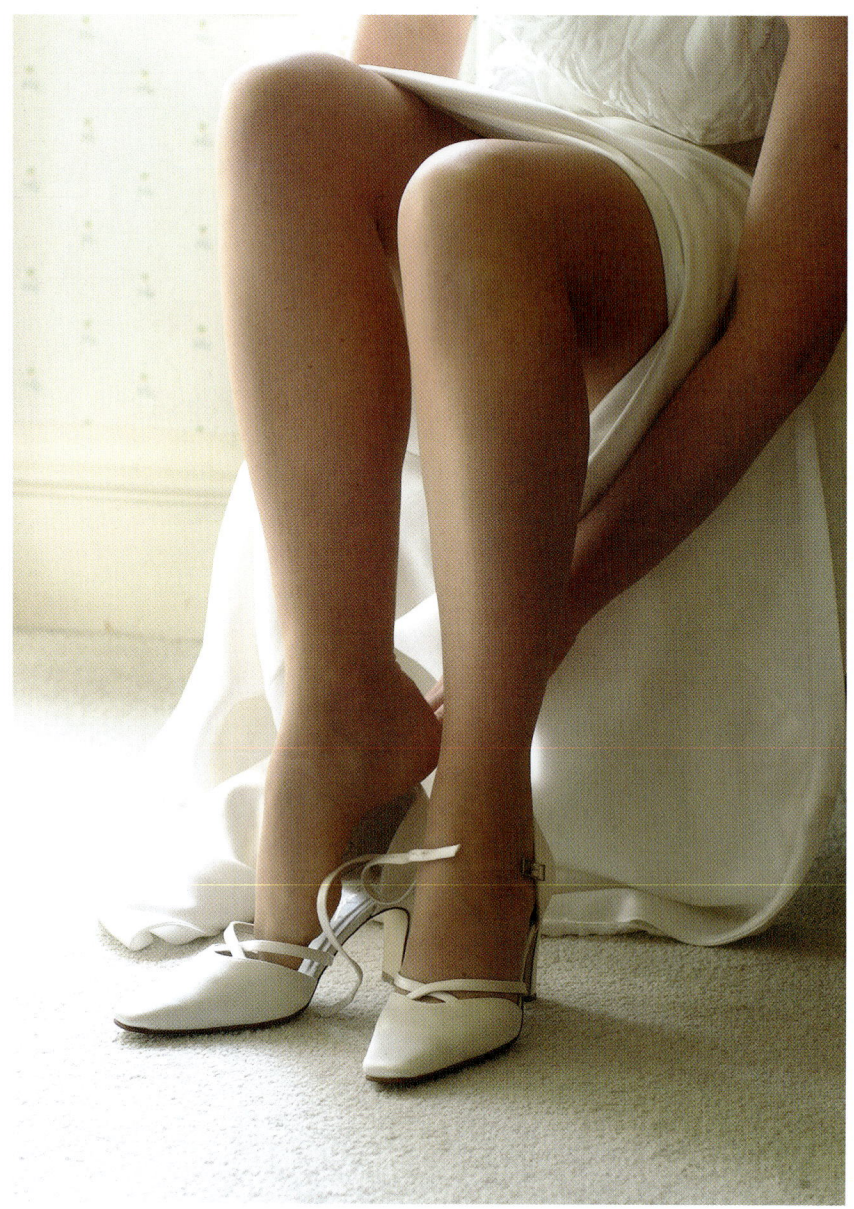

FIG. 6   ISO 800 f/4 at 1/125th

Shooting toward the window without using flash gave these legs a lovely rim light.

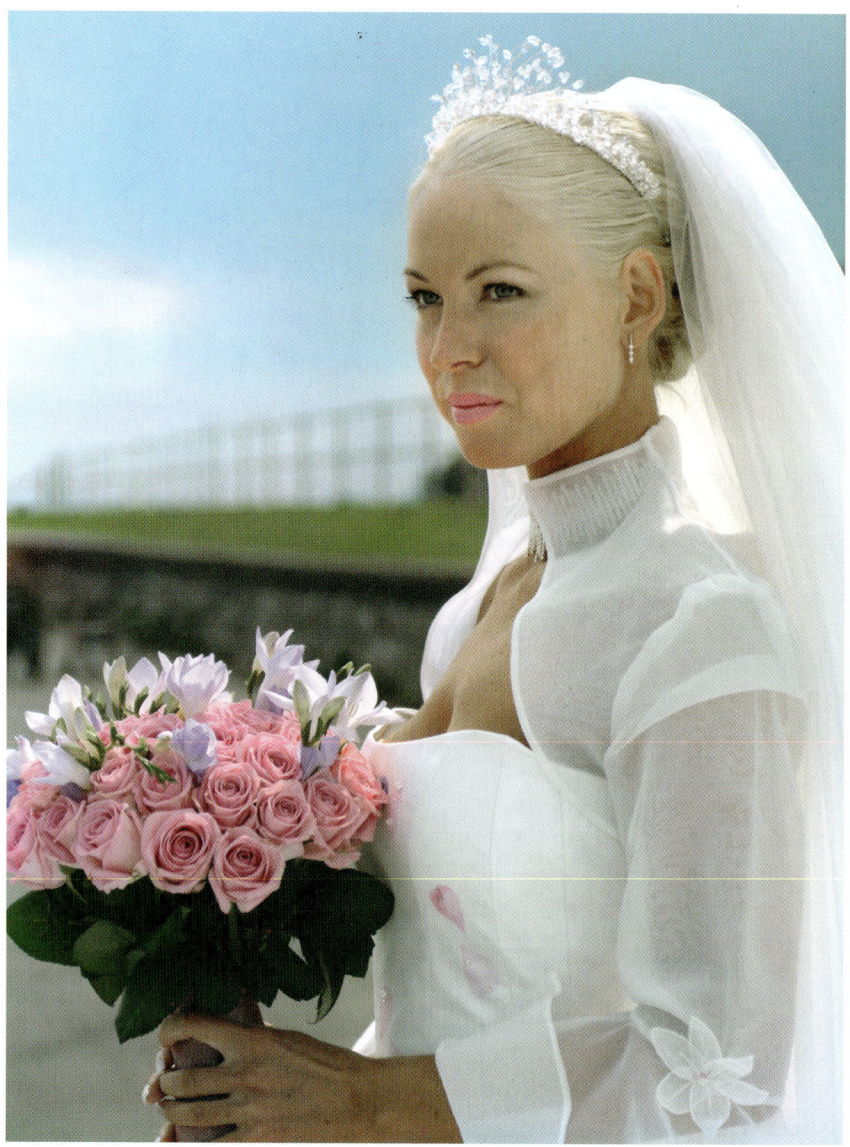

FIG. 7   ISO 400 f/4 at 1/3000th

Occasionally, changeable weather produces natural light patterns that can be used to great effect. Here, Julie posed the bride and shot into the light. The sky was of a dark enough tone to make an interesting backdrop.

FIG. 8   ISO 320 f/5.6 at 1/2000th

No exposure compensation was needed here to create this dramatic shot of the groom in early morning sunlight.

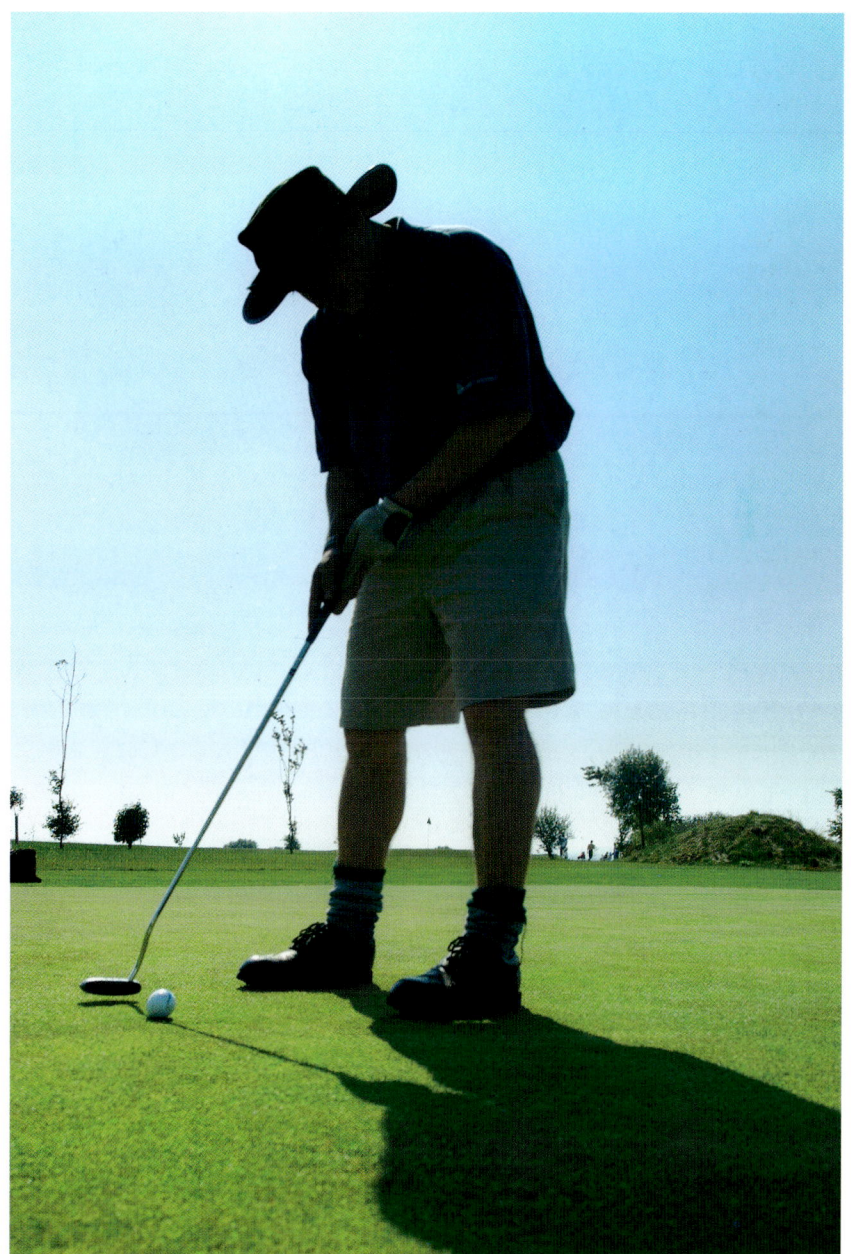

After assessing a lighting situation, we may decide not to use artificial light, but to go with the existing available light. In that case, several factors that affect the image quality need consideration: these include ISO, aperture, shutter speed, color, tone, and subject. Making 'natural light' pictures can be rewarding when everything comes together well. f/4 shooters like Julie and I use just enough depth of field to render our subject in sharp focus while maintaining beautiful out of focus backgrounds to support the final composition. The great reportage photographers have learned to *read* natural light well and produce some of their most dramatic images in what might seem like 'impossible' lighting conditions. Having a 'fast' 50-mm f/1.4 lens opens up a world of opportunity often overlooked by other photographers.

In the fashion, commercial, and illustrative photographic world a picture need not flatter the subject as long as it conveys

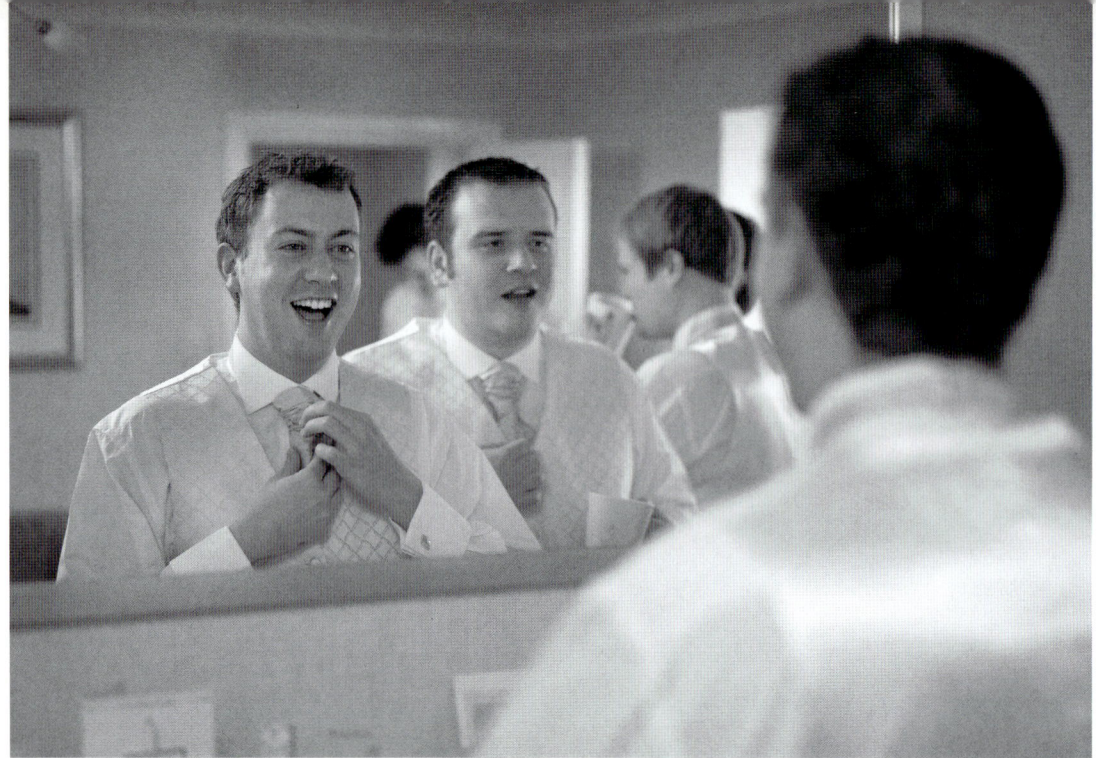

the right message. But for wedding photographers flattery is *everything*. Making a bride look great by lighting her from the 'right' side or angle is vital. A simple question I ask myself when I compose each image is 'Does the person I'm photographing look great in this picture?' If not 'why not?' Often the answer is simple. If a groom has a bent nose for instance, lighting his face from the same direction as the bend in his nose will cast a small insignificant nose shadow reducing the effect of the bend. Light him from the other side and wallop! his nose shadow scoots across his face and accentuates the bent nose.

The wedding make-up artist works hard to accentuate cheekbones and the jaw line; it's then up to us to take the process to the next stage. It's not difficult to take beautifully lit pictures, you just need to know what you are trying to achieve and how to do it. For example, you need to remember that

above

FIG. 9   ISO 400 f/2.8 at 1/60th

I placed my flashgun behind my back for this shot. It illuminated the room via the sidewall behind me. The resulting picture has a great light balance that has kept the back of the groom on the right at a sensible level.

opposite

FIG. 10   ISO 400 f/4 at 1/60th

For this picture of the same guys I used off-camera flash held above and to the right of me. I always point the flash upward and use a Sto-Fen diffusing dome. You can just make out the shadow of the ceiling lights. On another note, I asked the guys to remove their jackets as I thought their waistcoats would match the colors in the room.

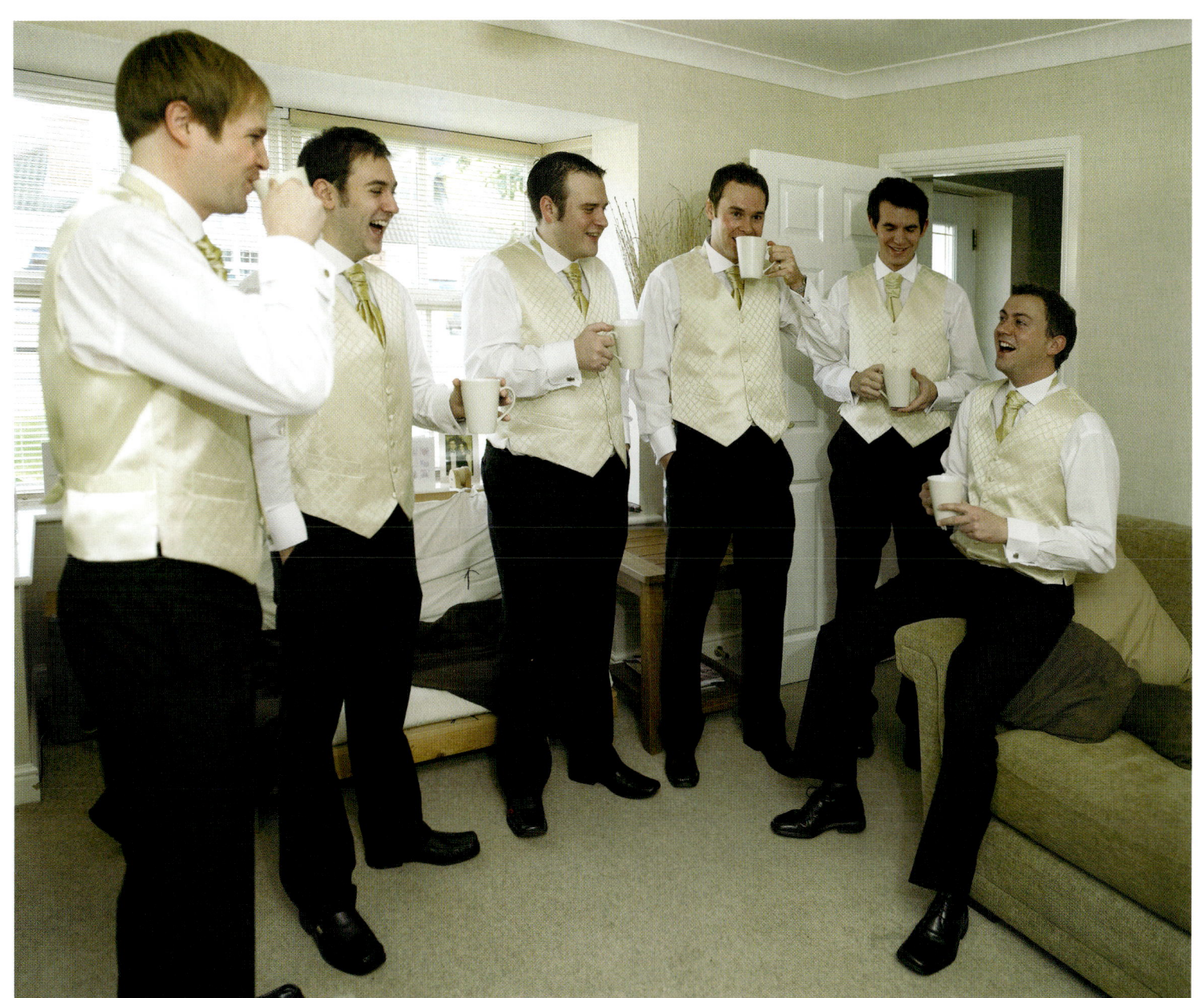

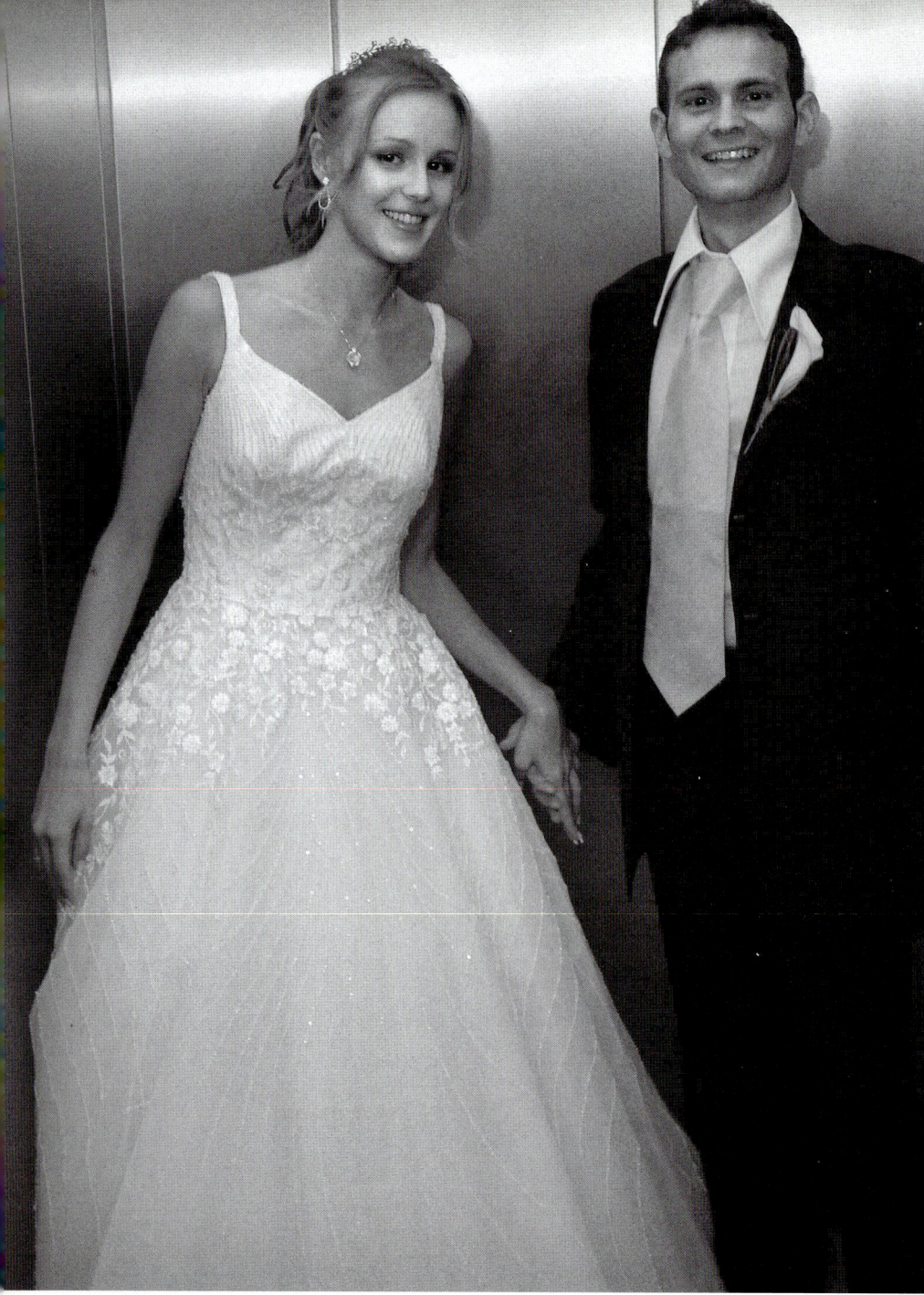

FIG. 11   ISO 200 f/4 at 1/60th

I used my flash off-camera in this stainless steel lift to capture this spur-of-the-moment shot. I like the kick back of light the background created.

FIG. 12   ISO 800 f/4 at 1/16th

I had to hold my camera very steady on a monopod to capture this picture using the ambient light in the lift. I had a three-floor journey to get everyone in the right positions and to hide my reflection.

attaching the flash to a camera removes the whole creative process of lighting. What this achieves is simply to illuminate the scene. On the other hand, using the flashgun off-camera while maintaining TTL functionality gives modeling to a face and is a technique Julie and I use extensively. But don't take our word for it. Experiment and find out what works best for you.

Try using your flashgun off-camera using either an infra red trigger or a coiled lead that supports TTL. Add a Sto-Fen diffuser or the one that came with your Speedlite. Have the flashgun in your left hand and your camera in your right hand. If the camera is too heavy for you to use in this way try using a monopod.

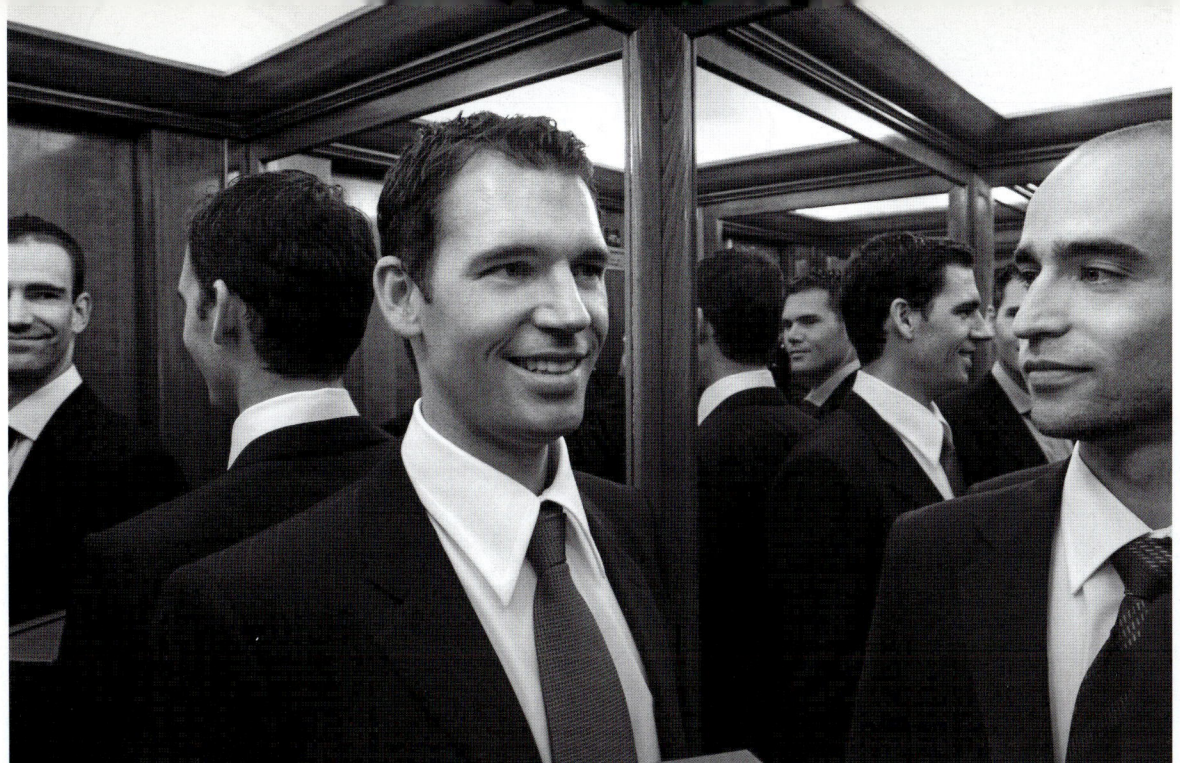

We certainly needed to change our working method several times before we hit upon a balance between aesthetic and technical quality. But whatever we do, the core principles of lighting still remain in our shots.

In classical portraiture, the key or principal light is usually a hard light source. The shape and size of the subject's nose and the depth of the eye sockets govern their position. There's nothing new about this. In fact, the artist Rembrandt is considered by many to be the founder of the principles for portrait lighting. He made a few mistakes by modern convention but went on to develop a formula that worked, and made it his own. The important point to note here is the key light angle and position are always determined by the position of the face of the sitter, and not the position of the camera (or the painter for that matter!).

> **TIP** When you are posing your subjects in ambient light, position their face toward the window, door, or light source. Aim to 'key' down the nose. If you are using off-camera flash aim this so that the flashgun is directly in line with their nose too. Where possible shoot into the unlit side of the face as it will be the shadow area of the face that will reveal its shape and make the picture interesting.

THE COLOR OF LIGHT

The various natural colors of light create opportunities to be exploited at weddings. In the days of film, I often had to filter light to get the correct 'look' that meant 'warming up' overcast

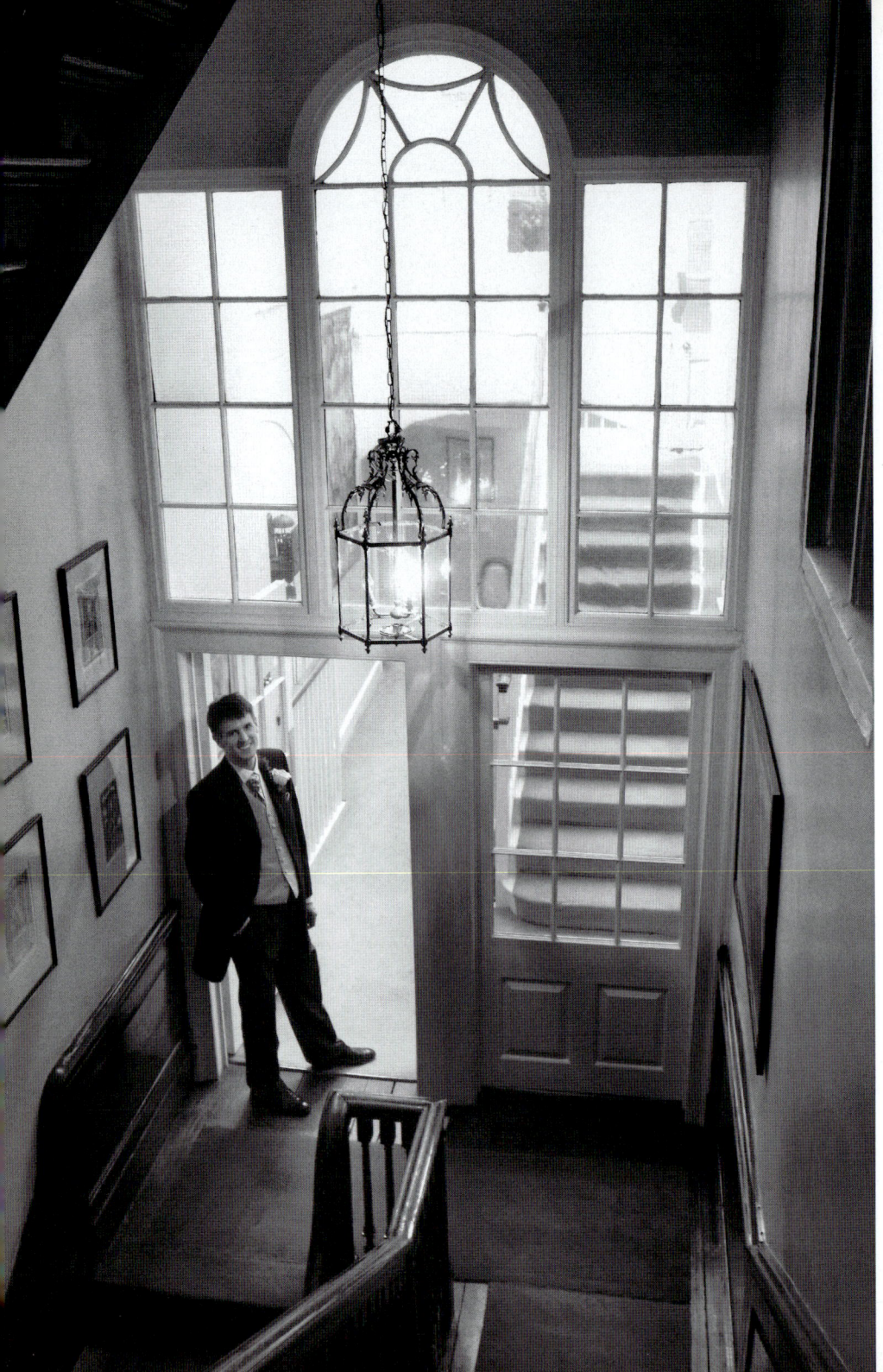

FIG. 13   ISO 400 f/4 at 1/16th

I used a monopod to steady my camera for this shot of the groom. Having the brightest part of this image the furthest away gave the picture depth.

light and 'bluing' tungsten-lit shots. Knowing and understanding color temperature was a must. Now, using digital capture, the white balance adjustments available in a camera or software can take care of that. In fact, I usually like to include as many light sources as I can in my pictures. UK winter weddings are hard work because of the sheer lack of light, but they offer wonderful opportunities for capturing a great variety of colored light in your pictures.

SHADOWS

Shadows reveal shape, light, and texture. What's more they're always available, easy to create, and very useful for adding graphical elements and interesting shapes to our wedding pictures. Try not to confuse the *hardness* of a shadow with its

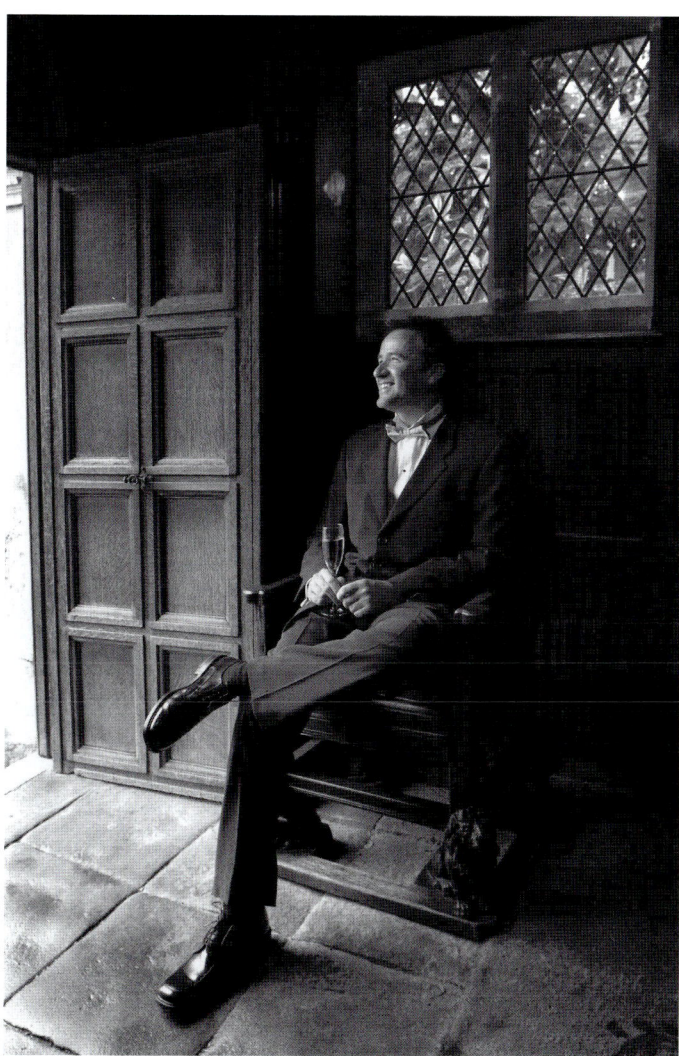

FIG. 14   ISO 800 f/4 at 1/16th

Minus two stops of compensation was needed here to keep the exposure under control in this low-key picture. I directed the groom to look at the best man I had positioned outside the door. This made the key light from the doorway work directly in line with the groom's nose. Shooting into the unlit side of his face revealed shape and form.

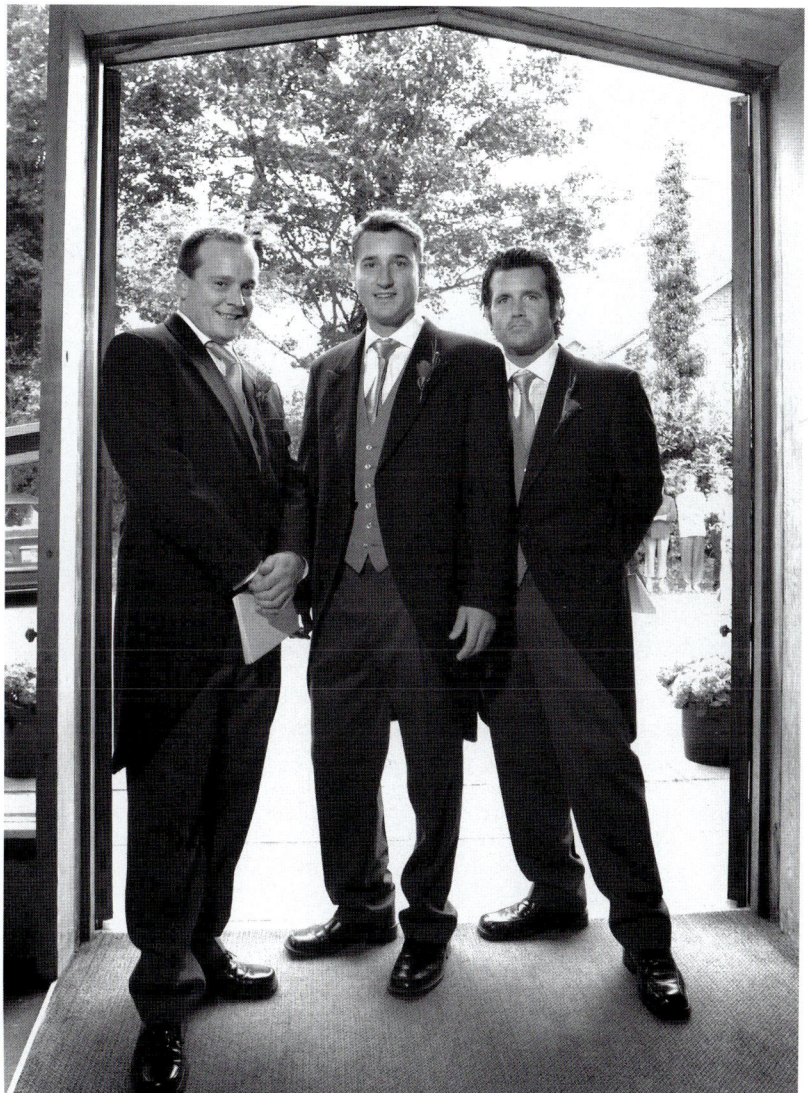

FIG. 15   ISO 400 f/4 at 1/125th

This church doorway provided a perfect frame for this picture of the ushers. A splash of flash held above and to the left of the camera provided the key light. I shot from below the guy's eye line to add drama to the picture.

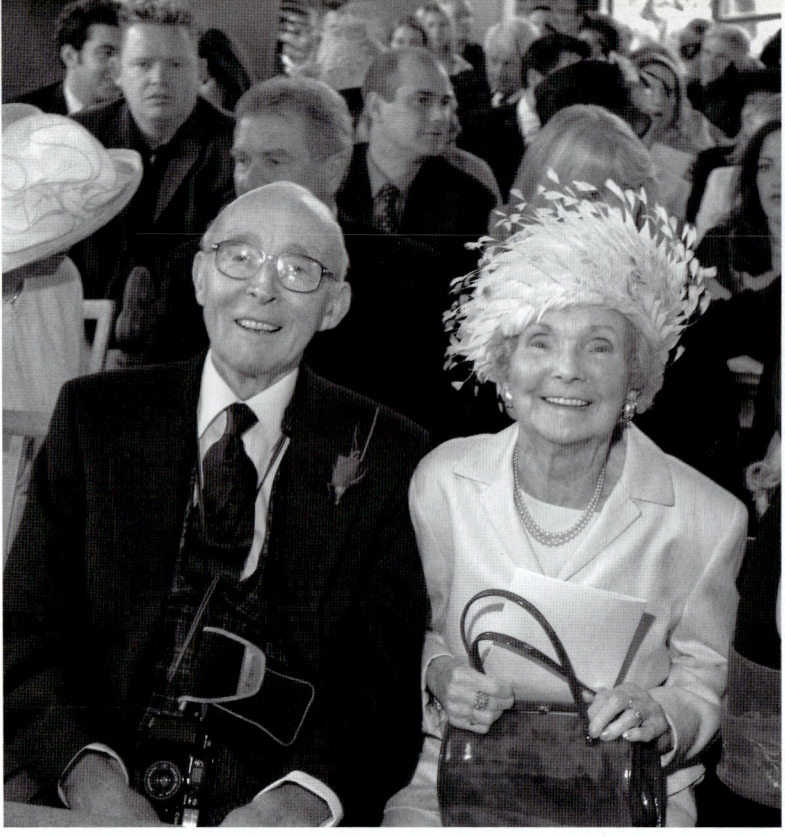

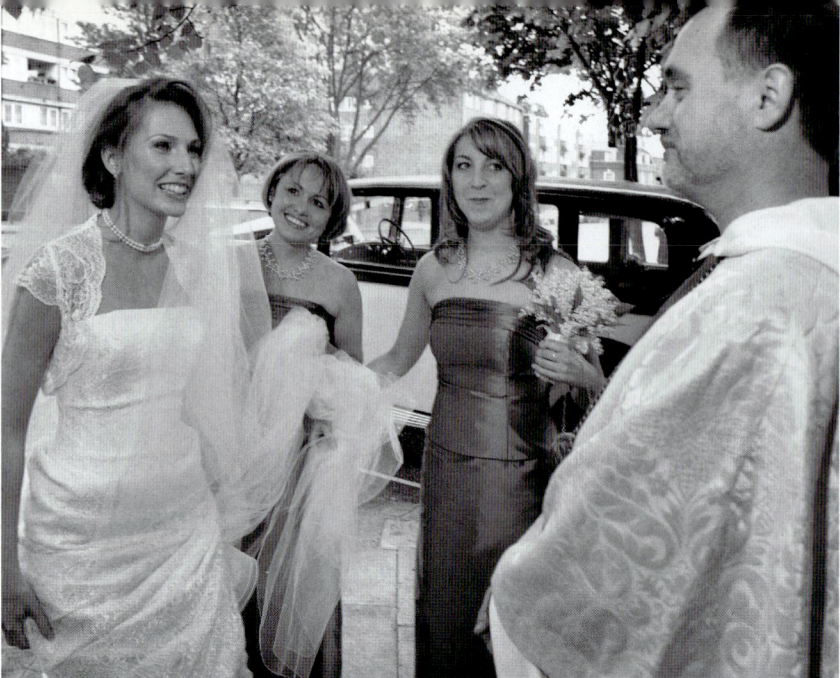

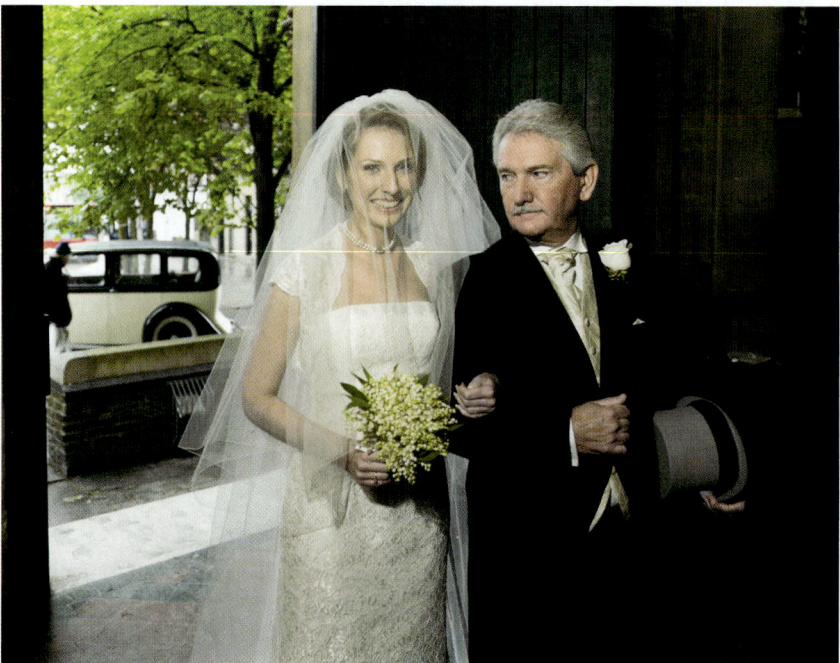

above

FIG. 16   ISO 400 f/4 at 1/60th

My off-camera flash technique was again used to capture this study of grandparents. I generated a rapport, created the moment, and captured it. Pictures like these are valuable to the whole family.

top right

FIG. 17   ISO 400 f/6.8 at 1/60th

I used a splash of TTL flash above and to the left of my camera to record this moment of the bride arriving on a rainy day. I exposed for the background and uncharacteristically added a bit more depth of field.

bottom right

FIG. 18   ISO 400 f/4 at 1/60th

A moment later, still with the flash attached, I opened the aperture to f/4 and caught this moment of the bride with her father. Having the bright horizon in this picture creates the depth that would be lost if the church door had been shut.

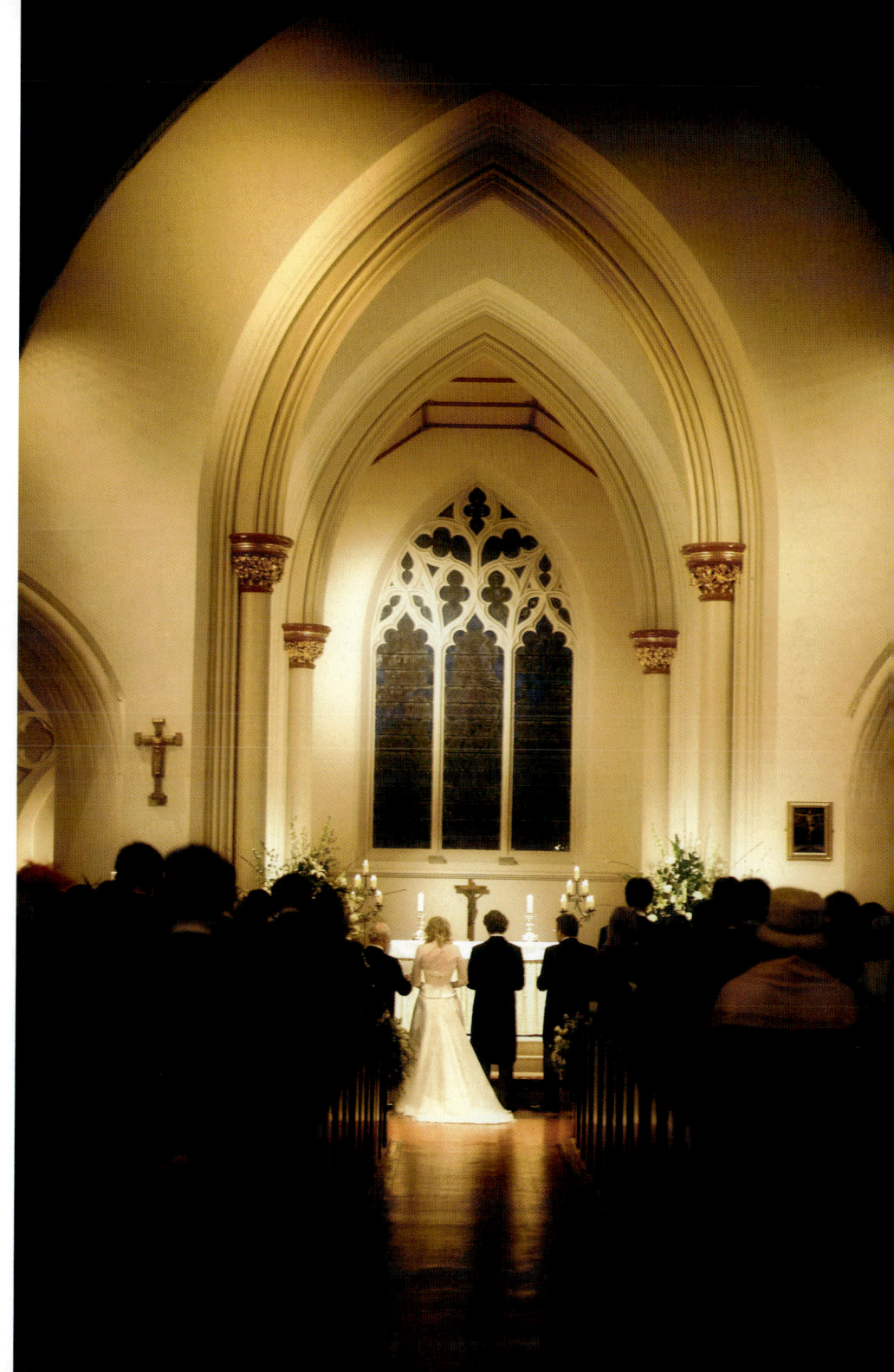

FIG. 19   ISO 400 f/2.8 at 1/15th

At night ceremonies or in the dark of winter I resort to long exposures with fast lenses to capture the atmosphere. I used a monopod leant against the font at the back of the church to keep the camera still.

contrast or *depth*. Hard shadows have crisp edges while soft shadows have diffused edges. When lighting faces or objects, it is worth noting that both hard and soft shadows reveal shape. In dark skin, it is the highlights and not the shadows that reveal shape. The contrast or depth of a shadow that is created is dependent upon the ratio of direct and indirect light.

It is important to realize that it is impossible to 'light out' a shadow. You can 'fill' a shadow to reduce its contrast until it becomes much less significant, but it will still be there. Press photographers use flash mounted directly on camera extensively but sparingly in daylight to 'fill' the shadows created by the sun and thus reduce contrast. On-camera flash used subtly in this way is a great hard-fill light source. But when flash is used as the key or principal light then *always* use it off-camera.

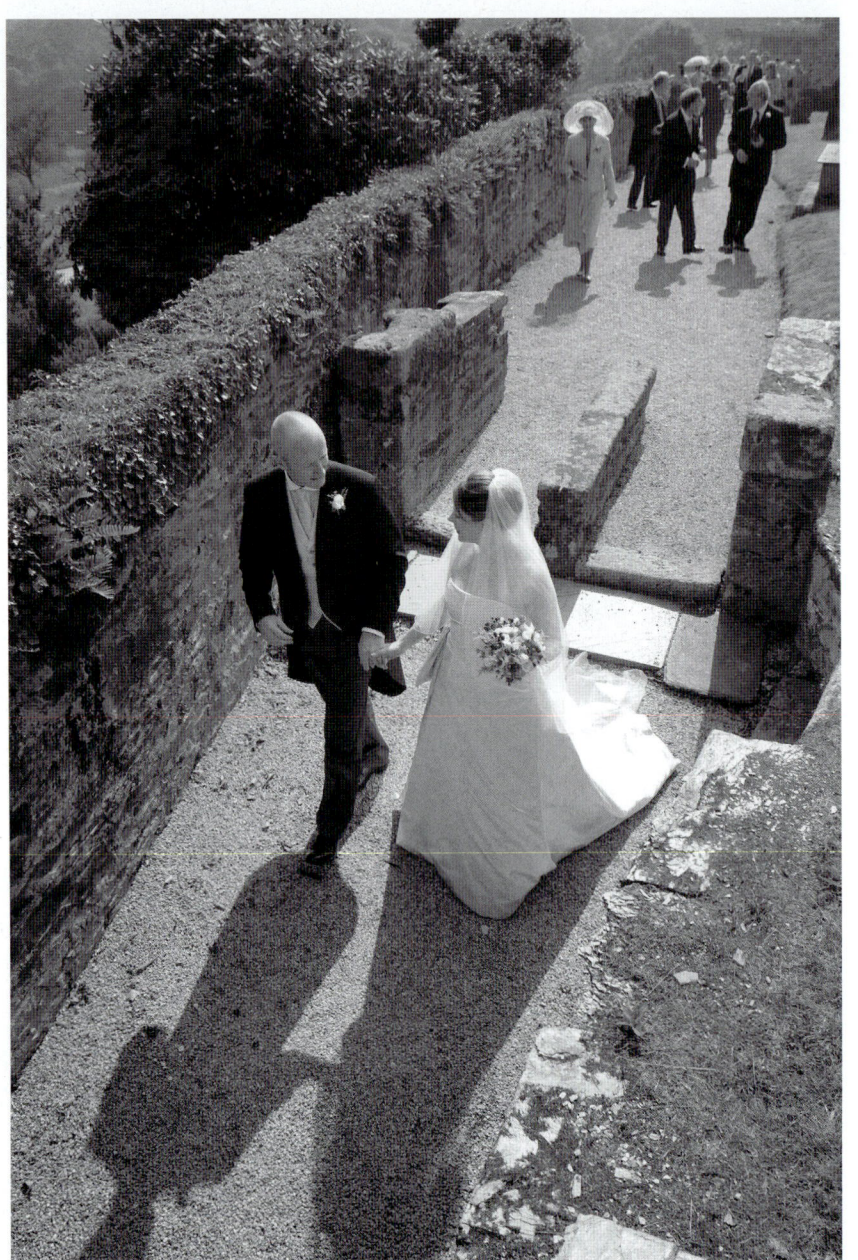

FIG. 20   ISO 200 f/4.8 at 1/1000th

A high vantage point together with the contra jour lighting made this picture work well. I held the interest at the top right of the frame and excluded the sky to strengthen the composition.

BRIGHT HORIZONS

Throughout the natural world the norm is for the brightest part of a scene to be the most distant. Take this, a most obvious scenario: you are standing on a cliff looking out to sea, the sun is shining, the sky and sea are blue. The brightest part of the scene (sun excepted) is the horizon. Throughout the world of fine art, from the old masters to the present works, this 'rule' of the distant being the brightest is used time and time again. This tonal variation linked to distance from camera creates depth in the image. Julie and I try and apply the same techniques on the wedding day itself where situations allow.

FIG. 21   ISO 400 f/2.8 at 1/20th

This spot at Babington House in Wiltshire is a favorite of mine because with plus two stops exposure compensation pictures really begin to sing. The rim light creates the separation between the bride and the hedge behind.

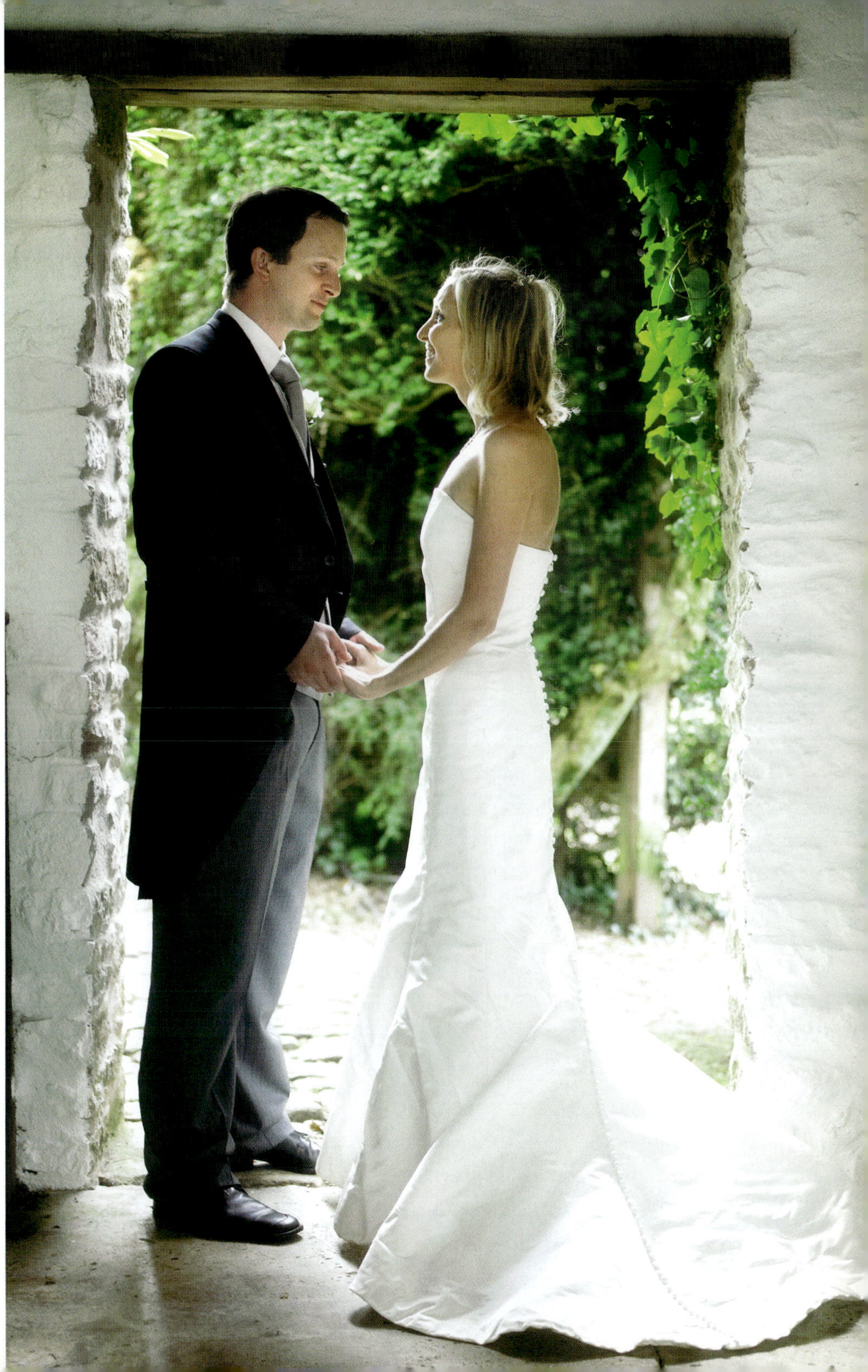

FLASH AND AMBIENCE

In a naturally lit world we expect to see room interiors darker at the top and lighter at the bottom. This is because light enters a window in a downward direction predominantly from the sky above. It is this simple truth that makes bounced flash pictures look so unnatural. A characteristic of bounced flash is for the floor to be the darkest part of the image and the ceiling to be the brightest – quite the opposite of the normal situation.

At a wedding, you need to achieve a balance when lighting interiors. Do you light the room and let the action happen or do

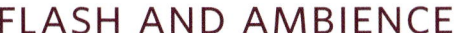

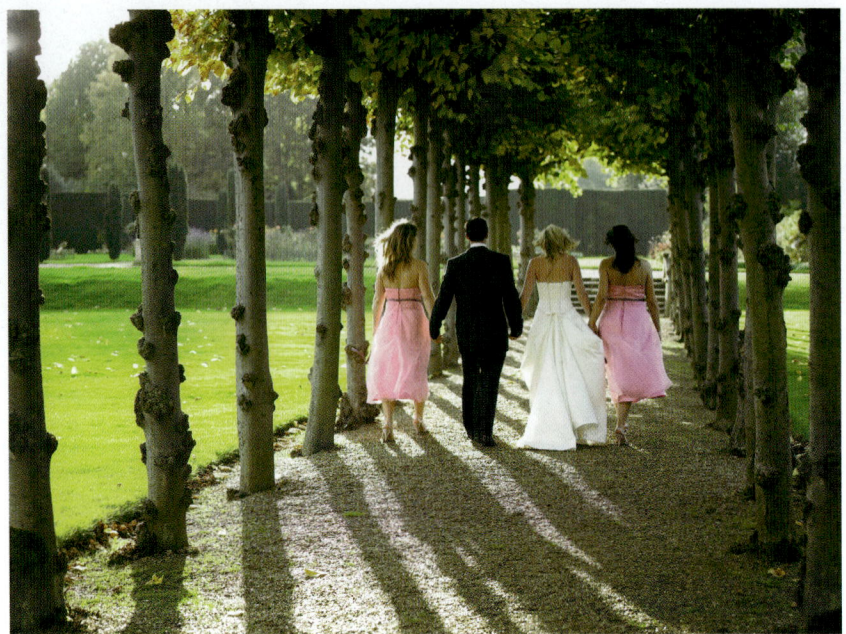

FIG. 22   ISO 400 f/4 at 1/500th

The shadows here form repeating patterns and lead-in lines. I chose an offset composition to favor the sunlit trees on the left.

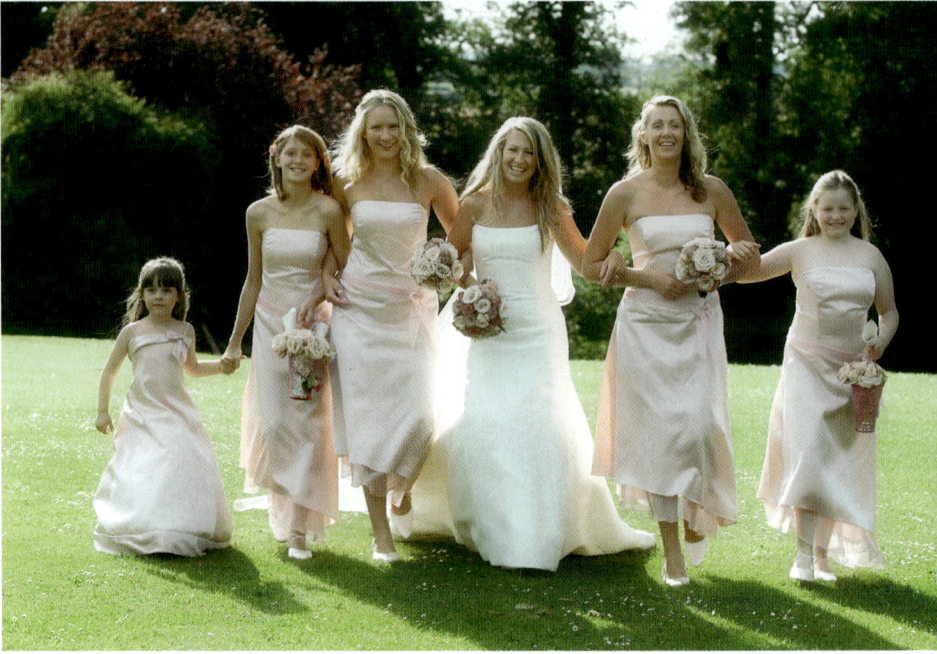

FIG. 23   ISO 400 f/4 at 1/1500th

I shoot group shots into the sun on long lenses whenever possible. The trick here is to avoid the sky in the composition and to use a hand to shield the lens from flare.

you light the people in the room and accept the ambience for the room? We do both, we expose the image so that the room's natural lighting prevails and then add flash or a tungsten spot to light the subject. Lighting the subject beautifully nearly always requires the light source to be away from the camera. Flash has the advantage of freezing the subject in the often lengthy exposures but is harder to control. Once a system that works has been adopted and learned, applying it is easy.

LOW KEY

Julie and I always try to avoid 'black holes' in our wedding pictures. One exception to this rule is when we want to shoot low key. Oak-paneled rooms and wet winter weddings pose their own problems but they also create opportunities to change the shooting style. One of the biggest problems we encounter is cutting flash output to avoid overexposure. Getting a bit of specula reflection of the flash in the background reveals

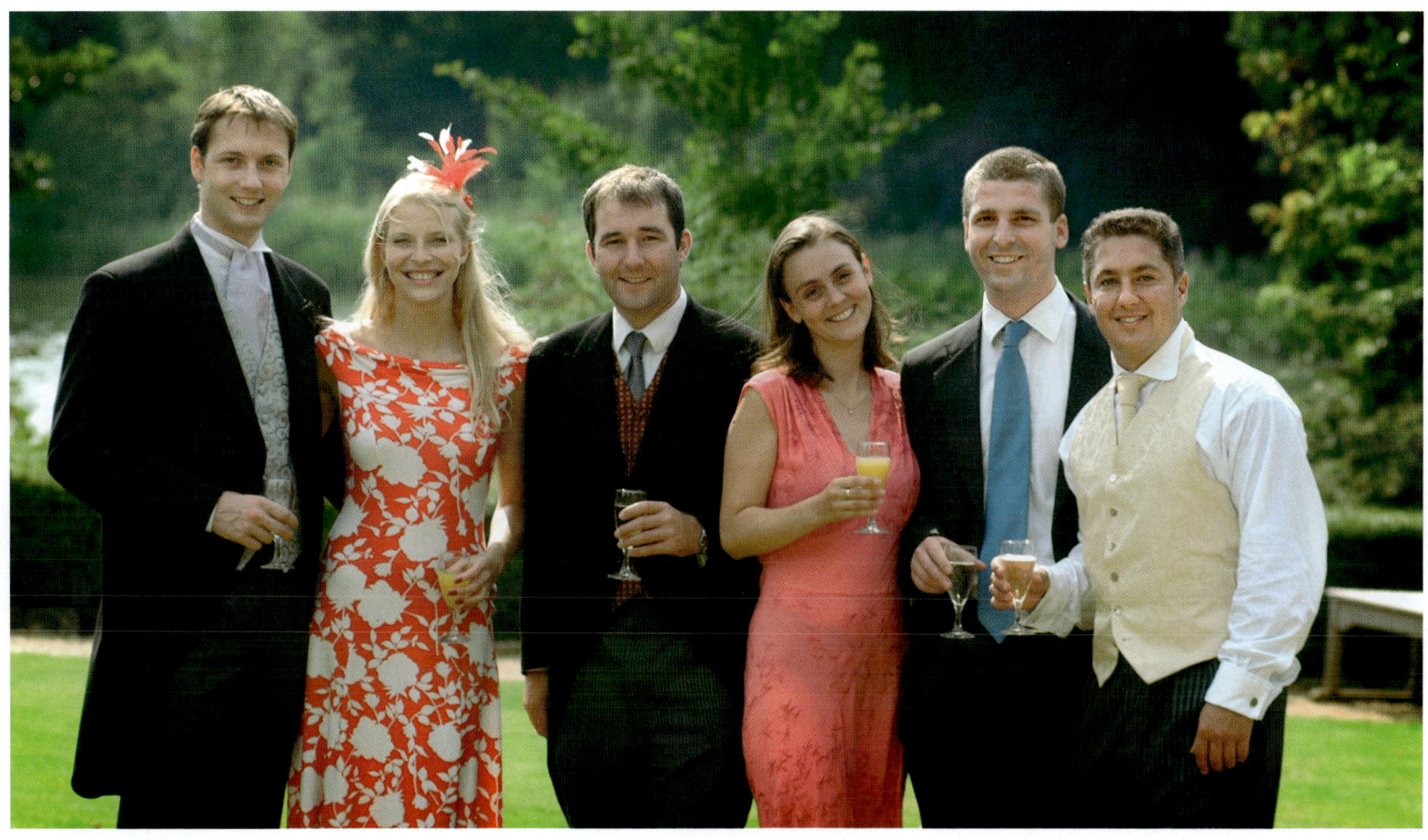

above

FIG. 24   ISO 320 f/4 at 1/1000th

Here is another group picture I took on a long lens into the sun. Simple line up groups like this work well if you create a moment and strike up a rapport with the guests. It's the expressions on the faces that determine if a picture is boring or not.

texture and brings the picture to life. If our pictures combine the ambience of the wedding venue and show detail and beauty of the clients then we have succeeded. Once you've decided on the lighting, then all that's left is to make the picture 'happen.' We nearly always create or stimulate the energy and fun in our pictures *after* the shooting techniques have been established.

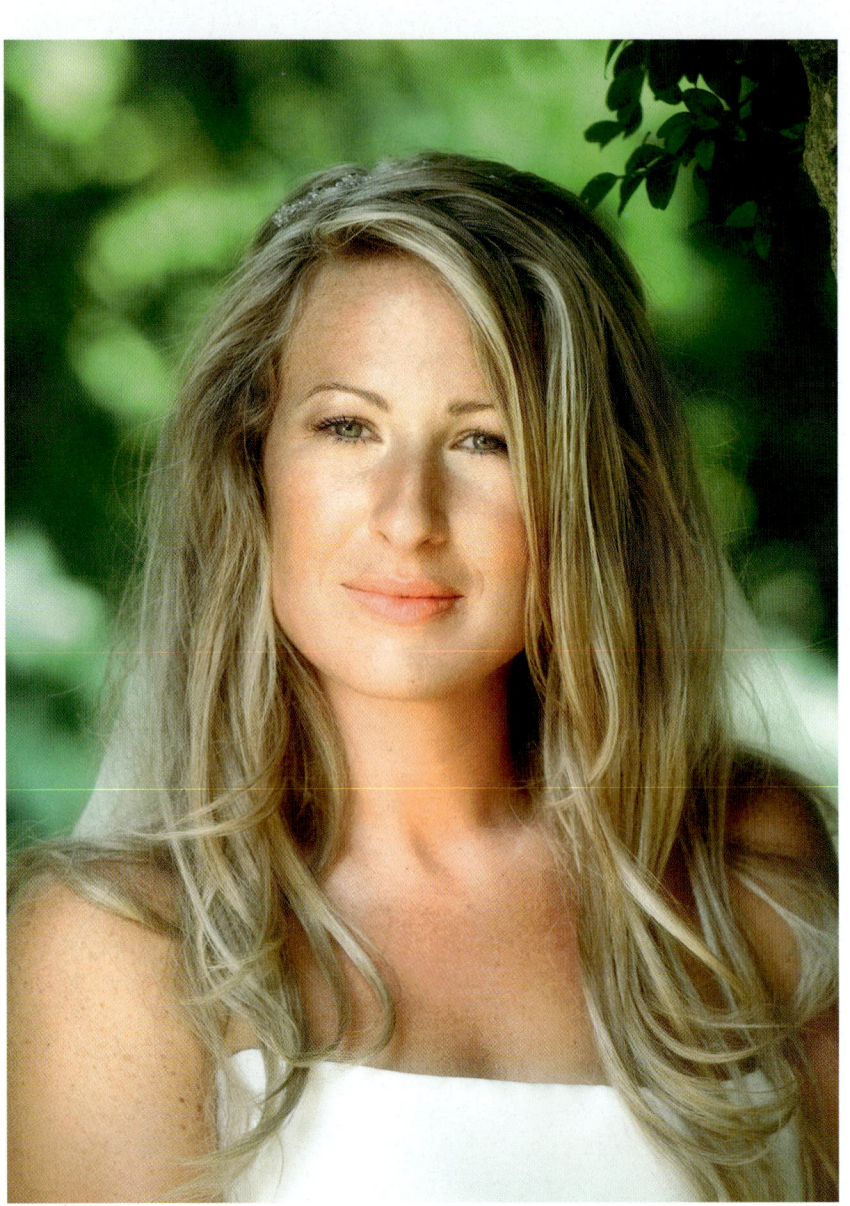

Fig. 25   ISO 800 f/4 at 1/350th

Reflected sunlight off a building behind me lit this bride beautifully. A subtle 'glow' was added in post-production to all the pictures from this wedding.

bottom

Fig. 26   ISO 400 f/4 at 1/1000th

Shot into the light on a long lens makes this a trademark Lovegrove picture. A hint of out of focus foliage in the foreground was unavoidable. Too much out of focus foreground would have made the picture voyeuristic.

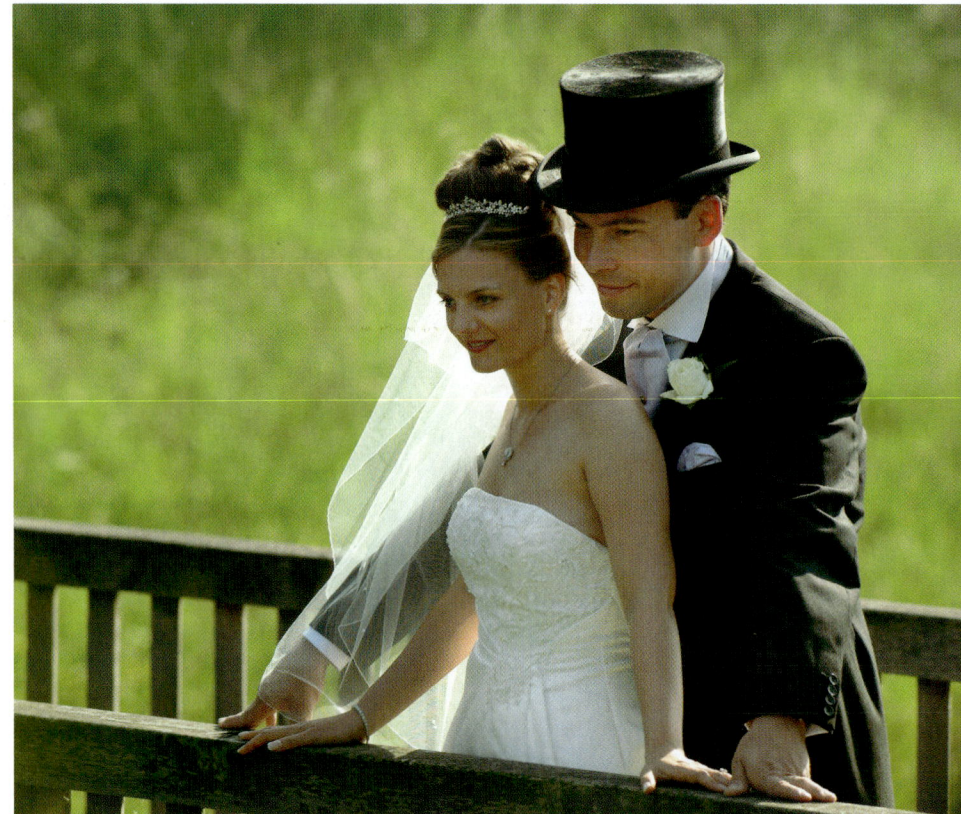

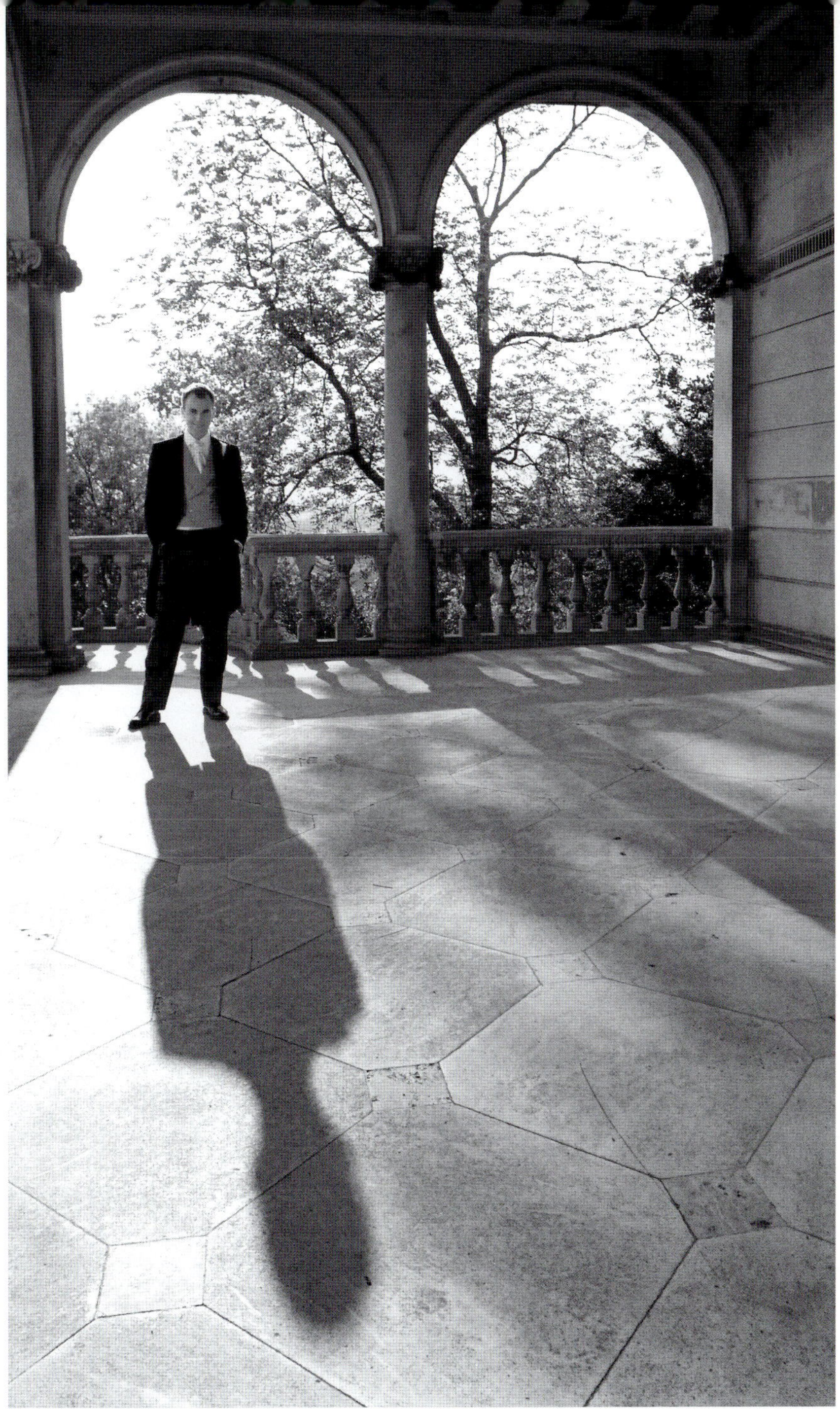

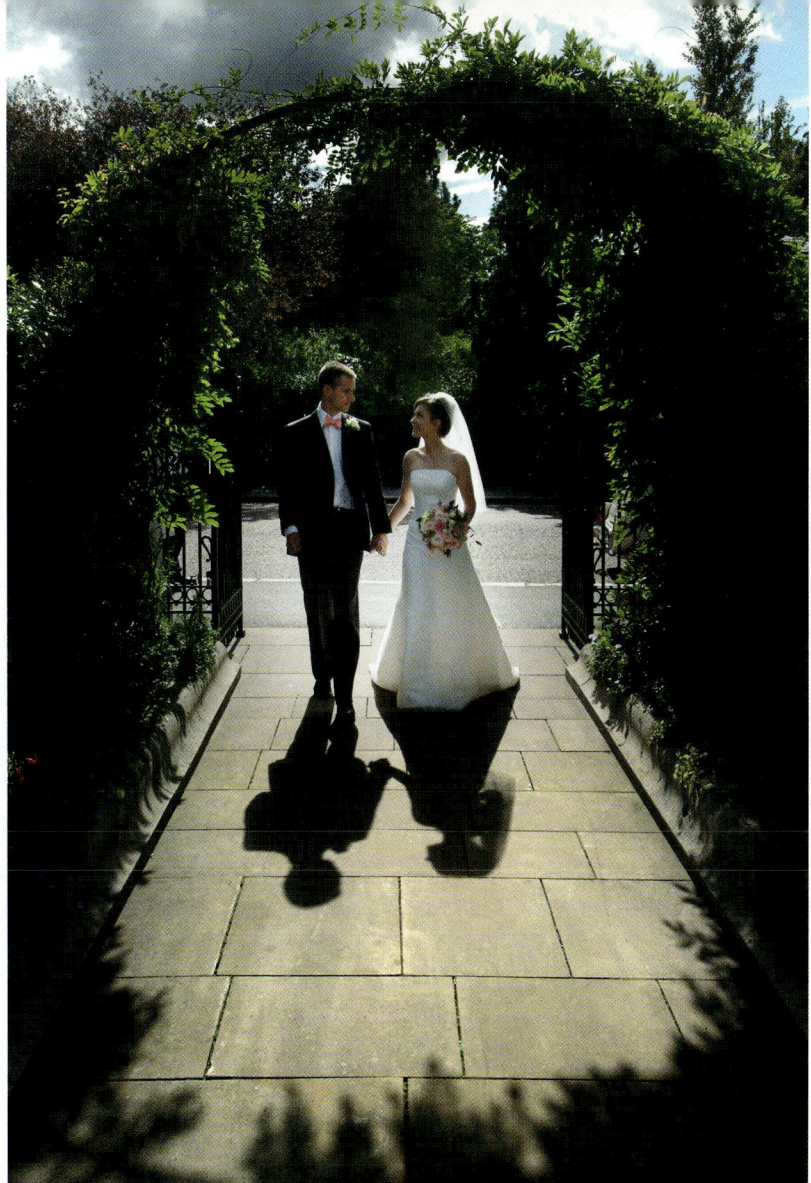

Figs 27 and 28   ISO 800 f/5.7 at 1/1500th and ISO 200 f/8 at 1/250th

A leading shadow and the two arches make a strong graphic composition, while the groom's casual stance makes the picture saleable. I was waiting for the bride and groom to appear around the corner when a guest came up the path toward me. I saw the shadows and immediately switched to a wide lens to capture this image. My only direction to the couple was for them to look at each other at the right moment.

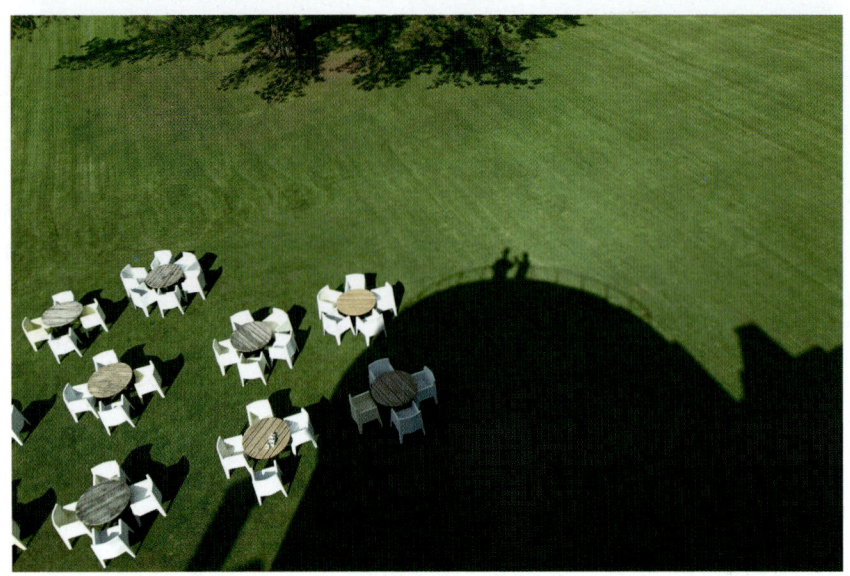

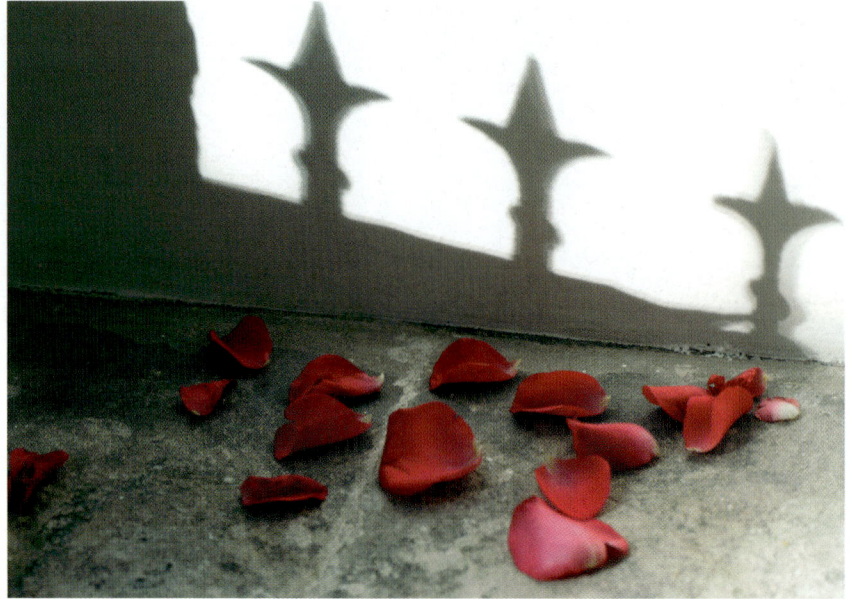

FIGS 29–31   All ISO 400 f/4

Have fun with shadows. These three pictures all made the wedding albums. It pays to have your eyes open to opportunity. In the first picture, I had to remove my shadow in Photoshop to leave just the groom and his best man.

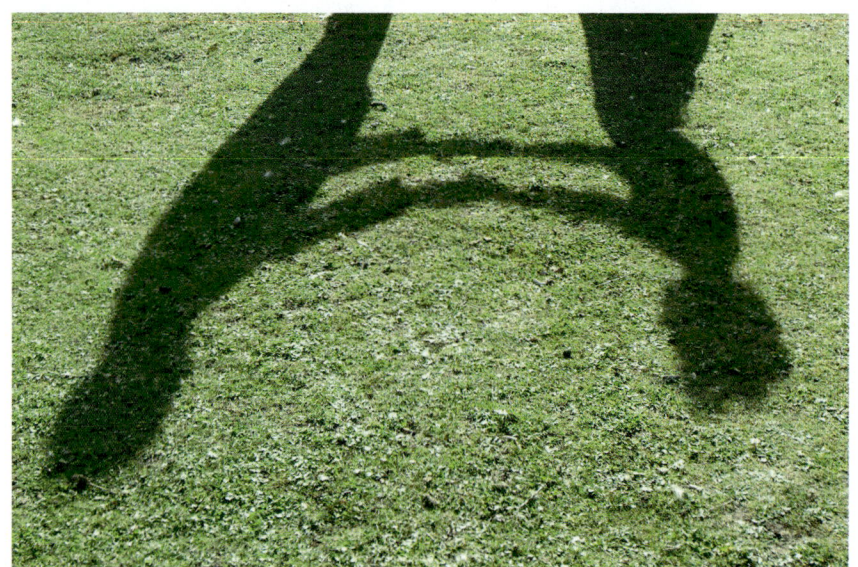

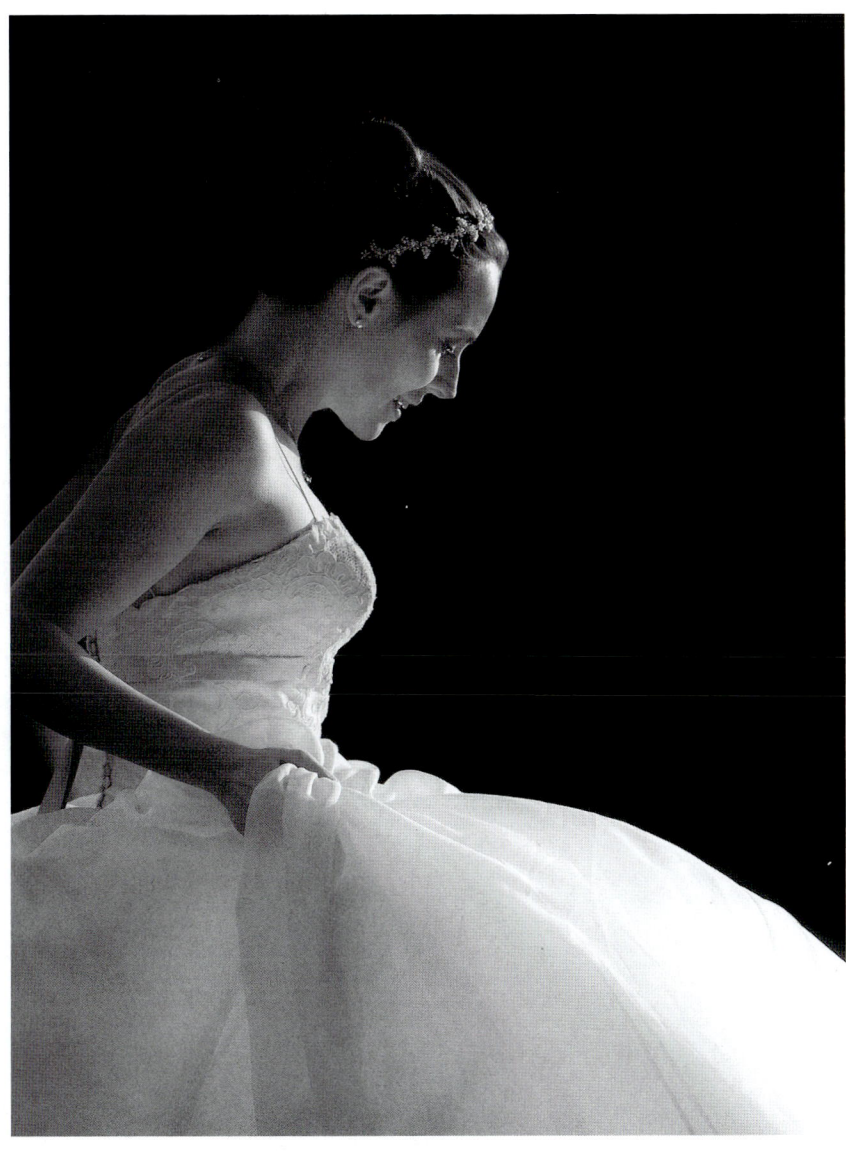

The direction and angle of light was perfect for this candid shot of the bride. The dark hedge beyond was printed down to black in Photoshop.

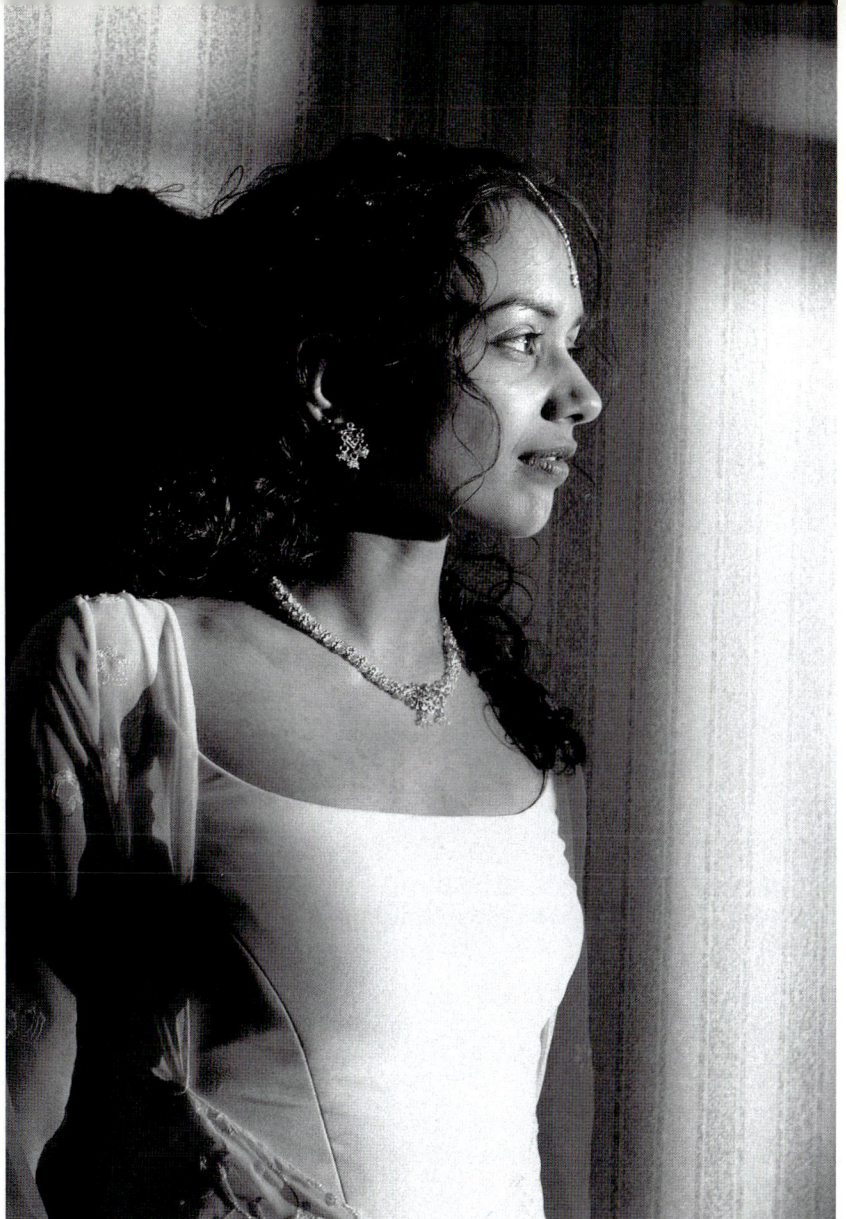

FIG. 33   ISO 800 f/5.7 at 1/90th

The pattern of the window shadow created by the setting sun on a hotel bedroom wall made this picture worth taking. I placed the bride so that her lit face was against the dark background. She is 'keyed down the nose' and I am shooting into the unlit side of her face. Notice how her wonderful cheekbones and jaw line have been accentuated by the lighting direction. Even the stripy wallpaper works in this shot.

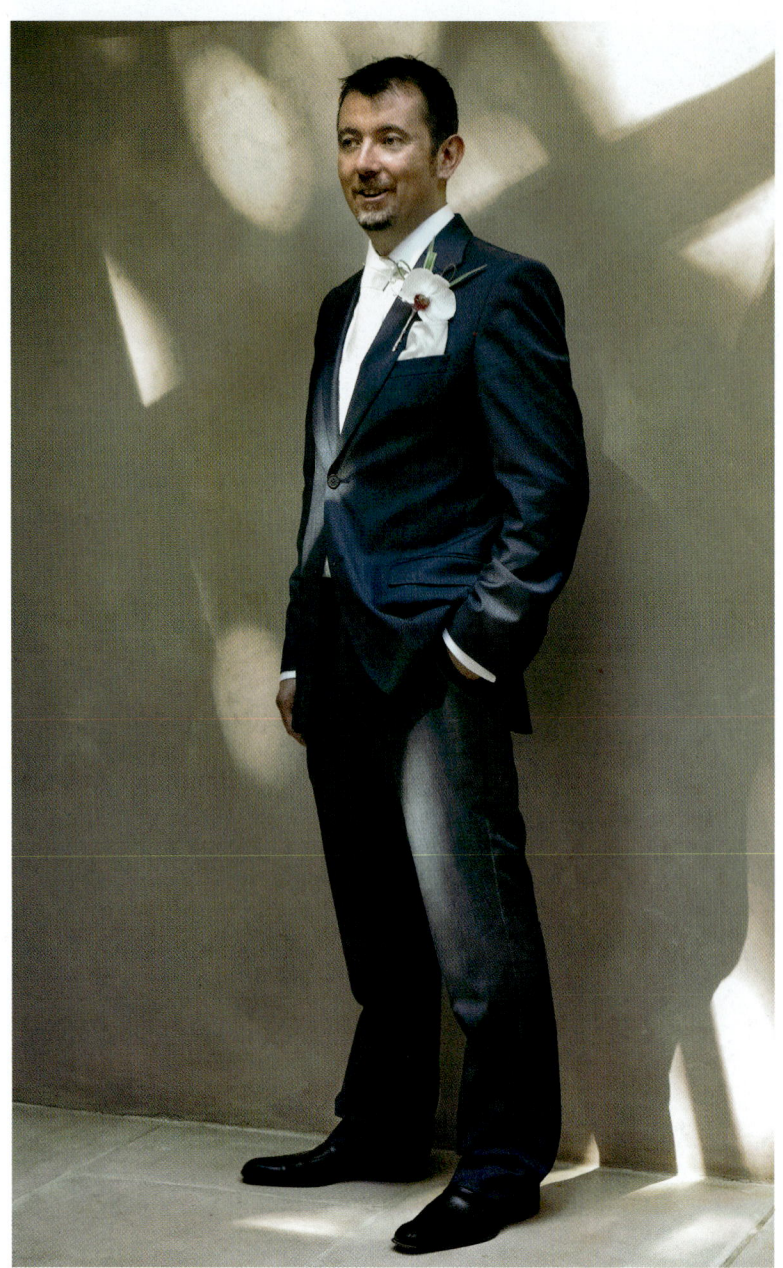

FIG. 34   ISO 400 f/8 at 1/20th

Dappled sunlight on this wall made a picture out of nothing. I nearly didn't get the shot because I forgot to put my lens back to f/4 after the previous picture. This error forced a long exposure but I used a monopod and I got away with it.

bottom

FIG. 35   ISO 400 f/4 at 1/750th

This bride is lit by a pool of light from a window 30 feet away at Wedderburn Castle in Scotland.

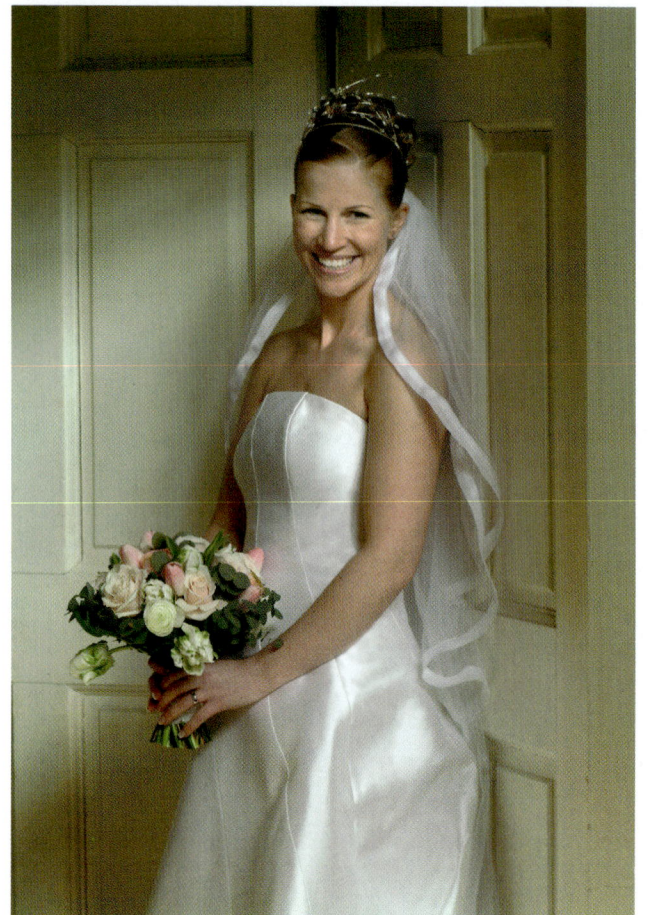

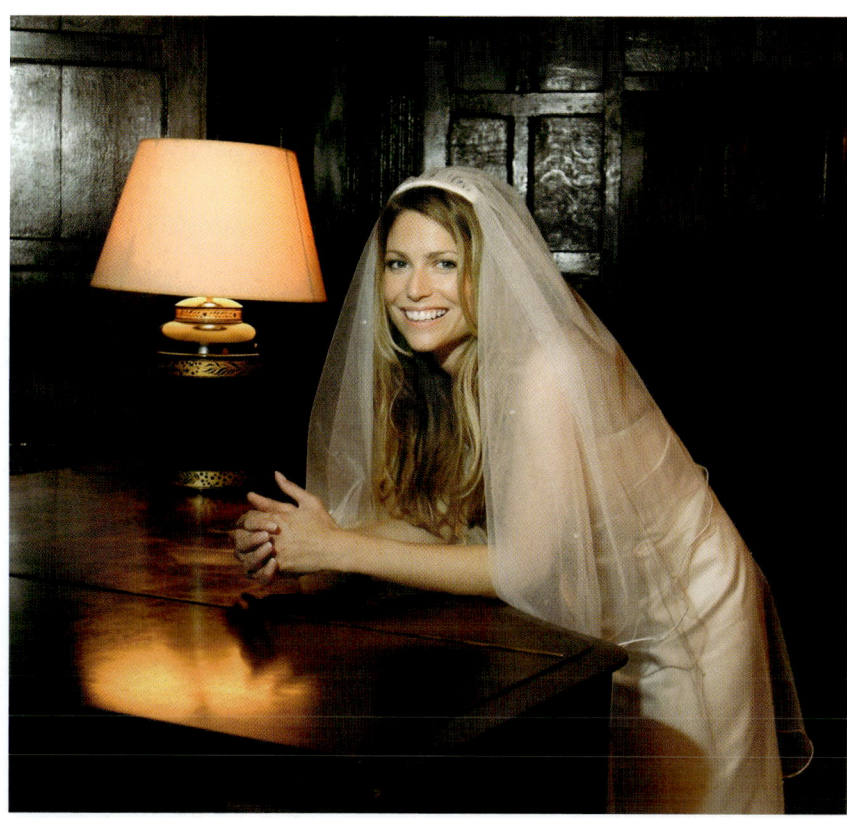

FIG. 36   ISO 800 f/4 at 1/10th

Winter wedding interiors in old houses with dark paneling are a speciality of ours. Here, I used a monopod to steady the camera, added a splash of off-camera flash, and exposed for the light from a table lamp. The flash reflected back off the shiny wood and the lamp reflected in the top of the piano avoiding the black-hole syndrome.

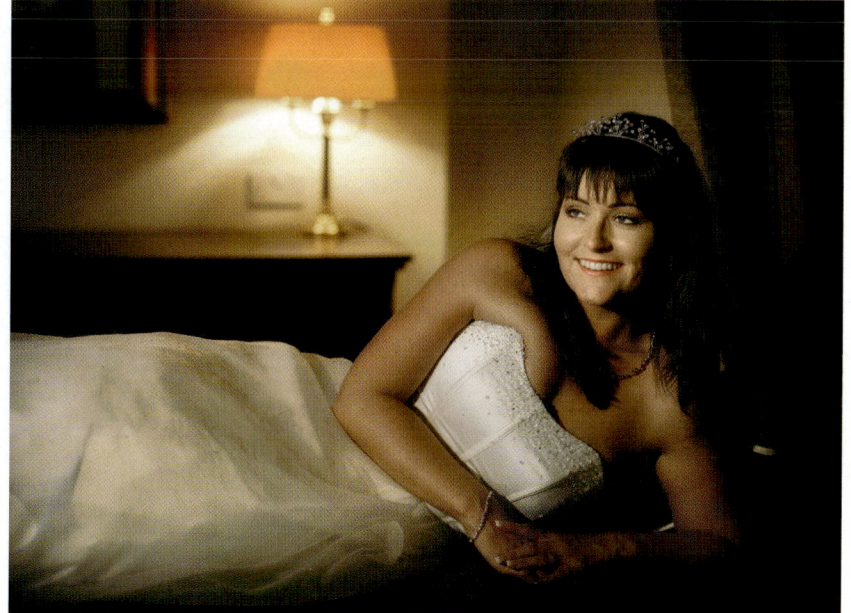

FIG. 37   ISO 400 f/3.2 at 1/90th

Julie and I used a Bescor battery video light from B & H in New York for this shot. Julie lit the bride 'down the nose' and I took the picture shooting into the unlit side of the face. I always make a habit of switching on the table lamps in hotel bedrooms because they give depth to a picture like this.

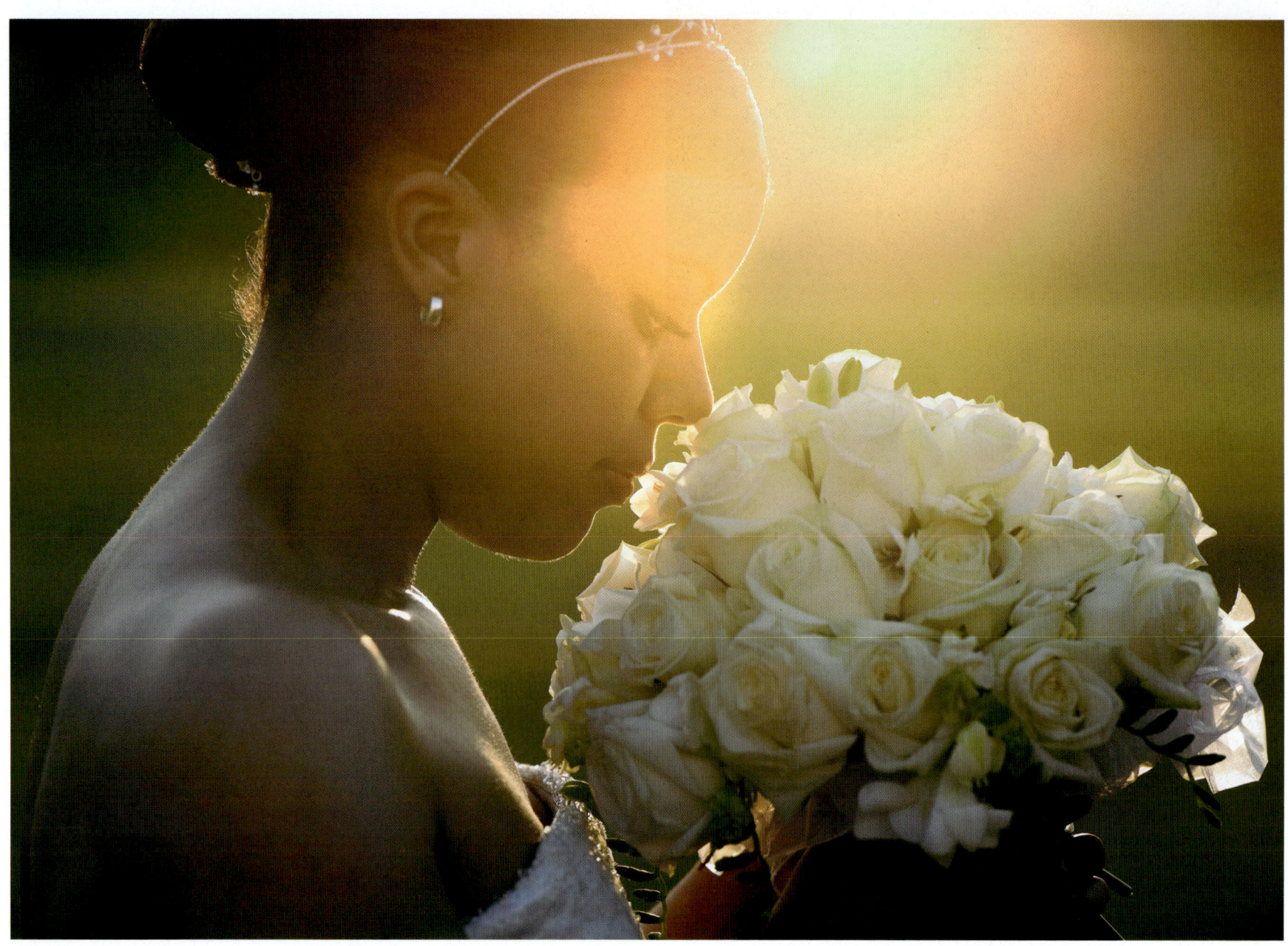

As the day becomes night there are a variety of picture opportunities that include the setting sun in the composition. Here are three that Julie and I have recently shot.

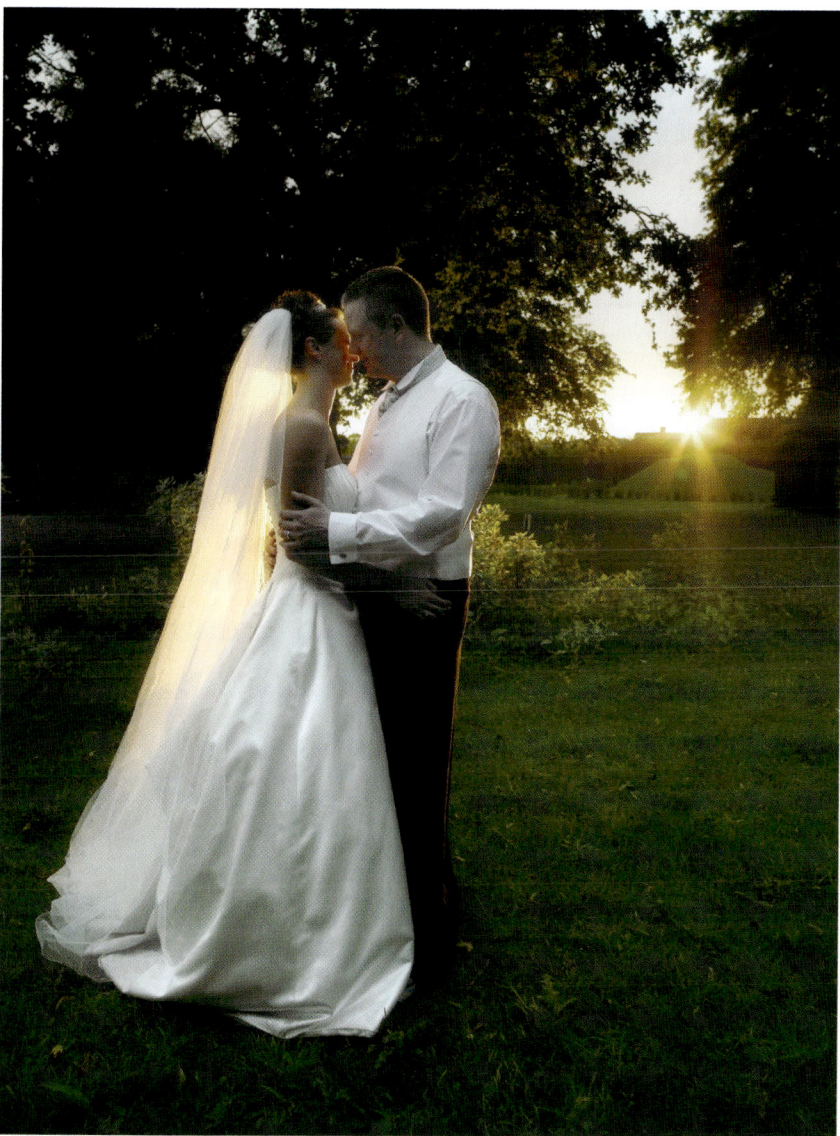

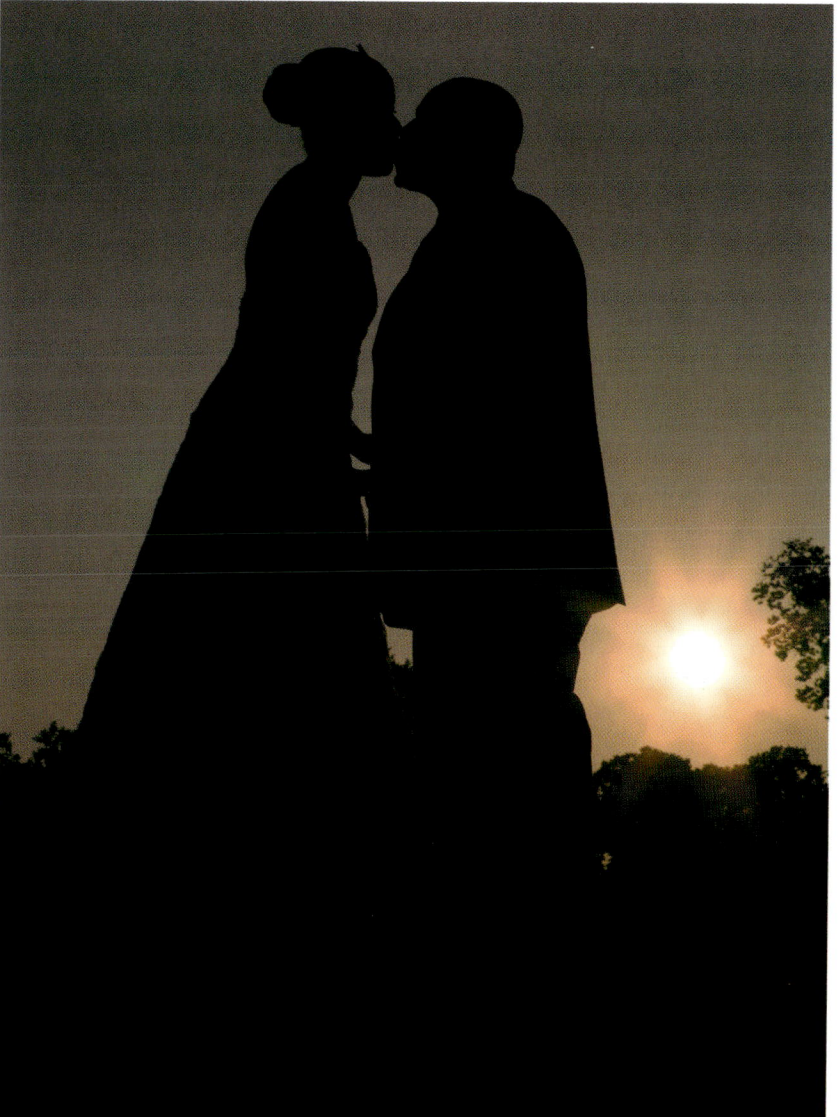

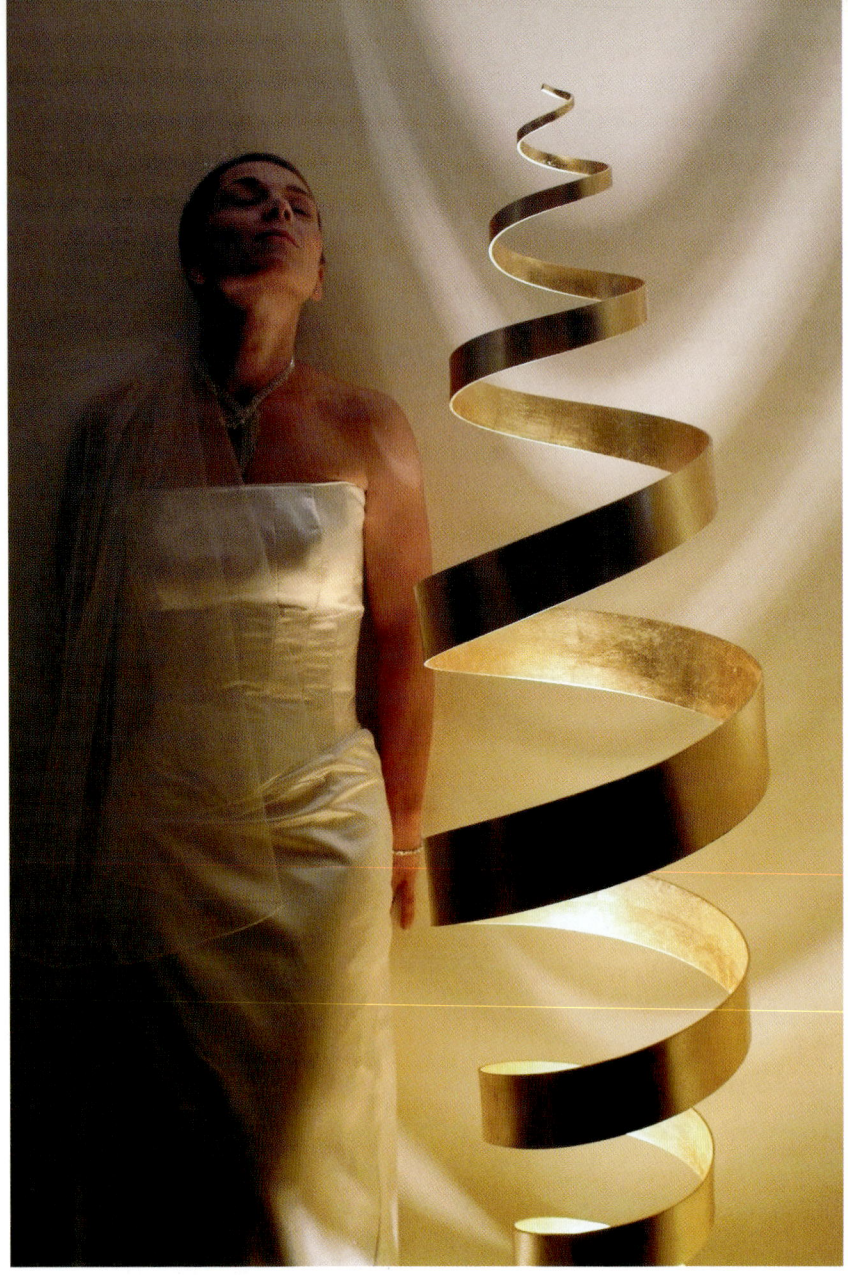

FIG. 41   ISO 800 f/4 at 1/25th

This fun light fitting made a picture. Props like this should not go unnoticed. I used a monopod to keep the camera still during exposure.

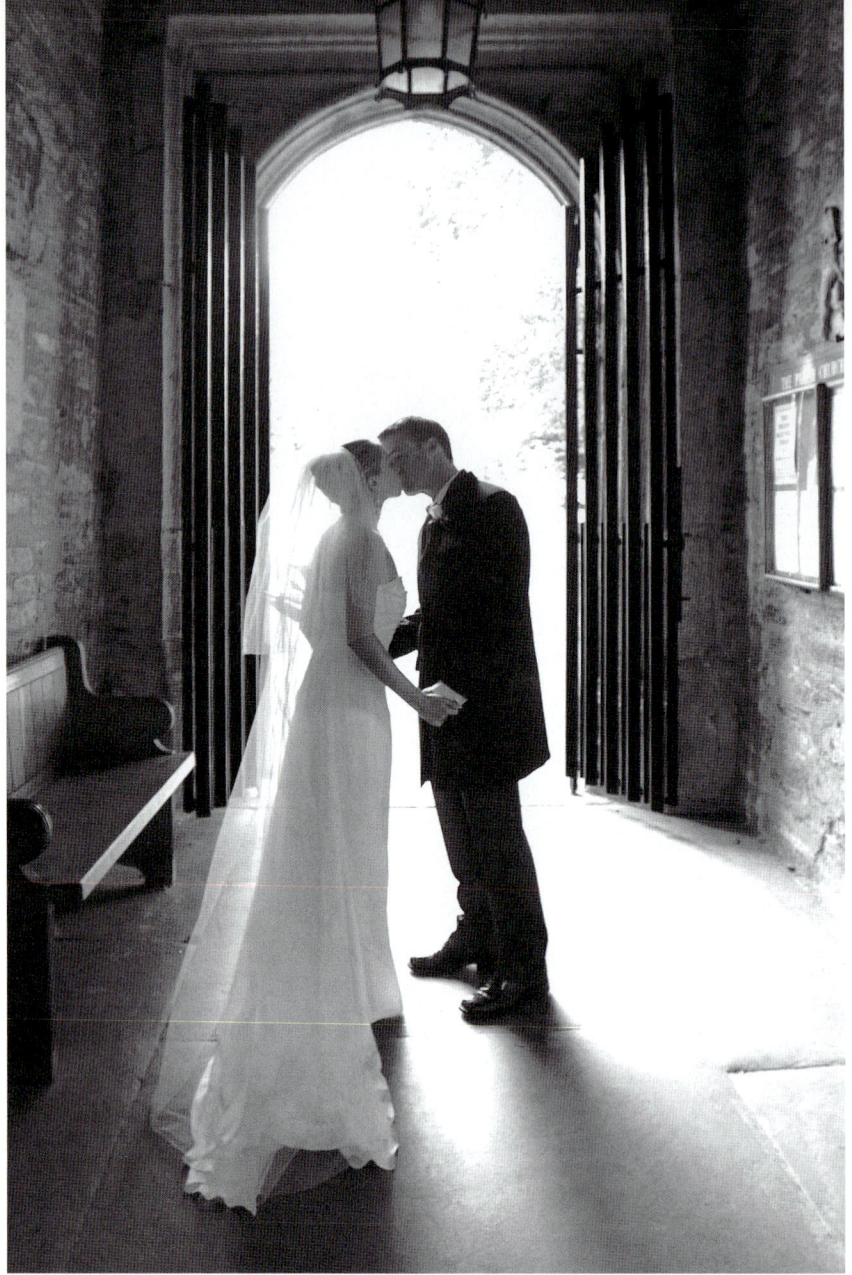

FIG. 42   ISO 800 f/4 at 1/60th

A near silhouette like this can be very effective. Leave the flash switched off and increase the exposure by a stop as a starting point.

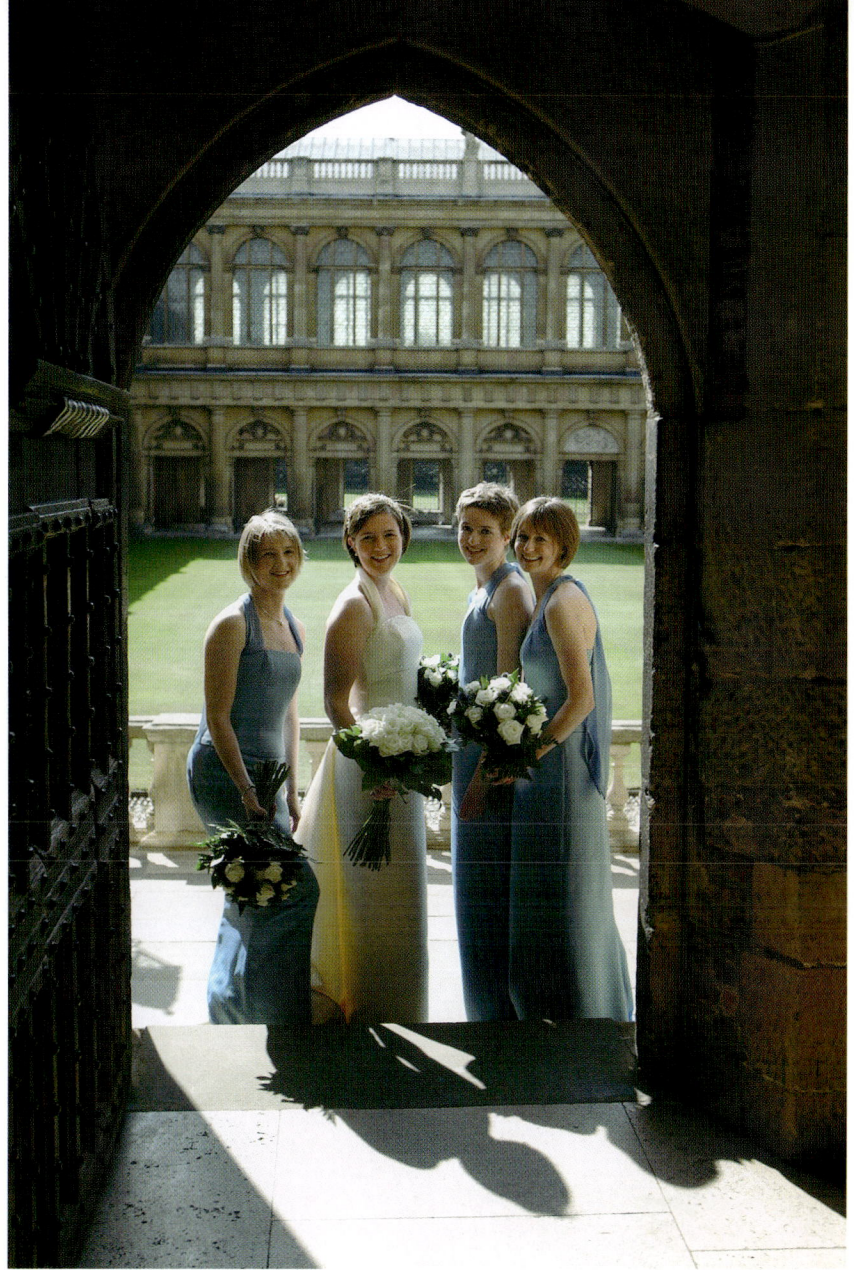

FIG. 43   ISO 320 f/4 at 1/850th

Asking the girls to step down a step allowed them to get some light from the walls either side of the archway. A risky shot but I got away with it. Trinity College, Cambridge.

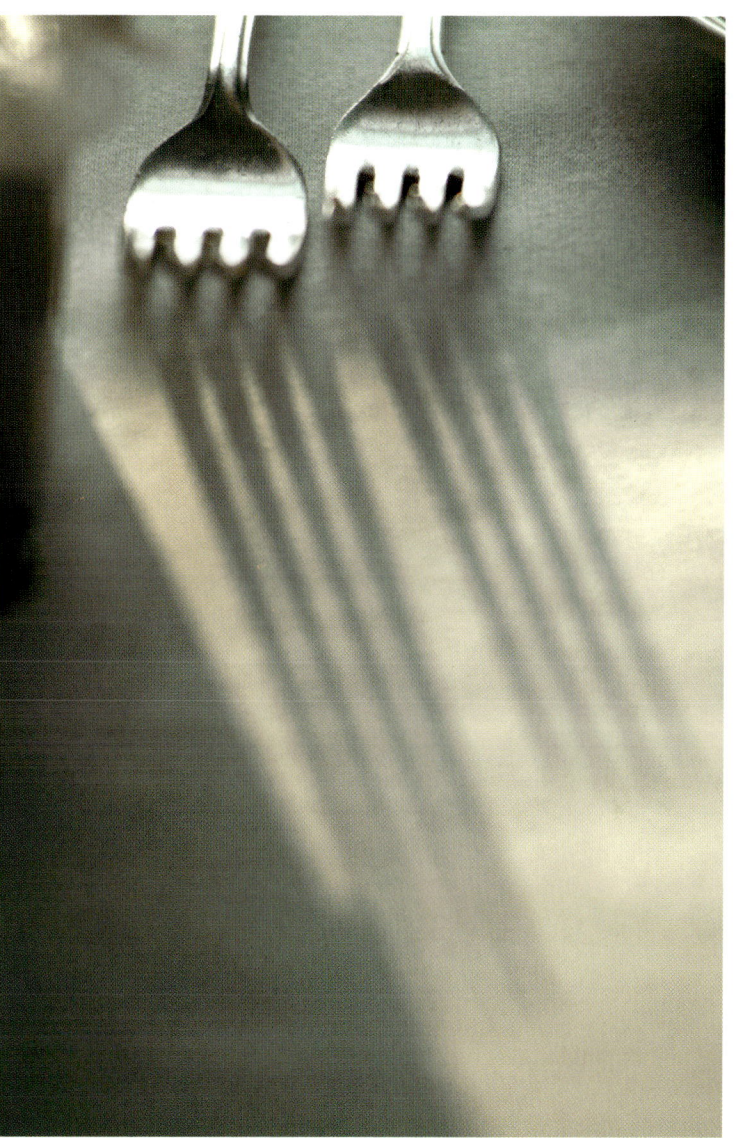

FIG. 44   ISO 400 f/4 at 1/500th

Very simple shots like this created by sunlight on the dining table have a charm of their own. Beware, you tidy them up a bit and the magic is often lost.

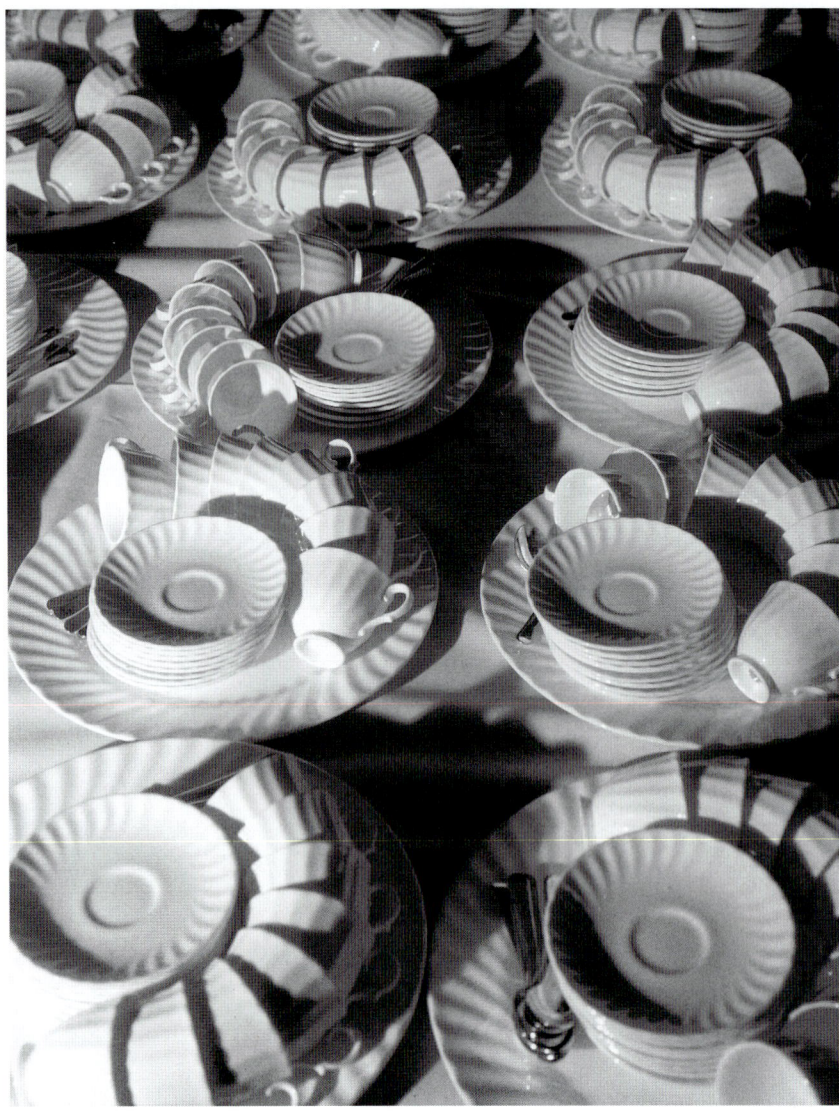

FIG. 45   ISO 800 f/4 at 1/60th

I saw these coffee cups and I couldn't resist a picture. I used a flash off-camera to create the dramatic shadows and emphasize the patterns. They look a bit like fossils now.

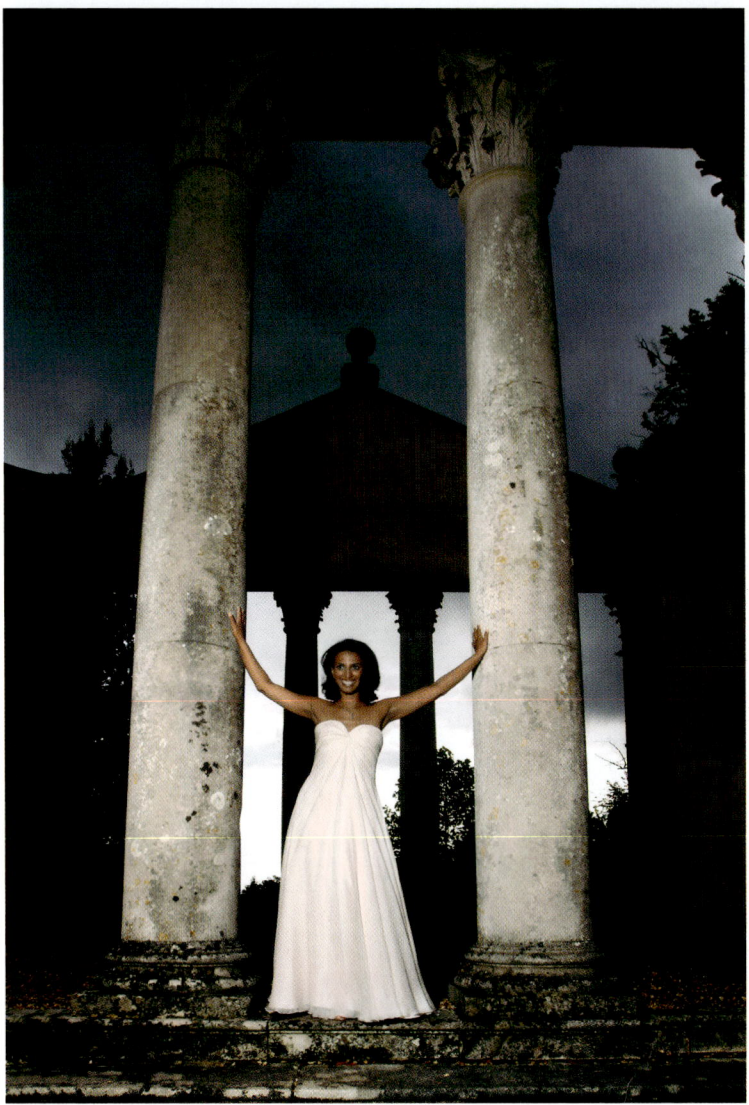

FIG. 46   ISO 400 f6.7 at 1/125th

Taken moments before the heavens opened and torrential rain came upon us. I used a small handheld flashgun on full power zoomed in to cover an 80-mm lens. Julie held this beside me as I shot on a wide lens.

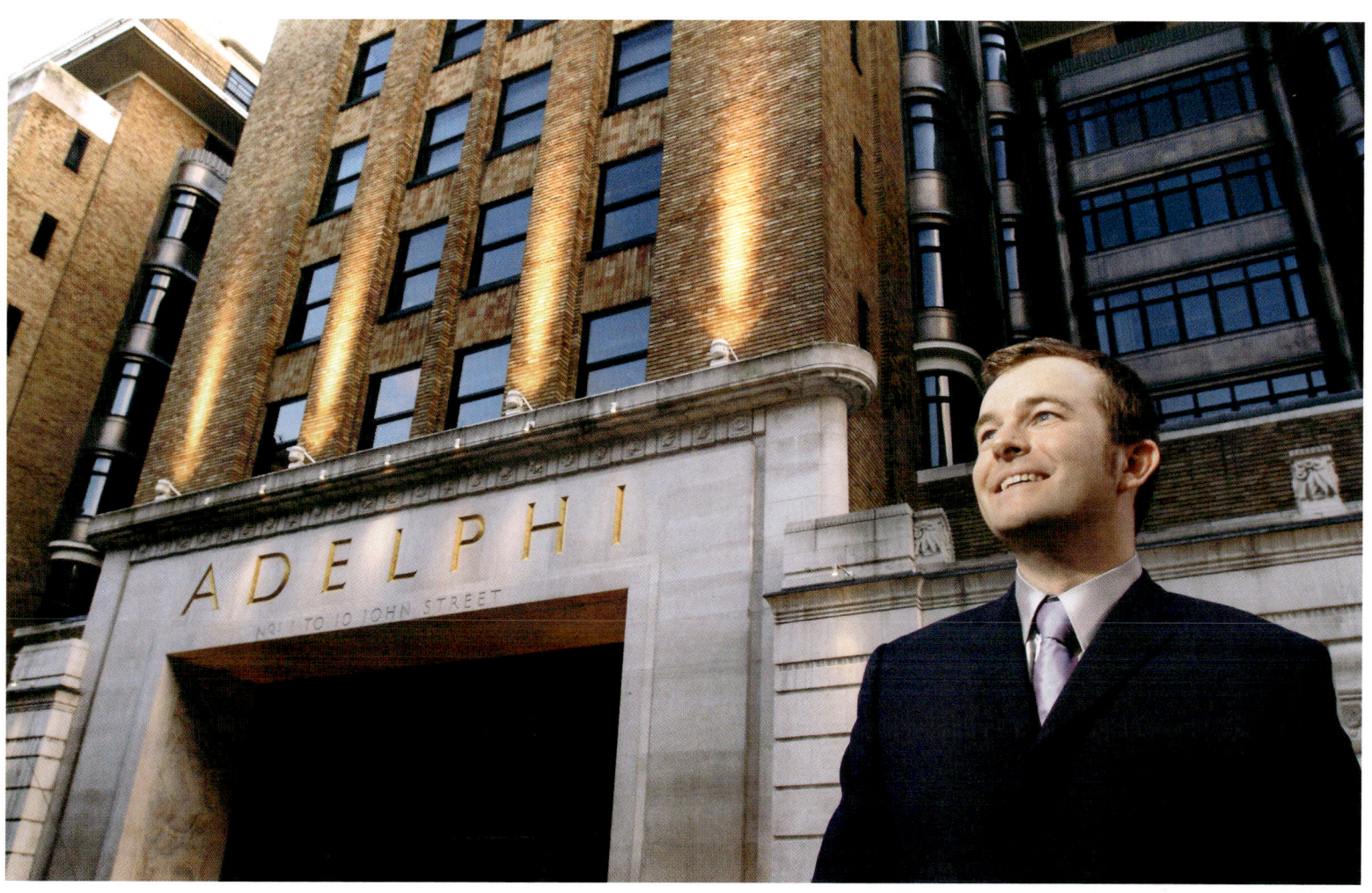

FIG. 47   ISO 800 f/6.7 at 1/60th

Julie held my flashgun so that this groom was lit straight down the nose and I balanced the exposure for the Adelphi building in the background. The color contrast with the yellow and blue further enhances this shot as does the low angle viewpoint.

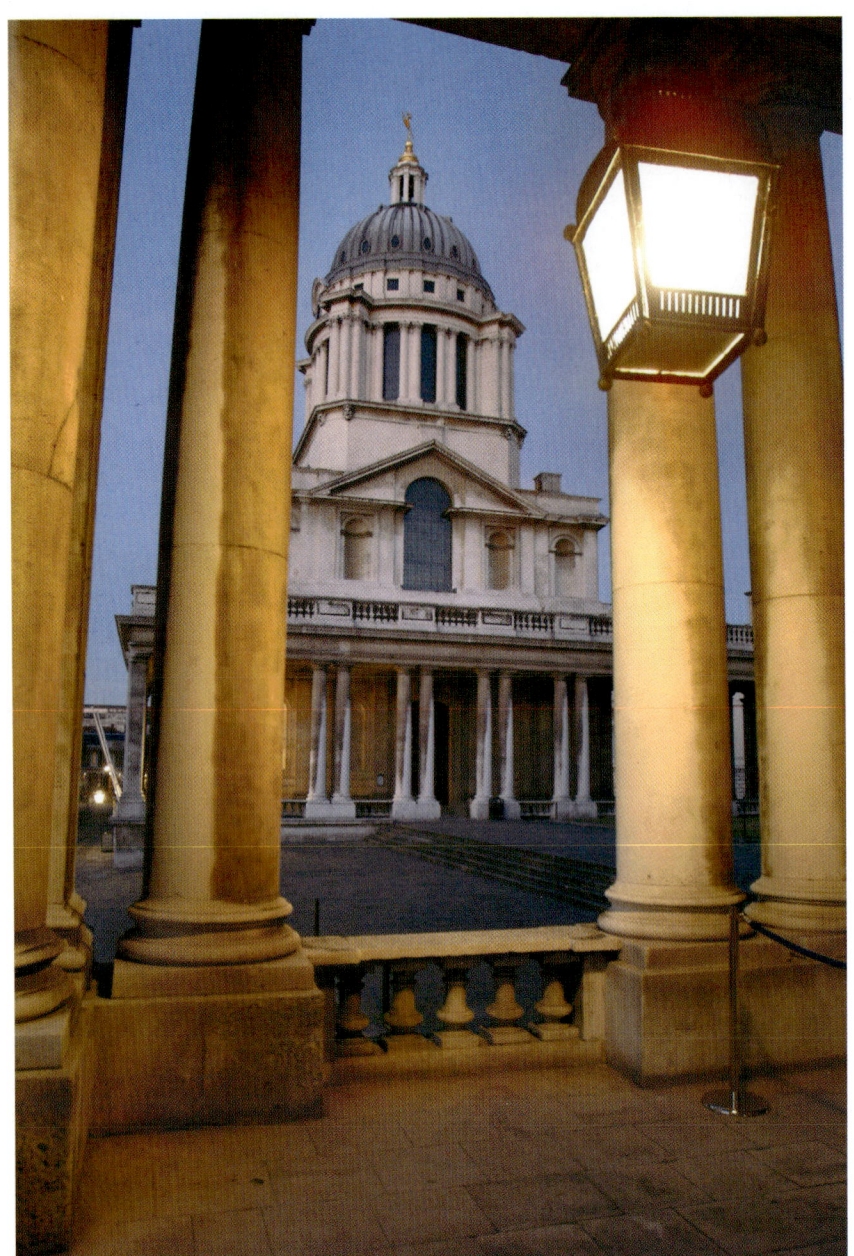

Mixing tungsten light and daylight at dusk is a firm favorite of mine. It doesn't matter what the weather is doing, great shots are nearly always possible. Shutter speeds get slow so be prepared to use a tripod.

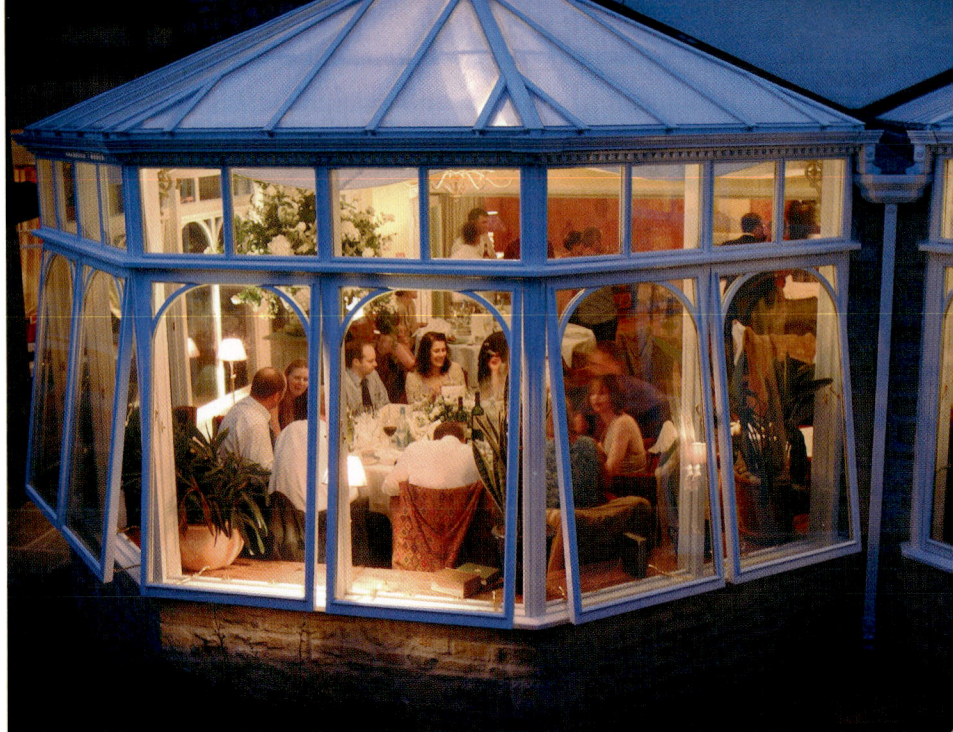

FIG. 50   ISO 200 f/4 at 1/2

Low pressure sodium light emits just one predominant wavelength and is therefore imposable to color balance correctly. I was about 10 minutes too late for this shot as I'd have preferred more light in the sky. The reflection is courtesy of a BMW 3 series sunroof!

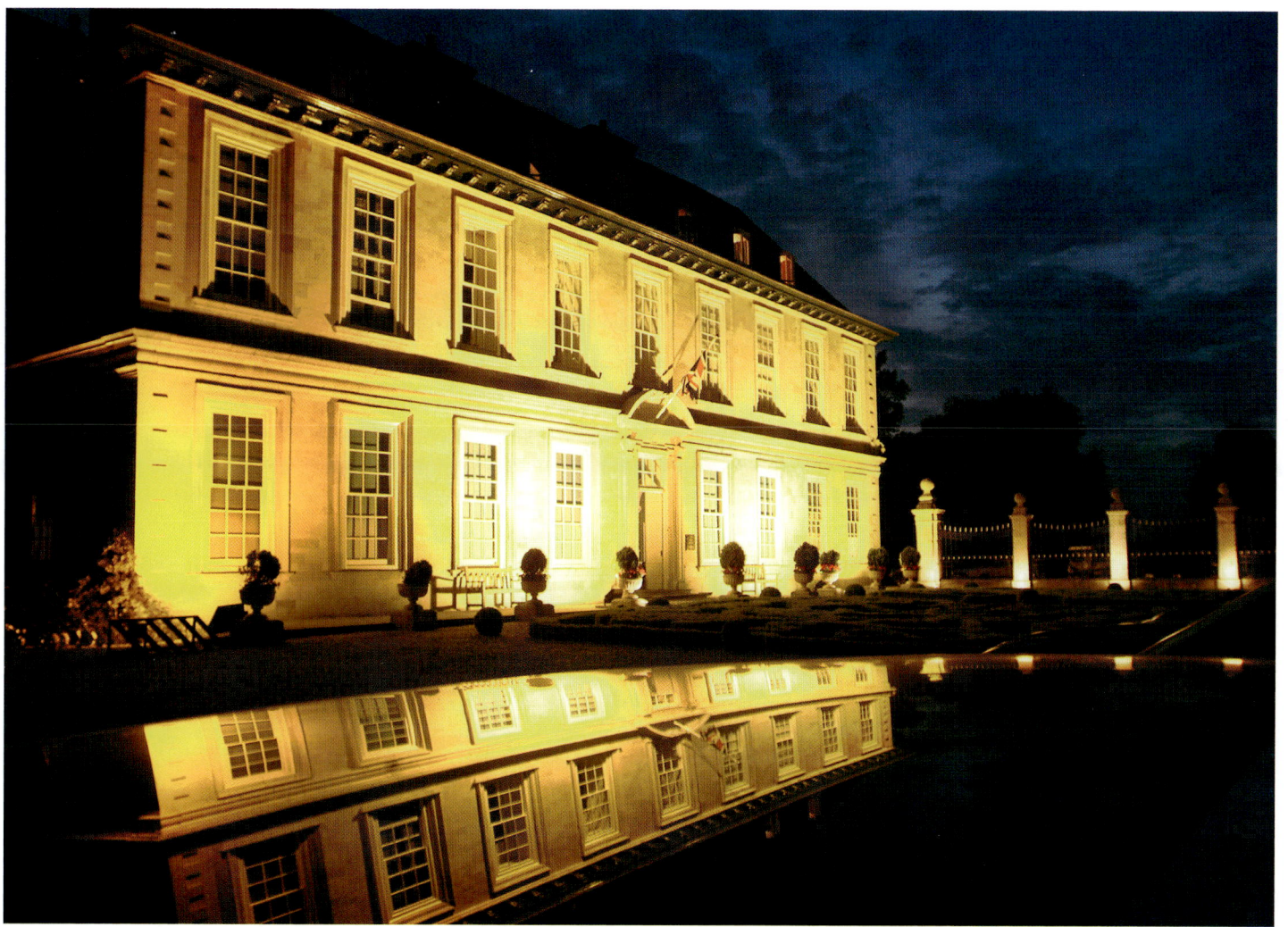

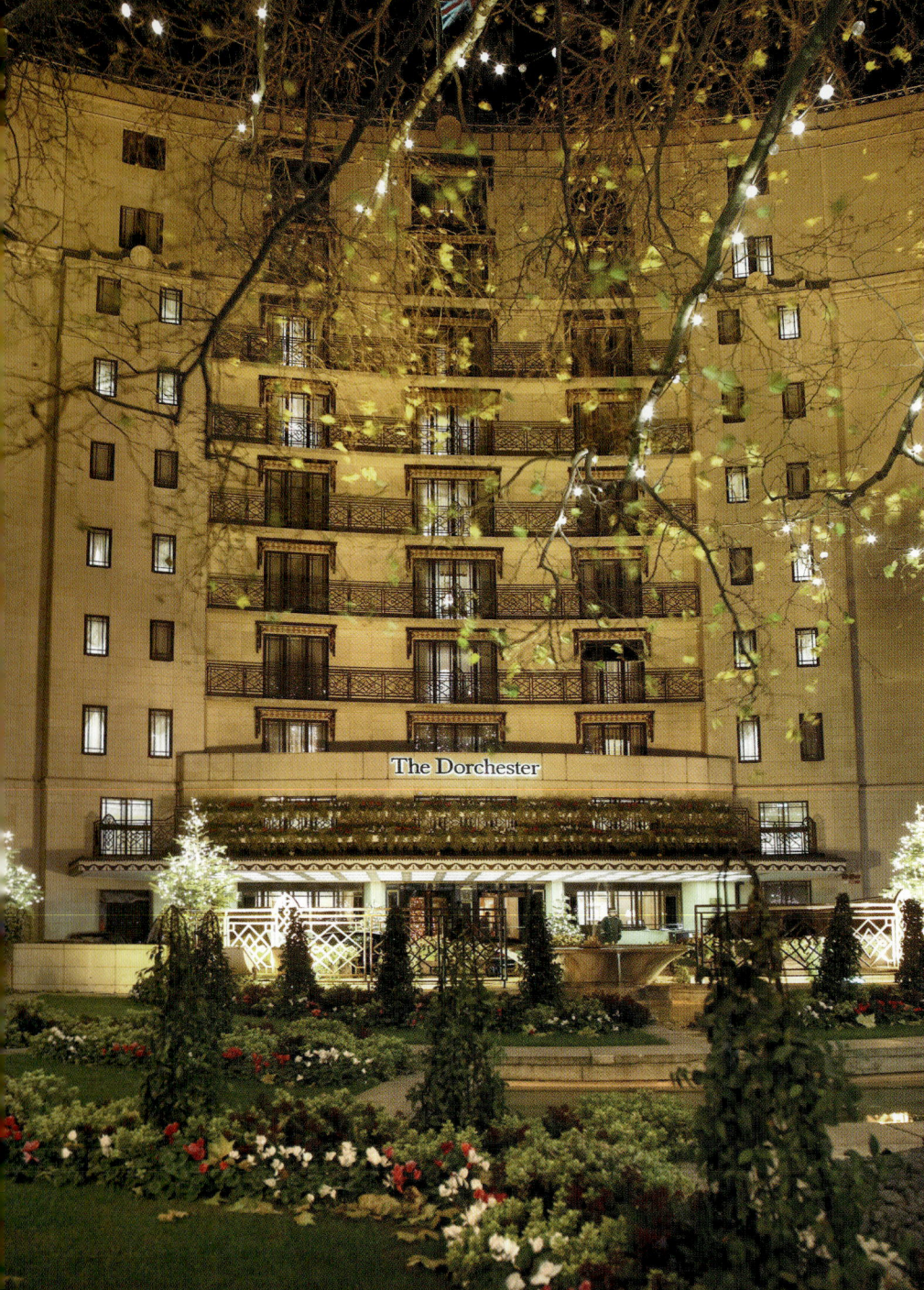

Fig. 51   ISO 400 f/4 at 1

This Christmas picture of the Dorchester Hotel in London makes a dull day look great. Night exterior pictures really lift a wedding album.

opposite

Fig. 52   ISO 800 f/4 at 1/30th

I had a few seconds to get the exposure spot on for this picture. I used manual focus and a tripod so I could concentrate on getting the bride and groom sharp and well exposed. I waited on until midnight to get this shot so I had to get a result.

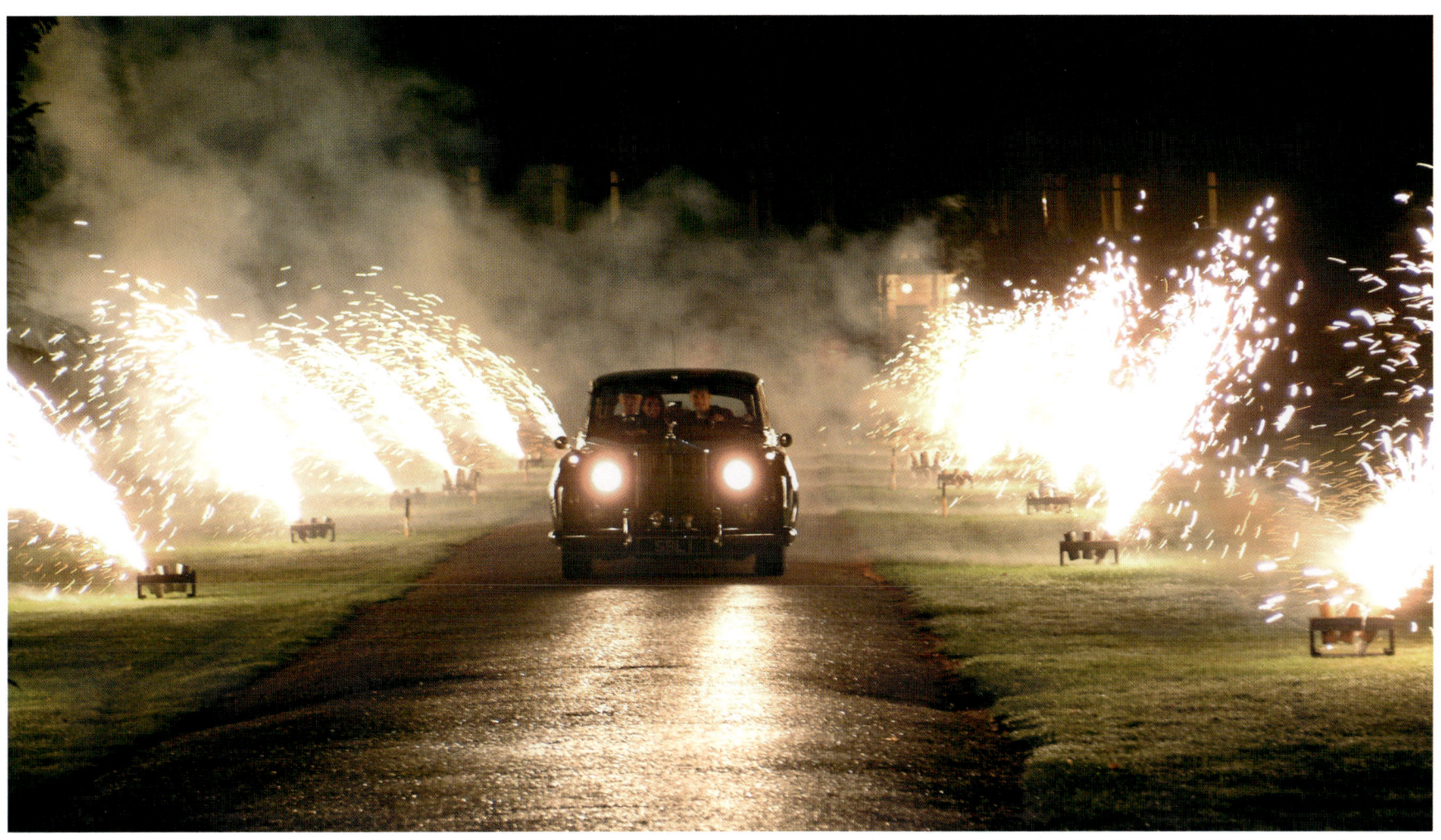

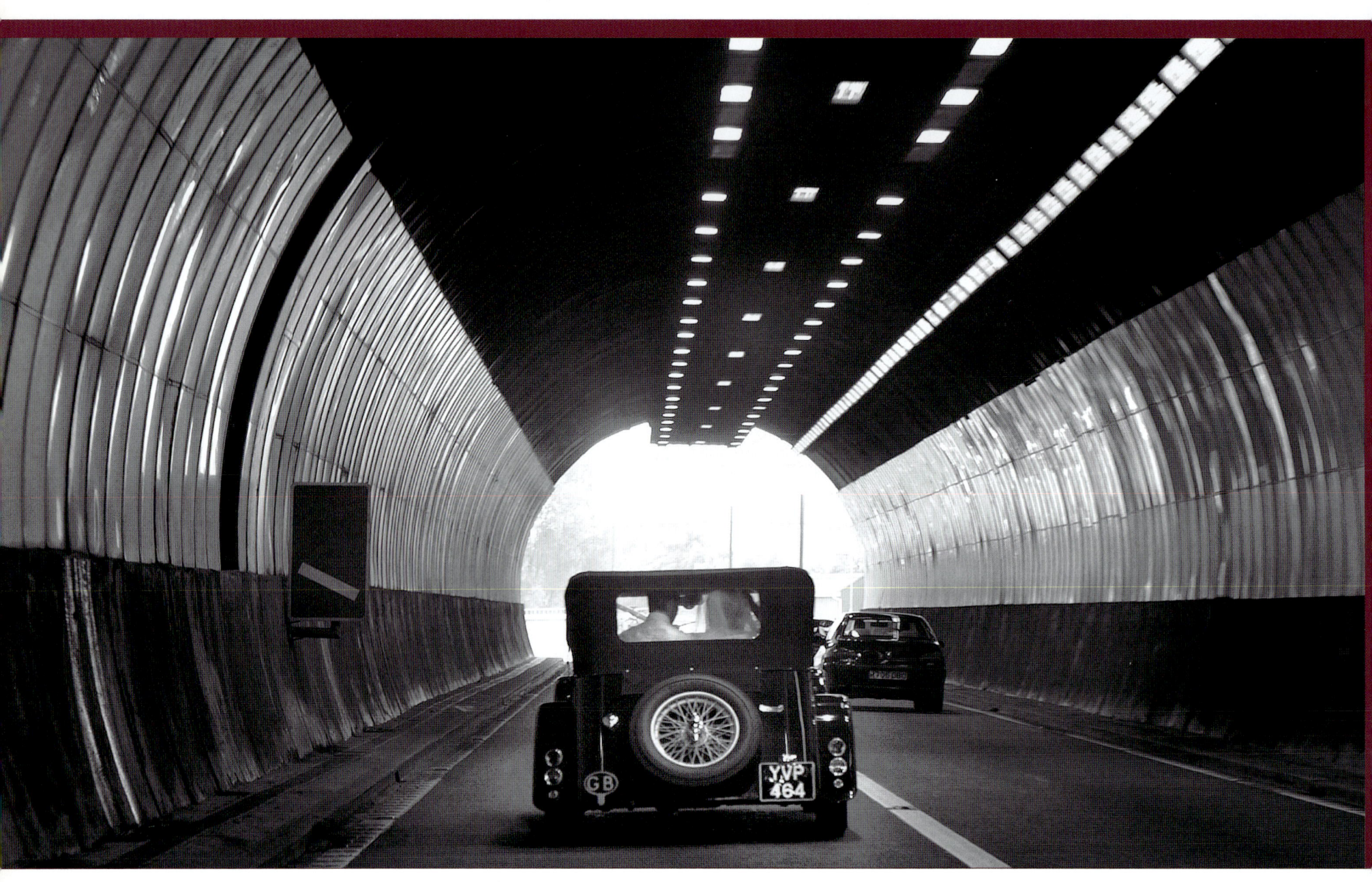

Chapter Four: Logistics – Planning the Wedding Day

4
Logistics – Planning the Wedding Day

PLAN AHEAD

Well before every wedding, Julie and I plan every detail of the wedding schedule and our involvement like a military operation. Why? First, because we want to achieve high standards we need to use our time efficiently and second, we don't want anything to take us by surprise. So instead of waiting for problems to happen, we try to identify them as early as possible.

For example, at our very first meeting, we might discover that the prospective bride and groom were planning to start the wedding day 100 miles apart. For us this would present a logistical problem, meaning we might need to take two cars – not an ideal scenario if parking at the church is tight or the wedding is a long

way from our base. Then let's say the wedding ceremony is already booked for noon. This might run to 1 PM after confetti and so on; factor in the 30-minute journey to the reception and the planned wedding breakfast being served at 2 PM. This would leave virtually no time to photograph the bride and groom or the formal groups. To achieve good coverage, clearly more photography time needs to be negotiated.

opposite

FIG. 1   ISO 320 f/4 at 1/100th

This tunnel shot was taken by Julie from the passenger seat as I drove the car. We knew this tunnel was on the route from the church to the reception and we cleaned the windscreen in preparation.

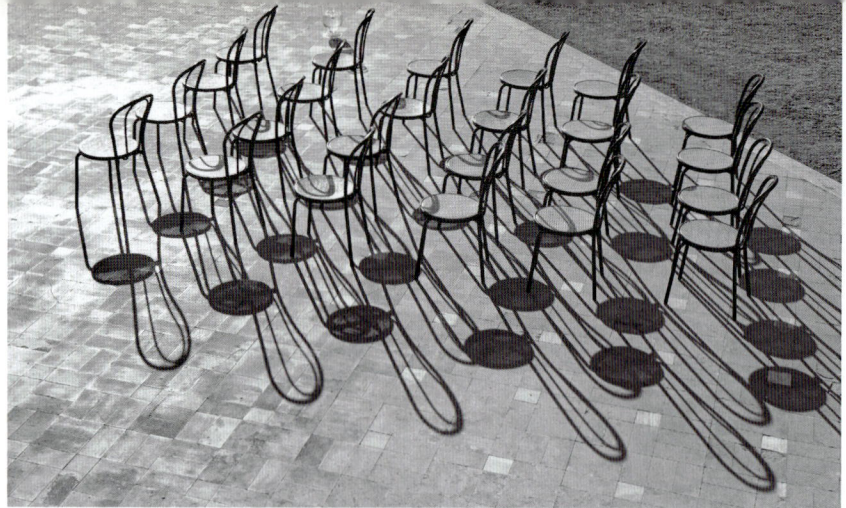

Fig. 2   ISO 200 F/4 AT 1/2000TH

I love simple repeating patterns like these chairs laid out for a wedding at Florence in Italy..

bottom left

Fig. 3   ISO 200 F/4 AT 1/125TH

If the couple have arranged video coverage of the wedding it is worth establishing a rapport with the crew before the day itself.

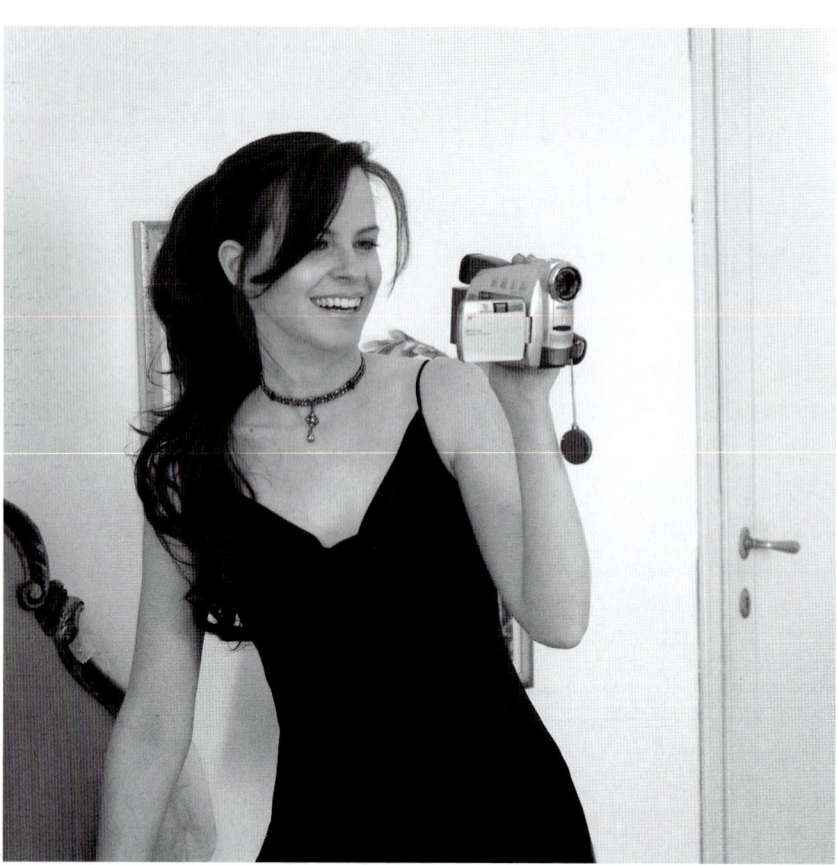

Looking at another scenario, a 4 PM ceremony at a Castle in Scotland in December probably rules out any pictures of the bride and groom together in daylight. If like us, you are happy to use available light or make your own, then this might not be a major problem. On the other hand, if you point out what exciting pictures of the couple you could take by daylight in the castle grounds, the bride and groom might be happy to be ready by 2 PM for an hour of photography before the guests start to arrive for the ceremony. Stay creative and open-minded at the planning stage and most problems will disappear.

But as a last resort, don't be afraid to say no to a booking rather than take on a wedding with a fundamentally flawed time plan. Setting yourself up to fail in this way will have a terrible knock-on effect that could pull you down emotionally. The psychological and financial effects of disappointing a bride can last for years.

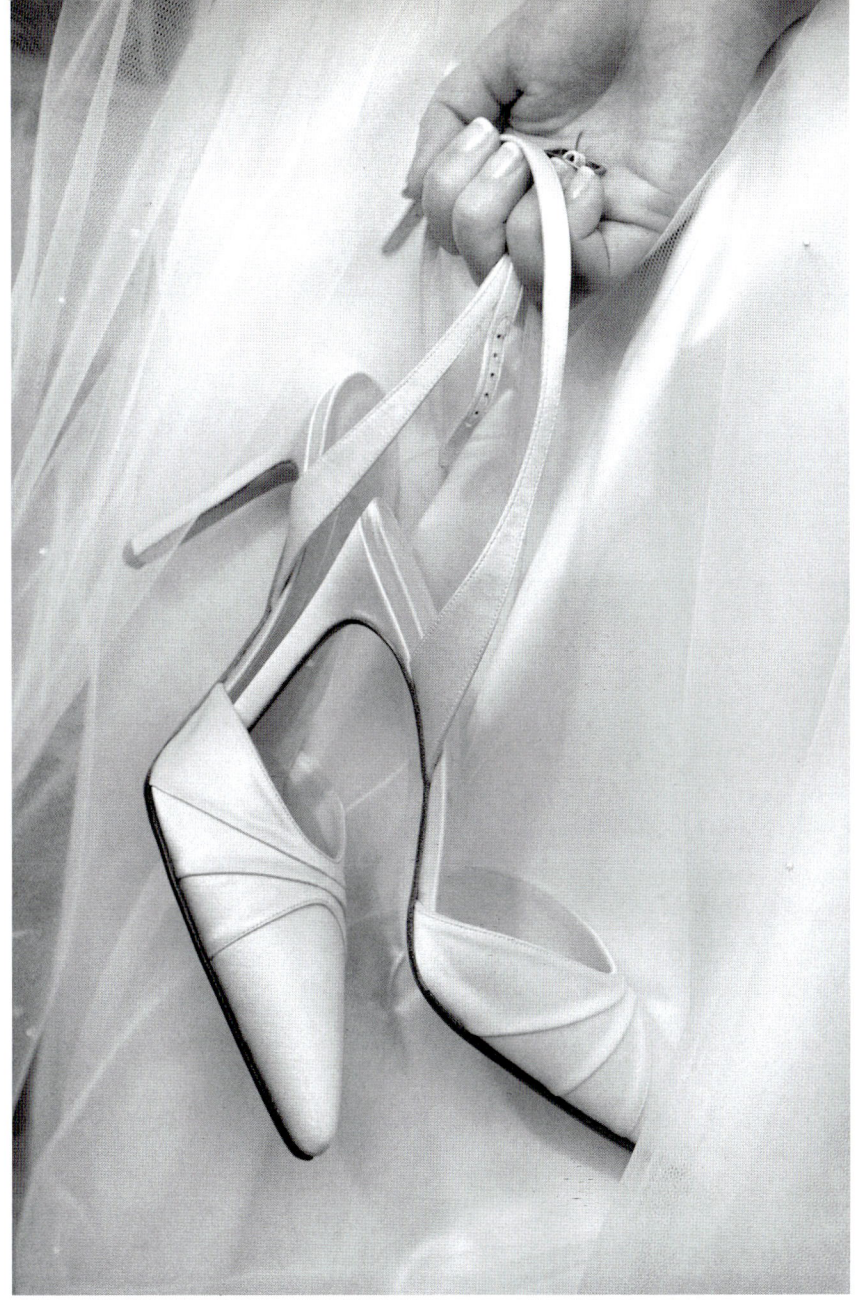

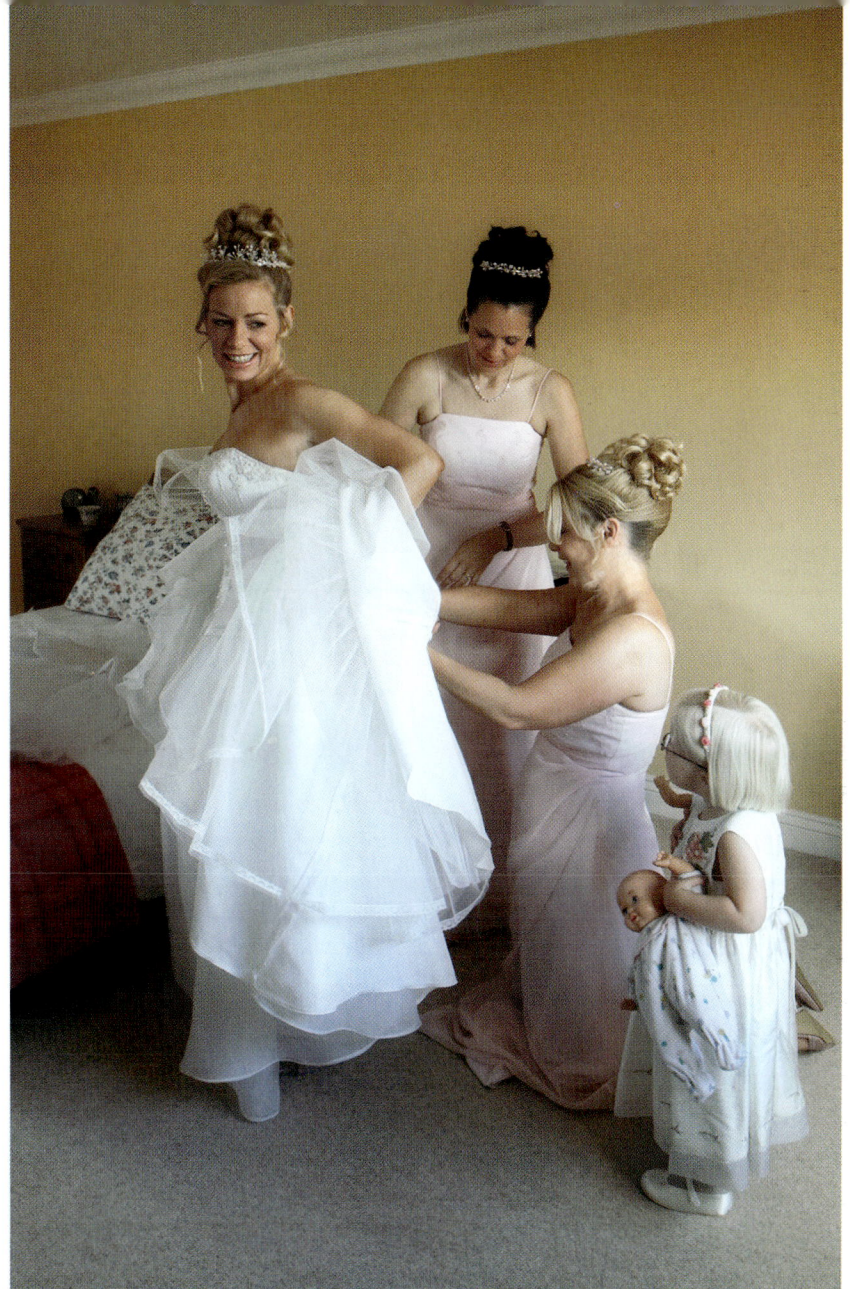

FIG. 4   ISO 800 F/6.7 AT 1/60TH

This simple picture of a bride holding her shoes was Julie's inspiration at one of our weddings. Keep coming up with ideas and you will stay creative.

FIG. 5   ISO 800 F/4 AT 1/125TH

It's all hands on deck for the final preparations. The cascade of girls in this picture makes a striking composition.

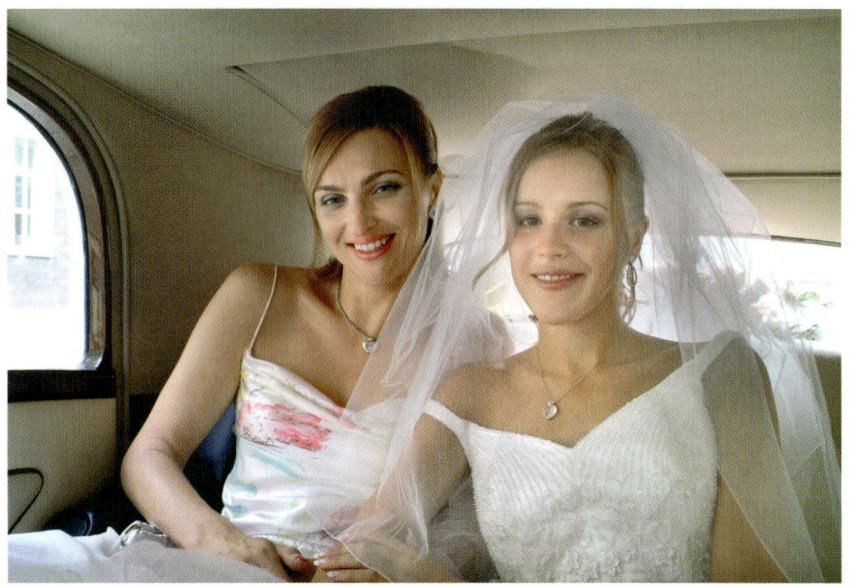

Fig. 6   ISO 800 f/4 at 1/60th

When Julie travels with the bride to the ceremony some great picture opportunities occur. Julie used plus one stop of exposure compensation for this shot of a bride and her mother.

TRAVEL ARRANGEMENTS

If our first appointment is more than 90 minutes from our home, Julie and I prefer to stay in a hotel close to the venue the night before the wedding. There are a couple of exceptions to this rule. If our start time is late in the day or we can drive to the wedding using minor roads that avoid congestion, we will travel on the day. The key principle for us is to keep stress at bay. Being stuck in a traffic jam on the highway behind an accident that could take hours to clear is not something I'm prepared to risk. Being late for a wedding is simply not an option.

So reduce risks, stay professional, and plan creatively. If the shooting day is 12 hours, or the combined shoot and travel time is more than 14 hours, we always stay the night of the wedding too. Driving at night when tired is not a risk we are willing to take. Always remember that you are your own most valuable asset, so look after yourself. Besides, a few nights away in a good hotel is always fun. Better still, this is a kind of fun that is tax-deductible!

Occasionally, it is more convenient for us to take two cars. Having two cars allows one of us to start later or finish early. If I am on a clay pigeon shoot with the guys at 10 AM and Julie doesn't need to start until noon, then taking two cars is to her advantage. On the other hand, I often stay on to photograph the fireworks or a special leaving ceremony at midnight, allowing Julie to head

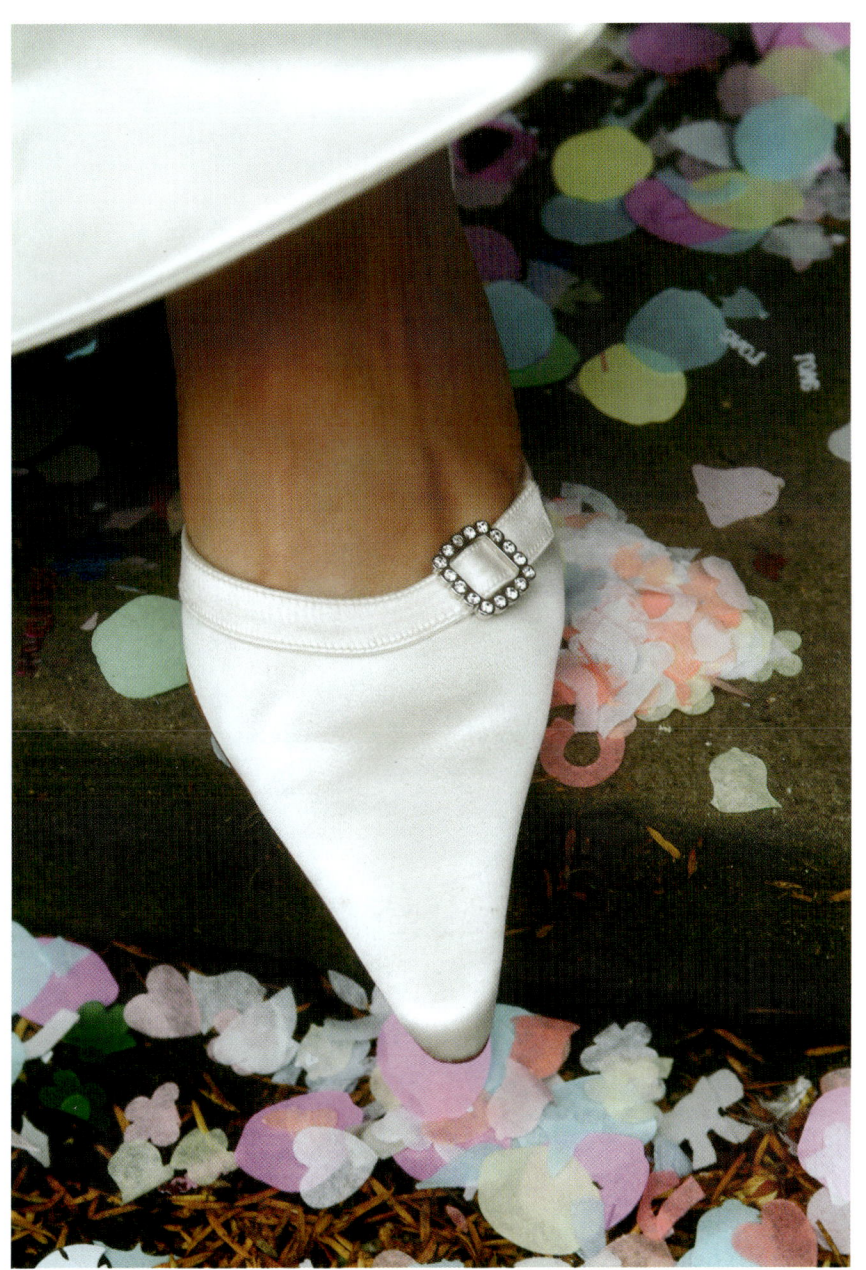

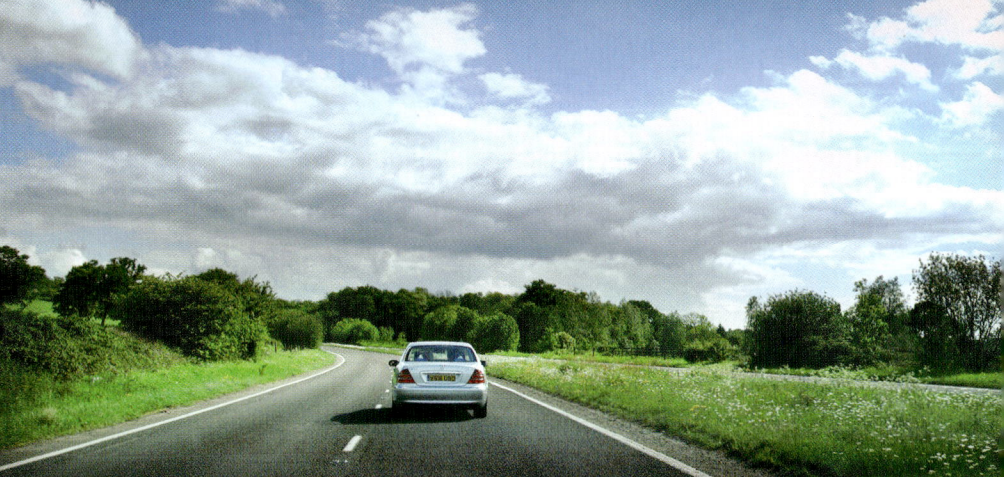

home or back to the hotel after the speeches at 9:30 PM. If parking is tight at the church, I'll leave my car at the reception venue and get a lift with the ushers. I've even taken the groom and the best man to the church in my car when it was the most convenient option. Having a clean car, inside and out, is obviously very necessary at weddings. Taking two cars to a wedding has its disadvantages too. It means twice the expenditure, and more importantly no champagne for either of us!

When you create a time plan for the day, be accurate with journey times. I've often heard a groom say something like, 'the reception is only about ten minutes away' only to find the journey takes us half an hour. Remember to factor in local events

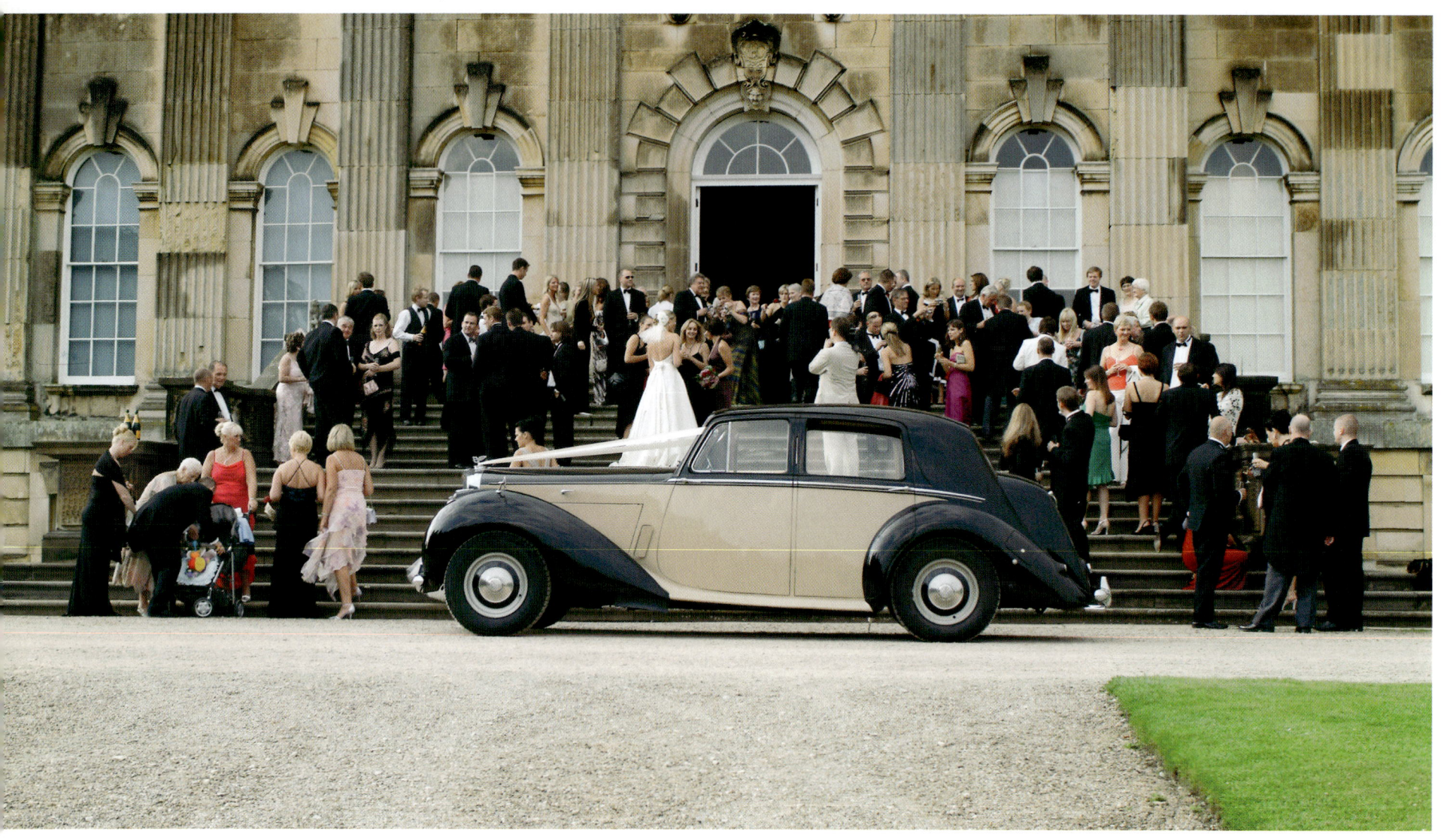

FIG. 9   ISO 400 f/4.8 at 1/1000th

When making this kind of picture, it is always worth the extra effort of walking some distance with a long lens rather than using a wide-angle lens from close in.

FIG. 10   ISO 320 f/4 at 1/650th

These girls play rugby and the surprise reveal of their socks and boots was part of the plan.

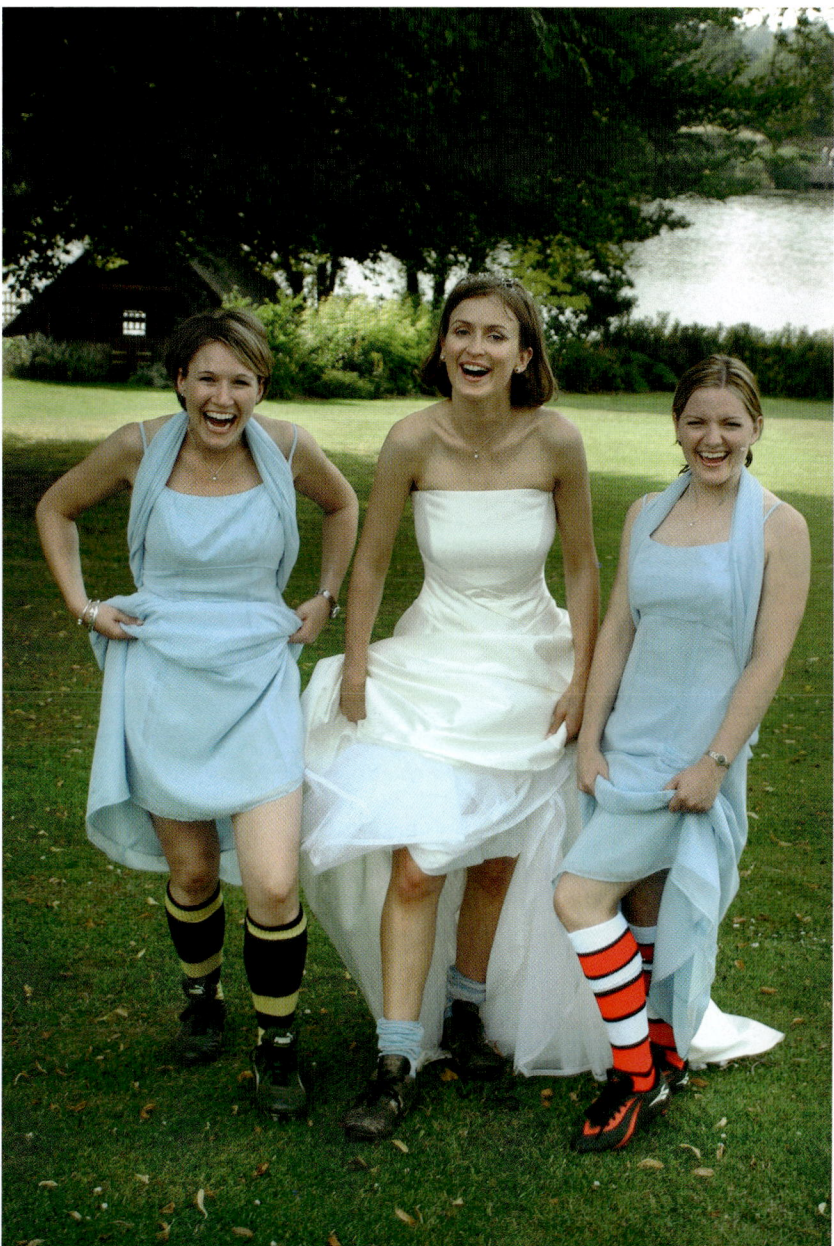

like major sporting fixtures and carnival parades as well as the usual traffic for that particular time of day. Use the Internet to research your journey and program a satellite navigation unit if you have one. Motoring organizations or local news media will provide you with the information you need. Once your logistical plan has been keyed in, always share it with the bride and groom. It might seem quite busy or unnecessarily complicated at first, but with the couples' help and offers of solutions or lifts, it will become manageable. Stay flexible! Right up to the morning of the wedding, plans will change. Rain may force the guys to cancel the golf or shooting. This will have a ripple effect and trigger plan B (if you've remembered to make one!).

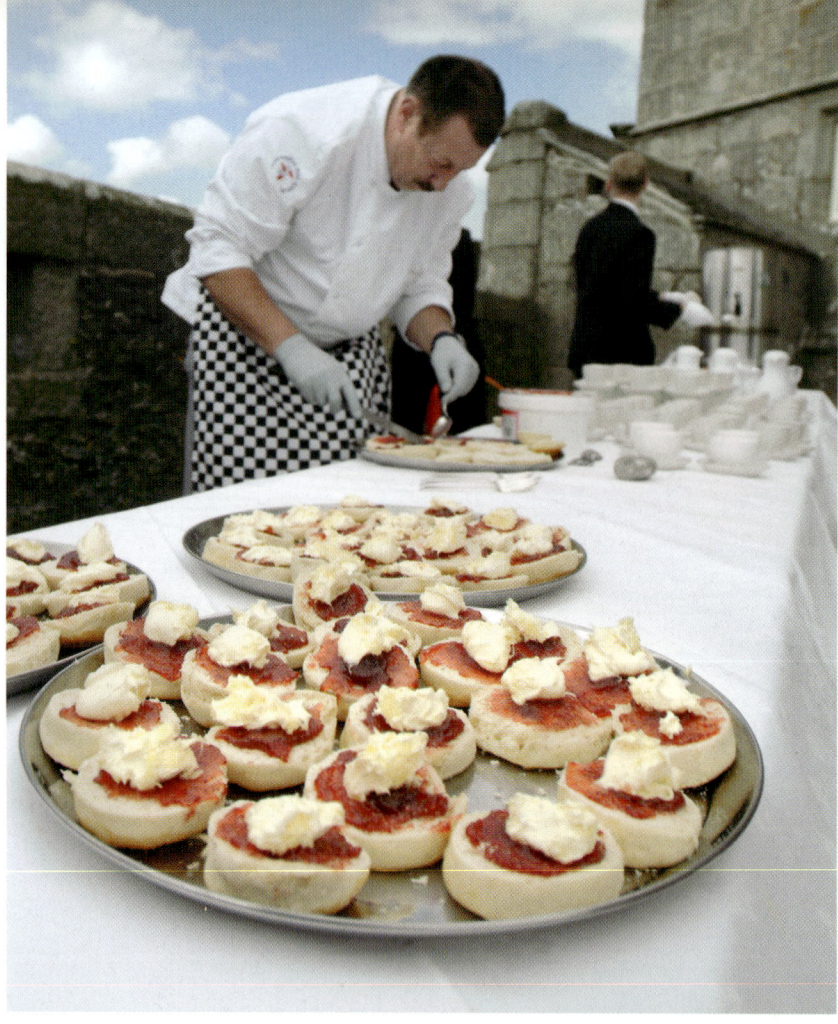

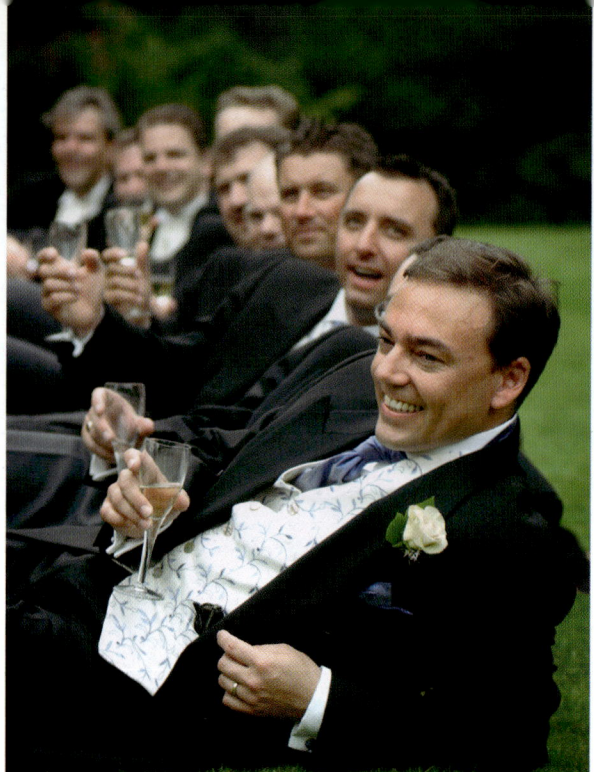

above

FIG. 11   ISO 400 f/4 at 1/4000th

Afternoon tea at Pendennis Castle in Cornwall wouldn't be complete without jam and clotted cream scones. Food preparation is all part of the story.

top left

FIG. 12   ISO 320 f/3.4 at 1/600th

Julie took this picture on a long lens down the line of guys while I took a wide shot from the left. Julie's picture made the album.

TYPICAL WEDDING TIME PLAN

(NAMES OF PEOPLE ARE FICTITIOUS)

RICHARD (THE GROOM):

10.00 Damien to meet Richard and guys for clay pigeon shooting. Smiths Farm, Combe Hay, near Bath, courtesy of Frank Shellard, Wellow Trekking Centre, Little Horsecroft Farm, Ford Road, Wellow. Meet at Wellow Trekking Centre BA2 8QF (1 hour from the Lovegrove studio)

1.30 Guys go to Richard's home: The Winding House. Wick Lane. Pensford. BS49 4BU (15 minutes drive).

1.45 All guys to get ready for the wedding and have a buffet lunch.

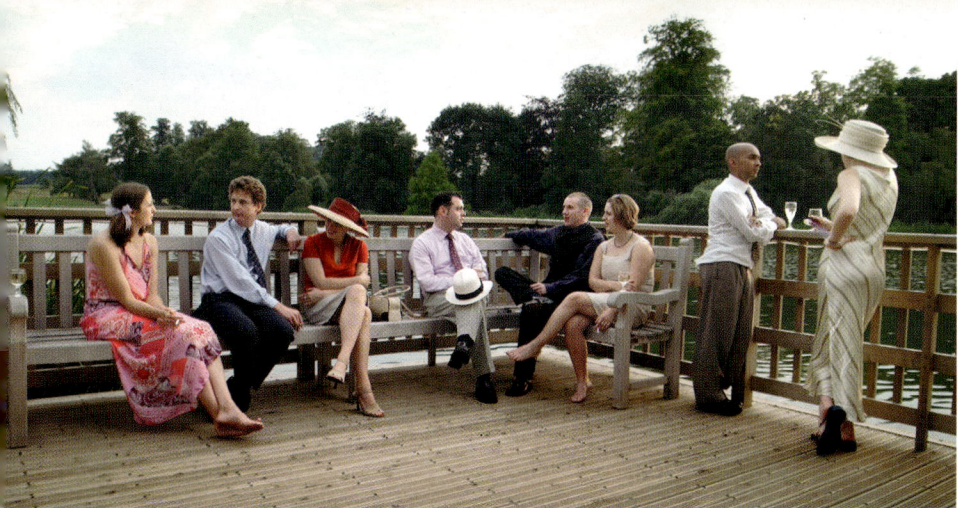

FIG. 13   ISO 800 f/5.7 at 1/250th

I came across this group of guests down by the water's edge. Their arrangement looks like a frame from a French art movie. I love the body language and chemistry in the picture, especially the couple on the right...

FIG. 14   ISO 800 f/5.7 at 1/1200th

...So I switched lenses, cut back the exposure, changed the shooting angle, and candidly caught them in this wonderful silhouette.

2.45   All guys to be ready for a few photographs and then leave for Babington House Hotel, Kilmersden, Somerset. BS54 3NJ (15 minutes drive).

3.15   Be at Babington for a few photos before greeting guests.

NICOLE (THE BRIDE):

2.00   Julie to be with Nicole and the girls at Babington House Hotel, Kilmersden, Somerset. BS54 3NJ (1 hour drive from the Lovegrove studio).

3.15   All hair and makeup to be finished.

3.40   All girls to be ready for a few informal photos.

3.45   Gather in the foyer for the procession to the chapel.

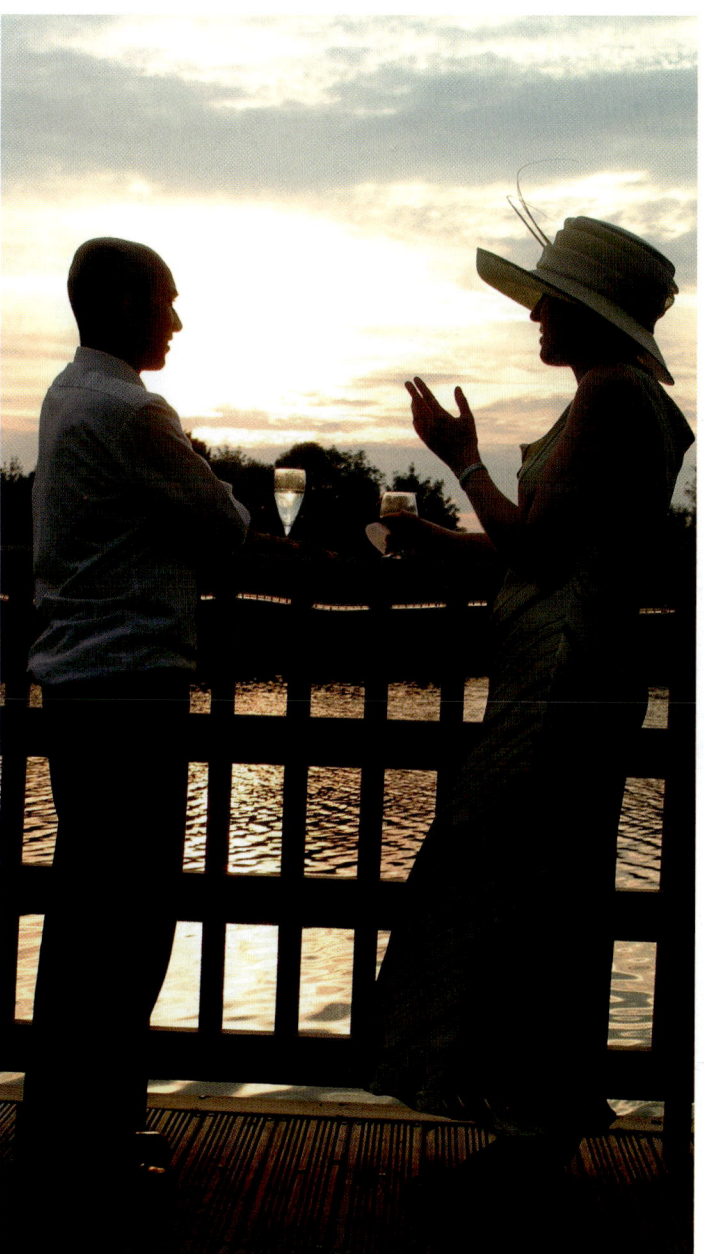

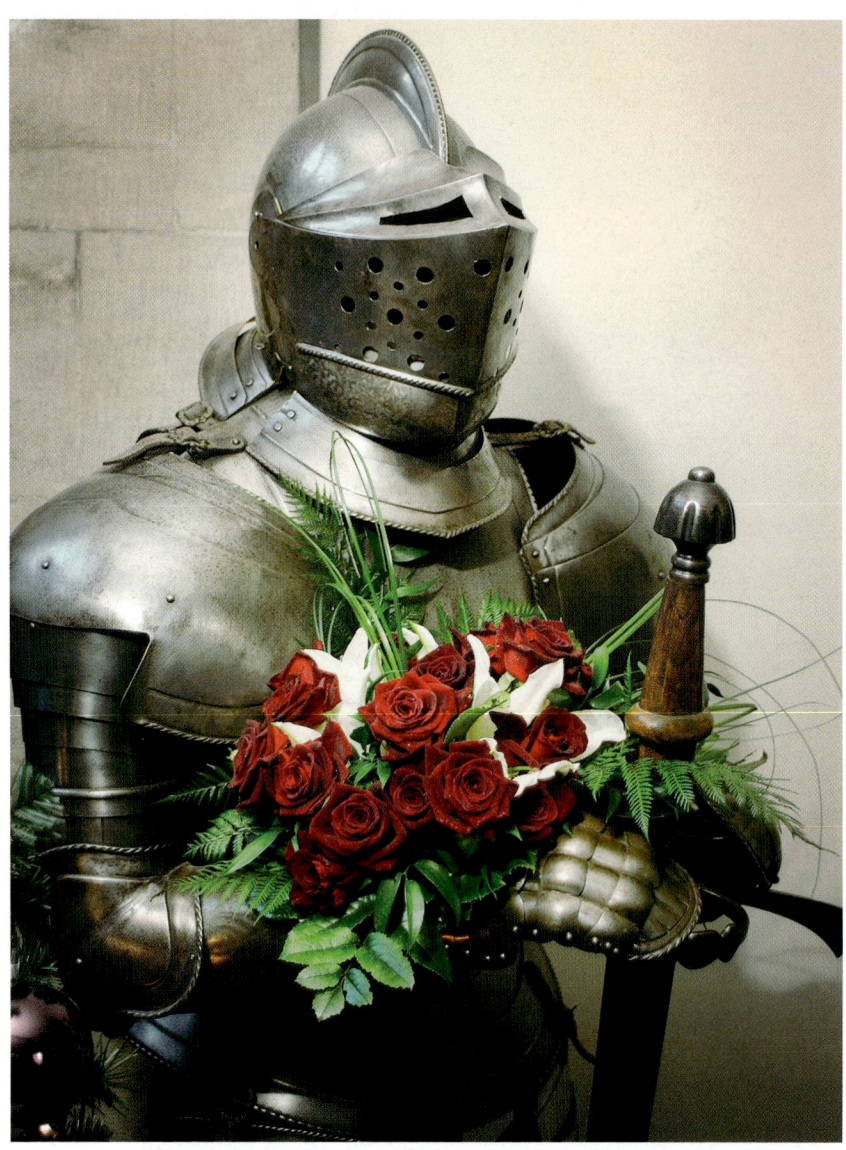

Fig. 15   ISO 800 f/4 at 1/60th

I had a bit of fun with the bouquet and the castle props while the bride was in another room. The surprise picture went down well at the viewing.

opposite

Fig. 16   ISO 400 f/5.7 at 1/60th

The best man was known for his love of beer so when I saw these barrels I knew I could put the two together for a bit more fun

Both:

4.00   Ceremony in chapel – John Mosley to give bride away.

4.45   Ceremony finishes. Confetti and milling outside chapel – Champagne and canapés are served.

5.00   Photos with Richard and Nicole only, away from the guests.

5.30   Group photos as per separate list (each usher to be given a copy).

5.40   Time to chat to guests while Julie and Damien photograph candidly, capture table details and terrace restaurant.

6.15   Ushers to gather all the guests onto the front lawn.

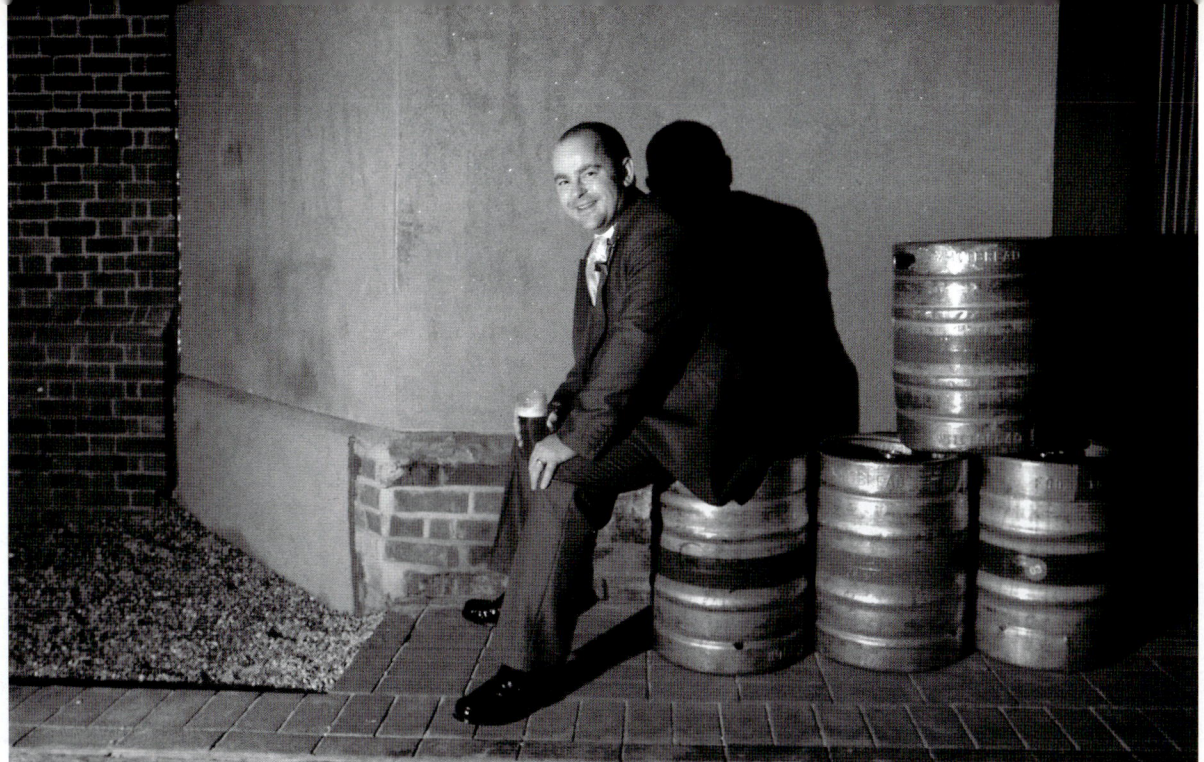

6.20 Big group picture of everyone on the front lawn.

6.30 Called through to dinner. Julie and Damien seated with the guests.

6.45 Speeches and cutting the cake immediately, followed by dinner.

9.30 1st dance in the bar area. Rock & Roll routine (surprise for all the guests).

9.40 Fireworks.

10.00 Belly Dancer in the bar (surprise for all the guests).

10.30 Dancing until midnight and beyond.

10.45 Damien and Julie to leave shortly after the party starts.

NOTES:

- Nicole's father died in 2002
- Mother of the Bride – Judith Collet
- Parents of the Groom – Jo & Colin Pearl
- Best Man – Chris Hammond (0789 4568760)
- Usher – Ben (Richard's son) & Gavin Young
- Chief bridesmaid – Katy Pearl (Richard's daughter) (0788 5643401)
- Bridesmaid – Tasha
- Ring bearer – Sam Patrick (Richards's son)
- John Mosley – giving bride away
- Flower girls – Georgia and Olivia Rowlands

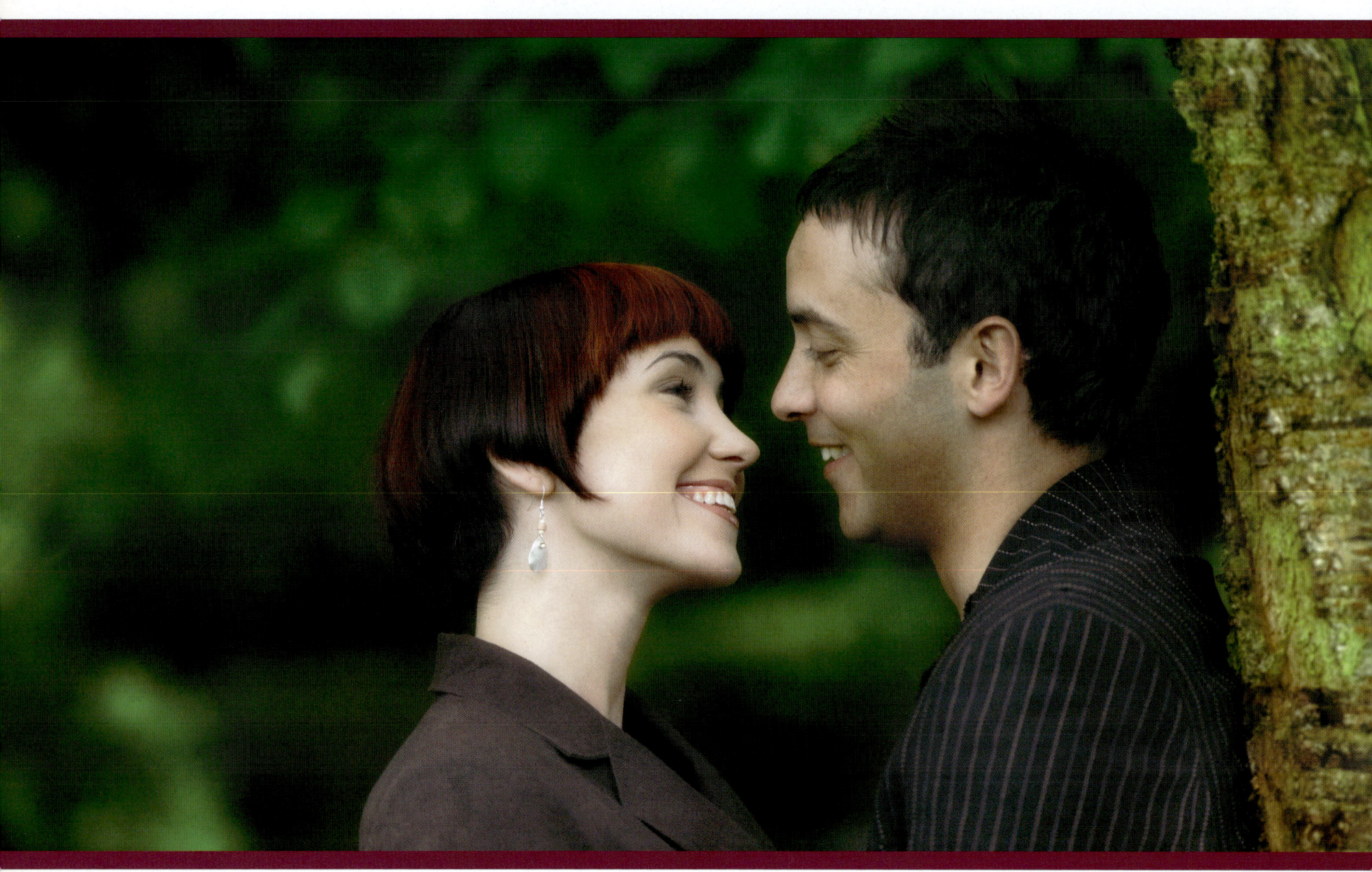

5 The Pre-Wedding Shoot

The idea of a pre-wedding shoot is not new – many wedding photographers offer either this service or an 'engagement sitting.' However, it is important to focus on the underlying objectives and benefits arising from such a session.

As we see it, the purpose of the pre-wedding shoot is:

- To further build upon the rapport established at the enquiry meeting. This rapport will prove vital to getting the cooperation and respect you require on the wedding day.
- To get to know how the couple behave in front of camera. Understanding what makes them tick, how 'touchy feely' they are, and how to take pictures that flatter them. Can they take a profile shot? What is the bride's best side to be shot from? Is the groom relaxed in front of camera? If not now is the time to change that, not the wedding day.

- To produce a set of pictures the couple love enough to rave about you. Having your bride and groom excited about you before the wedding is a great way to start your referral chain from this job.
- To make the most of the extra sales opportunity. You can add as much as 10% to your sales from each wedding client by selling pictures from the pre-wedding shoot.

We first discuss the pre-wedding shoot at the enquiry stage. We suggest that a spring pre-wedding shoot is ideal for a

opposite and next page

FIGS 1–4   ISO 400 f/4 at 1/40th to 1/180th

I took these pictures in the rain. I had the couple take shelter under a tree while I shot the sequence. F/4 gives a great look with a shallow depth of field and it also allows me to use a sensible shutter speed. I still needed my trusty monopod though.

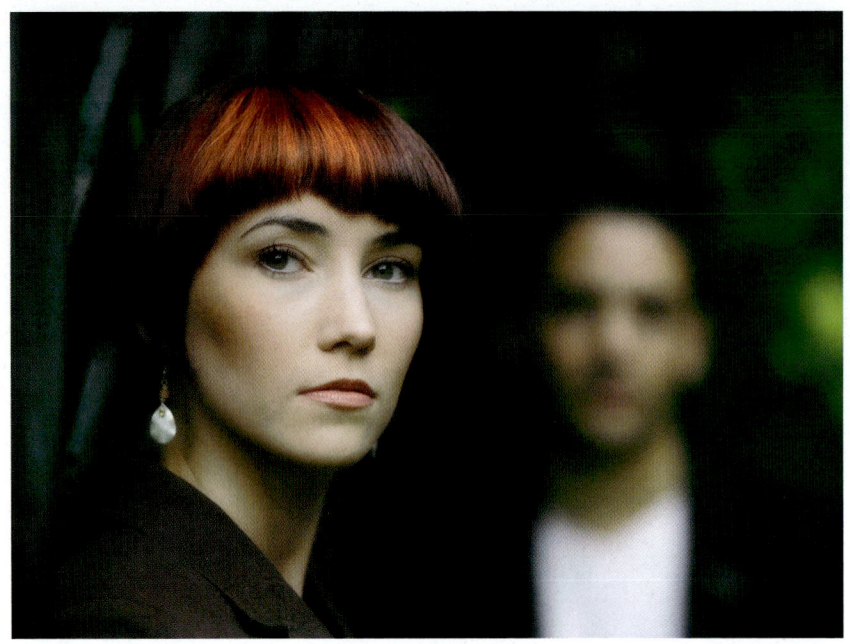

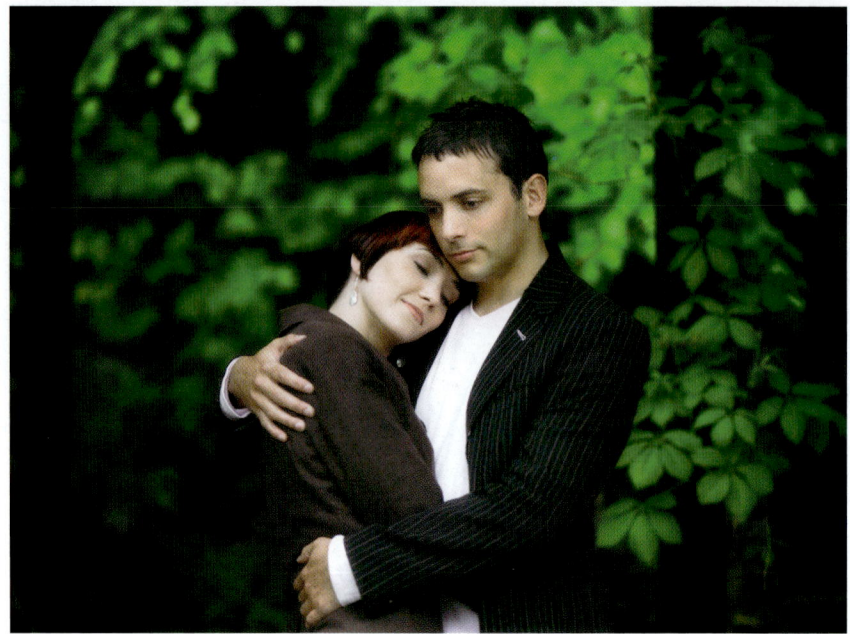

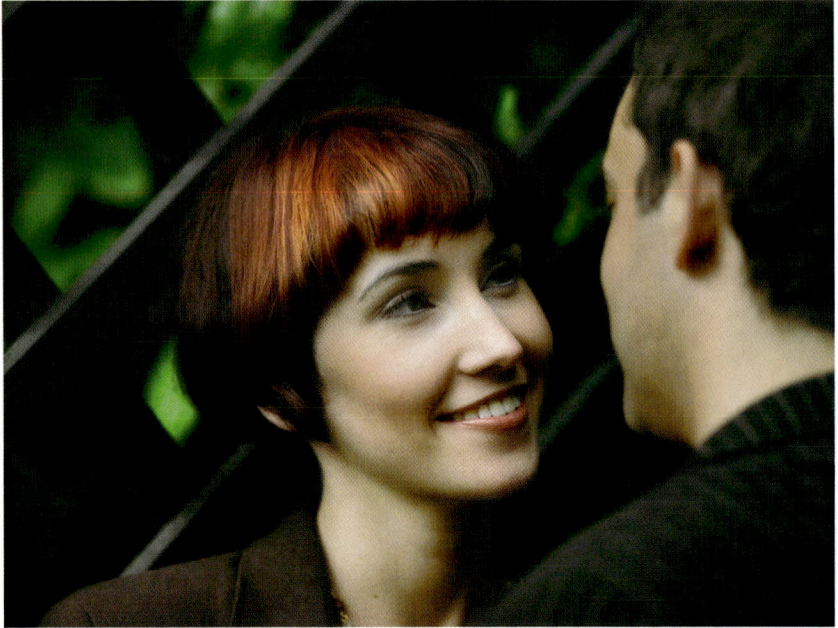

summer wedding. This is because you want the two shoots to be close enough for the rapport established to carry through, yet far enough apart for the couple to be happy to invest in the pictures without wanting to wait and see the wedding pictures before choosing pre-wedding shots.

I suggest you find a few locations that will be ideal for pre-wedding shoots. I have a couple in London, and one in Bristol. A good location is one that has a café or bar where you can meet the couple beforehand. It also provides washroom facilities and useful cover from a quick rain shower. If you are early or your clients are delayed by traffic you can relax with a cup of coffee

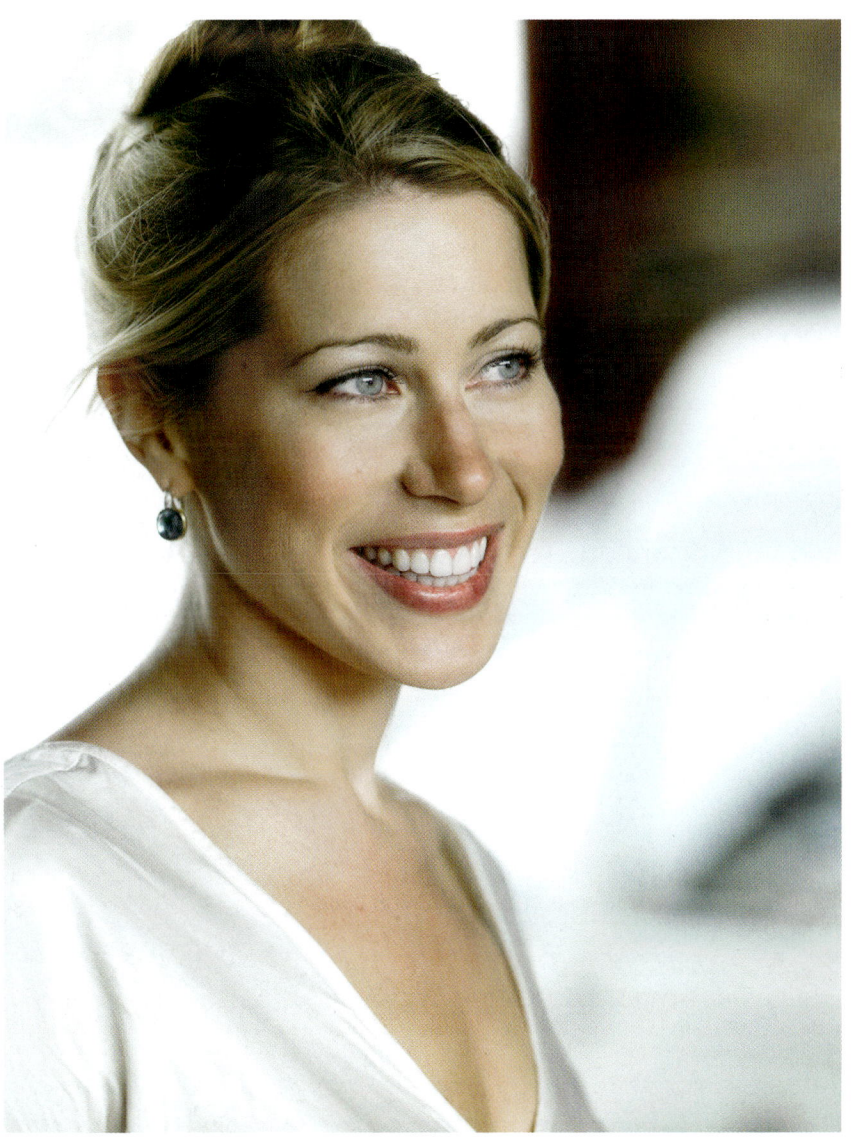

FIGS 5 & 6   ISO 400 f/4.8 at 1/180th

A trick I use to make portraits of couples is to use the out of shot partner to stimulate the emotion. This couple are looking at each other as I shoot. The fun and love in their eyes reflects the feelings they have for each other. All I had to do was change camera position to capture these two pictures just seconds apart. I choose my locations carefully as I want great natural light to work with.

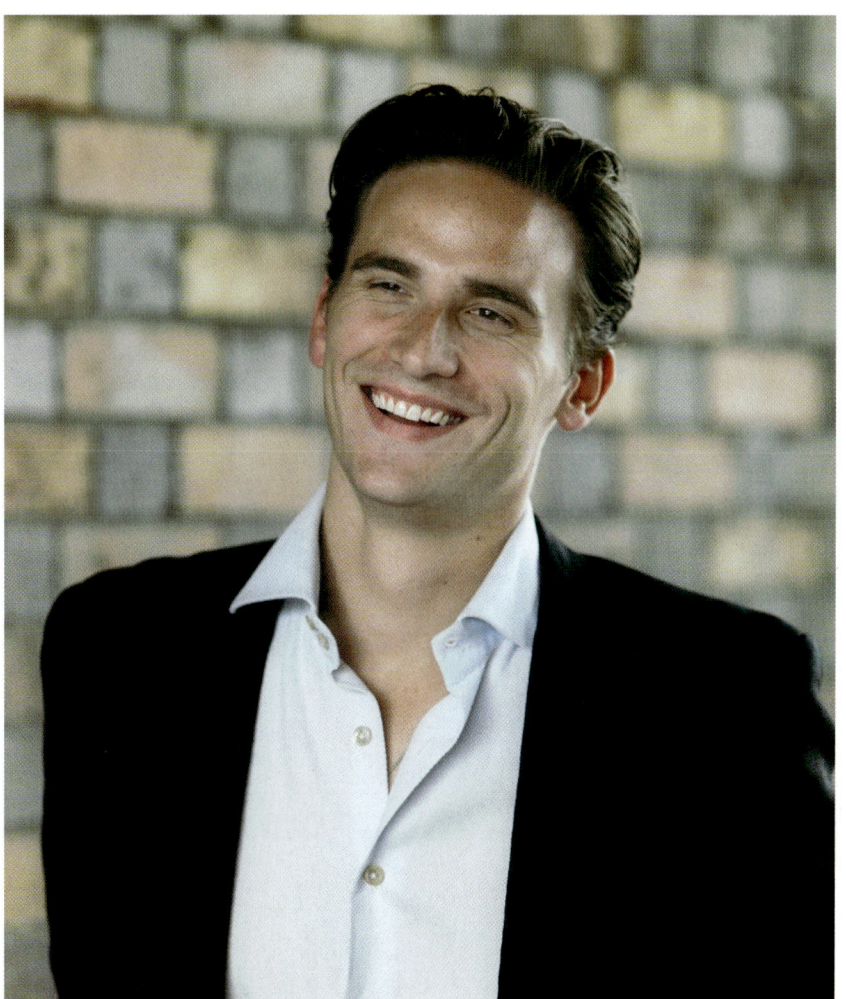

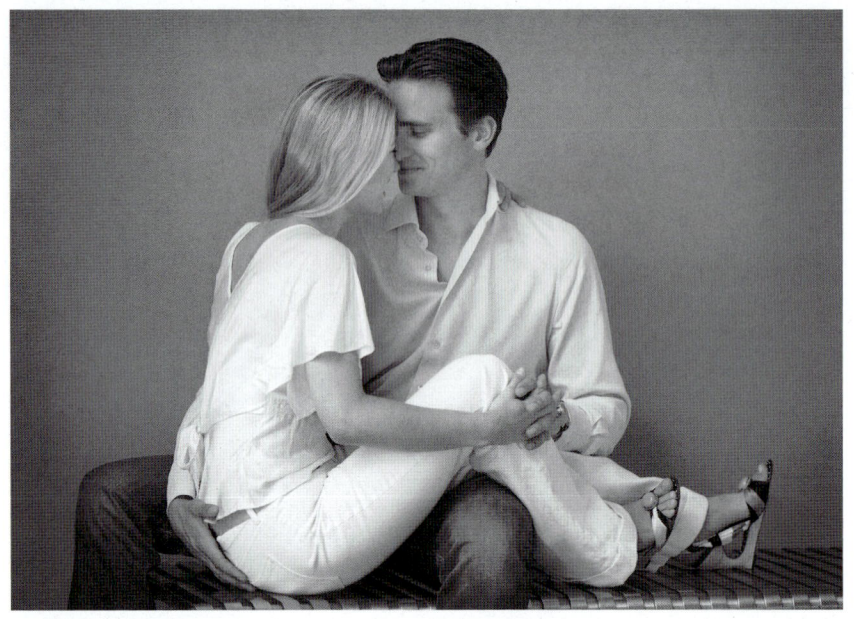

I shot this same scene from different angles and distances just like in my television days. Marko, our picture editor, chose to make one of the images black & white to help find out what the couple preferred.

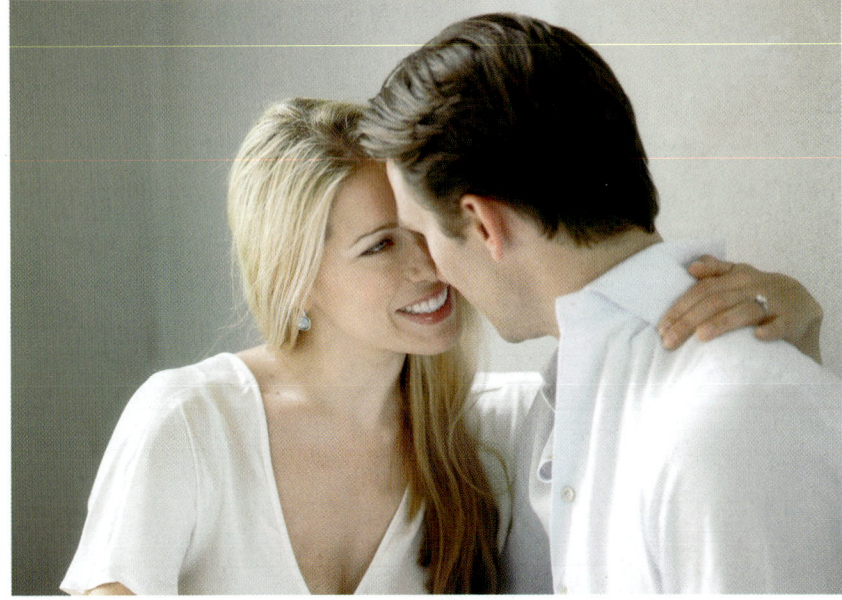

and wait in comfort. The photographic requirements of a good location are:

- To be able to shoot unhindered by officials. Some public open spaces like the royal parks in London are protected with bylaws and require you to buy a license to take pictures for commercial gain.
- Covered areas with natural daylight. A cloister or colonnade is ideal. Buildings with covered walkways also work well. If it is raining you can stay dry and use the wonderful sidelight this type of location provides.
- Open shady areas to shoot in on sunny days. Being able to keep the sun at bay is perfect. In the summer, leafy trees and buildings provide areas of shade to work in.
- Unpopulated shooting areas that give the couple some degree of privacy are ideal. (I'm also happy to shoot in busy areas if the couple are up for it.)

I take a simple kit of one camera, a monopod and two lenses, a 210 and a 35 mm, or occasionally an 80 mm instead. Traveling

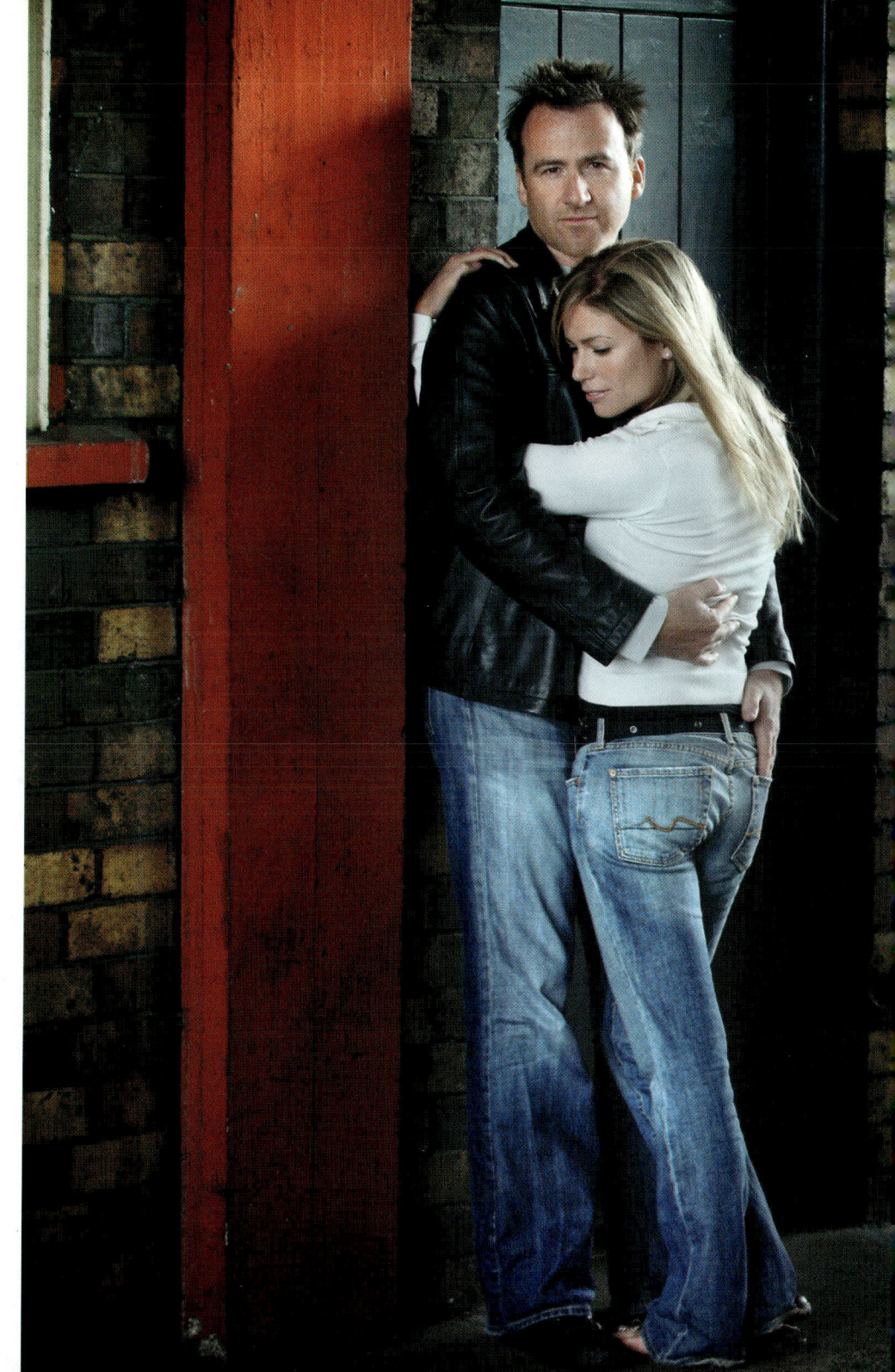

Fig. 9   ISO 400 f/4 at 1/125th

This location has the light quality and ambience of a film set. I placed the groom to be against the wall so that his head was in front of the light door. I asked his fiancé to drape on him. I turned her face toward the camera, brought her left hand up to his shoulder to form a graceful arc and placed his hand in her pocket. Relaxing her right leg and 'feel the love' were the last direction points I gave.

light is a good idea. My camera bag is often needed as a depository for a handbag, car keys, and a wallet. Keeping the couple's pockets clutter free saves time in Photoshop later.

Over the years, our pre-wedding experience has evolved into a super-slick event. We now have a smart studio in the country, just 20 minutes from Bristol, and we ask our clients to come to Bristol for their shoot. The day works something like this:

11:00 AM Meet at a waterfront bar in Bristol. Drink coffee and have a chat. I explain the purpose of the session, how I will work, what I expect of them and how much they will enjoy the session.

11:30 We leave the bar and go on a 'walk and shoot' tour of the old waterfront, Bristol docks area. The area is visually stimulating and provides a good experience for the couple. The shoot lasts from about 45 minutes to an hour.

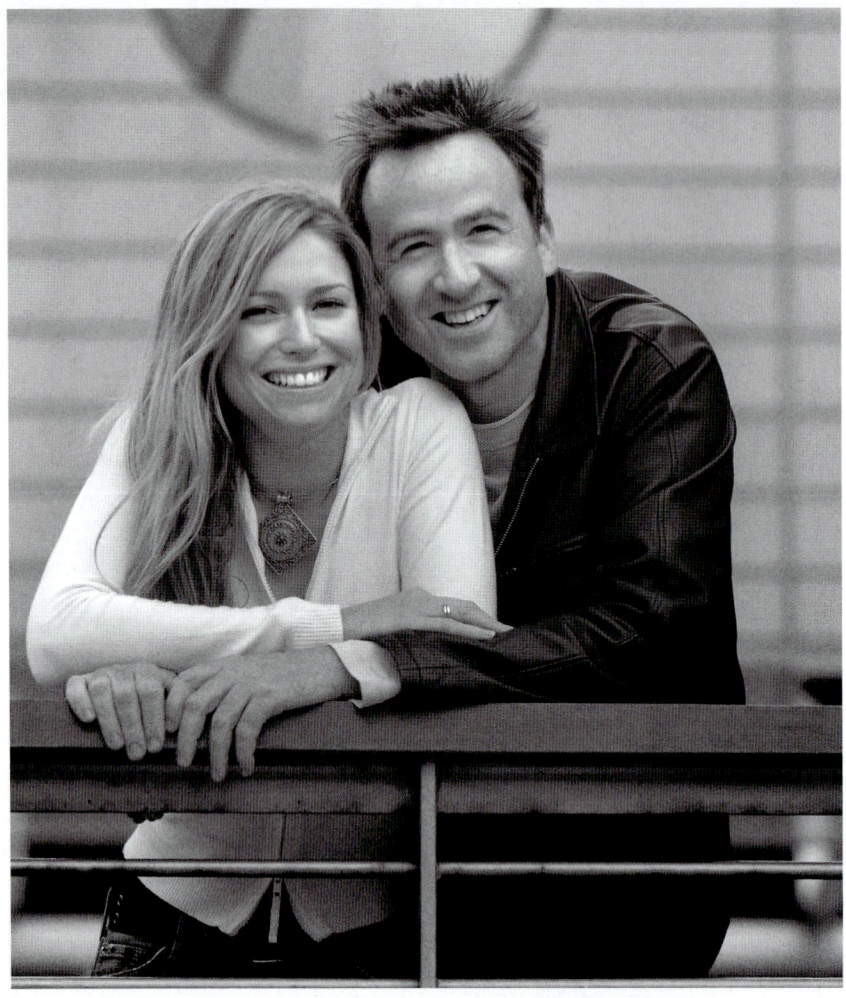

FIG. 10 ISO 400 f/4 at 1/1500th

Placing the groom behind the bride evens out their body mass in the picture. Bringing his head forward ensures that all their eyes are on the same focal plane. This is an important detail as I chose to work wide open.

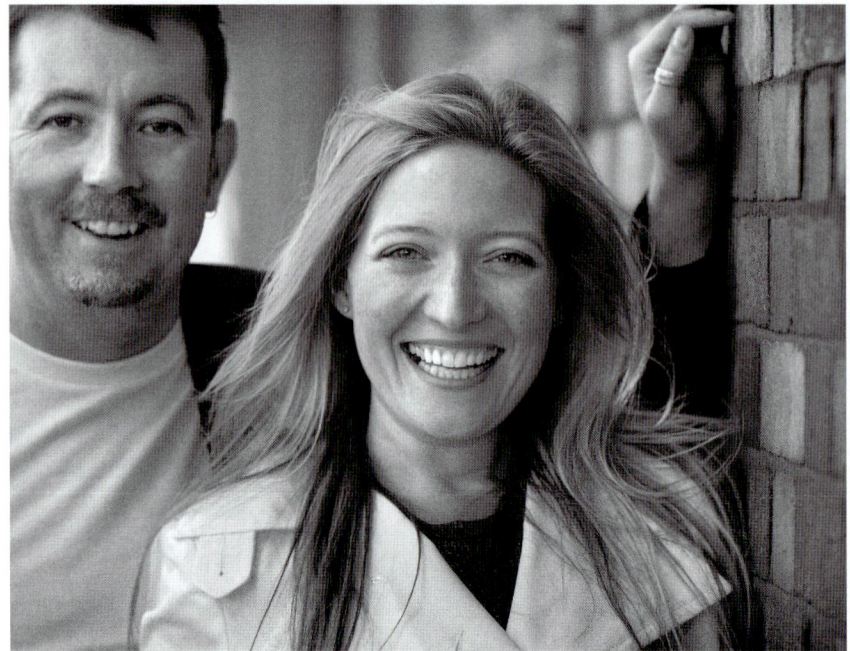

FIG. 11 ISO 400 f/4.8 at 1/320th

I love this picture. I saw it come together in my viewfinder and I just knew there and then that this couple were special. Their wedding was one of the most enjoyable we have ever photographed. Truly unforgettable for all the right reasons.

12:30 The couple go off to explore the area further and have lunch at one of the many fine restaurants on the harborside. I give them a map and directions to our studio and drive back to the studio with the Compact Flash card containing 100 or so images.

12:50 Julie loads the pictures into Capture One, selects the best ones, about 40 or so, using a tagging system, and passes the hard disk to Marko, our picture editor.

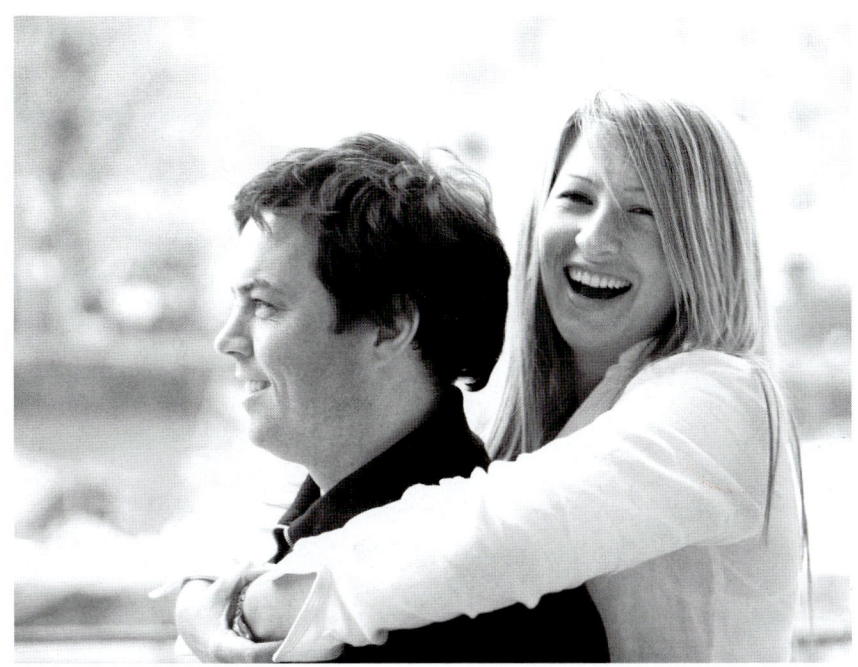

Figs 12 & 13   ISO 200 f/4 at 1/20th and 1/50th

It had just started to rain as we began to shoot but I made the moments fun and used a brolly to great effect.

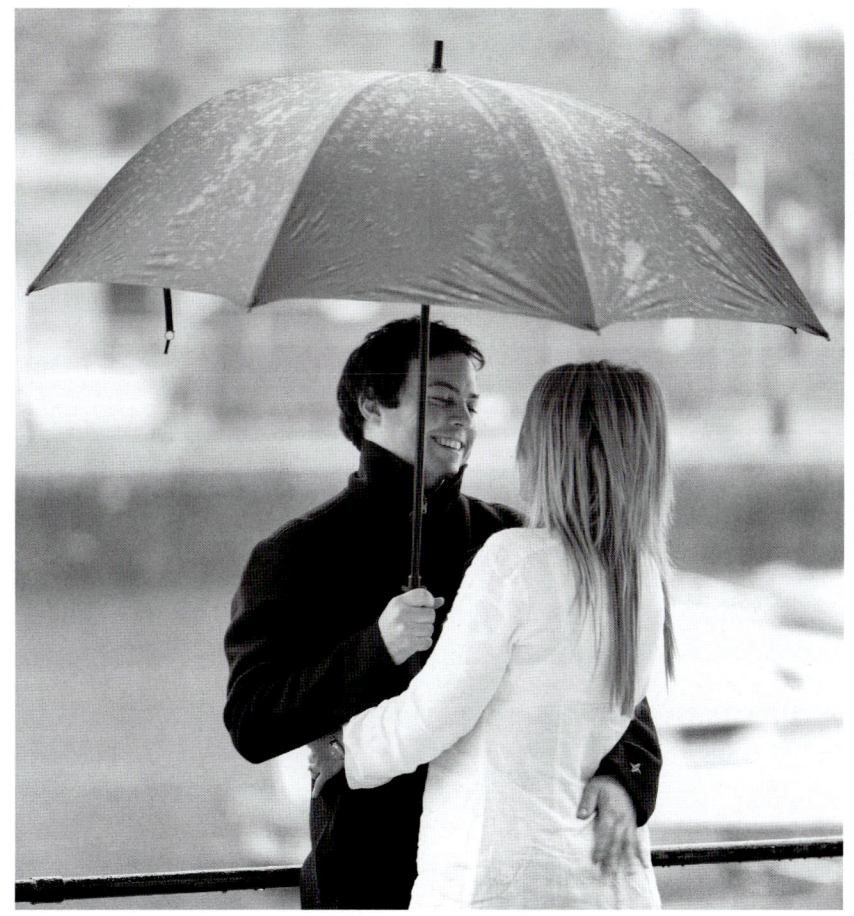

13:20 Marko makes any RAW adjustments to the files, processes the selected set to high resolution JPEGs and opens each one in turn in Photoshop for some spot tonal adjustments and cosmetic retouching and the like.

14:00 The couple leave Bristol having had lunch and make their way to our studio.

14:20 The couple are greeted by Julie who goes through the timings and details of their wedding day over a glass of

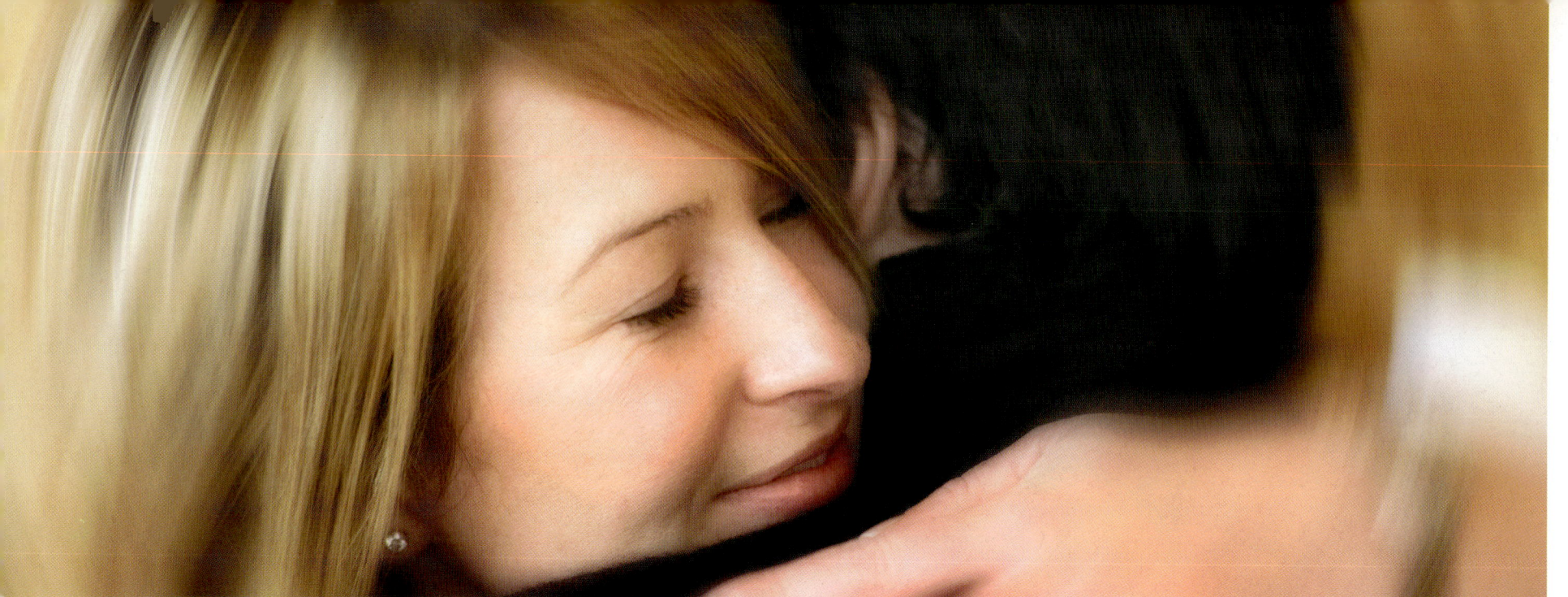

champagne. This discussion is a vital element of the wedding planning. It is our chance to re-confirm the logistics and opportunities we have for the wedding day itself. Julie will later key the time plan into her computer and email it to the couple.

15:00 Marko has finished editing the pictures and has created a set of viewing resolution files for Gemma, our sales assistant.

15:05 Gemma shows the couple the pictures using our projector in the sales room and takes their order.

16:30 The couple leave the studio and either make their way home or onto their hotel for the night. We aim to get them on the road before the evening rush hour.

The pictures I take are a combination of single shots – with and without eye contact – and couple shots. I usually keep the majority of the pictures tight, minimizing any distractions in the background. Isolation of the couple is my key aim, to produce striking portraits. I nearly always shoot at f/4 and at 400 ISO. The session is fluid and I try out new things as I go. I shoot from below and above the eye line to see what produces the most flattering pictures. I aim to shoot the emotions the couple have for each other and I will push them to their limits. Above all I keep the energy up and make the whole experience fun.

Julie's meeting is a chance for the couple to spend some time face to face with her. It may well be the first time they have met

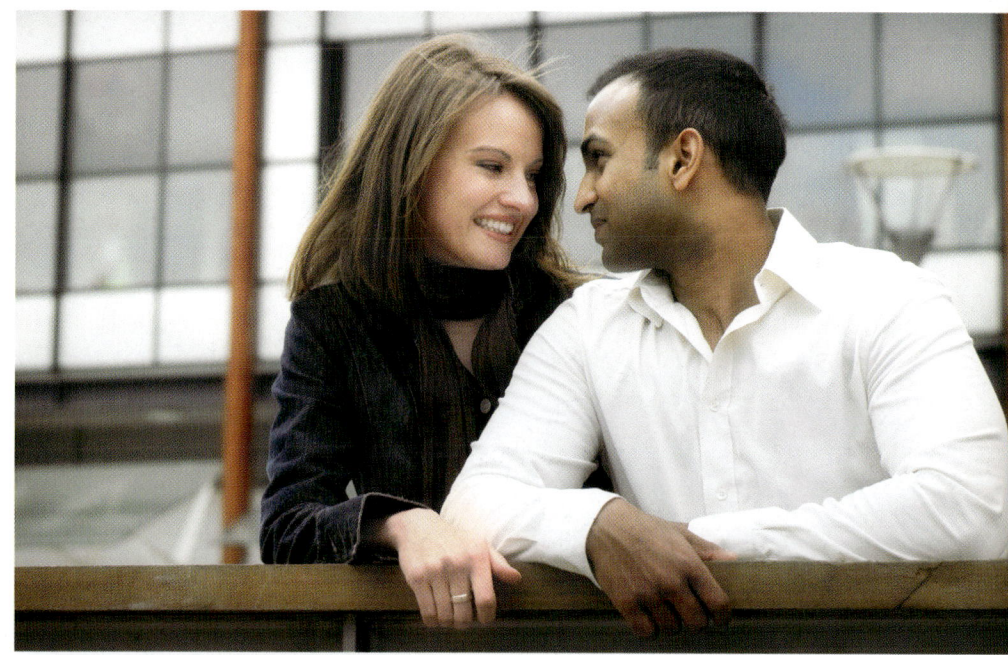

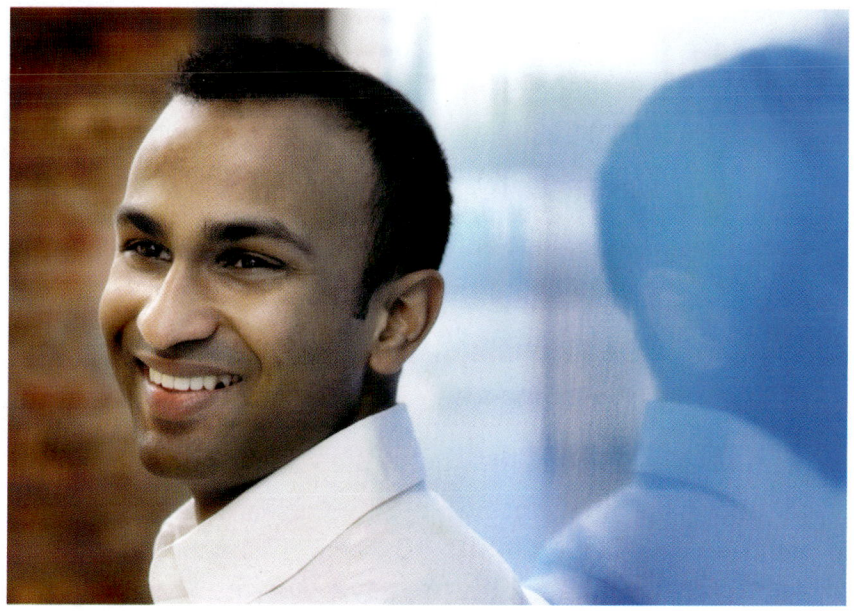

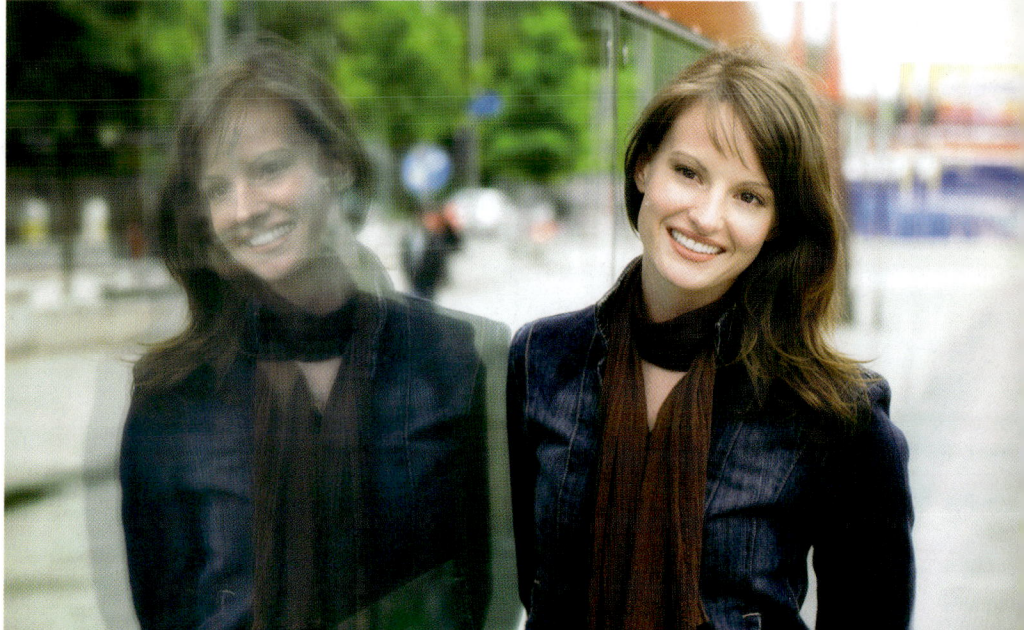

opposite

FIG. 14   ISO 200 f/4 at 1/30th

This image of the same couple was given a bit of treatment in post-production to see if they might like a funkier look to their pictures. As it turned out they were happier with a classic black & white look.

bottom and left

FIGS 15–17   ISO 400 f/6.3 at 1/250th ISO 400 f/8 at 1/500th ISO 400 f/5.6 at 1/200th

I switched my Hasselblad H1 to program for this shoot to see what settings the camera would choose. I was surprised at how different the images created by my 210 mm lens looked at f/8. I would have still preferred an f/4 look so I switched back to aperture priority and f/4 the next day and I have stayed there ever since.

in person and this is Julie's opportunity to cement the relationship that she has nurtured over the past months on the phone.

Gemma's viewing is more than a sales process. As well as taking the clients' order for pictures, she discusses the pictures in detail. Her aim is to find out exactly what the couple like and dislike about themselves in the pictures. They are made to feel free to discuss the pictures openly in a way that it would be impossible to do if I were showing them the pictures. Gemma's impartiality comes in handy. Her notes are shared with us all later. Marko needs to know how to edit the wedding pictures and Julie and I need to discuss shooting angles for the wedding day too.

An album containing 20 pictures and a framed print for each of the Mums is an ideal sale from the pre-wedding shoot. The pictures can be used on wedding invitations, websites, and even projected as a slideshow at the wedding reception. There are excellent opportunities to develop a product range to suit a set of pre-wedding pictures. Be creative with your product design and it will create its own sales.

One important spin-off from the pre-wedding shoot is a psychological one. This is often the time when the penny drops about just how many pictures they are going to want in their wedding album. If just 40 minutes of shooting by one photographer produced 20 'must have' pictures, then 12 hours

Fig. 18   ISO 320 f/4.8 at 1/850th

Here is a product idea for your pre-wedding images. Mount up a print of the bride and groom to display at the wedding and ask the guests to sign the mat. The size of the mount depends upon the number of guests at the wedding. It's a great memento for the couple and will hang on a wall in their home.

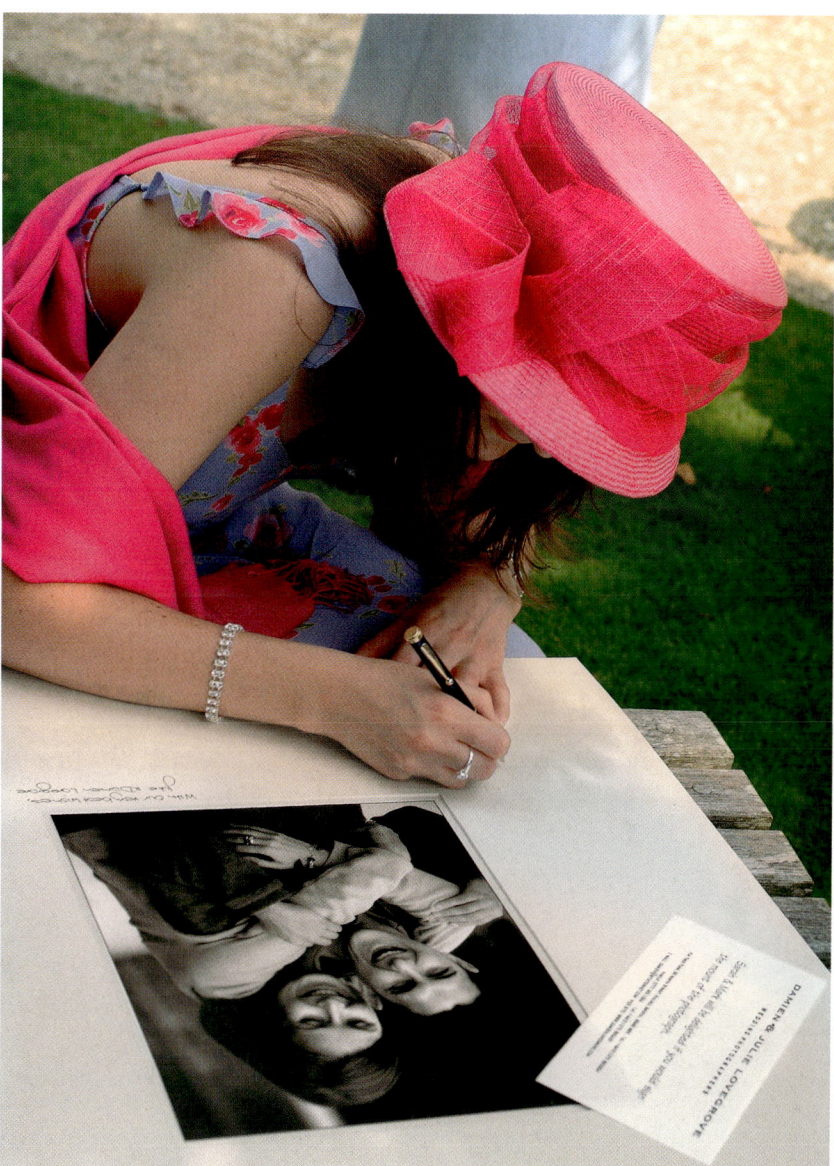

of shooting with two photographers is going to produce several hundred! We have already told them they will be shown three hundred or so pictures from their wedding and that they should expect to love them all. Couples often have a low esteem of themselves in pictures and they believe we can't possibly produce that many gorgeous pictures of them. The pre-wedding shoot dispels this theory and puts us firmly on the road to a big order from the wedding pictures themselves.

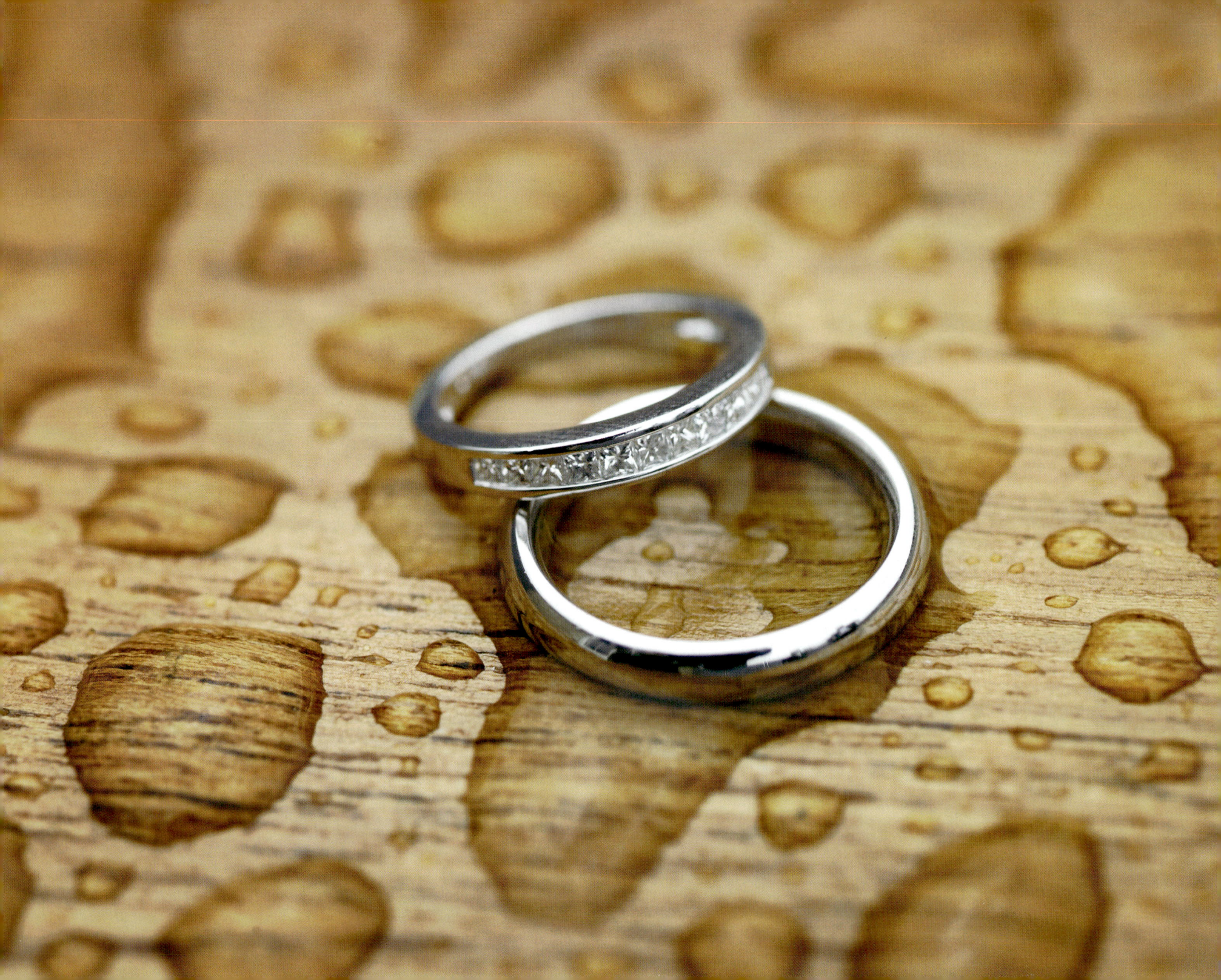

6
The Wedding Day

Well this is it – the Big Day. For the bride and groom it is probably the most important day of their lives. So we don't want to disappoint them. In fact we want much more than that – we want to make sure the pictures we deliver go far beyond their wildest expectations. How do we ensure this? By very careful planning, by hard work, by thinking on our feet, by drawing on our experience, and by building on the rapport we have already established with the couple during the pre-wedding shoot.

All set then? Here's a blow by blow account of a typical Lovegrove wedding.

EARLY MORNING

What better way to start your day than with a good breakfast? While you're at it, plan the rest of your day's eating arrangements too. On the way to your first rendezvous you may need to buy sandwiches for later in the day. We always carry an

opposite

FIG. 1   ISO 400 f/7.1 at 1/350th

Even on wet wedding days I look for opportunities to tell the story in a positive way. I stood on a balcony in the rain to get this picture while the groom was in the shower. The first he knew of it was at the viewing.

Clay pigeon shooting can be illustrated in so many ways. I like to use a more abstract approach at times.

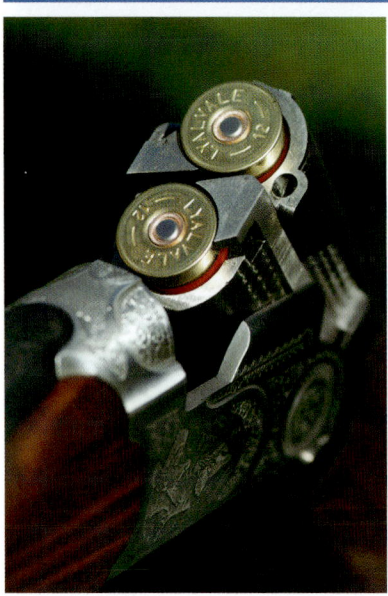

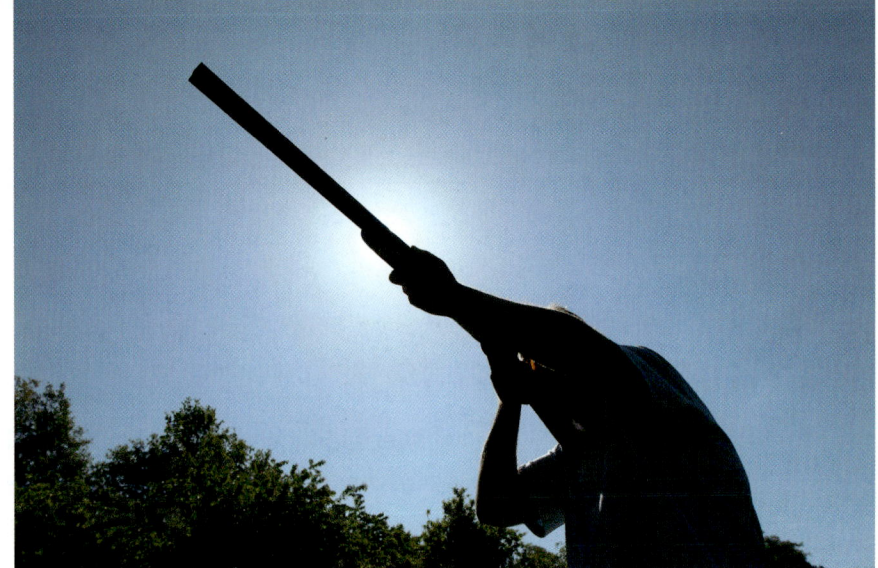

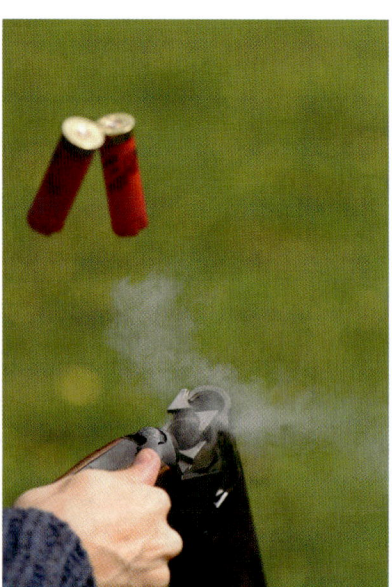

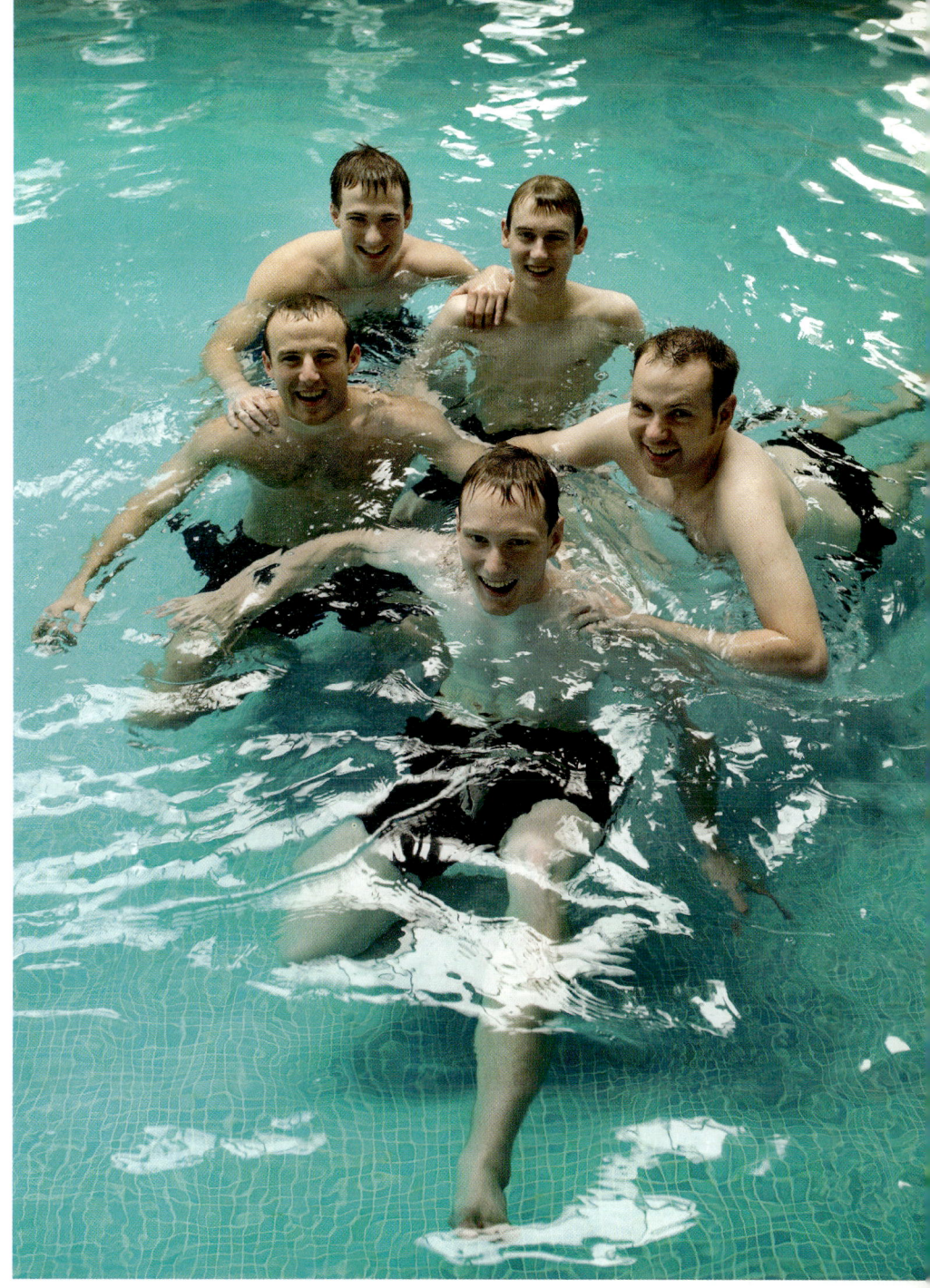

Fig. 6   ISO 400 f/5.6 at 1/90th

This group picture of the swimmers was taken right at the end of the swimming session. I had to leave my Hasselblad on a heater for 20 minutes before I could get pictures without condensation on the lens or the sensor. There was a male bonding process that went on to get this picture. A ring of body contact unites the group.

insulated cool box with us in the car for such eventualities. It's vital to keep up your energy levels for the whole day.

Next, carefully check your camera kit and load it into the car. This is a personal ritual that needs to happen every time. So create a system and stick to it. Repeating a set routine is less likely to allow you to forget a vital bit of equipment. Once we get to the hotel car parking lot, I always take one random shot and play it back. This proves to me that the camera has fully charged batteries, and that the settings are sensible. It also gives me confidence in my equipment and my ability to use it.

Julie and I then go through the running order for the day so that we are clear who's doing what, when, and where. (If we have a late start and the reception venue is nearby we might do a mini reconnaissance and have coffee there too. The reconnaissance

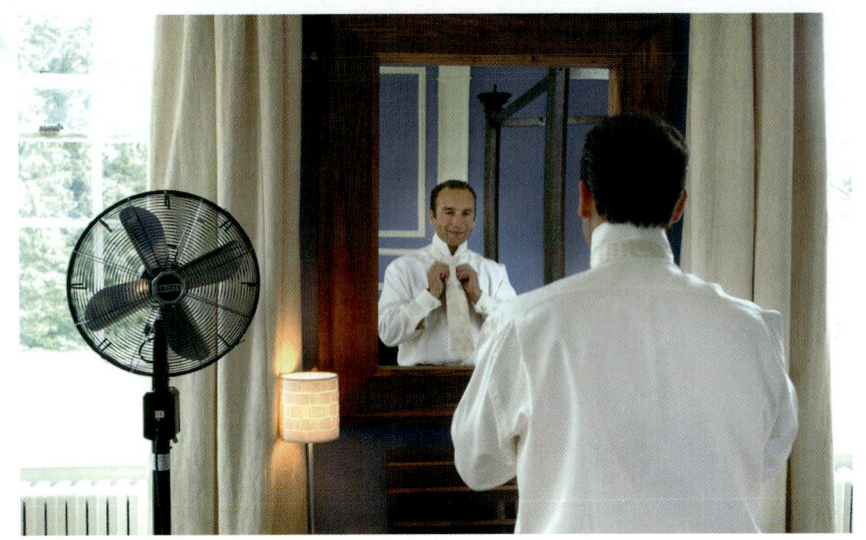

FIG. 7   ISO 400 f/4 1/60th

I have a habit of switching on table and wall lights in hotel bedrooms. The cool blue wall in the mirror balances the yellow glow from the lamp. The fan made a great prop so I moved it into the shot. The rim light on the groom's right shoulder from another window out of shot provided just enough separation of the light tones on the right.

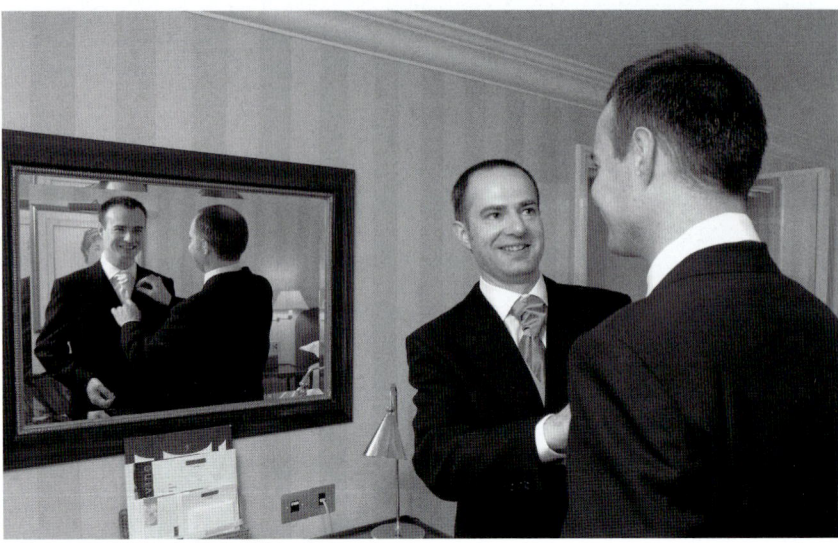

FIG. 8   ISO 800 f/4 at 1/60th

Another mirror shot lit with off-camera flash shows an interesting arrangement of viewpoints. I shot this from 6 inches below the groom's eye line to add drama.

will be to determine a good location for photographing the groups, establishing a rapport with the coordinator and checking that the catering time plan matches ours. It is not uncommon for the hotel to move the sit down time by half an hour to give them more time to clear a room after dinner for instance. Careful negotiation at this stage is vital.)

Once our checks are completed, we set up the day's venues on the satellite navigation system and head off to meet up with our respective parties. We always carry detailed maps as a backup. You never know when roadworks, an accident, or a police controlled incident may cause you to change your travel plans. Julie might drop me off at a golf club or at a hotel to meet up with the groom or I might drop her with the bride. These arrangements will have been planned for sometime. Once we have both arrived at our first meeting points and photography is underway, Julie and I often confirm all is well on the phone. Changes of plan or useful snippets of info gleaned are often relayed at this time. For instance, Julie might mention the bridesmaids are traveling in a black car rather than a horse and carriage and the oldest one will try and avoid the camera because she hates having her photograph taken. Armed with this info I will shoot candids with a long lens when the bridesmaids arrive at the church rather than shoot in close on the wide lens.

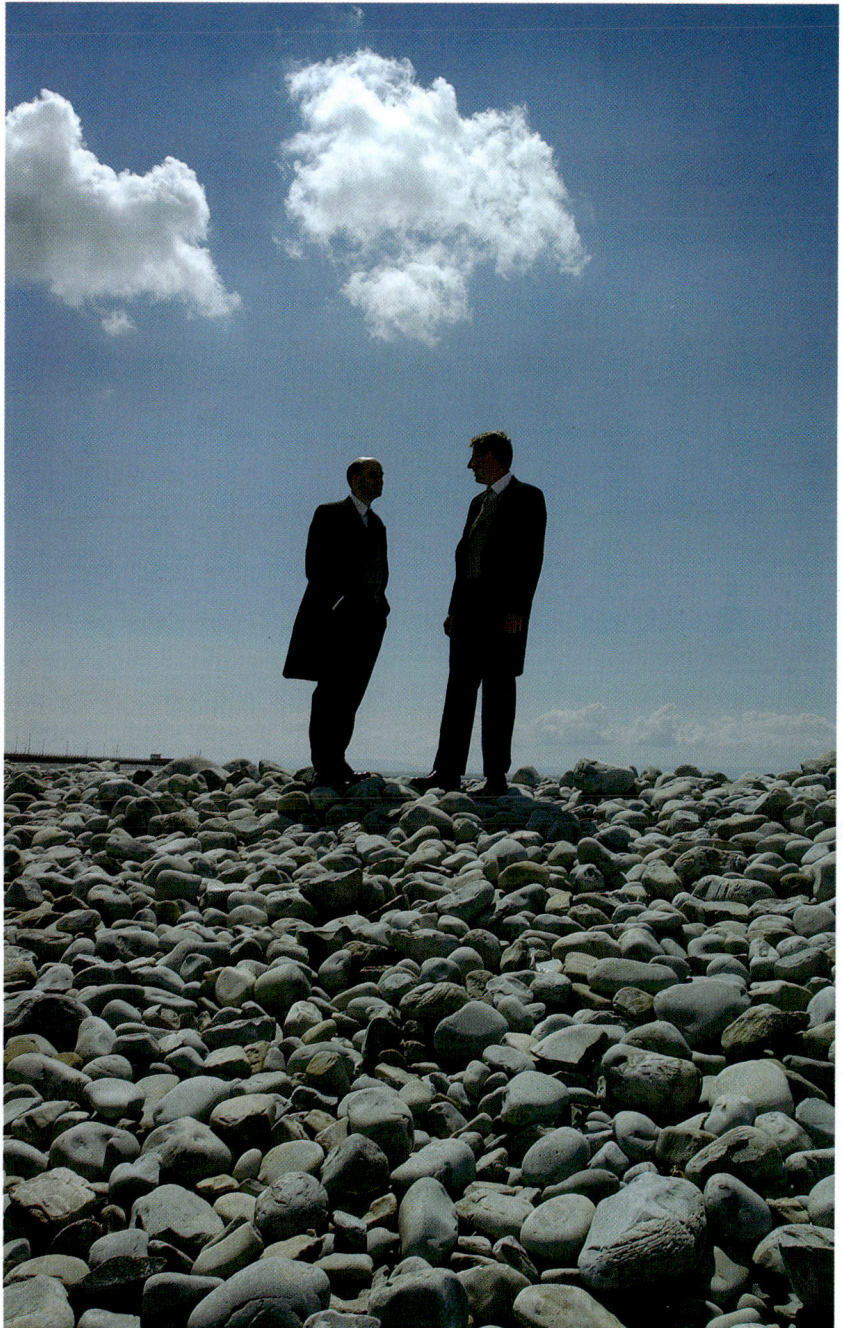

FIG. 9   ISO 400 f/13.5 at 1/700th

Two men, two clouds, and a pebble beach. I chose a low viewpoint to include more of the sky and to strengthen the foreground stones. I also chose to use more depth of field than usual and broke my own rules by doing so.

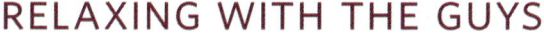

RELAXING WITH THE GUYS

Our objectives are clearly set for the first photography shoot of the day. When I meet up with the guys, my aim is to re-establish rapport with the groom and get to know the best man and the ushers and make sure they understand how I'm going to work. Only once I have something to photograph in front of me will I get the camera out. Every photographer's style is different. I choose not to hide behind the camera or be constantly fiddling with it.

I will often encourage the guys to start the day on the golf course or the shooting ground. If they decide to play nine holes, I'll arrange to meet them on the 6th green. This will give me three complete holes to get the shots I need. Bear in mind that while nine holes on most courses takes just under 2 hours, on

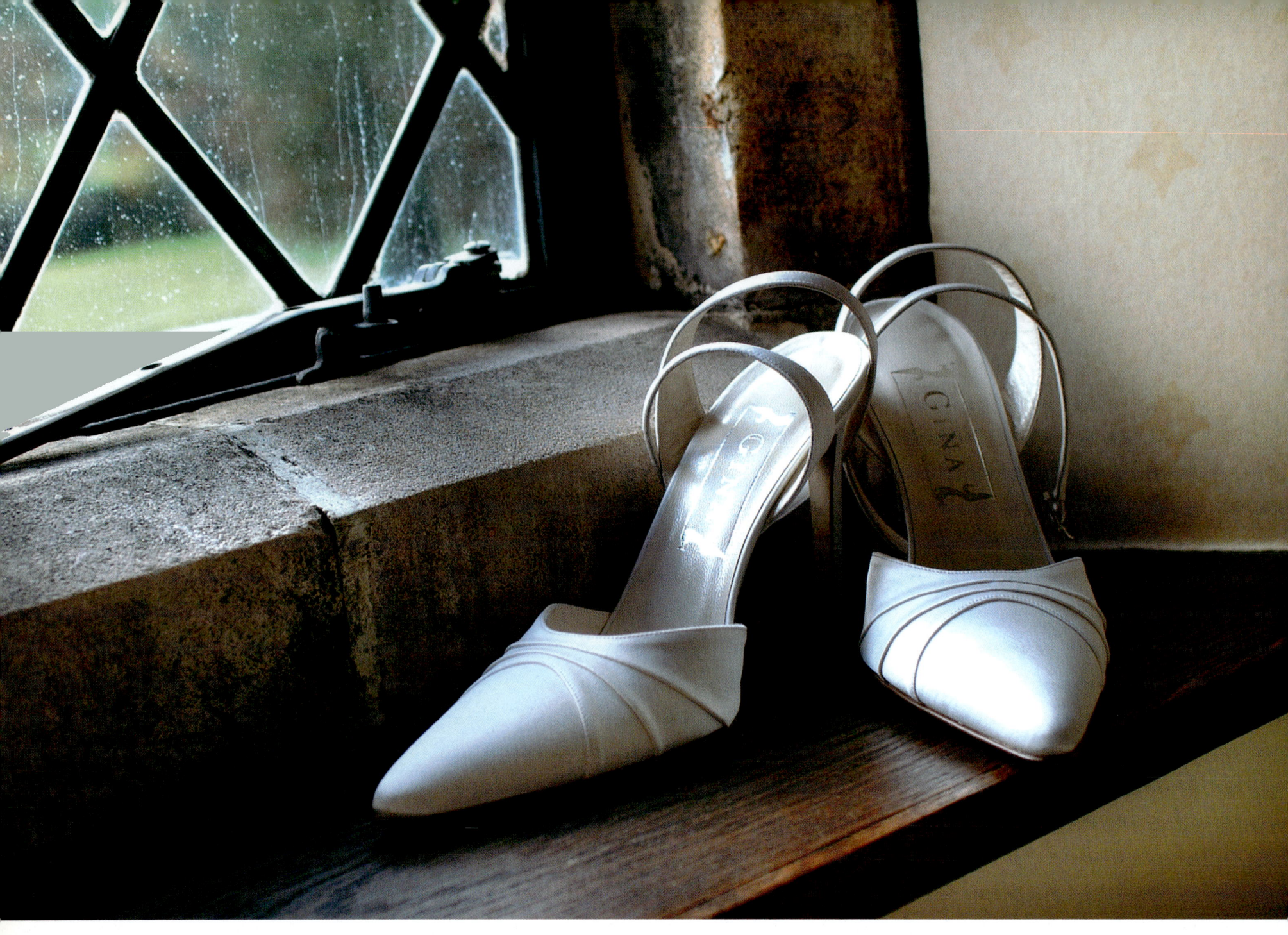

opposite

FIG. 10   ISO 800 f/4 at 1/125th

By including part of the old window in this picture of a bride's shoes Julie is setting the scene. It's the small details that say so much about a building.

FIG. 11   ISO f/4 at 1/45th

Wonderfully soft natural light gives this picture its charm. At light levels this low it is easy to resort to using flash. Resist the urge and better pictures often result.

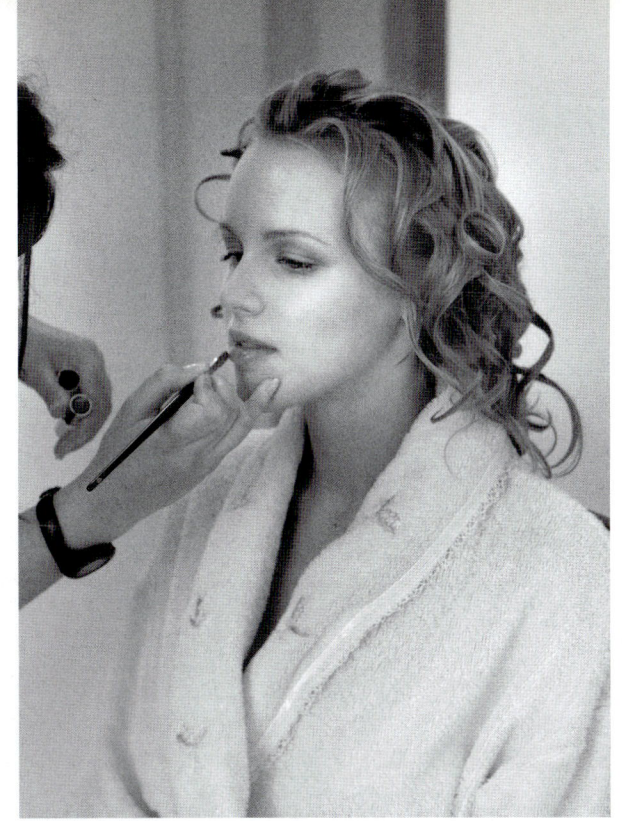

the wedding day morning the adrenaline alone is likely to whiz the guys round in about an hour and a half. So be prepared and arrive a good 20 minutes to half an hour early at the club house. The 6th green is often quite a way from the club house so I'll ask someone for a lift on a cart. I prefer to walk the three holes with the guys as it gives me a good opportunity to get to know them. I'm after just twelve or so shots from this part of the day.

The shots I want are the same if I'm at a clay pigeon shoot, a golf course, or at a health spa. I take wide shots to tell the story and establish the scene, closeups to show the detail and add drama, tight action shots of each person, arty silhouettes or reflections, and finally a group shot of all participants. The camera then goes back in the bag and once the activity is over,

we head off to the bar or next location. Do *not* over shoot. Have the end product in mind. Ask yourself, 'How many pictures of the golf or the guys swimming will make the wedding album?' Be realistic.

JULIE JOINS THE GIRLS

Meanwhile, Julie joins the bride 2 hours before she needs to leave for the ceremony. This gives her plenty of time to set up shots of the shoes, bouquet, veil, tiara, dress, and so on. Never forget that a small fortune has probably been spent on all the bridal accessories, so make sure you record them and handle everything with extreme care.

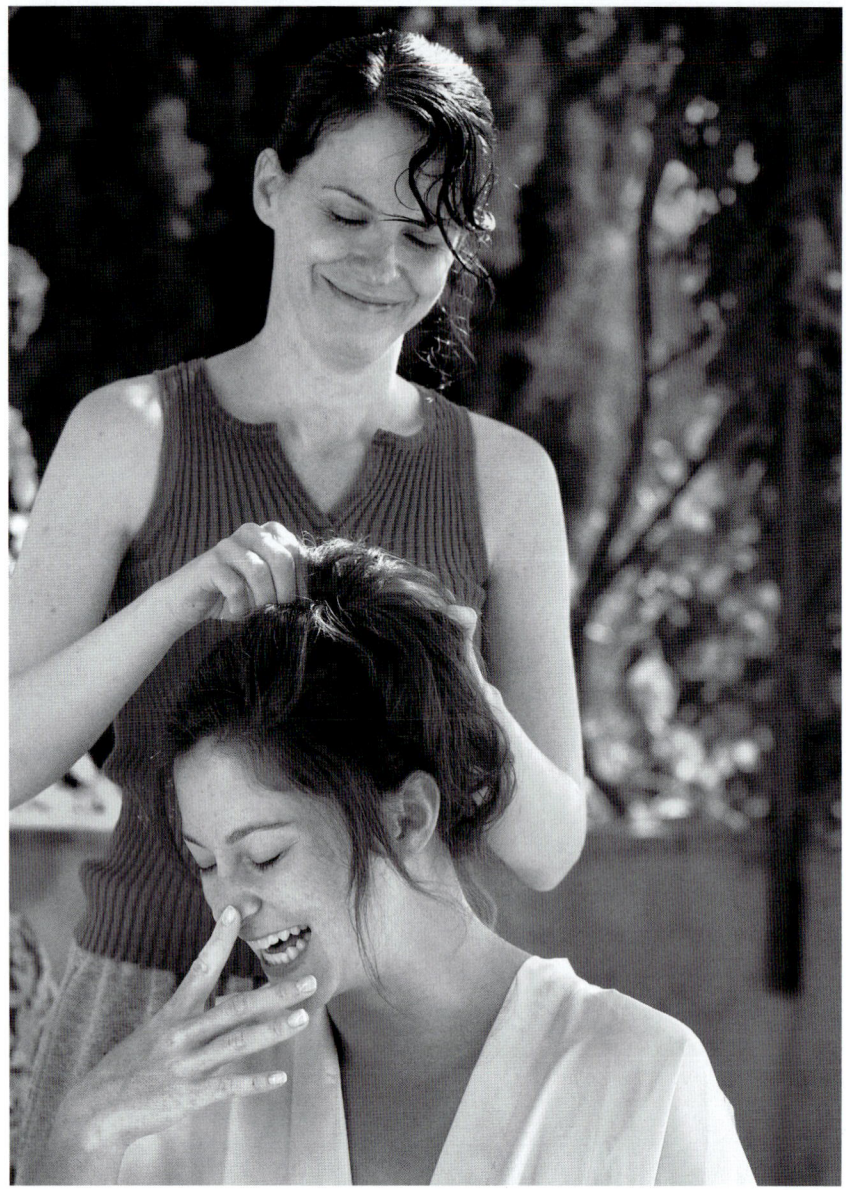

FIG. 12   ISO 200 f/4 at 1/360th

Fun moments like these are worth waiting for, but only once you have set the positions of the girls so you can shoot into the light.

If the flowers are delivered during this time, Julie will capture the moment when the florist first shows the bouquet to the bride – this often helps create a great reaction shot. Providing that the bouquet hasn't been delivered at the last minute (meaning time is tight) Julie will wait until the florist has left before taking the bouquet out of its box and photographing it. Although Julie takes the greatest of care with the bouquet, she doesn't want the florist telling her that she can't place it in a certain way in case the flowers get bruised or damaged.

With the shoes, once Julie has her 'safe' shot, she will often experiment with different angles and lighting situations to ring the changes – it's not uncommon for more than one shot of the shoes to make the album. Other details to be photographed at this stage are bridesmaids' shoes, dresses, bags, and so on. Julie

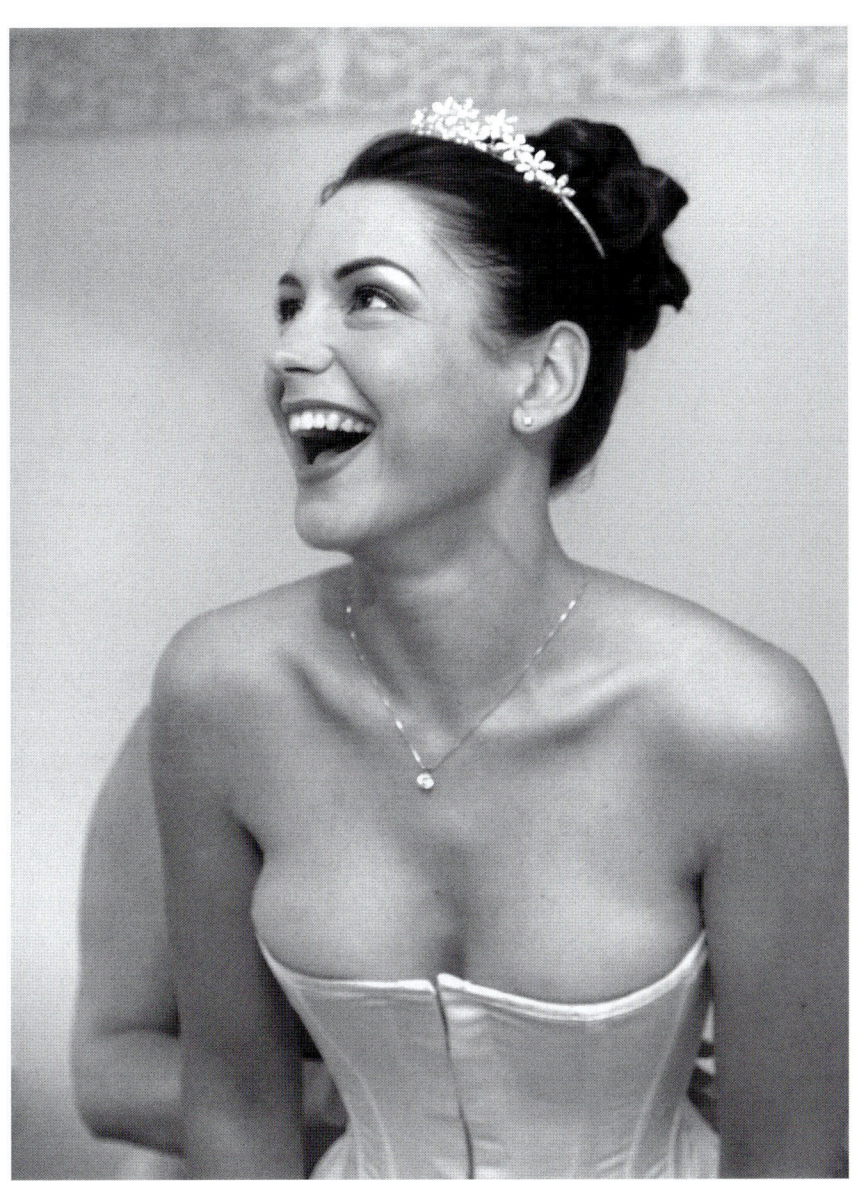

Julie used flash off-camera to capture this great moment.

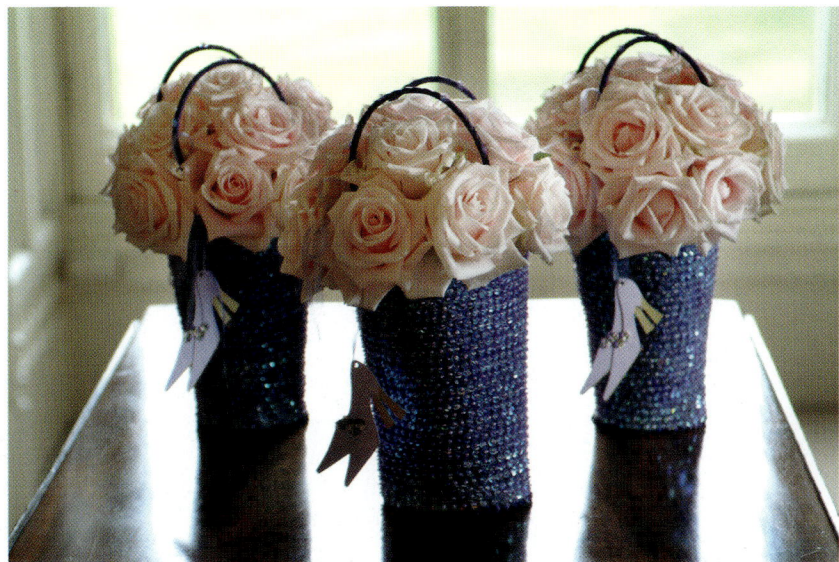

The best things come in threes. Julie shot into the light using a specula reflection off the shiny table to provide the drama. An increase in exposure compensation was needed to get this look in camera.

usually moves all of the above to a suitable location, sets up the shot, and then returns everything once it's been photographed. If all the bridesmaids' shoes are the same, she always checks that each one knows which is theirs – if there is any possibility that one girl may end up wearing the wrong shoes, Julie will write their initials inside before moving them.

Once all the accessories have been photographed, Julie will spend most of the remaining time building rapport with the bride, the bridesmaids and of course, the bride's mother, while their hair and make up is being done. She may take one wide

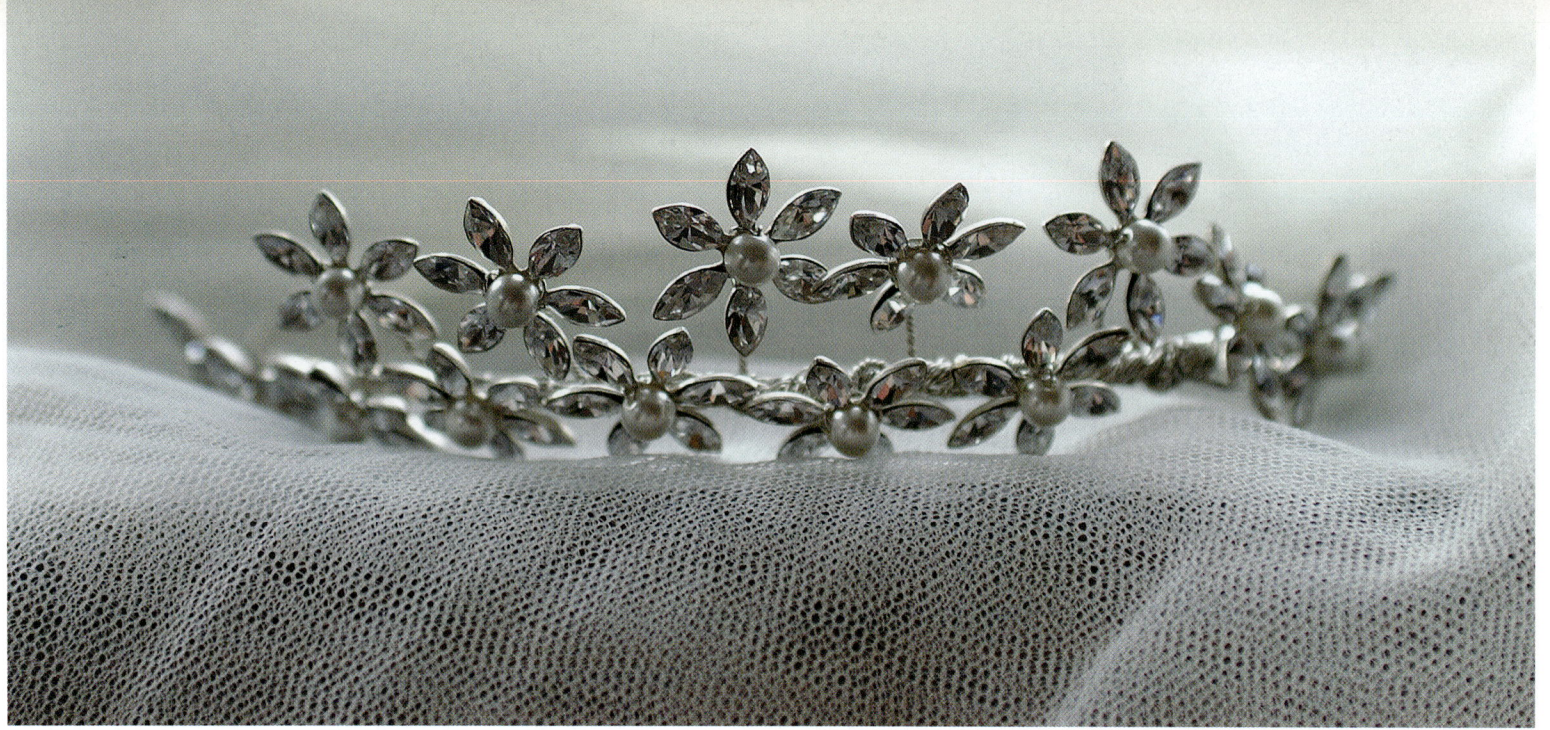

shot of the bride with her hair in rollers or very little makeup on, but often waits until hair and makeup is nearly finished before tucking herself in a corner of the room to photograph the bride head and shoulders. She's not shooting loads of frames – just the important ones such as lipstick being applied, or blusher being brushed on. If the back of the hair looks fabulous, Julie makes sure she has a shot of this feature before it's covered up with a veil. At this stage, depending on the background or available light, she may ask the make-up artist if she can finish off in a different place. It may only be a move of a couple of feet, but this can make all the difference to the photograph. This is also a great time to get some shots of the bridesmaids or the bride's mother in the room with the bride – it tells the story of who was there with her when she was getting ready.

BACK WITH THE GUYS

Meanwhile, back with the boys, I start to shoot my 'getting ready' pictures. While the groom is showering, I photograph the rings, his pocket watch, or anything else I can find that references the wedding. I look for cards or gifts from the bride, a set of speech cards or unique detail on his shirt or waistcoat. I used to have a dedicated macro lens but now I just use a +4 dioptre on my 100 mm lens. I keep the camera steady using my monopod and shoot into the light where possible. I don't shy away from high ISO, or slow shutter speed. These pictures rarely go bigger than postcard size in the album and I shoot as quickly and with as much efficiency as I can. A monopod allows me to shoot at three stops slower shutter speed and it keeps me relaxed because it carries the weight of the camera while I compose my shots.

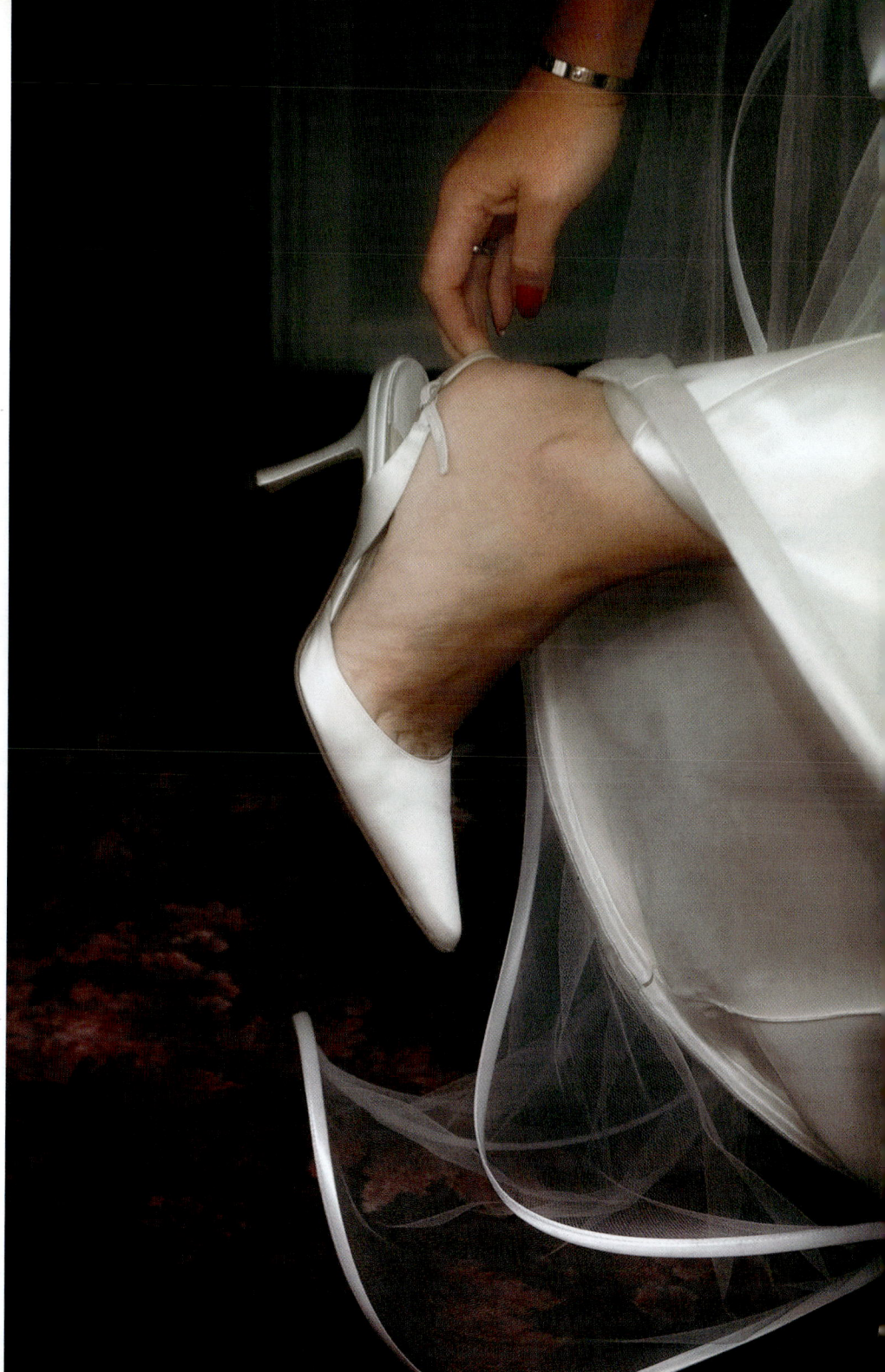

opposite

FIG. 15   ISO 400 f/4 at 1/280th

This tiara was placed on the piece of veil fabric Julie carries neatly folded in her camera bag. It becomes an instant studio background for still life pictures.

FIG. 16   ISO 800 f/6.7 at 1/60th

Pictures like this are gone in an instant so be ready.

There's a good reason for these shots. The more 'guy details' I can shoot, the more 'bride details' will make the album. Keeping the 'his and hers' sessions in balance makes for a better album and produces more print sales. Once the groom has a shirt and pants on, I concentrate on the camaraderie between the guys. I will start by arranging the area to be used for the pictures. This entails clearing away debris such as carrier bags and suit bags and opening the curtains if required. I like to see other light sources too, so I'll put on bedside lights where possible.

If the best man and ushers are getting ready in other rooms, I arrange for them all to meet in the groom's room before the cufflink and cravats stage. The fun generated by all the fiddling around, makes great pictures. Occasionally, I get shots of ironing, shoe polishing, and other male grooming. I usually try to get a

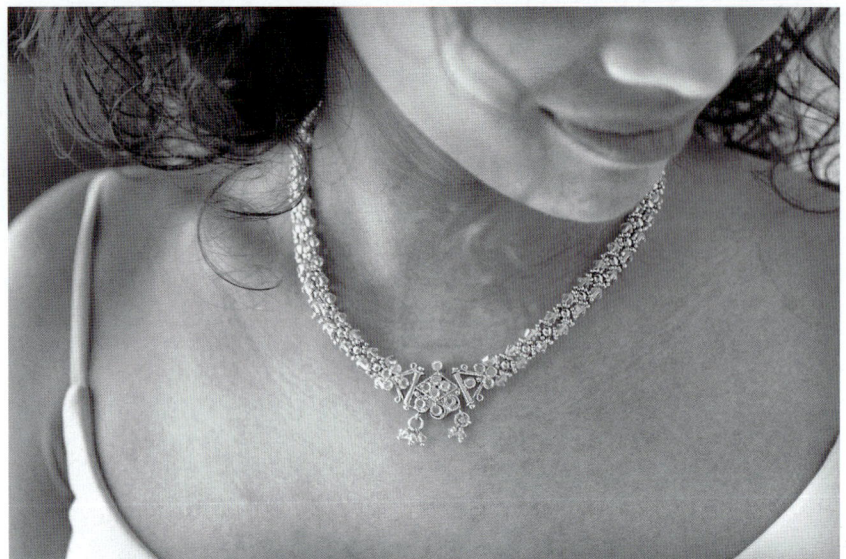

Fig. 17   ISO 320 f/4 at 1/140th

Details that include a key to the mood of the moment are more valuable than those that are inert. Including the bride's mouth in this jewelry picture even though it is out of focus was the right thing to do.

sequence of the groom with the best man. It is also important to shoot the groom on his own: a good setup is to have him putting gel in his hair or straightening his tie in front of a mirror.

Intimacy between men is rarely shown on the wedding day, so I help it along by getting the men to do each other's cravats or cufflinks. Ritualistic drinking of champagne, beer, or tea should also to be encouraged to create a feeling of team spirit and conviviality. I usually set this up as a group shot. A 'semi-casual' look – shirtsleeves or waistcoats – is ideal. I will take the same group outside the ceremony so I want this picture to be a bit different. Incidentally, I always leave the buttonholes until we arrive at the ceremony location: car seat belts can cause havoc with buttonholes and corsages.

It's a good idea for wedding photographers to have the skills required to tie Windsor, half Windsor, and Four-in-Hand tie knots. Knowing how to make a cravat look good and the ability to pin various types of buttonholes without ruining the line of a suit is very useful too. You can find all this information on the internet for free. In my camera bag I carry a sewing kit, the sort usually found in hotel rooms, a multi-utility tool, and a box of matches. These items are often needed in the morning at one time or another.

It's now time for the guys to get to the ceremony. I usually go through a quick checklist with the groom just before we pull away, to ensure we have everything: rings, orders of service, speeches, buttonholes, bottled water, money, and so on. The

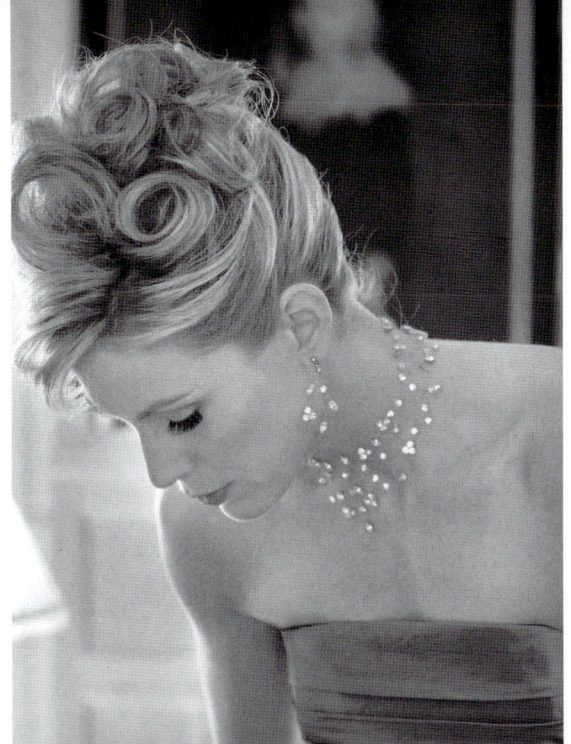

FIG. 18   ISO 800 f/4 at 1/90th

Fabulous hair, a beautiful bridesmaid, and wonderful light combined to great effect for this candid picture.

bottom right

FIG. 19   ISO 320 f/4 at 1/660th

Here Julie had a bit of fun with the flower girls at the bride's home while she waited for the cars to take them all to the church. The expressions on the girls' faces reflect on the moment Julie had created.

groom is usually both nervous and excited, so this can be a useful exercise often saving the day! This all goes toward the client experience and adds value to our service.

JULIE SHOOTS THE DRESS AND SPREADS CALM

Meanwhile, Julie is at the final bridal preparation stage. She will already have tidied away all bags, cases, boxes, discarded clothes and even made the bed if necessary. She will have decided exactly where she wants the bride to put her dress on, and moved furniture if necessary.

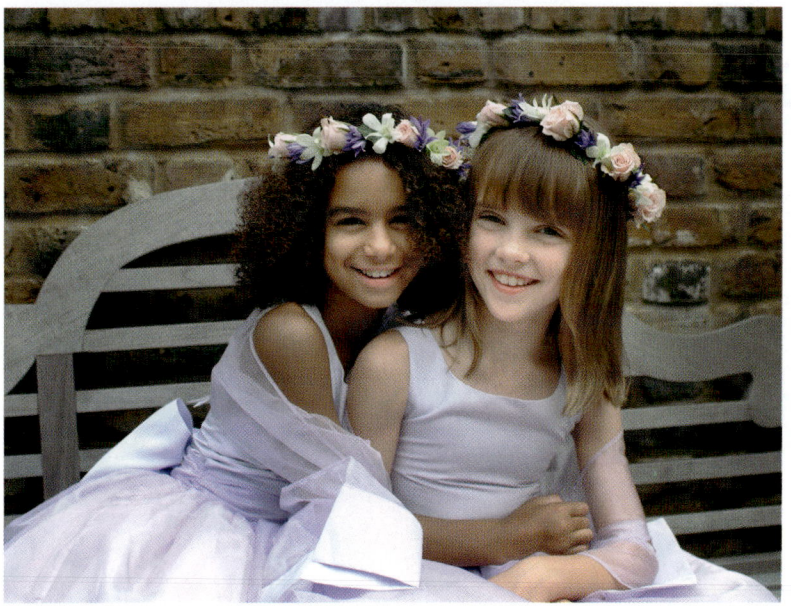

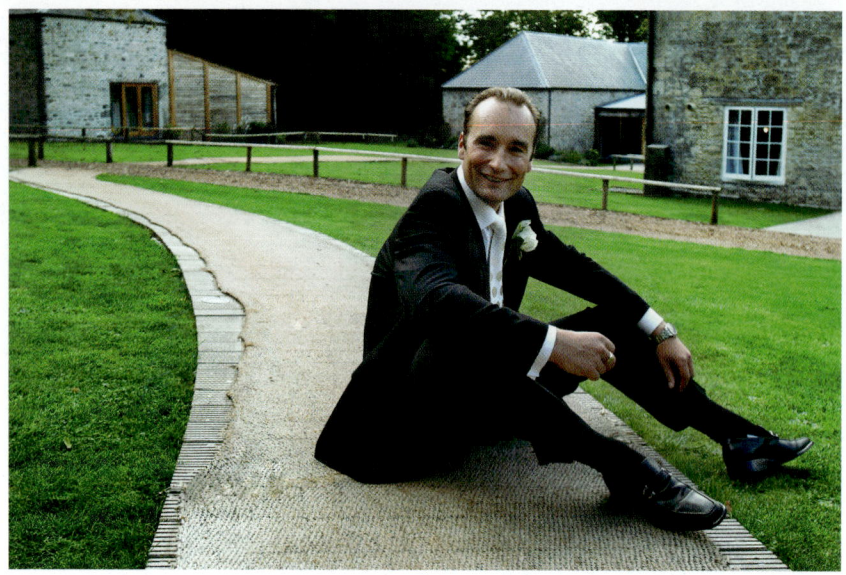

FIG. 20   ISO 200 f/4 at 1/180th

I chose to shoot this groom at ground level to make compositional use of the snaking path. This pose removed some of the formality that a standing picture might have had and it helped the groom before the ceremony.

bottom left

FIG. 21   ISO 400 f/4 at 1/250th

I like to get a picture of the groom and the best man arriving at the church. I was inside the church for this picture shooting out of the door on a 200 mm lens. I was lucky the focus didn't decide to go through to the background.

opposite

FIGS 22 & 23   ISO 800 f/4 at 1/125th and 1/470th

This groom was kept busy before the ceremony and I chose to keep my framing tight to add impact to the composition.

By now things may be starting to run late, in which case Julie's job is to gently move the proceedings along as quickly as possible – helping wherever possible. This often involves helping the bride to put her dress on and do up the buttons or laces as the bridesmaids or Mum have disappeared to get ready themselves. Julie only needs a couple of shots to tell the story, so if the bride is getting stressed she'll come to the rescue – that's much more useful than standing there with camera in hand doing nothing!

Finally, it all comes together and the relative calm of the previous hour and a half has now become a flurry of activity.

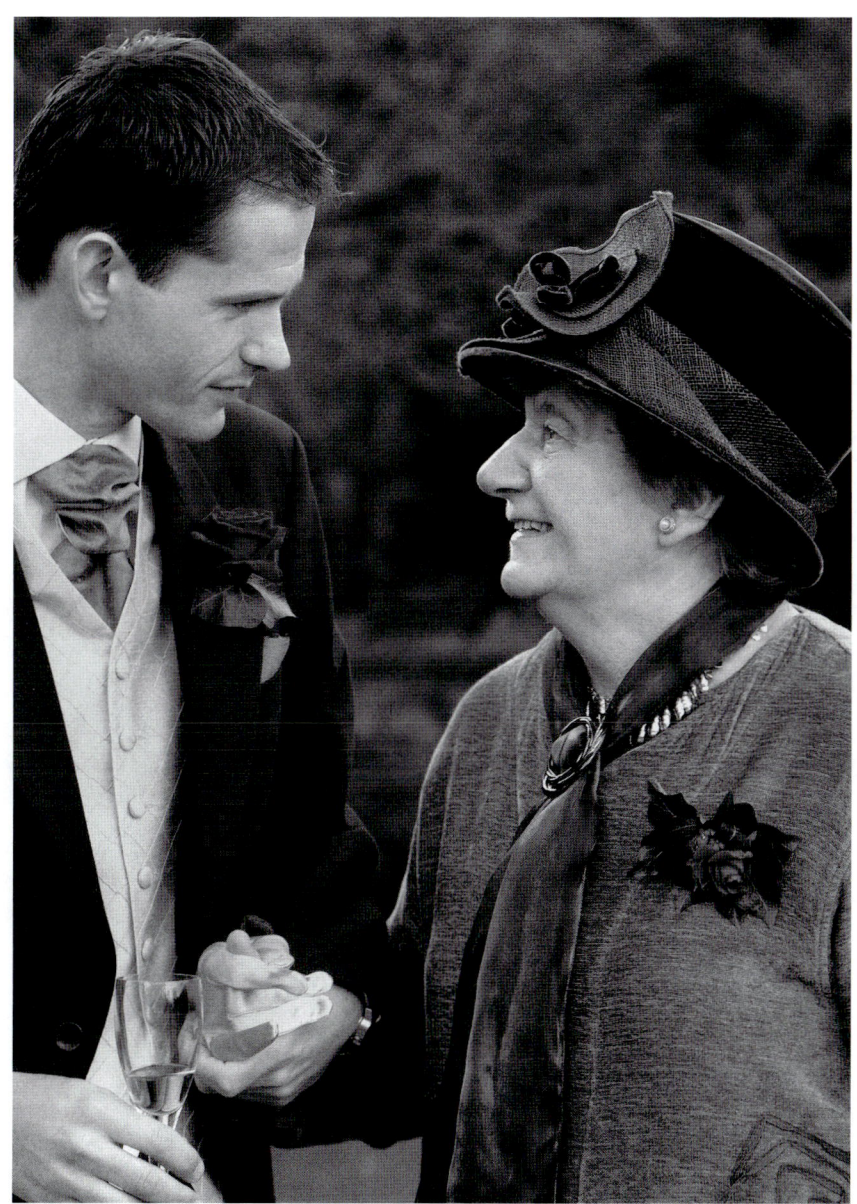
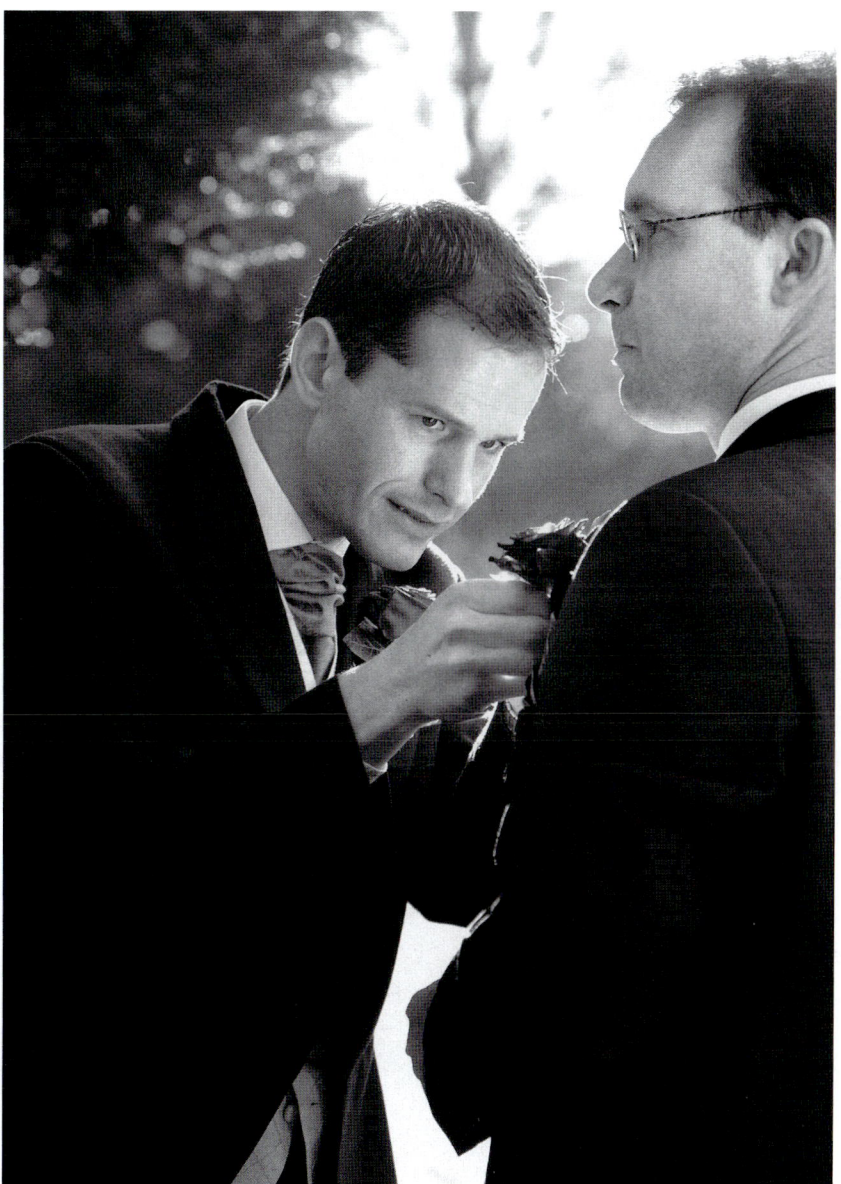

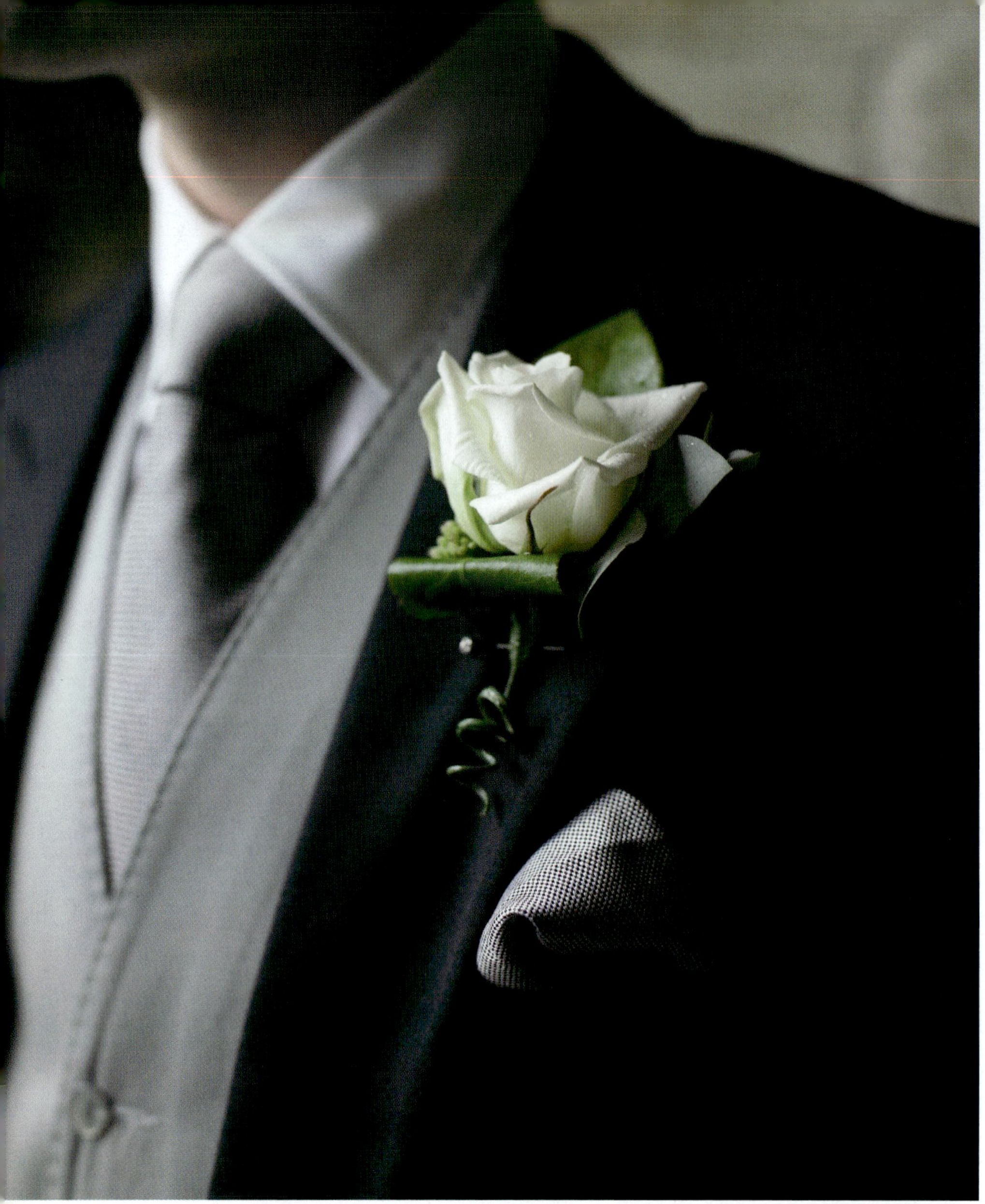

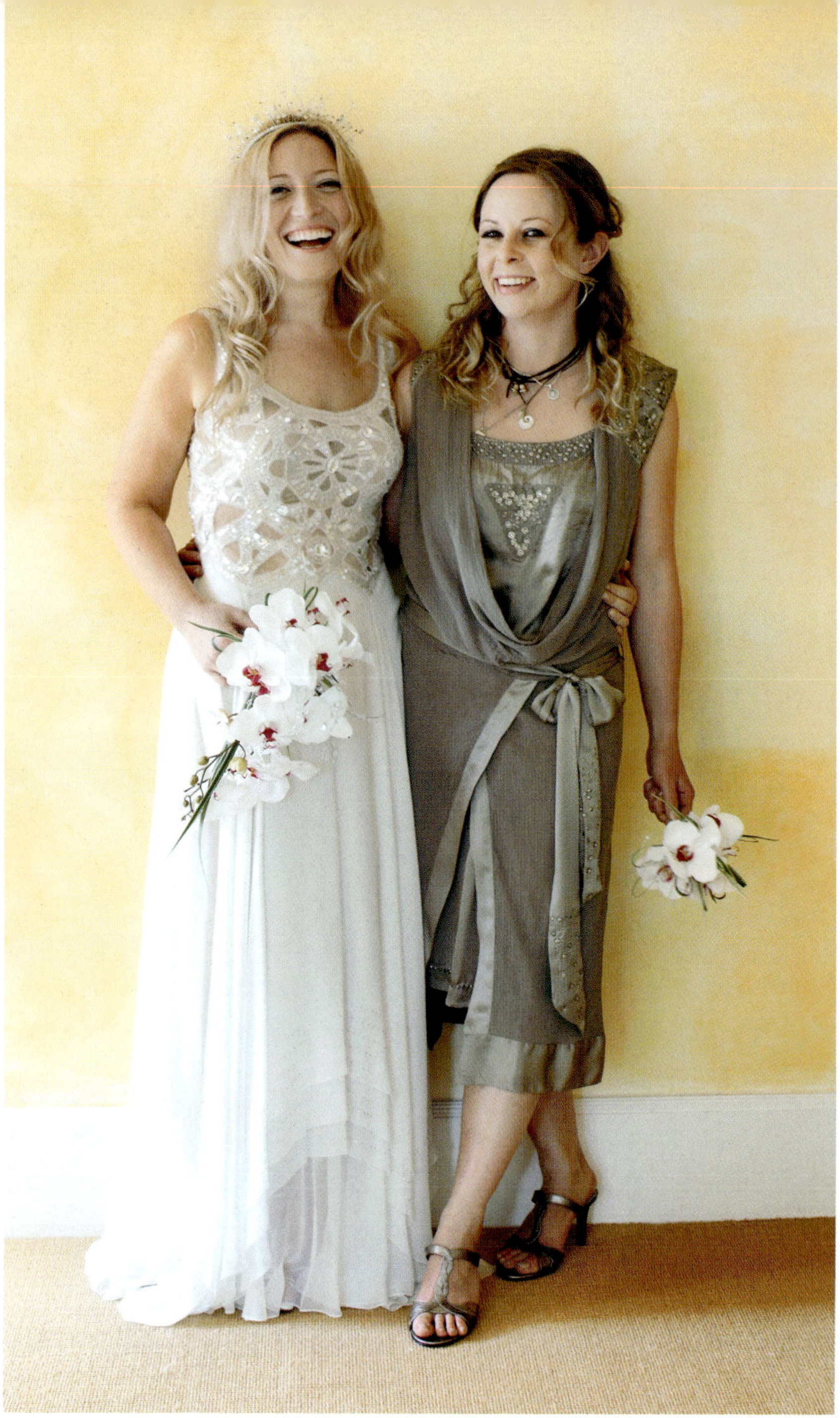

above

FIG. 24   ISO 400 f/4 at 1/160th

With tight framing like this pictures can have a broader appeal. The florist as well as the couple ordered this picture and it was used full page to illustrate an editorial feature in a UK wedding magazine.

opposite

FIG. 25   ISO 800 f/4 at 1/50th

Taken just before they left for the ceremony, this full length shot of a bride and her bridesmaid with their flowers was a must have for Julie. Pictures like this are easy to forget to shoot and are always wanted.

FIG. 26   ISO 400 f/4 at 1/45th

Predicting the action is vital to capture moments like this. Julie went round to the other side of the car and shot through the open door. Staying beside the bride would have been a big mistake.

The aim is for everyone to be ready 15 minutes prior to leaving as this ensures there is time for the following shots:

· Bride on her own, closeup and full length, arty shots, fun shots, and beauty shots

· Bride with bridesmaids, closeup, and full length

· Bride with siblings and family

If things are running late however, Julie will never add to the stress by setting up shots. It's more important to get the bride to the ceremony as quickly as possible – besides, if the bride is stressed, there is absolutely no point in taking photos of her as (a) she'll look stressed in the photos and (b) she'll remember the stress when she views the photo and won't buy it anyway. All these pictures can be taken during the reception so it's much better to be a savior than an irritation.

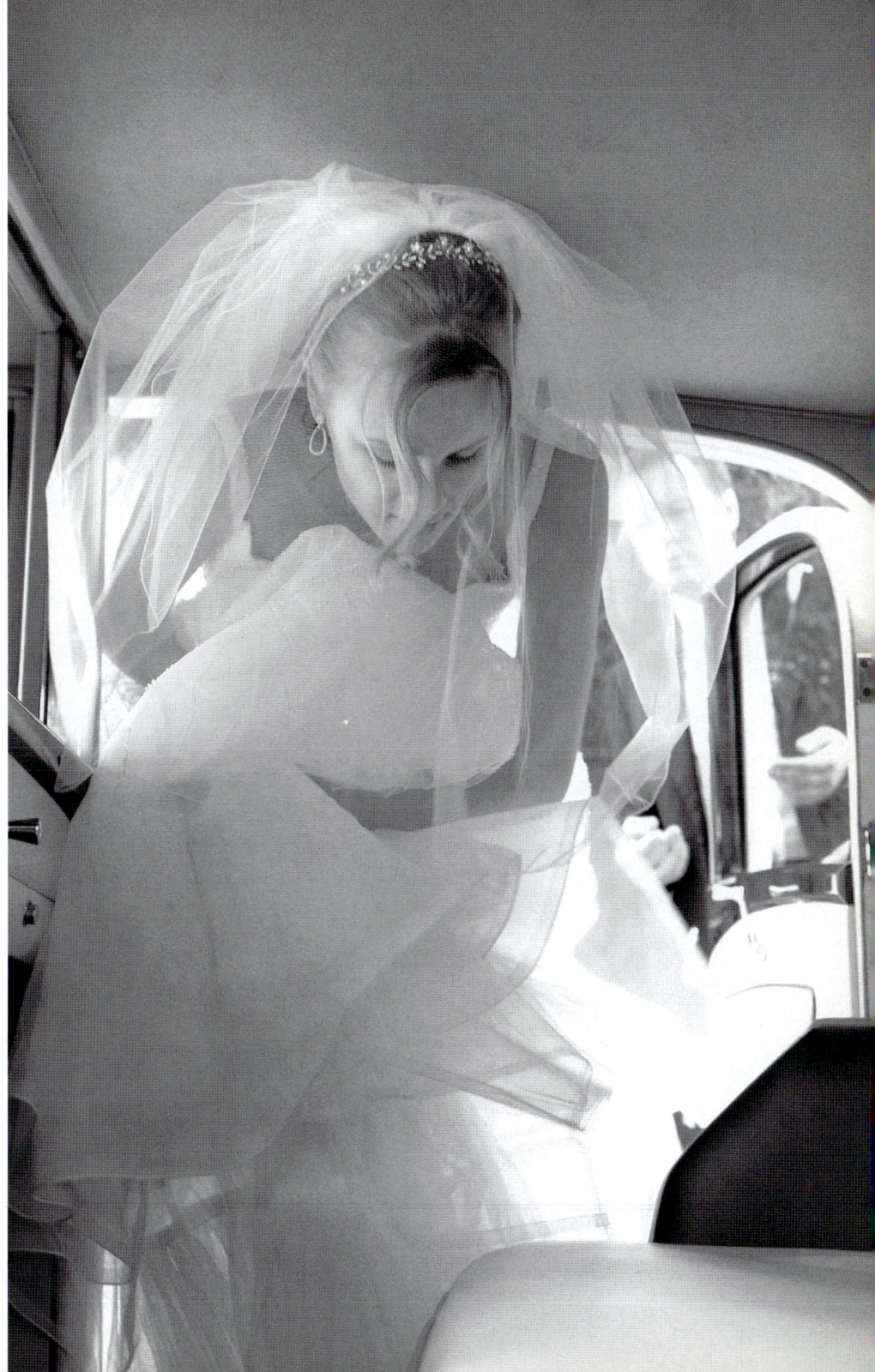

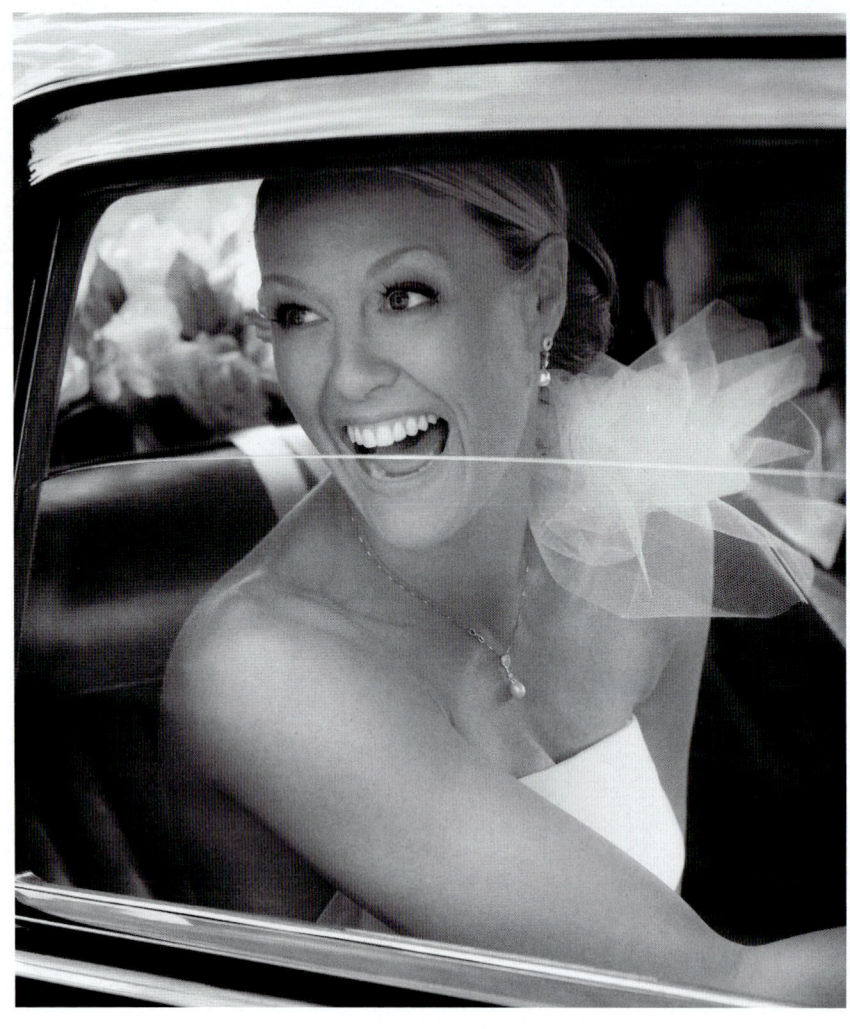

Fig. 27   ISO 200 f4.8 at 1/180th

Another great moment caught by Julie. It is often worth Julie hanging on until the last possible moment before she makes her way to the church safe in the knowledge I'm already there to capture the bride's arrival.

opposite

Fig. 28   ISO 800 f/4 at 1/360th

A well seen picture taken by Julie in Chelsea, London as the bride drove past the film advert poster.

Sometimes we will have a super-efficient bride who is itching to get into her dress an hour before she needs to. Julie will dissuade her from doing this, because once she has the dress on, the bride will not want to sit down, eat, drink, or do anything for fear of creasing it, or spilling things on it. This is where experience is invaluable – Julie knows how long it is likely to take to get dressed and can guide the bride (not to mention her worried Mum) so that calmness rather than chaos reigns!

OUTSIDE THE CHURCH OR CEREMONY LOCATION

At the ceremony location, I have several shots to get before the main event including the putting on of buttonholes. I usually get

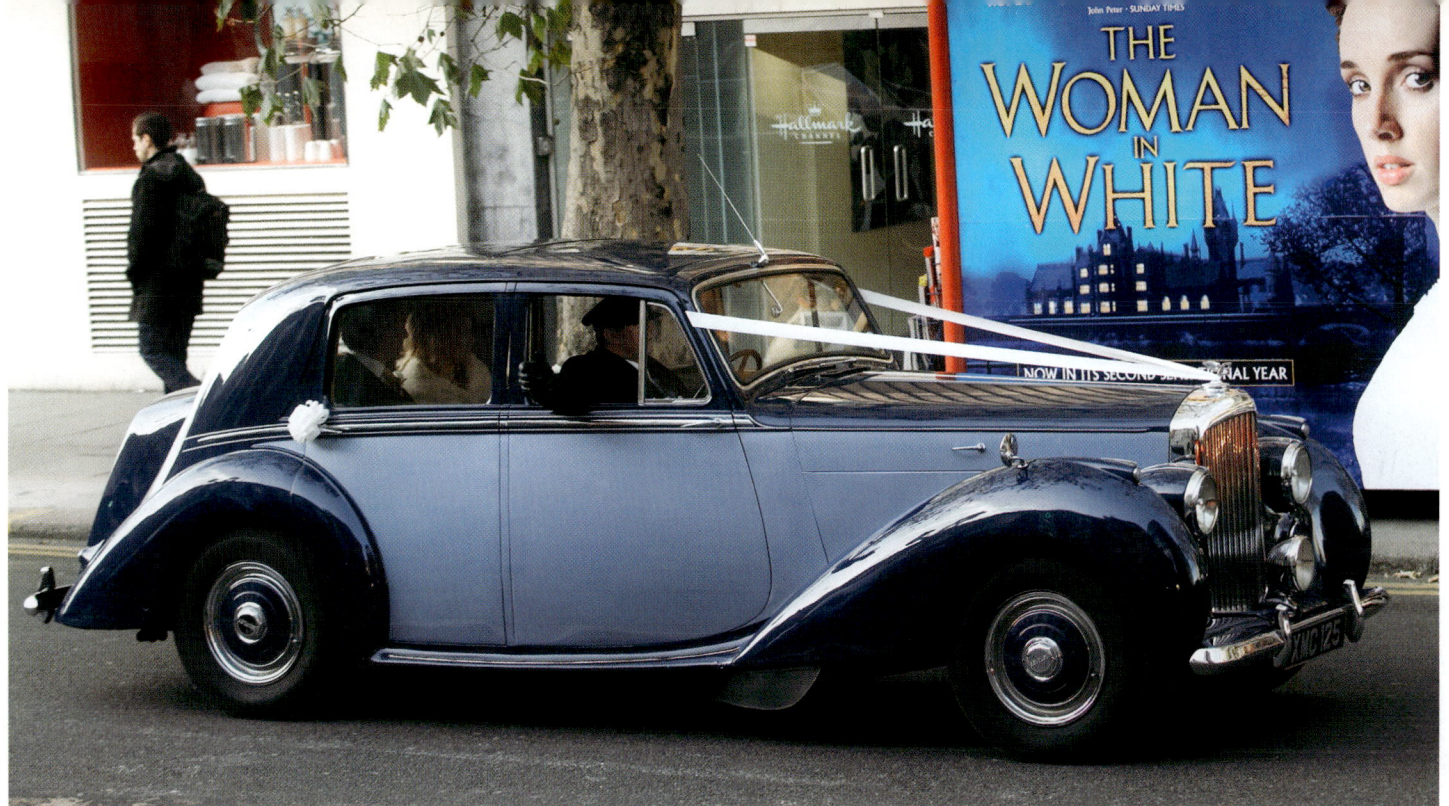

the guys to stand in the church or venue porch. This gives top cover and open shaded light. A wide shot sets the scene and closeups of the action follow. I shoot the wide on my 35mm lens and swap to the 100mm for the rest. Once the buttonholes are on it's time for a group picture before the ushers have to do their stuff. This group is quite formal. The guys may never look this good again!

Then come the long shots of the groom and best man and finally the groom on his own. I let the groom have a moment to himself as I go and find the priest, or officiator. My next role is to negotiate exactly where Julie can stand at the front and what coverage she can get: flash, or no flash, vows or not, and so on. Once the pleasantries are over and the deal struck, I'm off to photograph the flowers, candles, and other decorations. At the back of the

room I grab an usher for a picture with the orders of service. I then get an action shot of guests being greeted by the ushers.

With 5 minutes to go I get a picture of the groom at the front of the room waiting. I might quiz him about the girls being late and this prompts a look at the watch, which always raises a laugh when my shutter goes in unison! I wish him a good ceremony and leave him in the capable hands of the best man. I'll say Hi to the groom's parents and family before heading down the aisle and waiting for the bridesmaids. I keep my eyes peeled for interesting pictures. Gargoyles, the church cat, pageboys, and the ushers all make good picture opportunities. If there is a clock tower, I'll get a big wide shot a few moments before the ceremony starts. I have to keep my wits about me at this point because I am where the action is and I have to be ready

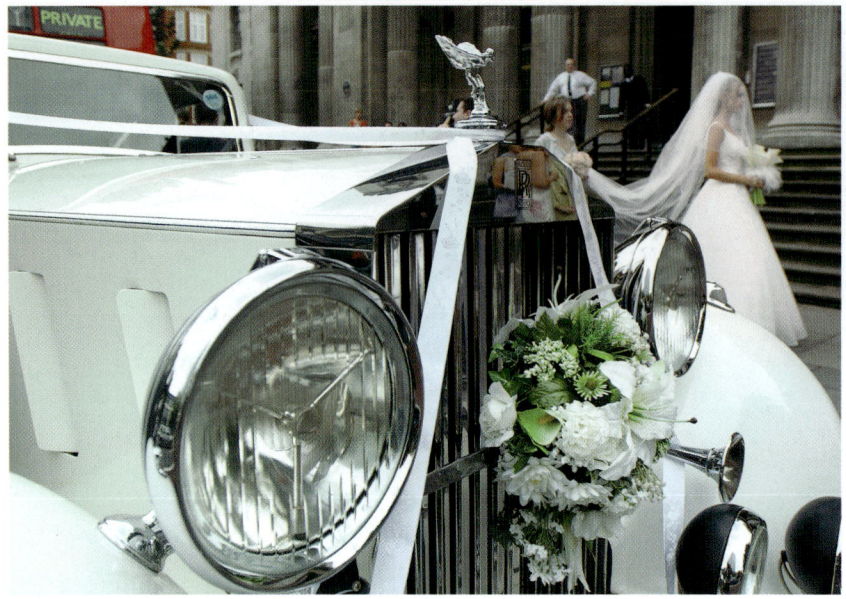

Fig. 29   ISO 800 f/4 at 1/2000th

I used a shallow depth of field to great effect here with my 17 mm lens. Split focus can be achieved with wide lenses if the point of focus is very close to the camera.

for anything. I keep my camera bag close at hand near the main entrance and venture off with my 100 mm on the camera. Having no zoom and using a fairly tight lens is risky but the pictures are worth it. At the BBC, the saying was 'If in doubt, zoom out.' (Meaning, if you lose focus, or the action is all around you, play it safe and use the wide-angle lens.) Playing it safe doesn't produce the great shots though, so I'm happy to take a few risks. If I'm having a confidence crisis I'll put the 35 mm lens on and keep back so as not to distort the perspective. Marko, our picture editor, can always crop in tighter later.

Now I await the bridesmaids. A few shots of them together looking at the camera and at each other and then I get ready to photograph the bride arriving. Julie is often just ahead of the bride. I'll quickly relay the instructions from the officiator and let her know what I've negotiated with regard to her coverage. I'll photograph the bride arriving in a reportage style, not stopping the action, just going with the flow. At the entrance I'll get a chance to take a few formal portraits of the bride and her father or the person taking her down the aisle. Next, I swap to the 35 mm lens to capture the bridesmaids fluffing the dress. While the 'meet and greet' is going on with the ceremony official and the bride, I slip past and take my place to the side at the back of the room. I attach my flash with Stofen via the coiled transistor-transistor logic (TTL) lead for the start of the procession.

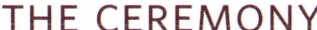

FIG. 30   ISO 400 f/4 at 1/125th

I used a splash of flash and a stop of exposure increase to get life into this picture. A photograph taken in a heavily backlit place like this is at risk of having a heavy, near silhouette quality.

THE CEREMONY

Julie has a clear view down the aisle with her 200 mm lens. And I get a shot with the wide from close hand. By now you will understand that we have a system. The key to our success is sticking to a procedure so that each of us knows exactly where we should be and what pictures we should get at each stage of the day. This still leaves room for creativity and during the ceremony is one place I like to exercise it.

Julie is static and to the right at the front with her Nikon on a Manfrotto monopod. Switching between lenses she gets the whole story in close detail favoring the bride. I shoot from the center of the aisle at the back. Once I have my wide shots I look for other shots of interest. I use minimal depth of field to record the flowers on the pew ends or I set up a still life of the order

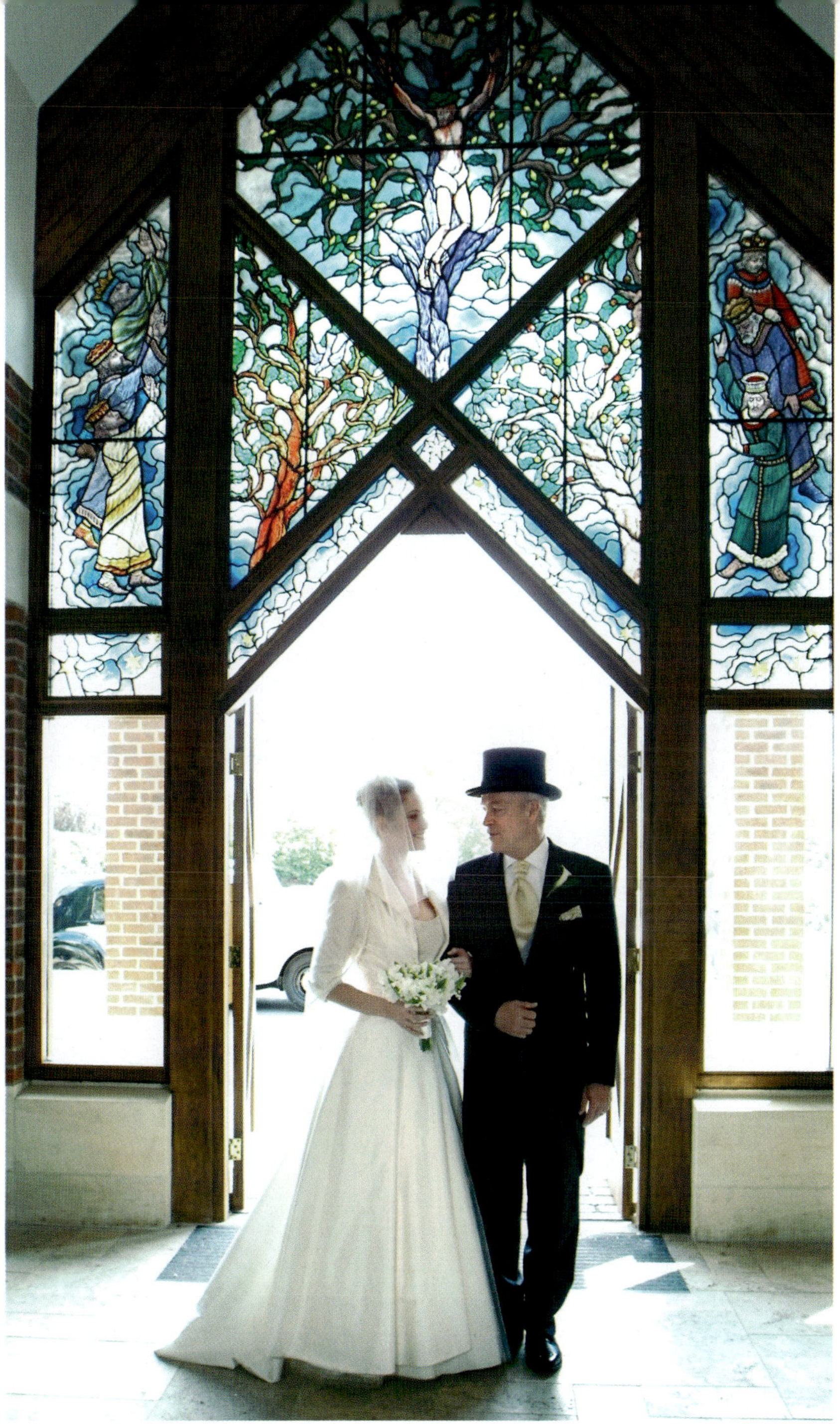

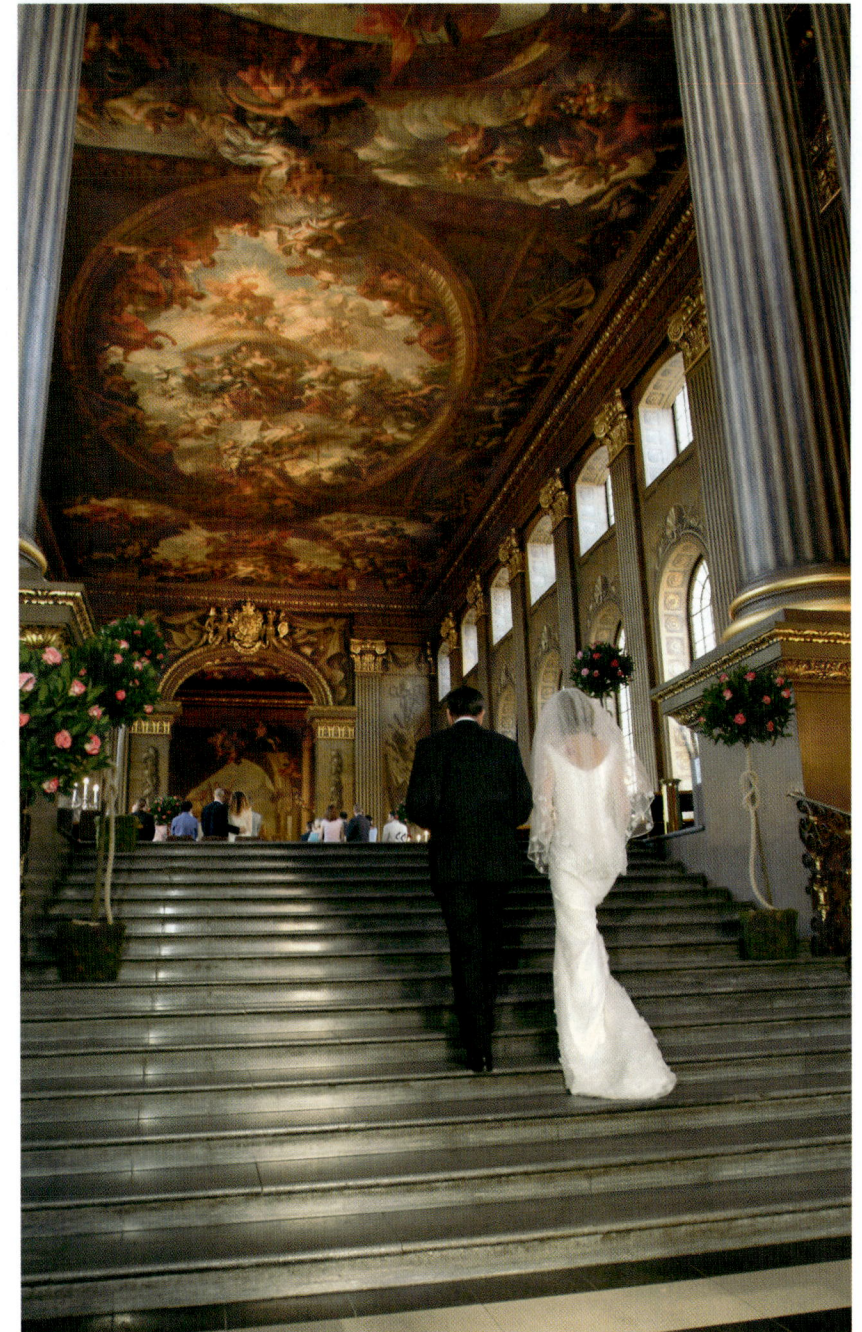

Fig. 31   ISO 800 f/4 at 1/45th

It's not often I consider taking a figure in the landscape picture like this of the bride and her father on their way into the ceremony. The sheer scale and grandeur of the Royal Naval College in Greenwich deserved such a picture. The wonderful reflected light on the risers of the steps leads the eye into the picture.

opposite

Fig. 32   ISO 800 f/5.7 at 1/30th

It is easy to see where I stand to take photographs during a ceremony in this picture of the painted hall in Greenwich. I am always behind the last row of guests and ready to capture the moments using either a wide or very tight lens.

of service or cones of confetti. I have about 20 minutes to be creative. A glance at the order of service will tell me when the readings are. I'll need to get pictures of the readings as Julie is not in the ideal place to cover these. I'll also get a shot of '... I therefore proclaim that they are husband and wife.'

After that, I'll pop outside and get shots of the cars or perhaps a horse and carriage. Arty exterior shots of the church are also on my list. Back inside, my next shot is during the signing of the register. I'll have my wide lens on with my flash to record any wide shots of the family or impromptu groups during the register signing. Julie gets the pictures of the signing itself. Once we have acknowledged to each other that all is well and 'in the can' I'll get a shot of the organist or soloist before heading to the back to get ready for the procession down the aisle. I pack

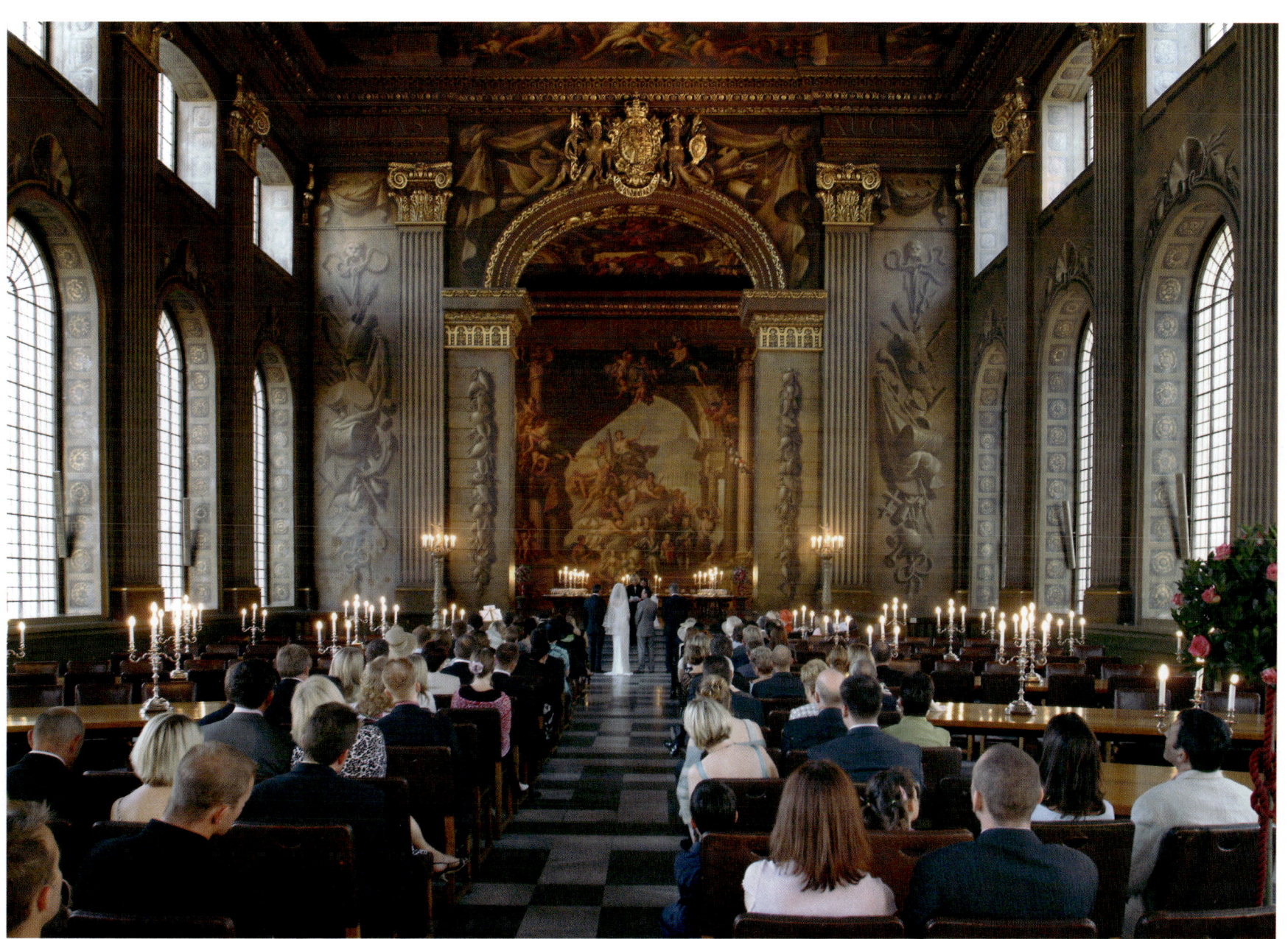

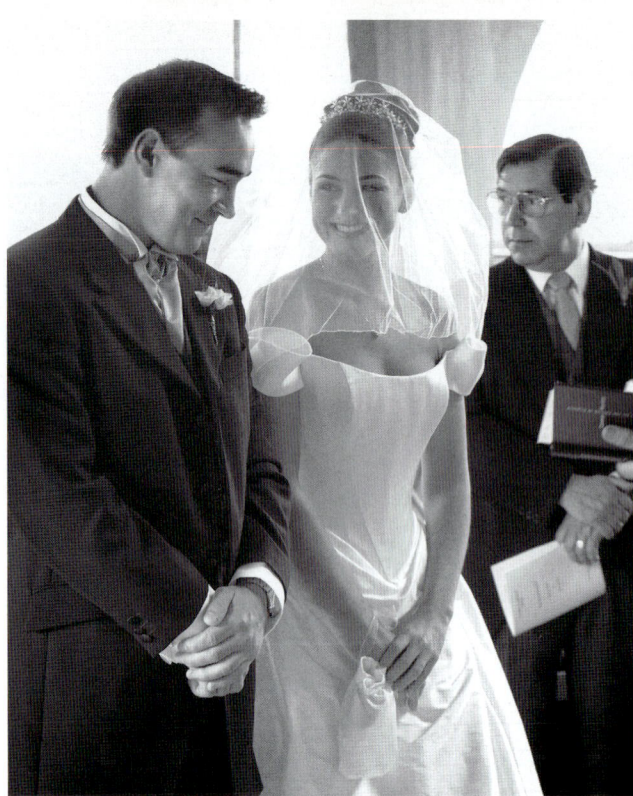

Fig. 33   ISO 1600 f/4 at 1/45th

Julie stands at the front of the ceremony room and to the right so that she is facing the bride when the couple look at each other. In this picture, Julie used plus two stops of increased exposure to counteract the intense highlights from the windows behind the bride.

below

Fig. 34   ISO 800 f/4 at 1/64th

It's okay to cheat. I took this picture of the organist while he was rehearsing some 30 minutes before the start of the ceremony. Getting this picture during the ceremony would have risked disturbing him and upsetting his performance.

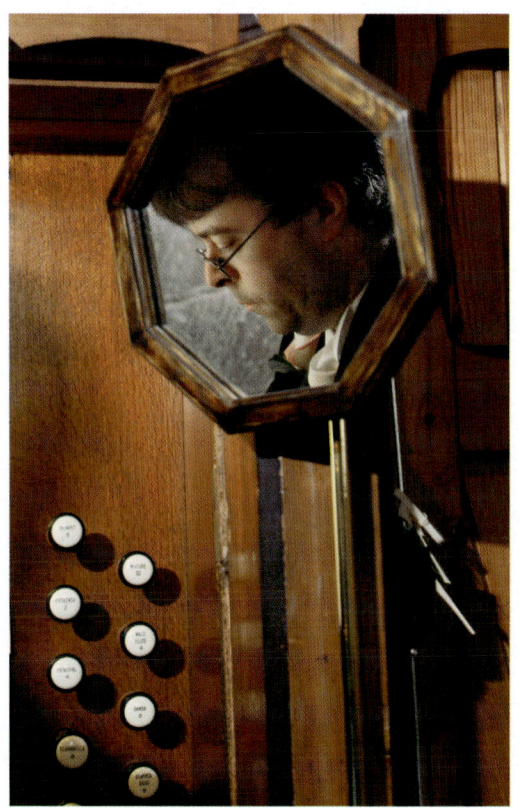

my camera bag neatly, collapse my monopod and rest it on top. I have my Hasselblad with its Phase One P25 digital back in my right hand with the 35 mm lens at f/4 and I have my Metz flash in my left hand set to TTL, attached to the camera by the Metz TTL lead. I switch the camera to manual focus and set the focus to 10 feet. The ISO is set to 400 and the shutter speed to 1/45th. I casually walk up the aisle to meet the bride and groom coming down toward me. When we are 10 feet apart, I back off, maintaining that distance while shooting at decisive moments to capture the action. Once a safe shot has been caught, I will go for a high-angle image by holding the camera above my head. A quick glance up at the screen tells me if I need to adjust my framing.

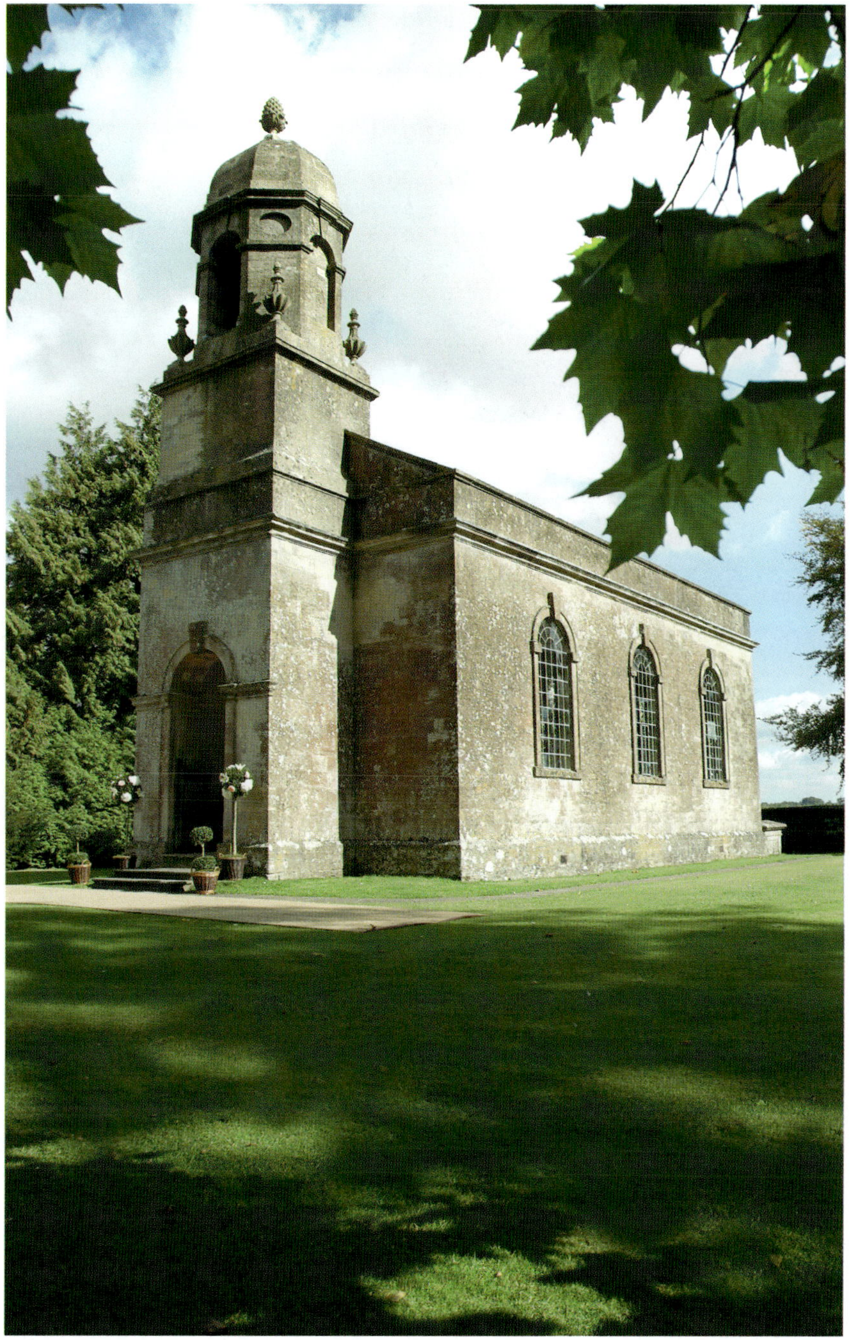

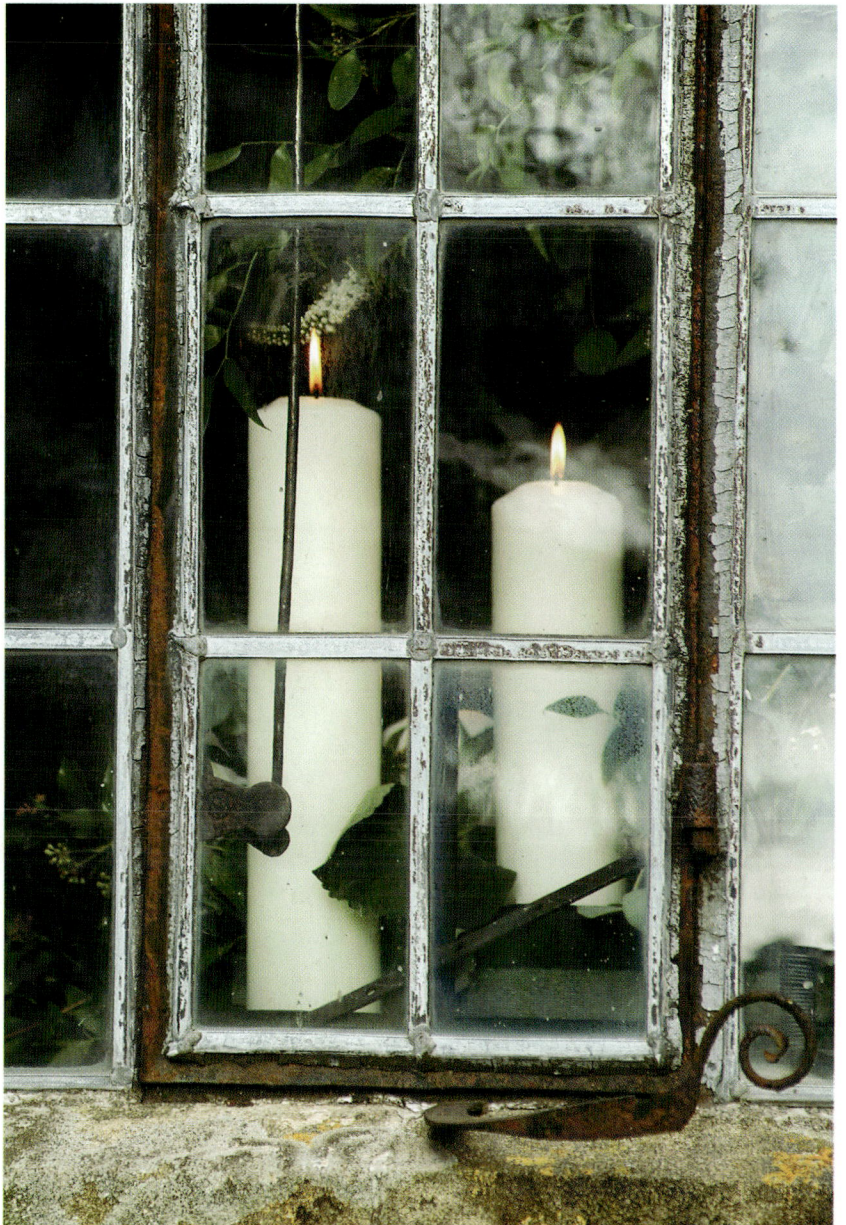

FIGS 35 & 36   ISO 200 f/4 at 1/500th

I went under the tree to use the foliage to help frame this chapel. I then went and shot the candles through the window from the outside.

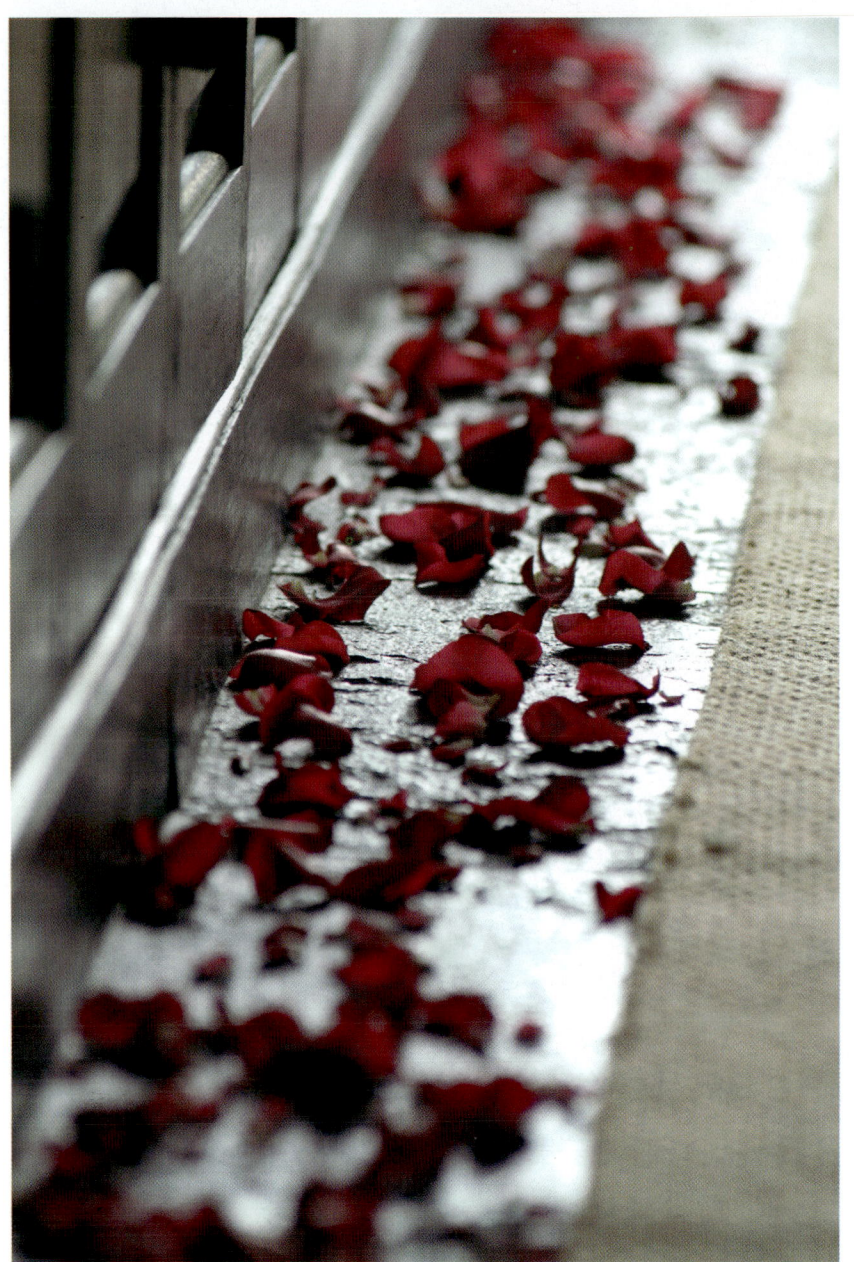

FIG. 37   ISO 400 f/4 at 1/125th

A long lens and shooting into the light made this a strong picture. The diagonal composition and shallow depth of field added interest.

OUTSIDE AGAIN

Julie in the meantime has made her way out of the ceremony and carried my bag with her. She has now set her camera to the settings required for the daylight outside. I step aside as the couple leave the church or ceremony room. Meanwhile, Julie is in place to get a clean picture as they exit the building. The next 5 minutes are very important. I take 30 seconds or so to set my camera to cope with the new conditions then I hoist it high above my head on my monopod for a self-timed exposure. This top shot is very popular and sells well. Julie steps back out of the shot, and uses her 200 mm to pick up candid emotions from relatives and friends of the couple. Between us we tell the story well. I shoot the wide shots and the intimate moments

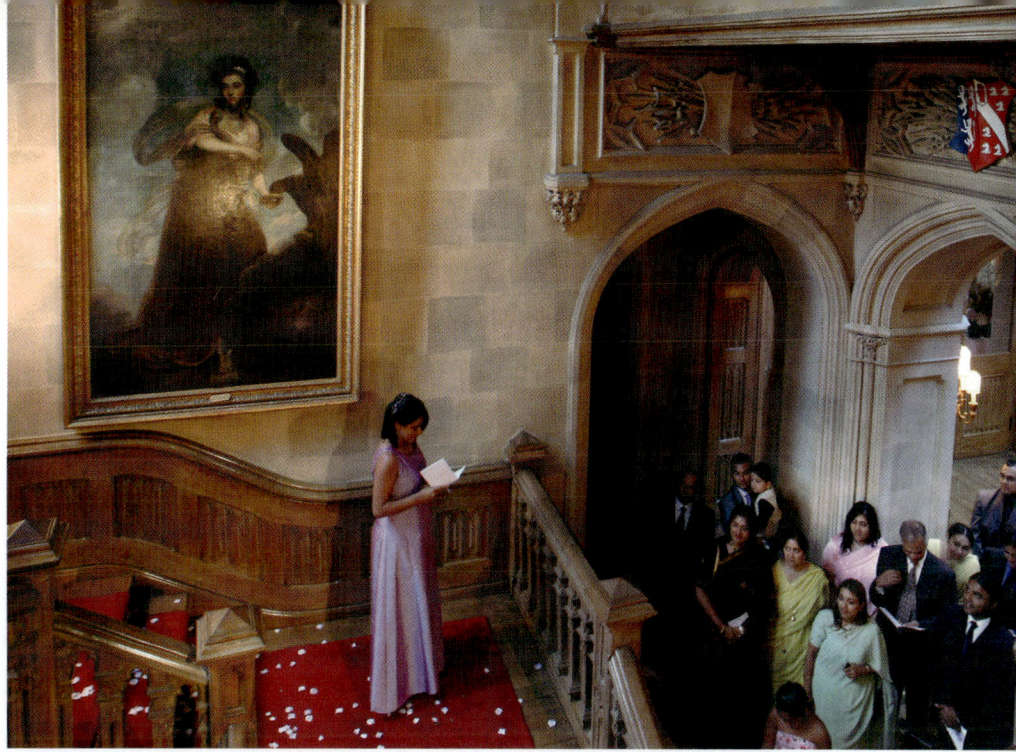

FIG. 38   ISO 800 f/4 at 1/10th

I used the balustrade of the staircase to rest my monopod against for this low light picture of a bridesmaid giving a reading. I wanted to include the background painting of the woman in my composition because it has harmony with the action. The low angle viewpoint the painter has used in his/her work gives the woman depicted strength and purpose.

bottom right

FIG. 39   ISO 1250 f/4 at 1/80th

Julie had to increase the ISO to capture this couple singing. An exposure increase was also necessary.

while Julie shoots the closeups and the people shots. We work quietly and efficiently knowing what is expected of each of us.

The confetti happens next. Julie and I often shoot this from opposite angles. I'm happy to include Julie in my pictures as we are part of the story too. Julie rarely gets me in the shots because she is on tighter lenses at f/4. After the confetti, either Julie or I go to get the car while the other one of us shoots the bride and groom preparing to leave.

Our car is poised right behind the bridal car with the engine running by the time the couple leave. I'll jump in and we are off. A great shot en-route is always a pleasant bonus if it happens. This is a good time for me to have a sandwich, while Julie drives. A wedding day shoot is like an action movie and we are halfway through. By this time we should have about 500 frames

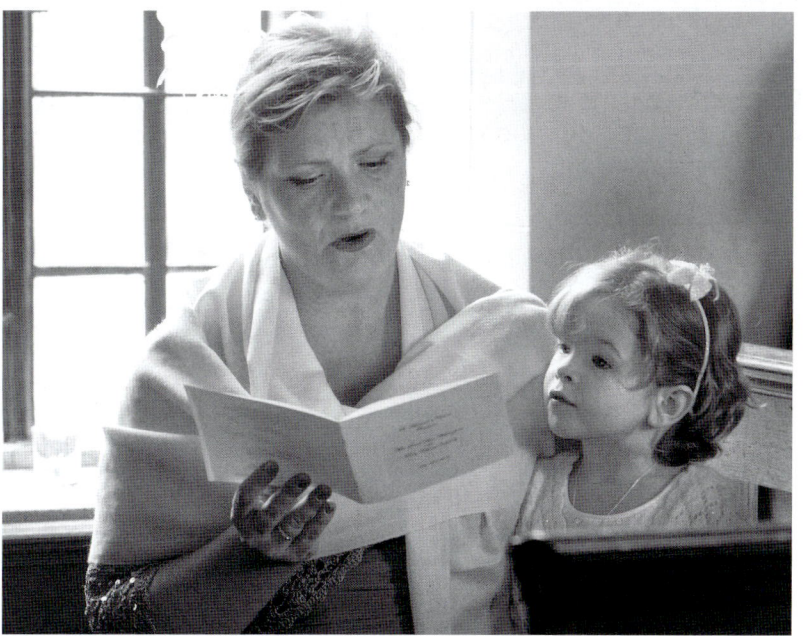

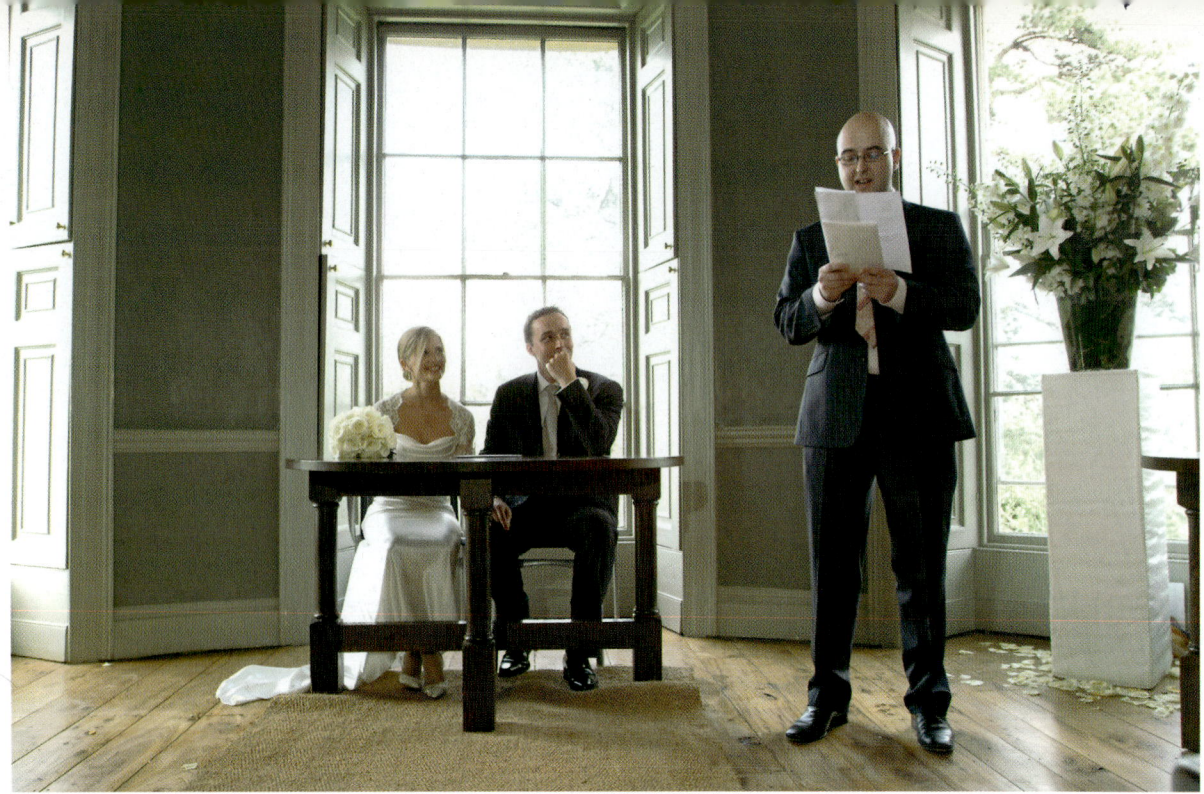

on our Compact Flash cards between us. Later, these will get edited down to about 175 to show the client and they will have about 90 or so in their album up to the end of the ceremony. An ideal ratio is about one in every four frames shot to make the book.

THE RECEPTION

At the reception our aim is to take the bride and groom off for a photo shoot virtually straightaway. While their guests arrive in dribs and drabs, park up, and powder their noses, we are working flat out setting up sequences and taking portraits. We will work as a team, Julie will set up shots for me, and I will set up shots for her. I have my 35 mm lens on the camera and Julie has her 70–200 mm. When we create 'as directed' action

we both shoot the same moments with about 45 degrees between us. These shots taken at the same time, from different angles, and with different lenses work very well indeed. We both shoot at f4 throughout and the sequence comes together seamlessly in the final album. We will work wherever the light and venue takes us. A 15-minute journey around the grounds or staterooms at this stage yields a strong set of pictures.

When the bride and groom rejoin the gathering, Julie and I start to explore our opportunities. We look around the back of the kitchens, beyond the boundaries and really come up with a plan for a second shoot. Gardener's sheds, old greenhouses, barn with tractors, stable yards, woodland, and formal gardens all make great opportunities for something a bit different. With the plan set we rejoin the main party. I shoot big wide shots and

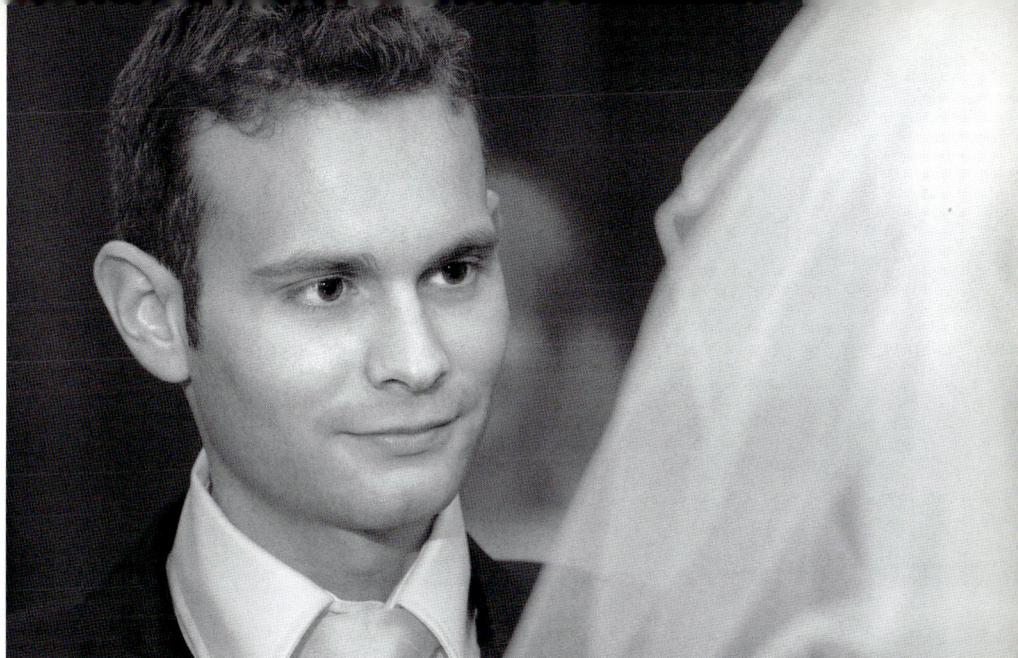

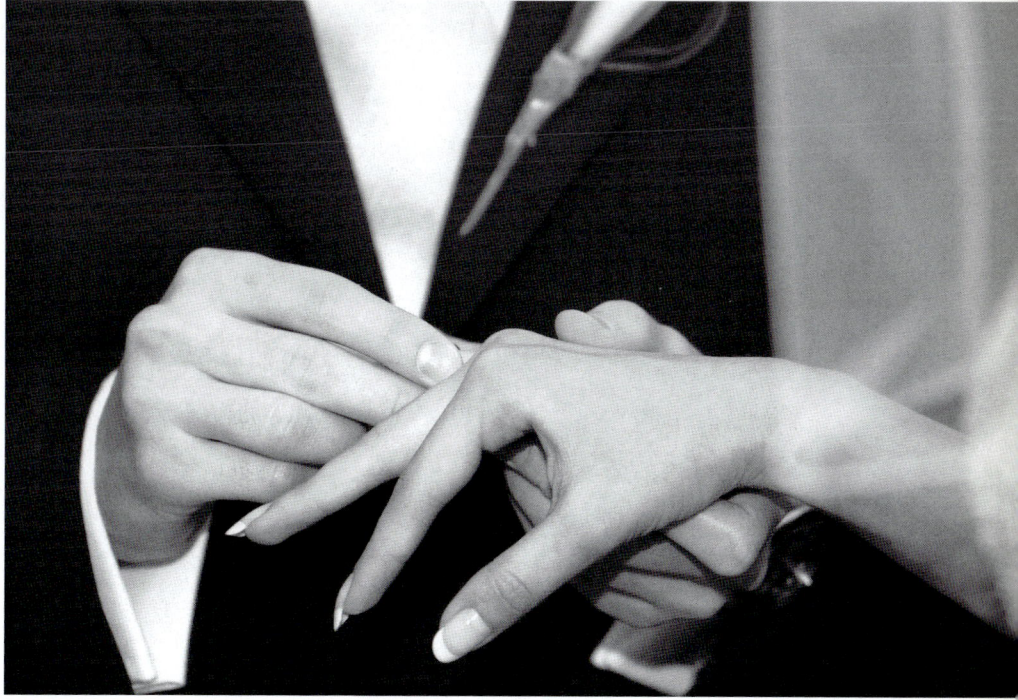

opposite

FIG. 40   ISO 800 f/4 at 1/125th

Some ceremonies seem to present challenging lighting conditions. With good lenses that resist unsightly flair a stop of exposure increase was all that was needed to make this picture.

FIGS 41 & 42   ISO 800 f/4 at 1/110th for both pictures

These two pictures were taken in very quick succession using a long lens. If I had used a wide lens to capture the whole scene some of the magic would have been lost: the look of love in the groom's eyes or the elegance of the bride's hands.

casual groups mingling while Julie shoots the details, canapés, champagne, and so on.

Once we have the story planned, we will take the bride and groom off on our little adventure. The next 10 minutes are spent 'going with the flow' creating striking couple shots and individual portraits. We will go to places the couple themselves haven't seen and we will be alone, just the four of us – no video, no bridesmaids, or hangers on. This is our time and our creative session.

Having had a load of fun, we return to the party. Julie enlists the help of the ushers and gives each of them a printed list of the group shots required. I set up for the groups shooting into the light, and avoiding the sky in the frame. If we are inside because of bad weather I will set up our Broncolor Mobil battery-

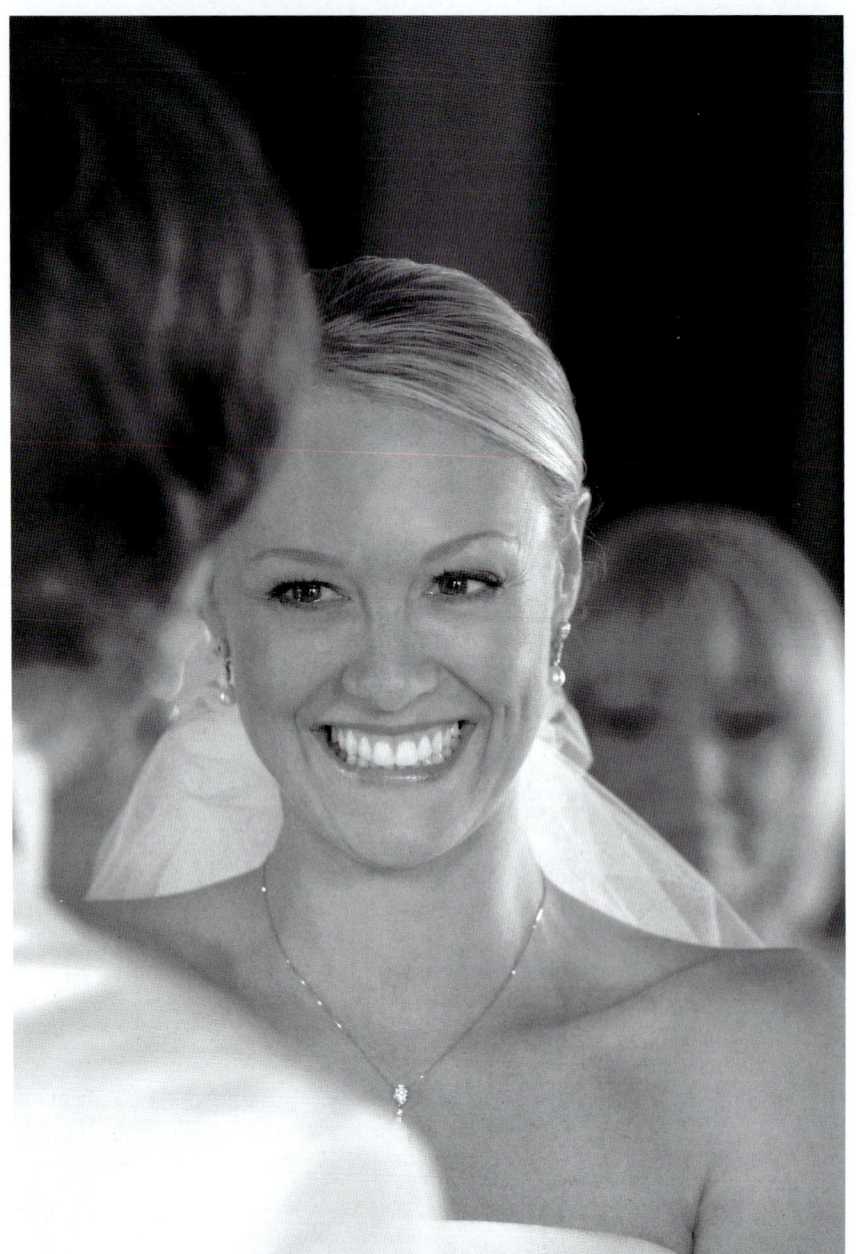

FIGS 43 & 44   ISO 800 f/4 at 1/60th and ISO 800 f/4 at 1/125th

Julie and I both took these pictures on tight lenses at 90 degrees apart. The light was excellent and the moment was wonderful.

opposite

FIG. 45   ISO 400 f/4.8 at 1/20th

This moment summed up the day of fun and celebration. The subject movement adds life to the picture.

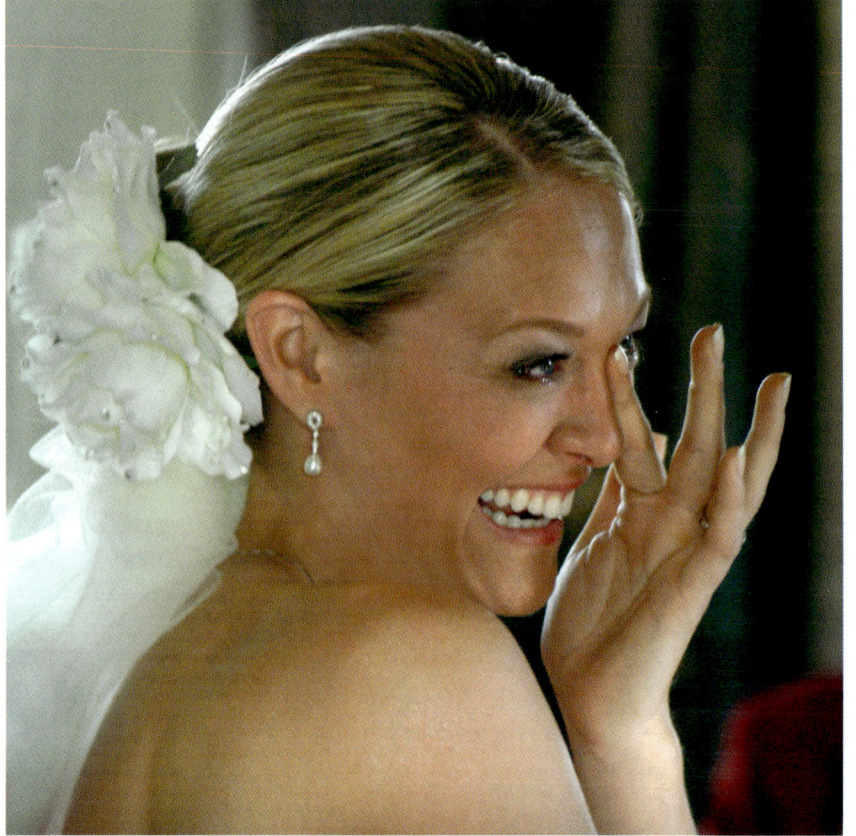

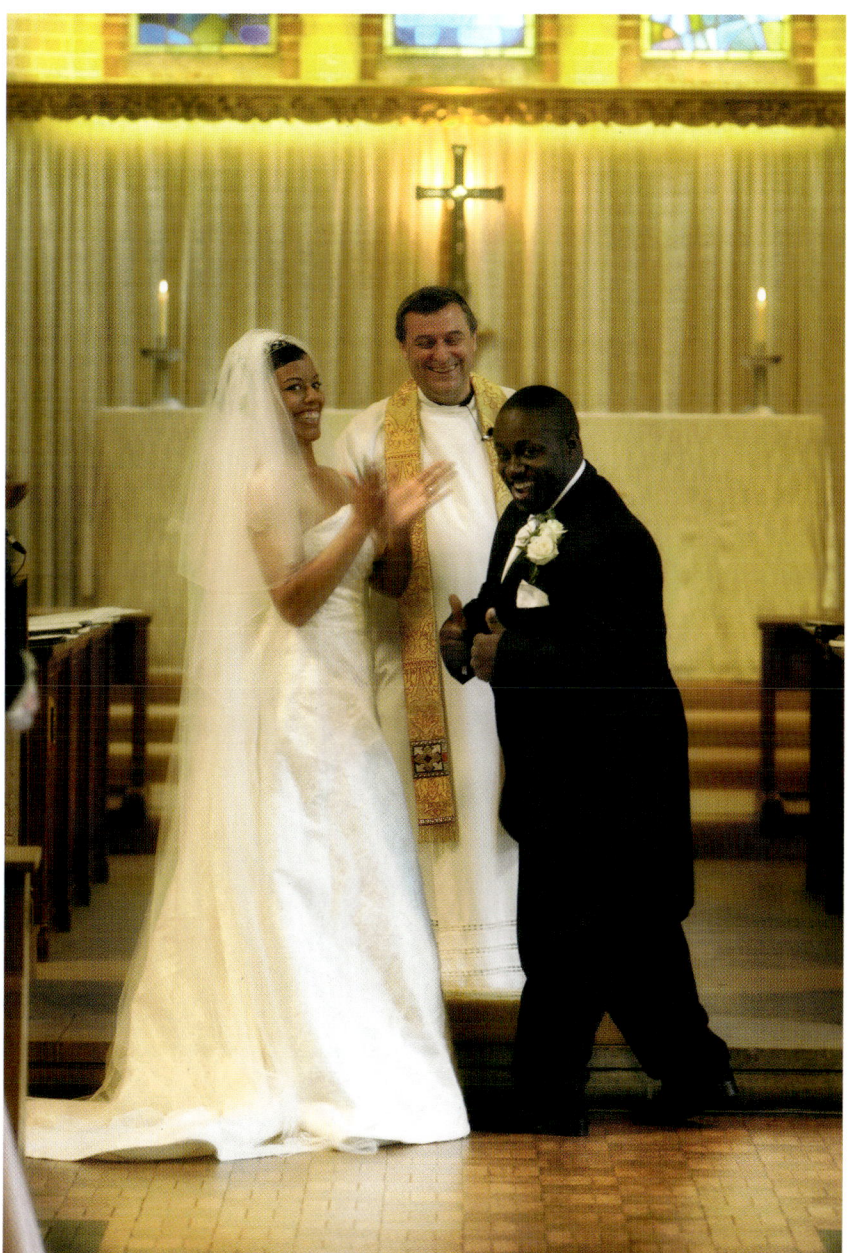

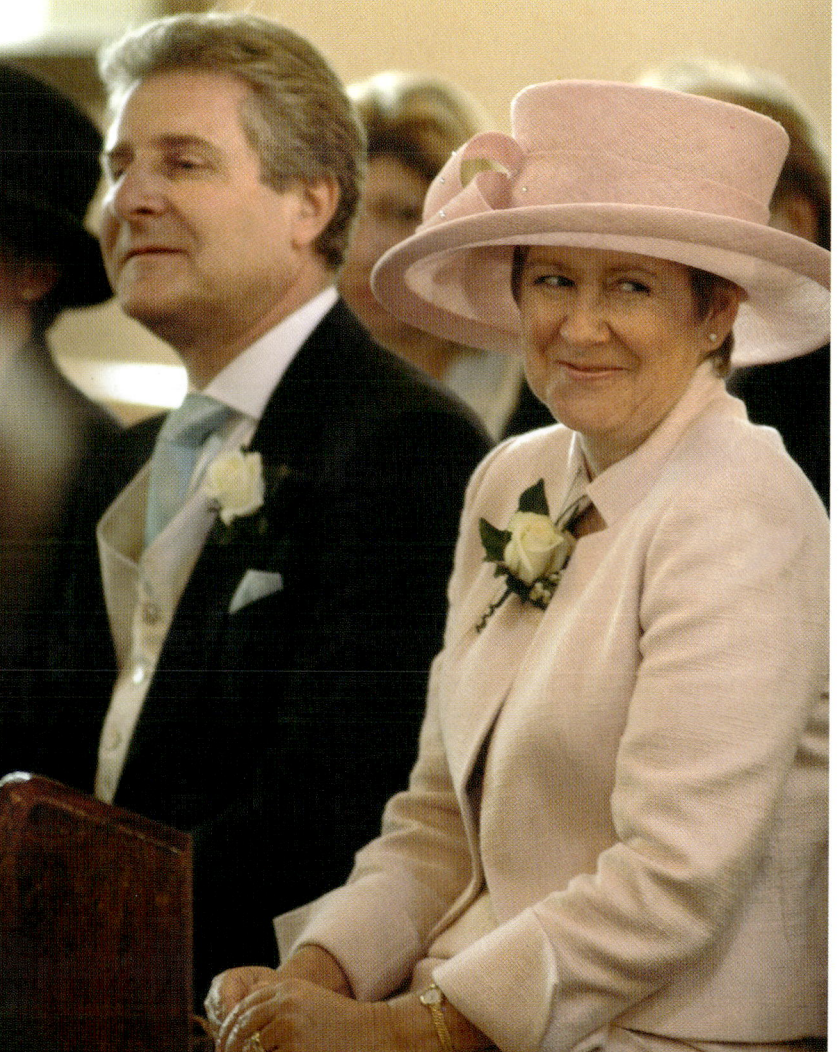

above

FIG. 46   ISO 1600 f/2.8 at 1/45th

The best moments often happen in dark places. I was on the limit of my Fujifilm S2 and my 200 mm lens to capture this great look.

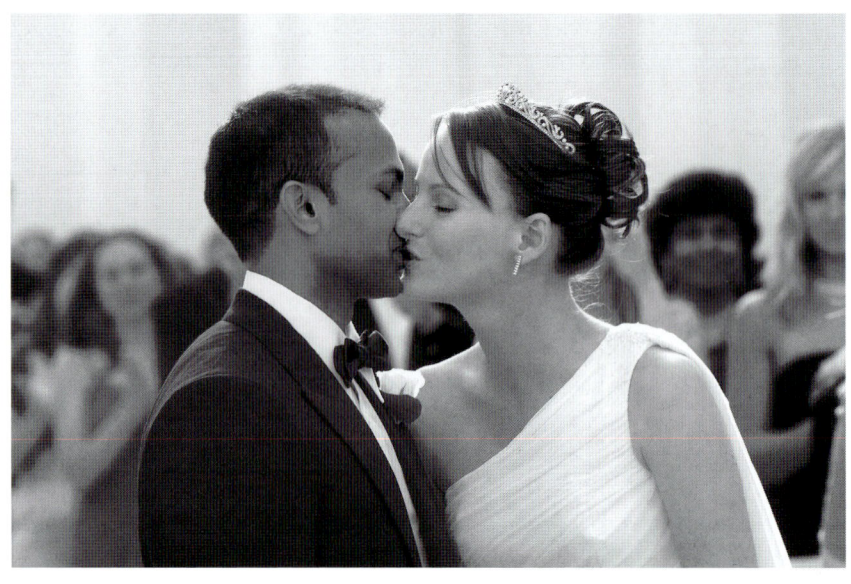

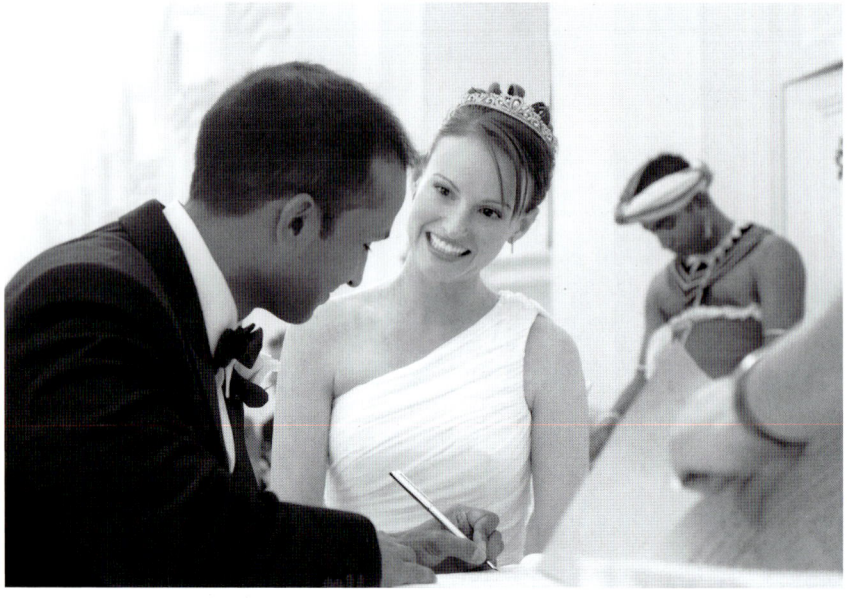

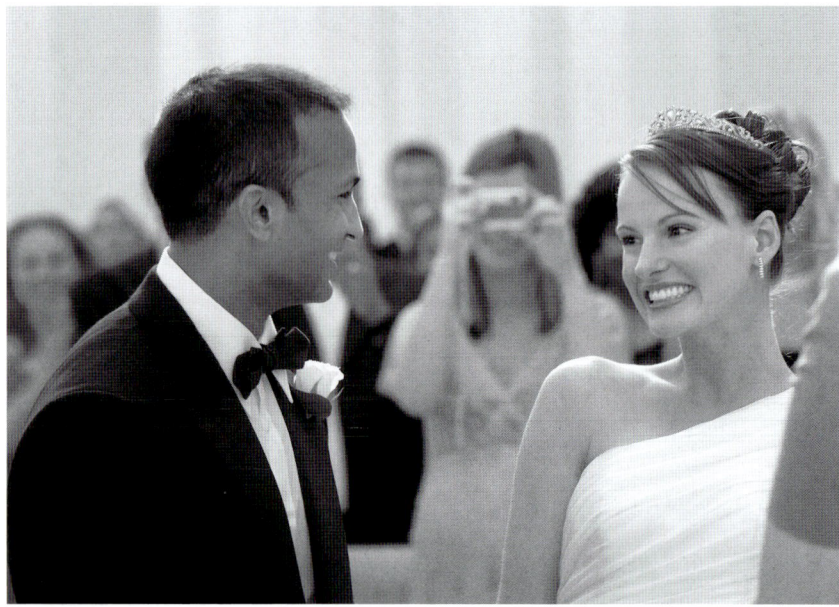

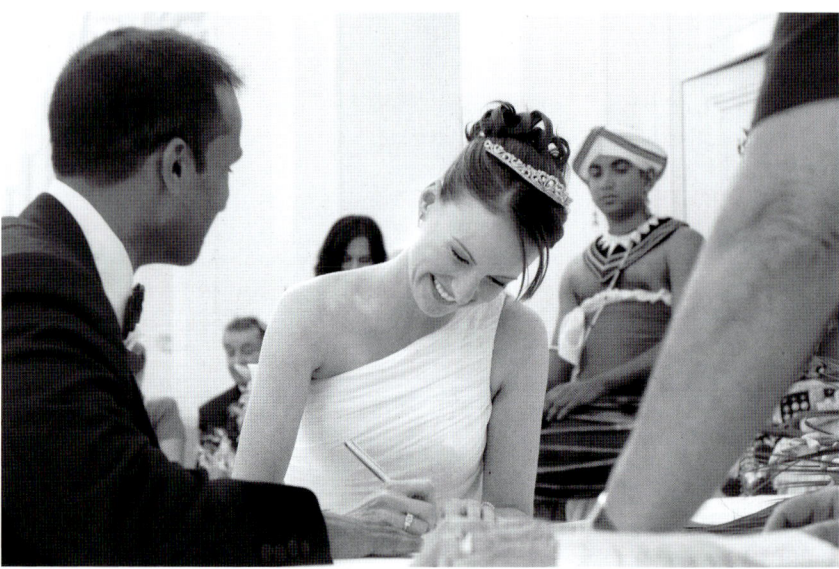

opposite

FIGS 47–50   ISO 400 f/4 at 1/180th

Julie's role at the front of the ceremony is to capture the moments as they happen. A great sense of timing is necessary to get the picture and I find I often miss the moment where Julie succeeds. It is primarily for this reason I leave the main role at the ceremony to her.

FIGS 51 & 52   ISO 800 f/4 at 1/90th

I held the camera way over my head to take this picture. It gives the couple a superstar look. I'm always on the lookout for new angles and ways of shooting things.

FIG. 52   ISO 400 f/4 at 1/60th

I take a straight shot too for safety but I make sure to choose my moment. More recently a shot like this will be full of guests' cameras

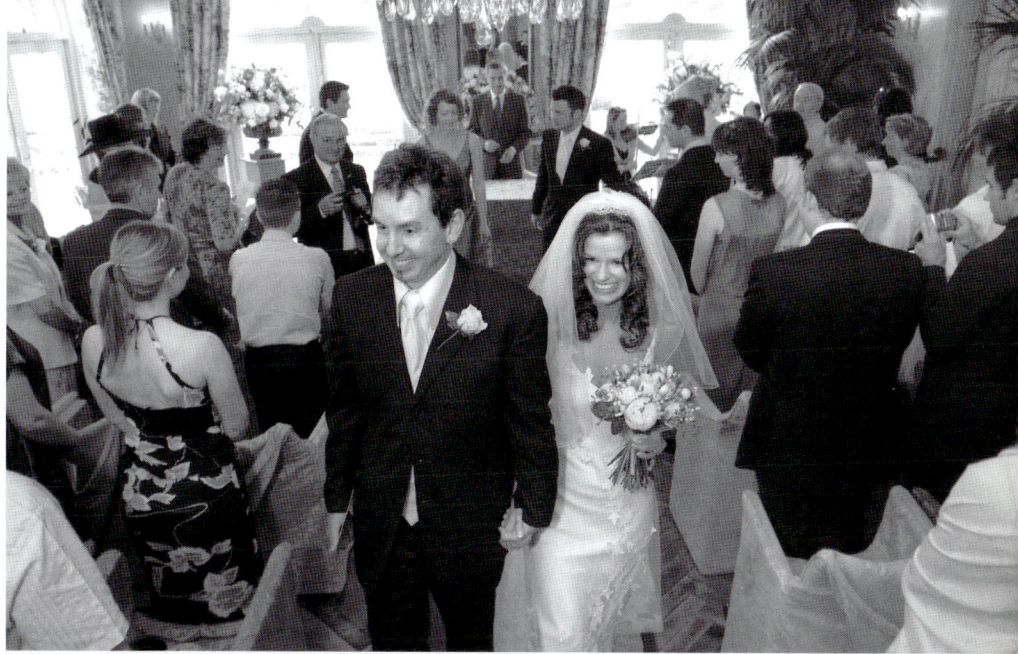

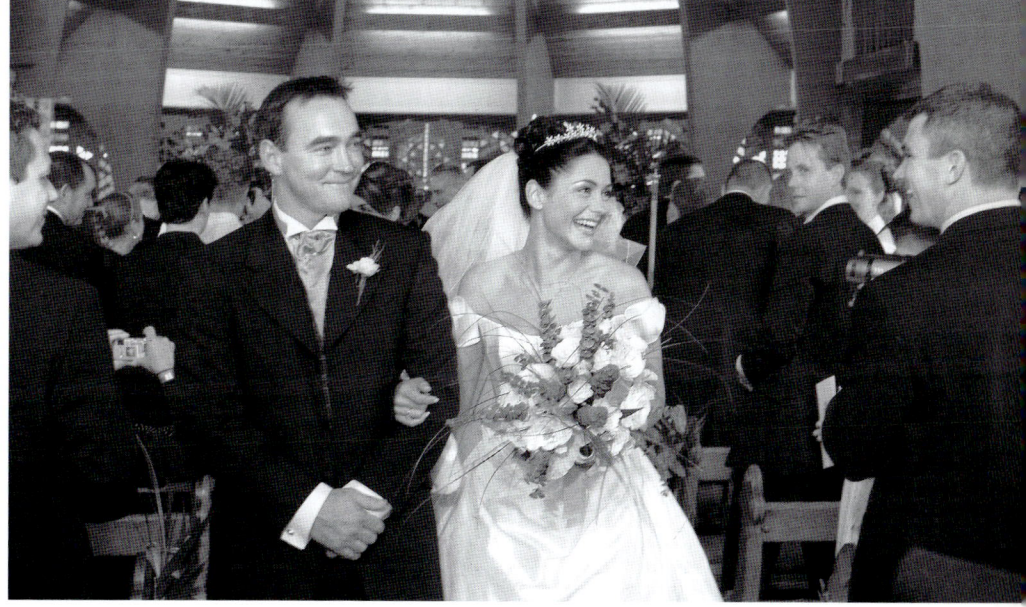

powered flash with a brolly on a tall Lowell stand. Staying self-powered is a good thing; it avoids trailing cables, working with unknown power supplies and the risks they bring.

It is the ushers' role to gather the people required for the groups. The lists they have were printed by us a week ago or so from the details sent through by the couple. We give them a 10-minutes warning saying something like, "In 10 minutes time at a quarter past four, can we please have all the people listed here, over there at the far end of the lawn." This gives the ushers time to get Uncle Harry out of the bar and Aunt Ethel wheeled into place. By utilizing the ushers in this way we are not the ones demanding the attention of the guests.

We work through the groups quickly and efficiently. I always invite other family and guests to take their pictures first once I

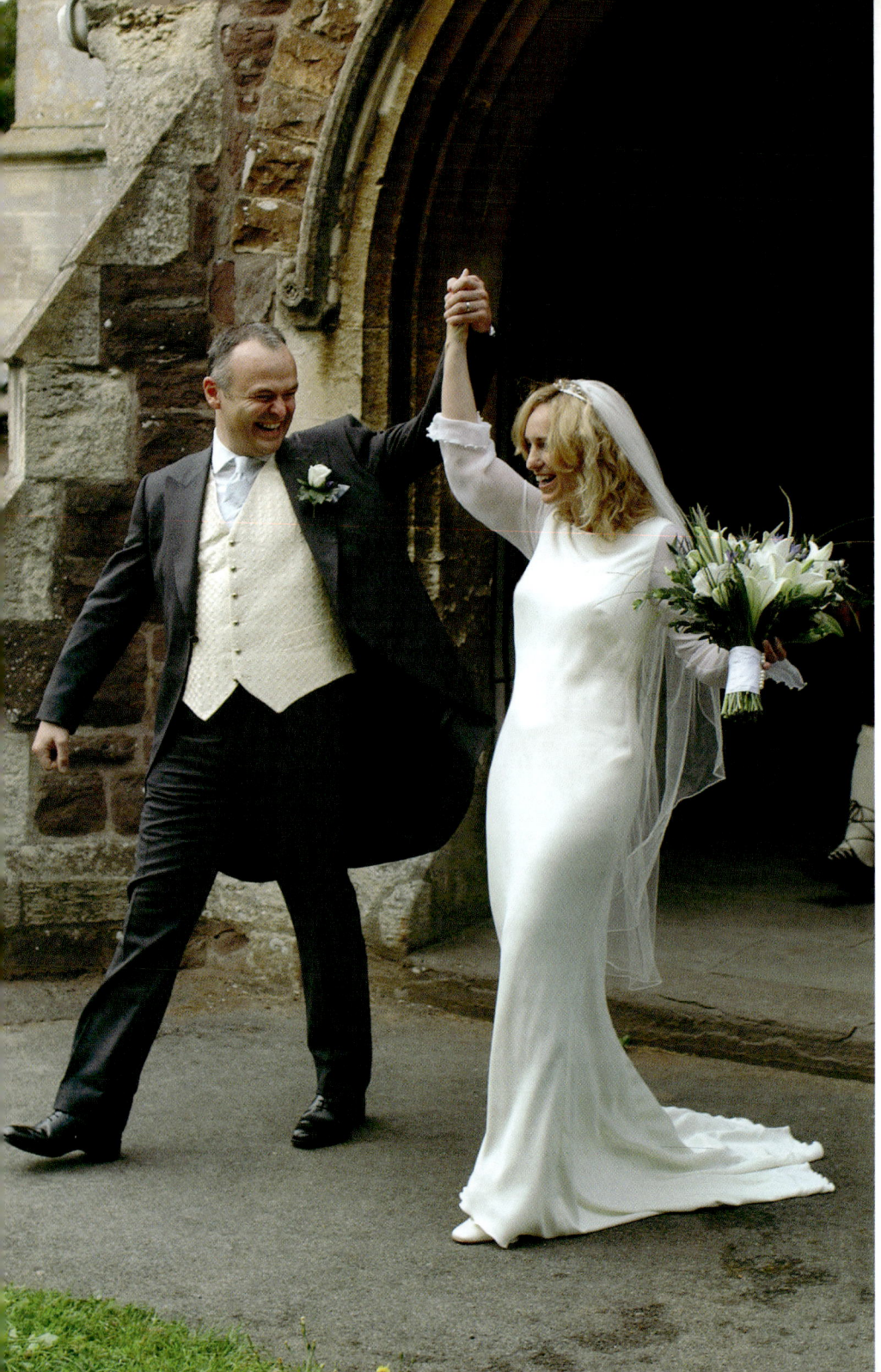

FIG. 53   ISO 400 f/4 at 1/1000th

After the signing of the register Julie slips out of the church and is ready to capture the exit of the bride and groom. Julie will shoot from one side allowing me to get a shot from inside without us seeing each other.

opposite

FIG. 54   ISO 400 f/8 at 1/320th

The sunlight rimming the couple adds to the picture of this wonderful moment.

have set up the group. I then ask everyone in the group for their attention. If I catch eyes wandering off I politely ask that no one else takes pictures at that time because of distractions. This is rarely needed if they have already taken their shots. Once I have everyone's attention I create a fun moment and take the picture. I'll take a couple of other frames too while looking around the group working with individuals to bring out the best in them. My camera is always on the monopod and I might stray to f/5.6. Marko will combine a few of the frames to make a group without compromise.

Teenagers need a different sort of encouragement to their parents or young children, so I create several moments aimed at different parts of the group. This is just part of the service that keeps our product that bit special. I will only arrange a group

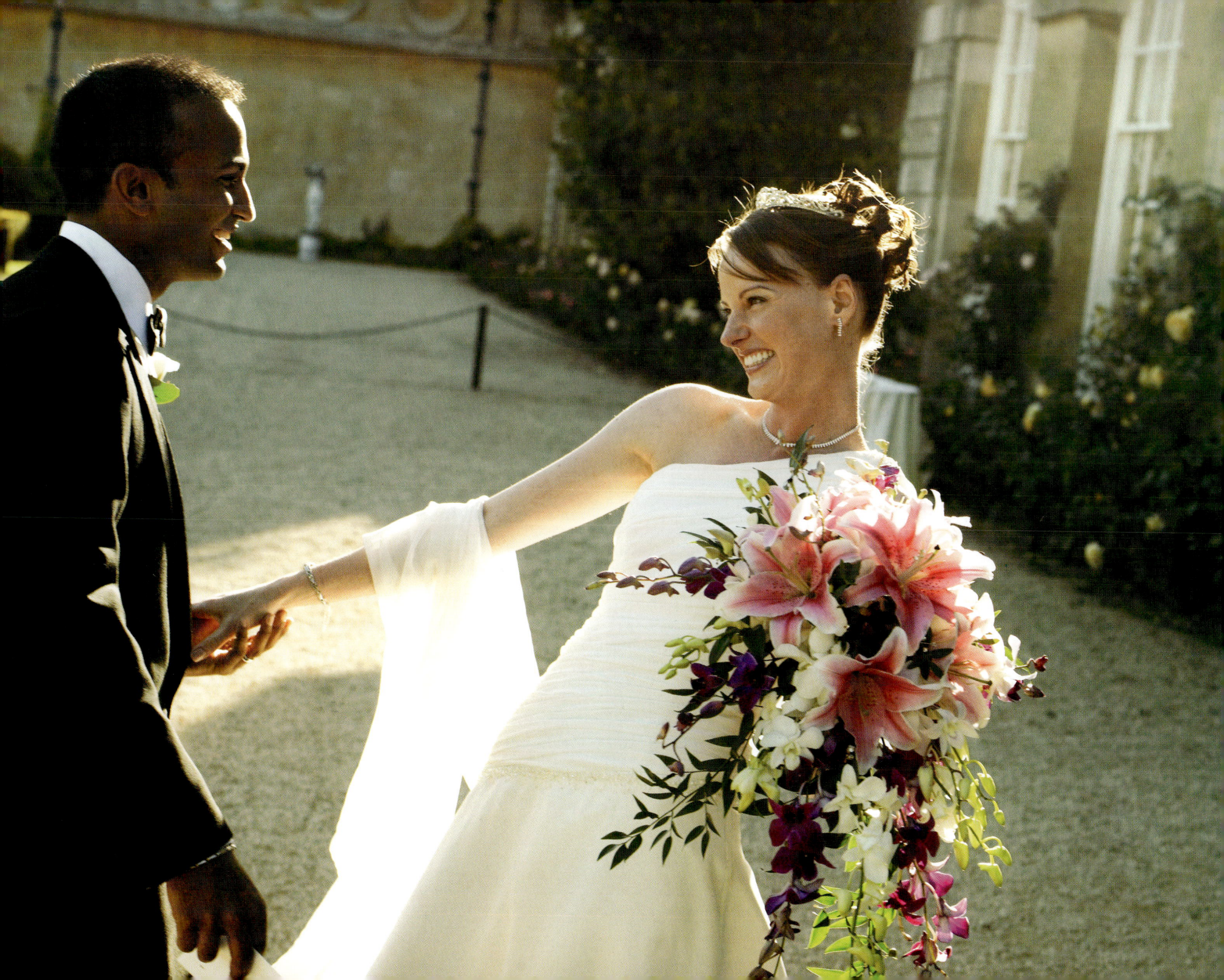

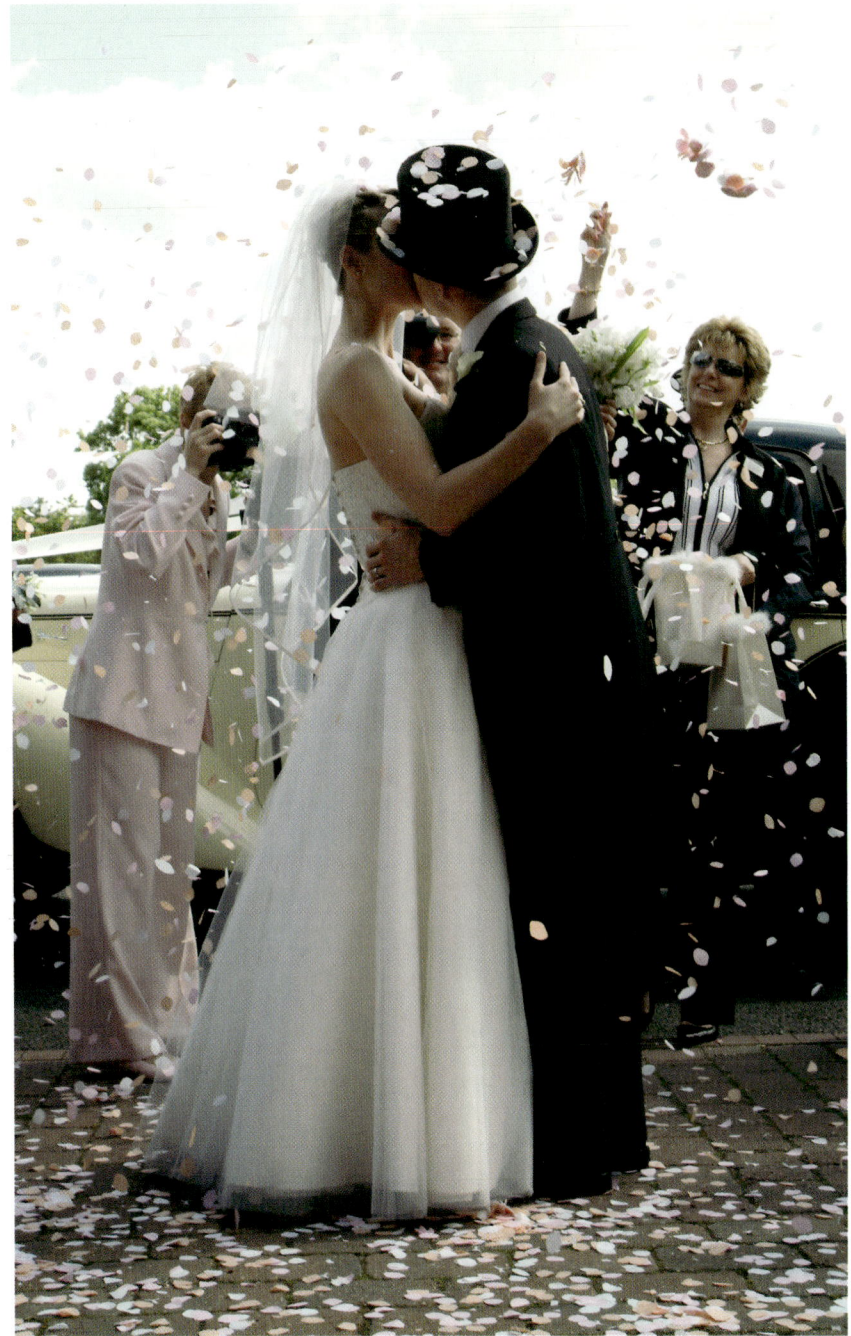

FIG. 55   ISO 400 f/9.5 at 1/320th

Julie, in pink is in this picture. Occasionally, we shoot 180 degrees apart for a confetti sequence. We are part of the day and it makes sense to be part of the album too.

once all the required people are present, this way they will not be getting bored with me and they can carry on chatting. Julie shoots from about 45 degrees to me, to pick up singles of important family members and guests using her 200 mm lens. Once she has good frames of the right people, Julie will go and photograph the table settings, the cake, and the room where the reception meal will be served.

I will put my 210 mm lens on my camera and shoot couples having fun, bridesmaids and pageboys playing, and other key elements that create a visual record of the day. Soon it's time for a glass of champagne. I love champagne, and a few salmon canapés go down well too! At this point we'll devote a few moments to spot checking the running order, ticking off the shots we've done, checking the time and generally gathering our

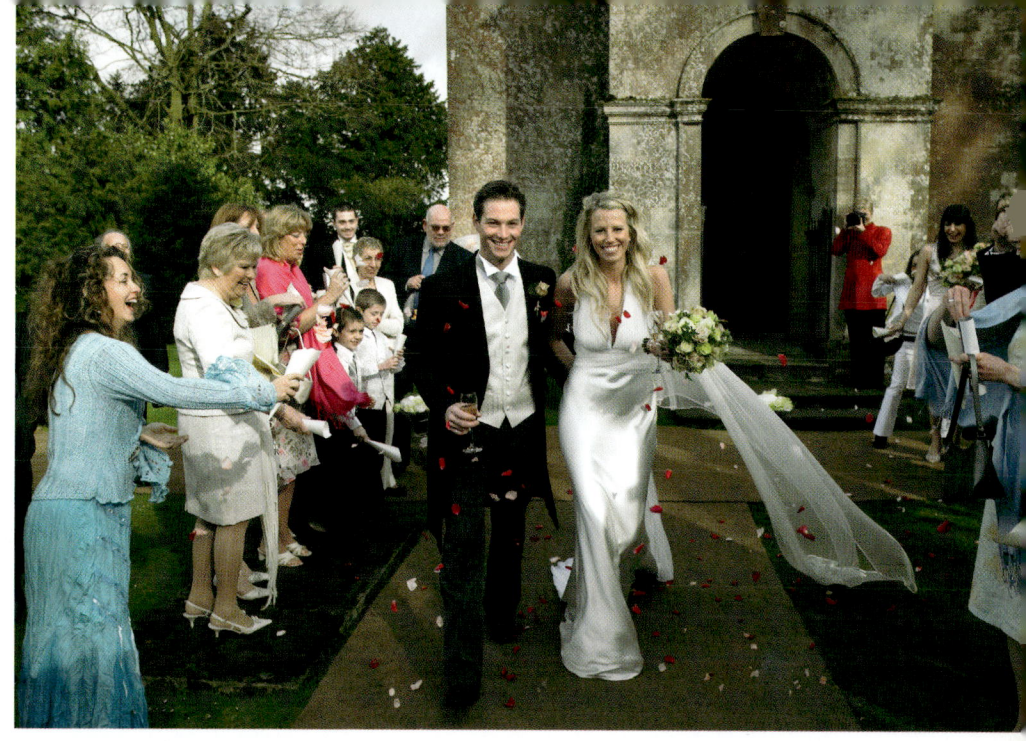

FIG. 56   ISO 400 f/6.3 at 1/640th

Julie is in red in this picture and I'm walking backward in front of the bride and groom.

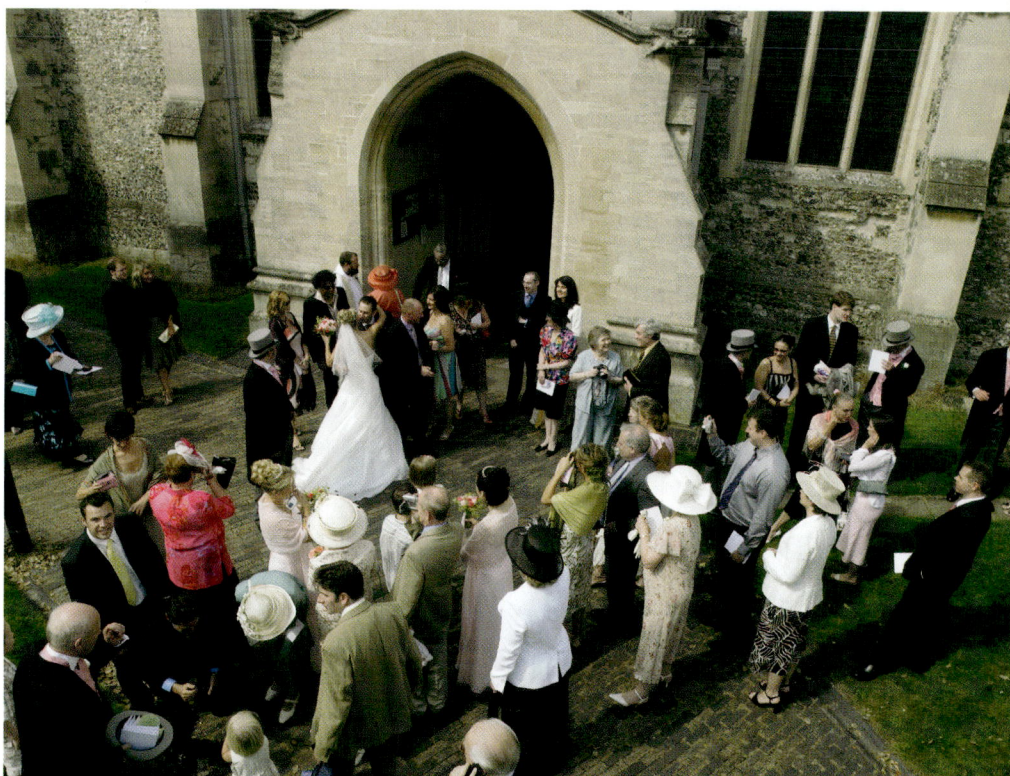

FIG. 57   ISO 200 f/10 at 1/250th

This shot was taken on my Hasselblad at the top of my monopod using the self-timer set to 10 seconds to trigger the shutter. It takes a bit of madness to hoist $40,000 of camera, lens, and digital back above your head on a top-heavy pole. Disclaimer – 'Don't try this at home.'

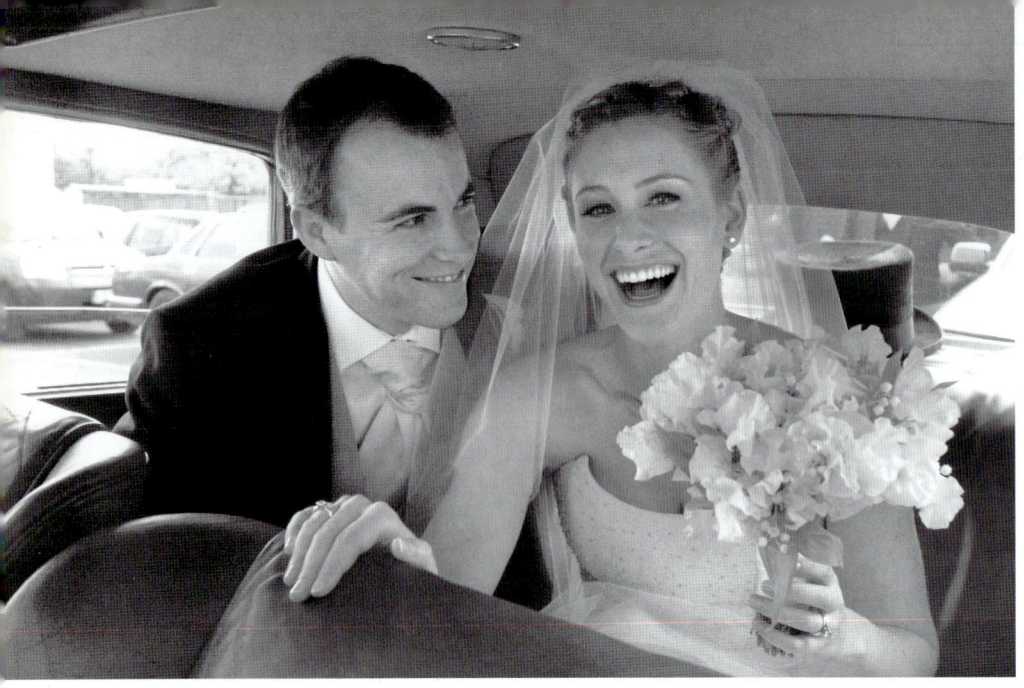

FIG. 58   ISO 400 f/4.8 at 1/90th

A delighted bride, a loving groom, a top hat on the parcel shelf, and great light come together in harmony.

below

FIG. 59   ISO 100 f/4 at 1/90th

Celebrity weddings can attract a bit of a crowd so be prepared. I took this picture with the camera held above my head.

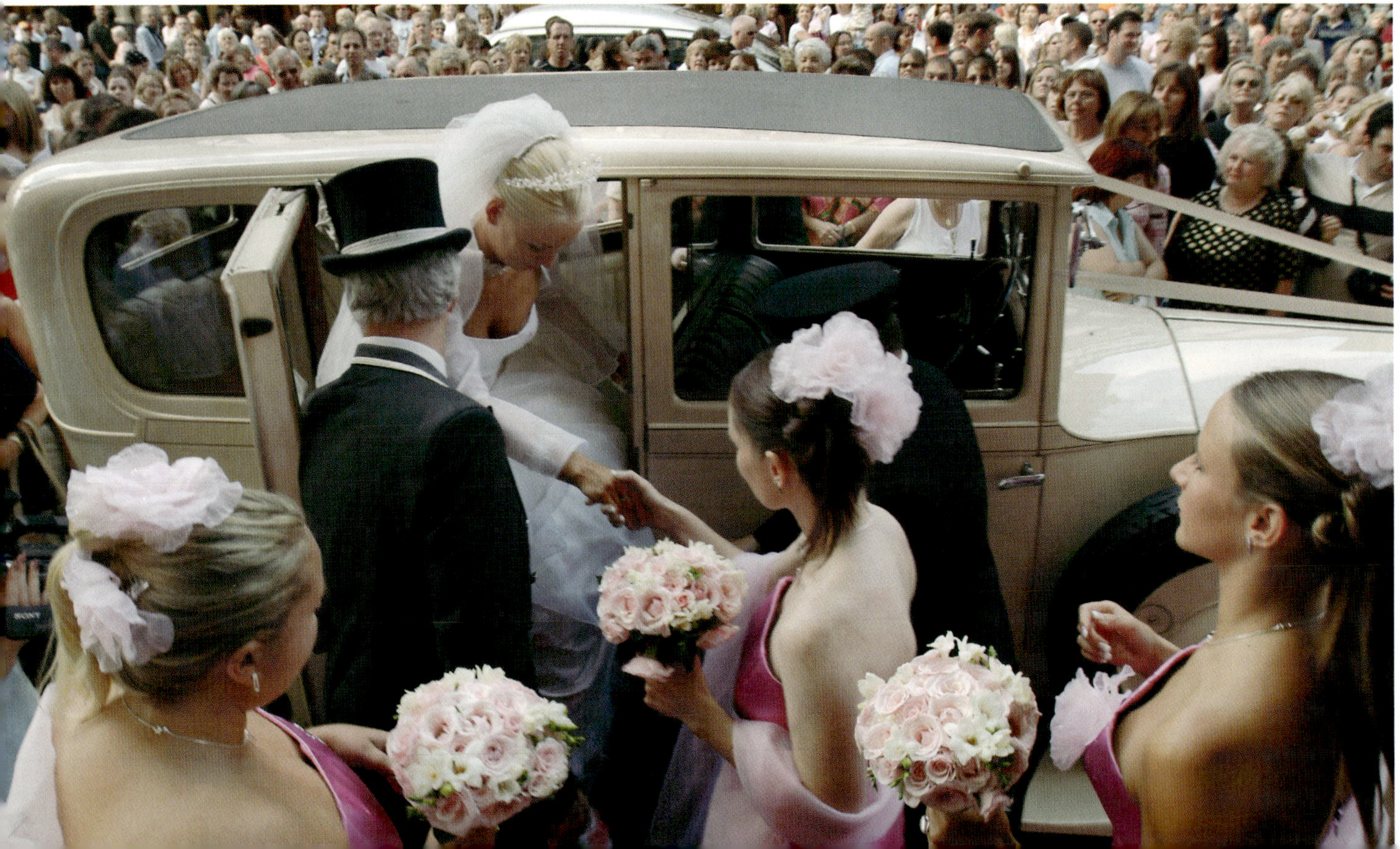

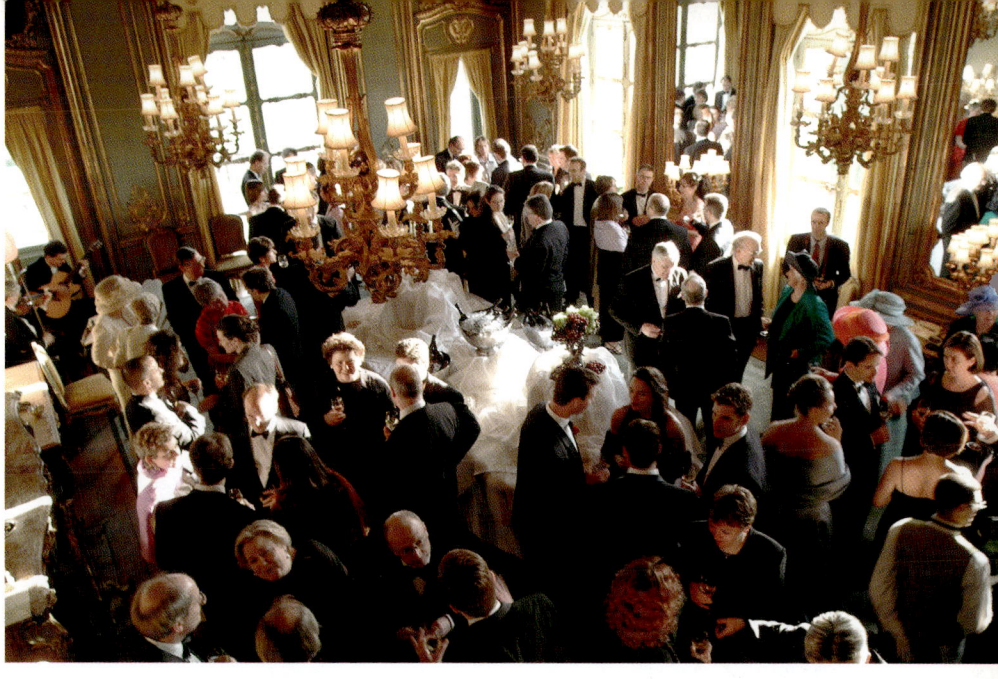

Fig. 60   ISO 320 f/4 at 1/20th

Here is another top shot taken with my camera on the monopod resting high up against the wall in the corner of the room at Cliveden House.

bottom

Fig. 61   ISO 320 f/4 at 1/1200th

Establishing wide shots like this one taken by the summerhouse of Sherbourne Castle are always favorites for our clients. The color and ambience tell the story so well.

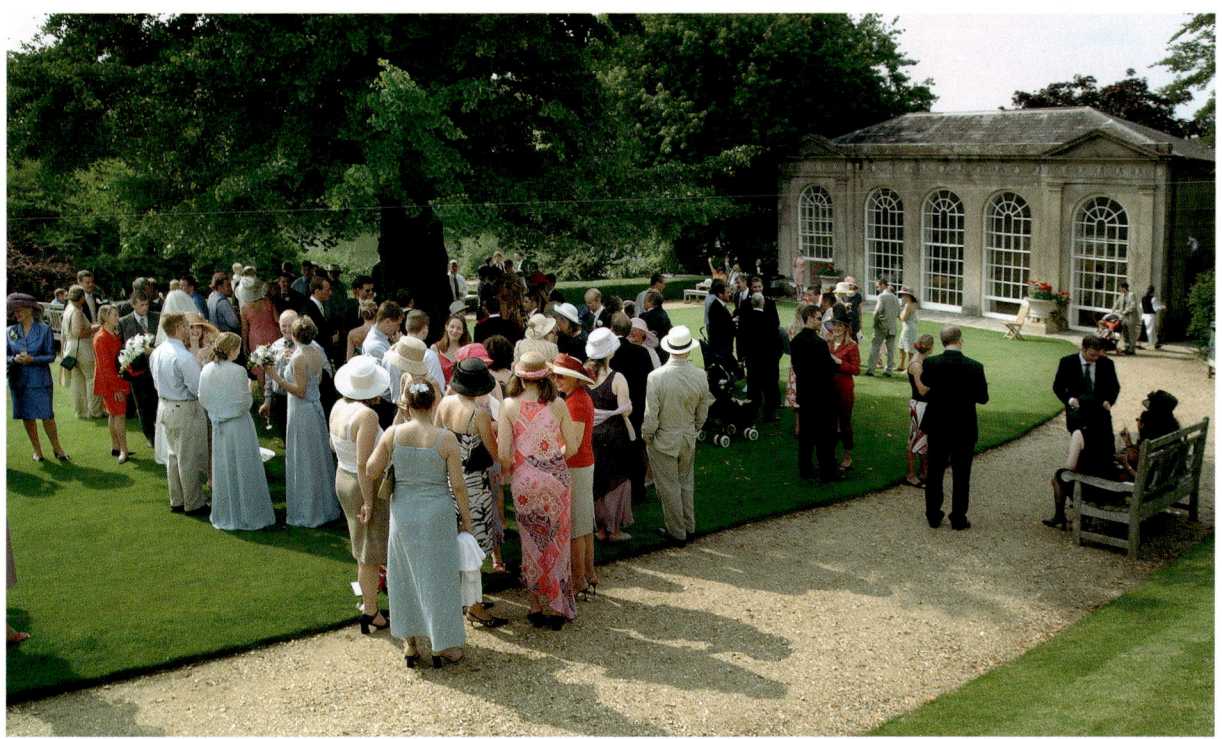

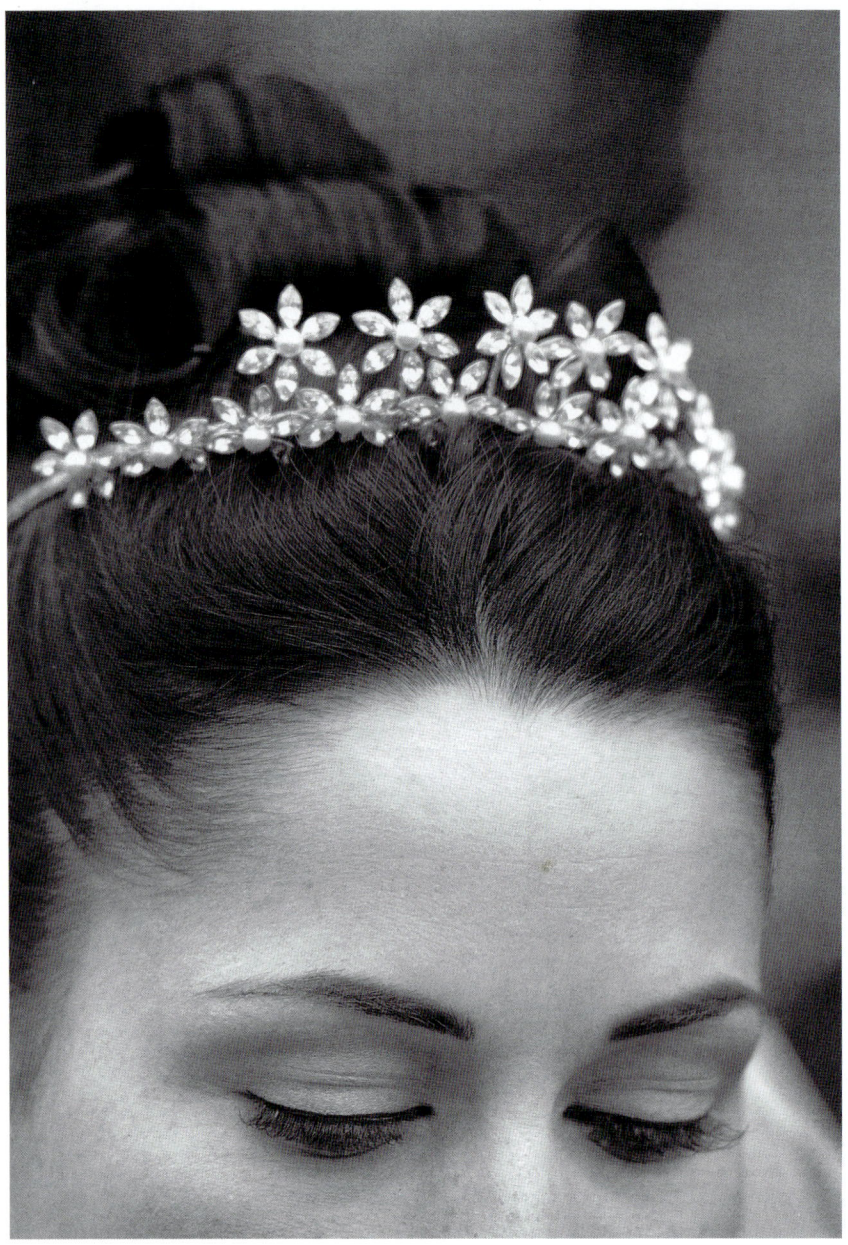

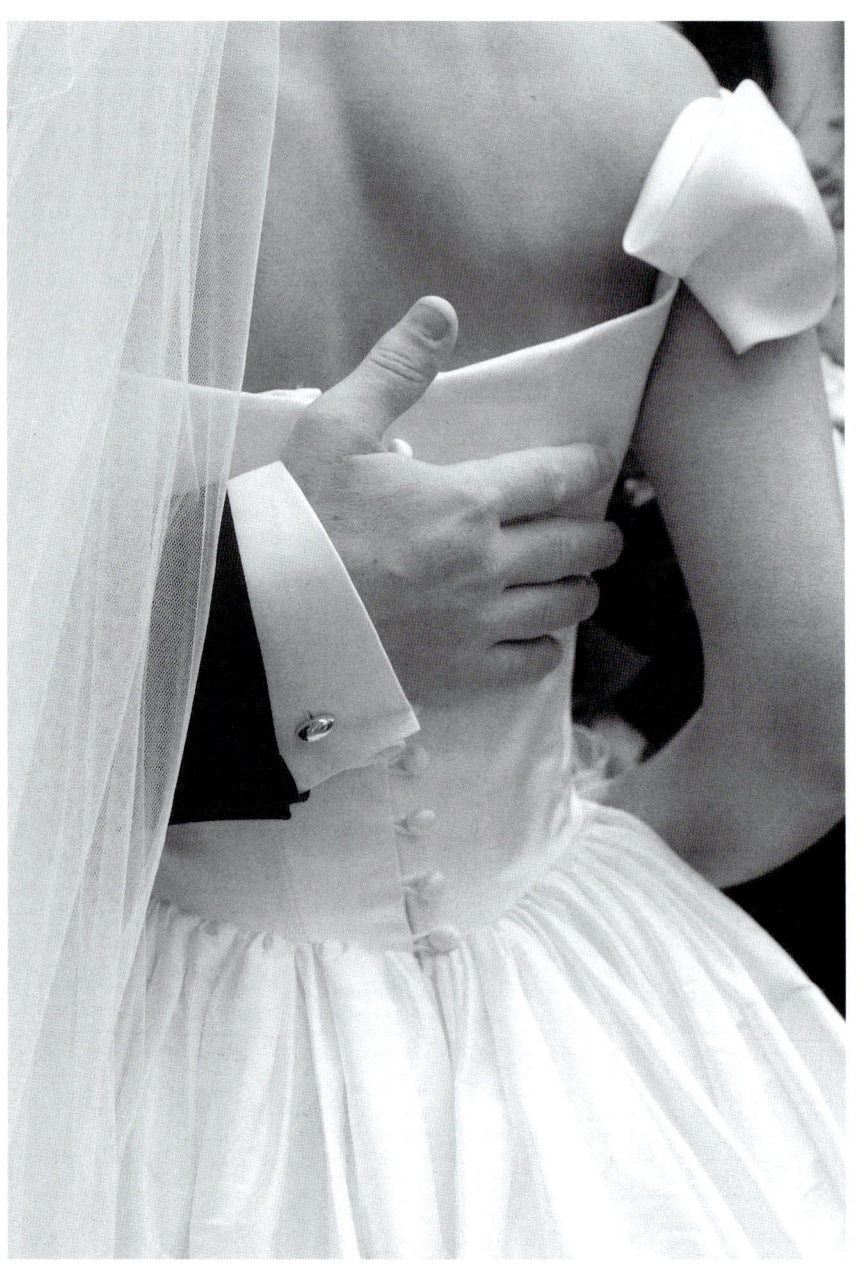

FIGS 62 & 63   ISO 400 f/4 at 1 250th and 1/550th

Julie captured both the tiara picture and the hand on the back of the dress picture candidly using a long lens. Staged closeups rarely look natural.

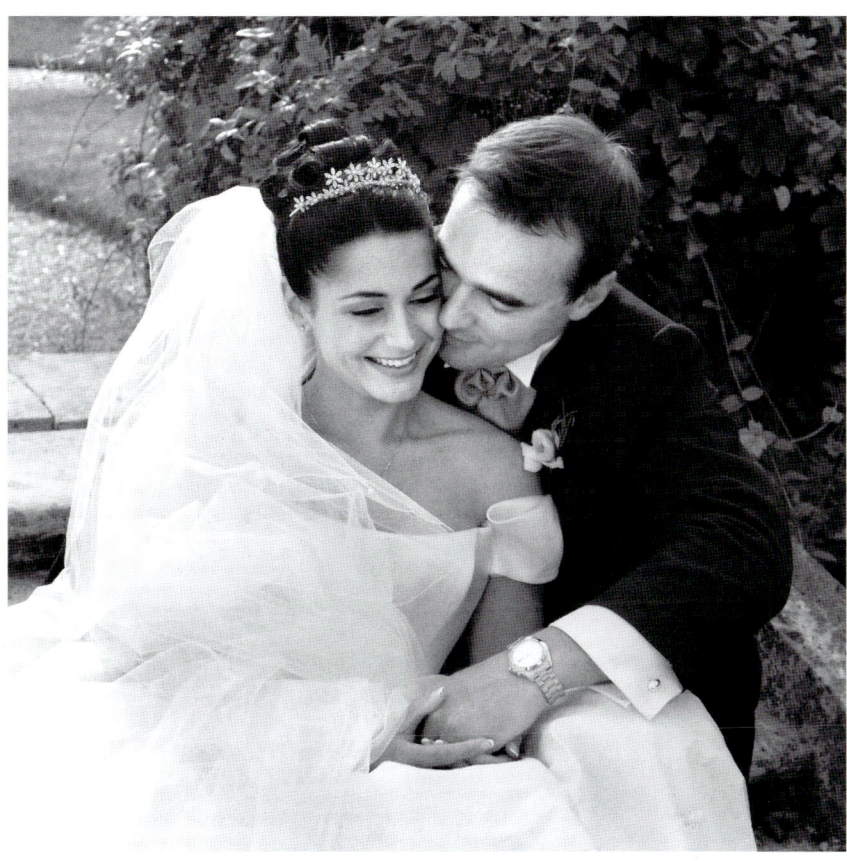

Figs 64 & 65   ISO 400 f/4 at 1/1450th and 1/650th

I shot the wide and Julie captured the closeup of almost identical moments. Both pictures made the album. My exposure was a stop less than Julie's because I had to hold the detail in the dress.

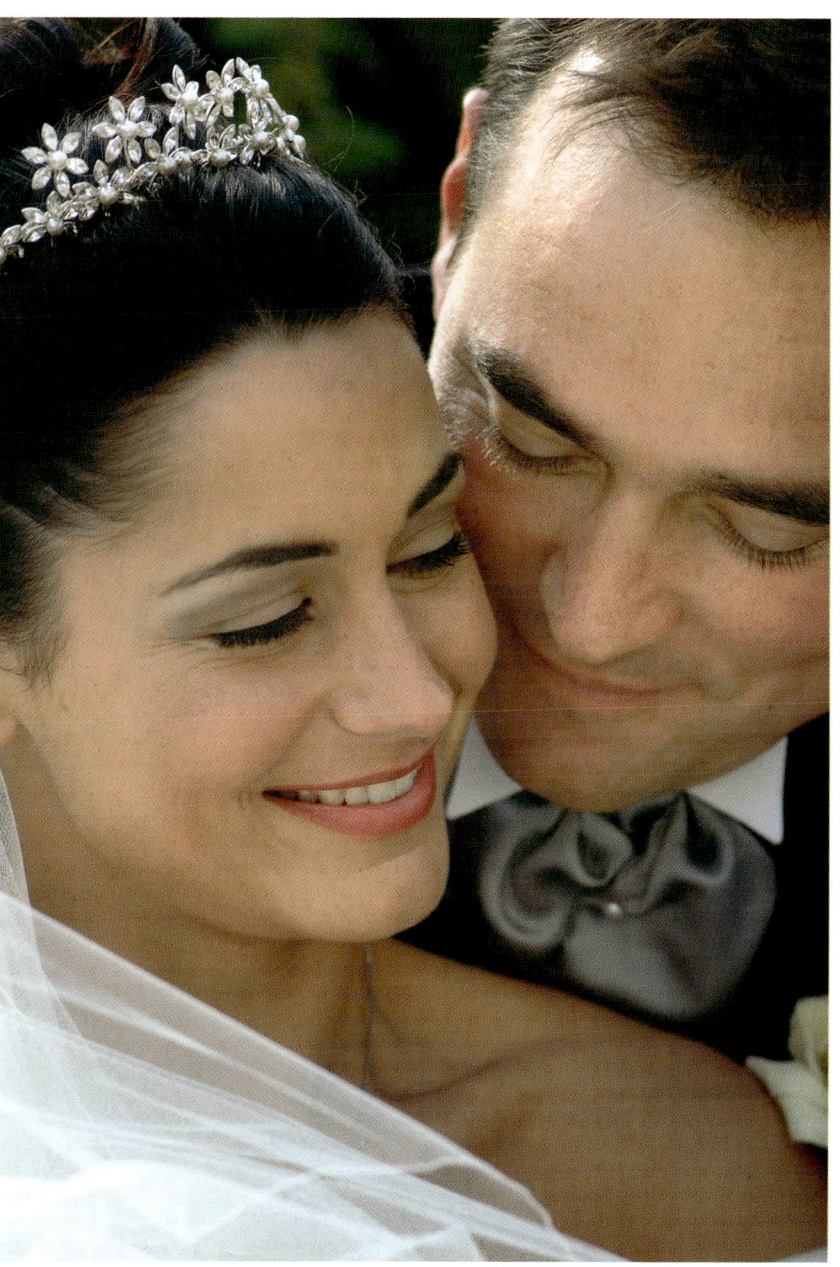

ISO 400 f/4 at 1/500th

I asked the groom to hop up on the pillar and I shot these two frames into the light.

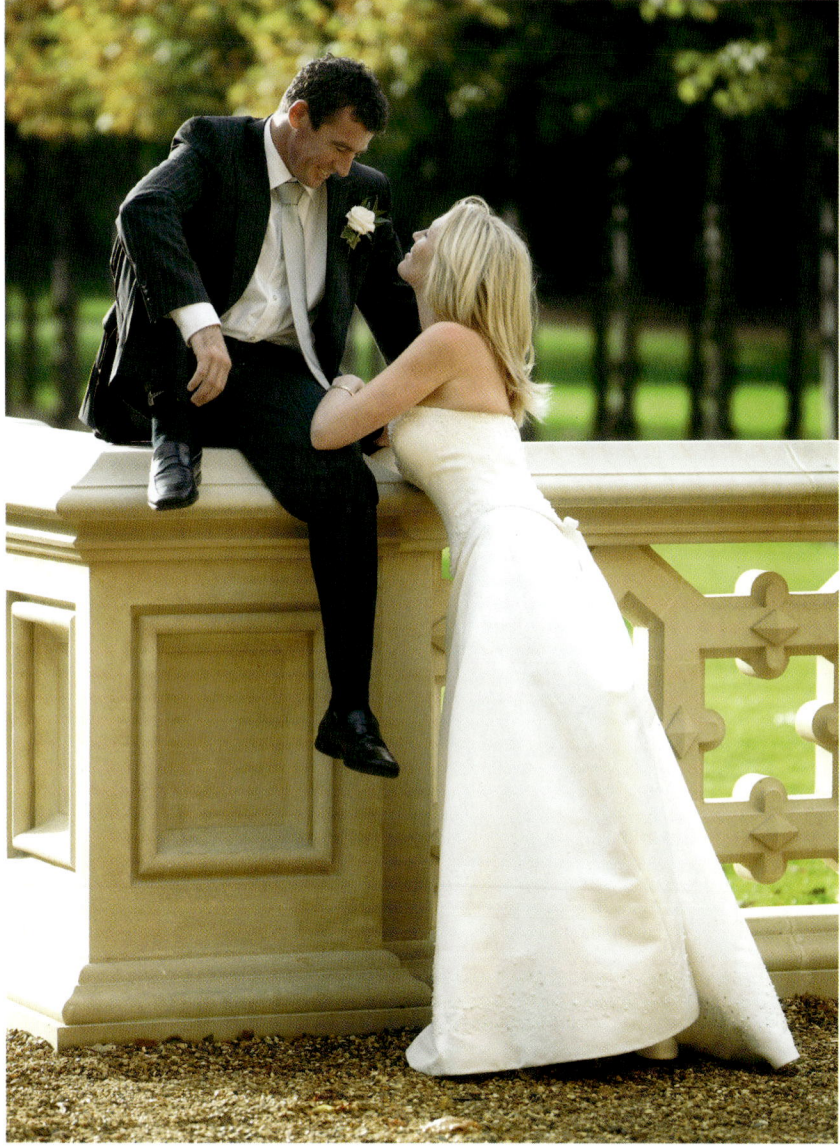

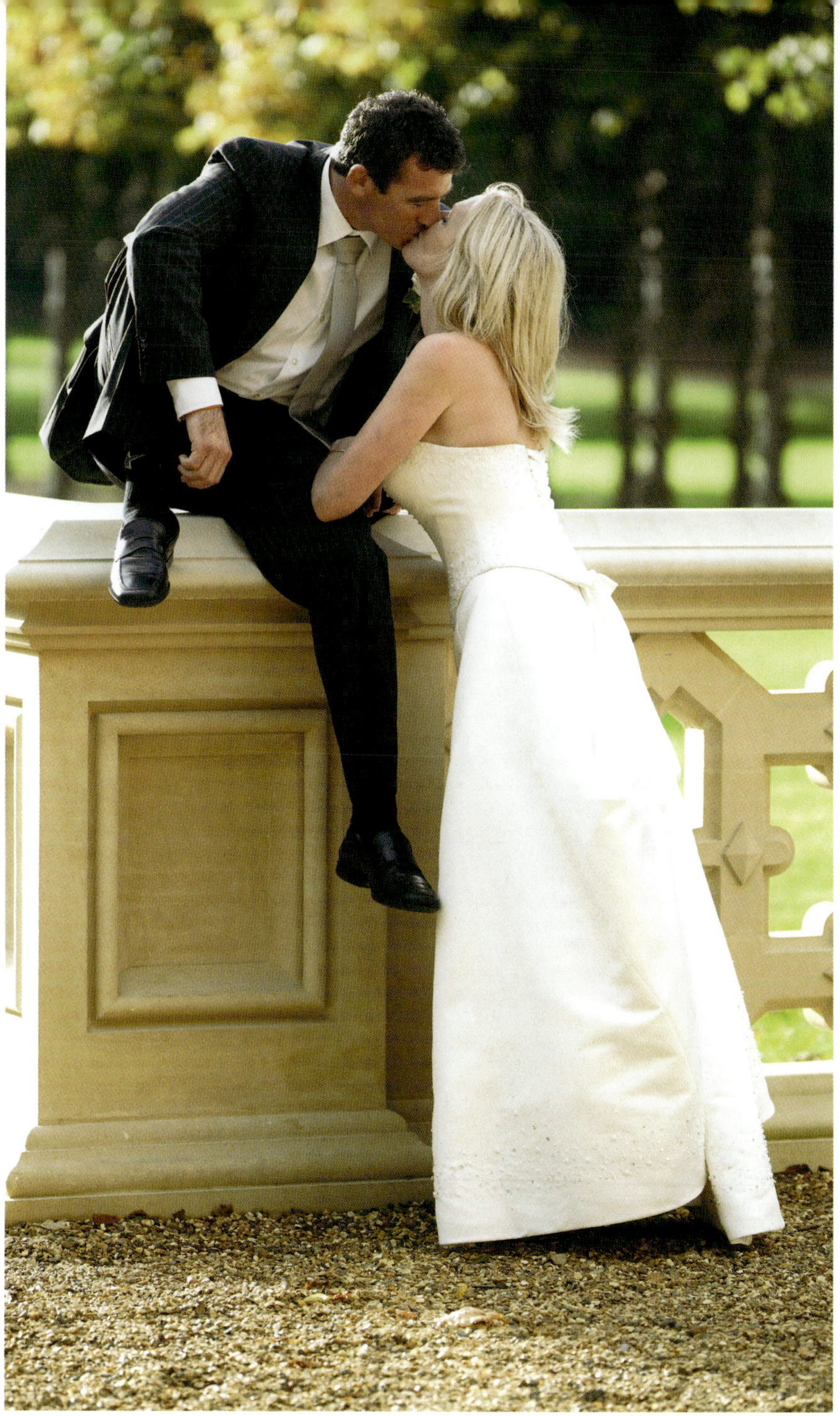

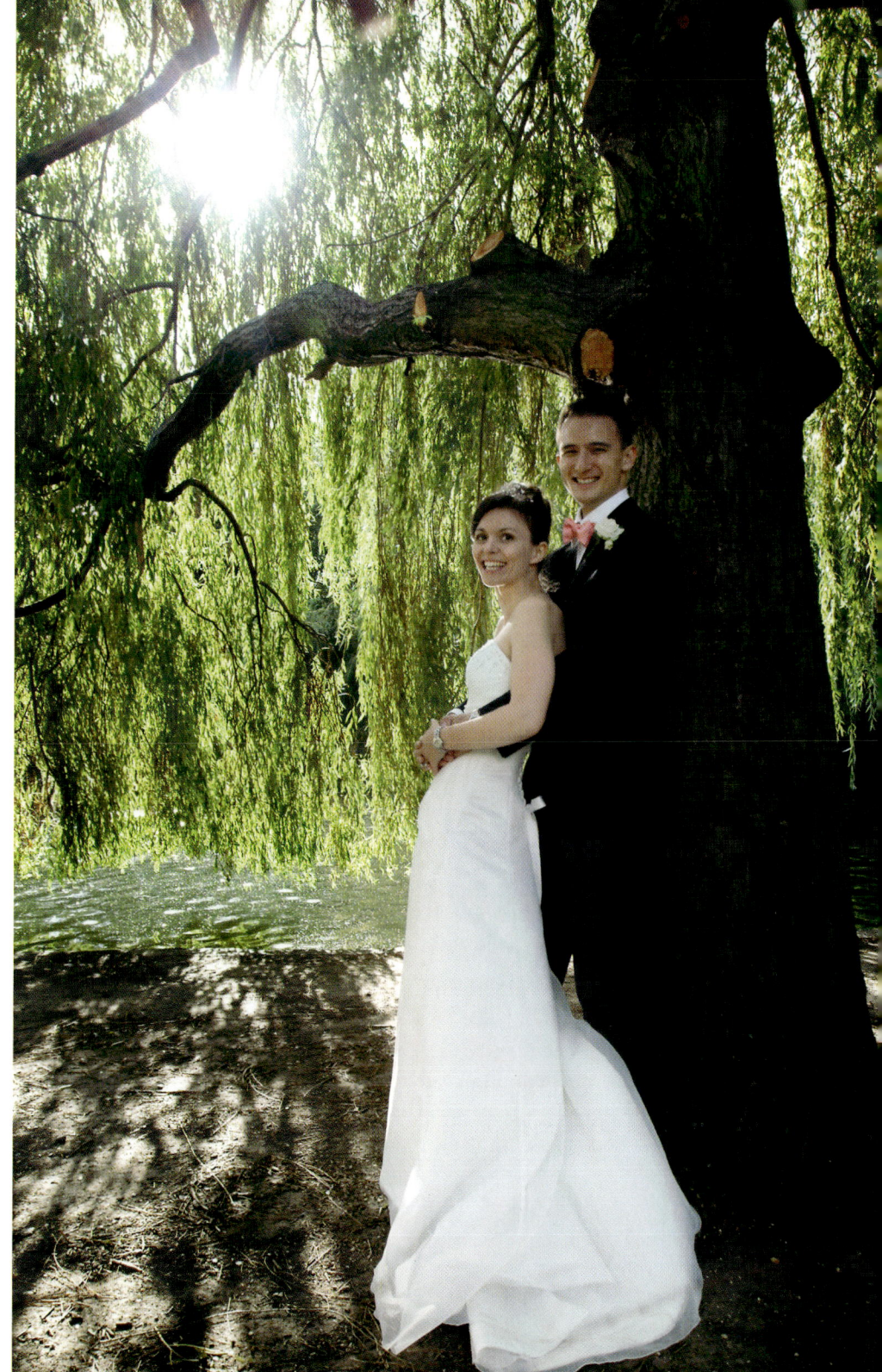

Fig. 68   ISO 400 f/4 at 1/250th

A bit of spot flare from the sun works in this picture in St James park in London.

thoughts together. We like to keep an overview of what's going on and how we have done. Julie might say 'get a good picture of the bride's mother now that she's relaxed. She looks petrified in all the shots I took of her earlier.' This is just the time to do it.

The next big event is often the big group of all attendees. I try to get some height for this shot and when possible, I liaise with the venue to get a key to an upstairs room overlooking the lawn. I aim to shoot this picture just 5 minutes before the guests are called in to sit down for dinner. That way, once I have taken the picture I can hand over to the best man or wedding coordinator to announce dinner. The whole party are in one place and this system works well.

Both Julie and I shoot the entrance of the bride and groom. We shoot from different angles and keep out of each other's way. I

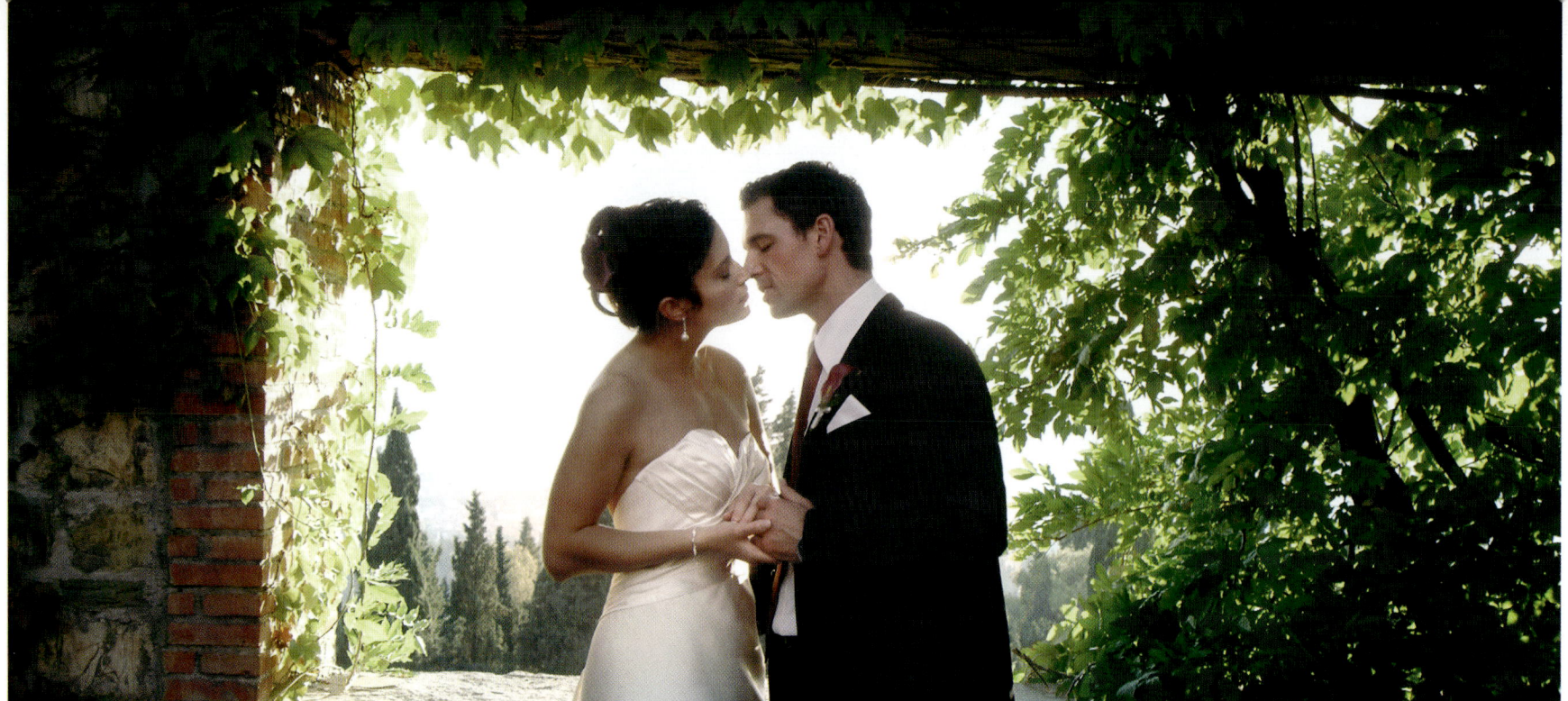

Fig. 69   ISO 200 f/4.8 at 1/90th

It's not possible to spot the sun in this picture as it is completely blown out. Plus two stops exposure compensation was needed for this picture taken in Florence, Italy.

like to take an overhead shot. It adds a sense of royalty or movie star quality to the picture. We then place our camera equipment near the table where we are seated and join the other guests for dinner. We can relax for an hour or so knowing we have every shot we need up to that point.

After the starters and before the main course, Julie might nip out and set up the laptop in a backroom away from prying eyes. Here she will start the download process. There will probably be three or four Compact Flash cards to download by this stage. Capture One pro is the software we use on our MacBook Pro. We create the session on an external bus-powered 120Gb Firewire external hard drive. This will allow us to hot swap the files with other computers back at the studio without the need

opposite

Figs 70 & 71   ISO 800 f/4 at 1/250th

We found some shade for this shot and asked the couple to practice their first dance. The look of love on their faces is fabulous.

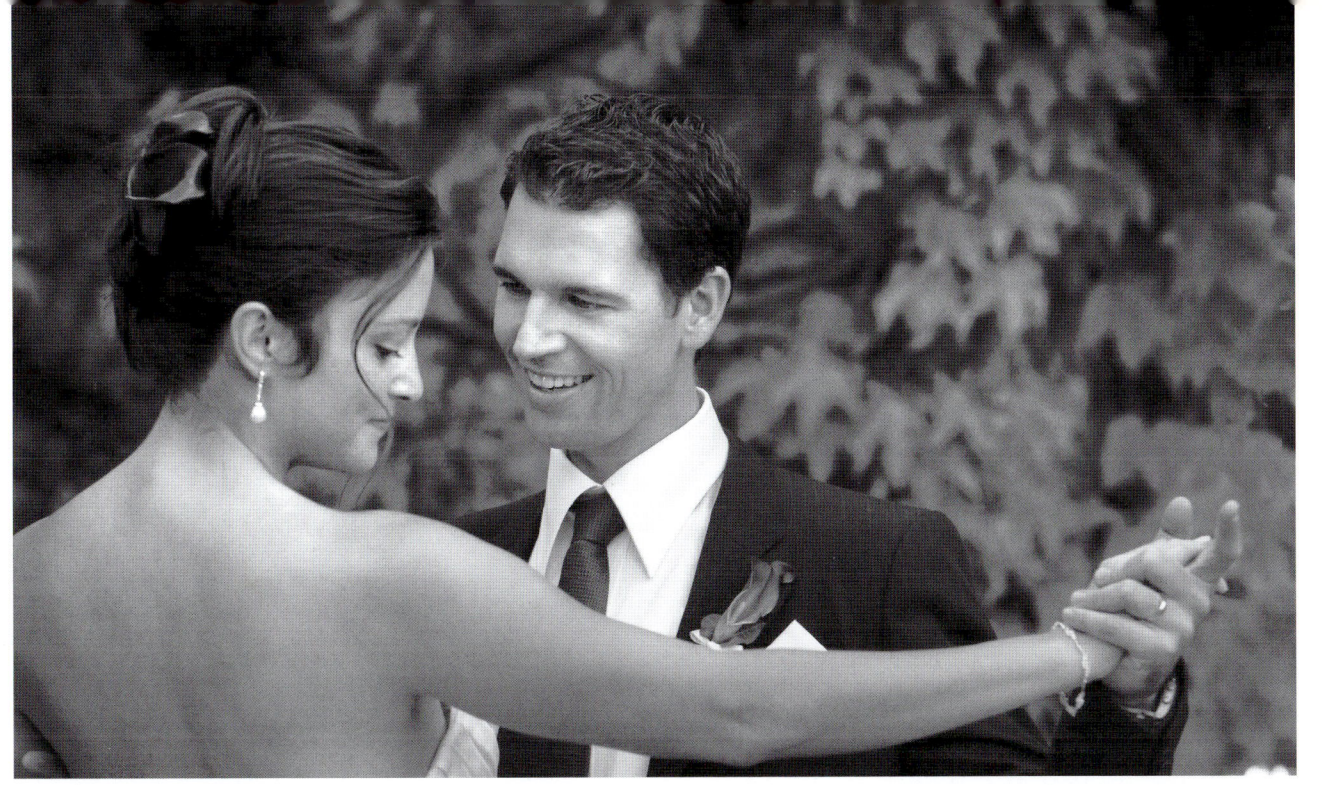

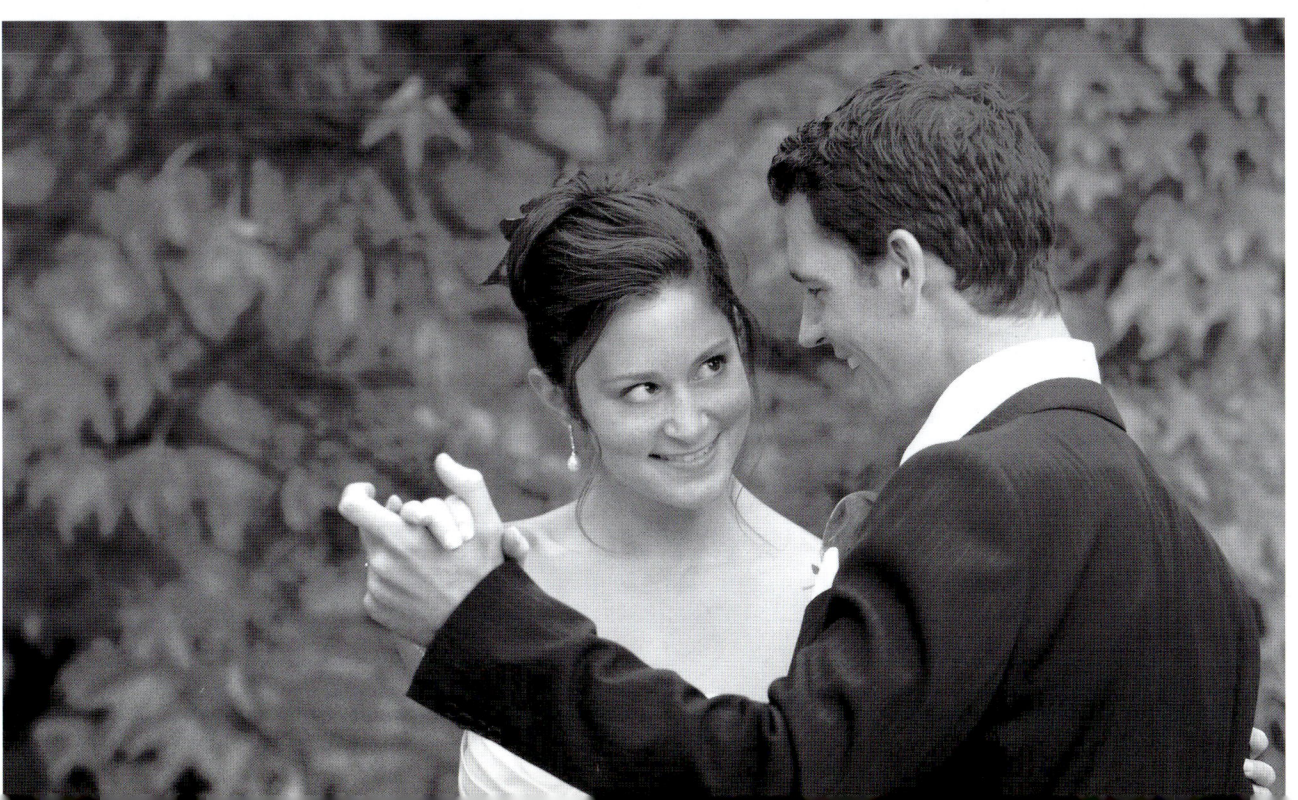

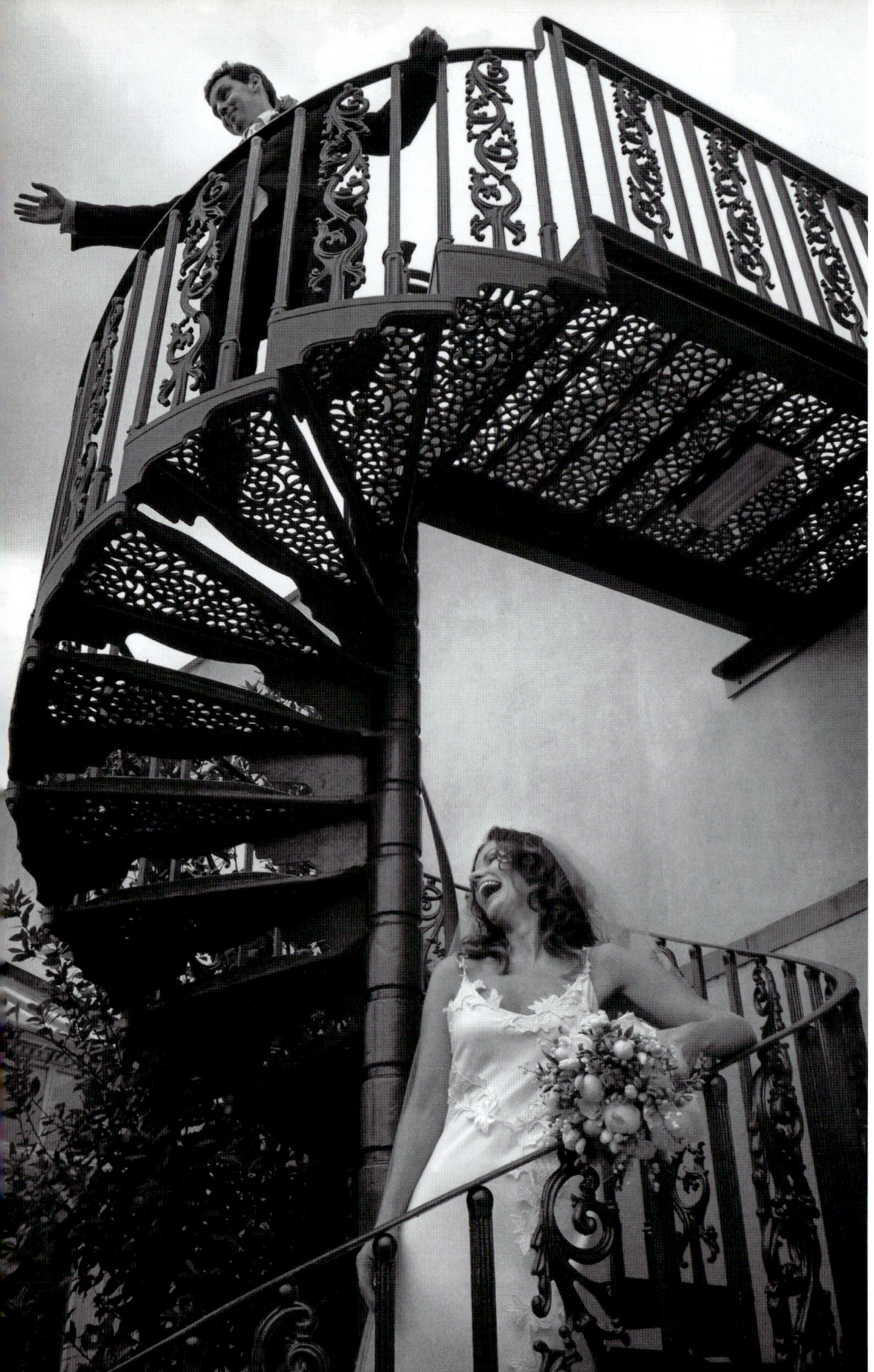

FIG. 72   ISO 200 f/6.7 at 1/180th

Spiral stairs are always a good place to take pictures even if they are just a fire escape as in this picture.

for duplication. The images are also left on the flash cards at this stage.

If the food looks great, is well presented, with elegance and design, I capture it. I take pictures of my own plate using my Metz flash held off-camera to create low angle interesting sidelight. With the lens at f/4 and the camera set to manual, I get a shot suitable for a recipe book. Once the image is right, I'll eat the food with the feeling I've earned it!

Our next big task is to photograph the speeches. As you might expect, we have a system for this. Just before the speeches commence, we tidy the top table. We place bottles of water down beside the table and remove the table name or number if it obscures anyone. Floral arrangements may also have to go temporarily. I shoot using TTL flash off-camera, ISO 400 f/4 at

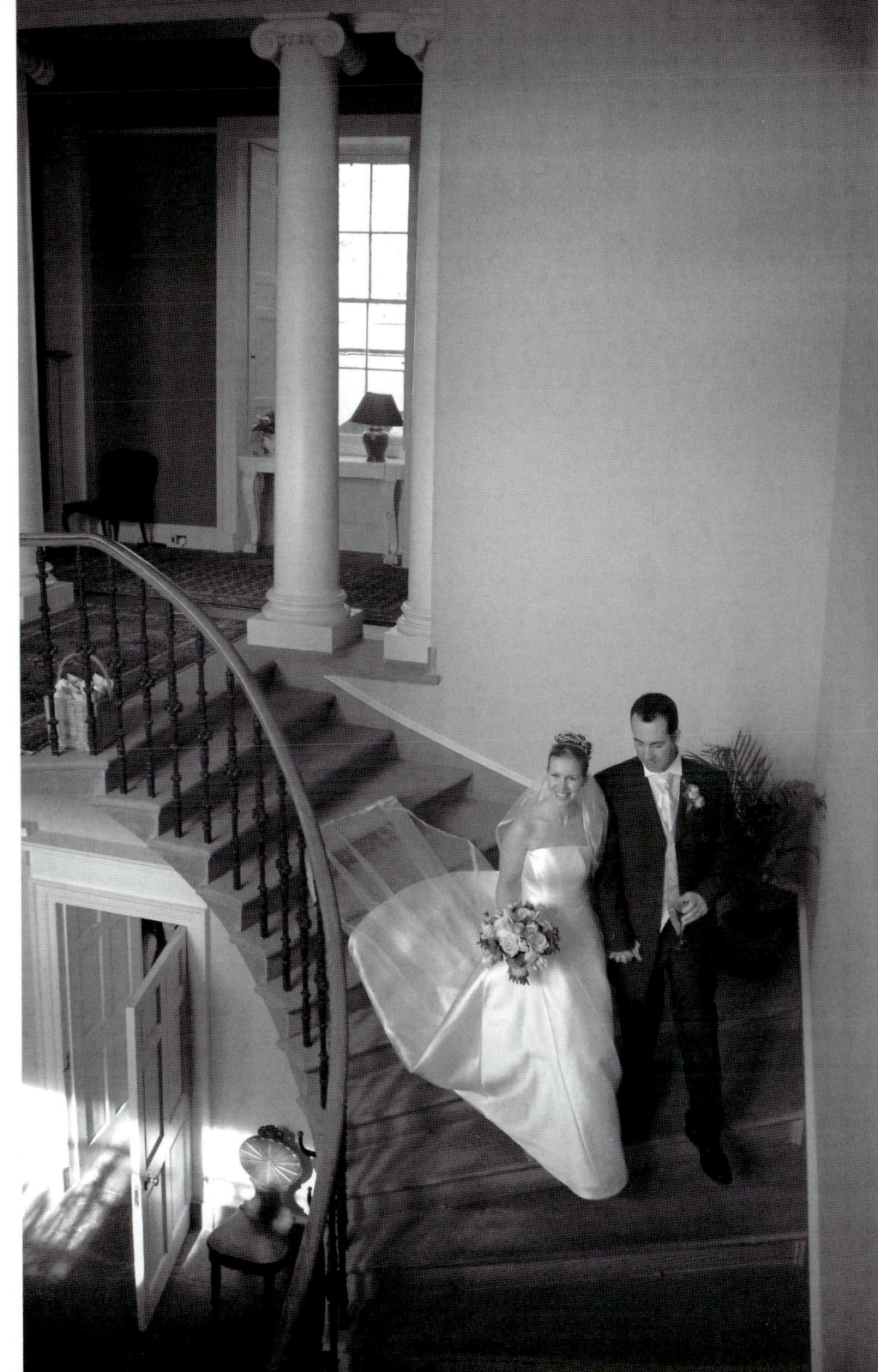

FIG. 73   ISO 400 f/4 at 1/250th

There is always a minor risk element that kicks in to your train of thought when you go away from the action to pursue a better vantage point. I had to get through several rooms and onto the balcony in time to catch this frame of the couple on the stairs. I kept the camera upright and chose to place the bride and groom in the bottom third of the frame. This avoided diverging verticals and showed the scale of the entrance hall at Wedderburn Castle in Scotland.

1/45th second and a 35 mm lens. I am like a jack in the box. I sit on the floor in front of the top table, and pop up to take pictures at opportune moments. Julie is always toward the back of the room using TTL flash off-camera and settings of ISO 800 f/4 at 1/60th second with a 70 to 200 mm lens. The important fact is we try very hard indeed not to block the vision of any guests. During one of the speeches, I will nip round behind the speaker to get an over the shoulder wide shot view of the room. This sets the scene. Julie will duck out of the way for this shot. I also take top shots with the camera held above my head during toasts or applause. The sequence of speech pictures in the album can often run to 20 or so prints. With over 10% of the album shot at this time we take this section very seriously indeed.

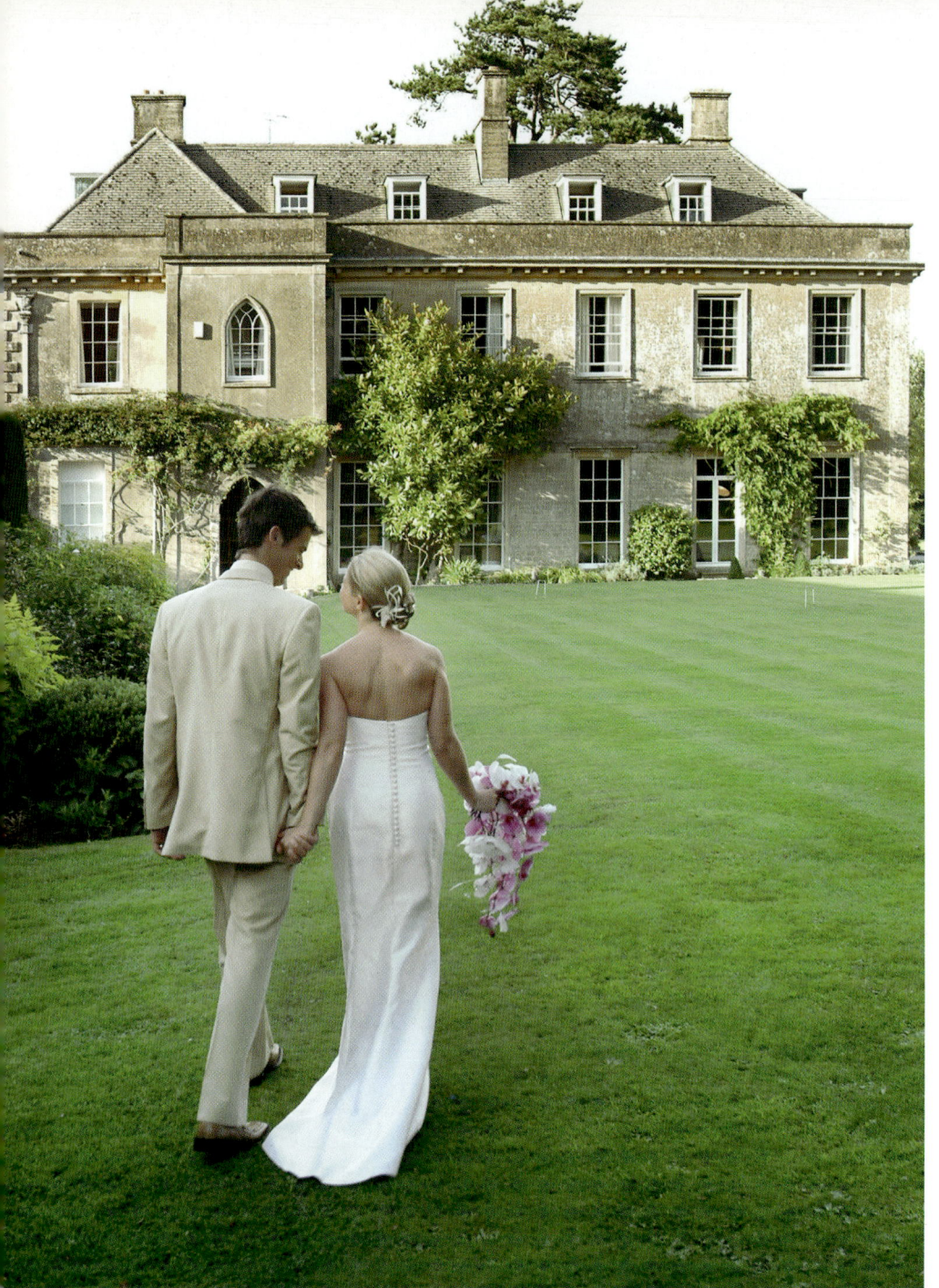

Fig. 74   ISO 200 f/4 at 1/125th

Placement of the bride and groom in the bottom left of the frame together with the distant Babington house in sunlight made this picture an ideal wedding magazine front cover. This is the kind of publicity that venues and photographers thrive on. Remember, there is often a wider use for your images than the wedding album. Couples and their families often enjoy the added publicity magazine coverage brings them.

After the speeches comes the cutting of the wedding cake. Not all weddings are the same of course and some don't have a cake to cut, but if they do it's usually my task to cover the moment. I stick with my 35mm lens and get in quite close. I often have to direct the couple a bit to get them behind the cake to one side. I ask the groom to place his hand on the knife first so he doesn't crush the bride's hand. I count them down and conduct a cheer from the gathering of onlooking guests. I get a couple of frames at the right moment and keep down out of everyone else's shots.

Capture One builds previews as it goes, so while I'm covering the cake cutting, Julie has the opportunity of checking the shots from earlier in the day. This is especially useful as she might notice that in the one shot we thought we had of the bride's

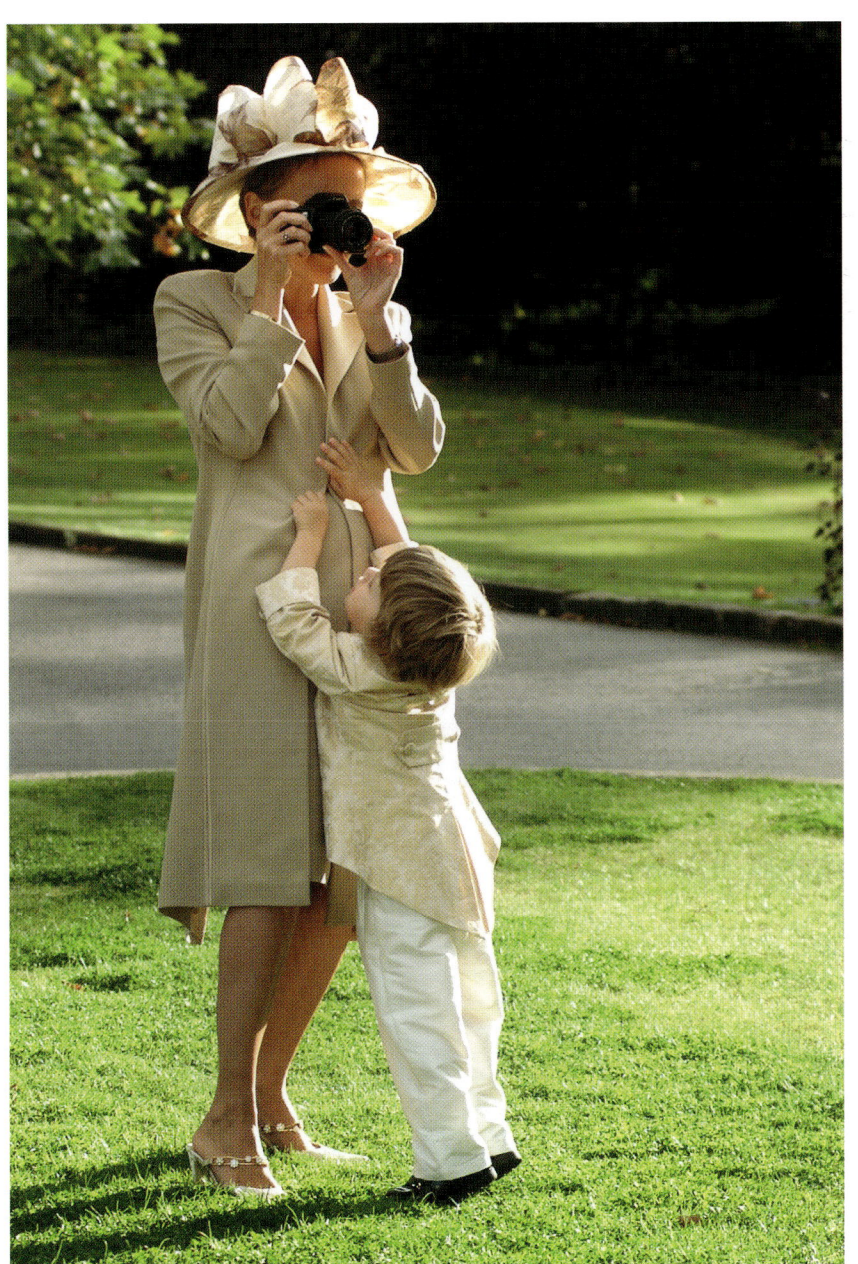

Fig. 75   ISO 400 f/4 at 1/470th

This is a common site at today's weddings. Even the children want to be involved with taking the pictures, and so they should. The inexpensive digital SLR has rekindled the hobby of photography at a higher level among amateurs. I took this picture into the light and I managed to keep out of her picture.

below

Fig. 76   ISO 400 f/4 at 1/1000th

I like to take pictures of parents, and other key friends. Julie will often invite couples to be photographed by me and within a few minutes we can have been a very prolific team. I exclude sky and I shoot into the light, always at f/4.

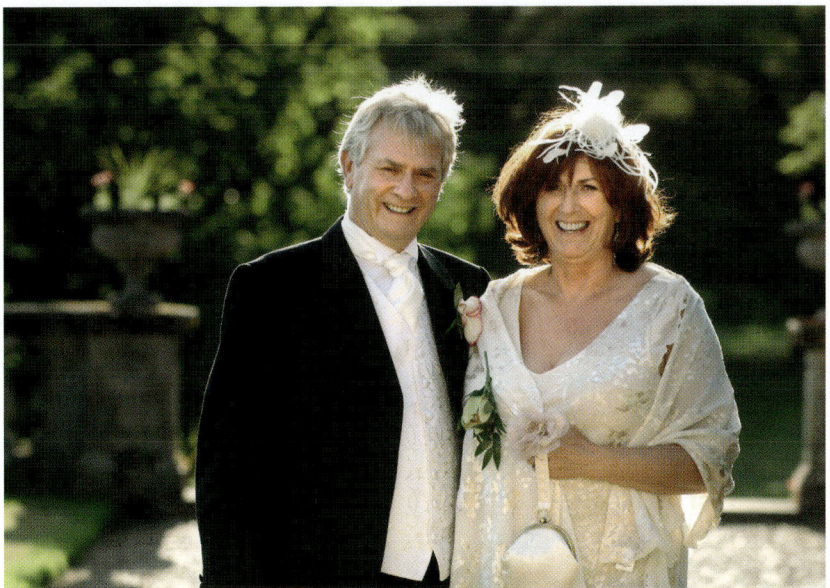

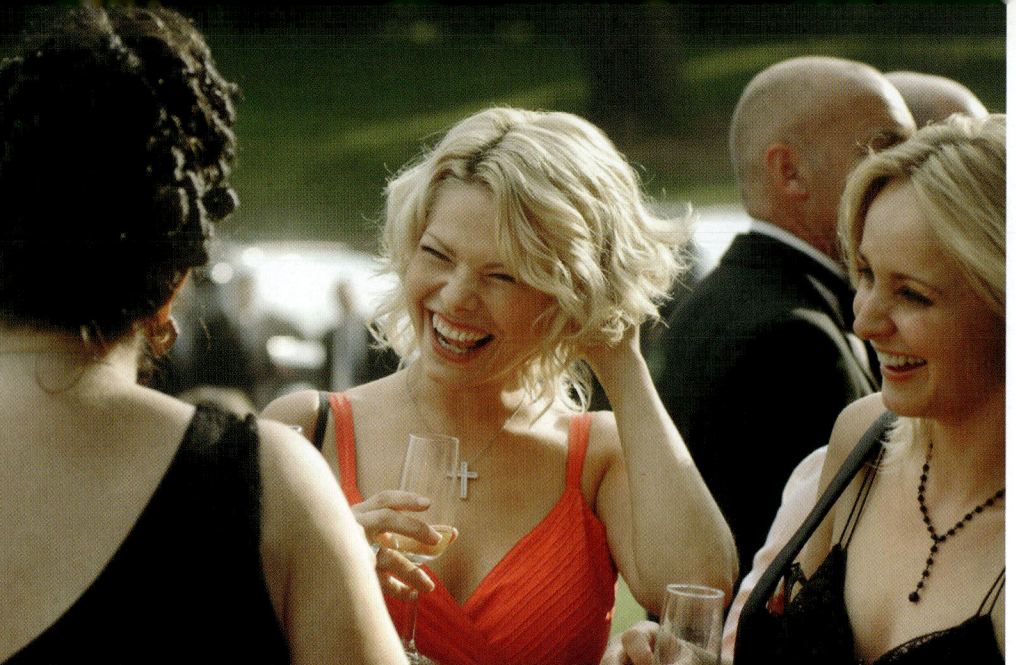

FIGS 77 & 78   ISO 200 f/4 at 1/725th

It is easy to be attracted to take pictures of a pretty girl in a red dress but I am always aware of the value of a balanced coverage. A lot of fun can be had taking a picture of long-established family friends like these three ladies. I was shooting a series of family group pictures into the light and I glanced round to capture this picture of the bride's mum's friends.

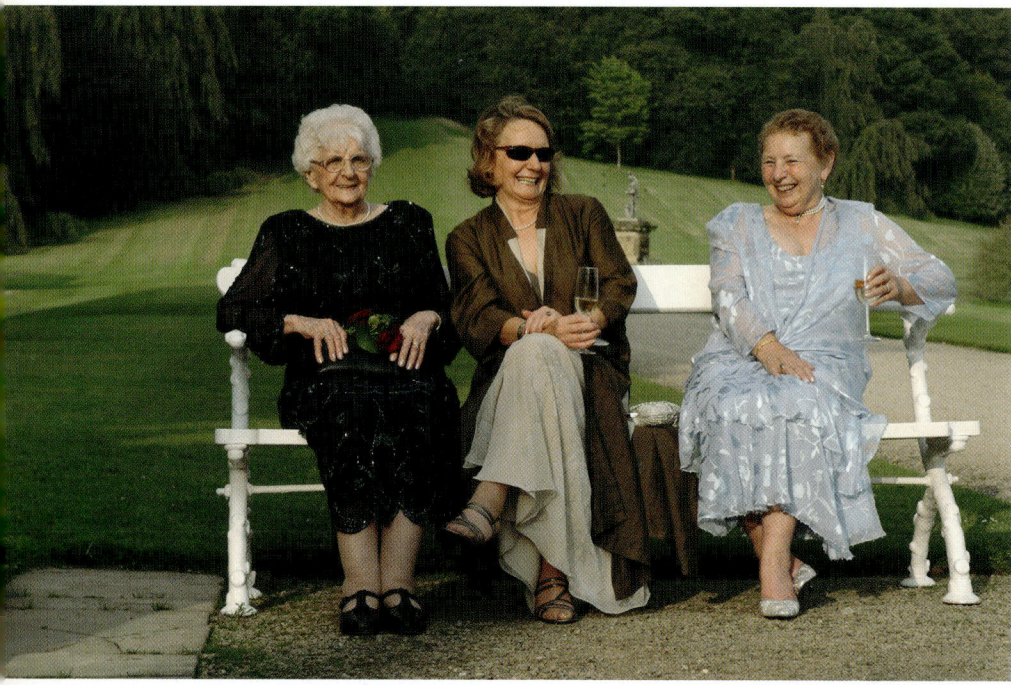

brother, he is half blinking. This kind of thing is normal and it will be my job to whisk him of for another portrait later on. If this moment is handled well, it can really add credibility to our professionalism. I often make the re-shoots seem like they are just our way of giving personal attention to important guests. We will go into the reception area, outside, or perhaps into an adjacent room to take these pick up shots. Occasionally we get spotted and a few impromptu groups happen. Sometimes the children have made new friends and I photograph them on the stairs or in a 'group hug.'

Meanwhile, I'm keeping my eye on the light outside waiting for the right time to take an external dusk picture. Even if the weather is bad and it's raining, a wide shot of the venue at dusk is always a winning picture. I'll get the tripod from the car and

Fig. 79   ISO 320 f/5.7 at 1/250th

The shade from this cedar tree was a very welcome location for this informal group shot on a hot summers day. I'm glad I took the decision to place the bride at the back of the group and the groom on the left as it makes a far more interesting layout than the more obvious symmetrical option.

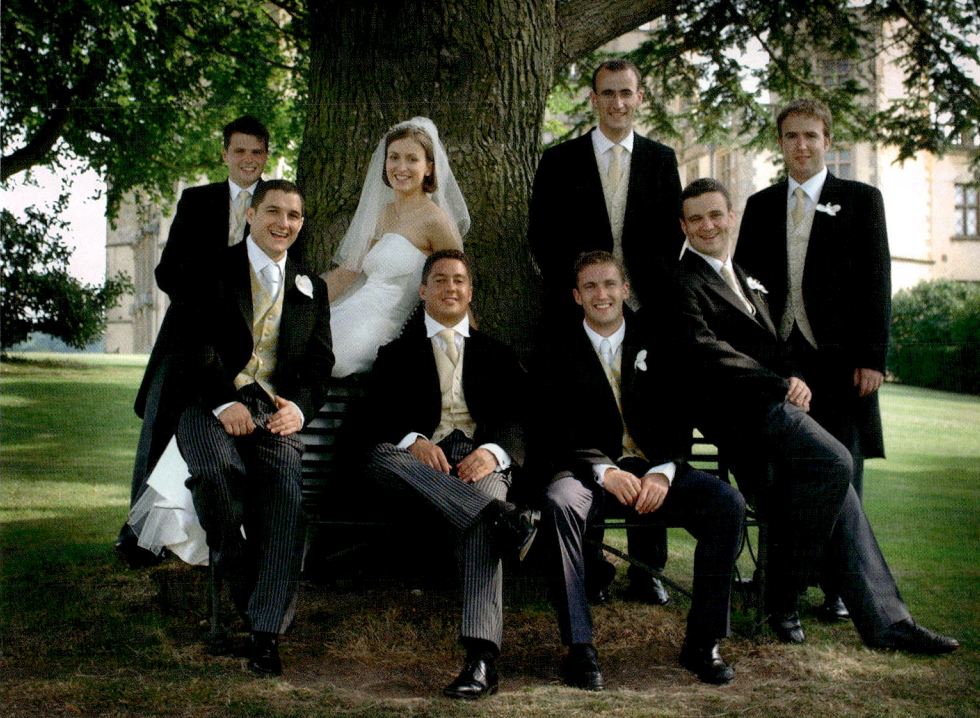

below

Fig. 80   ISO 400 f/5.7 at 1/1000th

I love taking the opportunity to play at recreating movie scenes. I staged this picture to be taken on a long lens.

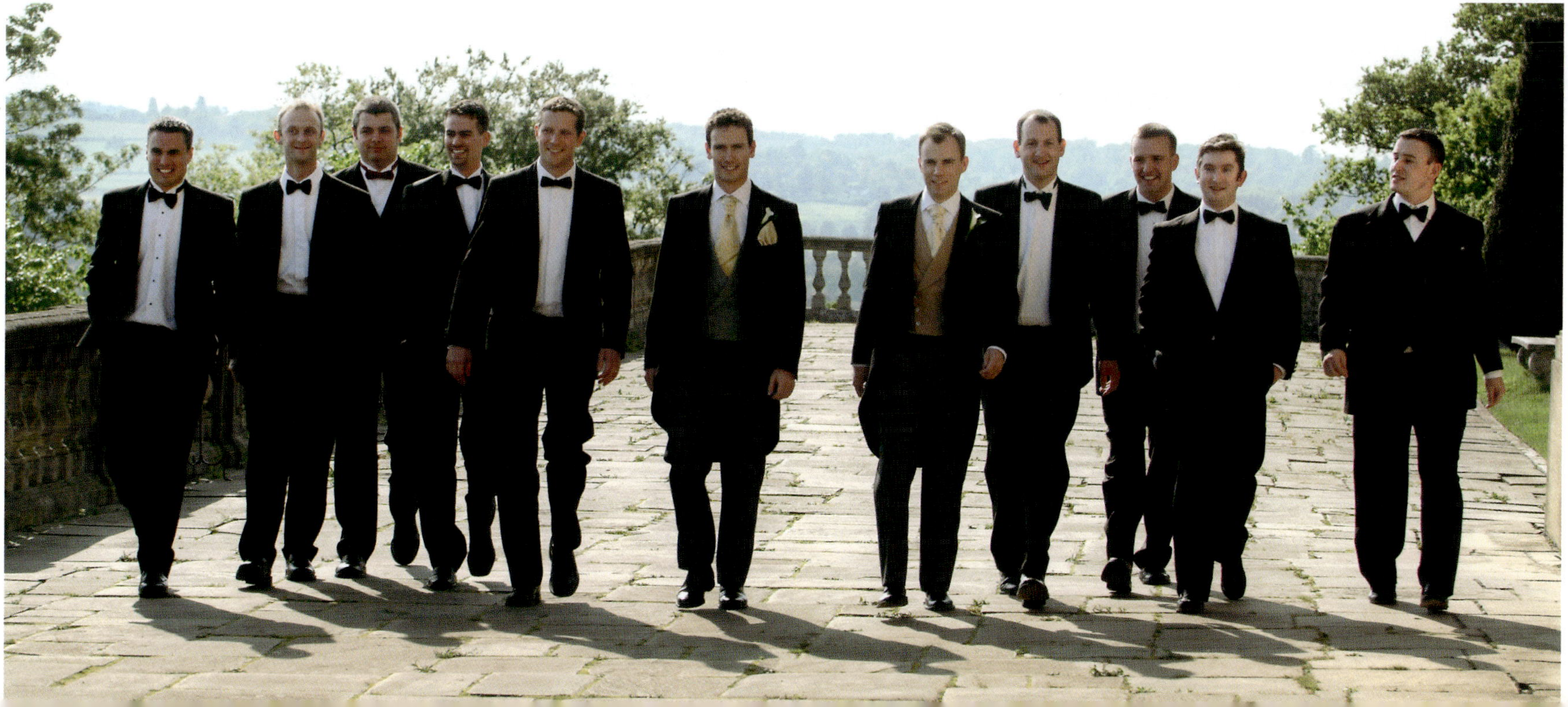

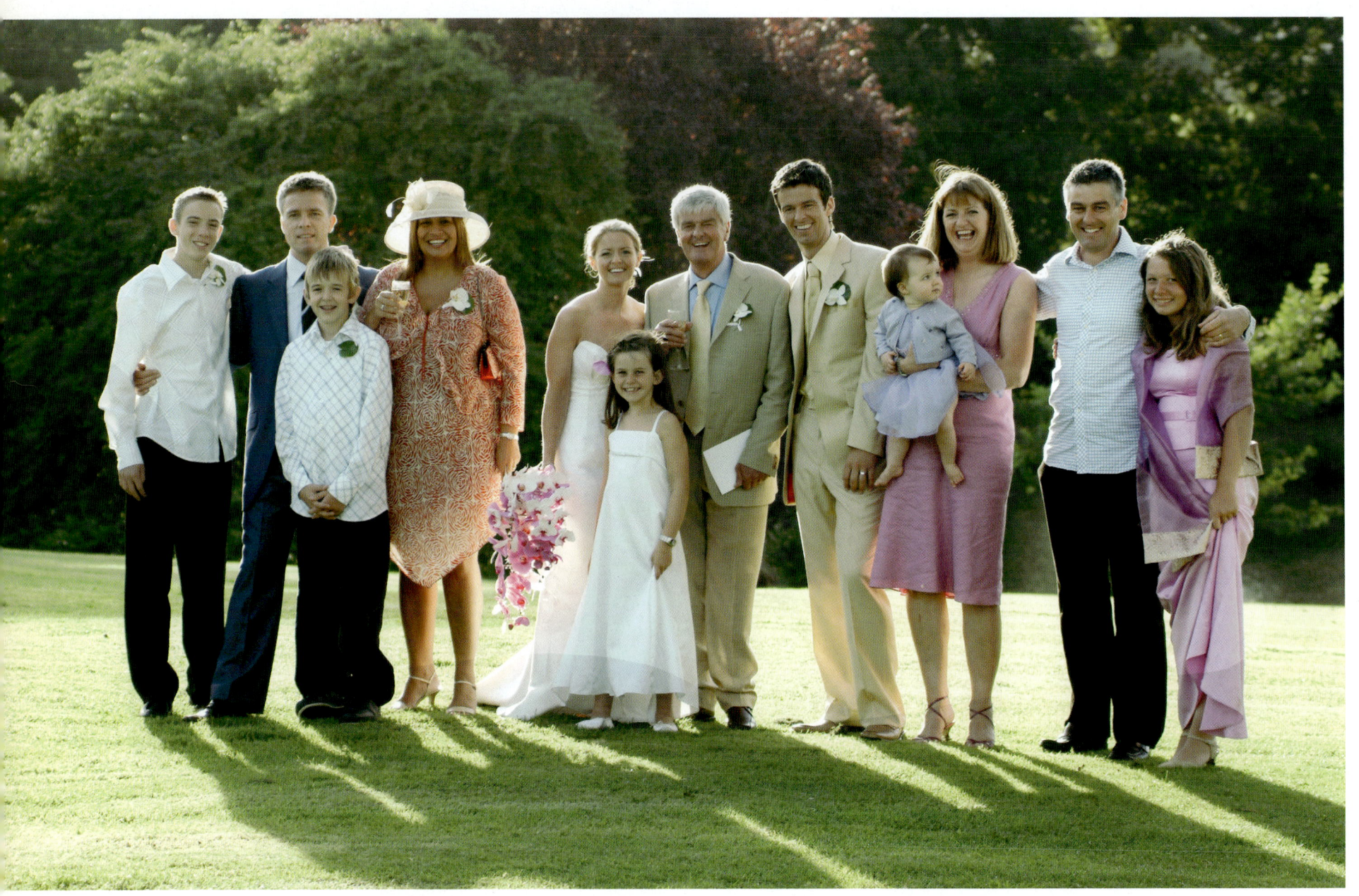

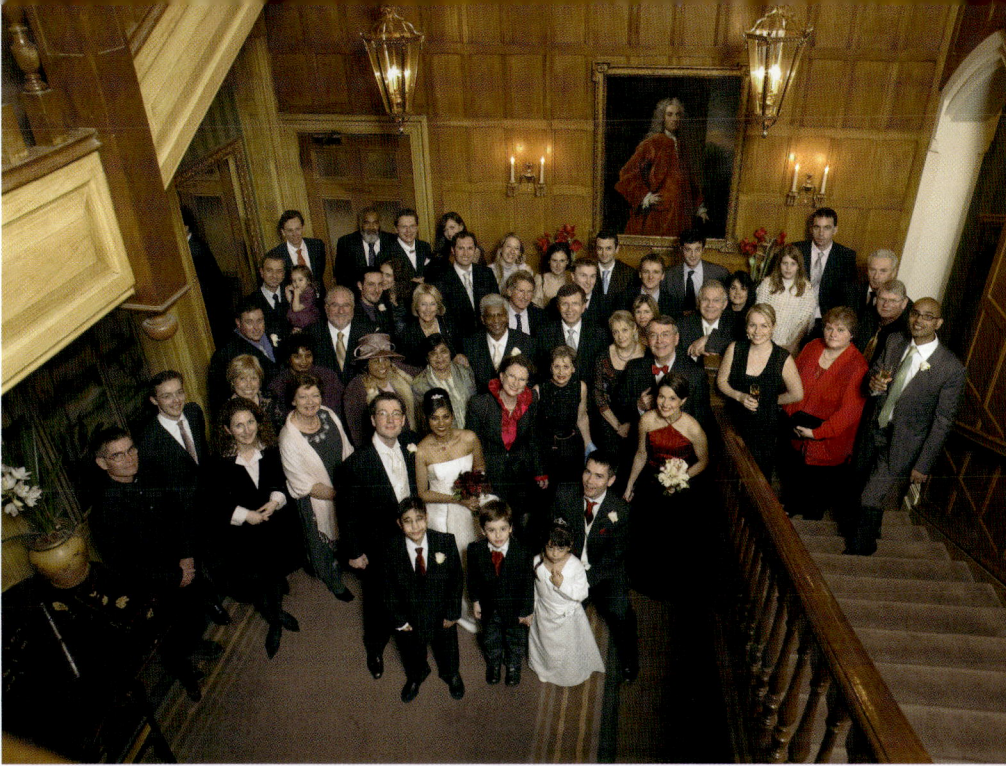

opposite

Fig. 81 ISO 200 f/4 at 1/360th

Another group shot taken into the sun. This time, I placed the guests in their subgroups and made the bride's father the star.

top right

Fig. 82 ISO 200 f/7.1 at 1/4

When it's too dark to shoot outside or the weather is bad I set up the groups inside using a 1200 W battery flash and an umbrella. I took the decision to keep the aperture closed to f/7 to have enough depth of field for the group. I then decided I wanted to use a maximum of ISO 200 to keep the image quality as high as I could get. This left me with an exposure of 1/4 second to record the wall lights. I relied on the short duration of my Broncolor flash to freeze any subject movement and I used a tripod to steady my Hasselblad.

bottom right

Fig. 83 ISO 800 f/4 at 1/90th

This little bear was on the chair and I decided to prop him up on the table and to turn the label over to capture the personal message. Even bears get the contre-jour treatment.

use up to 30 seconds exposure to record the last fading light in the sky contrasting with the warm glow of the interior lights. I find the calmness outside and the fresh air reinvigorating. Ten minutes too late and the shot will be gone. The timing is critical.

Once it is dark and the band are ready it's time for the first dance. Julie and I work together on this using different techniques to record the event. I love 'flash and burn,' that's a technique taught to me by the photographer Andy Earl. It involves combining a long exposure of perhaps 1/4 second with a splash of flash and a healthy amount of camera movement or shake. Julie prefers to use a long exposure without flash. I will get a few 'safe' shots captured too, just in case the couple want a clean look to the dancing pictures.

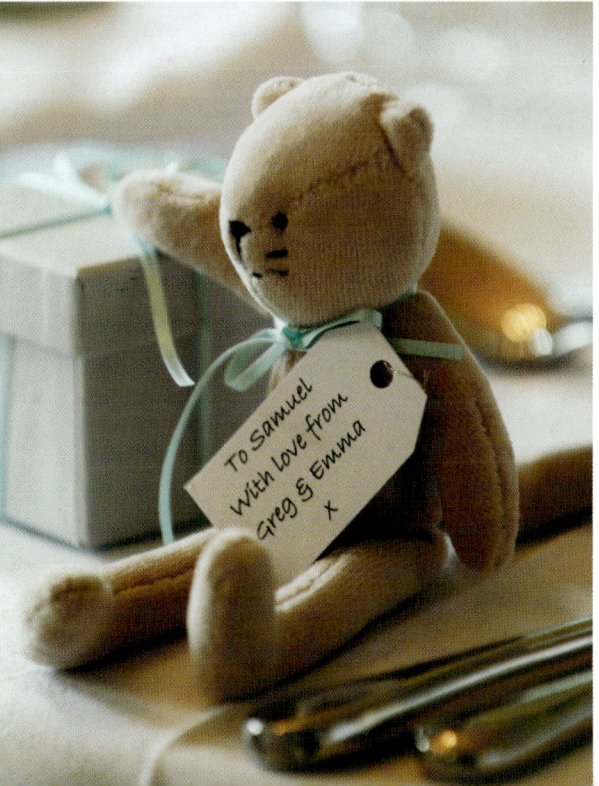

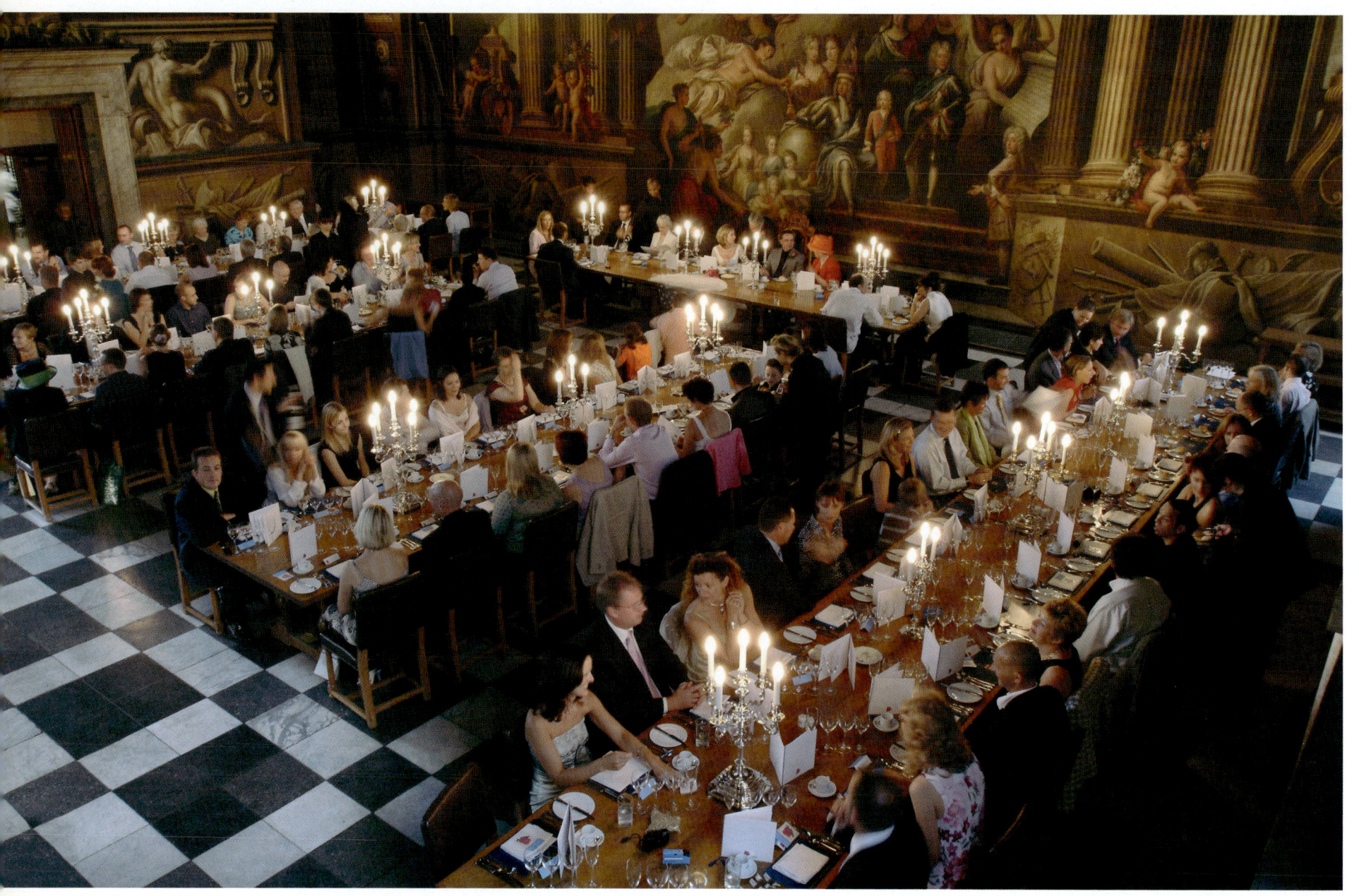

Fɪɢ. 84   ISO 200 f/8 at 1/

I hoisted my camera high up against the wall on the top of my monopod for this time exposure.

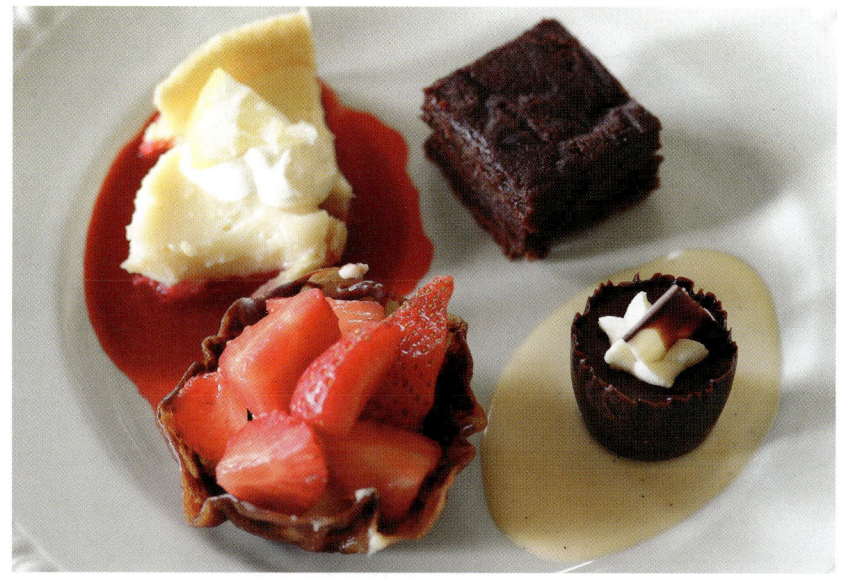

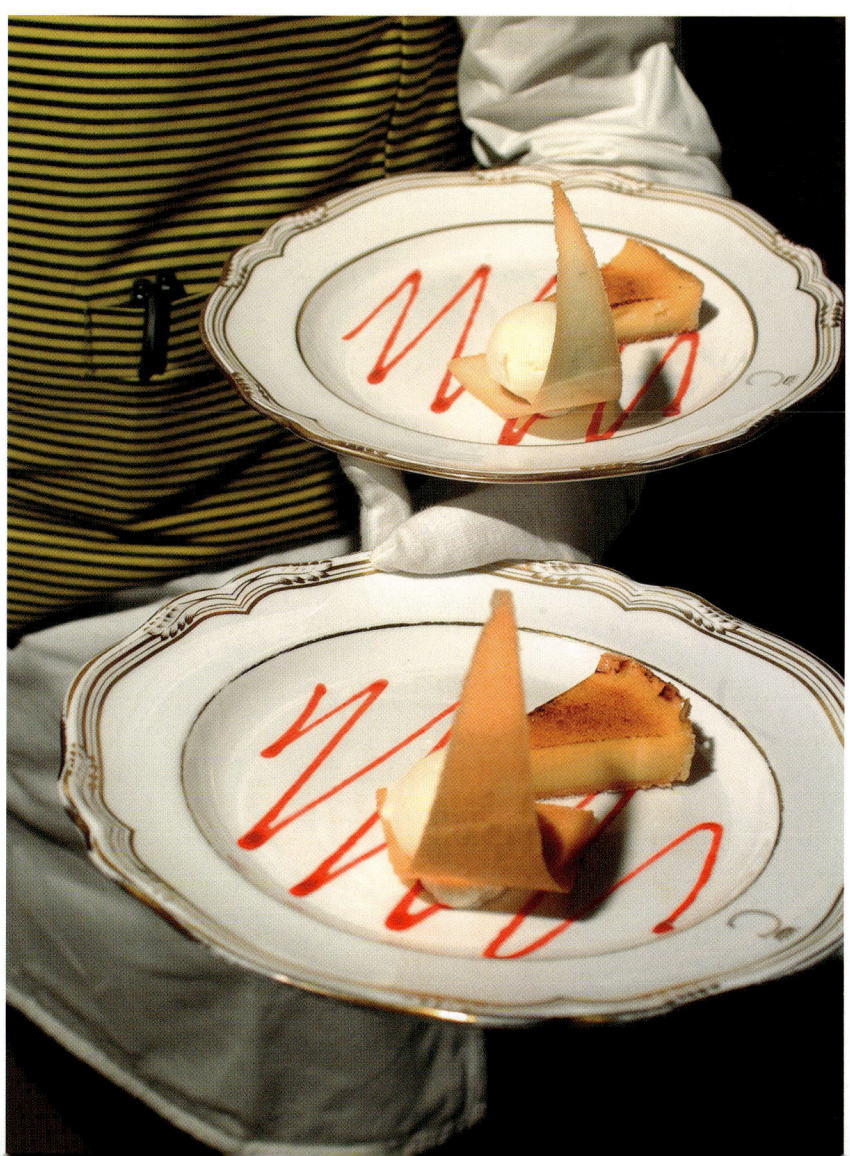

left

Fɪɢ. 85   ISO 320 f/5.3 at 1/100th

This grab shot of a passing waiter was entirely lit with off-camera flash.

above

Fɪɢ. 86   ISO 800 f/4 at 1/80th

This was my dessert and I chose to hold the flash at a low angle to make some fun shadows. My dinner was my just reward.

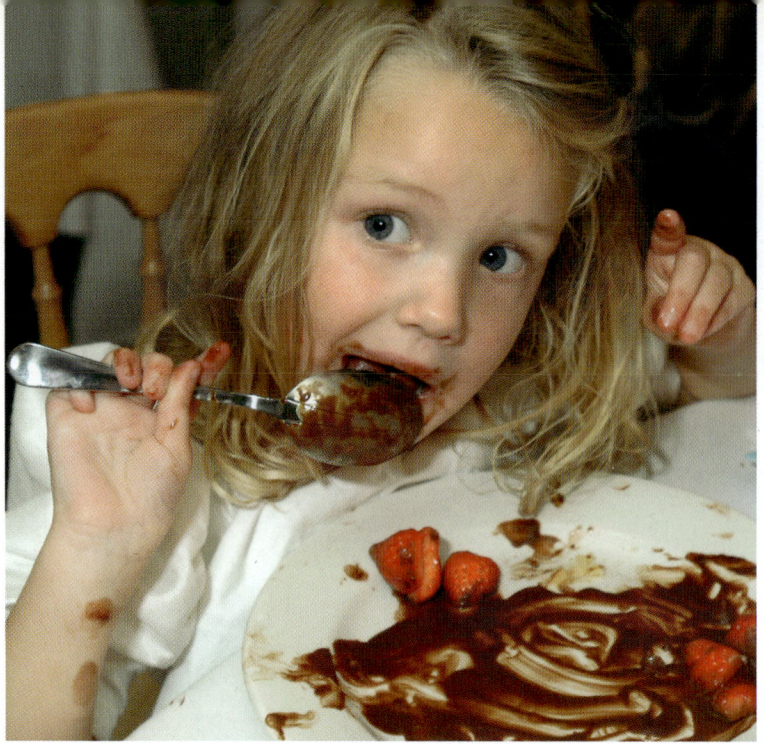

Fig. 87   ISO 800 f/4 at 1/45th

Pictures like these will be enjoyed for many generations to come.

bottom

Fig. 88   ISO 800 f/4 at 1/30th

Sometimes it's what you leave out that makes the picture.

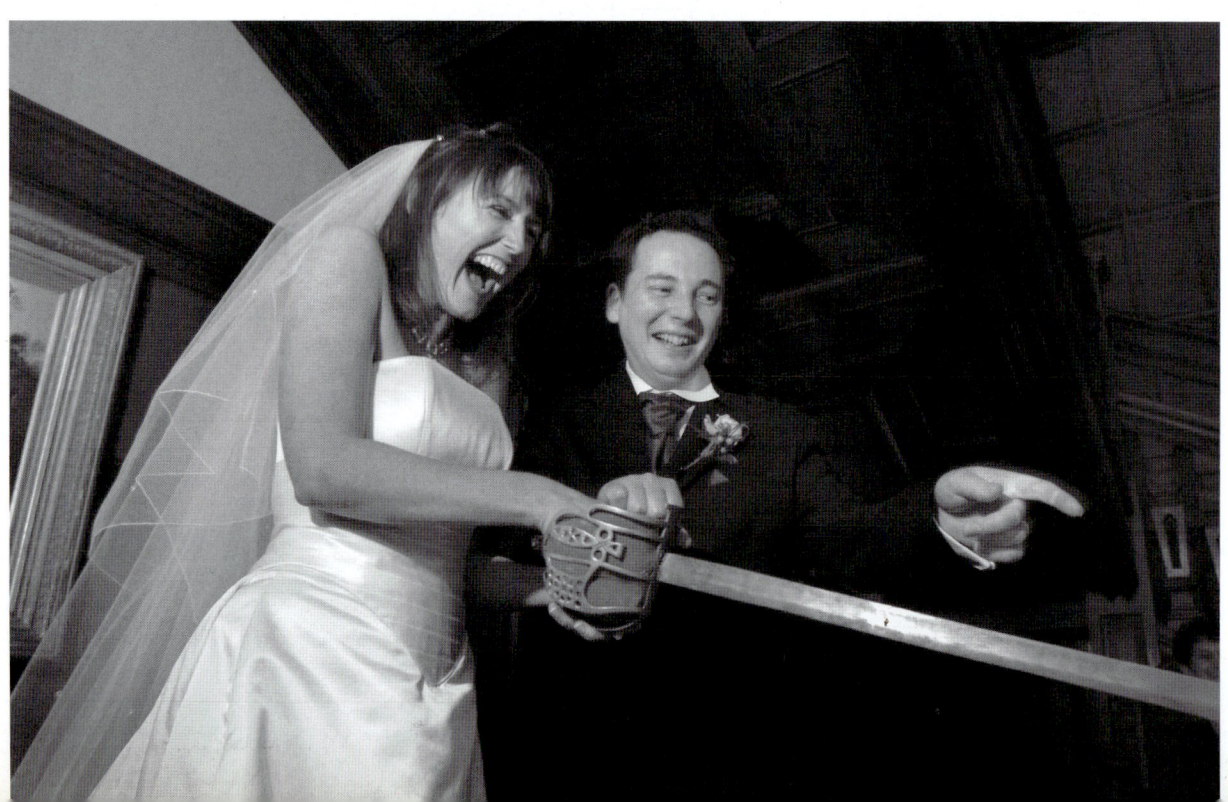

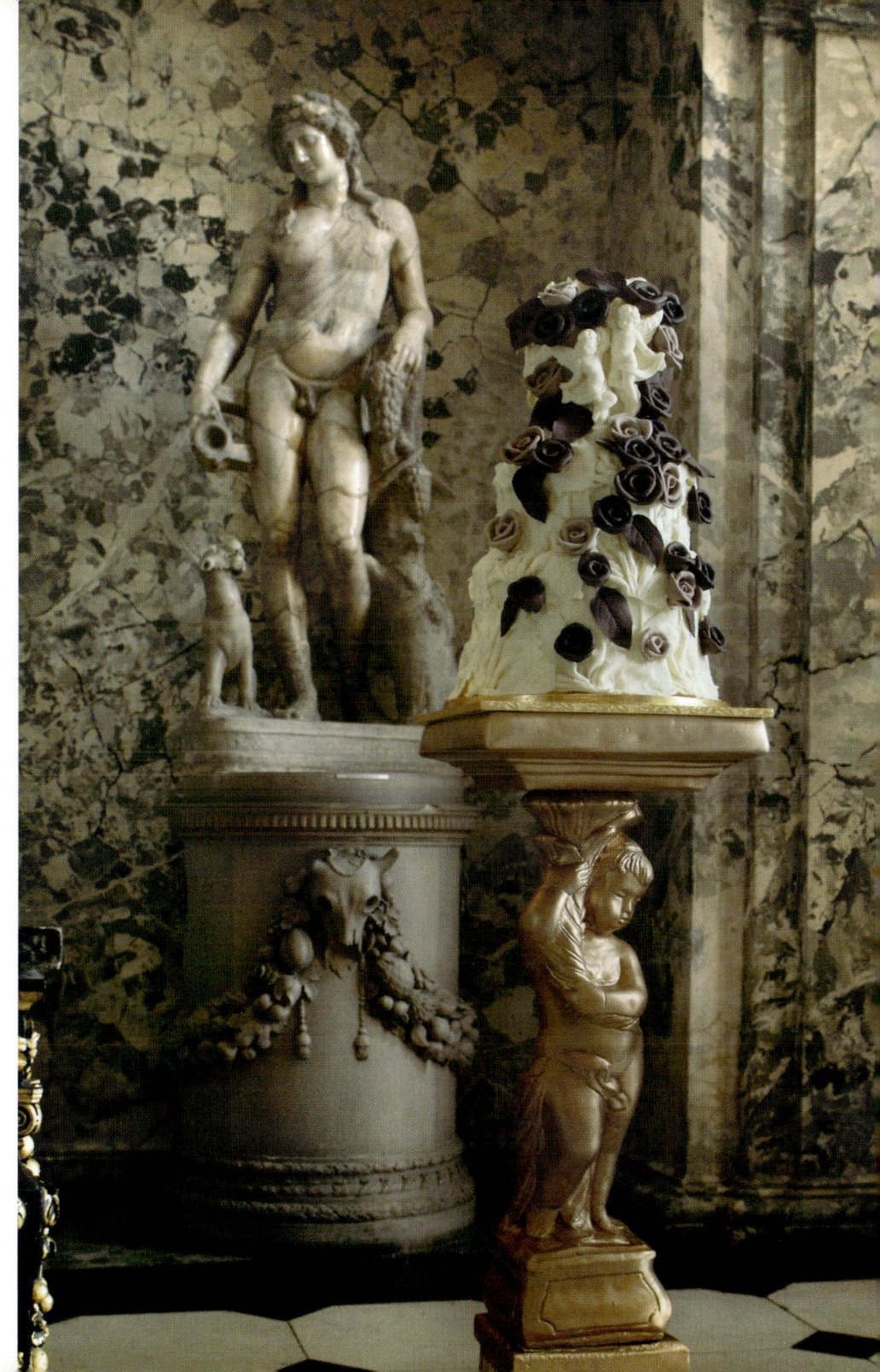

Fig. 89   ISO 800 f/4 at 1/30th

I think this wonderful cake has met its match in these opulent surroundings.

Once everyone else joins in the dancing I aim to capture a few wide shots showing the scale of the fun and a few closeups of key guests letting their hair down. These might be the last shots of the night depending upon the schedule. Dancing shots finish an album off nicely.

Occasionally, our clients put on a display of fireworks. I use a tripod to record the fireworks. First, I like to shoot a base to the picture that can be recognized. Then, I aim to get a few great aerial bursts to give Marko enough images to combine to form the final set of pictures. Meanwhile, Julie is sticking close to the bride and groom, and takes shots of them from behind looking skyward, and from the front with the other guests gathered around them.

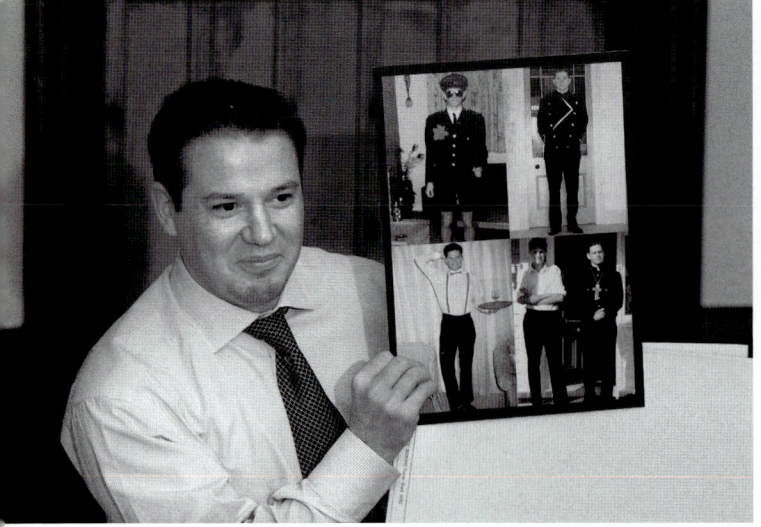
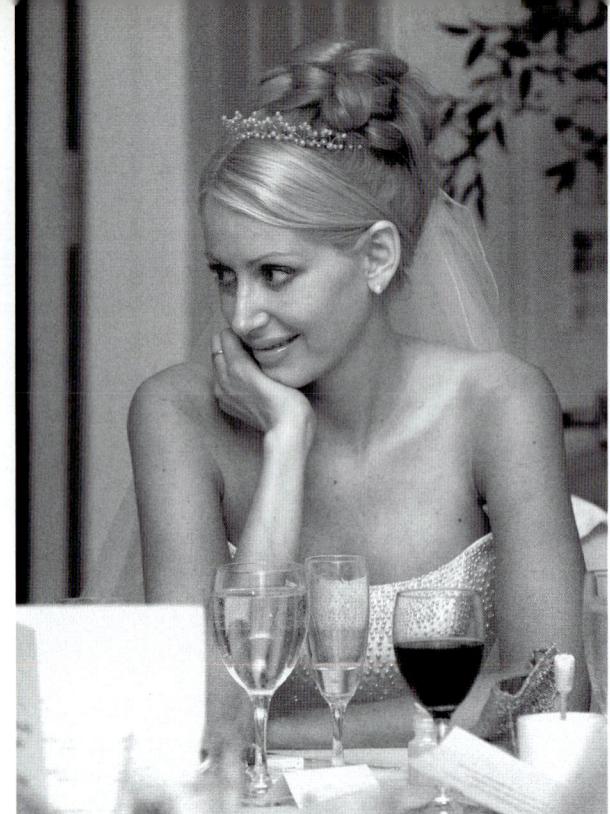
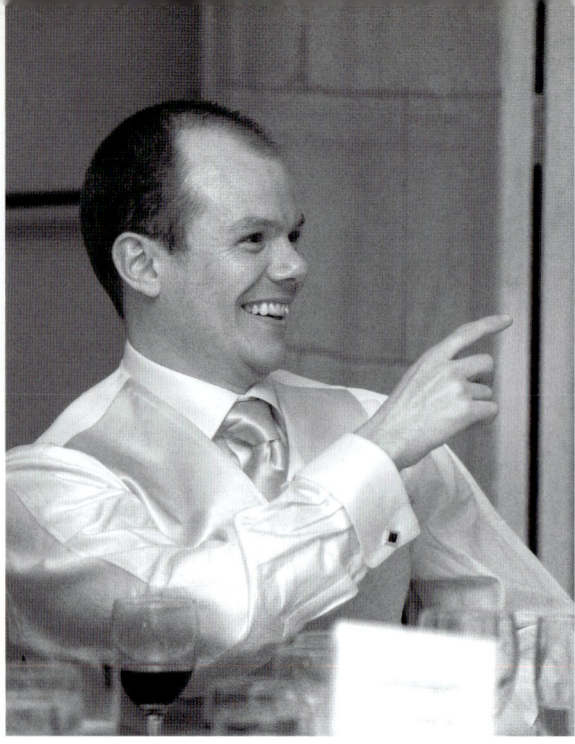

FIGS 90–96 INCLUSIVE   ISO 800 f/4 at 1/60th for all the pictures

Sequences of pictures during the speeches really tell the story well. Notice the ratio of speaker to reaction shots. Once you have got a good picture of the speaker concentrate on everyone else.

FAREWELL

Once that's in the bag, we say our goodbyes and head back to the car with the rest of our gear. By this time the wedding coordinator has long gone, so we concern ourselves with the guests with whom we have struck up a rapport. Finally, we thank the bride's parents for dinner and we are gone.

Once back at our hotel it is my task to finish downloading the remaining pictures and confirm we have all the pictures shot. I

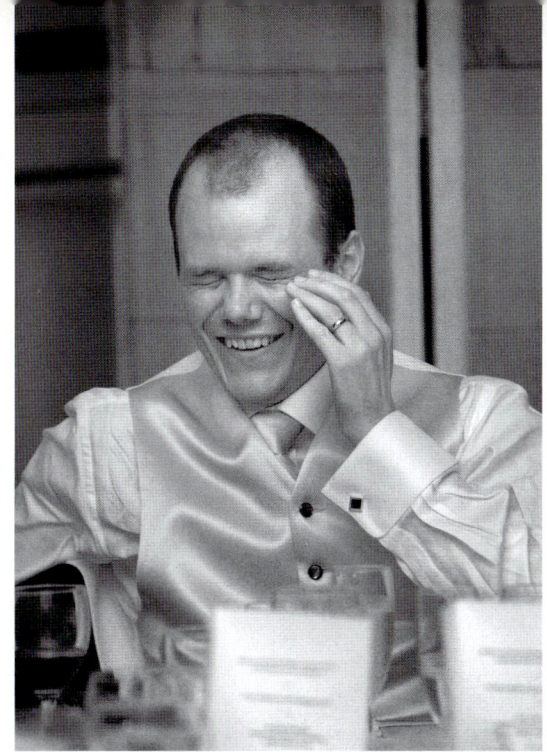

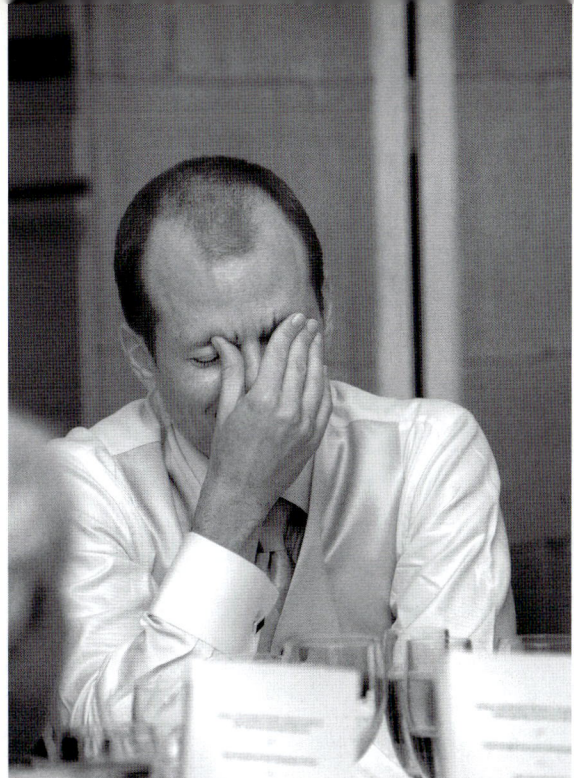

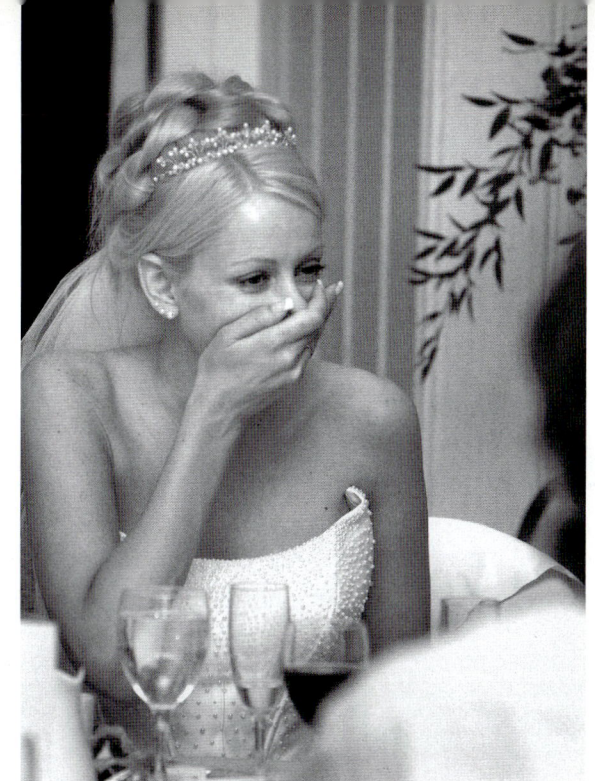

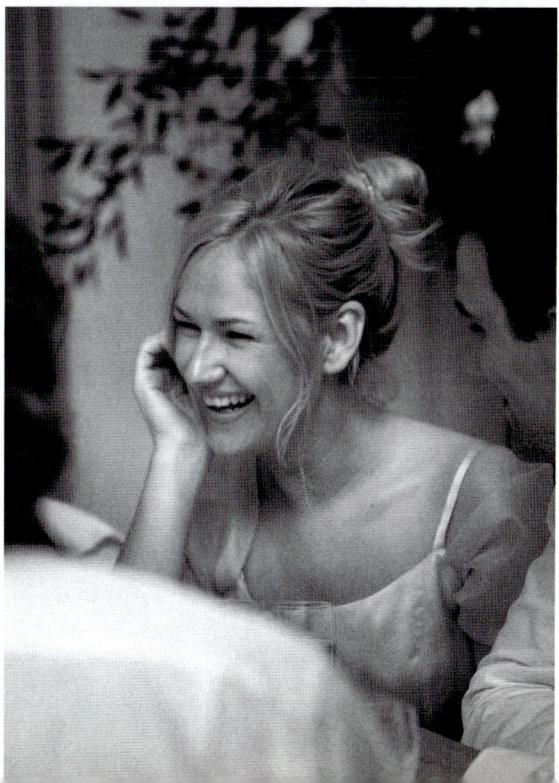

sort them by 'time taken' and this puts them in chronological order. Once all files are present and correct I switch off, shut down, and crash out. It can be as late as 1 AM before my head hits the pillow. I sleep very well indeed knowing that we have a great set of pictures from the wedding.

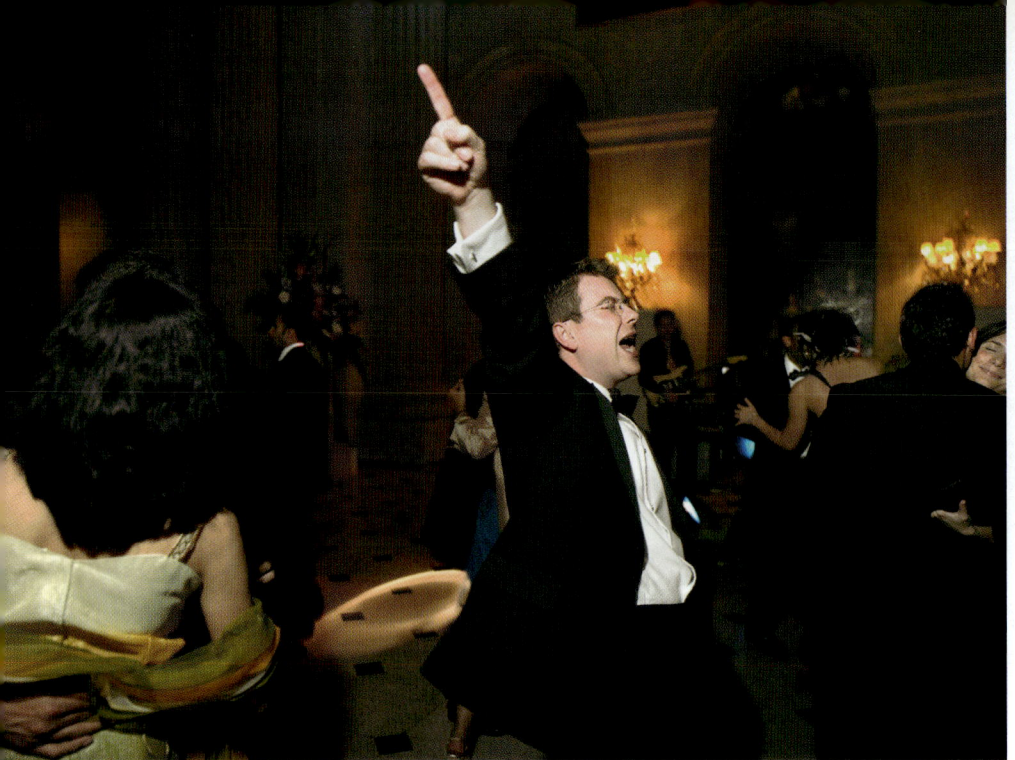

Fig. 97   ISO 400 f/4 at 1/8th

Sometimes it really is very dark indeed. I always extend the exposure time enough to get the background to record. Nothing is worse than a black hole for a background.

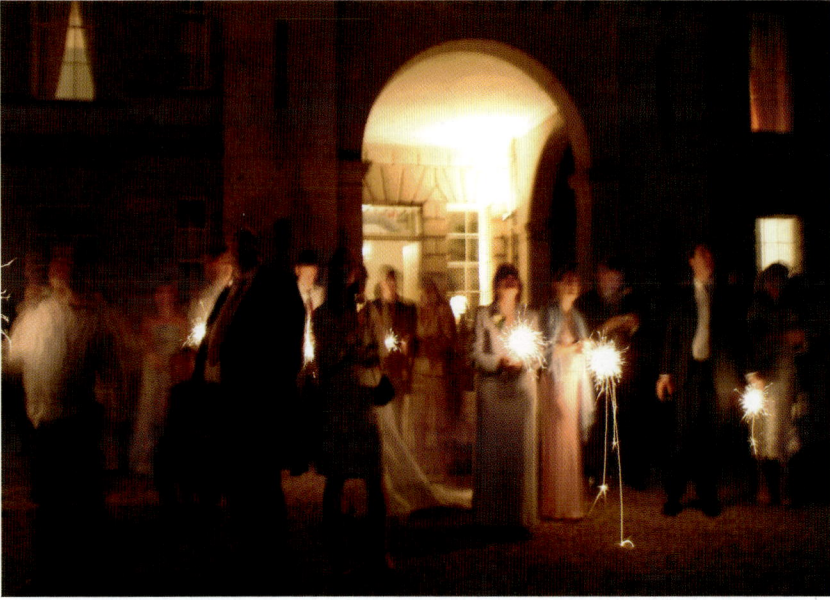

Fig. 98   ISO 800 f/8 at 3 seconds

A 3-second exposure was just right to record the atmosphere here.

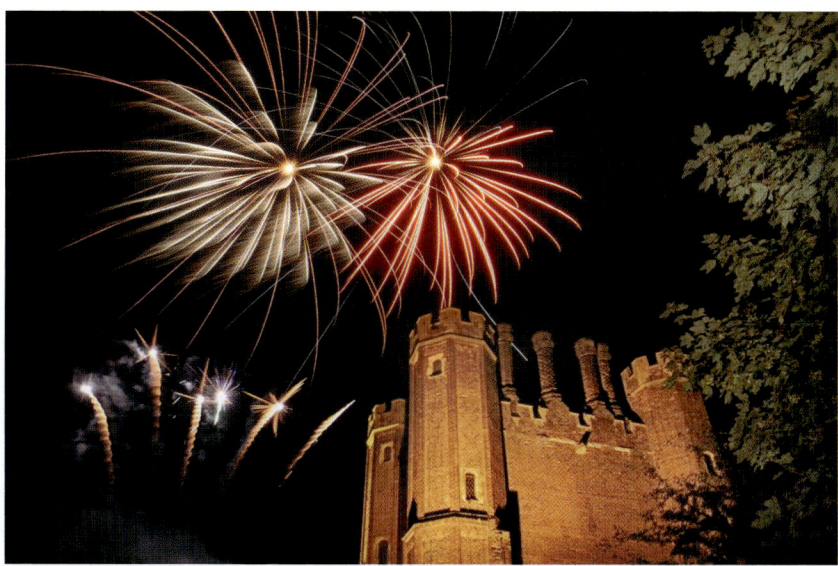

FIG. 99   ISO 800 f/22 at 4 seconds

I used a tripod and a long exposure to record the fireworks in this shot.

FIG. 100   ISO 800 f/8 at 1/60th

Julie always gets a shot like this from behind the bride and groom. It is quite easy to add the odd burst from my shots if required.

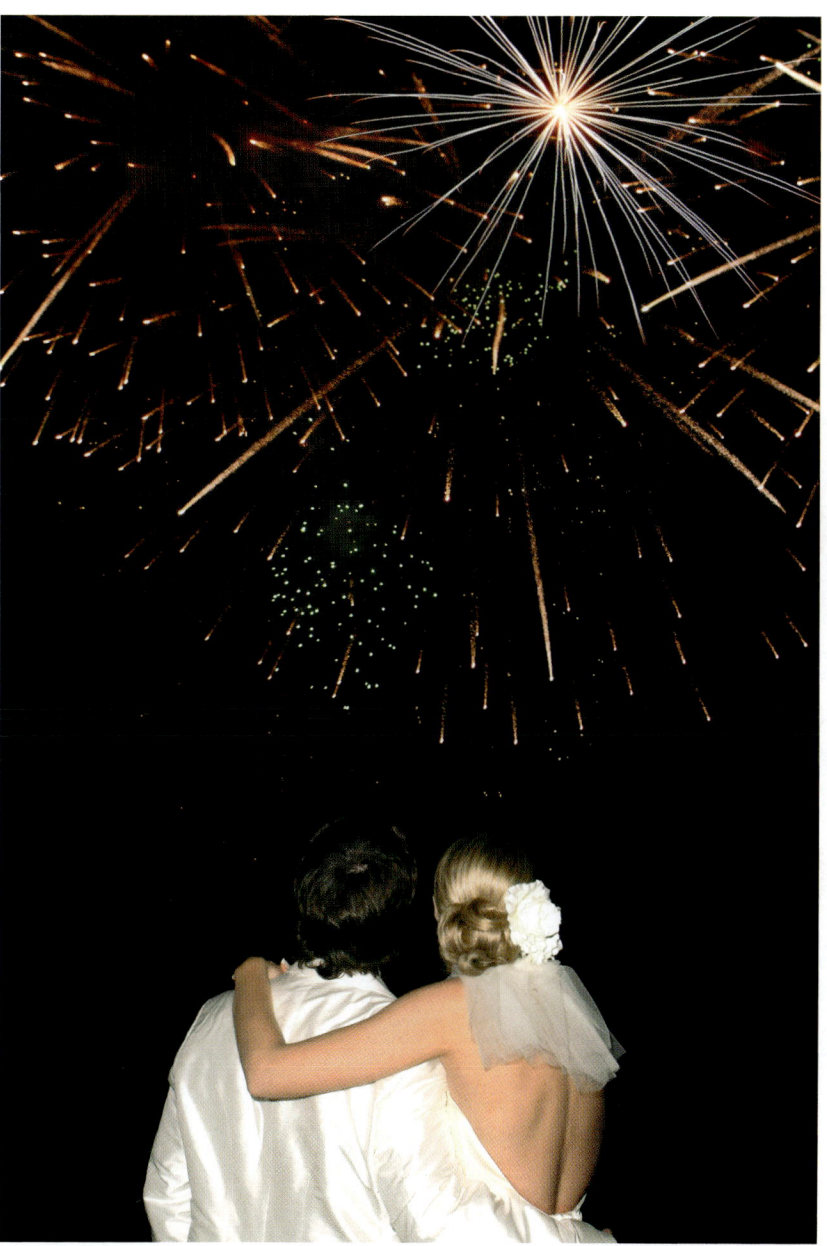

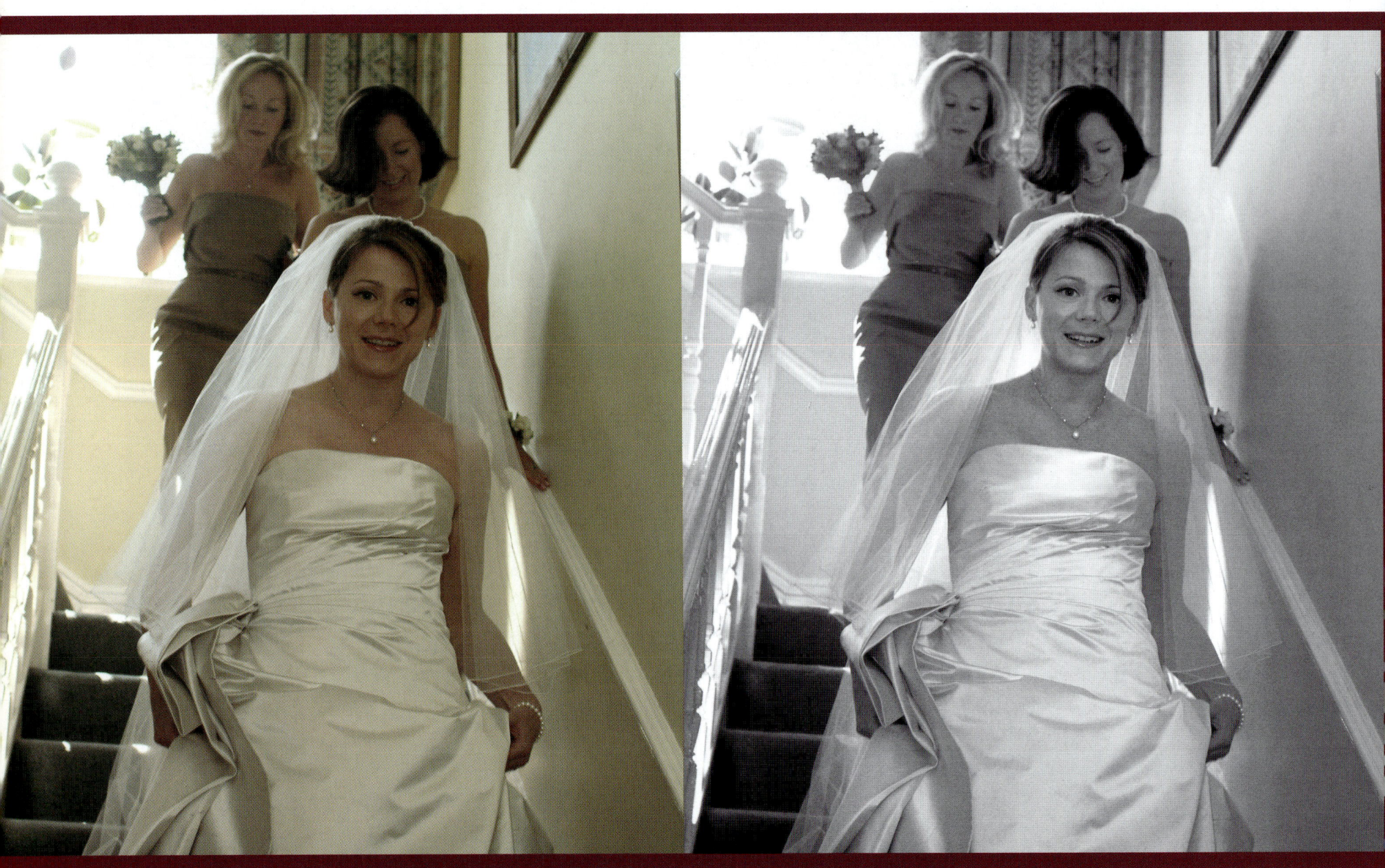

7

Digital
Post-Production
Workflow

Digital 'post-production' is now a standard procedure for most digital wedding photographers. But because image manipulation and enhancement can be beguiling, it's easy to get *too* involved – leading to wasted time. What you need is a good ratio between time in and value out. Every minute spent in Photoshop must be rewarded with a corresponding income.

So you should question everything you do, measure the time it takes you to complete tasks, assess the finished results, and ask yourself, 'Could I charge *more* for my pictures if I spent *more* time working on the files in post-production?' Equally valid is

the question, 'If I cut the time in post-production, would it affect the amount I can charge for the prints?' There are obvious 'no value added' stages in any workflow that need careful scrutiny to achieve optimum efficiency. When you are dealing with a thousand or more files with each job, it's easy to waste time on nonessential or duplicated tasks. You need to protect the

opposite

Fig. 1A & B   ISO 400 f/4 at 1/125th

The camera-generated JPEG was lacking in contrast and there was no color information worth keeping. Marko adjusted the black level for the whole picture before adding contrast to the bride. Notice how her dress now has a silky sheen.

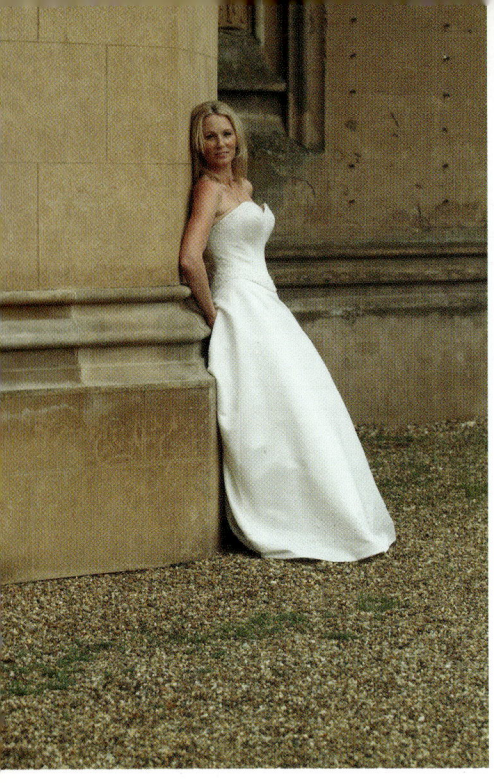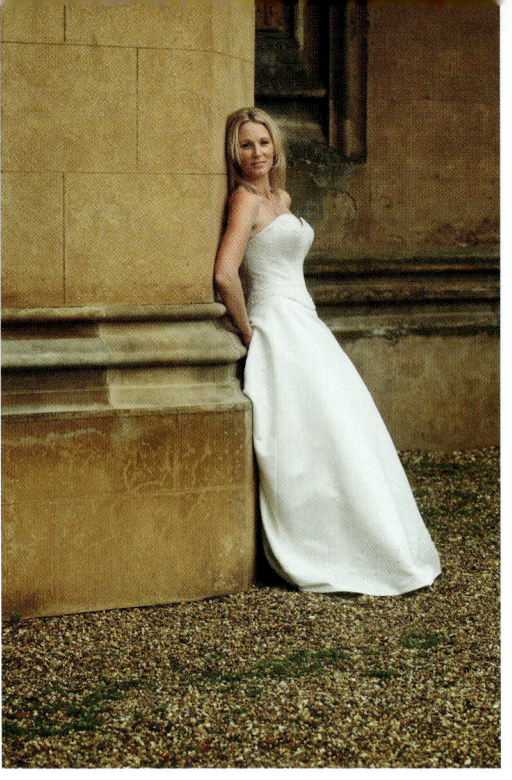

This file needed just minor tweaks to become wanted by the bride. Marko tucked the bodice back to meet the bride's chest and removed the nails from the back wall before adding an overall punch to the picture.

bottom left

This dancing shot was void of any endearing qualities so a little help in post-production was needed to prepare it for the viewing and subsequently the album too.

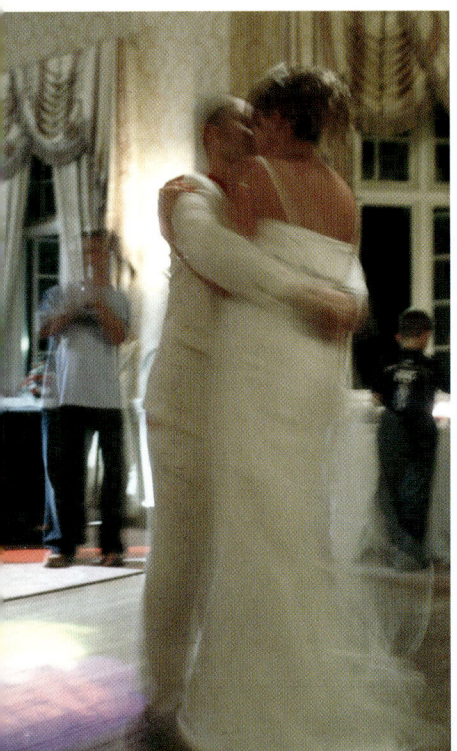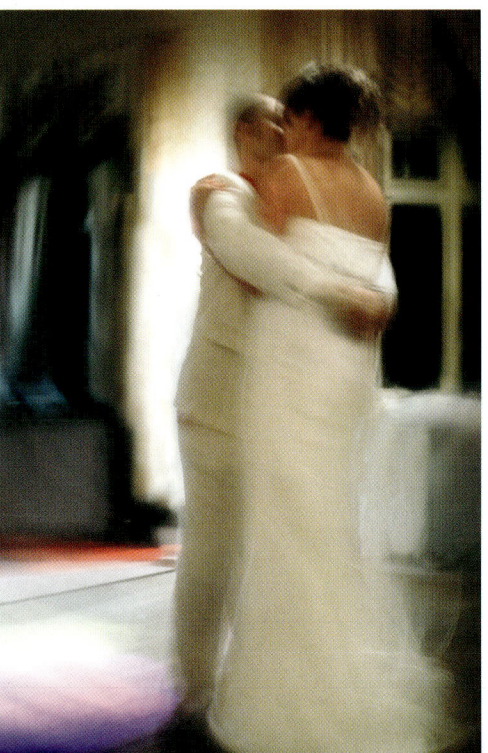

integrity of the files, back up the right data, and avoid repeating the same tasks on the same image.

Here's another time-saving tip: never hang around waiting for the computer. If you keep seeing the hour glass (PC) or beachball (Mac) it's probably time to upgrade your computer, buy it a bigger memory chip, or review any processor-intensive tasks. Time is money, or in some cases, the difference between having a life or not.

As for the more mundane jobs, there are many ways to do most of the picture editing or sorting tasks. But you need to ask whether the methods you use are the quickest and produce the best results? Explore alternative systems rather than just sticking to what you know. Having an open mind will lead you to time-saving opportunities like programming the function keys on your

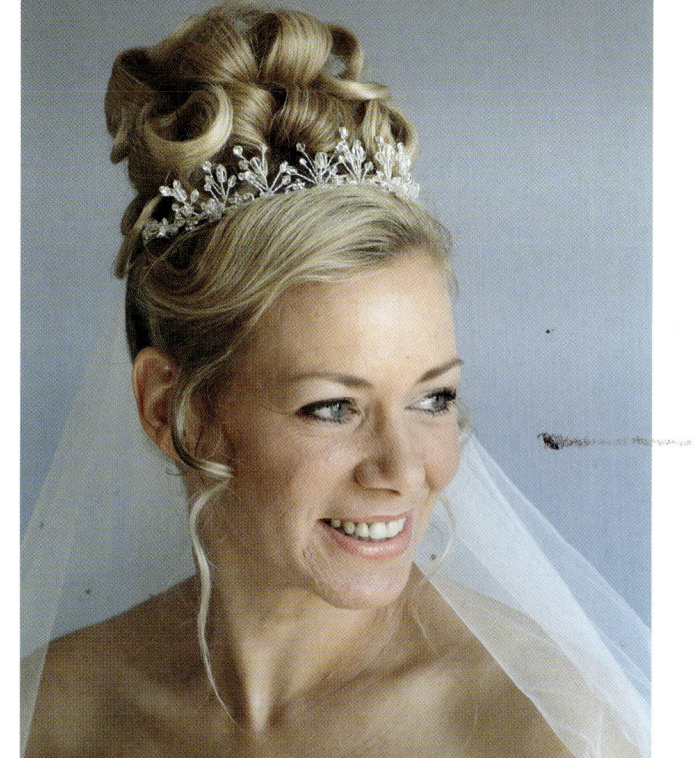

This beautiful bride wanted some complexion softening and a smaller nose. It is important for our clients that their true character remains. Over blurring of skin can ruin a picture.

keyboard or using actions and scripts more effectively. When I started using Photoshop back in version 3, I used the color balance, levels, and brightness/contrast controls. On version 9, Marko and I use the curves tool to do all these tasks and more.

When should you upgrade your computer??

We upgrade the principal editing machine at every camera change. That happens about every 2 years. At that point, the old editing machine becomes the new server, the old server becomes the new admin computer, and the old admin computer becomes the new home computer and so on. So with one upgrade everyone is happy. We started shooting weddings digitally on 3.2 megapixel cameras, then after 2 years we moved on to 6 megapixel cameras. This change doubled our

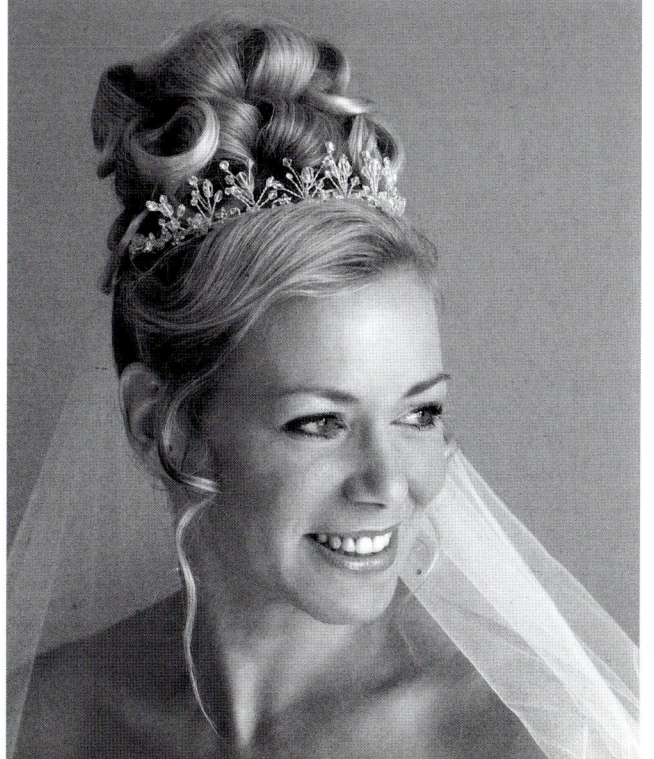

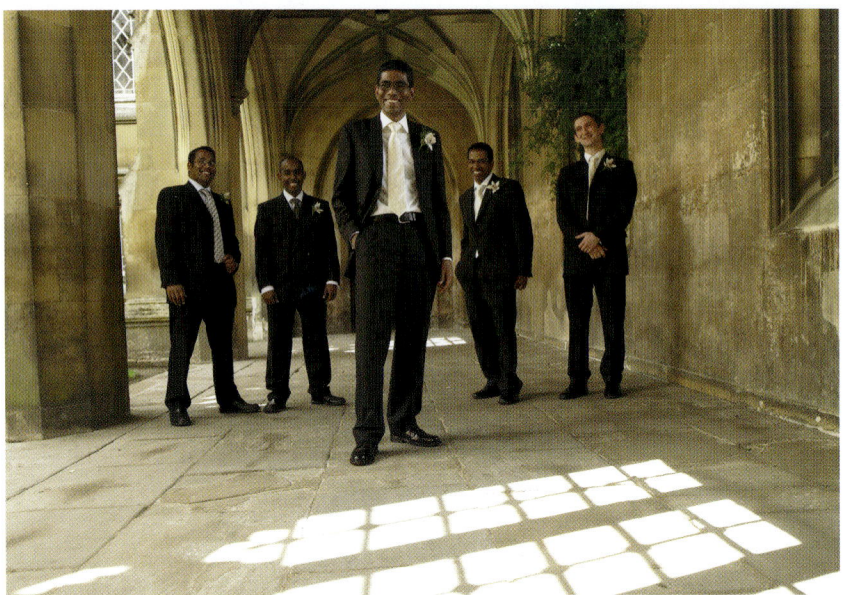

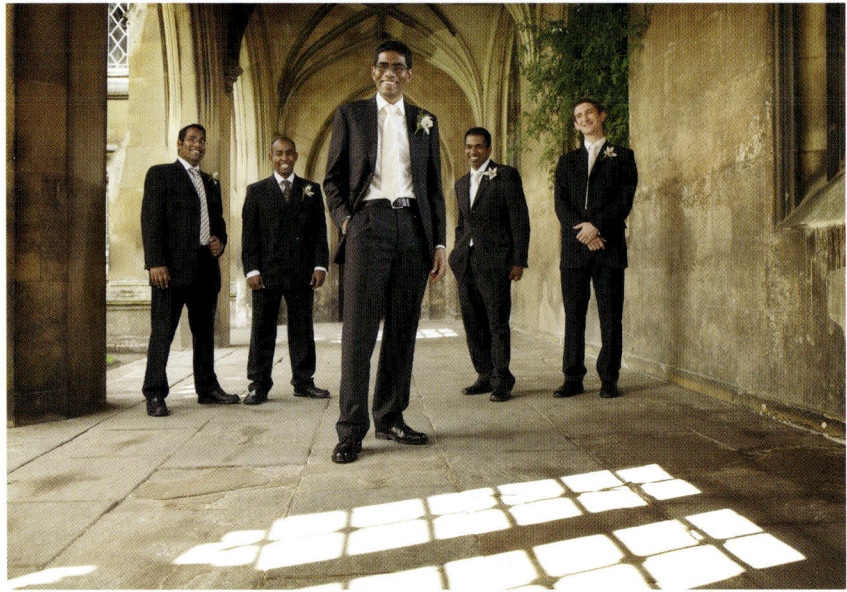

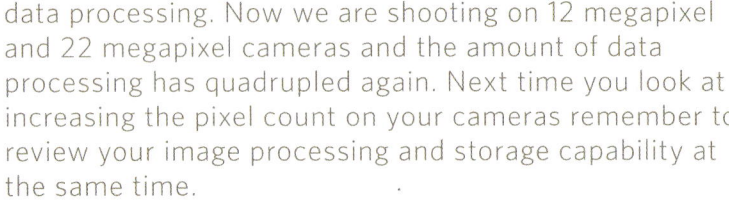

data processing. Now we are shooting on 12 megapixel and 22 megapixel cameras and the amount of data processing has quadrupled again. Next time you look at increasing the pixel count on your cameras remember to review your image processing and storage capability at the same time.

Let's take a look at our workflow for a typical wedding. Julie and I shoot between 1000 and 1200 pictures on the wedding day. We usually start the download process to a small 120 Gb bus-powered USB2 drive at the wedding in the evening. We create a new session on the drive using Capture One software and the Compact Flash cards are downloaded one at a time. This process is completed in our hotel room after the wedding or at home the next morning.

Once all the cards have been downloaded we have two copies of all the pictures. One copy is on the 120 Gb hard drive and the

FIG. 5A & B ISO 200 f/6.8 at 1/60th

This Phase One file had a slight green cast when it was processed from RAW. Marko sorted the color, the tonal range, and the verticals in Photoshop. Just 90 seconds was all that was needed to prepare this picture.

other is still on the Compact Flash cards. It is a good principle to have more than one copy of your work at all times. Julie then spends about 3 or 4 hours the next day using Capture One to select the 350 or so files to keep and writes notes for Marko for the pictures that require combining. The selection process is made using the tagging tools in Capture One. The unselected files are dragged to the trash folder within the session. Marko, our picture editor, then plugs the hard drive into his computer and adjusts the image settings on the 'keepers.'

SCREEN CONSISTENCY

It is worth bearing in mind that all our screens are calibrated with a Gretag Mcbeth Eye One device. Marko's screen – a 22 in CRT – is the best quality we have.

First of all, Marko arranges or sorts the files by size. This separates Julie's and my shots as we use different cameras. He sets a global change to all of Julie's files to increase contrast and remove a slight warm cast. Then he selects my shots and adjusts the film curve to minimize the differences between the two cameras. Next, he arranges the files by capture date. (When we prepare the kit before a wedding, we always synchronize the clocks on all our cameras including the spare bodies.)

With the files now sorted chronologically, Marko makes the changes necessary to ensure a great, consistent-looking set of images. This process takes about 2 hours for the 350 or so pictures. This process could be done more quickly but with less accuracy. Marko ensures all the detail we need in the files is present and the color is spot on, which saves time in Photoshop later. These settings are saved on the run by Capture One and

opposite

FIG. 6A–C   ISO 400 f/8 at 1 and 3 seconds, respectively

Sometimes it is necessary to combine firework pictures to get a true reflection of their intensity. Here, Marko used a lighten blending mode in Photoshop to quickly merge these separate frames.

are stored in the session ready for use at any time. The whole set of images can be processed on any of our computers that are available. Our server has plenty of processing power to spare so we usually get this computer to do the processing for us, leaving Marko's machine free for other tasks. We process the files to JPEGs at the highest quality, 100% size, 254 dpi, and with the Adobe 1998 RGB color profile.

'Why JPEGs?' I hear you ask. 'Why not?' is my reply. JPEGs are the most universally accepted digital image format. You can do anything with a JPEG, use it online, in spreadsheets, page layout programs, image editing software, on iPods and so on. TIFFs on the other hand are about eight times the size, and less versatile. Our aim at this stage is to get a set of color accurate 'digital negatives' that hold all the detail information we need. All the JPEGs will fit on one disk for archiving. There are other

advantages of JPEGs, as you will discover. One such advantage is time saving when each of the files are opened in turn to do further editing or when the files are written to DVD. With in-camera image-processing becoming better all the time there is a lot to be said for capturing in JPEG from the start and missing out the raw conversion work all together. Many of the world's finest wedding photographers use a JPEG capture system, and for very good reasons. My Phase One P25 digital back only captures in RAW hence we are forced to use a RAW workflow.

Once a set of JPEGs has been created, Marko combines the files that need 'head swaps' or merges the files he has processed twice for high dynamic range reasons. An image with high contrast can be processed in Capture One twice with very different exposure settings, one dark and one light. By opening both images in Photoshop and dragging one on top of the other

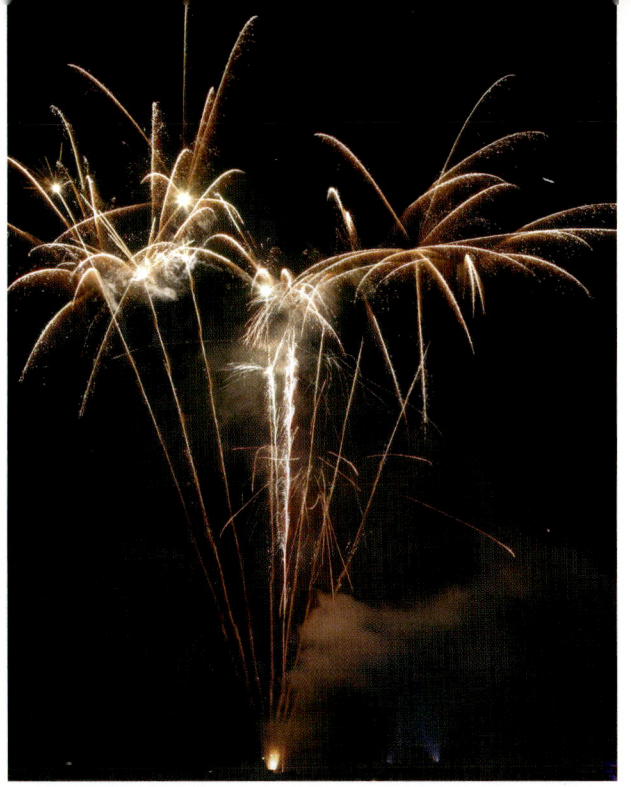
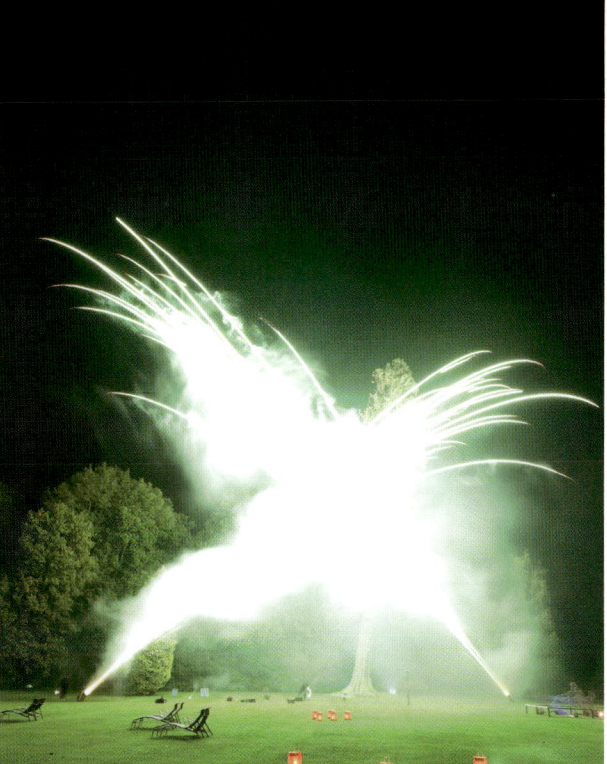
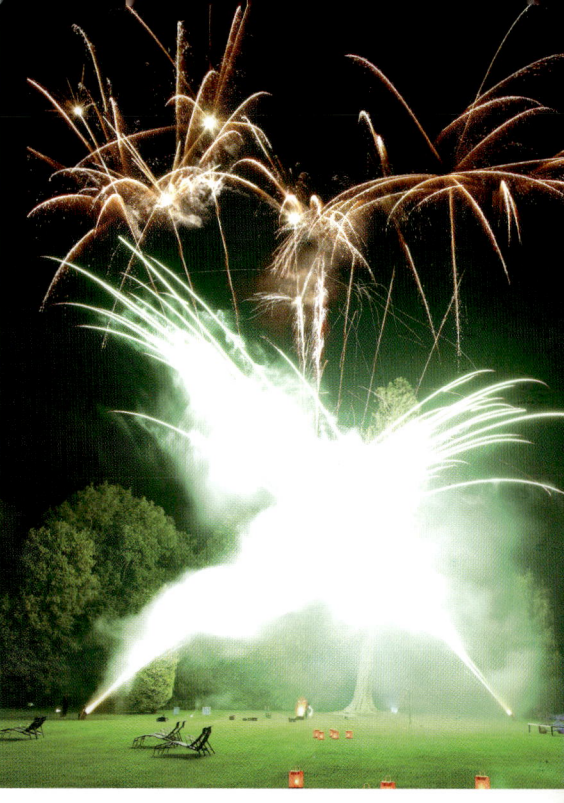

while holding down the shift key, you get a two-layer image in perfect register. By painting with black in a mask on the top layer you can reveal the detail from the layer below, thus combining the two images.

Marko then passes the final set of JPEGs – still on the same 120 Gb drive – to Julie who loads them into Iview Media Pro, building big previews at the same time. JPEGs load quickly and easily in Iview Media Pro, and within minutes, Julie is able to drag and drop the images into the final order that we want to show them to the client. The files are nearly in the correct order already because she has chosen to sort them by capture date. Some pictures were taken out of sequence; the table settings for instance and others will be jumbled especially the ones taken earlier in the day. Julie may remove a few 'similars' too.

Once Julie is happy that the set of images is in the correct order, she will renumber them like: smith001.jpg to smith350.jpg using the batch rename command.

The resulting set of JPEGs is considered our 'digital negatives' folder and from now on the file names of all images will stay the same. Julie backs up this set of JPEGs onto one DVD and that gets stored at her parents' house as the 'official' off-site backup. The Compact Flash cards are then cleared down and the JPEGs are copied onto Marko's main external computer drive. This is a 1Tb raid formatted, Firewire2 disk array.

If we ever need to return to the original JPEGs, we know that all the detail is there and the color is right. All the RAW files except the 'trashed' ones get thrown out at this stage. You may decide to keep your RAW files, it's up to you. We only keep the

Just a few simple adjustments helped this picture. Some correction of the verticals and a tidying up of the background was dealt with before the black and white version was created.

trashed RAW files until after the viewing when they too finally get thrown out if the client is happy with our coverage.

The next process is to bring the 350 or so chosen pictures to life. Marko does this using our 'speed editing' technique. Speed editing involves opening the JPEGs 10 at a time and working on selected areas using curves to add drama and a little cosmetic retouching. Occasionally some files need perspective correction or a little tidying with the clone tool. The aim is to get the pictures to 95% of their potential within 2 minutes each. Some will need 5 minutes while others are fine straight from Capture One. Over 2 days the whole set will be transformed by Marko. Each file is saved as a layered 8-bit TIFF. When Marko decides to make a file black and white, the color image is edited first, then it is duplicated on a new layer before making it monochrome using the channel mixer. Keeping the layers separate ensures

both color and mono versions are always available within the file without further editing. Any effort put in at this stage to improve the pictures is reflected in the value of the whole set. Having a consistently good set of images at the viewing will result in a big order. We never show a picture that is not flattering, so cosmetic changes always get done before the viewing.

Once all the image enhancements have been done, an action is run on the edited set to create a set of viewing files. A viewing file is made using Photoshop's 'auto fit' function to match our projector's resolution of 1280 pixels by 1024 pixels. It is flattened, sharpened, and has a 2 pixel white stroke applied to the inside edge before being converted to the standard RGB (Red Green Blue) color space. The next part of the action saves the files as JPEGs at quality 12 in a new folder. The folder of JPEGs is then loaded in a new Iview Media Pro catalogue

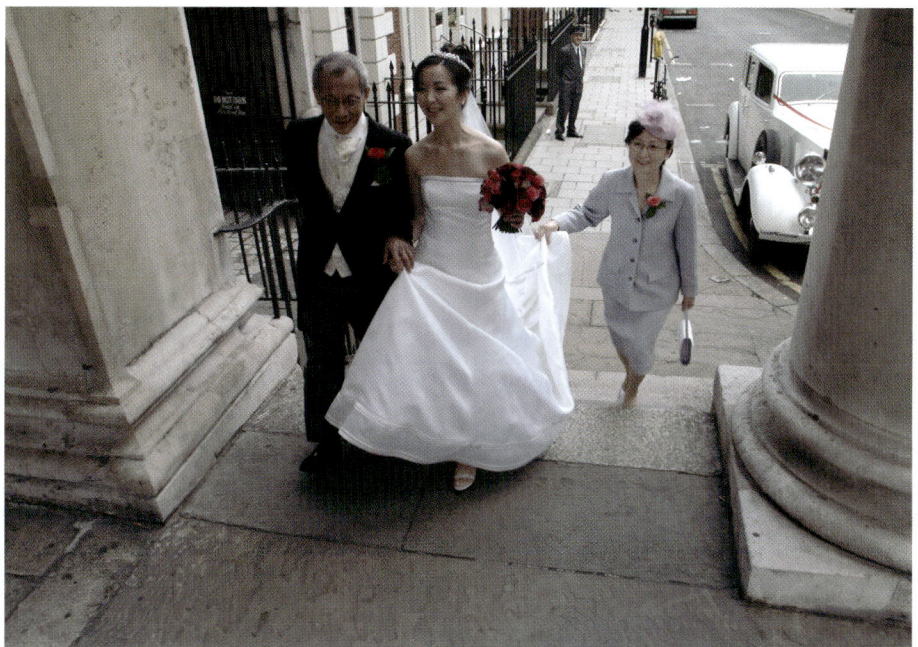

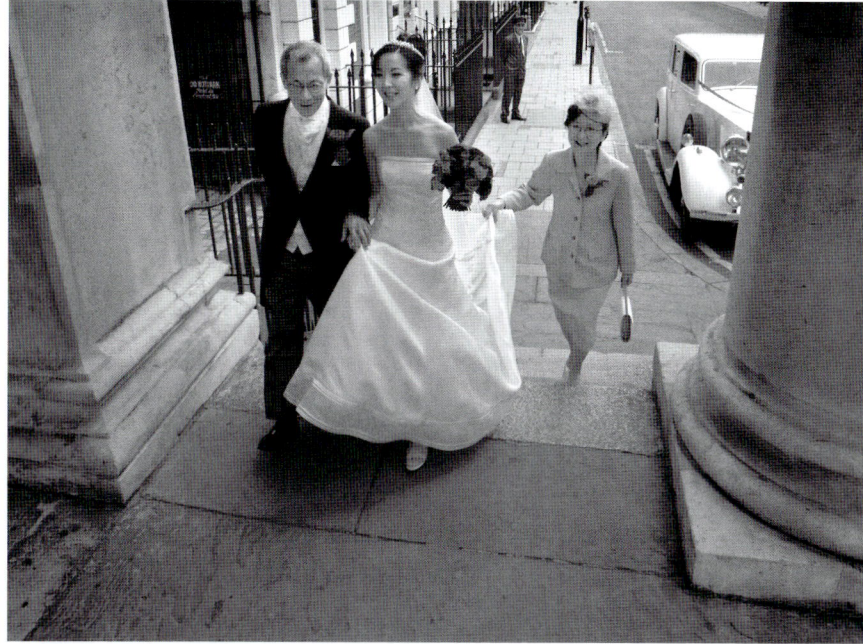

ready for the viewing. Each viewing file is between 1 and 2 Mb in size. These small files require less processing by the viewing room computer when making slideshows on the fly than full resolution pictures. This allows both smooth transitions and fast full screen previews during the viewing process.

For the viewing session our aim is to create separate sets of images for each of the wedding albums and picture frames ordered. We use the 'catalogue sets' feature in Iview Media Pro for this purpose. Unlike tagging, catalogue sets allow each image to be in as many places as you want. We may have as many as seven sets after a viewing:

- Bride and groom's album
- Bride's Mum's album
- Bride's Dad's album

- Groom's parents' album
- Multiframe for the kitchen
- Folder prints for thank you gifts
- Internet set for upload to our site
- Delete set, images never to be seen again.

Any additional editing requested by the clients at the viewing will be carried out on the high-resolution files. Occasionally, there will be requests for Marko to do his magic: straightening teeth, dropping dress sizes, putting hair back on the men, or taking years off the bride. This, along with other editing Marko sees fit, will be done prior to creating any album designs. Marko will only do further work on the files that have been bought. The album sets will be recreated with the high-resolution files by duplicating a selection of the original edited files into newly named folders.

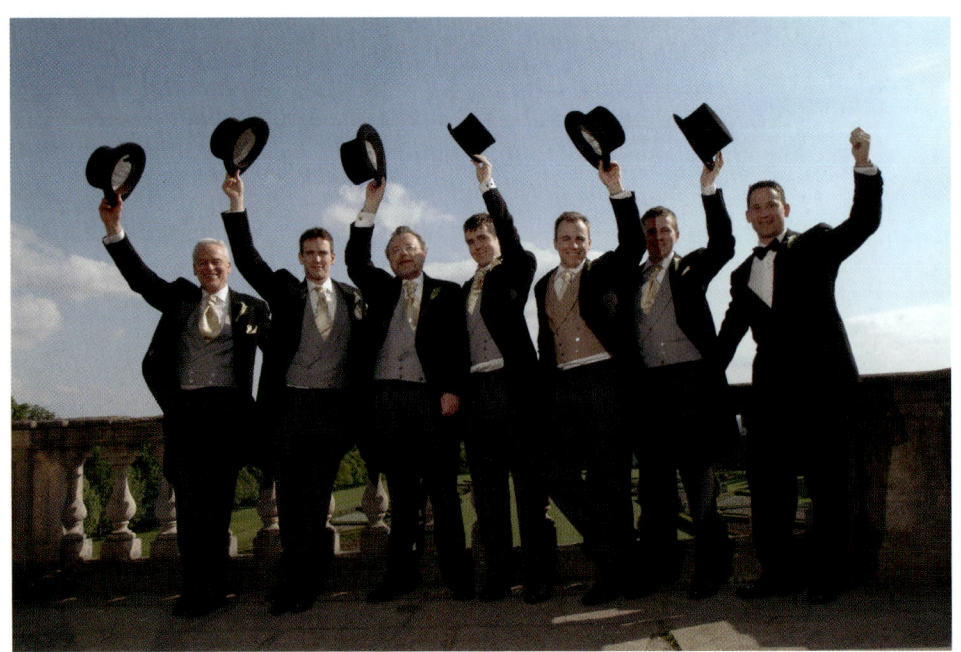 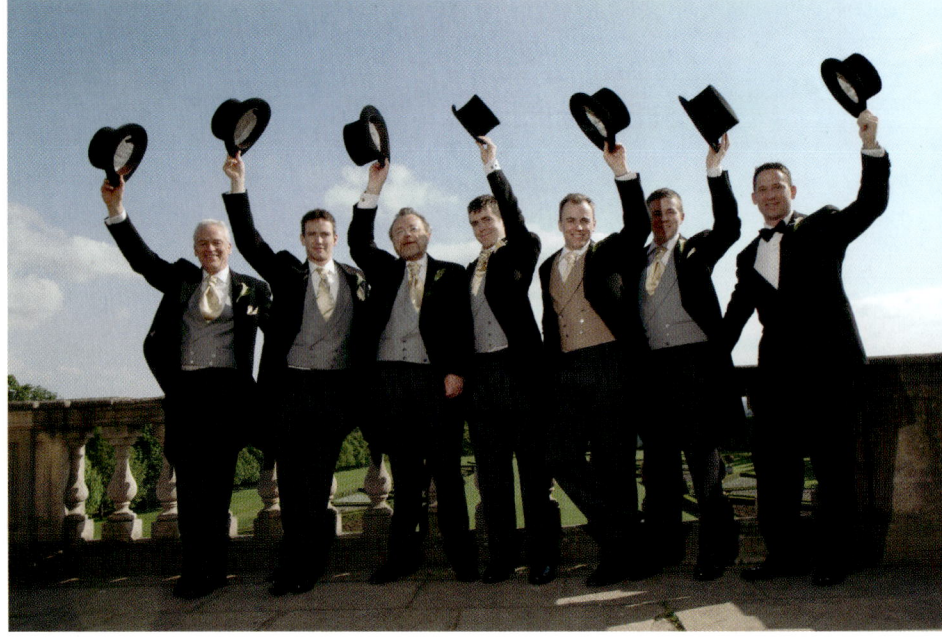

Marko now designs the albums for the clients using Jorgensen Album Designer (JAD). Once the layouts have been created he emails the clients with PDF versions of the plans for approval. After any required changes to the album plans have been made, Marko uses JAD to output the printing files as complete sheets for each page. The pages go through another Photoshop action to prepare them for print by our lab. This action shrinks the files very slightly to compensate for linear gains in the print process. It also sharpens the images and applies a small color balance tweak and finally a gamma adjustment using curves before saving each file as a flat sRGB JPEG. Each digital output device has its own characteristic. We create a new action for each device or lab we use to ensure we are getting the same look in our prints that we have on our calibrated cathode ray tube (CRT) screens. Our printing files are sent to our lab over the Internet using FTP software.

SHRINK TO FIT

Most commercial labs enlarge images to give their paper cutters some bleed to trim. If your album designs have print borders revealed under the overlays, or multiple images whose layout position is critical, the size of the borders and position of the prints on the page will vary unless some pre-shrinking has been applied to the files.

Fig. 8a & b   ISO 200 f/16 at 1/125th

The ushers were all in morning suit and one of the men was in a dinner jacket and without a hat. I asked him to pretend he had a hat and Marko did the rest back at the studio. I lit this picture with a splash of flash and as my flash sync speed on my Fujifilm S2 was just 1/125th I had to use f/16 to get the required exposure.

Once all the printing is complete, the job goes through to the album and frame construction phase. The digital files for the job get archived to DVD and the 1Tb hard drive eventually gets cleared down. The archiving is the last very important step in the post-production workflow. We archive the following files:

- The original untouched JPEGs (our digital negatives).
- The edited high-resolution multilayer TIFFs.
- The Iview Media catalog from the viewing.
- The JAD album designs.

These files are about 20 Gb in total and fit on four or five DVDs. The DVDs are consecutively numbered and their contents are entered in our dedicated Filemaker Pro database. We currently archive about 1Tb of data each year. We periodically spot-check our archive to ensure there is no deterioration of the data. Even our 10-year-old CD-Rs seem fine at the moment. All the disks are stored in a cupboard in the studio, and each disk is in a paper sleeve with a clear acetate window. Our backup disks containing the 'digital negatives' are at Julie's parents' house for safekeeping.

Other systems to consider when designing your back-up procedure include: using fireproof safes, magnetic tapes and readers, hard drive arrays, and online server space. Alternatively, if your product includes all the files at high resolution on disk, you could of course let your client take care of their own archiving.

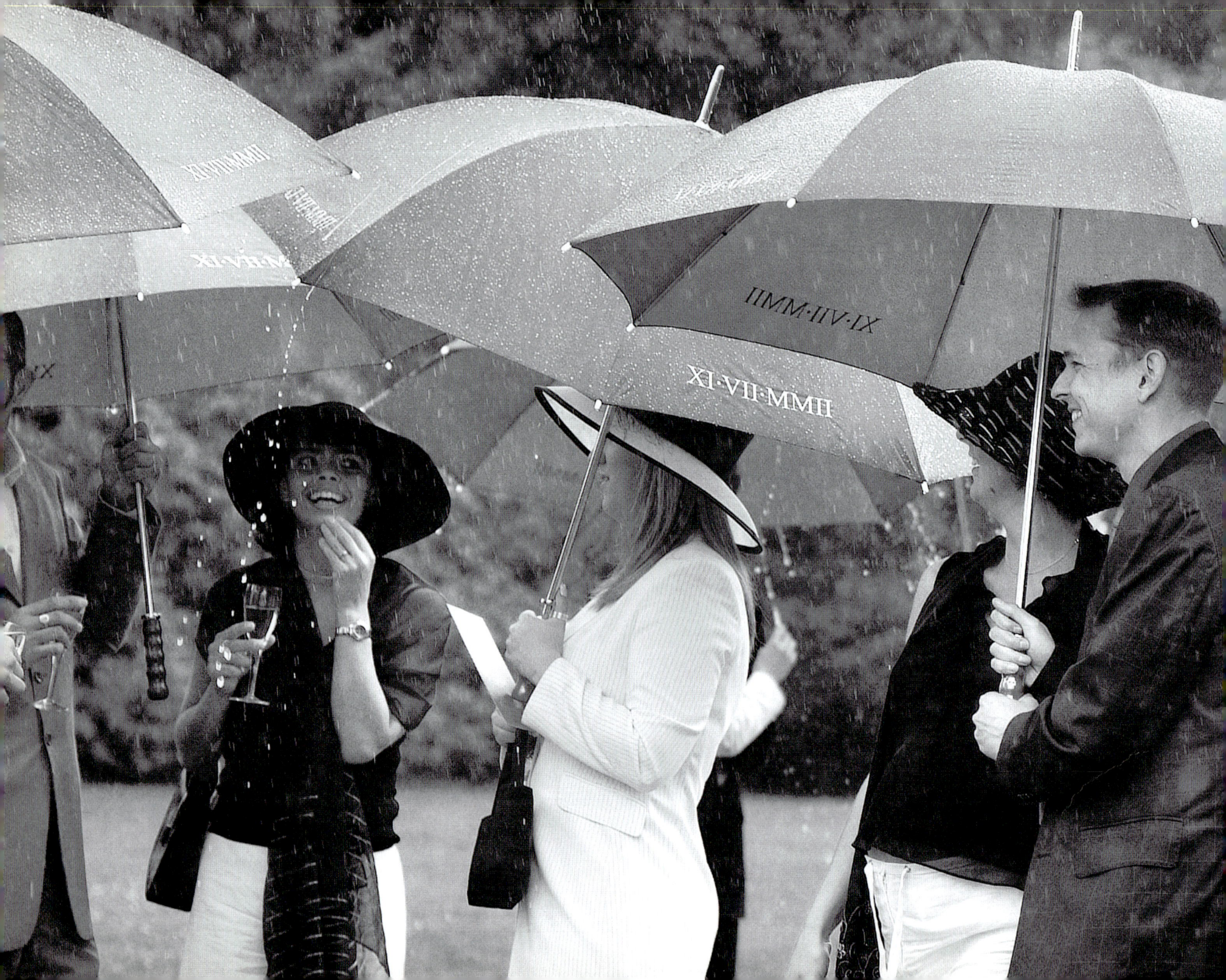

8
Life and Business Strategies

In this chapter, I'm going to lay my cards on the table. I'm going to tell you our story – with as much honesty as possible – how we struggled at the beginning, what we did to overcome our inexperience, and how we plan to achieve our goals in life. Theory is all very well but ultimately what counts are the actual choices we make and the lessons we learn along the way.

What is it that attracts people to the world of professional wedding photography? Like me, they have often come from settled careers that have allowed them to explore photography as an enjoyable hobby. Then, as their skills increase, they start to dream. Could photography be a way out of the rat race – a chance to earn good money doing something they really enjoy? Wedding photography is in constant demand and is considered easy pickings. Sometimes redundancy is all the excuse needed

for a new professional photographer to emerge from the crisis. This is the first part of the journey.

Everyone has their own story but this is ours. It goes in four stages, taking us well into the future.

STAGE 1: TAKING THE PLUNGE

One day I came home from my secure job at the BBC and told Julie that I had handed in my notice. I can see now that it was selfish of me to plunge us both into chaos, but I really expected

opposite

Fig. 1   ISO 800 f/4 at 1/470th

Rain happens in the United Kingdom. With a positive mental attitude even a wet wedding can be great fun.

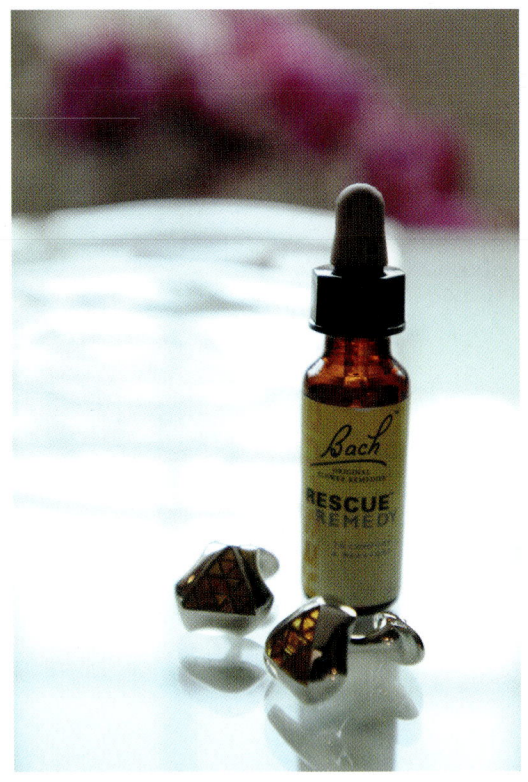

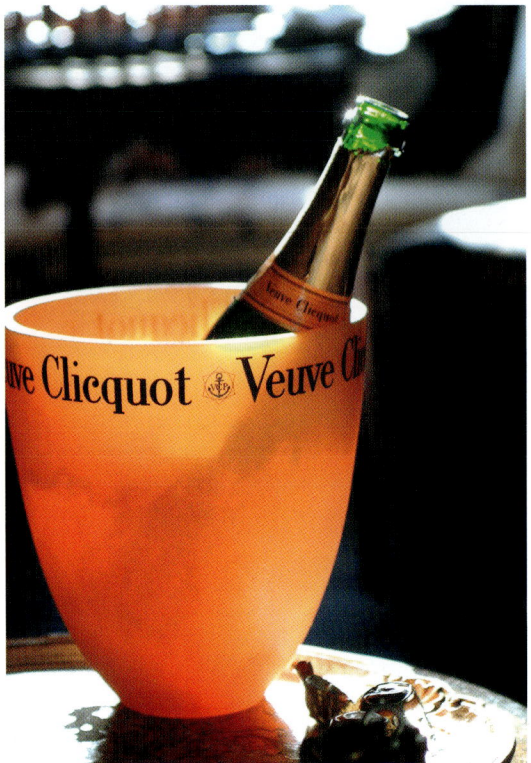

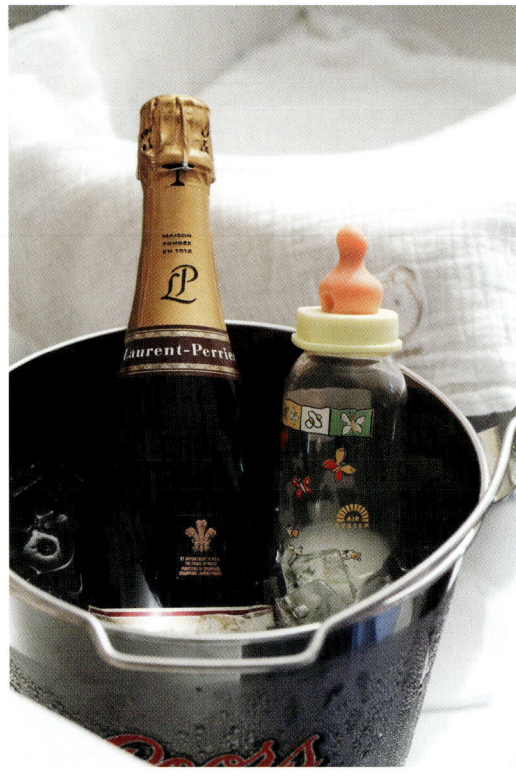

left

FIG. 2   ISO 800 f/3.4 at 1/180th

The cufflinks and the rescue remedy were on the grooms bedside table. I placed them on a glass coffee table to get this shot while he was in the shower. We all need help when the going gets tough.

middle

FIG. 3   ISO 1600 f/4 at 1/470th

This casual backlit shot of a champagne bucket set the mood in the album. Sometimes it pays not to interfere and tidy up a shot too much. The composition works well with the bucket resting on the left edge of the frame.

right

FIG. 4   ISO 800 f/4.8 at 1/45th

The baby's milk was a bit hot so into the ice bucket it went to cool down for a few seconds. It was there just long enough for Julie to capture this amusing picture.

FIG. 5   ISO 400 f/4 at 1/60th

This beautiful picture captures a great experience for the little princess.

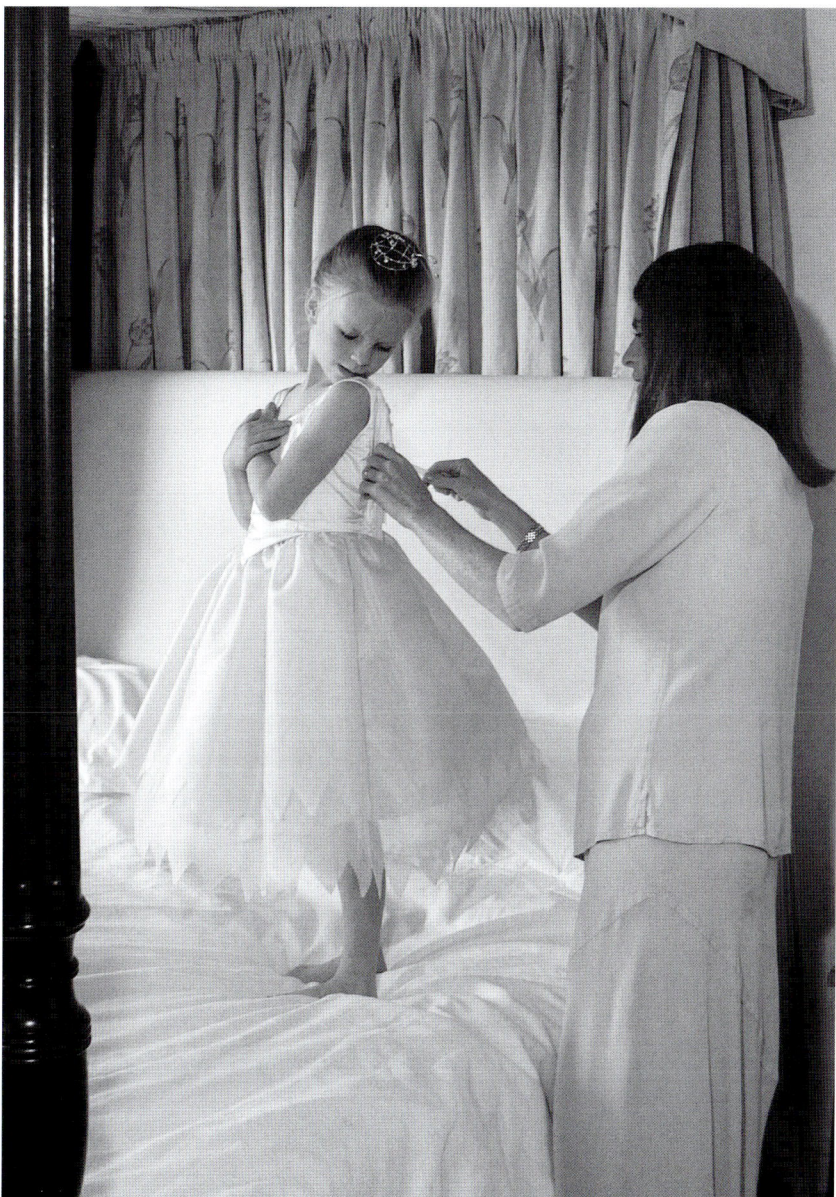

to make easy money as a photographer. I had a modicum of talent and I'm certainly no shirker. But – and this was a very big 'but' – I was totally unaware at that time how little I knew about business in general and especially about the business of photography.

We soon went deep into the red – £40,000 overdrawn – before I began to pull us into a profitable position. The turnaround came as a result of training. In fact, we invested £8000 of our bank's money on business training. Did it work? Absolutely. It was like a light being switched on. From day one, I learnt something that I'd never really considered: that I was in retail. I also had guidance in the form of a mentor: Catherine Connor refocused my perspective, taught me about the customer experience, setting goals, and more, far more.

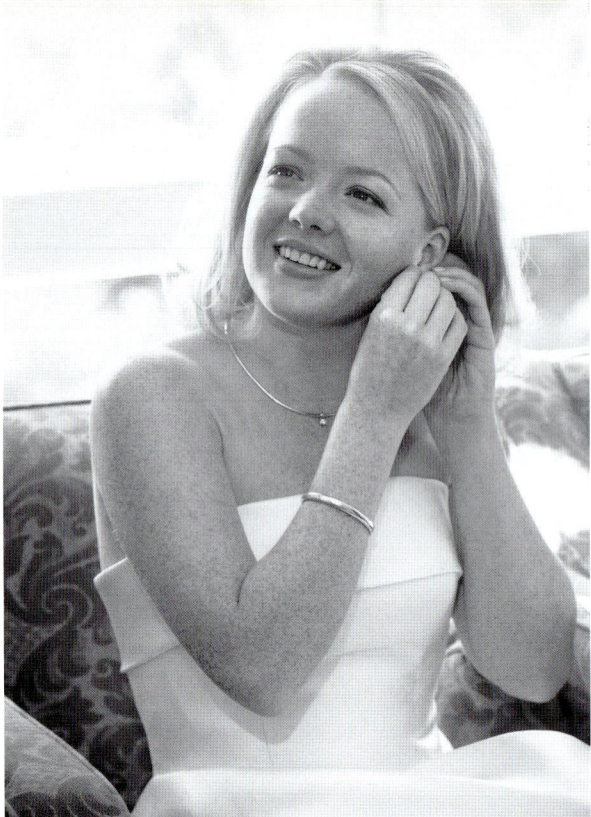

Fig. 6   ISO 400 f/4 at 1/60th

A splash of flash from a flashgun held above the camera gives this picture its clarity. Julie chose to increase the ambient exposure setting by one stop to keep the bright background light.

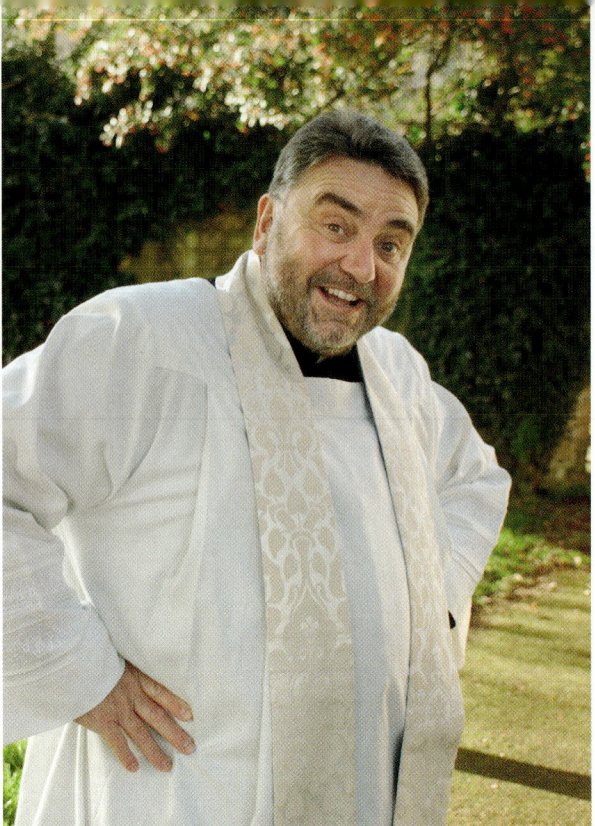

Fig. 7   ISO 800 f/4 at 1/750th

Creating a rapport with the priest is a good idea to help the ceremony flow. I had been previously asked by the bride to take a picture of the priest on the wedding day. He was flattered and kindly obliged.

STAGE 2: EXPANDING THE TEAM

Then came the next stage in the familiar path of a wedding photographer. Having learned to plan ahead, sort tasks, and manage personal time, it became obvious that we needed to expand our team. Taking on two full-time staff in year two saved me from the 2:00 AM finish each night. This is a scenario that so many start-up business managers go through. With two new staff on the books, our fixed costs hit new highs and throughput of work had to rise dramatically to feed the beast our business had become. So we grew from 25 weddings per annum up to 40 weddings. Julie became a photographer in her own right, and had a meteoric rise through the ranks to the top echelons, much to the annoyance of some 'old school' fellows. Within a year she was 'wedding photographer of the year' and setting new standards. I was a lucky guy. Not only did I have a wonderful partner, I had one who really appreciated photography! A greater percentage of our workload was now spent taking pictures. Our staff handled the darkroom duties,

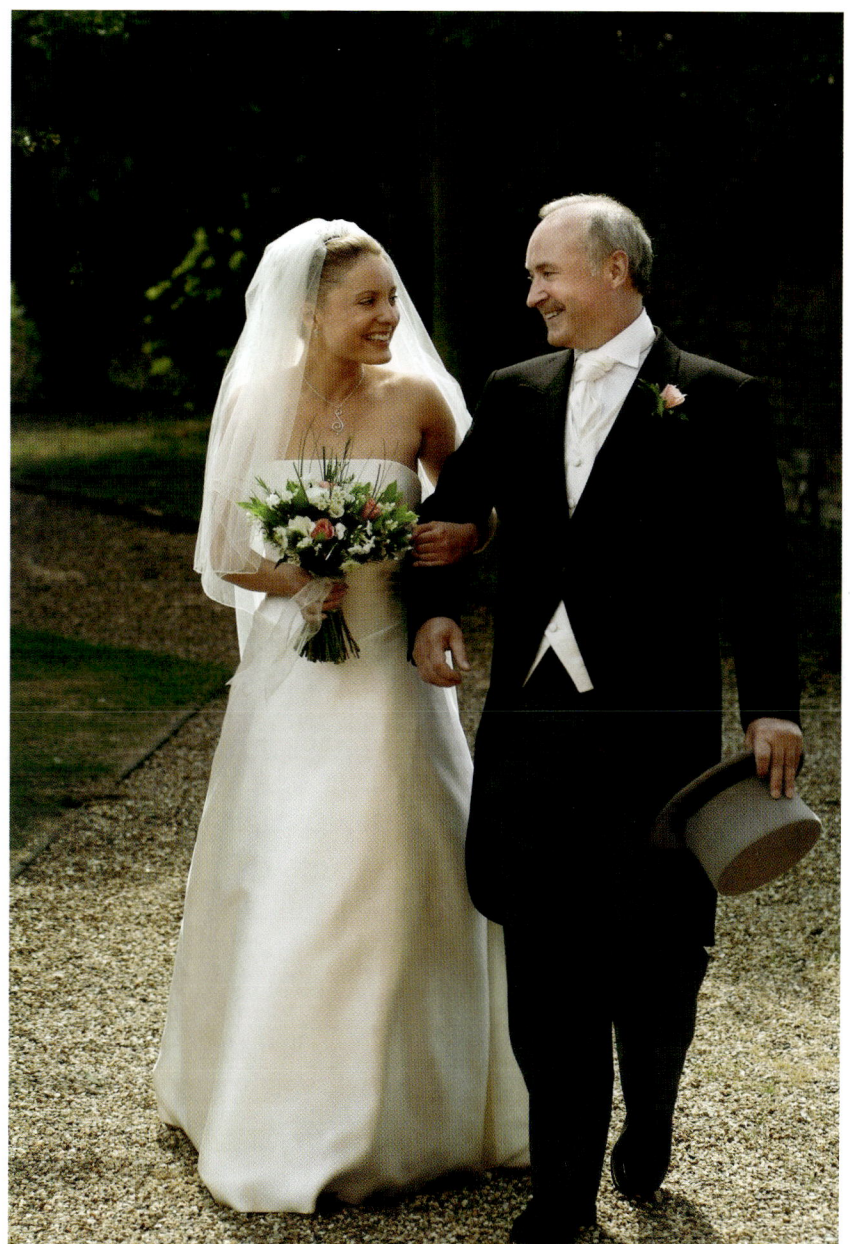

FIG. 8   ISO 200 f/4 at 1/500th

I knew this shot was going to happen and I was ready and prepared when it did.

ordering stock, gluing and sticking of the wedding albums, and most of the general office tasks.

STAGE 3: A DEDICATED WORKSPACE

We had to move. Having staff working in our home was not fun – we needed our own space – somewhere to think or cry! Clearly a dedicated workspace was required so that we could entertain clients and so that our staff could perform their duties in comfort and with pride. The simple things like having a dedicated production area for album construction is a must. Working on tasks like that on the kitchen table is not recommended, especially if you have children.

OK, so you've done it. You've become good at your job and built up the business. Additional staff now allows you to concentrate

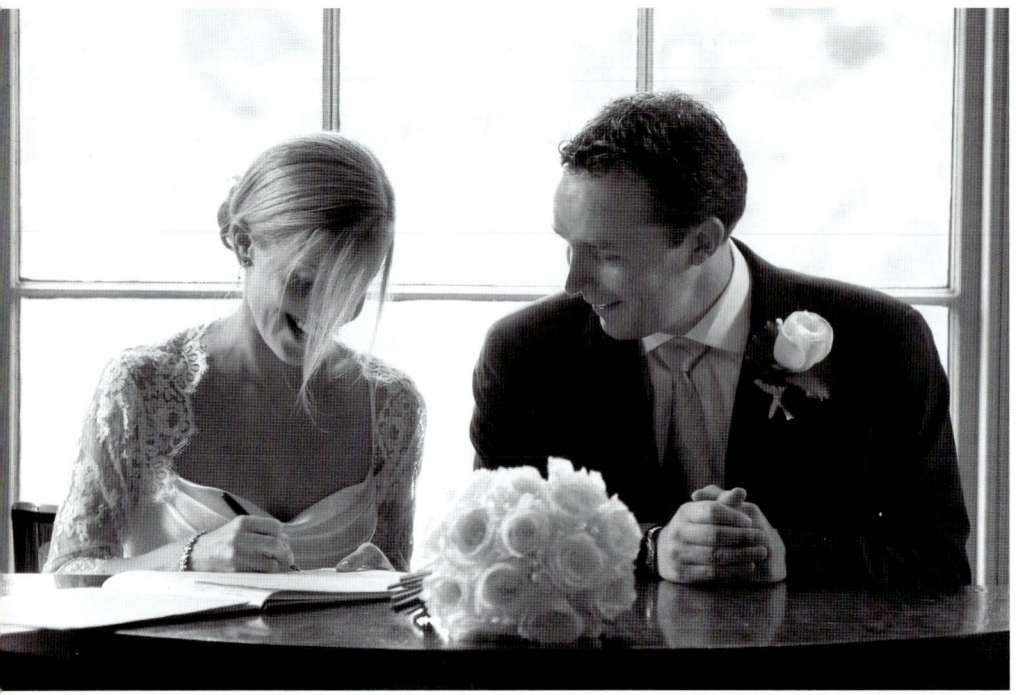

Fig. 9   ISO 800 f/4 at 1/125th

One stop of exposure compensation was needed to capture the delightful expressions on this couple's faces.

on the creative stuff. You've moved to premises that allow a dedicated workspace. Is it enough? The majority of social photographers seem to think so. They've got their name over the door and are considered successful. As the years go by, a succession of staff come and go until one day, retirement looms. But how many have managed to plan an income for the next 30 plus years in retirement?

The truth is that for decades, rather than owning the business themselves, the business has owned them! It's far too easy to think that you have arrived when your name is in lights above the door of your studio and your photography is in demand from your local community. But even with this level of success, taking extended holidays is expensive because if you're not shooting, you're not earning. Ill health is a big risk too and some sort of income protection insurance might be a wise purchase. At this stage in a career, if Stage 4 is to be reached, some forward thinking is needed.

STAGE 4: THE GOLDEN AGE

The lucky few photographers who used Stage 3 to plan an exit strategy, will build a business with real value. They will own the business and not be a slave to it. Stage 4 is the golden

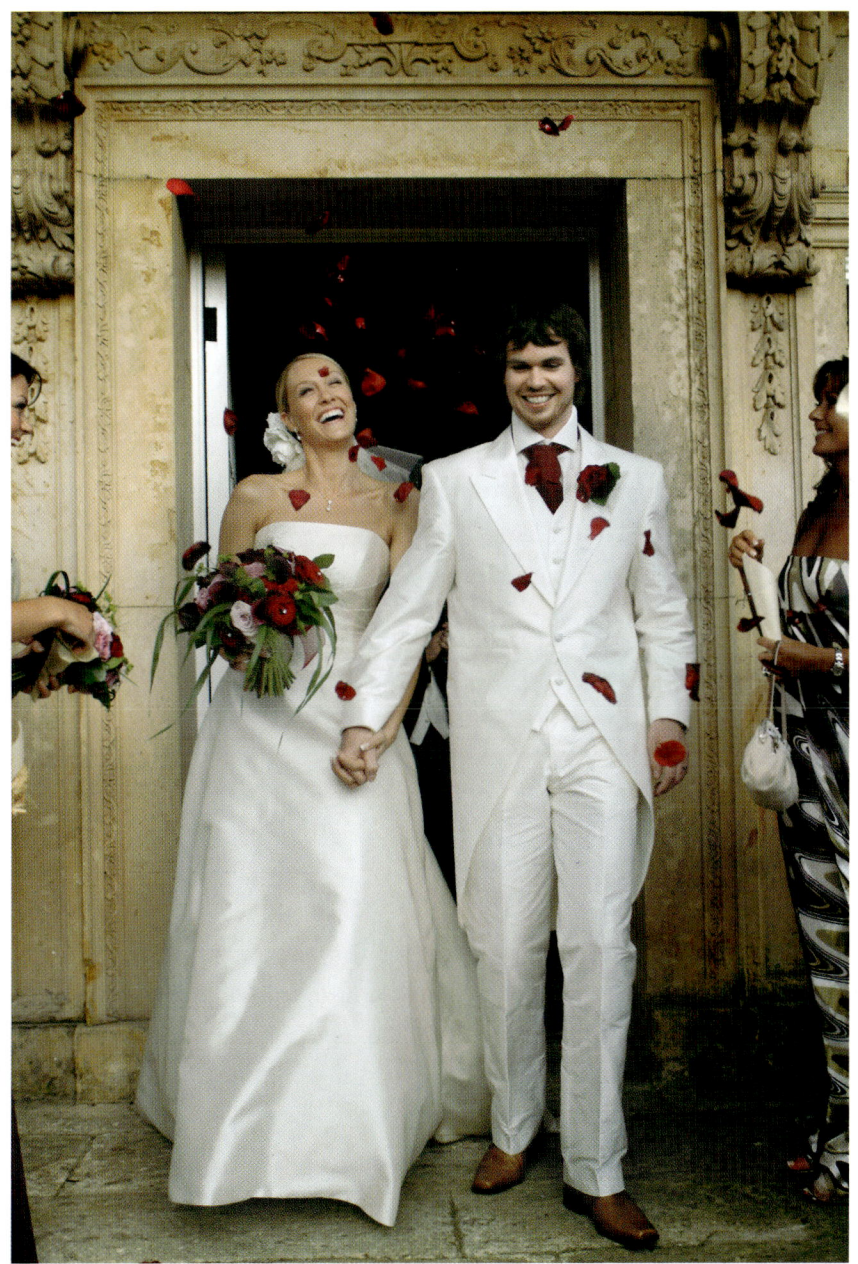

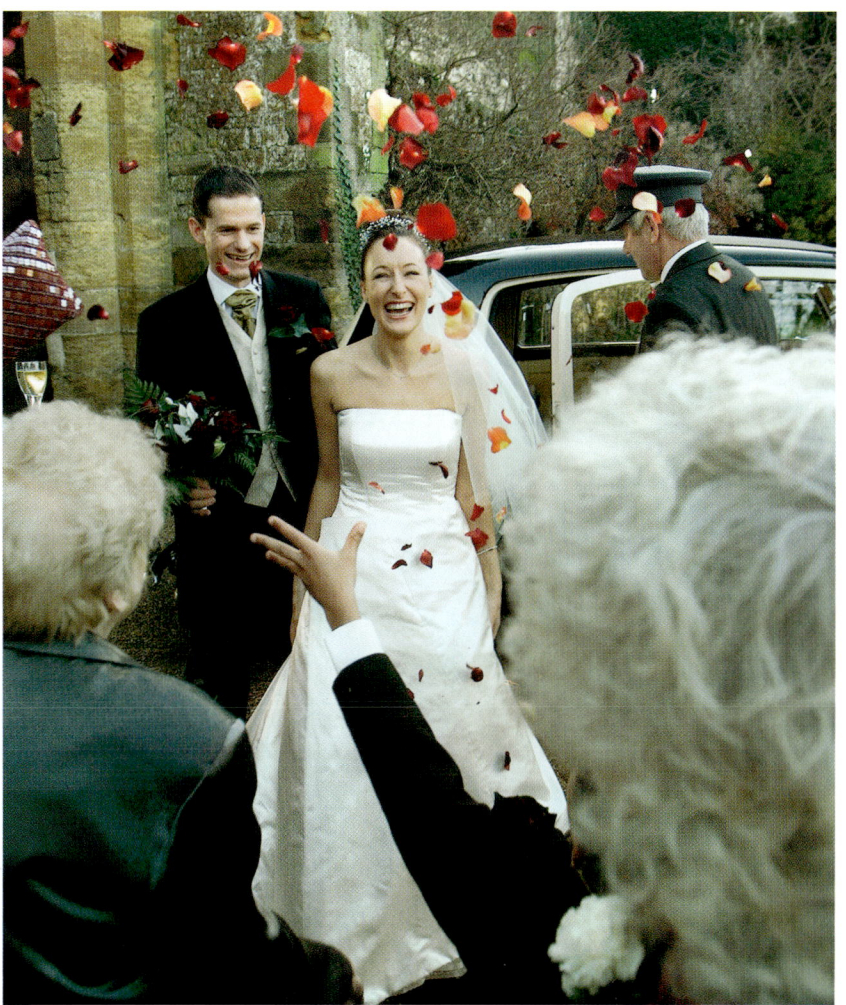

FIGS 10 & 11   ISO 400 f/4 at 1/1000th and 1/450th respectively

These two pictures illustrate very different approaches to photographing a similar situation. I set up the first picture by asking the guests to form two lines with their confetti. I walked backward as the couple came toward me. In the second picture, I chose to mingle in the crowd and shoot the moment in a reportage way. The guest point of view is an interesting one to shoot but beware of overdoing it. Out of focus backs of heads in the foreground of images are rarely attractive.

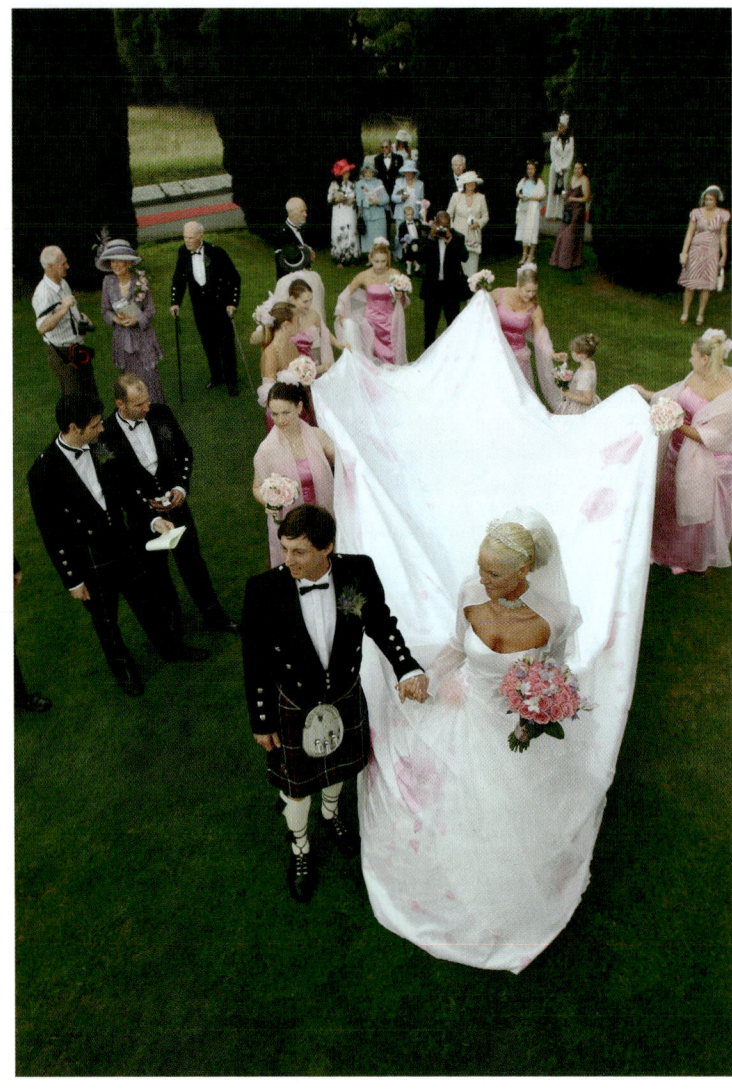

above

FIG. 12   ISO 200 f/4 at 1/360th

I used my camera on my monopod held way up high trick to get this picture of the bride's dress. I used an air release to trigger the shutter.

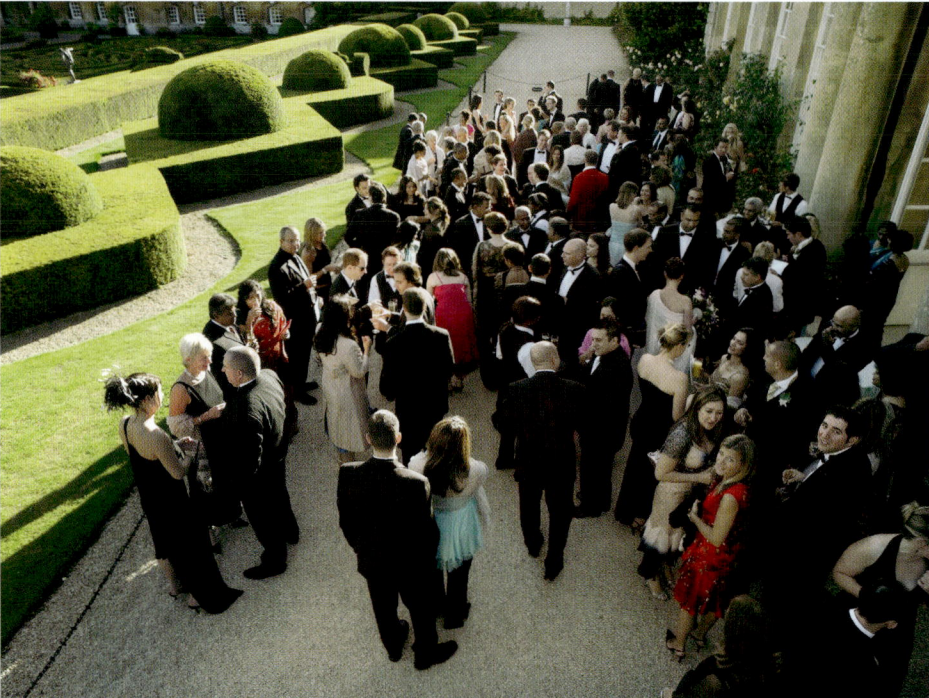

FIG. 13   ISO 400 f/9.5 at 1/125th

High viewpoint pictures like this are always in demand by our clients. This is a scene-setting picture that allows a series of milling pictures to follow in the album.

age. Imagine this, you have created the ultimate moneymaking machine; you have the right staff, including photographers you have trained, and a manager in place at your studio. You can let the business run itself!

At this point getting out becomes a real option. For example, you could pass the business on to a son or daughter to run while maintaining a directorship. This is a good way to secure an ongoing income well into retirement – assuming that your

Fig. 14 ISO 800 f/9.5 at 1/360th

Some clients like creative intervention. I set each guy in their own place in turn and asked the bride to 'drape.' I held the camera above my head to get a slightly higher viewpoint. I took the picture and then immediately checked I hadn't chopped any limbs off by accident.

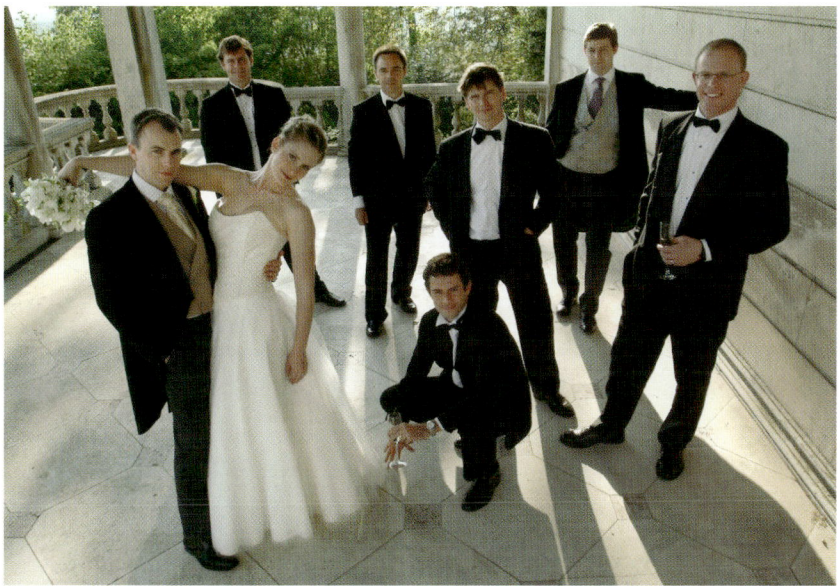

children are ready for the responsibility. Another option is to sell franchises or set up licensees. For this to work, you will need to have created an exceptional business with repeatable systems, a business model that can be easily duplicated. Another option is to sell the business. If your business has had three consecutive years of growth and will run without you, it has real value and someone will buy it. By now you will be aware that Stage 4 is all about options. These choices later in life are valuable, and if you start to plan your exit strategy now, you too can have options when you want out.

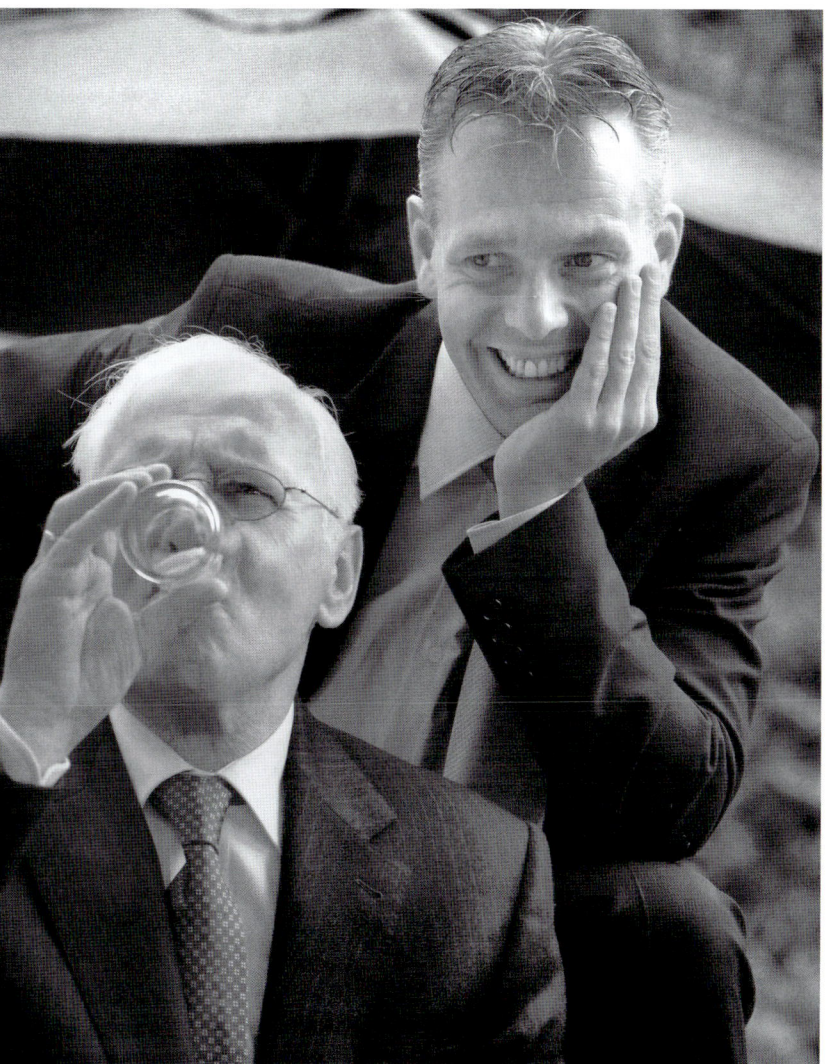

above

Fig. 15 ISO 800 f/4 at 1/725th

This picture of a dad and his son at the reception was one of those seen moments that needed a lightening reaction to capture.

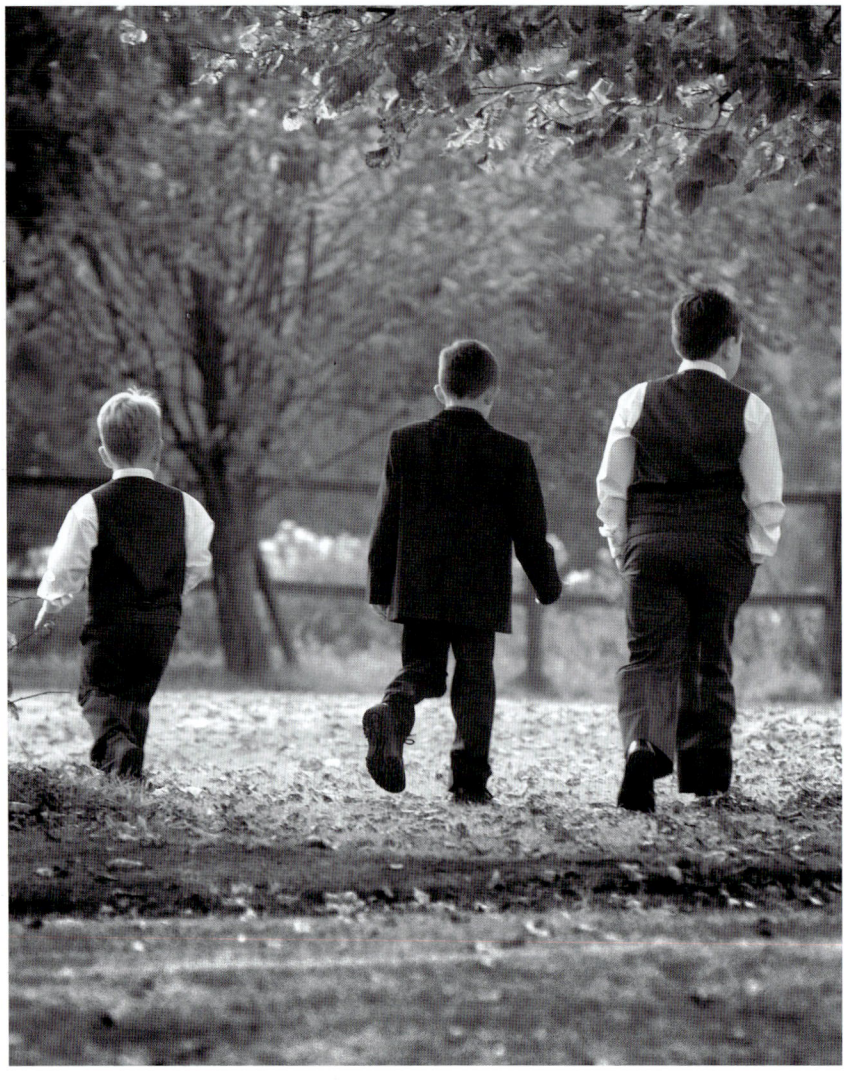

above

Fig. 16   ISO 400 f/4 at 1/210th

I saw these boys wander off and I had time to swap my lens to a 200 mm zoom to capture this lovely shot.

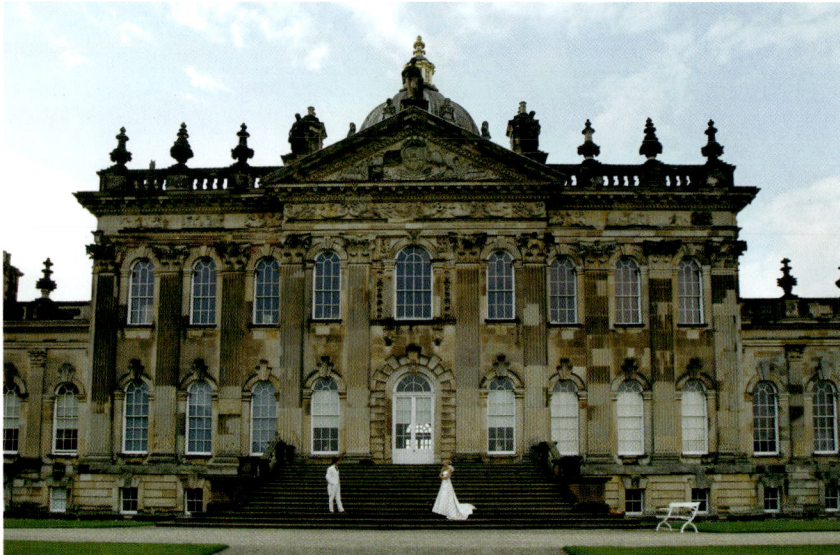

Fig. 17   ISO 200 f/4 at 1/250th

Sometimes the best way to show scale is to go for a jog with a telephoto lens and to shoot from a distance. I placed the couple against the dark steps to show off their white clothes. It's a brave thing to have done but the picture is worth it.

But what about us? There we were, stuck in Stage 3 with a studio, staff, overheads, and a full diary of commitments. We were on the treadmill with no way off. What would happen if we became unable to shoot weddings? Did we own the business or did the business own us?

Clearly, it was time for some further training. We needed to become entrepreneurs, in charge of our own route and keeping the long-term in mind. After all, I wasn't expecting to be shooting weddings in 25 years' time. It was at this time that Gregory Haddock, better known as 'The Profit Doctor,' became our business coach and sounding board for all my whacky ideas.

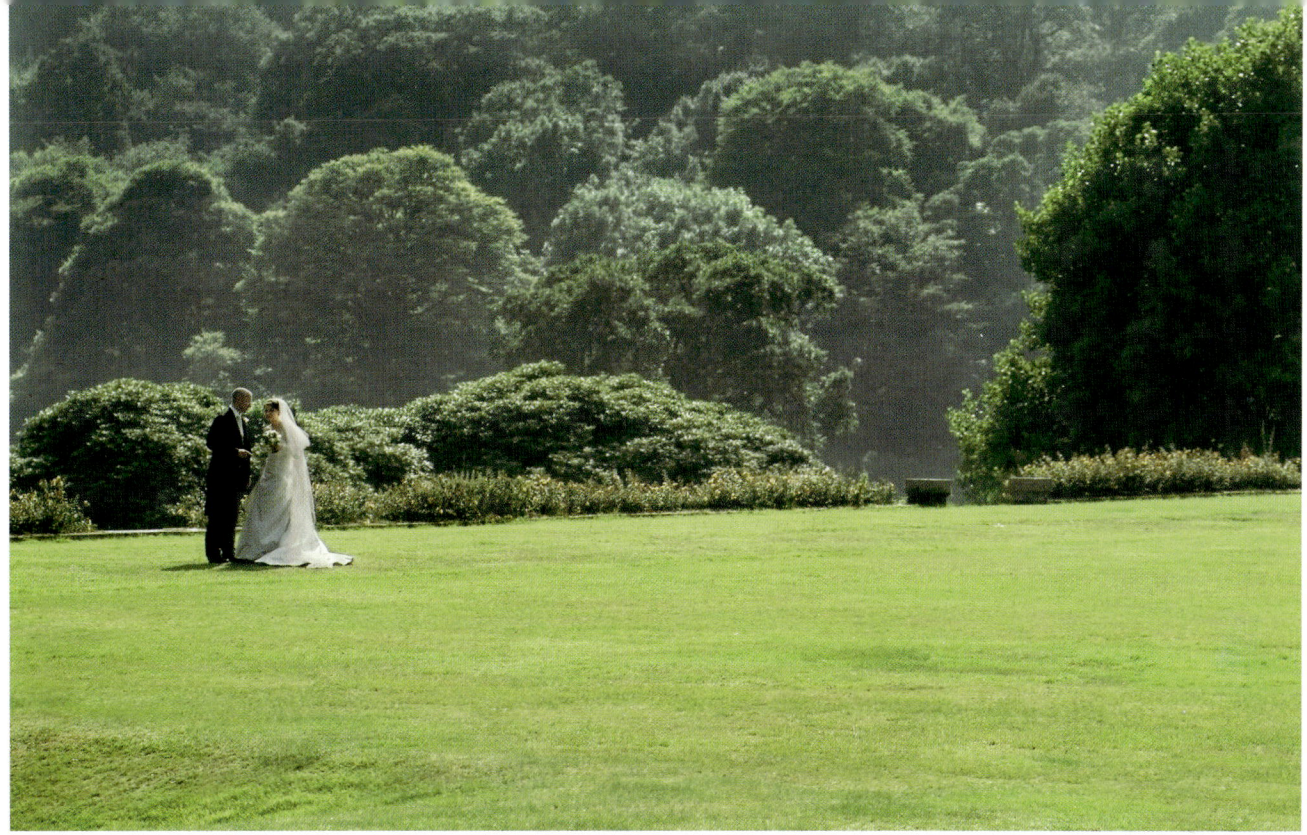

Fig. 18 ISO 200 f/4 at 1/3000th

This is another figure in the landscape shot taken on a long lens to exclude the sky.

He guided us through the transition and toward Stage 4. For a multitude of personal and financial reasons, this was no easy task. He set out a simple strategy that Catherine Connor had begun 5 years before. Catherine was our mentor and coach from Years 2 to 4 and remains a good friend and source of inspiration to Julie and me to this day. Let me share their strategy with you.

PERSONAL GOALS

First, you'll need to write out your personal goals. Do this at least annually because in life, priorities and circumstances are apt to change. So decide what you *really* want and write it down. The process can be very therapeutic. Take a look at our goals from early 2007:

- Have more time at weekends for Francesca, our 10-year-old daughter.

- Reach a financial comfort zone, without a mortgage and with a continued income by 50. (Have enough assets at work so that our lifestyle is affordable and work itself is optional.)

- Have more family weekend breaks, and a better quality of leisure time.

- Travel the world and have at least two great trips a year.

- Have a long-term offshore base for 3 months of the year in 8 years' time.

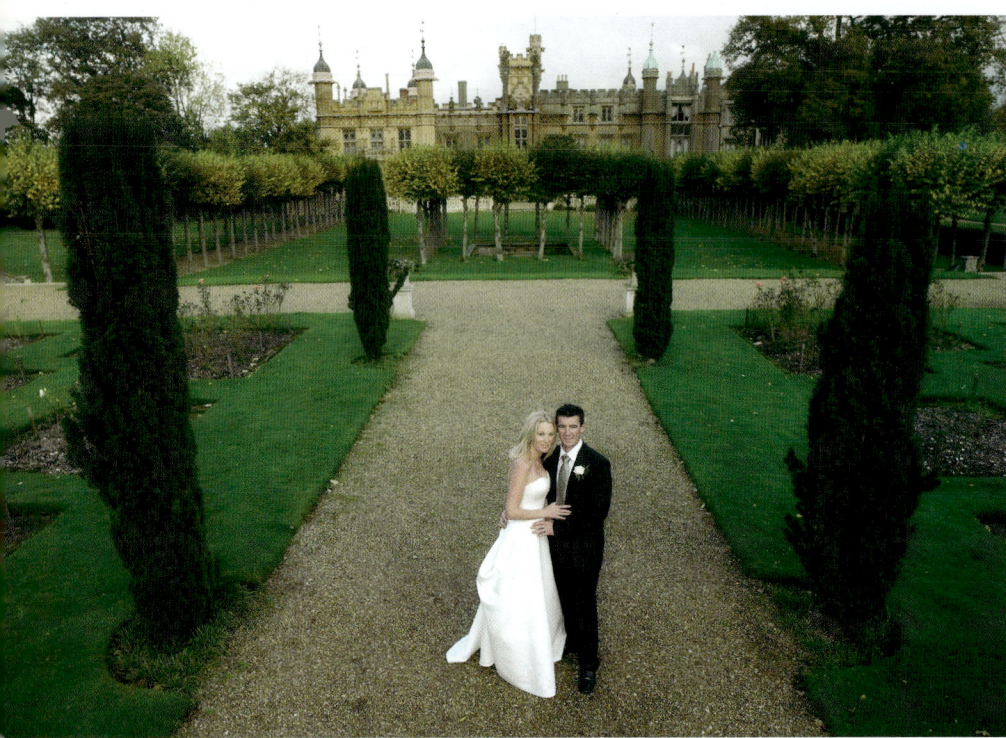

Fig. 19 . ISO 400 f/9 at 1/200th

To get Knebworth house in the background I had to hoist my camera above my head on the monopod and guess the framing. By exposure three I had it spot on. This process relies on trial and error using the image on the back of the camera as the feedback.

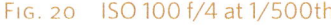

Fig. 20   ISO 100 f/4 at 1/500th

I used a low viewpoint for this beautiful bridal portrait. The Queens gate to St James Park in London made an ideal setting and contre-jour sunlight did the rest.

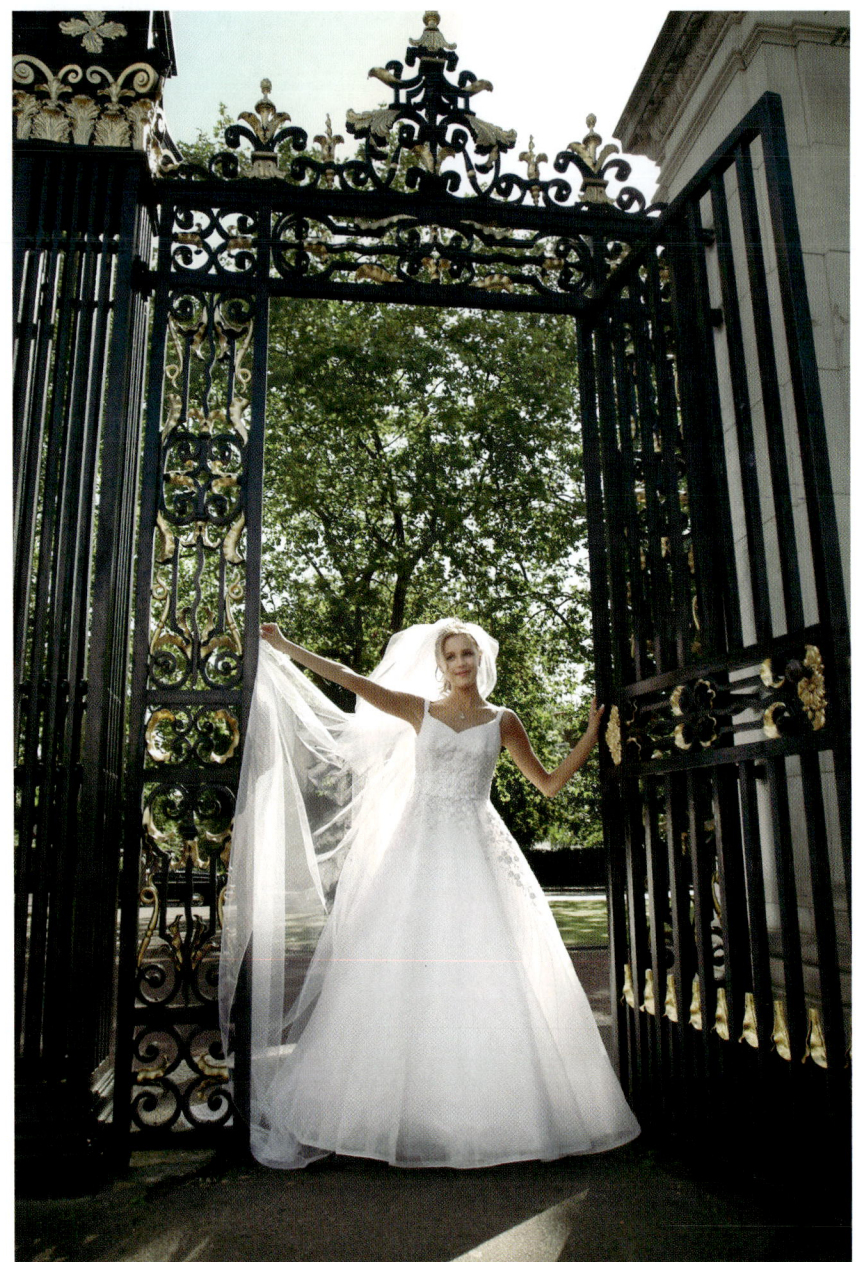

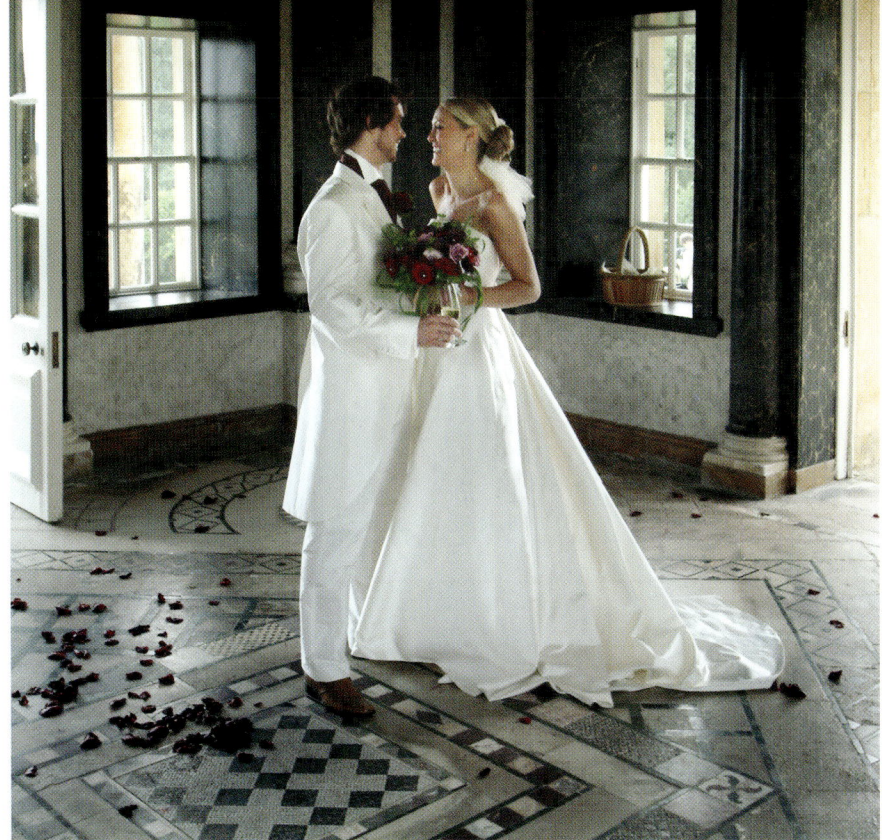

FIG. 21   ISO 800 f/4 at 1/60th

The couple's position is critical in this picture. They are symmetrically set against the dark panels and rim lit from two sides. The bride's wonderful expression makes this picture sing.

This seems quite a simple list and most of the items are obvious. Writing them down helped polarize our thoughts and gave us a horizon to aim for. When we reach that point there will be another horizon in front of us with a new set of goals that may include grandchildren for instance.

BUSINESS GOALS

The next task is to set out your business goals. Business goals are designed to deliver the necessary resources to meet personal goals. Here are the business goals I set out in January 2007.

- Improve cash flow and make more consistent profit in the portrait business.
- Eliminate all remaining business debt in 2007 (studio build overspend –oops!).

- Build the portrait business up to the planned four shoots a week level. Two baby or pregnancy shoots for Julie and two family or child shoots for me.
- Double the size of the www.lovegroveconsulting.com arm of the business by running more workshops and training events.
- Engage licensees to shoot weddings. This will free up most of our weekends for Francesca. It will enable us to reduce the number of weddings that Julie and I shoot personally while maintaining our brand position.
- Finish the Wedding Book and start on the Portrait Book.
- Offer our digital picture editing services to other photographers around the world.
- Damien to become a freelance writer contributing articles to four magazines on a monthly basis. This will help to maintain our brand position and provide personal income to finance travel ambitions.
- Julie to explore her opportunities to offer consultation services to one sector of the property market.

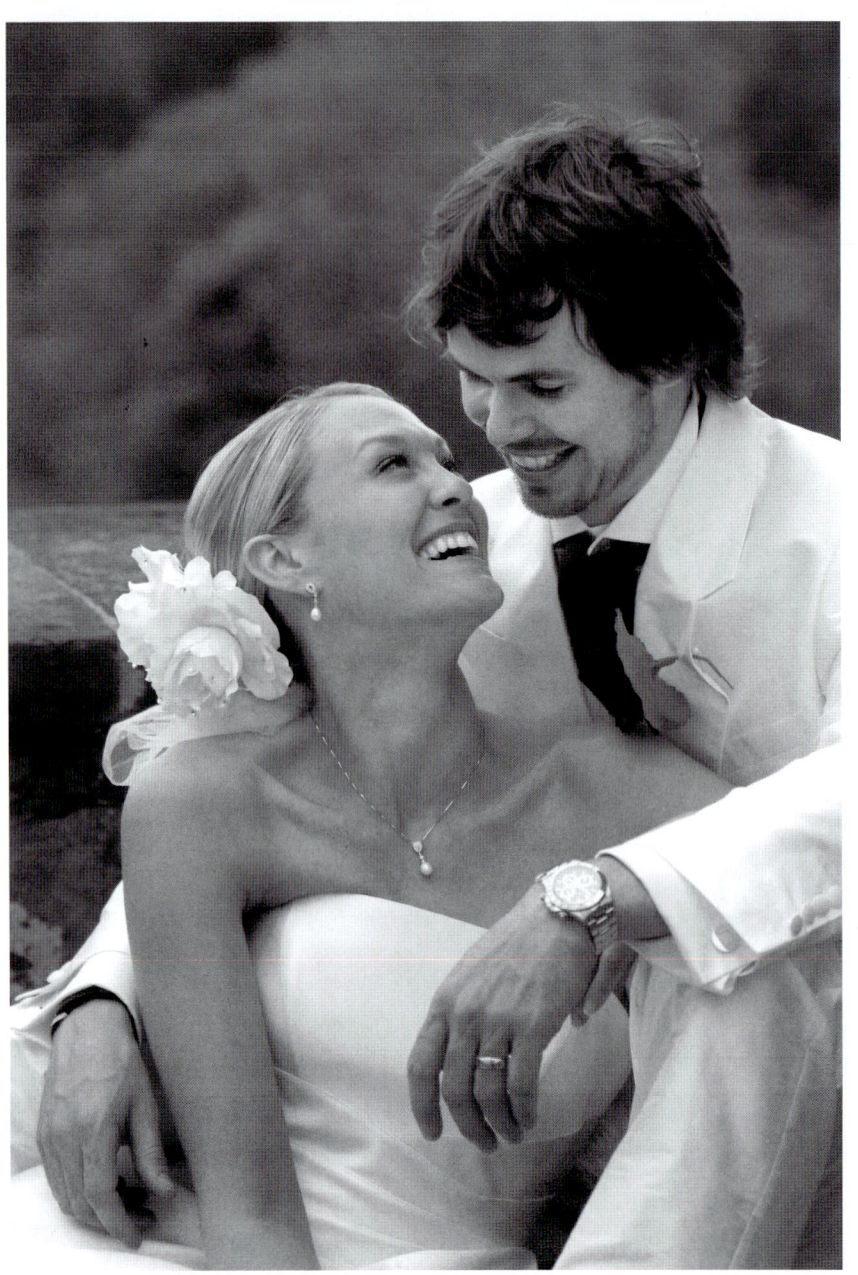

Fig. 22   ISO 800 f/4 at 1/1440th

I used a set of steps to offset the couple's heights in this image. It was one of a series of four pictures taken on the steps. The love and fun evident in the picture does the rest.

opposite

Figs 23 & 24   ISO 400 f/4.8 at 1/500th and ISO 200 f/4 at 1/30th

I was on the inside looking out and Julie was on the outside looking in for these two pictures taken just moments apart.

This set of business goals shows diversification. On the other hand, it may be more useful for you to narrow your trading scope. For instance, if you photograph both portraits and weddings and you find the portraits use a lot of your resources without delivering good profit, you might decide to focus your energies on further developing your already successful wedding business. This is exactly what Julie and I did in Year 2. By Year 3 we had almost dropped portraits all together. Then in Year 5 we built a purpose-made studio with portraiture in mind and restarted our portrait business from scratch. Portraiture is now a major sector in our business portfolio.

I suggest you get a pen and paper and start setting out your own goals. Begin with easy-to-achieve targets and focus on the issues and opportunities you have at the moment. You may find

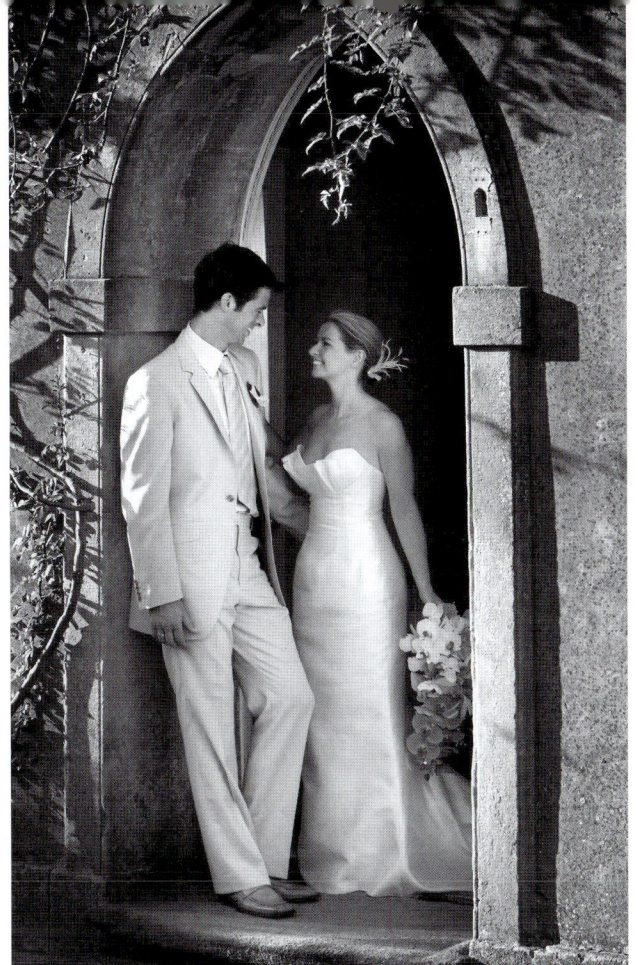

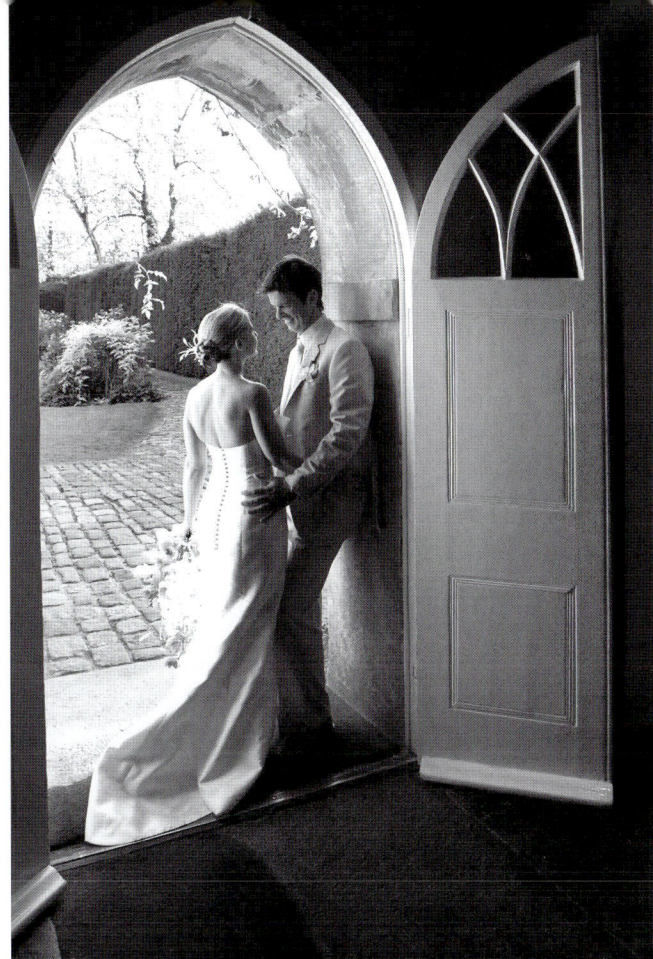

it easier to time stamp your targets with Year 1 goals, Year 2 goals, and so on.

S.W.O.T.

This stands for Strengths Weaknesses Opportunities and Threats – the four most useful indicators that a business can build on. You can divide a sheet of paper into four equal rectangles by drawing a line across the centre both vertically and horizontally. Label each of the sections accordingly and start writing. If you want to split sections of your business or personnel then do a separate chart for each.

Strengths and weaknesses can be virtual or abstract as well as physical. Don't hold back or be too optimistic when doing your analysis.

A good repertoire of poses and shots that work to convey different moods and emotions is vital to be able to capture the spirit of the day. There is no eye contact with the camera in any of these pictures.

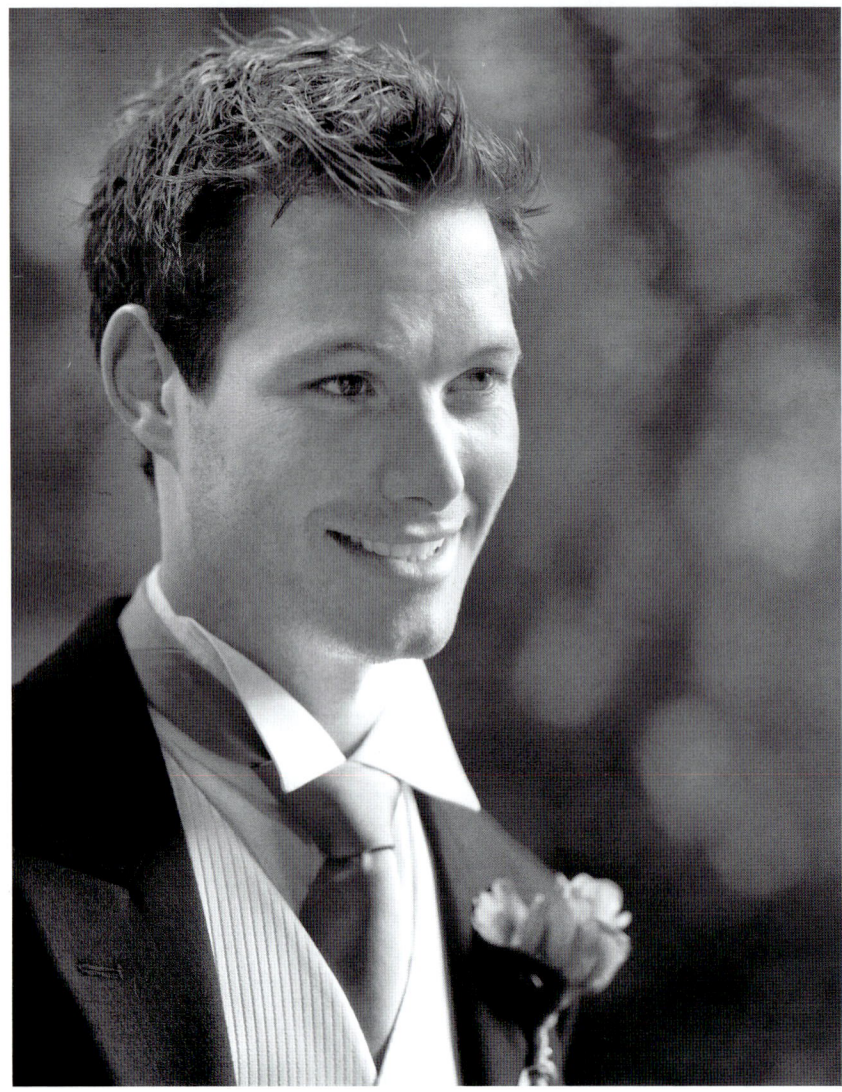

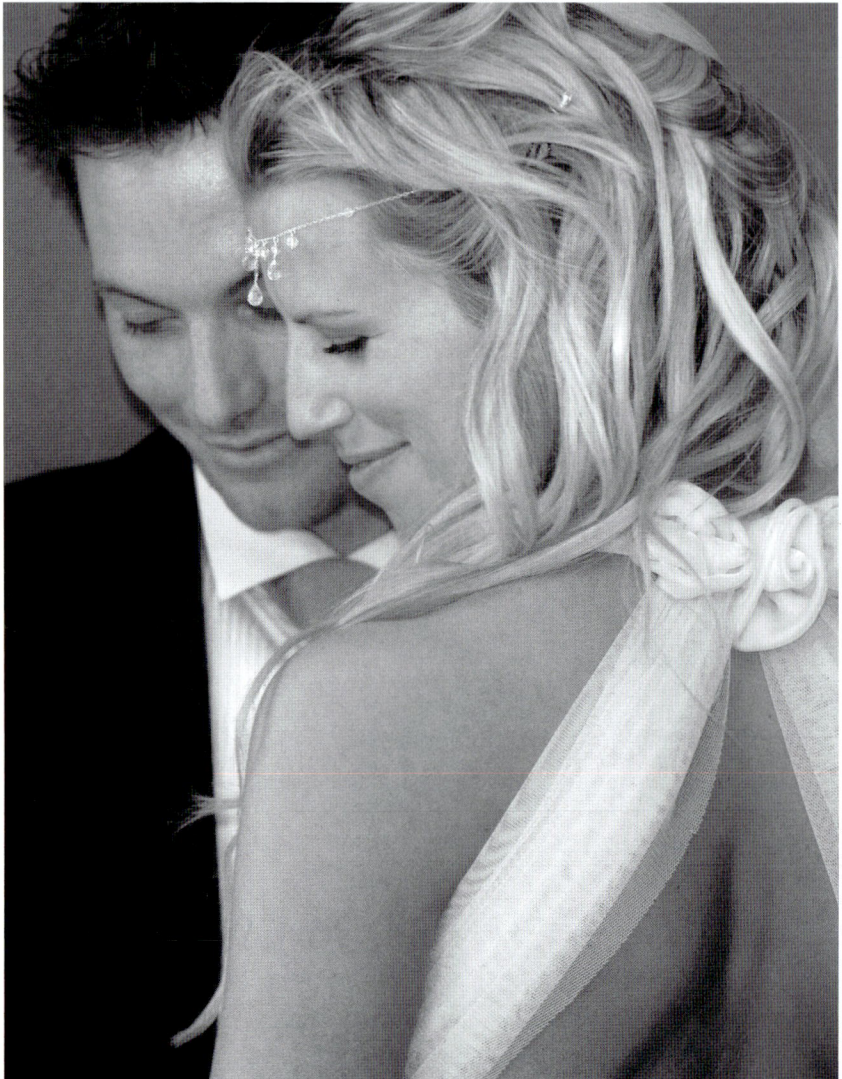

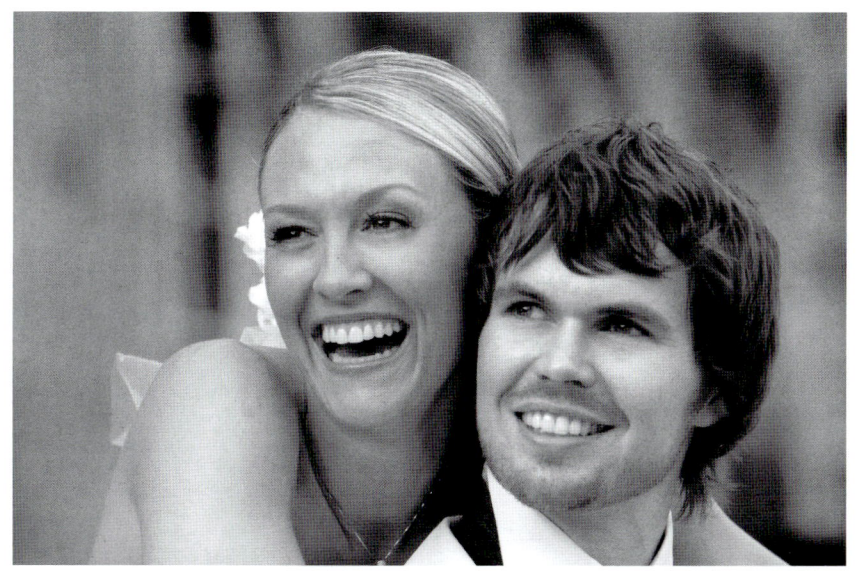

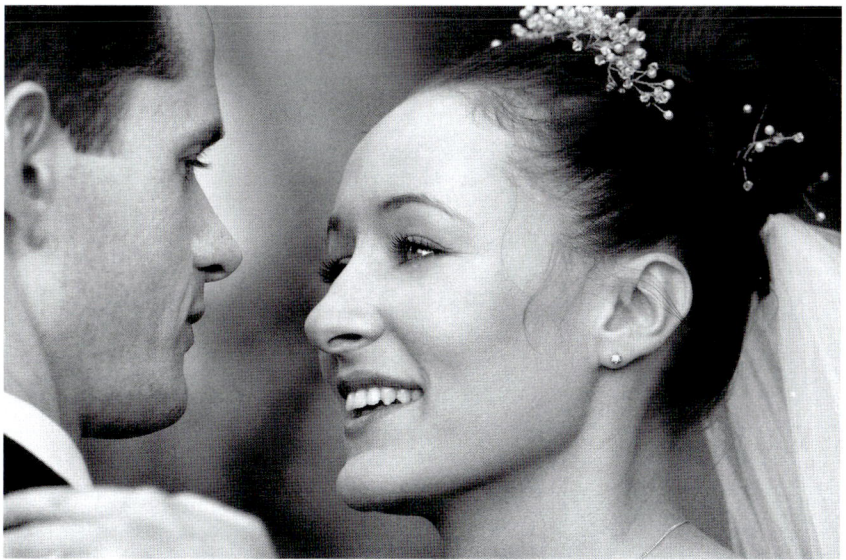

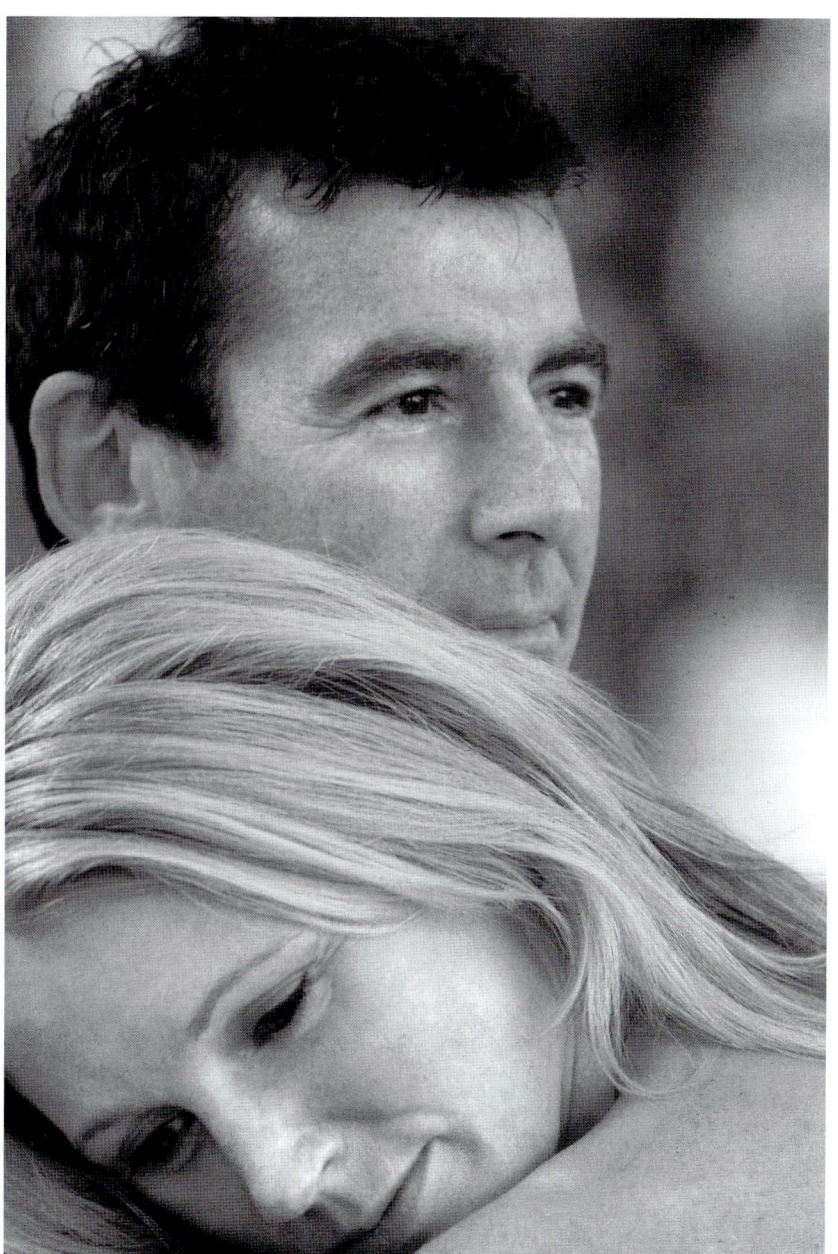

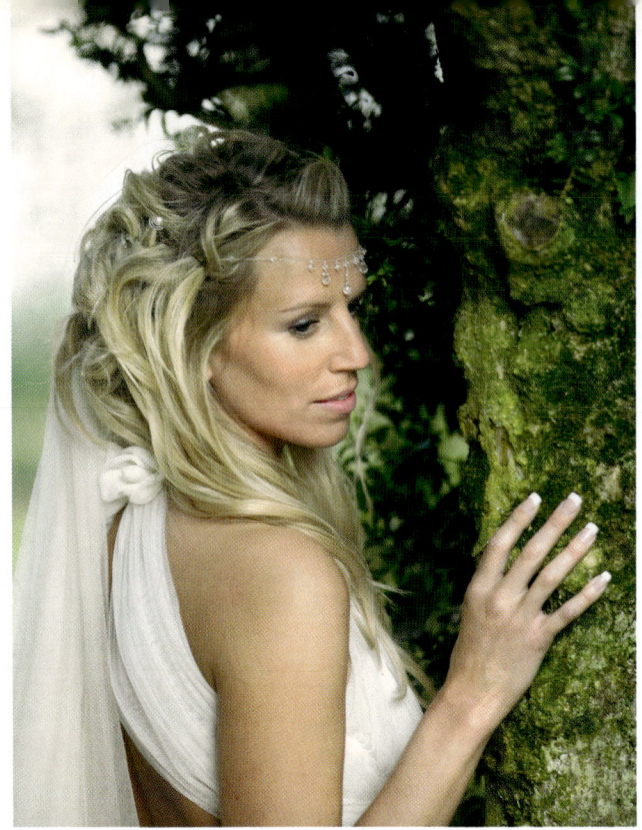

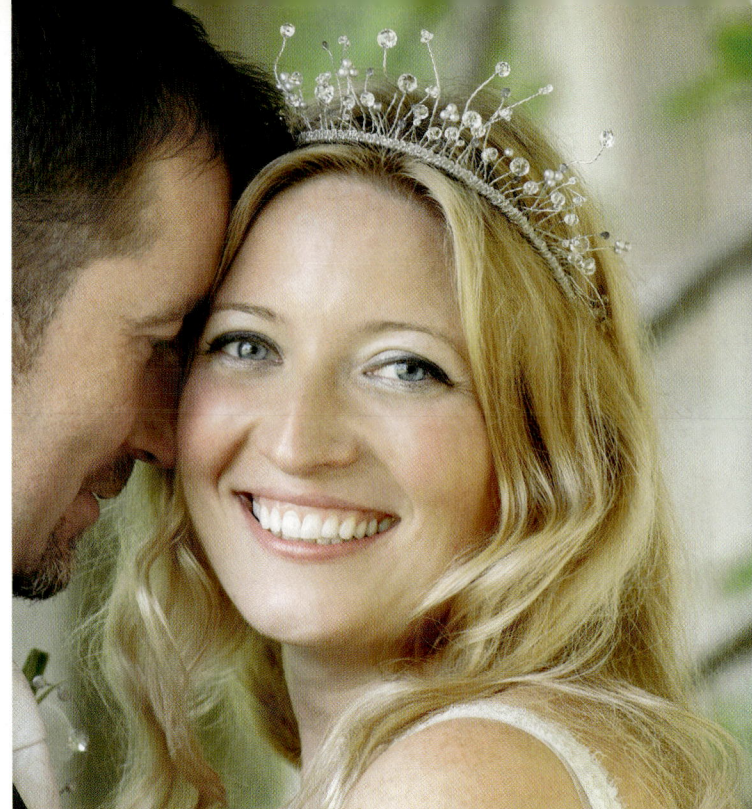

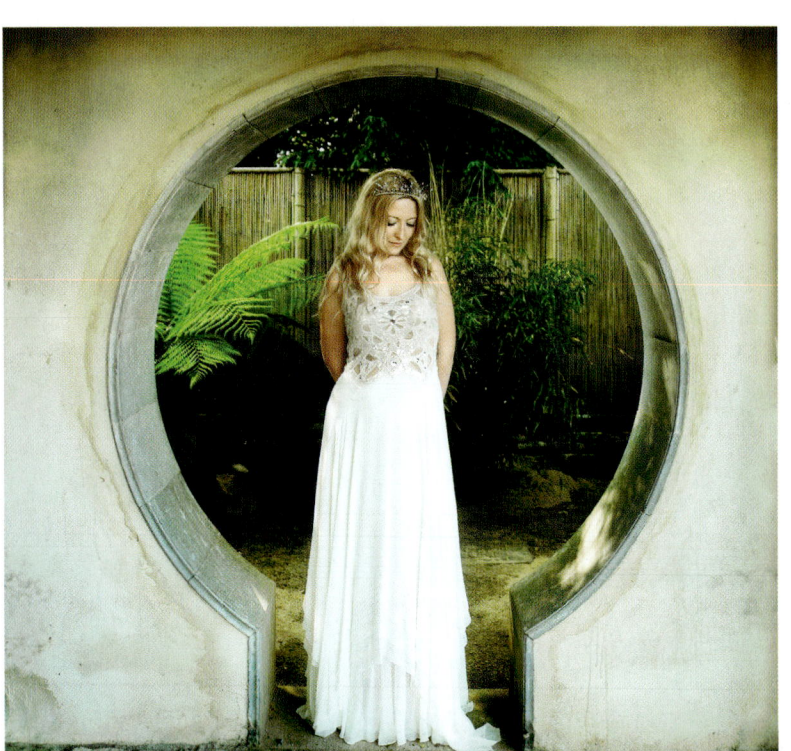

top left

FIG. 30   ISO 400 f/4 at 1/80th

An old moss-covered tree was perfect as a location prop for this bridal portrait. It's the kind of spot that is easy to dismiss at a venue.

bottom left

FIG. 31   ISO 400 f/5.6 at 1/45th

This keyhole gate at Matara in Gloucestershire sets a calm mood for the picture. I asked the bride to glance down and place her hands together behind her back for a simple elegant pose.

above

FIG. 32   ISO 400 f/4 at 1/80th

This bride is radiant. Go in tight when the moment is right and you will be rewarded.

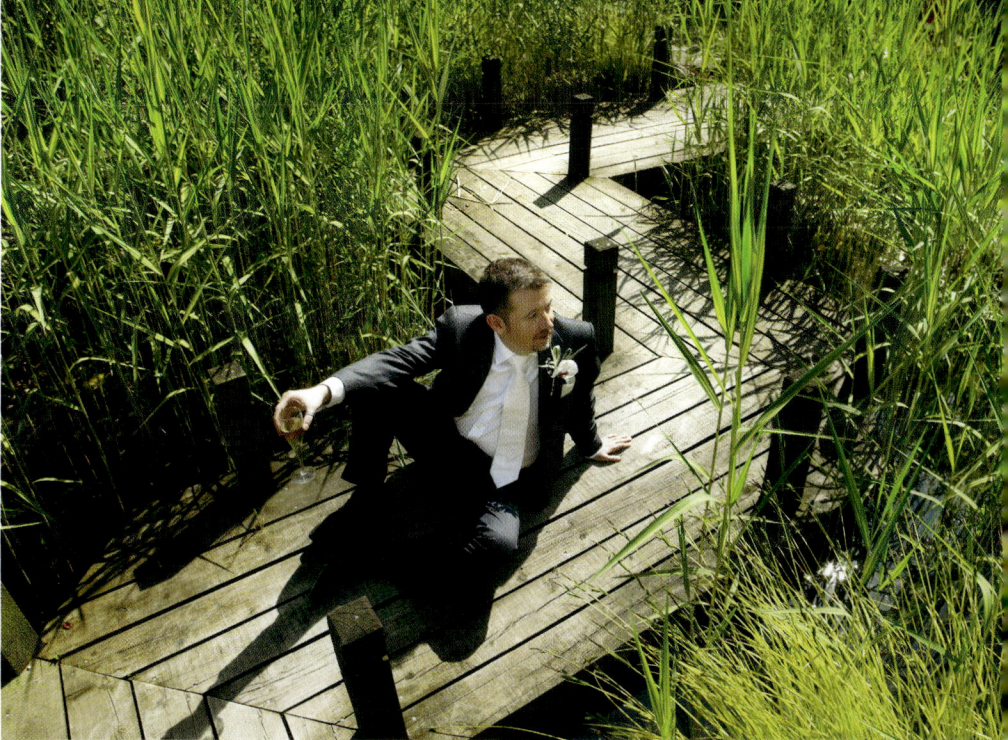

Fig. 33   ISO 200 f/8 at 1/250th

My monopod was used to great effect again for this aerial shot of the groom showing the zigzag decking.

Typical *strengths* could include:

- Dedicated and determined to succeed
- Positive mental attitude
- Enough start-up capital to get the business going
- Great product and service
- Good studio location with passing trade
- Good health

Typical *weaknesses* could include:

- No real unique selling points
- Not enough hours in the day to develop the business
- Lack of brand credibility and experience
- Lack of suitable tools to do the job efficiently
- Not enough cash flow to sustain growth
- Tired display products holding back the product value
- Partial color blindness means reliant on outsourced picture editing

Typical *opportunities* could include:

- Establish a good rapport with the coordinators at local wedding venues
- Make a parents' album sample to encourage further after-sales
- Submit the best weddings to date to magazines for free editorial coverage
- Enter competitions and other PR-friendly activities
- Get trained in craft skills to maximize picture quality
- Hire a professional graphic designer and a copywriter to revamp the website
- Create a database to handle client and job information more efficiently

Typical *threats* could include:

- Uncle Harry with his new Digital SLR camera at weddings
- Local competitors at a low price-point with good products
- A possible downturn in the economy
- Ill health through sickness or accident
- Lack of financial mastery

Lovegrove Weddings

SWOT ANALYSIS at January 07

STRENGTHS	WEAKNESSES
Established company and brand	Business debt
Price and market positioning	Lack of extended financial mastery
Evidence and testimonial bank	Erratic cash flow
Systems and procedures	Dependency on Damien & Julie
Creative and artistic abilities	Geographic spread of clients
Wow! Factor inherent	Building could constrain growth
Charisma & vast experience	
Age, energy, and health	
Supportive partnership	
Customer experience	
Website design	
Website statistics	
Use of technology	
Our financial investment and commitment	
Profitable	
Healthy gross margin	
Current team	
• Right people	
• Right jobs	
• Attitude & impact on clients	
Existing client base	
Sales and marketing expertise	
Management skills	
Marketing collateral	

OPPORTUNITIES	THREATS
Licensees or franchises	Larger team – damaging reputation of company
2007 weddings (delegate)	Lack of work through complacency
Russian millionaire connections	Damien & Julie (sickness, accident, death)
You & Your Wedding magazine partnerships	Lack of continued business development
Book will add credibility and secure bookings	Fashion and social trends
	Downturn in economy

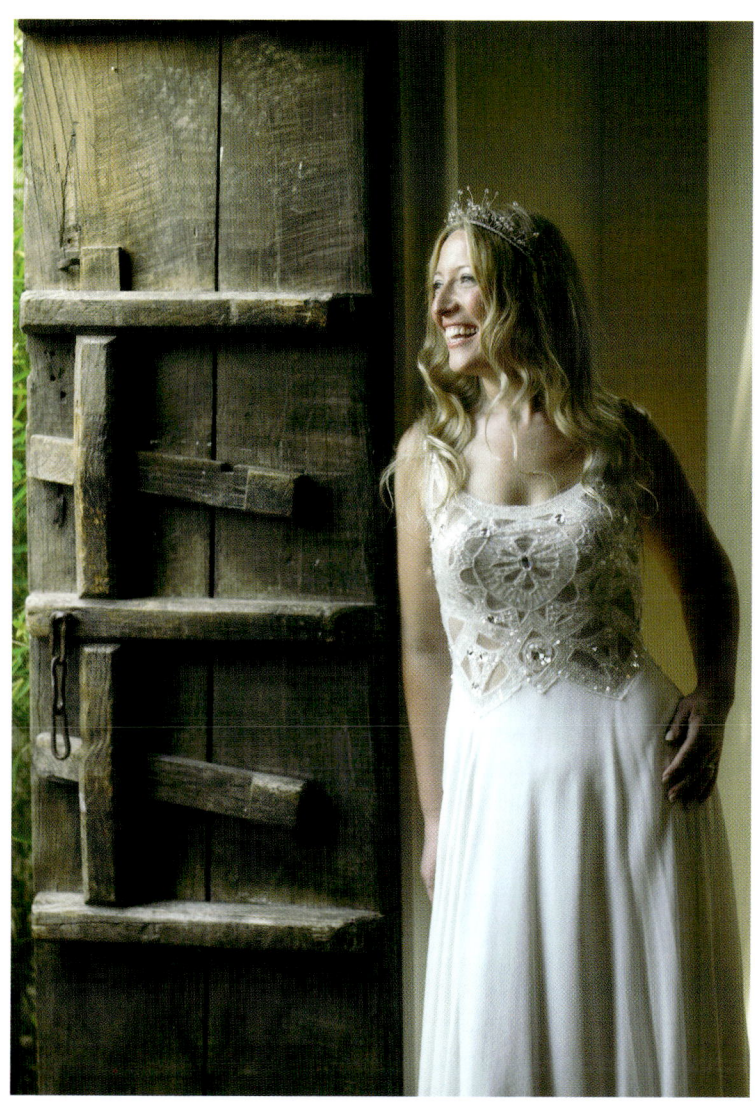

FIG. 34   ISO 400 f/3.4 at 1/100th

The bride is looking at her groom in this setup. Triggering a natural emotion is key to the success of this kind of picture. The moment will be remembered as being fun and the picture will have more value as a result.

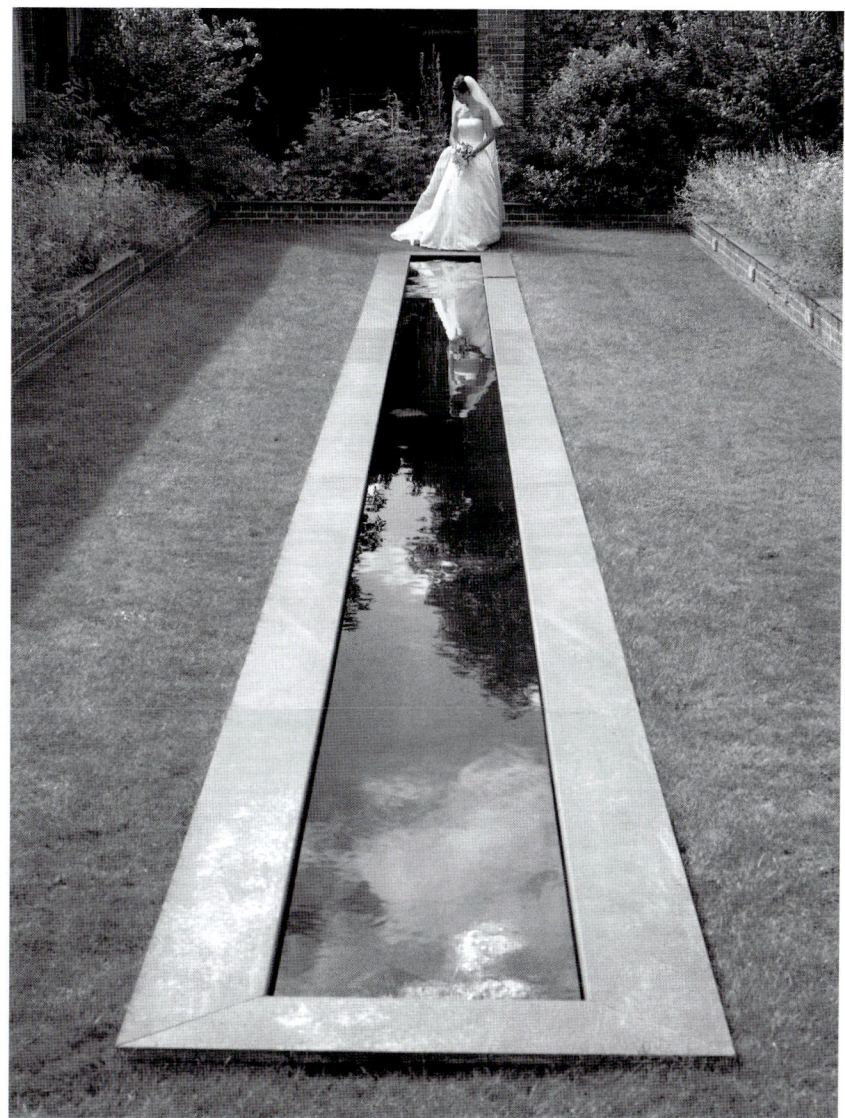

FIG. 35   ISO 400 f/9 at 1/750th

Mad architecture and design create instant opportunities for a picture.

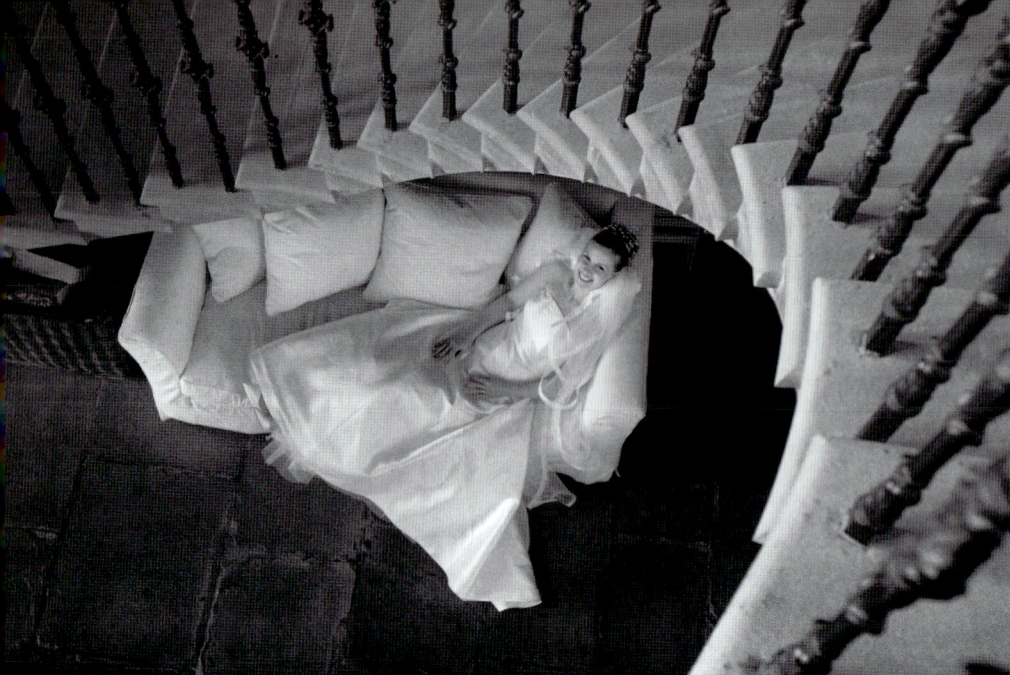

FIG. 36   ISO 800 f/4 at 1/90th

I always try to include the sweep of the stairs in my compositions. I take extra care not to drop the camera in these situations.

Once you have completed your S.W.O.T analysis, you can list your priority actions and start to plan your diary to put in place your strategy for success. There is one other piece of information I need to share with you. If like me you are always busy, you may be asking how can I possibly fit more tasks into my workload? Managing your time well will free up the necessary opportunities and resources you need to be able to take action. Action is like a powerful drug and speaks louder than words. So make things happen and act sooner rather than later!

TIME MANAGEMENT

As I go through life, certain people have the most incredible effect on the way I think and do things and they don't even know it. Stephen R Covey is one of them. In his book *The*

Seven Habits of Highly Effective People he dedicates a chapter to time management. This really made me rethink my life and I personally recommend you get the book. I downloaded my copy from iTunes and I play it in the car from time to time. I'll leave you to discover Stephen's simple system of sorting your tasks.

Meanwhile, here are my own thoughts to get you thinking creatively about time management. Time is worth *more* than money. When you're running a business, time is your most precious resource. Many people will tell you that *time is money* but it is far more valuable than that. You can usually sell some equity, get a loan, or use one of the numerous other ways to get some money but you can't create time. There are short-term answers to the *not enough hours in the day* problem. You can spend less time with your family and friends, or you can sleep less and work until 2:00 am 7 days a week for a short time. But these are *not*

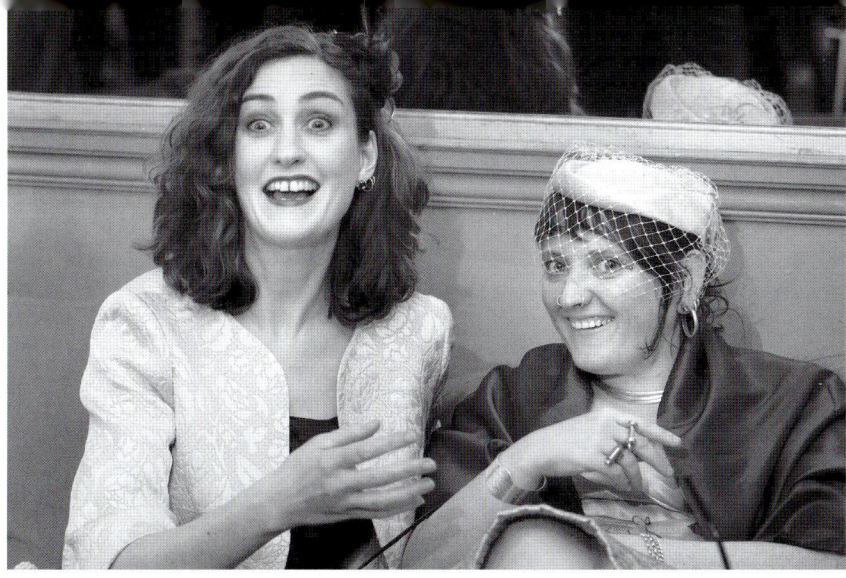

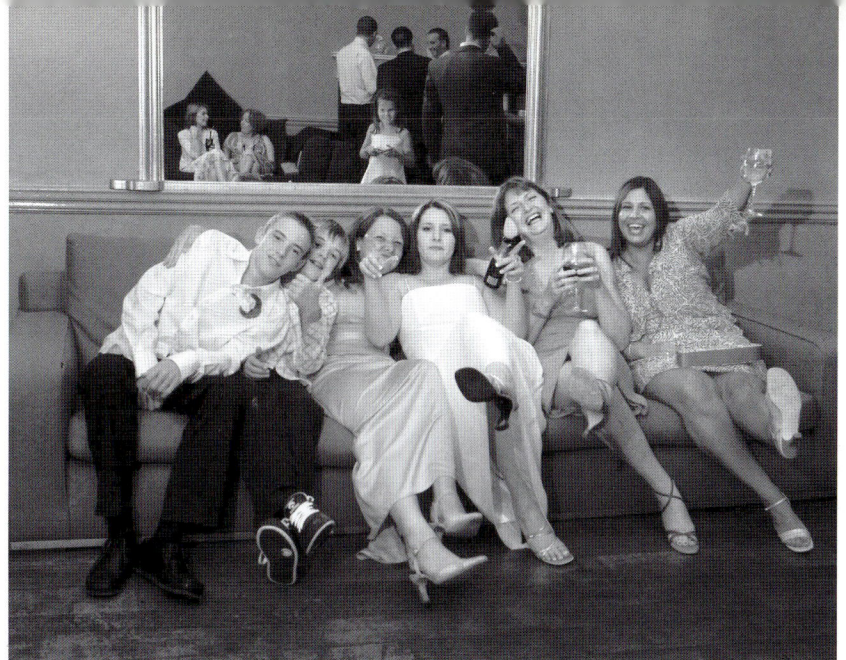

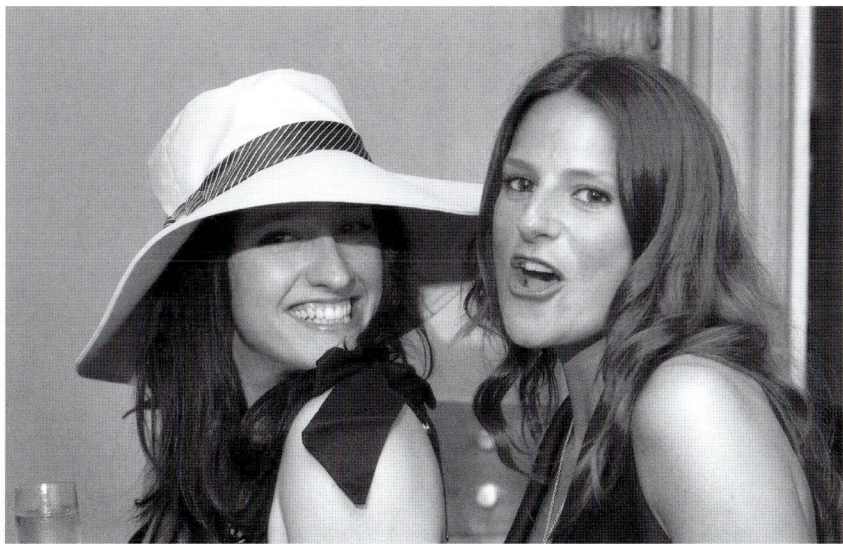

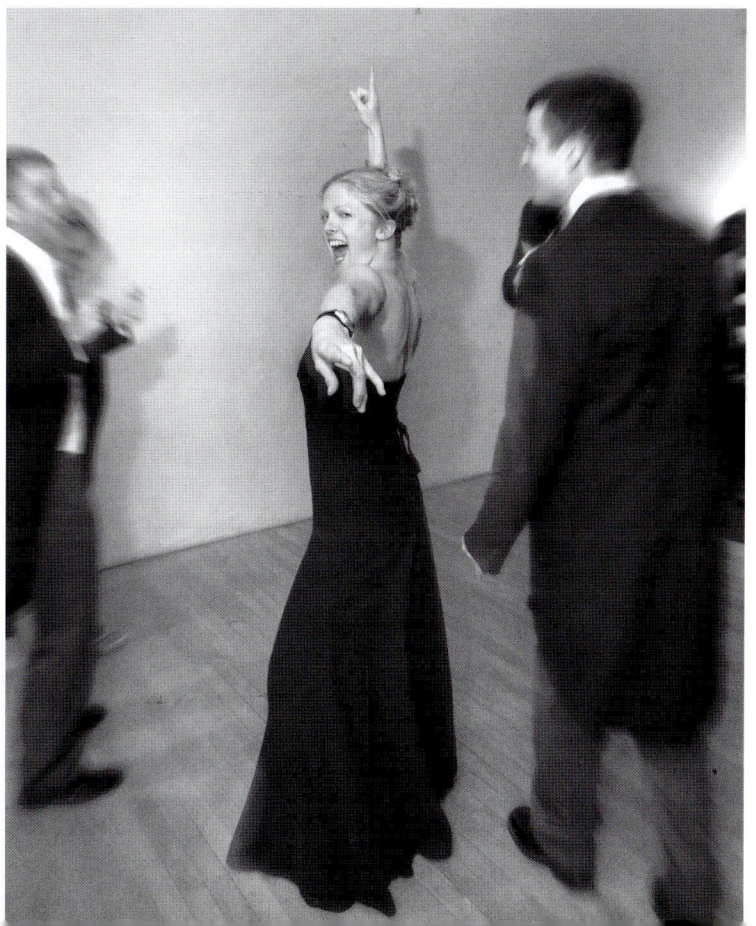

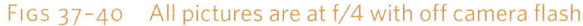

FIGS 37–40   All pictures are at f/4 with off camera flash.

All party pictures I take get the TTL flash off the camera treatment. I will create moments and interact with wedding guests to get the best pictures. Rarely does a reportage approach yield as many saleable results as this method of engaging the revelers.

long-term solutions. To run a small business well, you need to make the most of the time you have available to you.

Steal an hour to create a list of all the tasks you undertake as part of your business and all the activities that make up your leisure time. Put these in column A on a spreadsheet. Over a period of a week or so, log a time for each activity and task as it happens in adjacent columns. Straightway you will begin to see areas where economies can be made. If you keep up the time logging for a month or so, you'll get a more accurate appraisal.

Now act on the information you have discovered. For instance, you may have spent 8 hours doing bookkeeping during the month and you might be able to outsource that task to a local bookkeeper who will come in for one morning each fortnight (and as a bonus, they may well do a better job than you!). You

may have spent 12 hours browsing forums. That's a task with very little benefit to your business and if you stopped using the forum altogether, your business probably wouldn't suffer. You have to identify the tasks that are important to the continued success of your business and those that are urgent. Redesigning your website maybe important for your continued success but it is not urgent. By not urgent, I mean if it's not done this month, it won't matter too much. An urgent task is one that has to be done now or at a specific time at whatever cost. Photographing a client's wedding is one such task. Dealing with a customer complaint is another. If a task is not important to your continued success then consider dropping it altogether or delegate it. Holidays and family time are important and non-urgent activities, so too are product design, website design, personal training, and business planning. These are the tasks you should do more of at the expense of the non-important tasks.

Plan your activities at the start of each day. It's easy to be deflected from the tasks you initially set out to do. Common distractions for most of us are the phone ringing and a constant stream of emails. Any unfinished tasks at the end of the day should be at the top of the next day's list. Focus on the tasks that are most important rather the trivia. Give yourself a good number of short-term goals. Set timeframes for the completion of tasks. For instance you might set yourself 1 hour to update and revamp a webpage. With a specific timeframe you'll be far more focused on completing it in that time. If you don't give yourself that deadline it can drag on for hours. Of course, you need to learn to give yourself a realistic amount of time for each task in the first place. At just one page a day, by the end of the month your overhauled website will have become a reality.

Finally, when you're trying to maximize the effectiveness of your time you must be aware of the heavy price of perfection. Striving for perfection is a commendable aim, but when you're running a small business, perfection is often unrealistic and ultimately damaging. It makes more sense to consistently aim high than to try and achieve perfection every time. The time you spend on progressing a task from 'high quality' to 'perfect' is rarely time well spent. The return you get for investing your most valuable resource in making such a small gain is just not worth it. Once it's good enough, stop and move on to the next job on your plan. It will be time better spent.

Further reading to help bring out the entrepreneur in you is *The E Myth* by Michael Gerber and if you want to get thinking on another level after just 90 minutes then get a copy of 'The Secret' on DVD from www.thesecret.tv.

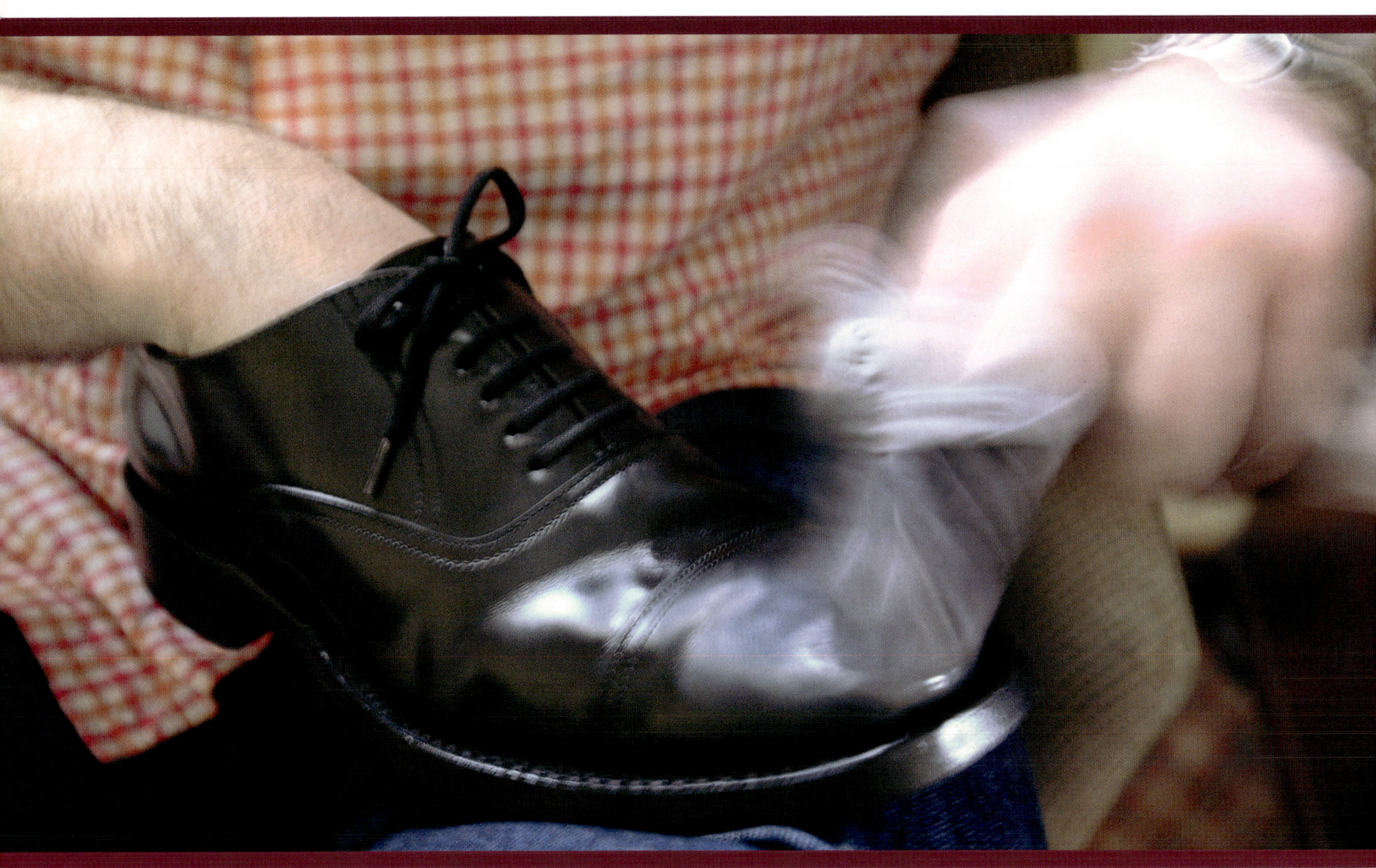

Chapter Nine: Marketing

9
Marketing

Many people's idea of marketing is rather vague. Something to do with promoting your business? Yes, but let's get more focused than that. Marketing is the process of *generating qualified leads*. A qualified lead can be described as a couple who are getting married, on a date that you have available, within your coverage area, who like your style of work, and can afford your services. From now on I will refer to a qualified lead as a *prospect*. It's worth noting that the business of converting prospects into clients is the *sales process* and is covered in the next chapter.

First let's get one thing straight. *Marketing ideas are useless unless acted upon.* To put it another way, marketing effectiveness is directly proportional to levels of action or activity. If you have read the section on time management then you will realize that marketing effort is firmly in box two.

So where do we start? It's all too easy to focus all your advertising on yourself or your business and not on your prospects. We've all done it, just look at any ad and ask yourself, who is the ad really talking about? Is it talking about the *prospect* or about the *photographer*? You must focus ALL your marketing communications on the prospect. Your ads, your brochure, and your website must NOT be self-serving. Your sales and marketing

opposite

Fig. 1   ISO 800 f/4 at 1/10th

Simple creative use of a slow shutter speed adds drama to an otherwise ordinary picture. I steadied my camera on a monopod.

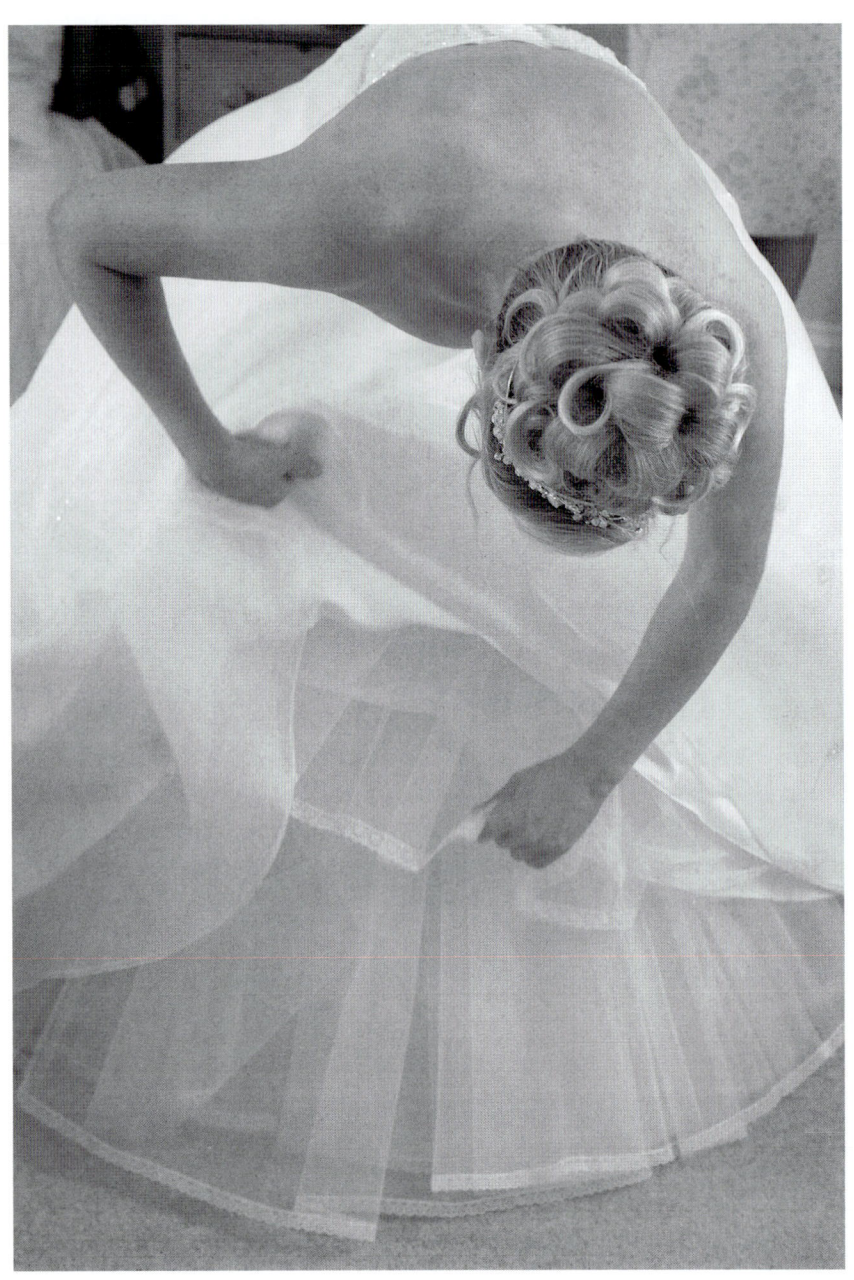

Fig. 2   ISO 800 f/4 at 1/180th

This tight composition of Julie's excludes all unnecessary background distractions. It has a strong composition combined with the primary subject elements of hair style and wedding dress design.

opposite

Fig. 3   ISO 400 f/5.7 at 1/2000th

With a dress this long it is hard to get it all in the frame at times.

literature must pass the 'So what?' test – every time. Remember the prospect is interested in one thing and one thing only: what's in it for them! Forget about how great your photography is, how many awards you have won, save that for later. Instead, begin with your focus on your prospects and their needs.

The more you know about your prospect, the easier it will be for you to convince them that they need *you* to photograph their wedding. Ask yourself, why someone should book you? What are the benefits to them? When you've found some answers, use them in all your marketing communications. It's that simple. A true 'benefit' differs greatly from a 'feature.' Features are about the product; benefits are about the prospect.

Next come your USPs, Unique Selling Points. These are the key elements that make what you offer – your product and

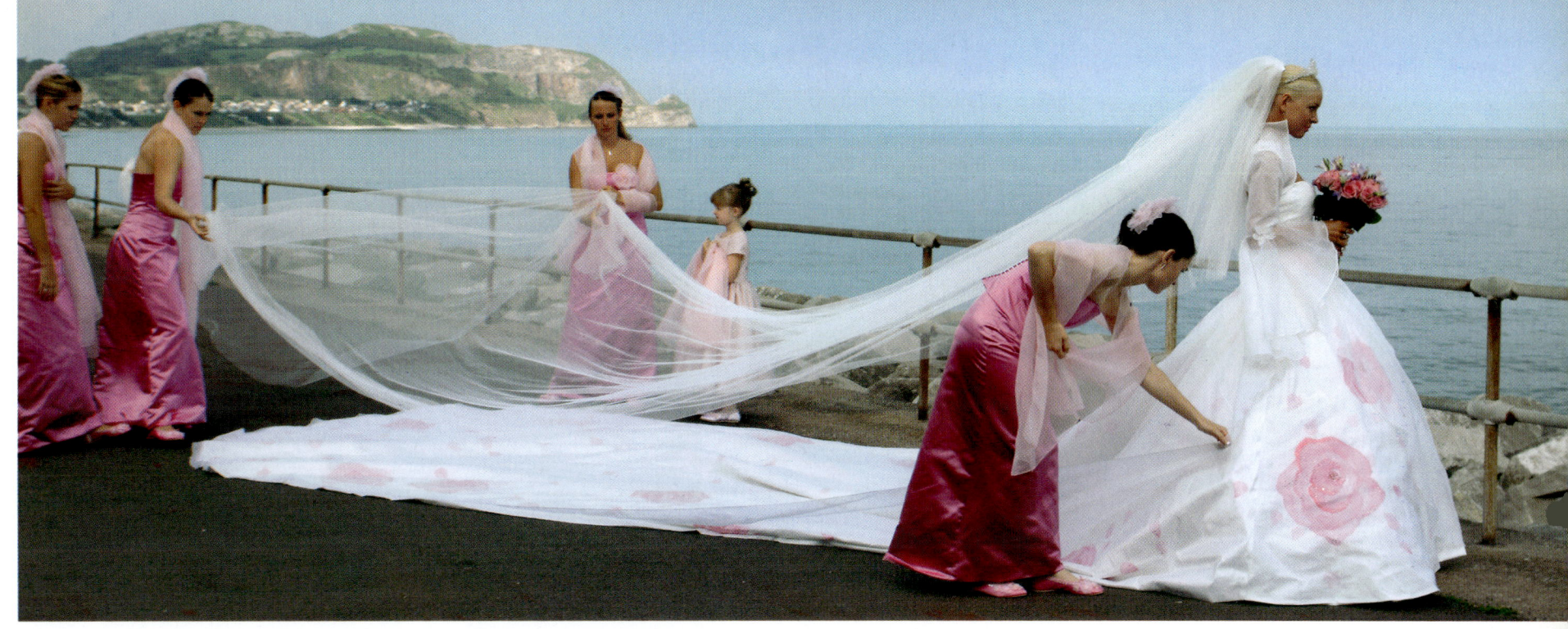

service – different from what your competitors offer. Brainstorm you ideas for USPs with your team and write them down. You will need them when you design your adverts, website, or brochure.

ADVERTISING: IS IT WORKING FOR YOU?

AIDA is the acronym to remember. The four key steps to designing a great advert, brochure, or website are: Attention, Interest, Desire, and Action.

Attention.   Start with an attention-grabbing headline – that's the first rule of good advertising. Get the headline right and you immediately have your reader's attention. Writing a good headline is a creative process. There are several different approaches. You could use 'risk reversal' as the principal element

for your headline: 'Perfect wedding photography – guaranteed.' This is a very strong statement and attracts brides who worry about getting pictures they dislike. It's a powerful statement and will demand the viewer reads on. Alternatively, you could use a question as a headline; 'Are you worried about high reprint prices?' Or 'Would you like to own your wedding pictures on disk?' You could use the power of 'new': 'New – pictures on disk at full resolution for every bride.' You could use a client quote. By using a testimonial, your headline gains instant credibility. Instead of it merely being a 'claim' that needs supporting and convincing, it becomes a 'fact' and is therefore instantly believable. 'Our Lovegrove wedding album was the best investment we ever made' – Julie & Steve Henley.

Interest.   Encouraging your reader's interest through the headline or body copy is the second key element of a good advert. 'When

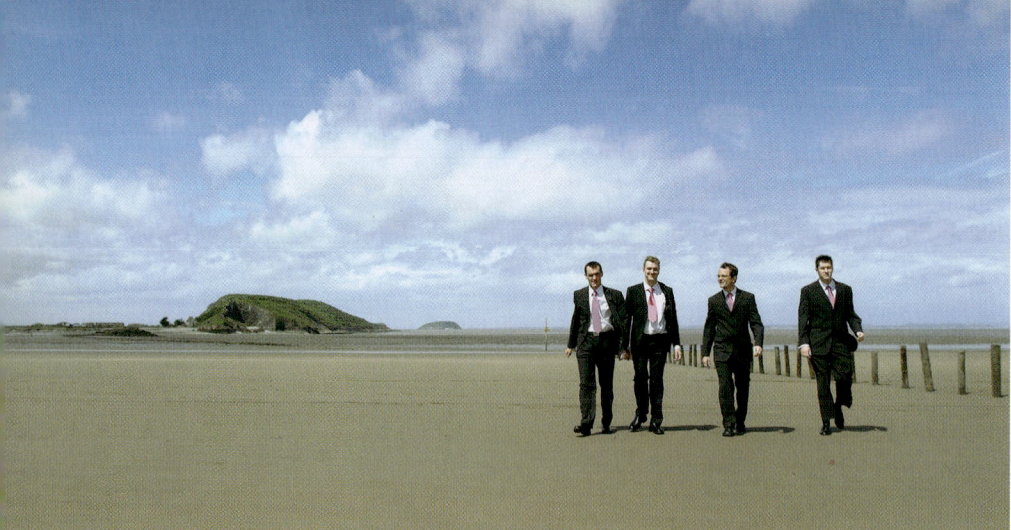

above

FIG. 4 ISO 320 f/4 at 1/2000th

Glancing sunlight on faces is less of a problem with figures in landscape shots like this taken at Weston Super Mare. The range and balance of colors make this shot work so well. The blue of the sky is opposed by the yellow sand and the green hill is opposed by the pink ties.

FIG. 5 ISO 400 f/6.3 at 1/90th

Flash would have killed this picture. I love the opportunity to frame pictures with doorways. The detail of the door on the left leads the eye to the group of girls.

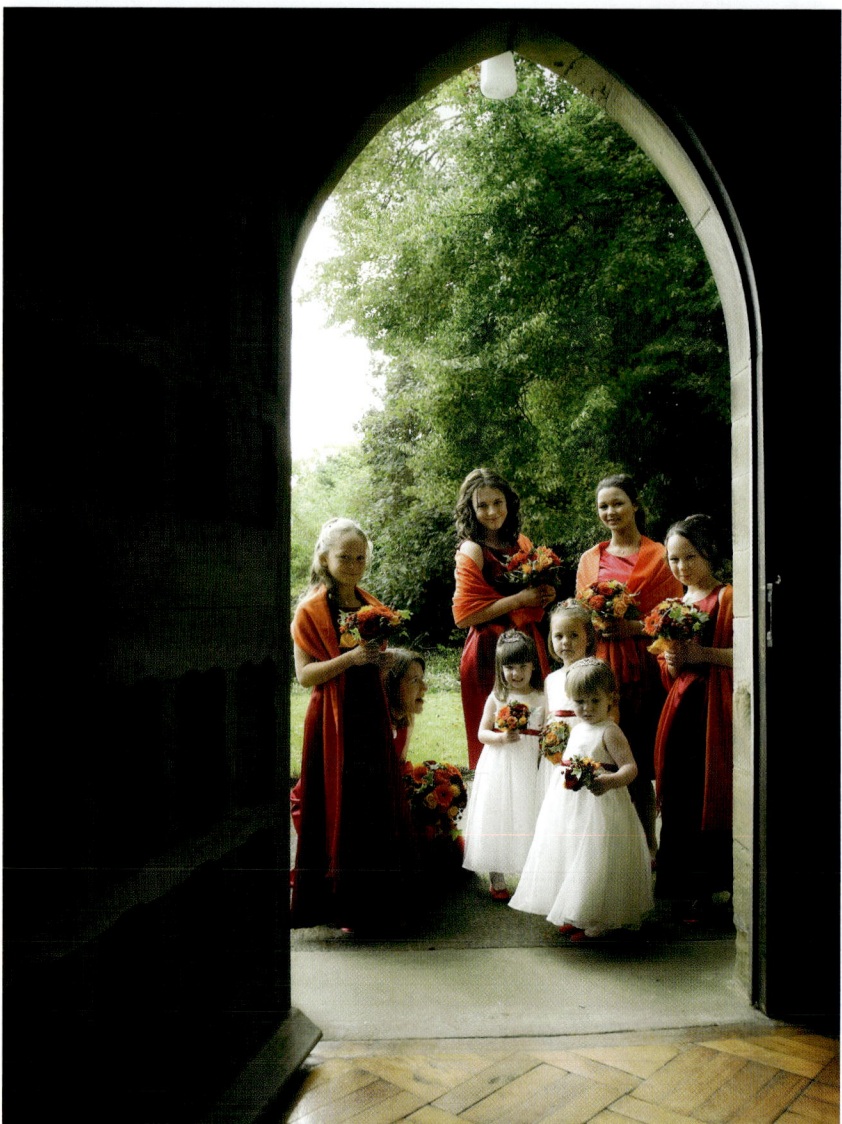

choosing a wedding photographer, watch out for hidden extras. At Lovegrove Weddings, the price you see is the price you pay.' Giving free advice is always a good way to maintain interest.

Desire. Creating desire is probably the easiest of the four elements to fulfill. Images are our weapon. Great images that show love, friendship, fun, romance, humor will create the desire we need in our advert. Avoid stock poses that other photographers may use. Use pictures that will appeal to a bride, not a photographer. Use images that make people look attractive, avoiding unflattering 'exclamation' shots of brides with their mouths wide open, for example. Your choice of images in your advert should reflect your USPs if possible. If you have a certain post-production look that your brides love, then use it in your adverts. If most photographers are using black

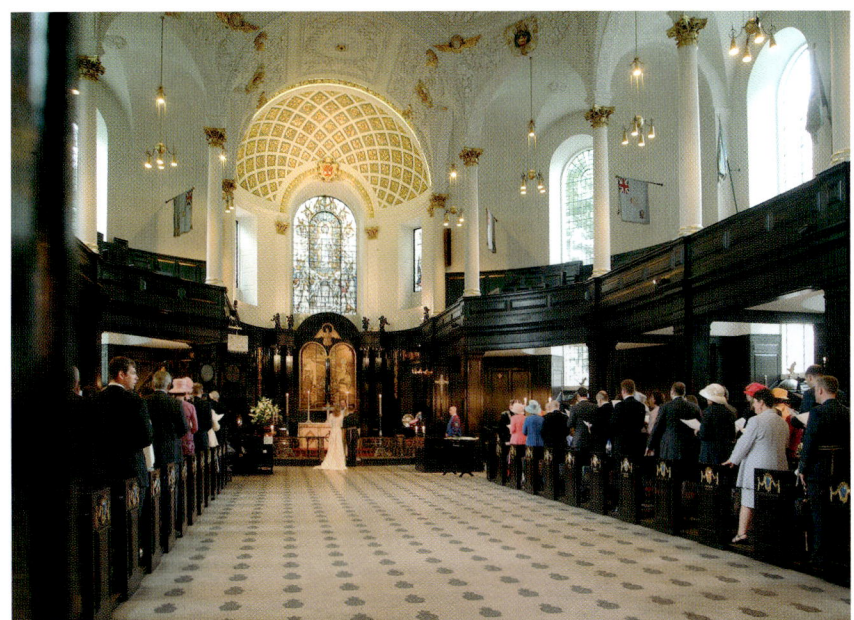

Fig. 6   ISO 800 f/4 at 1/10th

I had to sneak this interior picture of the beautiful and famous St Clement Danes Church in London. Occasionally you will come across a power hungry official who does not allow any interior photography, at any time, whatsoever. You just have to do your best when faced with such obstacles. My camera was on my monopod resting up against the door frame and I used a self-timer to take this picture while I looked the other way. The Church bells are featured in the children's nursery rhyme 'Oranges and Lemons.'

below

Fig. 7   ISO 400 f/5.7 at 1/125th

I included the background balustrade in this picture to help set the scene at Clearwell Castle in Gloucestershire.

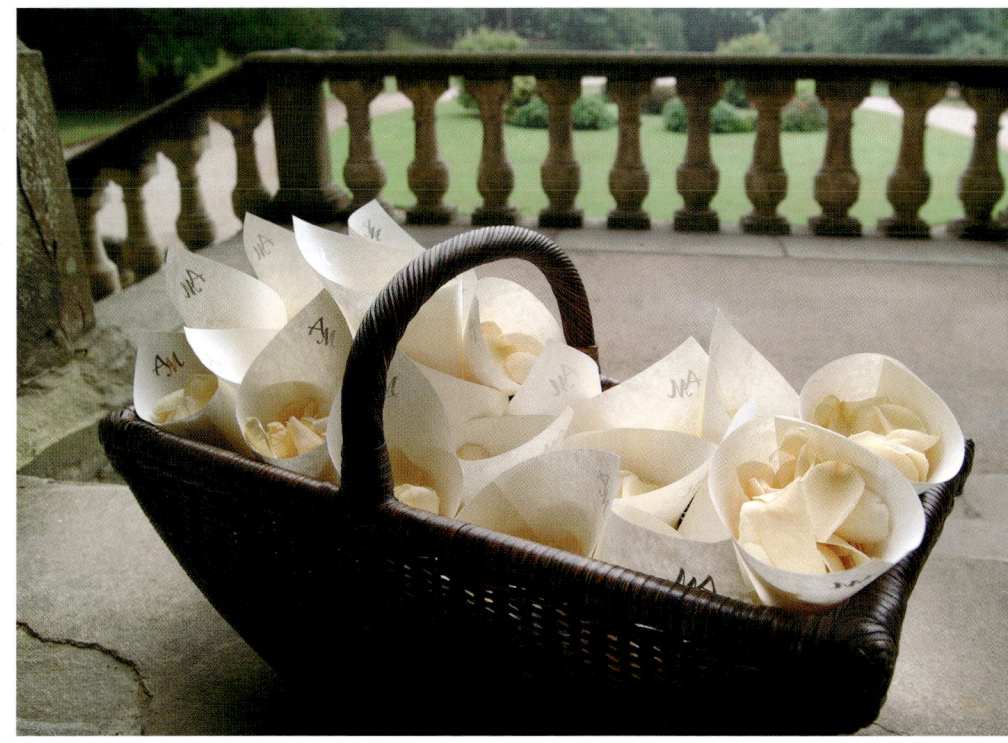

and white images in their adverts, use color. Be different and let your advert stand out from the rest.

Action.   A call to action is the final essential component that makes a great advert. The aim is simple: tell the reader what to do. Make it definite, and explain how taking action will benefit them. Make sure your call to action passes the WIIFM test: 'What's In It For Me?' For example, a call to action can be used to set a price point. A supermarket might combine a call to action with a time-limited offer; 'Visit your Tesco store today, chickens half price. Hurry, offer must end Thursday.' The use of the word 'your' is a clever ploy of granting ownership to the reader. 'Half price chickens' is the WIIFM and the use of the word 'hurry' is a reinforcement of the call to action. Another supporting phrase is 'while stocks last.' Calls to action in

Fig. 9 ISO 400 f/4 at 1/90th

If you are ever faced with strong repeating patterns like this avenue of trees use a long telephoto lens to compress the perspective. Place and pose your bride carefully. Julie was just out of the frame chatting to the bride while I ran back to get the picture.

below

Fig. 8 ISO 400 f/4 at 1/90th

By offsetting the composition Julie included the rear dress detail in this candid shot.

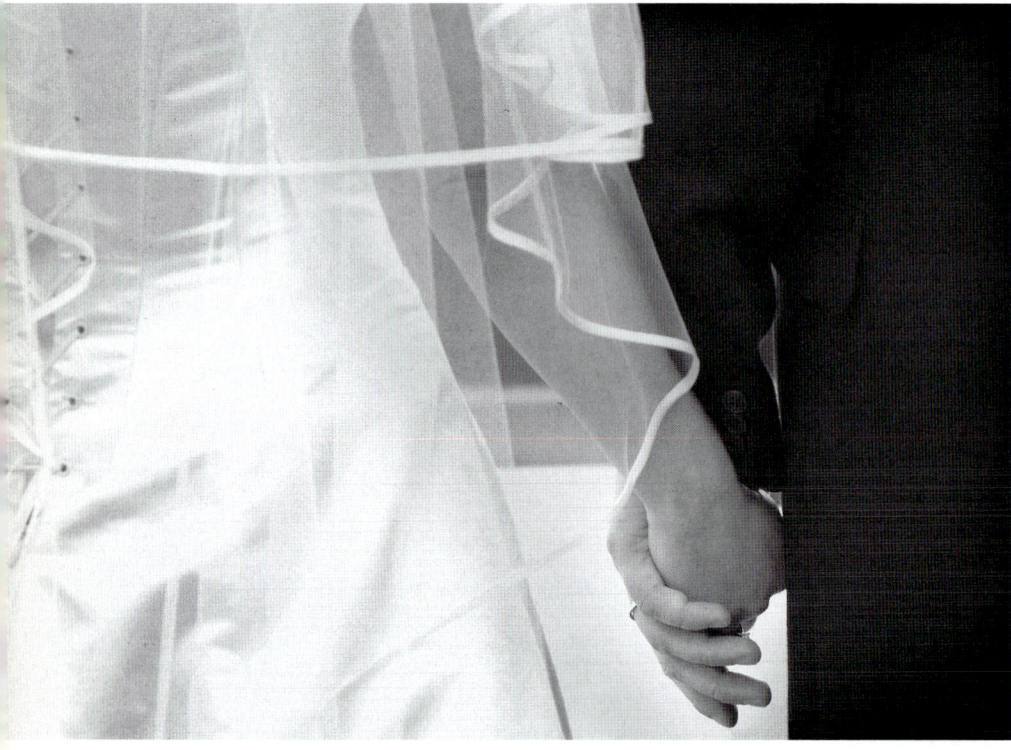

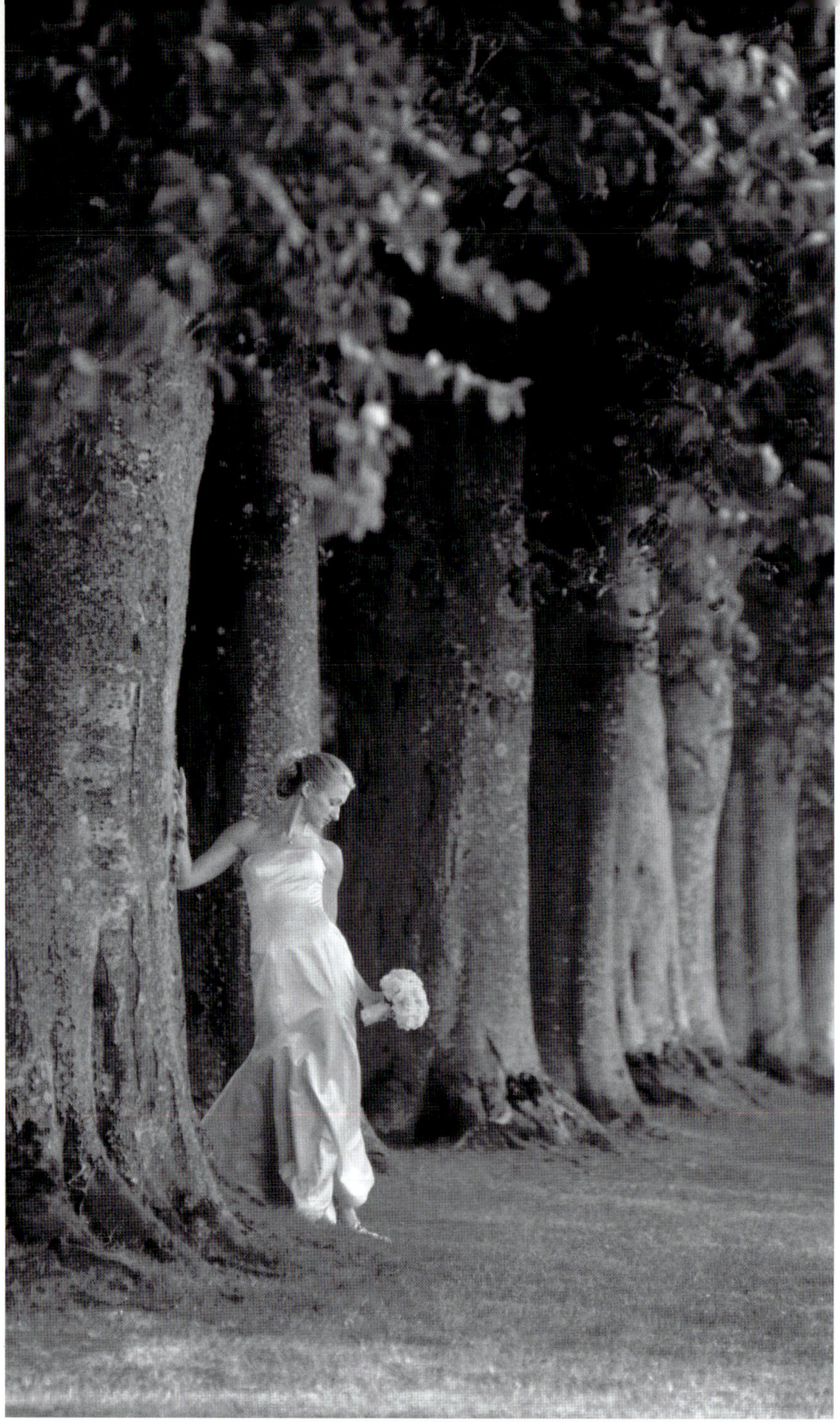

Fig. 11   ISO 800 f/4 at 1/2000th

Fig. 11   ISO 800 f/4 at 1/2000th

I saw this hour glass detail in the gate and had the instant idea for this fun picture.

below

Fig. 10   ISO 200 f/5.7 at 1/125th

Radiant beauty, fun, and verve are the key ingredients of this portrait. I placed the bride on the thirds with a window detail to balance the shot. The tunnel effect natural light completed the picture.

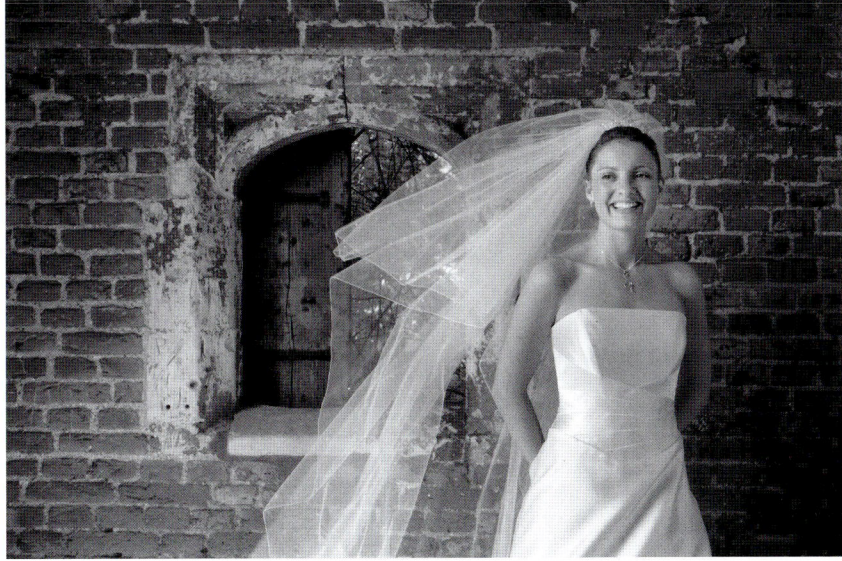

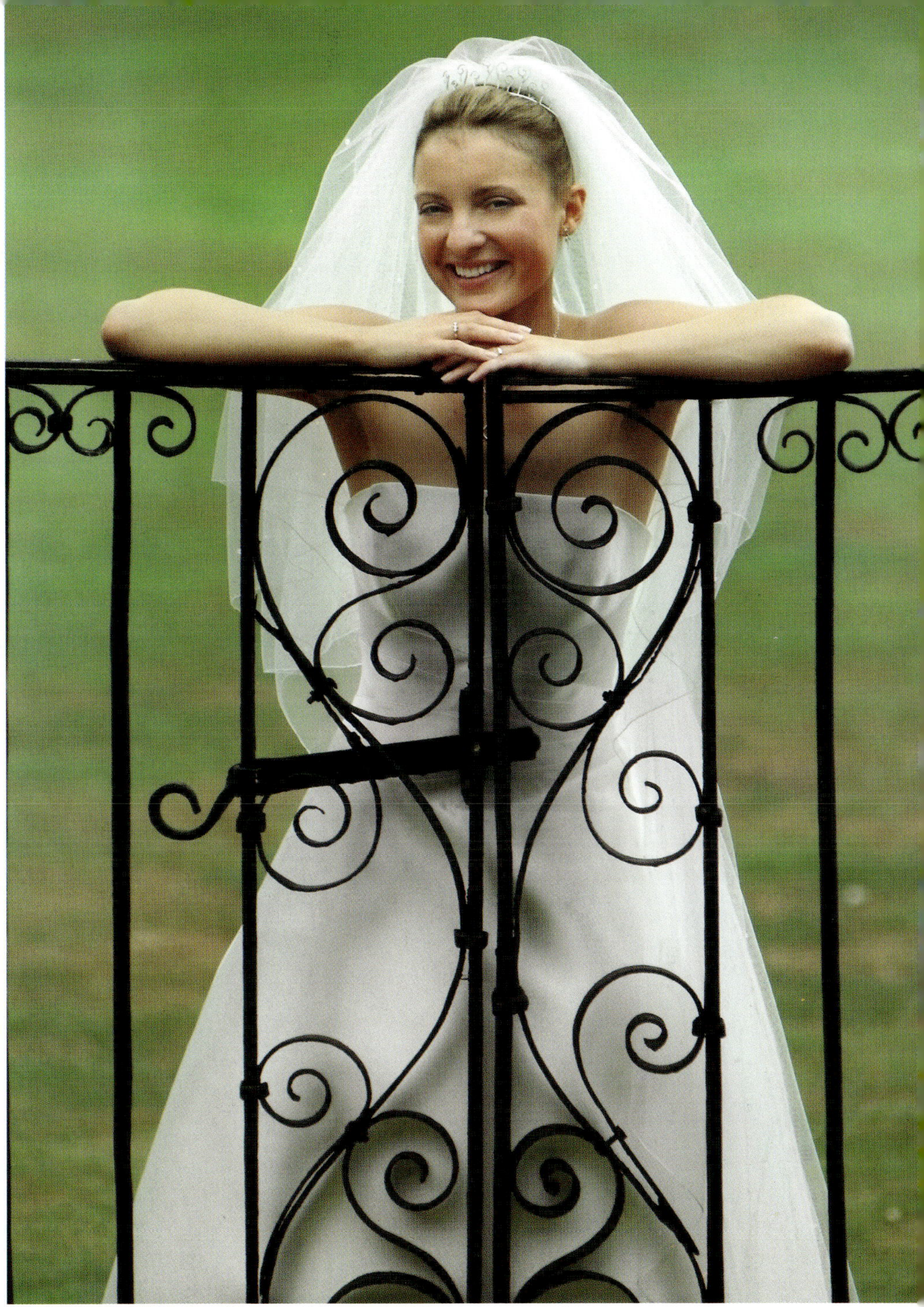

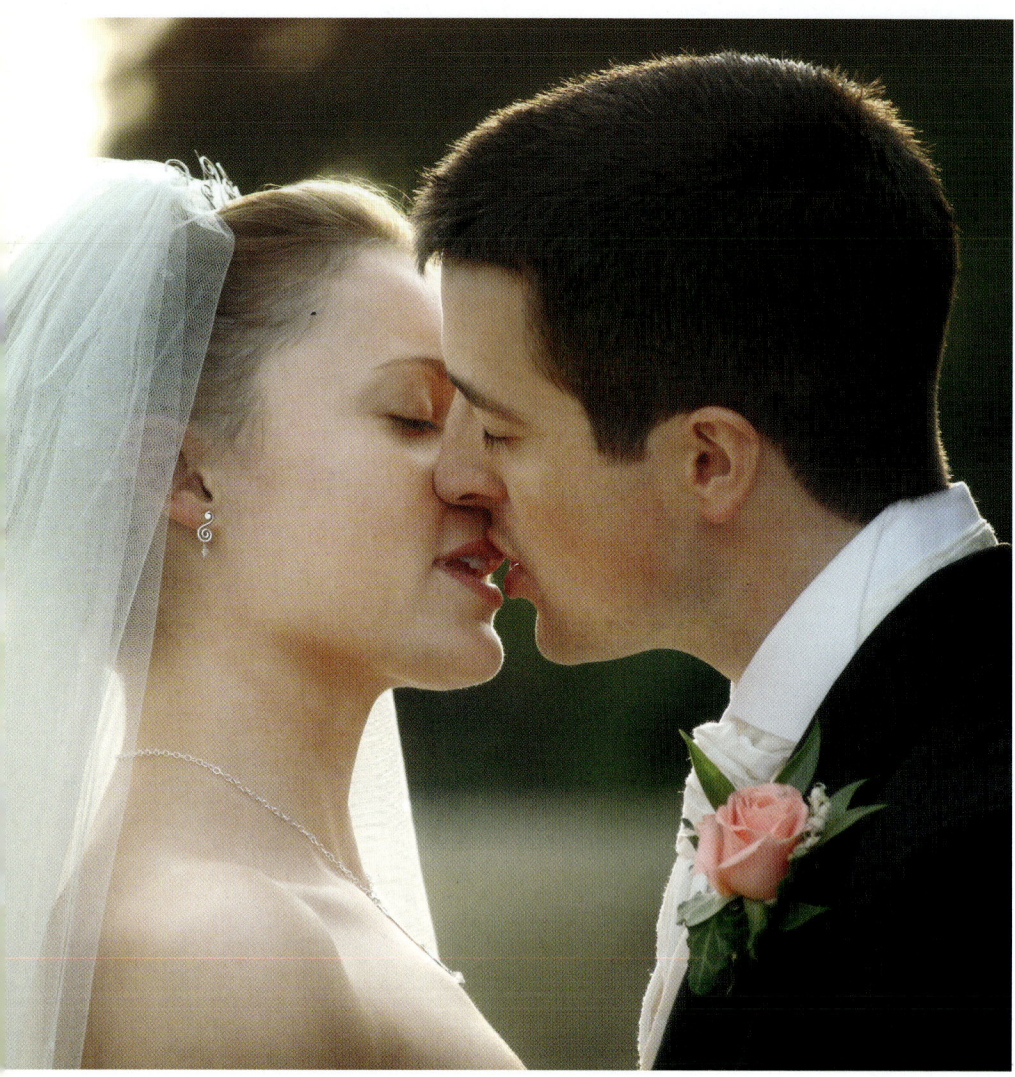

Photographing a kiss well is a tough thing to do. Rarely does the picture convey the intimacy in a sensual way. This picture shot into the light has all the magic elements required for success.

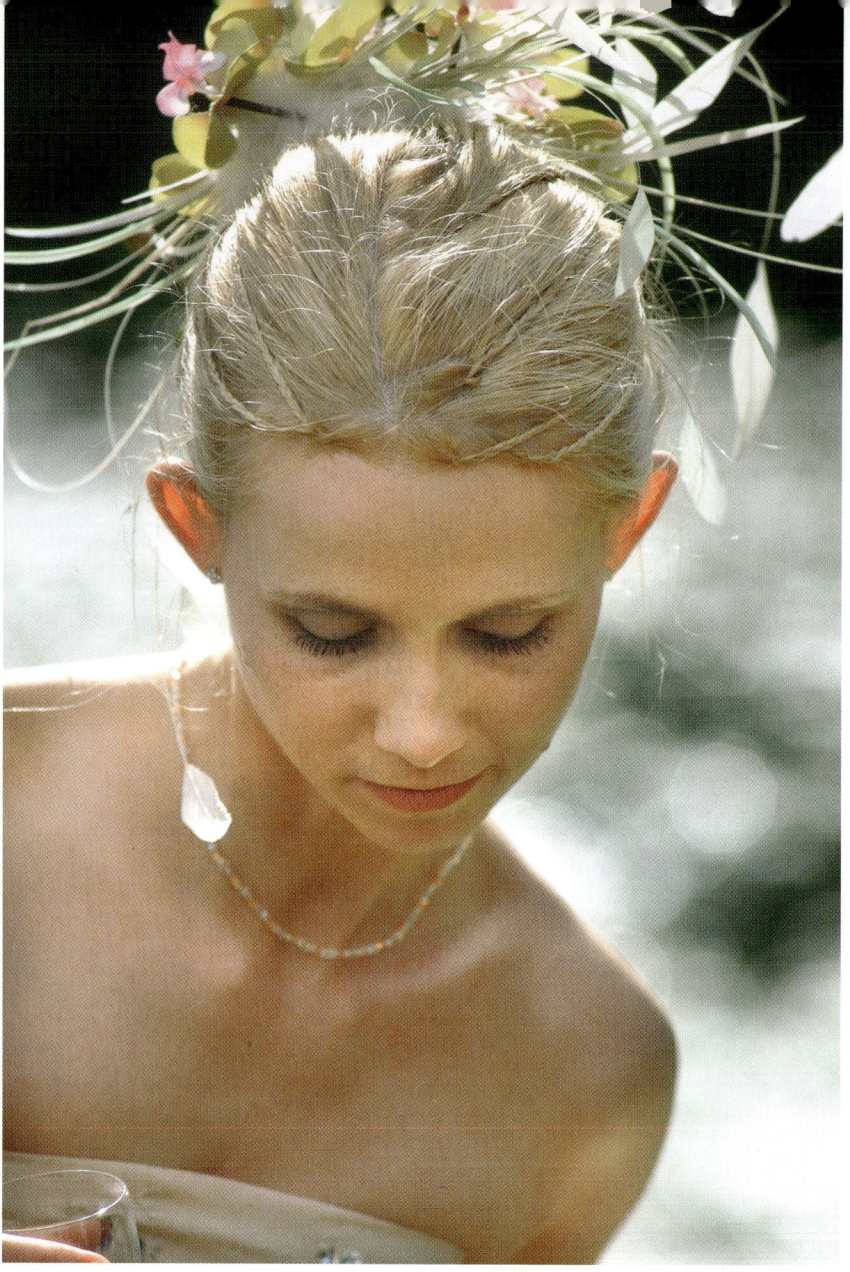

At f/4 what you see is what you get, so composing out of focus backgrounds is easy to do. At f/11 this picture would have been full of competing distractions. The glance down makes the picture a Lovegrove.

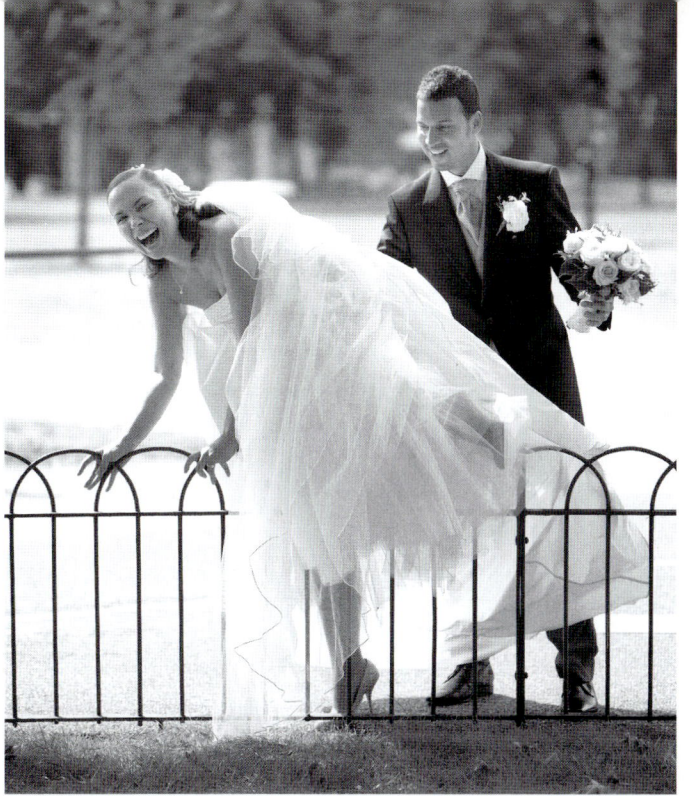

Fig. 14   ISO 400 f/4 at 1/800th

This moment was easily predicted as we left Hyde Park in London. I held back, switched to my 210 mm lens and shot into the light to capture this bit of fun.

bottom right

Fig. 15   ISO 320 f/5.7 at 1/1800th

The Cornish coast is a wonderful backdrop for wedding pictures. Julie and I spent 20 minutes shooting this couple on the beach and I remember there was not one shot of the couple's faces in the final set. None were needed.

Lovegrove Wedding adverts have included: 'All the advice, ideas and inspiration you need to plan your perfect wedding are online now at www.lovegroveweddings.com' and 'Treat yourselves to the world-class photography of Lovegrove Weddings. Request your copy of their inspirational new brochure and showreel, either by visiting www.lovegroveweddings.com or calling 01275 853204 today.'

Why not try this yourself? Next time you write an advert, design a brochure or create a flyer, make sure it meets the AIDA criteria.

TEST AND MEASURE

Advertising budgets can run away with you if you don't test and measure. A simple guide to remember is that every £ or $ spent

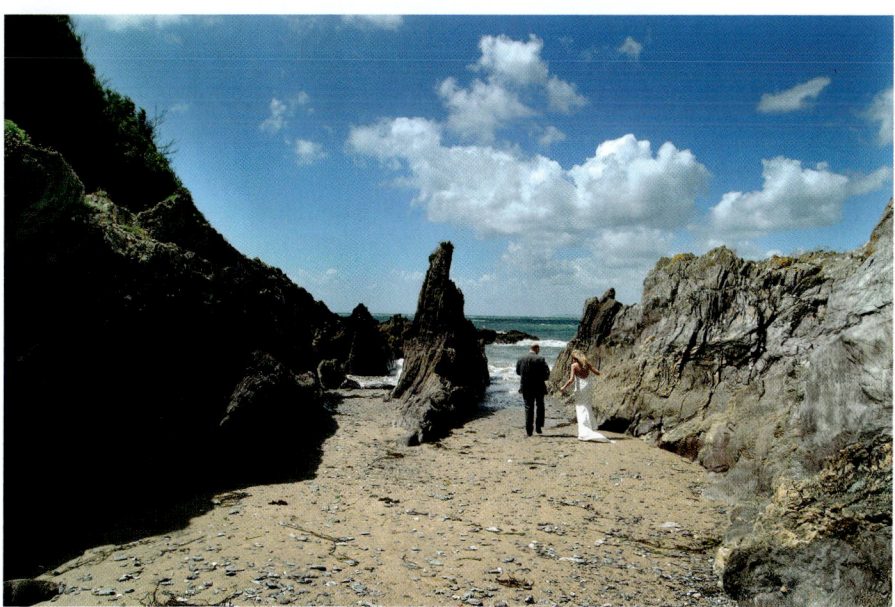

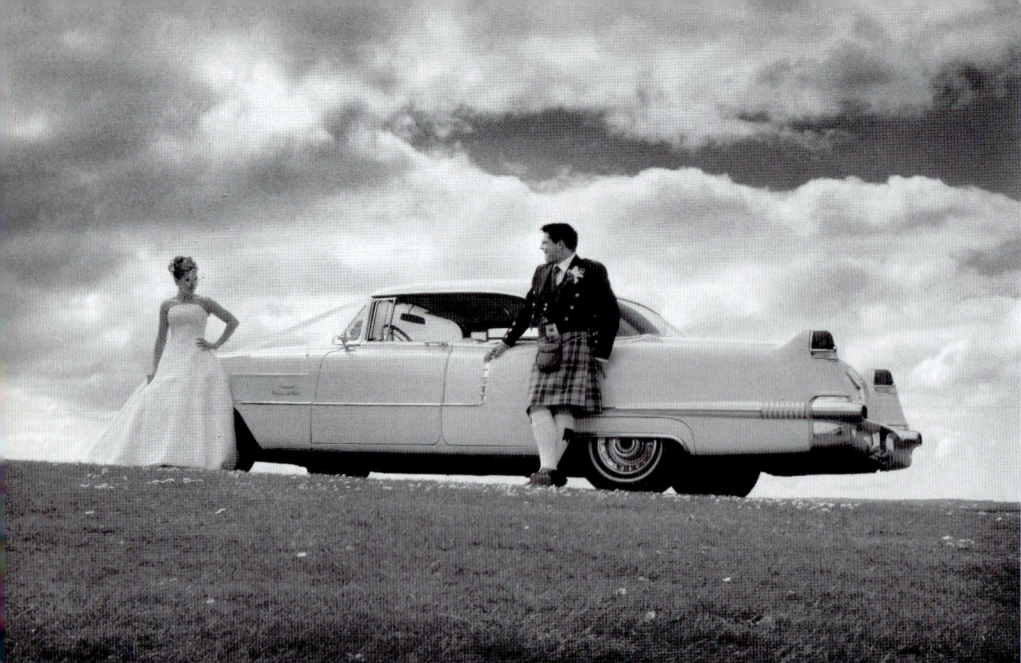

Lying on the ground often gets a great viewpoint but is not so good for my Armani suit.

bottom left

FIG. 17   ISO 160 f/9.5 at 1/360th

A rich heritage of fine country houses helps provide great surroundings for UK weddings. However, I often find myself craving for the simplicity of clean modern design. The grass is always greener on the other side. Highclere Castle in Royal Berkshire.

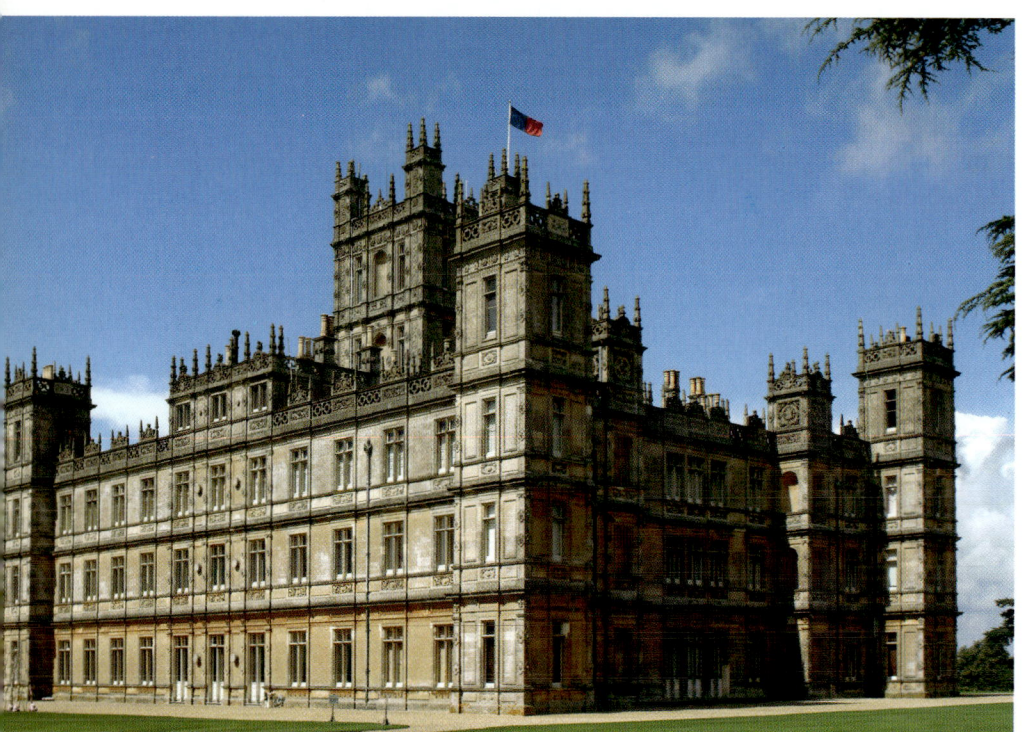

on advertising should bring in £10 or $10 of business. Work with that 10:1 ratio in mind. If an advert fails to deliver this response there are several possible reasons. It might be that your advert does not follow the AIDA system. Your advert may be in the wrong magazine or in the wrong place in the right magazine. A competitor's advertising may have eclipsed yours. Try this simple test: ask a female friend you trust to look through all the photography adverts in a particular wedding magazine and tell you which photographers she would contact and why.

When Julie and I want to check how effective our advertising is at getting response, we use a system known as 'web or email redirect.' The call to action in one magazine will say 'visit www.lovegroveweddings.co.uk for inspiration and advice on planning your perfect day.' The same advert in another

FIG. 18   ISO 400 f/4 at 1/75th

I love spiral stairs. Great pictures come easily when you have repeating patterns together with a diminishing perspective and strong geometric shapes. I positioned the groom and the ushers to allow the viewers' eyes to travel through the picture..

bottom right

FIG. 19   ISO 800 f/4 at 1/4000th

Boys will be boys.

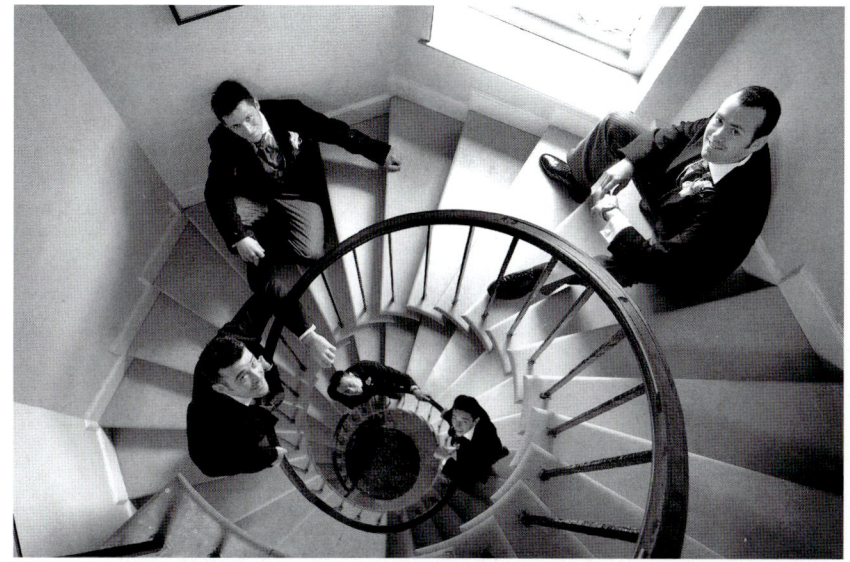

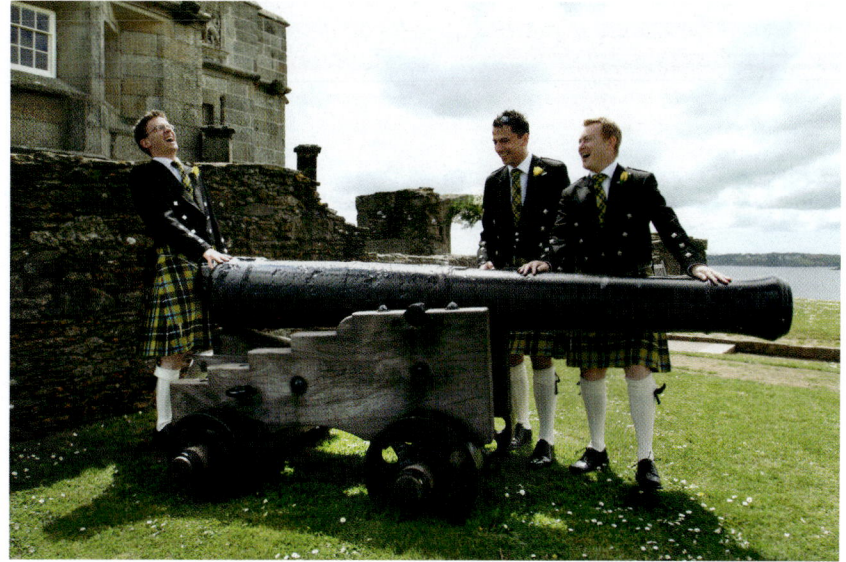

magazine will use 'visit www.lovegrove-weddings.com.' Both addresses will redirect to our main site at lovegroveweddings.com. This makes it is easy to see the number of referrals each advert generates. You can use email addresses the same way. 'Email studio@lovegroveweddings.com' or 'info@lovegroveweddings.com.'

But remember, the results given by your statistics software will not indicate the amount of *eventual business* generated. This system just records the *activity* the advert generates. For a more comprehensive test, you will need the prospect to tell you *where* they first became aware of you and *what* made them take action. We cover this within our online enquiry form. Later we also confirm the information they entered. Once a prospect books you and becomes a client, ask them what magazines

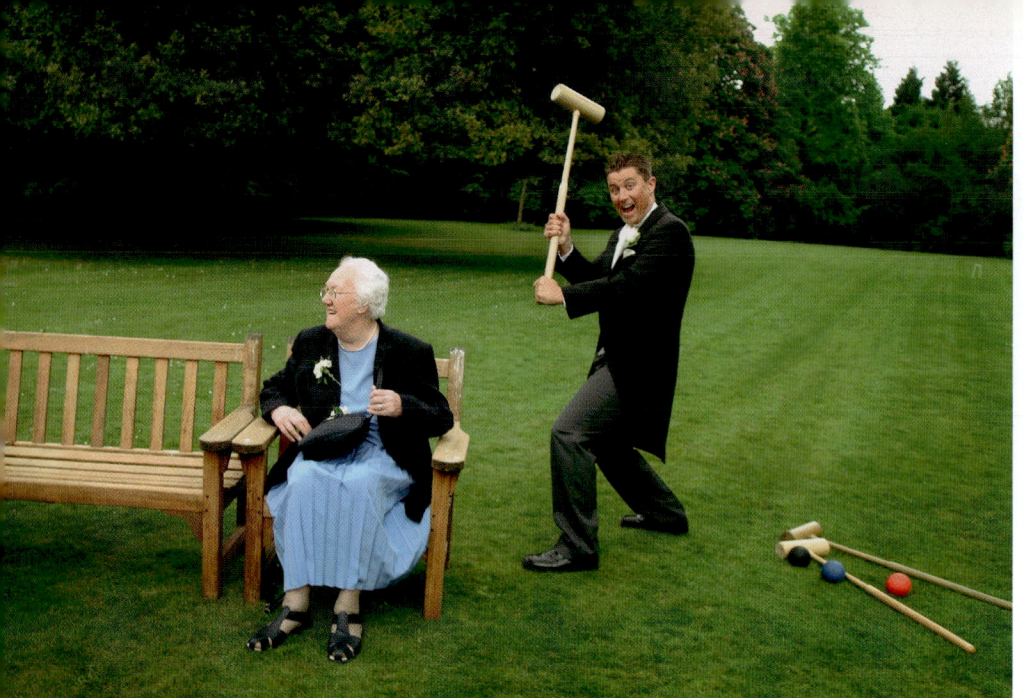

FIG. 20   ISO 320 f/4 at 1/400th

Leave space in your work for humor. The gravity of responsibility as the principal wedding photographer must not block your ability to see an opportunity for a fun picture.

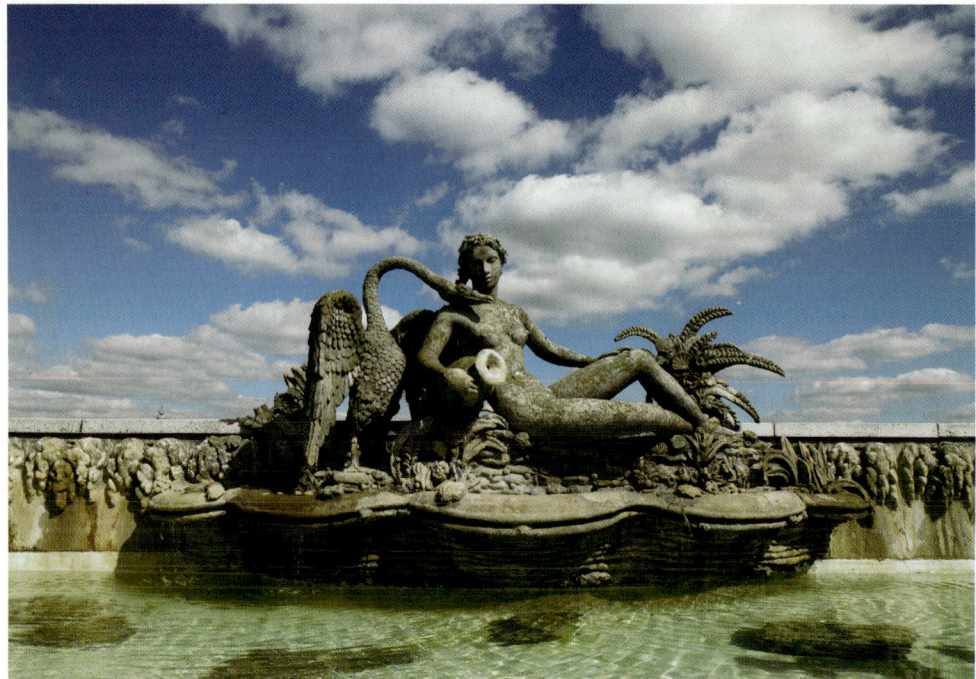

FIG. 21   ISO 400 f/13 at 1/500th

I used a wide lens to pull in the sky and water for this picture of the water feature on the balcony of the penthouse suite of London's Dorchester hotel.

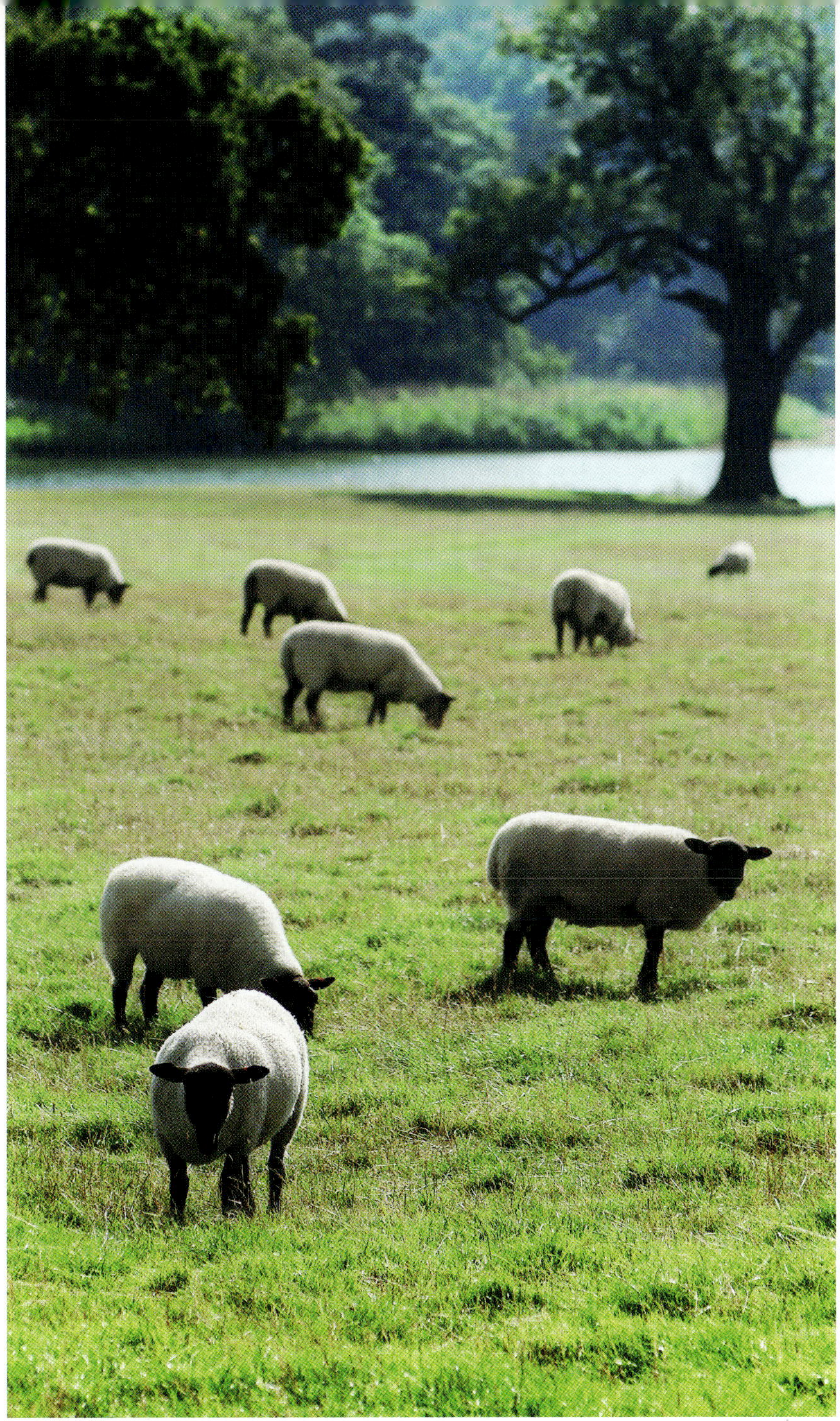

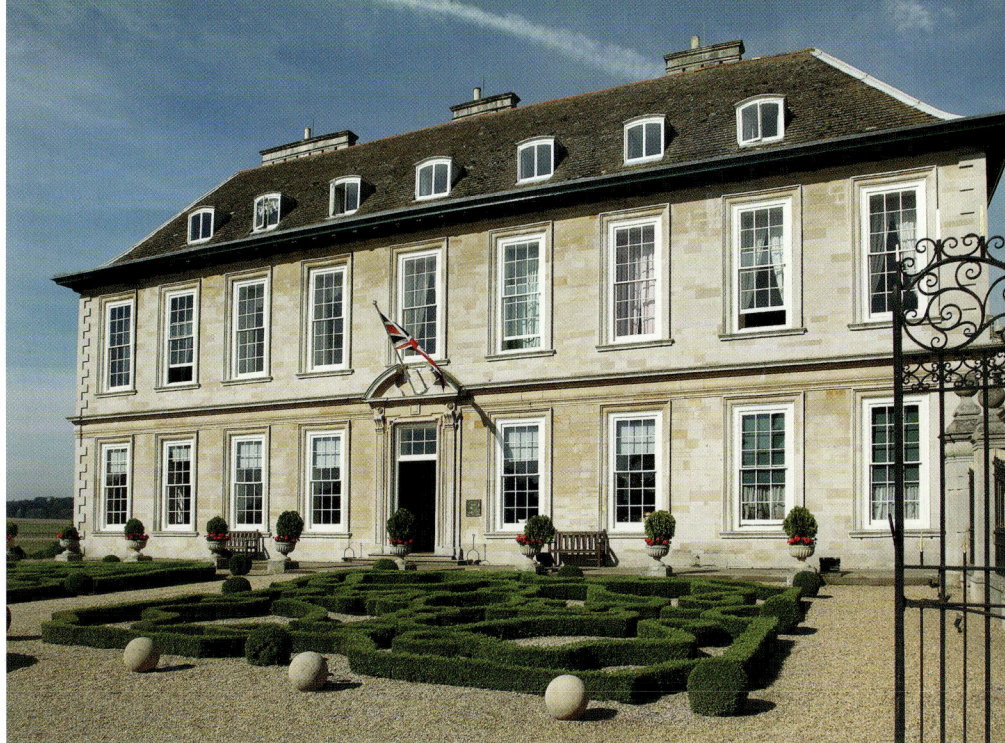

above

FIG. 23 ISO 200 f/4 at 1/3000th

Stapleford house itself looks fantastic in the morning sun.

left

FIG. 22 ISO 200 f/4 at 1/2000th

The sheep in the grounds of Stapleford Park were 'cute' according to the bride. This picture made the album as a result. Tip: If you clap your hands the sheep will lift their heads and look at you for a moment long enough to get a picture.

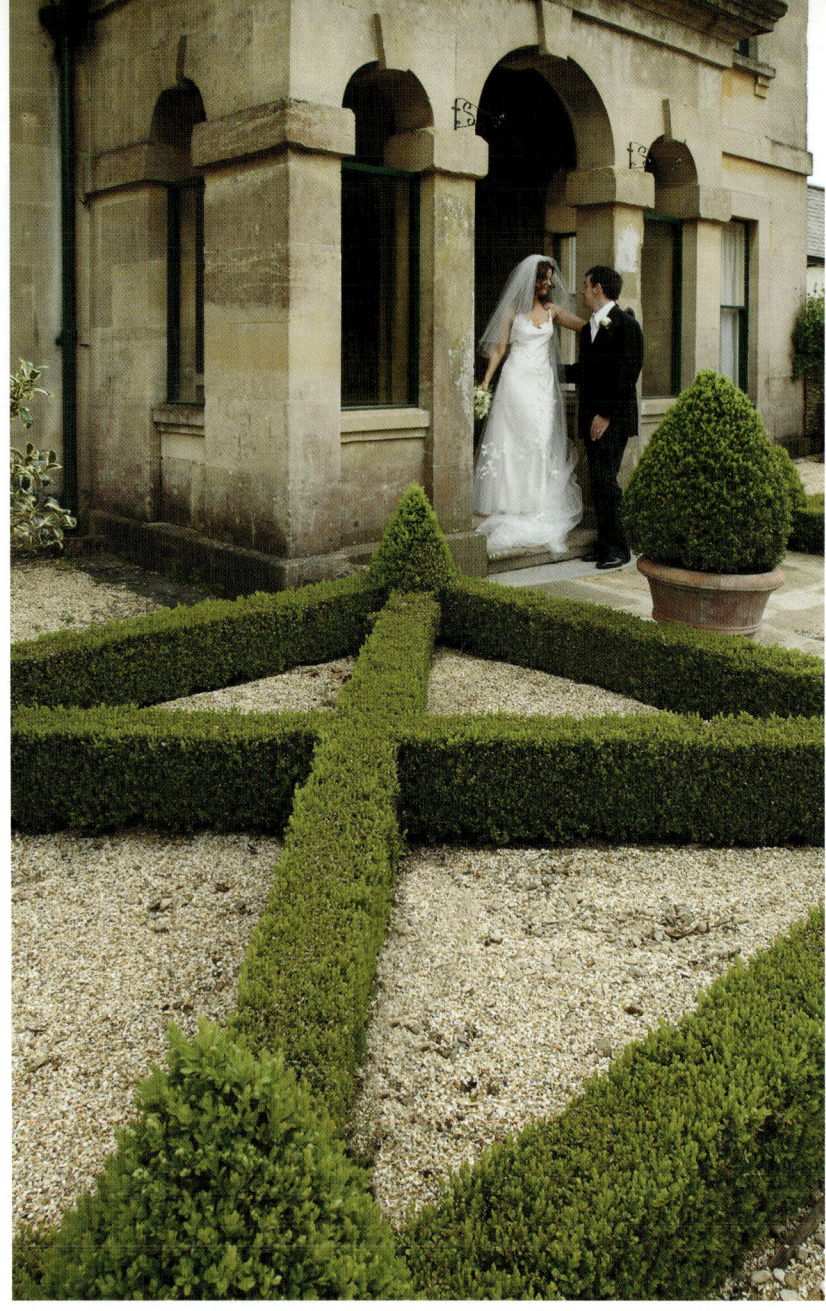

FIG. 24   ISO 200 f/6.7 at 1/180th

The formal hedges at Charlton House provided a strong lead in to this simple picture.

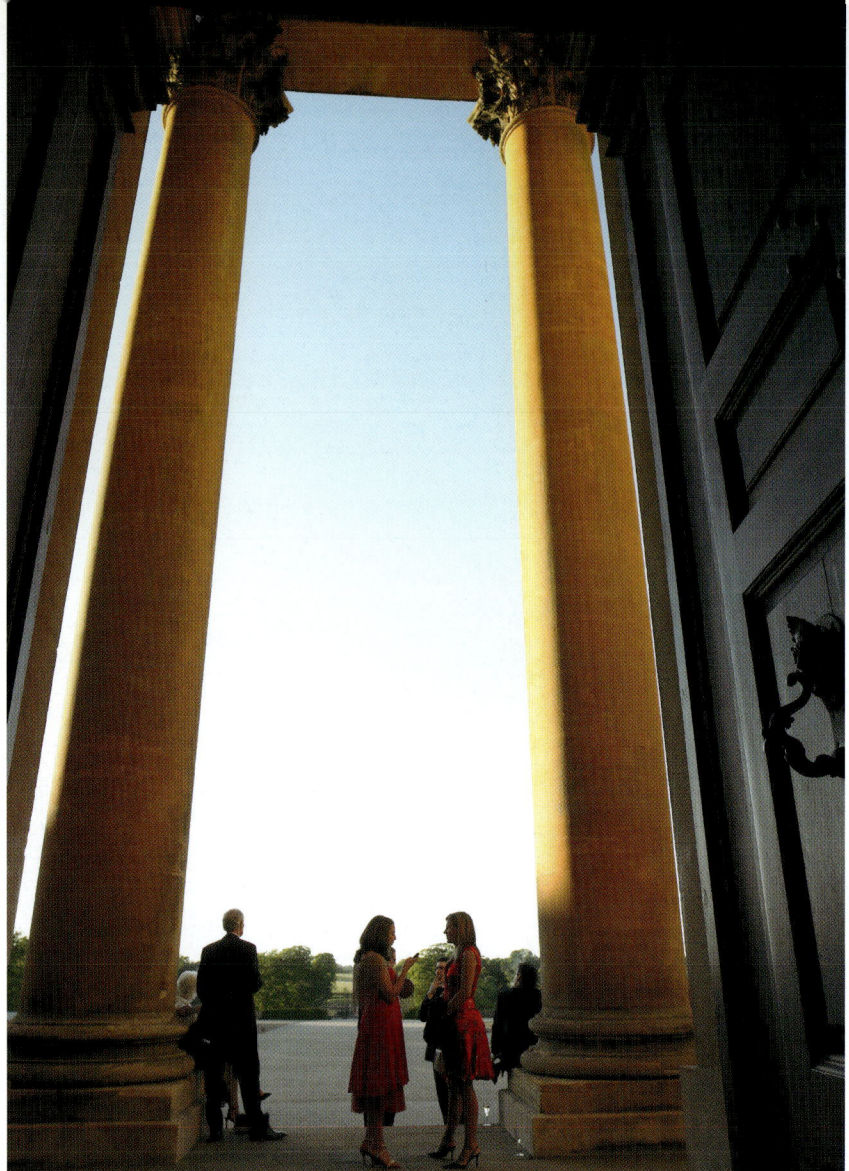

FIG. 25

I love the sense of scale using a wide lens has created. The doors of Blenheim palace are shown in all their magnificence. A splash of red makes a picture like this leap out of the page. The blue of the sky, yellow of the sandstone and green of the foliage complete the primary color line up

Fig. 26   ISO 400 f/4 at 1/360th

Old architectural details combine easily with contemporary floral design by Johanne Shipp at Passion Floral Design in this picture. Plus two stops of exposure composition brought out the color of the orchids

they like best and why. When you have gathered this valuable information, act upon it.

If advert 'A' cost £1000 and generated 30 hits leading to 4 clients, while advert 'B' at £1000 generated 20 hits that led to 6 clients, you can deduce that advert 'B' is 50% more effective than advert 'A.' It sounds obvious, but the extra activity generated by advert 'A' may fool you into thinking it is having a better response. If you need 40 clients and each magazine is bimonthly you might decide to have a run of four adverts in each title. After all, a one-month sample is not a great indicator of future advertising performance. In the United Kingdom, we have found the best times to advertise are September to November and January to April. Keep checking the effectiveness of your advertising and stay in touch with your clients, to identify

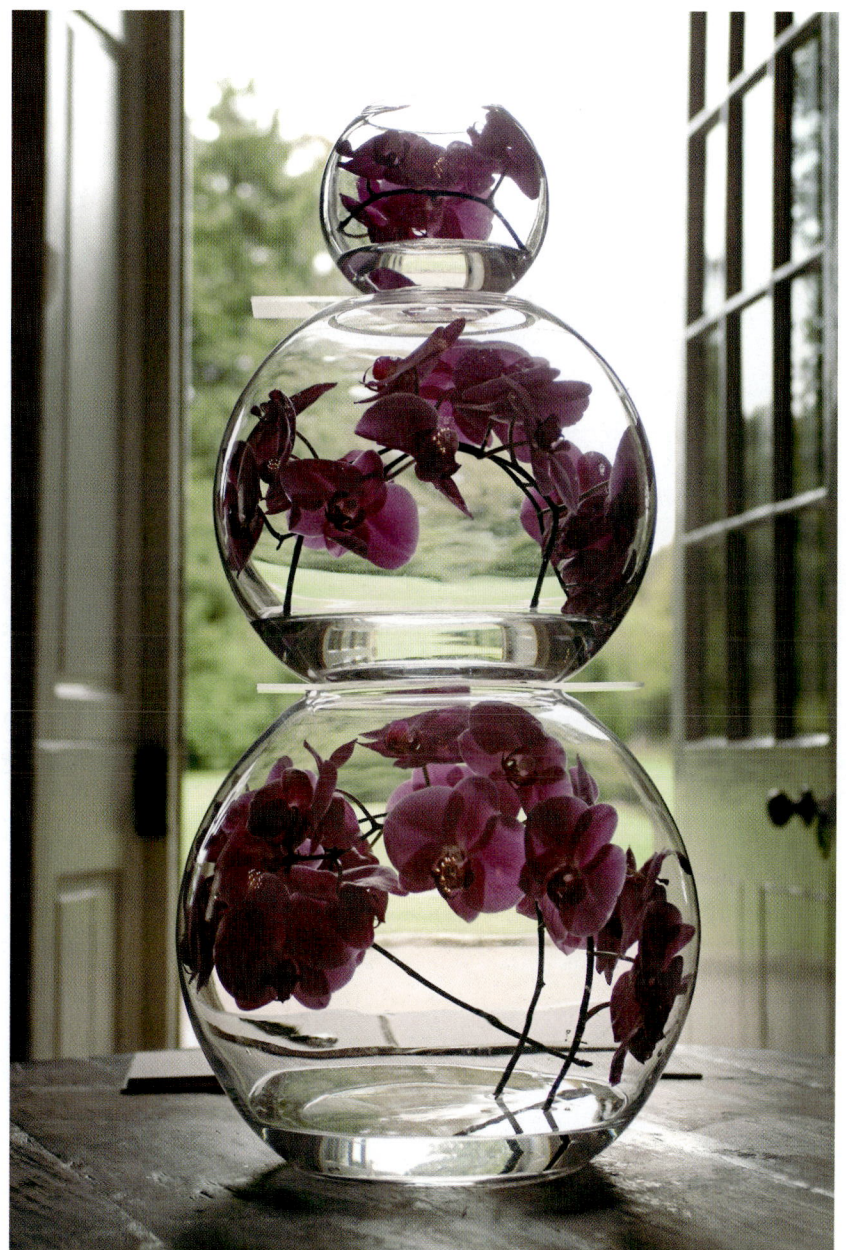

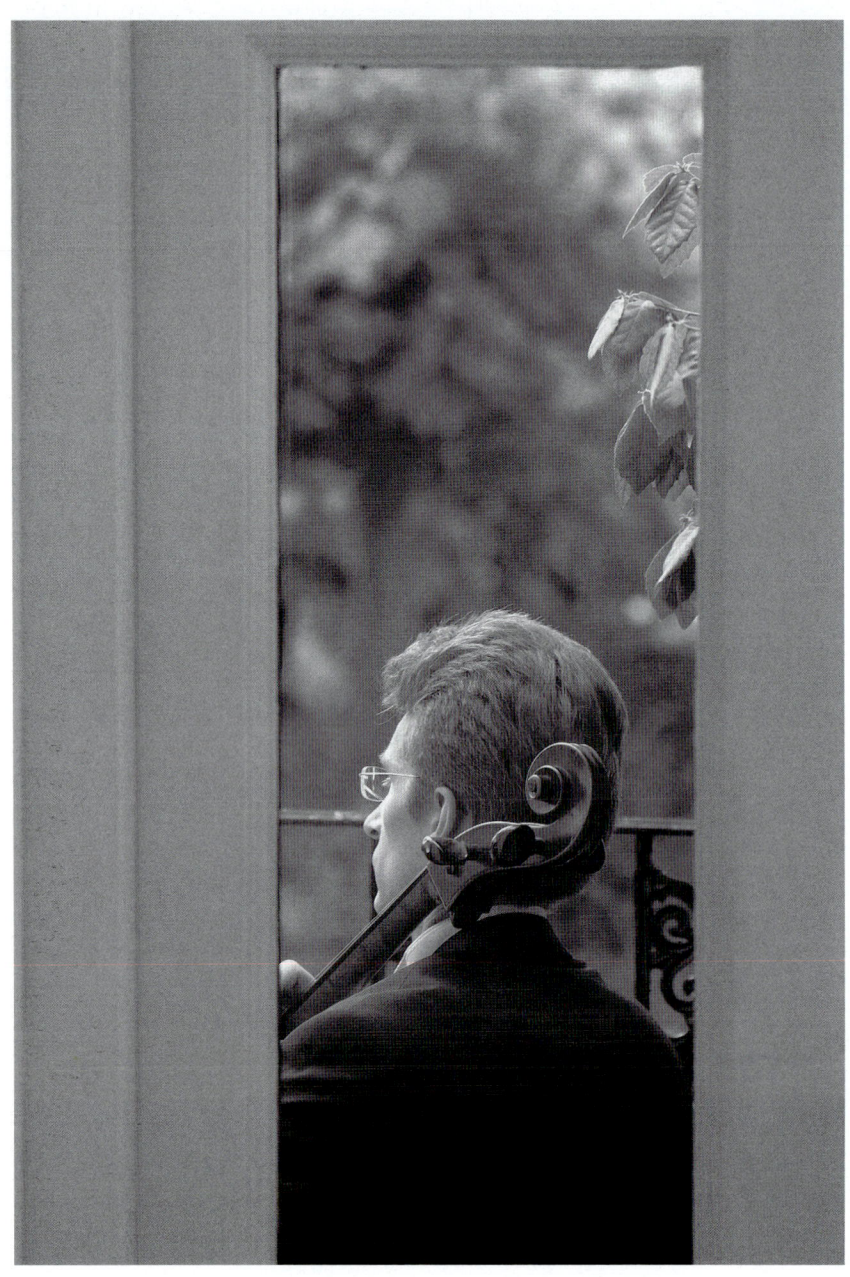

Fig. 27   ISO 320 f/4 at 1/100th

Less is more. This is my picture of the string quartet at a Hempel Hotel wedding.

market trends. Ask what online forums or directories they visit. It will open your eyes to further opportunities.

WHERE TO ADVERTISE

Selecting places to advertise takes lot of common sense and a bit of research. The vast majority of brides-to-be read wedding magazines. As a result, bridal magazines can charge high prices for their advertising space. If you want to know what magazine to advertise in, ask your brides. Or, if you are just starting, go to a busy newsagent and while browsing the pages of your favorite photography title, keep an eye out for who picks up what wedding title. Lunchtime on a Monday is the best time for this exercise. Look at the magazines yourself. Ask yourself a few questions. If I were to get married would I choose my

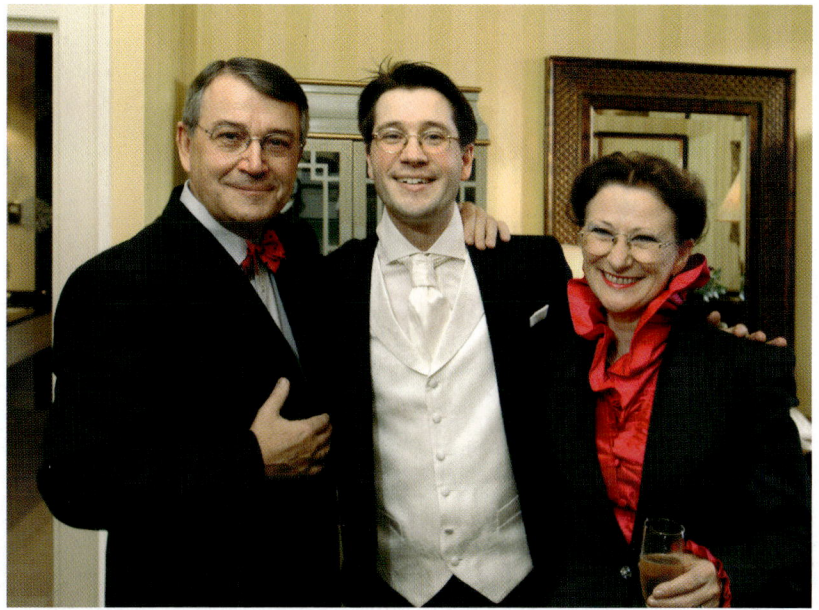

FIG. 28   ISO 400 f/4 at 1/60th

Creating a great rapport is essential to capture a picture like this. The expressions of the groom and his parents are a mirror of mine.

photographer from the adverts in this magazine? Do you find the magazine inspiring? Does the cover price reflect the quality of the content? What is the coverage of the magazine, national or local? If you are only offering to photograph local weddings, then don't advertise in national magazines, as the vast majority of readers are likely to be outside your territory.

The internet is another useful place to advertise. You can buy advertising from search engines in various ways. You can pay for a banner on another supplier's website. 'Pay per click,' is the system in common usage as I write this book but the internet is evolving so fast that I expect 'web real estate' will soon be sold in other guises too. Keep asking clients and prospects what forums and websites they visit. When you do advertise online, test and measure thoroughly. Ask fellow photographers where they

advertise and ask how effective their advertising is, then study your options. Search engine optimization is a system that may well generate more 'hits' to your site. But hits don't mean clients so beware of companies wanting to charge big sums to 'optimize' your site. You can do it yourself with the help of one of the many free online guides. Remember, your website is a brochure, so don't fill it with search terms designed to increase your hits, fill it with useful information that brides will want to read.

NETWORKING

It will pay you to cross promote with other wedding suppliers. A good place to start is to ask your clients and prospects what suppliers they are using. It may surprise you to find that the same names keep cropping up. An initial telephone

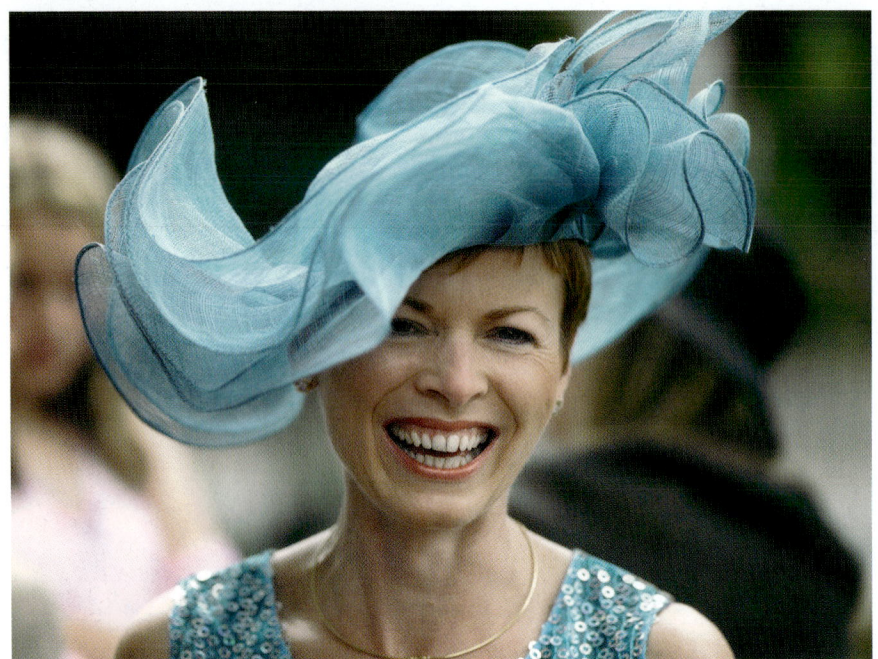
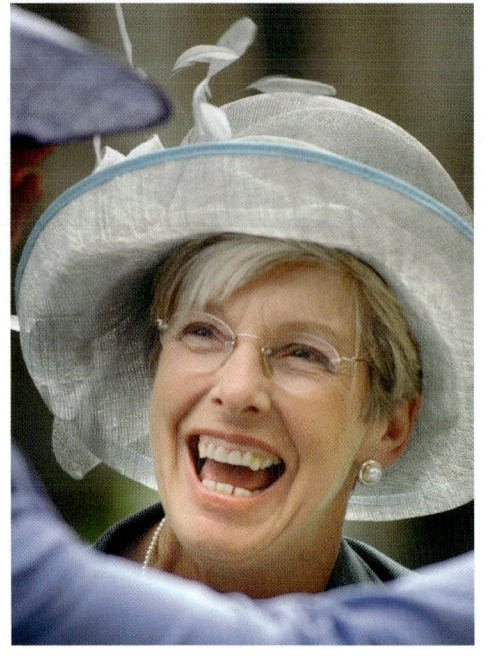

call will open up opportunities. 'I understand from my client, Penny Dollar, that you are the florist for her wedding. She is so excited about your creative ideas. I would love to come and see you. Can I treat you to lunch next week?' At the meeting have a clear objective of what you want to achieve. Before the meeting, write down on a sheet of paper an ideal outcome, then a worst-case scenario. Next, detail any history you may already have, shared past clients, venues and so on. It's always good to reinforce your mutual alliances in this way. Think through what you can do for the florist. Perhaps you can offer him or her complimentary pictures of their flowers from every wedding you work on together. If you have yet to work on a wedding, then offer them a half-day to shoot their brochure. Your name will be credited on their website and in the brochure that goes

out to all their enquiries. In return ask them to mention you to all new leads. The process of shooting a brochure should be a fun rapport-building exercise. Do this type of networking with as many partners as you can. Always be sure to make detailed notes after each meeting and use the information wisely. Soon, your name will be the talk of the industry.

You should also approach wedding coordinators – they too are always hungry for pictures. Some coordinators are members of professional organizations and are bound by their codes of conduct. Others are happy to take 10% of your fee for a referral. Keep them happy if you want to work with them. Coordinators at hotels are often not very well paid, so it is always worth offering a tip, or giving them a gift if they recommend you. If

FIGS 29 & 30   Both pictures f/4

Candid pictures of ladies in hats having fun always make the album. They are a principal part of the glamour of the day.

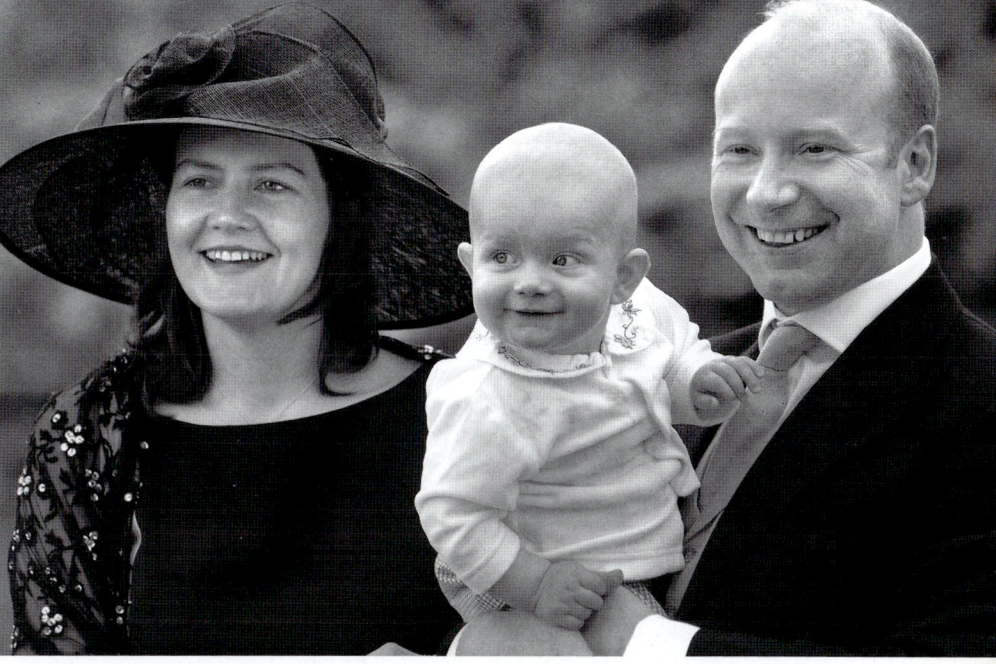

FIG. 31   ISO 400 f/4 at 1/400th

This charming family portrait shows all the qualities of a Lovegrove moment. I created the fun and held the young family's attention while Julie captured the action.

you like the hotel and the coordinator, reward them with a gift even if the recommended bride doesn't book you. That way you will get the next referral. Once you have become established at a venue it may be worth having a display album on view there. If you decide to go down this route make sure the pictures were all taken at one wedding at the venue in question. When you get your next lead from the venue, ask 'Were you shown my album?' If not, follow it up. Keep testing your system.

Dress designers love photo shoots. Offer your services to them, get into their brochure and get mentioned in their store. A simple letter after a wedding saying 'How lovely Penny looked on Saturday. Your dress made her sparkle and it shows in my pictures. Please accept these pictures on CD with my

compliments. I have checked with Penny and she is happy for you to use them for marketing purposes. Please credit me if you use them, Thank you.' Then follow up a week later with a call. The object of the call is to arrange a visit to their shop. If you get on well with the designer and they have lots of wall space above the hanging rails, offer to give them display materials. Framed pictures or display graphics with joint branding will add credibility to your company.

Great customer experience along with a high quality product converts clients into raving fans. An army of raving fans is the holy grail of marketing. It generates leads and so the cycle continues. When you reach the point of generating all or nearly all of your business by referral you have cracked the marketing system!

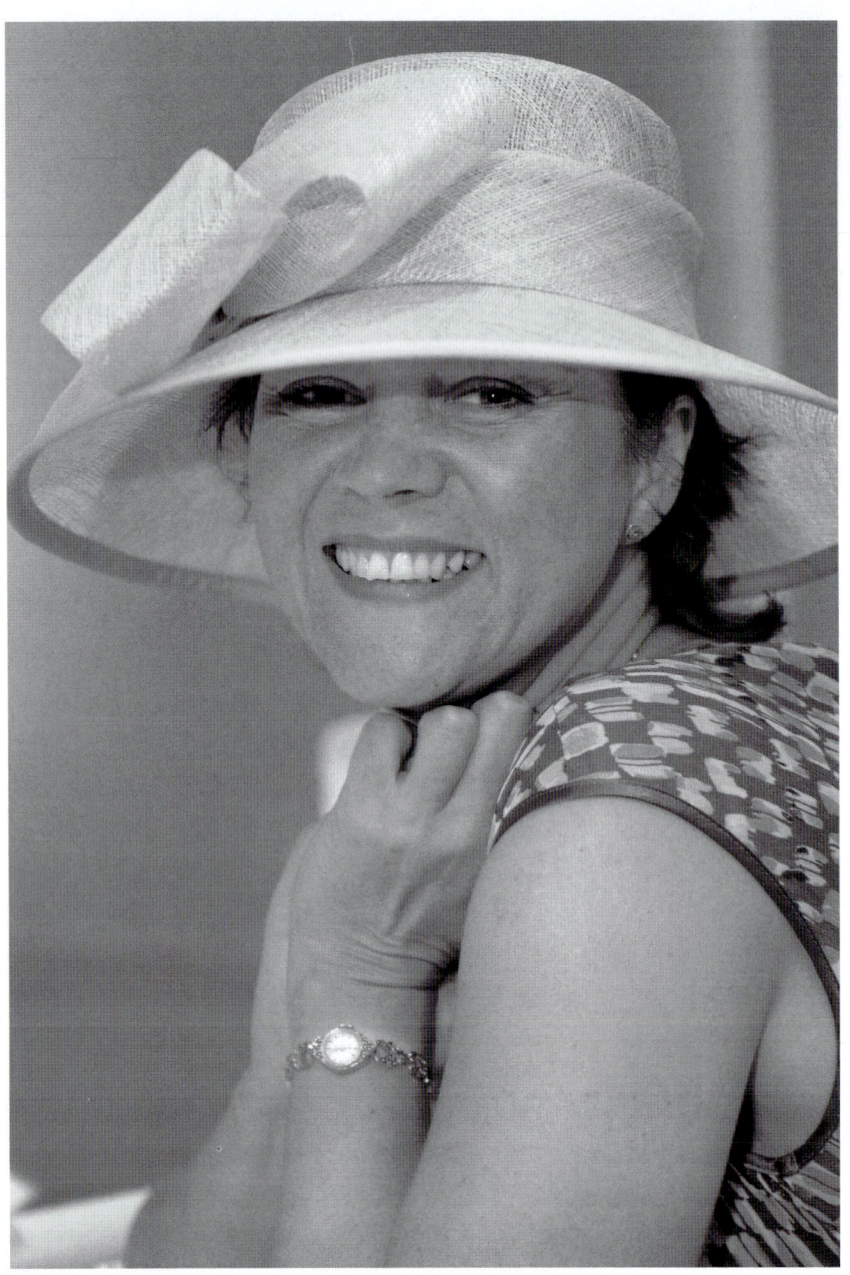

FIG. 32   ISO 800 f/4 at 1/60th

This picture shouldn't work but it does. The shadow from the lady's hat cuts through her eyes. Her hands are in an unattractive position and her shoulders are hunched. It is the radiance that shines through and makes this an attractive picture.

THE VALUE OF A BRAND

In this book, we often mention 'brand.' But what is it and how does it differ from 'product'? Imagine two pairs of bridal shoes. They may have been made in the same town in Asia, with the same materials and to a similar quality; yet once the brand labels have been sewn in, one pair might be worth over twice the price of the other.

Never underestimate the value of a brand. A brand must be nurtured and protected. The best way to do this is by delivering a consistently high quality product right down to the finest detail. Make sure you back this up with *everything* you produce. For example, the Lovegrove website indicates that we specialize in wedding photography, with no mention of commercial, portrait,

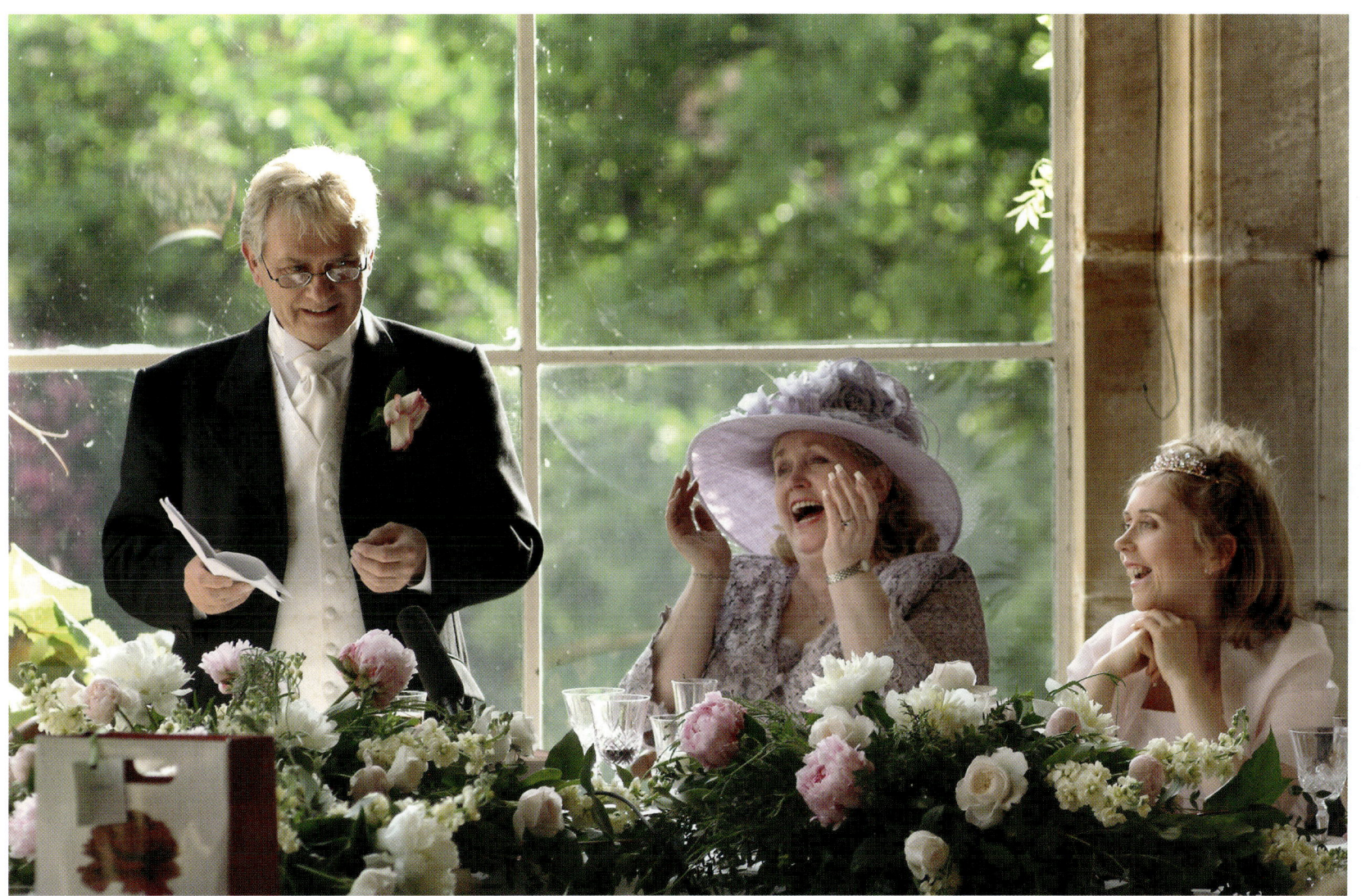

Fig. 33   ISO 400 f/4 at 1/250th

To capture a great moment like this requires good timing. Julie is far better at capturing the decisive moment than me. It is for this reason that she shoots the speeches.

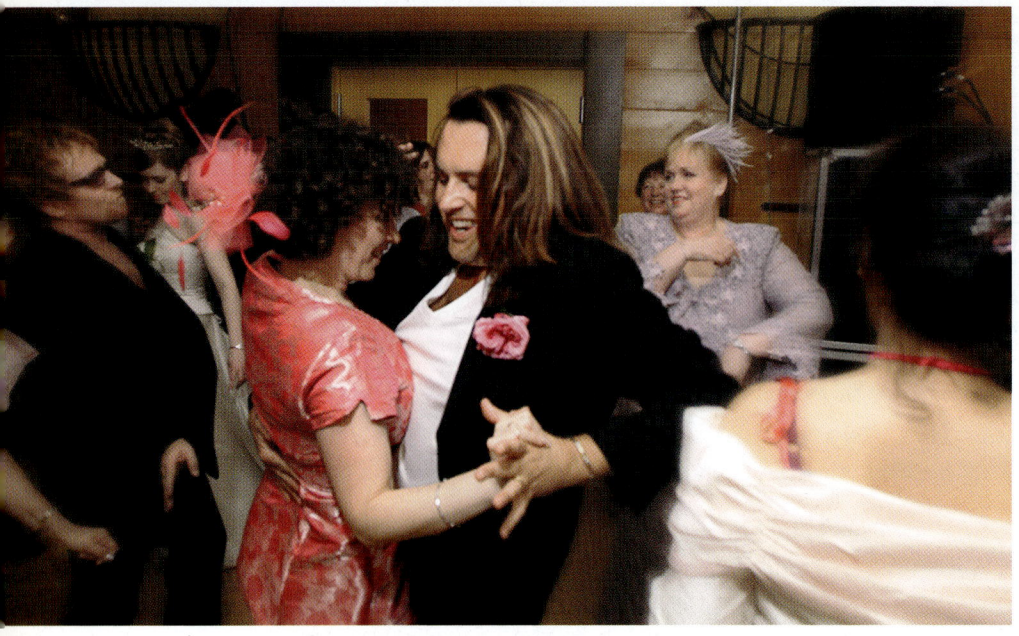

FIG. 34   ISO 800 f/4 at 1/60th

A little bit of motion blur around the perimeter of this picture added to the drama of the moment.

opposite

FIG. 35   ISO 200 f/4 at 1 second

This hamlet was lit up at night as part of the Ravello arts festival in Italy. This view from the wedding reception restaurant was fantastic.

or other photography services. This makes Lovegrove Weddings a dedicated specialist provider. The 'click path' through the website is planned to educate and entertain potential prospects and encourage them to appreciate the Lovegrove product. The website utilizes testimonials and quotes from past clients and photographers alike to reinforce our core values.

Our advertising follows a structure too and this reinforces our brand. Advertising the brand rather than the product is a great tactic to employ from time to time. Coca Cola do this all around the world. Getting our brand name in the editorial pages of the top wedding magazines has got to be one the easiest and most rewarding brand building activities we have ever undertaken. And it is better than free! I say that, because we have given wedding pictures to magazines to publish with our credits

clearly shown and we have received free or heavily subsidized advertising in return. Another brand building opportunity is to associate your company with another strong brand. We did this in 2005 with both Estée Lauder and *You and Your Wedding* magazine. The exercise started with a trip to London where I took the editor of *You and Your Wedding* to lunch. Other team members joined us and we brainstormed the whole idea. Carol Hamilton, the editor at the time, managed to get Estée Lauder on board as they were launching a range of bridal cosmetics, and we provided the prize. The system was simple: we ran a joint competition to find the 'UK bride of the year.' The payback was enormous credibility through association with a top international brand, while the massive exposure generated in the media and in stores gave our own brand yet another boost.

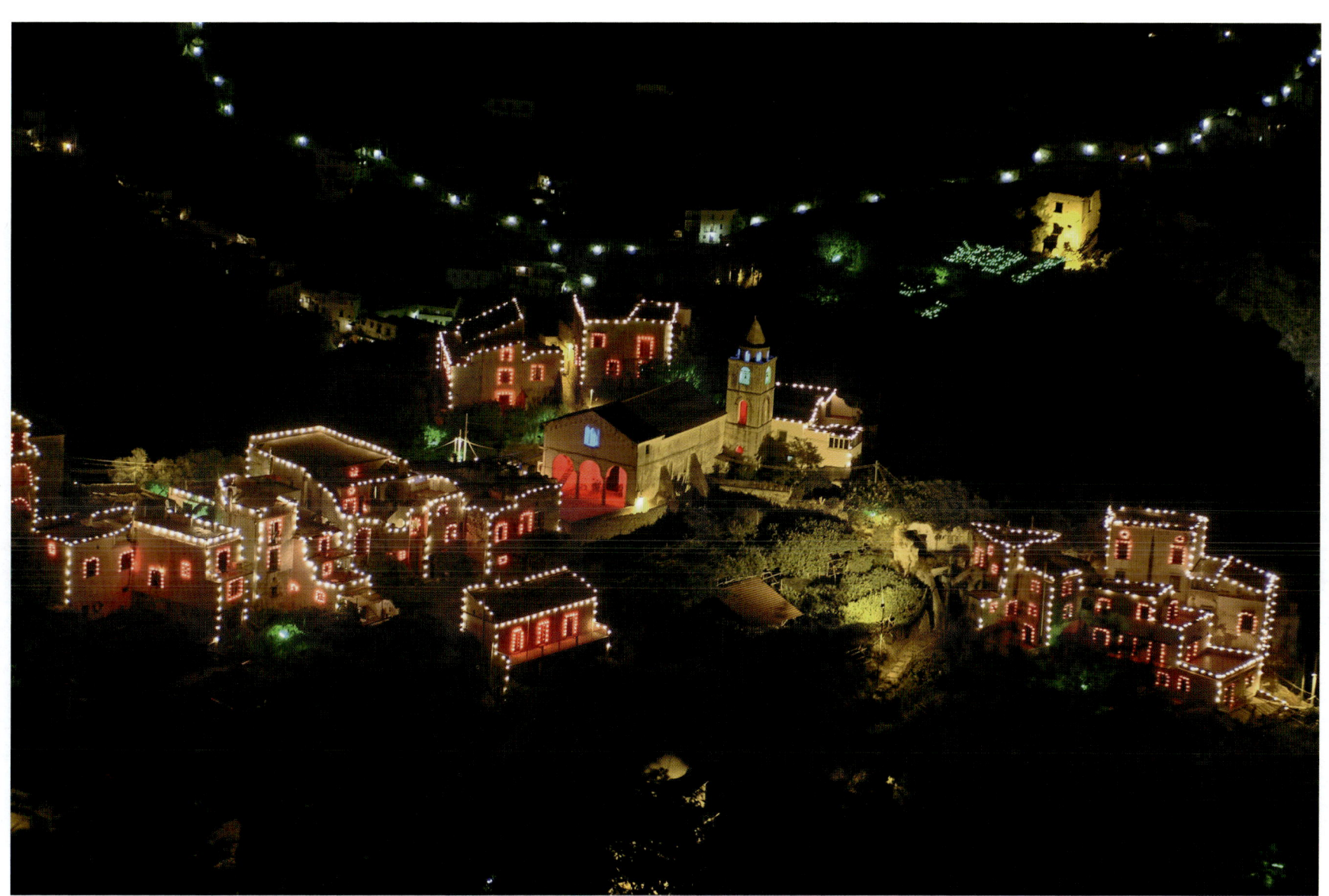

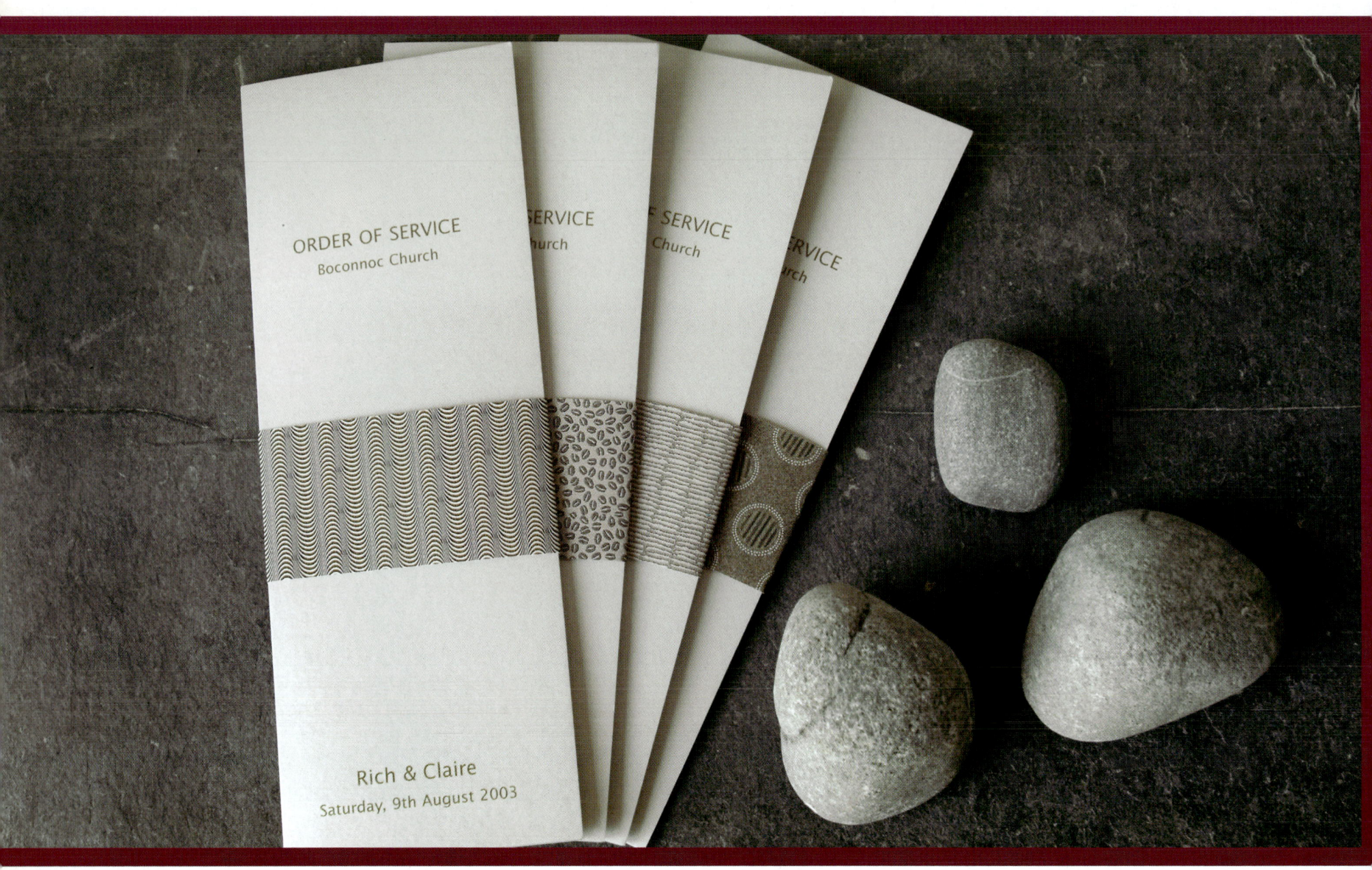

10
Sales

What is it about photographers and selling? Even some of the very best photographers are not good at selling. Possibly, it embarrasses them to sing their own praises. They would probably prefer to stick to photography. That means if they want to maximize their sales – get paid what they're worth – they'll need to find someone else to do the selling for them. In this chapter, I will tell you how *we* do it and why we feel comfortable with our system even though we are photographers not 'sales people.'

But first let's take a look at what our clients expect. Sales strategies come and go like wedding photography styles and it's important to keep up with the trends in retail sales systems. Your clients are subjected to these 'new' systems every day so you too must be in tune with what triggers today's buying decisions. Nothing is really new in sales, it's more a case of some things are 'in' and some 'out.' They either work or they don't.

It wasn't long ago that the dominant sales tactic in our industry focused on an 'up-sell' strategy. Up-selling is the process of pre-selling a cheaper package and then later convincing the client to spend more than they intended. The public have wised up to this and now the tide has turned. Let me explain...

opposite

FIG. 1   ISO 400 f/6.7 at 1/180th

I was made very aware of the importance to the bride at this wedding of attention to detail. I neatly arranged the four orders of service and found three pebbles to balance the picture. I like doing this kind of thing and it is always appreciated.

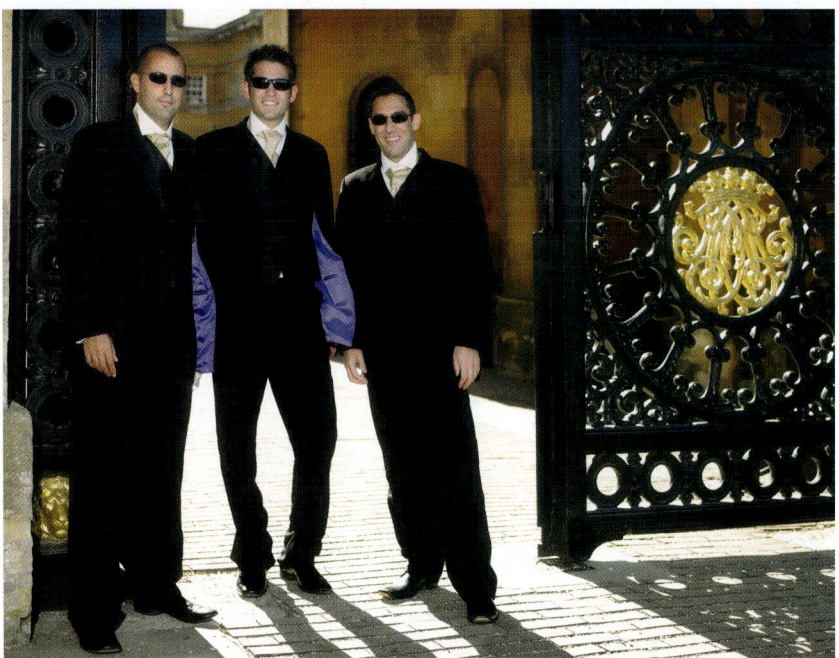

FIG. 2   ISO 200 f/5.6 at 1/320th

The strong backlight and the gate detail make this an interesting picture further enhanced by a gust of wind revealing the purple lining of the ushers' suit.

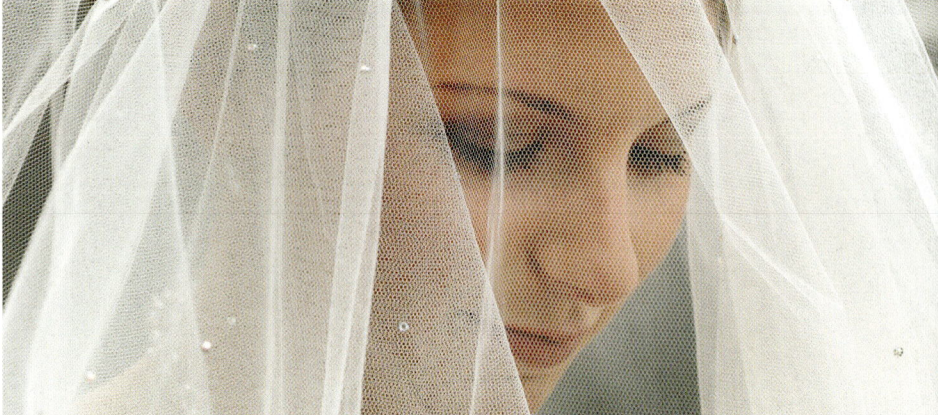

FIG. 3   ISO 320 f/4 at 1/2000th

A classic picture like this is timeless. Julie arranged the veil to reveal the bride's face. A glance down completed the look.

In the 1990s, clients of wedding photographers often went to a viewing to see their pictures, quite unaware that they were going to be subjected to an up-sell session. Worse still, the only way they could have the pictures they wanted, in the album they wanted, was to pay a lot more money to the photographer. Often, this sum was as much as the original fee or even more. I know it sounds ridiculous, but the public became used to the 'up sell' and tolerated it. Photographers justified the system as a means of performance-related pay. This is the sales model that was used at the booking stage:

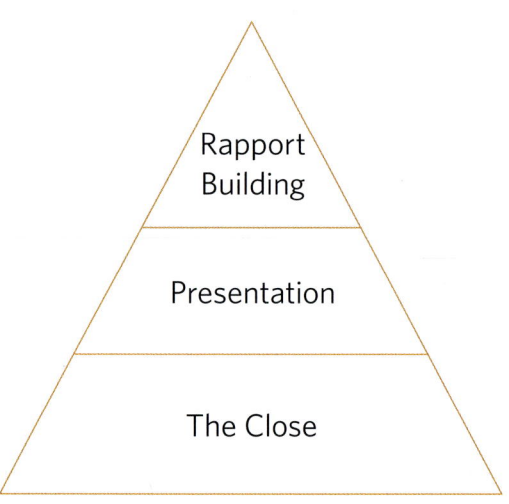

Rapport Building

Presentation

The Close

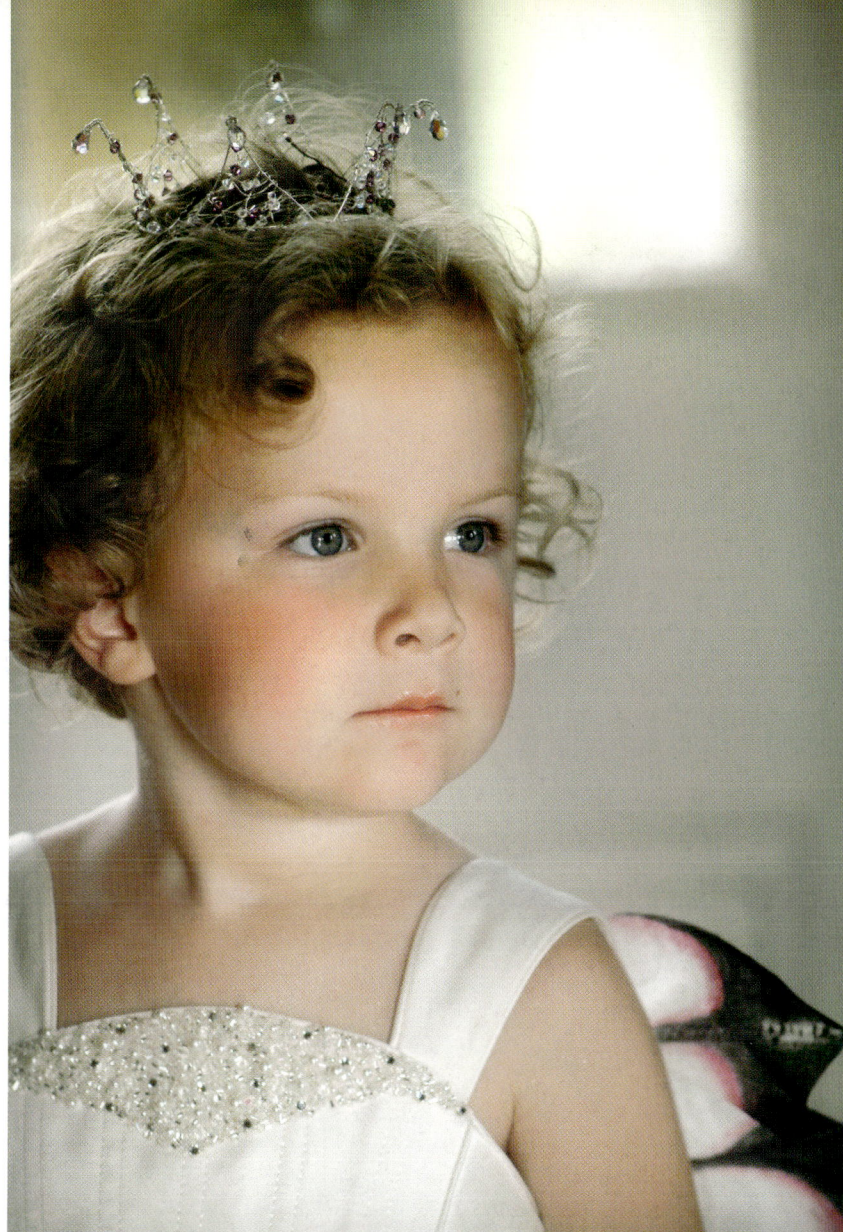

FIG. 4   ISO 800 f/4 at 1/250th

A radiant glow in this child's face, the rim light, and the neutral expression makes this a beautiful picture.

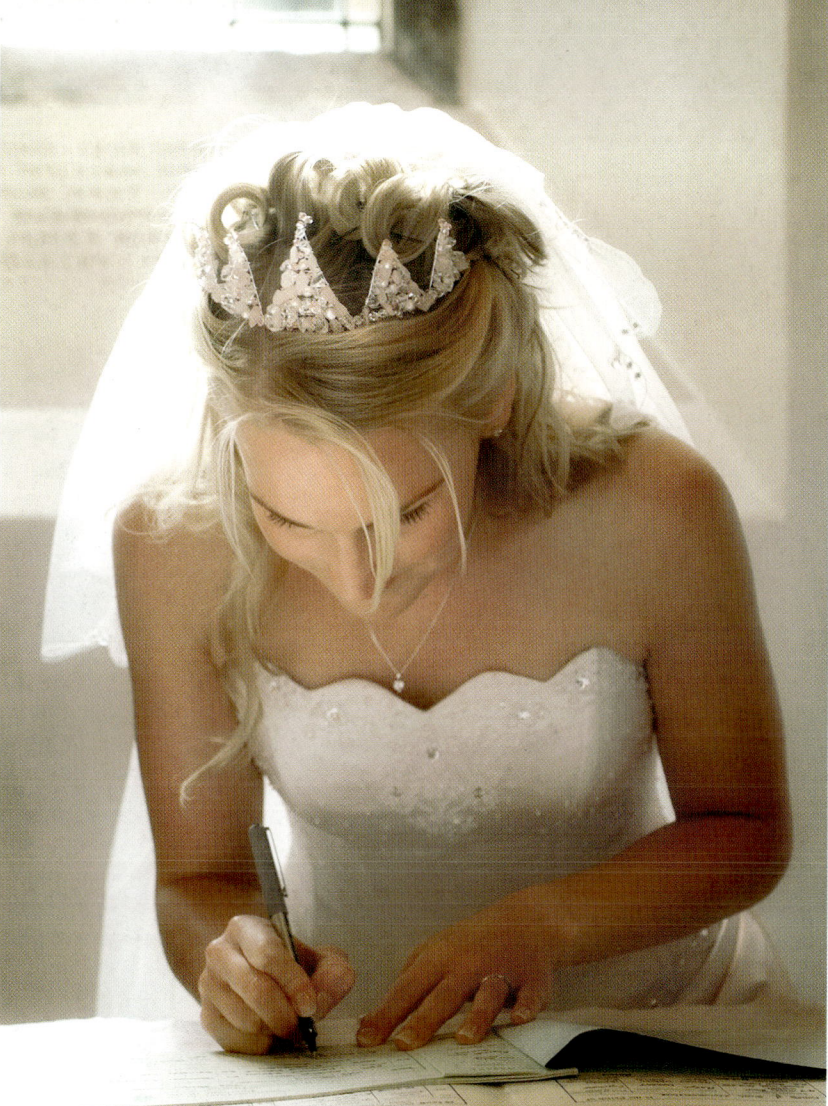

FIG. 5   ISO 800 f/4 at 1/60th

Wonderful light and a beautiful bride are a great start to making good pictures. This is a picture of the bride signing the register but it is also a picture that shows the coordination of fashion elements. The tiara perfectly compliments the bodice of the dress. Never underestimate the importance of capturing these details in your pictures.

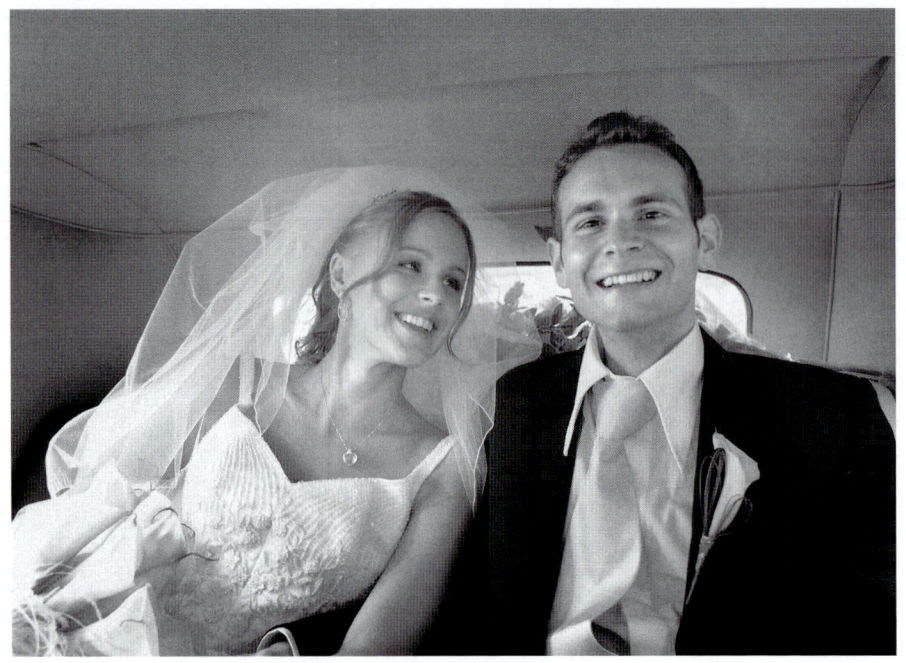

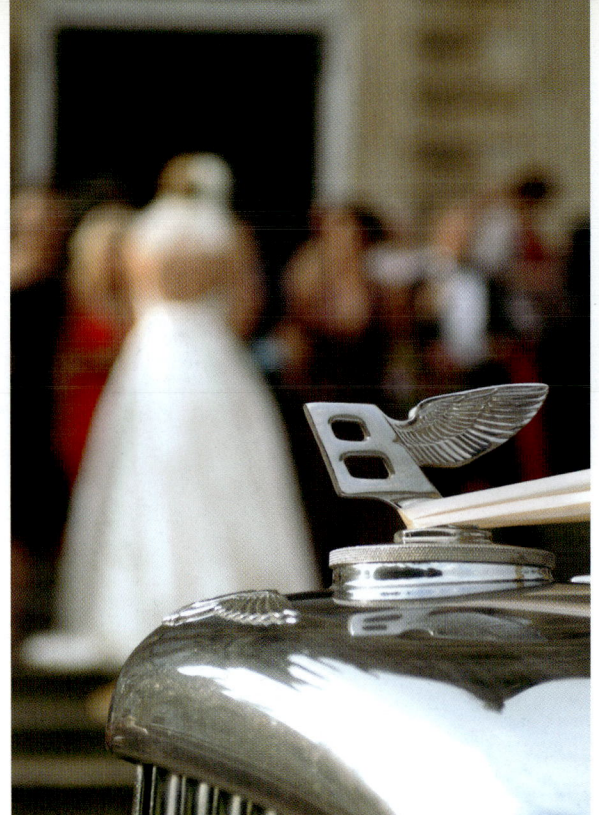

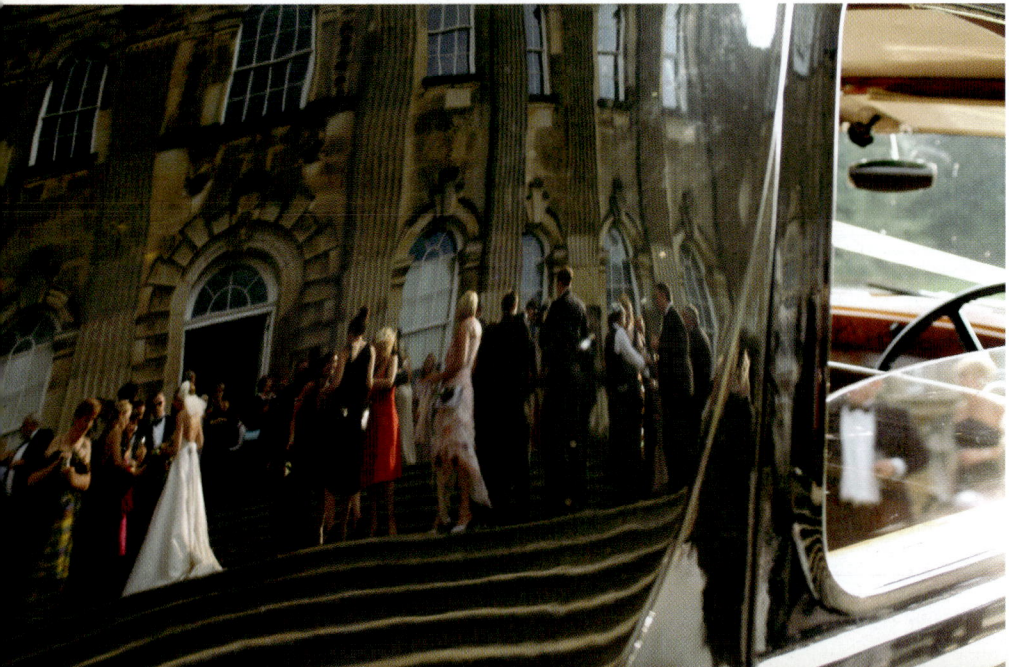

top left

FIG. 6   ISO 800 f/4 at 1/60th

A lovely moment captured by Julie. This couple have gone on to become great portrait clients of ours.

top right

FIG. 7   ISO 400 f/4 at 1/100th

I like to have fun with split focus and I find f/4 is a perfect aperture setting.

left

FIG. 8   ISO 400 f/4 at 1/125th

This is a clever picture well seen. Including part of the car is vital to give the reflection meaning.

Arches are a strong design statement. I like to shoot from the dark into the light. I place my sitters carefully to compliment the composition. I use the camera screen to asses the exposure and compensate as required.

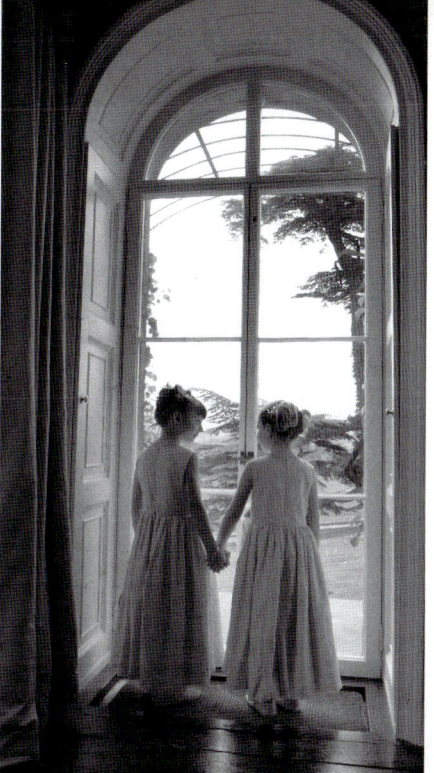
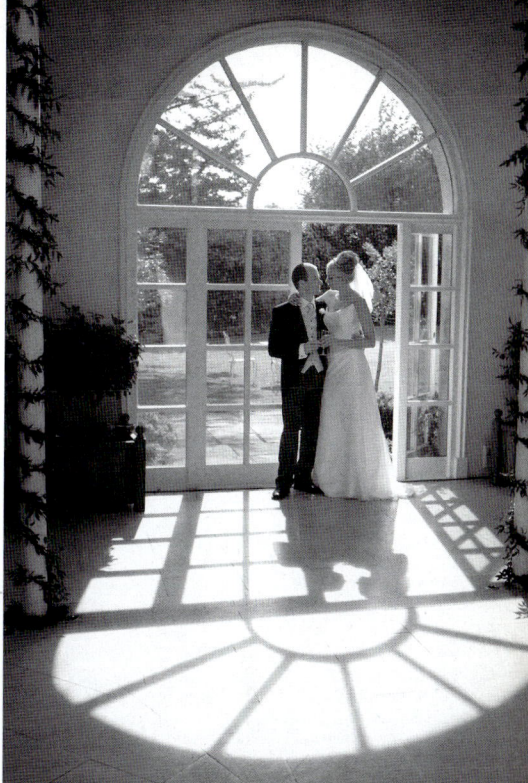
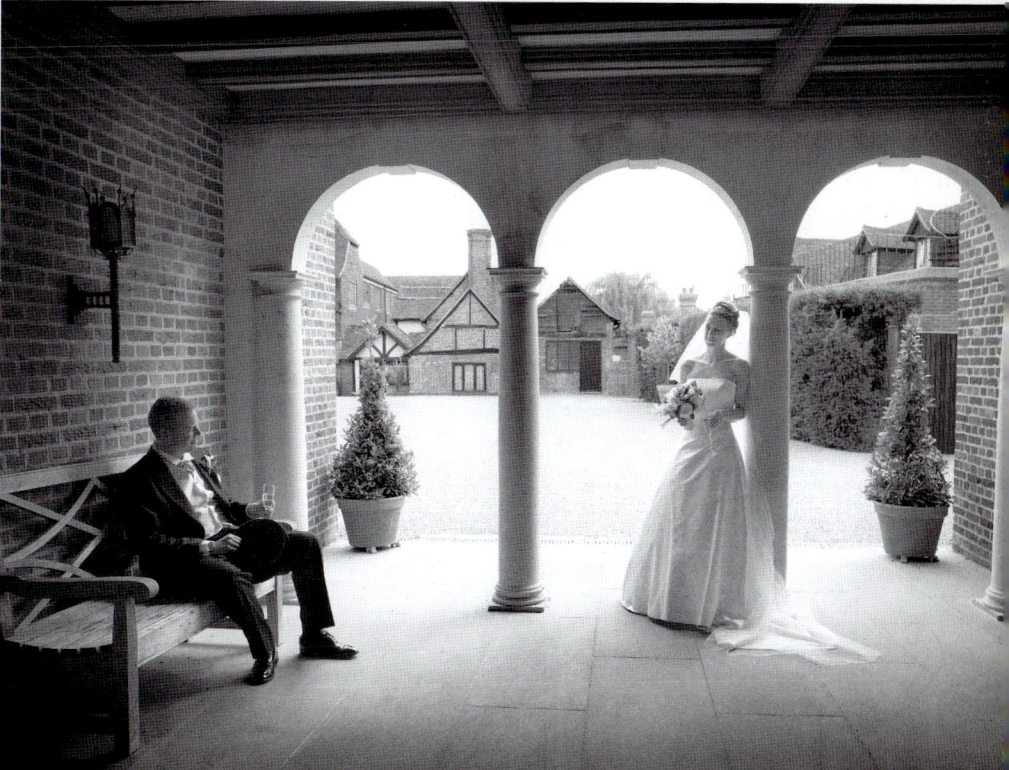

The rapport element (greeting) of this sales model is a well-rehearsed handshake with eye contact, a gentle but positive nod of the head, and a welcoming gesture. Offer hospitality and link swiftly into...

The presentation. This is where the salespersons deliver a slick presentation of the services and products they have to offer. This presentation is delivered in an environment where the salesperson holds court and is in control.

Next comes the close. This is the process of manipulating the prospect until a buying decision is reached. Persuasive techniques are used, such as dealing with each obvious objection in turn and then seeking out hidden objections and dealing with them too. This is followed with a 'trial close,' and if still not successful a few more haggles later, a 'full close' is sought. A trial close might be 'What color album would you like?' To

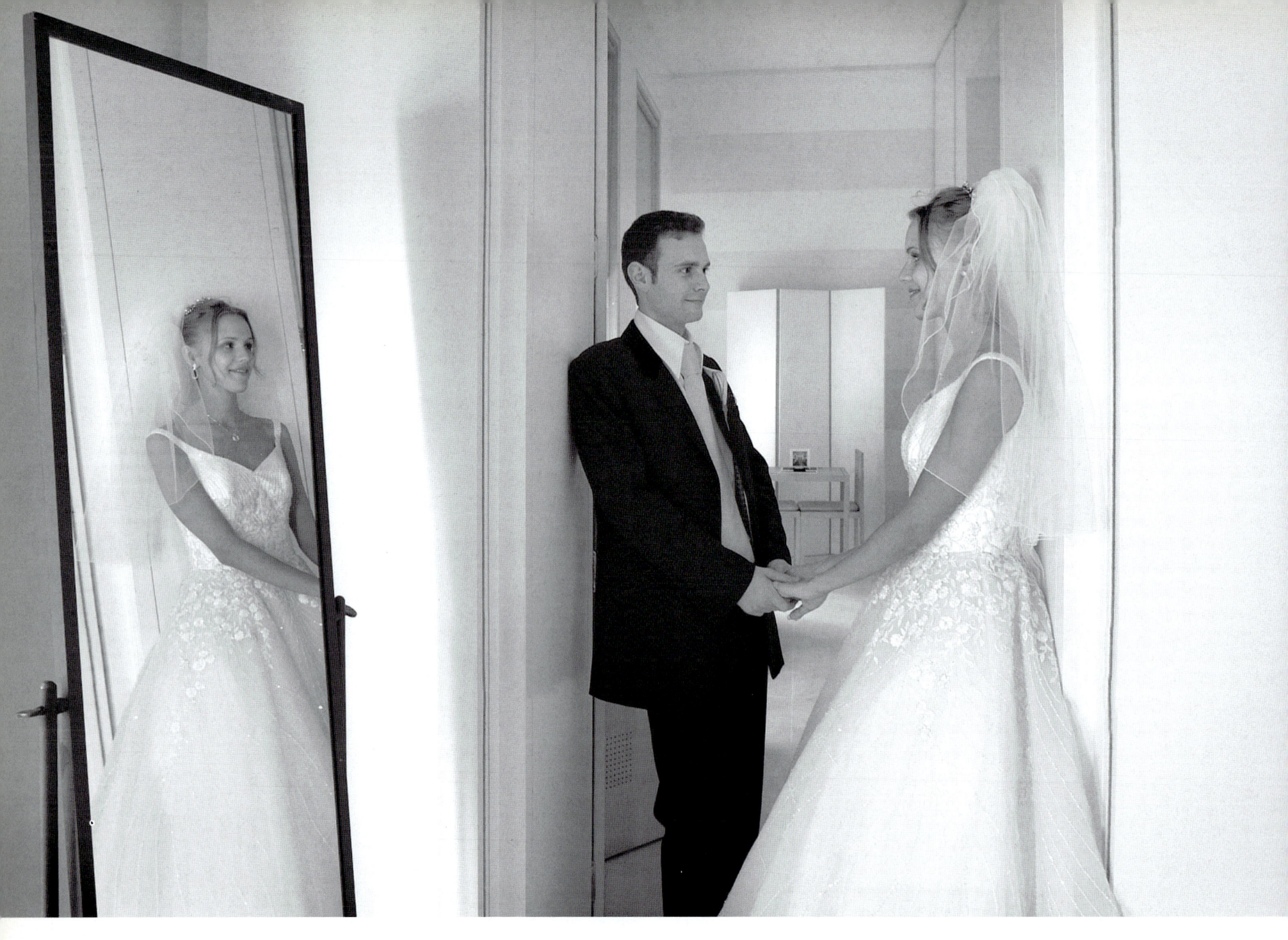

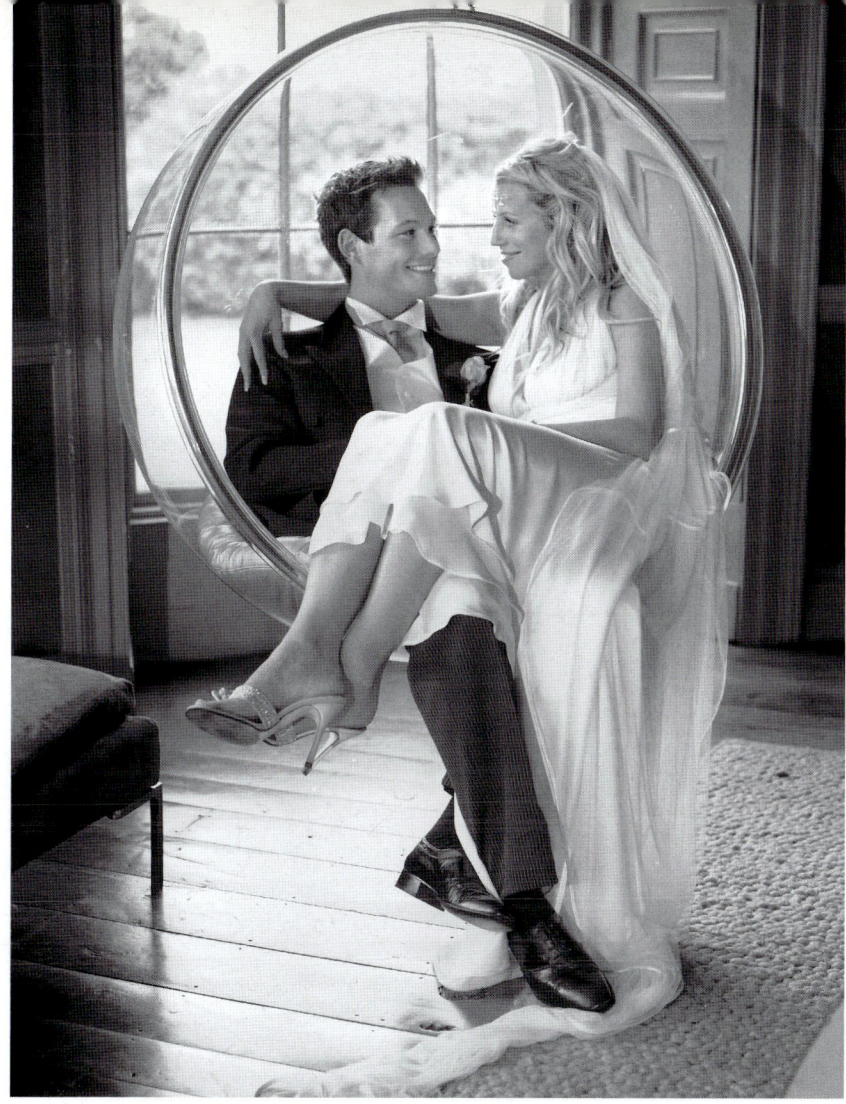

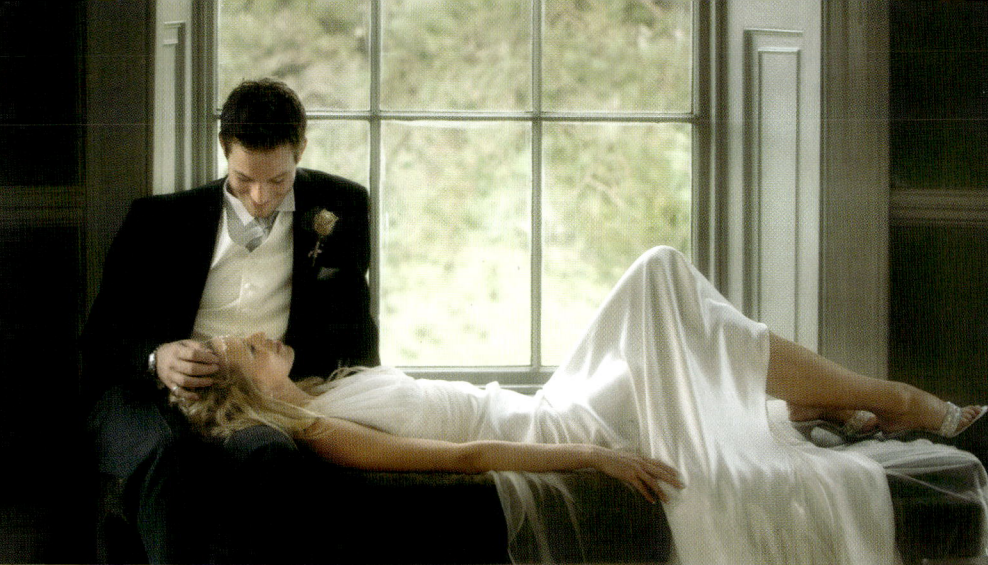

Figs 13 & 14   ISO 400 f/4 at 1/60th

The 'playroom' at Babington House presents many opportunities to create graphically strong compositions like these.

which the salesperson hopes to get a response like 'We'll have a black album please.' This would trigger a close response, perhaps the line 'How would you like to pay; credit card or check?'

The viewing session sales model is similar but with a few more manipulative techniques thrown in. Pitching husband against wife was a classic one, with the salesperson saying something like 'If you let Mark have those car pictures you can have the extra shoe detail shot that you know you want.' Another killer technique was through customer profiling. If the clients arrived in a mainstream regular car the salesperson might say "Everyone loves this album, it's so classic yet current." If, however, the client arrived in an individual car that was not mainstream the sales pitch for the same album would be 'This album is different, not to everyone's liking but shows an individuality through a unique design.' And so on... You get the picture.

opposite

Fig. 12   ISO 800 f/4 at 1/60th

Classical photography is here to stay. I angled the mirror carefully and ensured I could see the full length of the room. This picture was taken at ISO 800 on the wonderful Fujifilm S1 camera with just three megapixels. Pixel count bears little effect on image quality. It's the lens that makes the image.

below

FIG. 15   ISO 400 f/3.4 at 1/40th

This is another classical composition again with depth. The Lovegrove style is to include a bright distant element to add a three-dimensional quality.

FIG. 16   ISO 200 f/5.7 at 1/125th

The horizontal spars on the left of the frame lead into the picture. The couple are well placed and it's up to the vibrant colors of this Hunstanton beach hut to make the picture come alive.

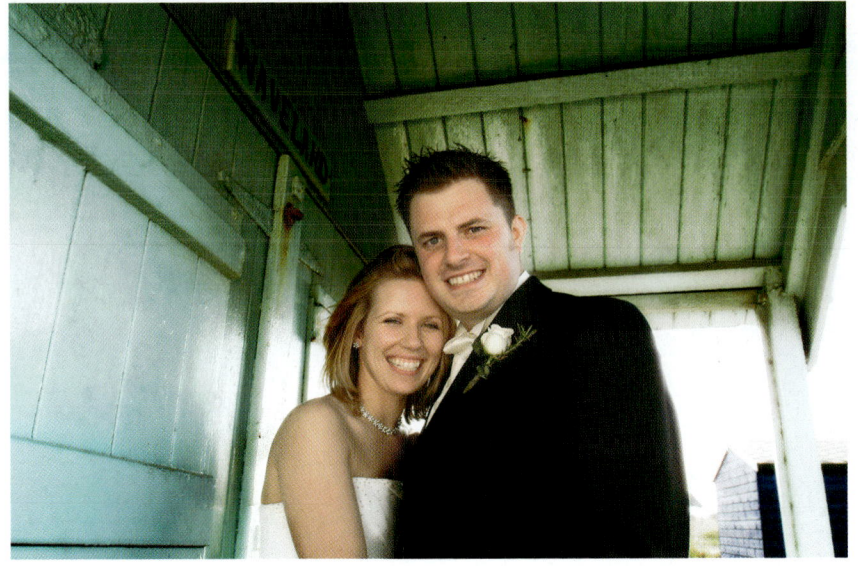

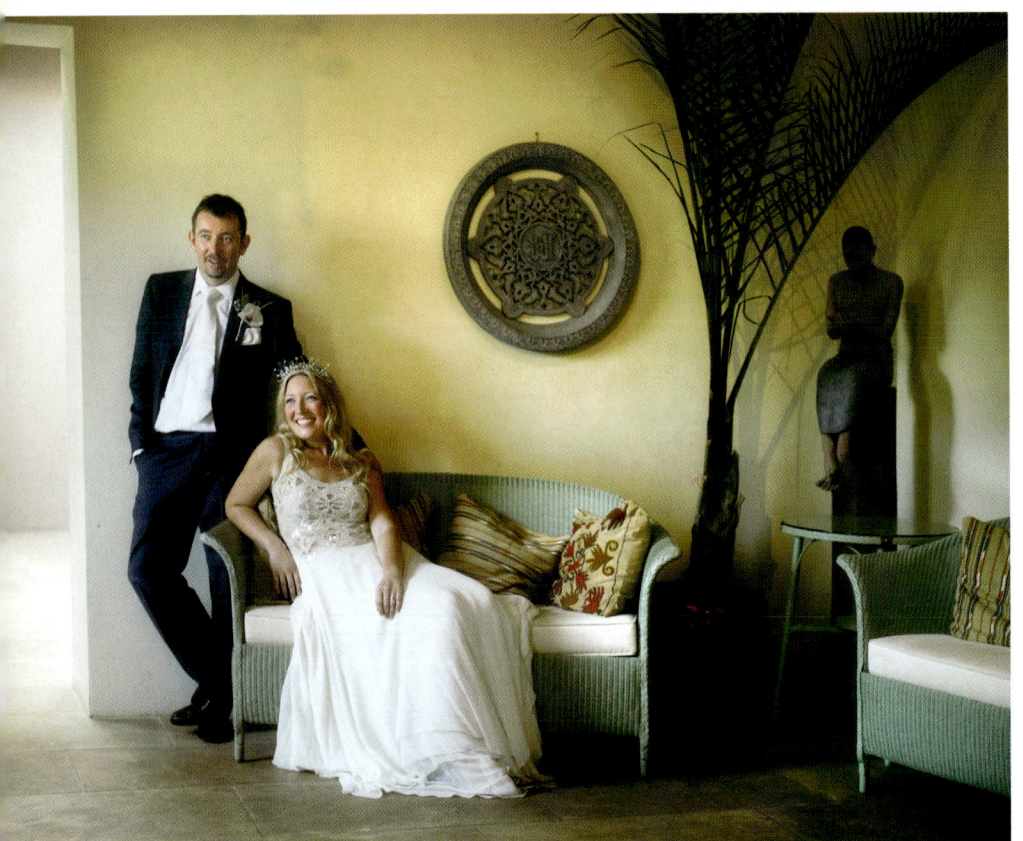

In the current era – the 'noughties' – clients have wised up to manipulative sales techniques and now the most successful strategies are based on a motivational and consultative system.

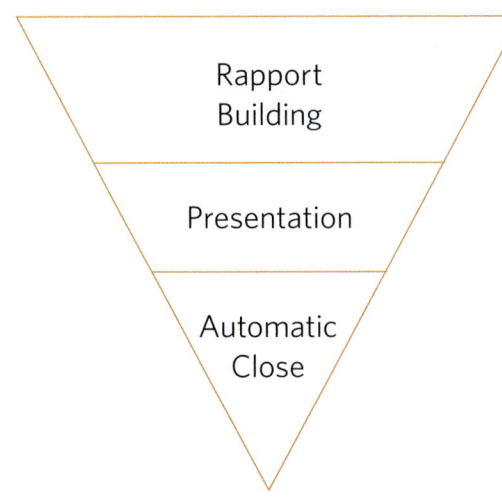

Rapport Building

Presentation

Automatic Close

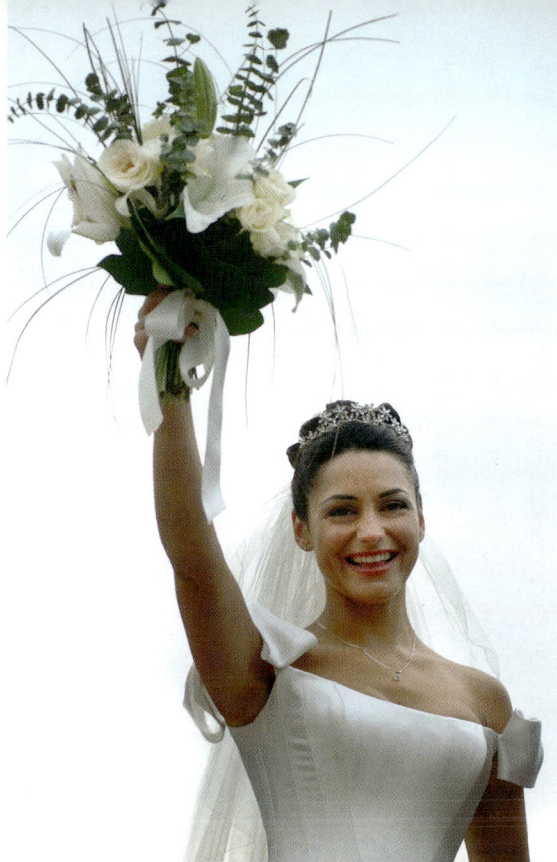

FIG. 17   ISO 400 f/4 at 1/800th

This is my statue of liberty shot. The poses found in the world's art masterpieces are fun to recreate.

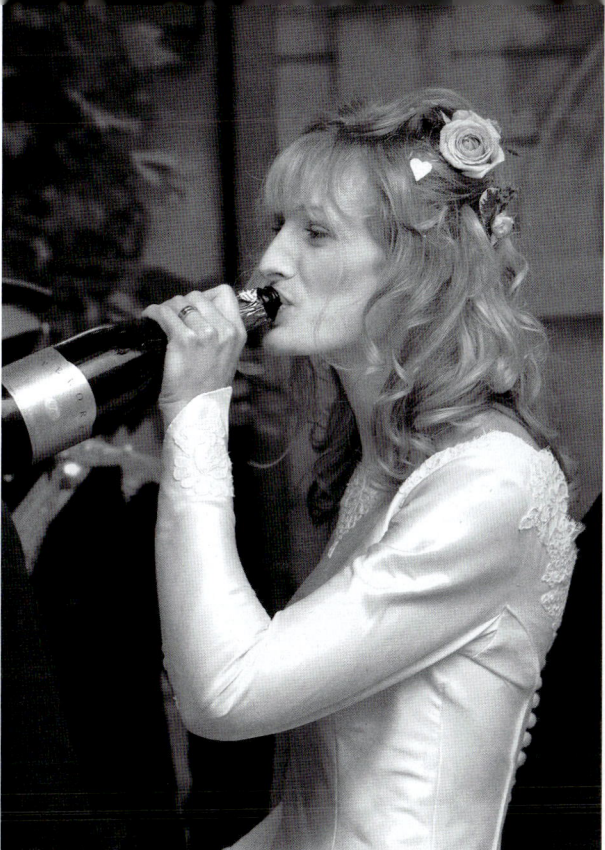

FIG. 18   ISO 1600 f/5.2 at 1/250th

There are times in life we come across people whose wonderful spirit of adventure and down-to-earth character leave a lasting impression on us. This candid picture reminds me of one such bride.

The emphasis is on creating a sincere rapport and trust. This part of the process takes much longer than in the previous model. That's because it involves listening to your client and delivering goods or services that meet their needs. It's a much less stressful system that can be delivered by anyone without the need for special training. So if you don't consider yourself a salesperson welcome to sales in the noughties! It's fun, uses genuine principles, and builds long-term relationships with clients. Sales

happen up front at the enquiry stage. A prospect is listened to and their needs are fully understood. Then a package that meets their needs is offered and all likely extras are disclosed. The close is an automatic procedure that follows. A typical phrase used by the salesperson during the presentation stage might be 'Damien & Julie will take hundreds of pictures at your wedding and you will love them all. Expect to spend an extra £2000 on pictures in your album plus another £1200 for parent's albums. (Trial close)

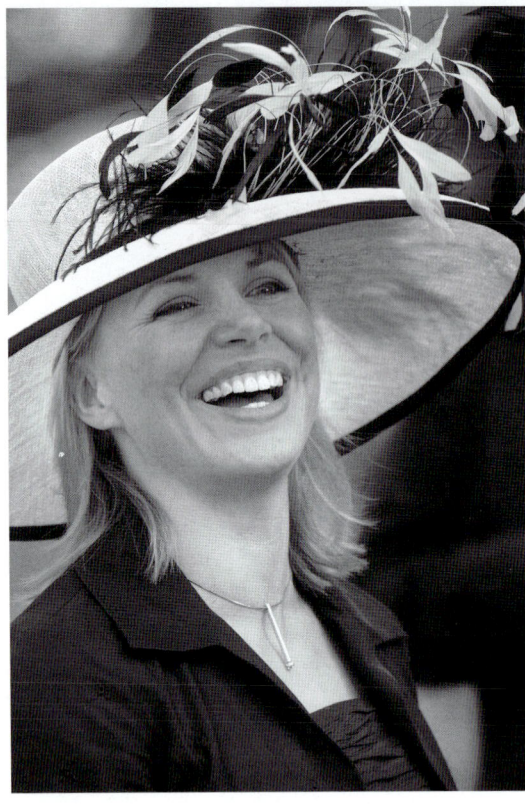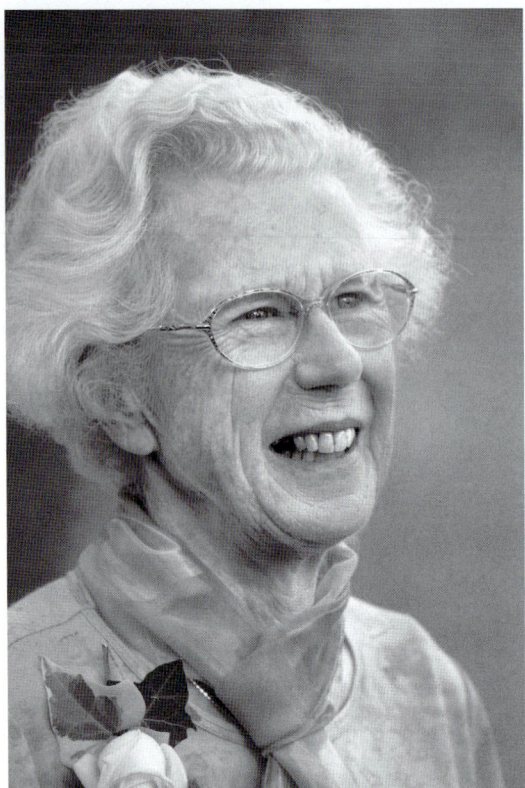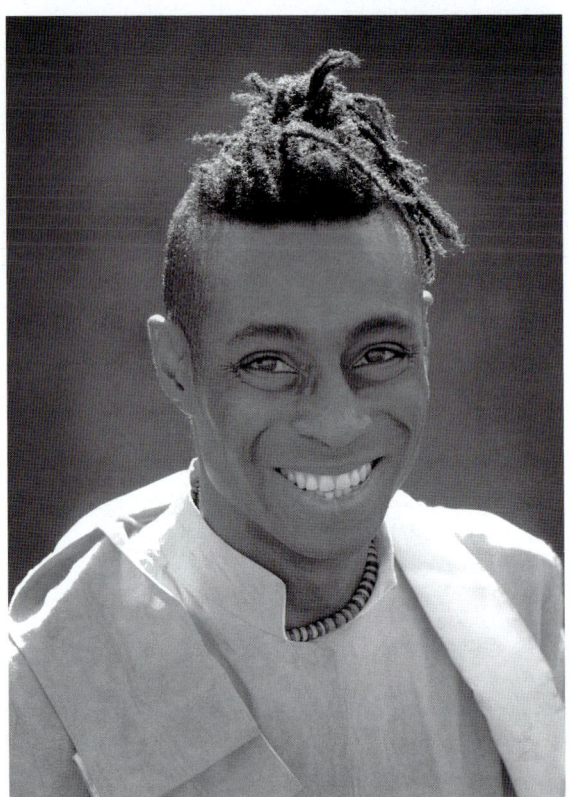

Are you happy with this?' If the answer is positive, the clients are then guided through the contract.

The viewing where the clients eventually get to choose their wedding pictures then becomes an order taking process instead of a sales session. A more subtle use of music, and a low pressure, fun atmosphere allows clients to relax and really enjoy the process without the sinking feeling the next day of having been ripped off. Ask, rather than sell, is the key to this system. When a client tells you what they want, the close is automatic. Then if you go on to exceed their expectations, they become your friends for life. The one tip that is universally suited to all retail and service-based businesses is 'under-promise and over-deliver.' Do this at every stage of your client experience and you too will soon have an army of raving fans.

opposite

FIGS 19–21   ISO 400 f/4.2 at 1/300th to 1/500th

I always shoot into the light to capture beautiful portraits of the wedding guests of all ages.

FIG. 22   ISO 200 f/5.7 at 1/250th

A simple plot for a shot by the bridesmaid to reveal the bride's garter created this moment. I shot into the light and excluded the sky.

HOW WE DO IT

The initial follow-up

This is the first step on the road to converting a prospect into a client. Remember, a prospect is a pre-qualified lead. They can afford you; they like your work; and you are available to photograph their wedding. It is important to get the opportunity to speak directly with either the bride or groom as early as possible in the sales process. Prepare well before picking up the phone. Have all the details about the wedding to hand. Have

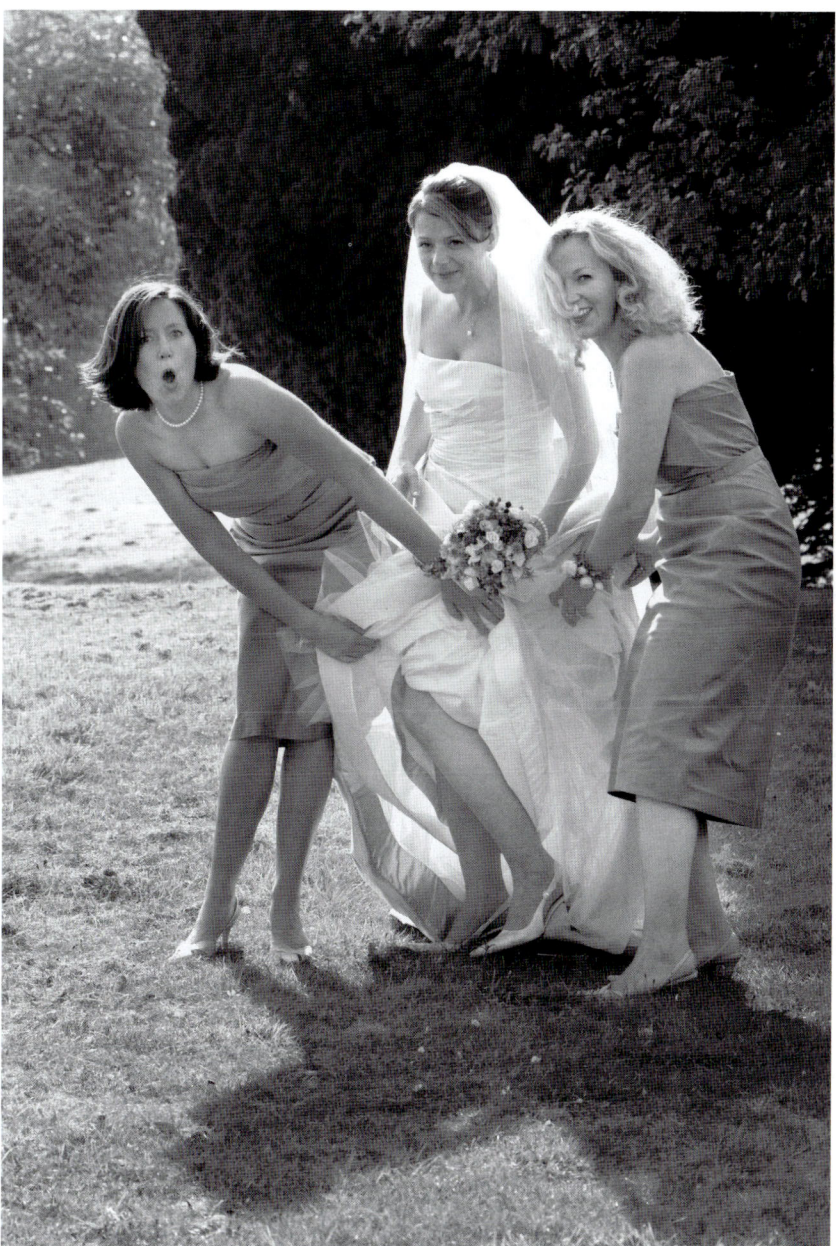

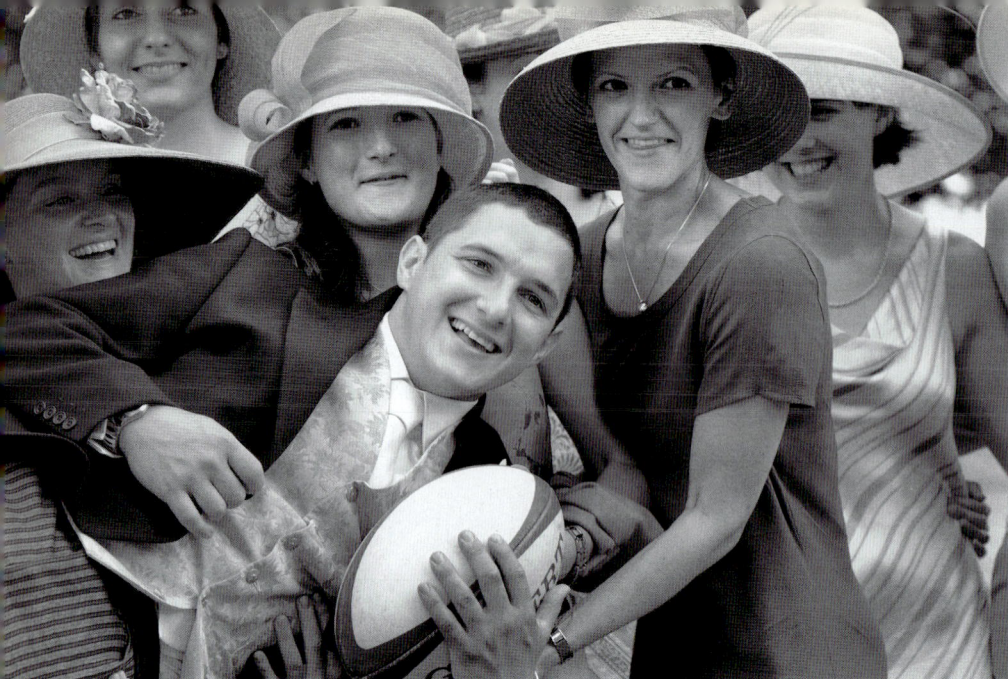

Fig. 23   ISO 320 f/4 at 1/360th

It's okay to crash in on a group shot and go for impact. There were a few stragglers on either side just out of the shot but I went for the main action that was fairly concentrated.

opposite

Fig. 24   ISO 200 f/6.7 at 1/180th

For this group shot of RAF colleagues plus the best man I went for a long lens approach and a carefully set pose.

your diary open at the relevant page, have a pen and paper and most importantly have plenty of uninterrupted time ahead of you. This phone call will often last half an hour or more, so plan for this carefully. Julie always makes the initial follow-up calls for us. This has allowed her to become an expert at this stage of the process. Start with the end in mind, have a clear objective and a route you want the conversation to take.

Introduce yourself and ask if it is convenient to talk. If it isn't, ask for a time and a contact number when you can call back. Above all, sound enthusiastic and 'smile down the phone' because successful selling is often considered to be the transfer of enthusiasm. If it's a good time to talk, start by congratulating the bride or groom on their decision to get married. That's a remark they'll be used to by now, and shouldn't be overlooked.

Be genuinely interested in their wedding and ask questions about the details and run of events. Listen carefully, making notes as you go.

There are certain messages you should be picking up on and holding back for later in the conversation. If for instance the ceremony is at noon, the guests will be expecting to eat shortly afterwards and the time between the ceremony and the meal will be tight. This may cause problems and restrict your opportunities. If the reception is in a marquee in the garden of the bride's parents' home you need to qualify what arrangements have been made for photography in a wet weather scenario. This will determine how high photography is on the couple's agenda. Group pictures in marquees rarely look spectacular, especially if the majority of the marquee is full of tables laid up

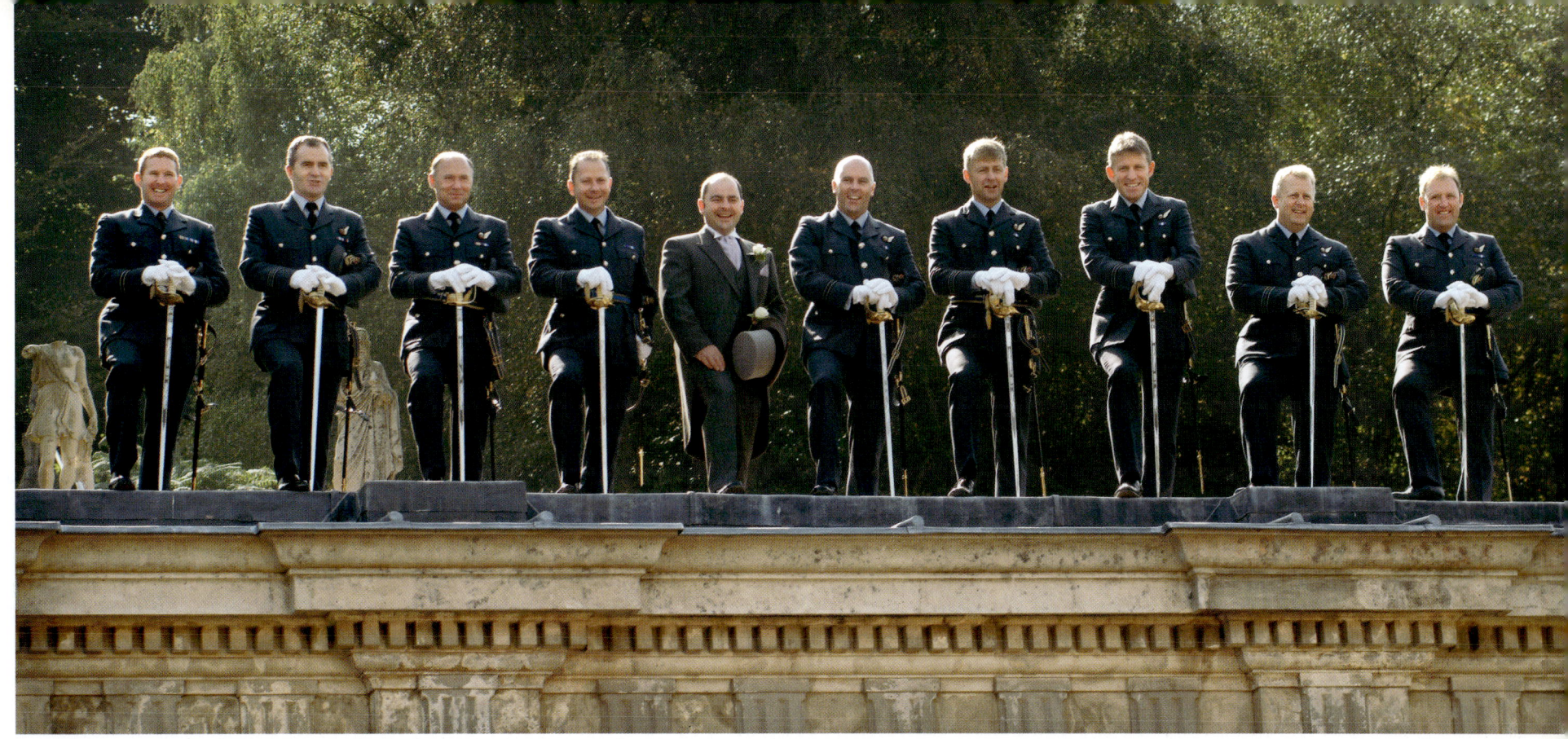

for dinner. Equally, the bride's parents' home has little relevance to the groom's family and might be out of bounds to muddy feet anyway. There may be other solutions you can suggest like making use of a neighbor's hay barn or the function rooms of a local golf club en route from the church to the reception. Stay positive and think creatively and you'll be able to provide free valuable information. If the timings of the wedding day are set in stone and make it difficult to take the pictures you know are needed, then don't be afraid to suggest that the couple try another photographer. Say something like 'I know how important photography is for you and under the circumstances of your wedding day, it is going to be very difficult for us to exceed your expectations. I therefore suggest you have a look at the work of other photographers who specialize in your kind of wedding. You may find you can save yourselves some money in the process and allocate this to other aspects of your day.' Do not make specific recommendations, however, because this still associates your brand with the wedding and it may have repercussions.

When the wedding details sound favorable and you have managed to strike up a good rapport then it is important to take the conversation further down your route. Your objective is to

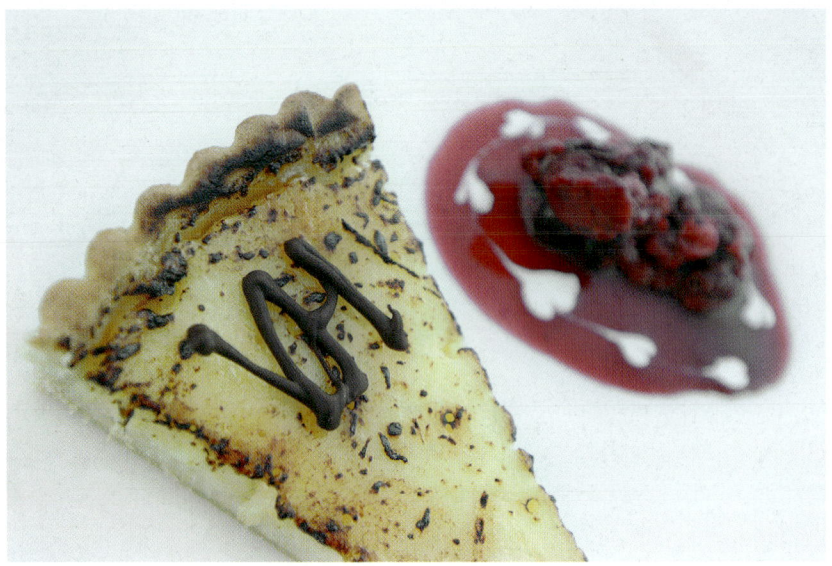

I always aim to photograph the dessert, especially if it has been personalized.

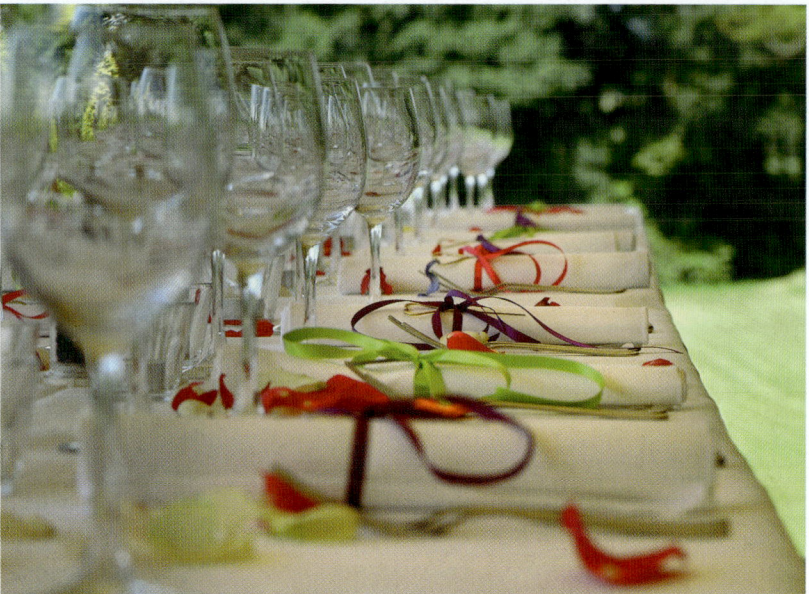

This picture was taken in a marquee with the sides open. I used a long lens down the table to capture the repeating pattern and to show the various colored ribbons.

re-confirm the qualifying criteria by asking 'Have you seen our prices? Do you know what is included for that sum? Do you like the pictures you have seen of ours so far?' If it's yes, yes, yes, go on to arrange a meeting in person. Only have a meeting in person if all qualifying criteria have been met. Protect your valuable time and theirs.

The enquiry meeting

This is stage two of the sales process. Careful preparation is vital. Make the couple do some work. Arrange a meeting at your studio or if you work from home and don't have a suitable place to meet then use a good hotel. Never go to a client's home for this meeting. You will have to compete with their telephone or television, and you may feel you resemble a traveling salesman. At a client's home you will be the guest and will not be in control of the environment. Before we had our studio, I'd use hotels as a base for an enquiry meeting. You need to employ a well-rehearsed system.

Take the following items with you:

1. Two complete weddings in albums. These should be relevant if possible to the style of the prospect's wedding. Winter wedding or church ceremony for example.

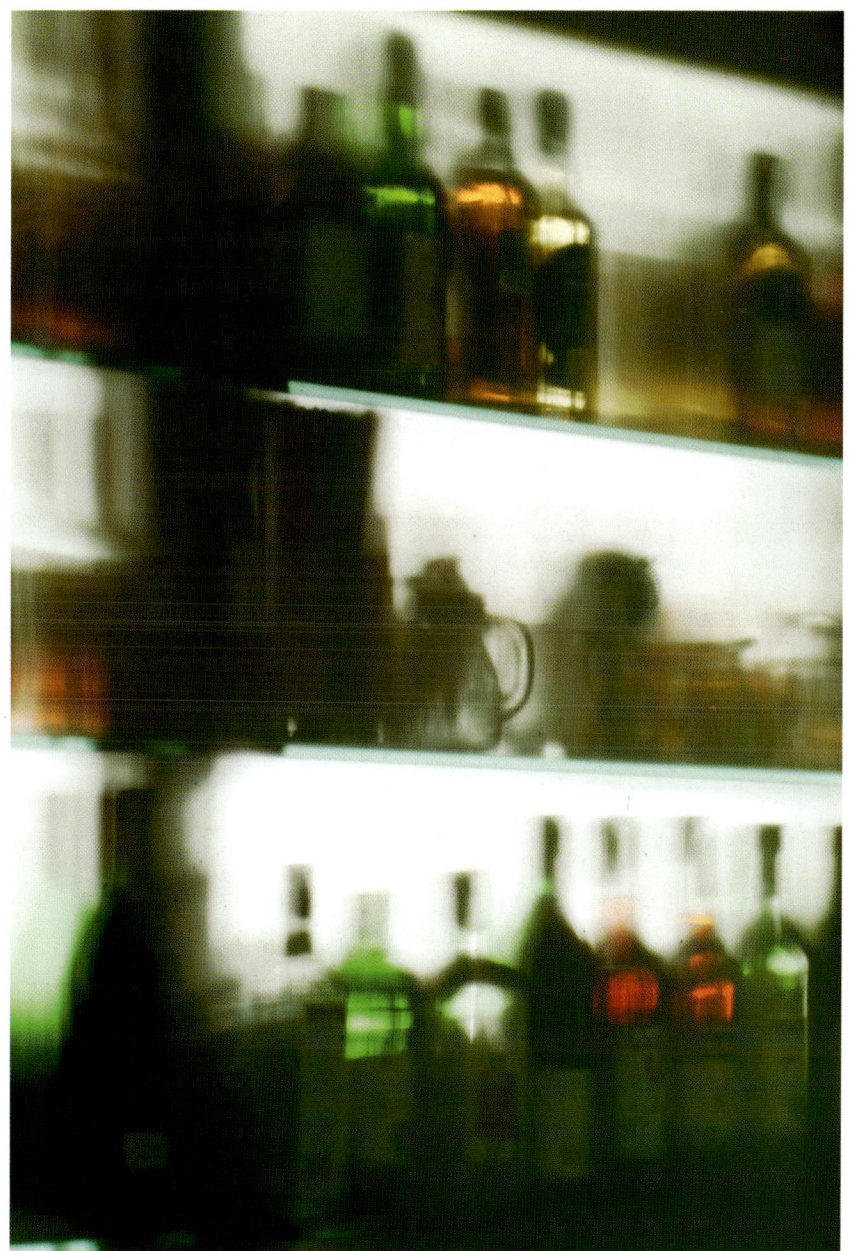

Fig. 27   ISO 400 f/4 at 1/90th

In the storeroom behind a hotel bar there was this shot to be had. It never made the wedding album but it would be good for a drinks invitation. I just don't stop looking for pictures at a wedding.

2. A printed out form with all the client's details you have gathered to date, plus spaces for the extra information you need. You should have printouts of any emails and mobile phone numbers.

3. A pen and a smart clipboard.

4. A contract, FAQ's, brochure, show-reel, or other marketing collateral you may have.

5. Cash to tip the waiting staff.

Arrive at the hotel of choice at least 45 minutes before the meeting. Dress appropriately for the establishment and decide where you want to sit with your clients. A coffee lounge is ideal. You may need to hover at a nearby table until the best place becomes available. Explain to the waiter that you are going to be joined by some friends and that you would like to pay for all hospitality. Open a tab and leave a credit card plus a healthy tip. When your clients join you, the waiter will automatically come

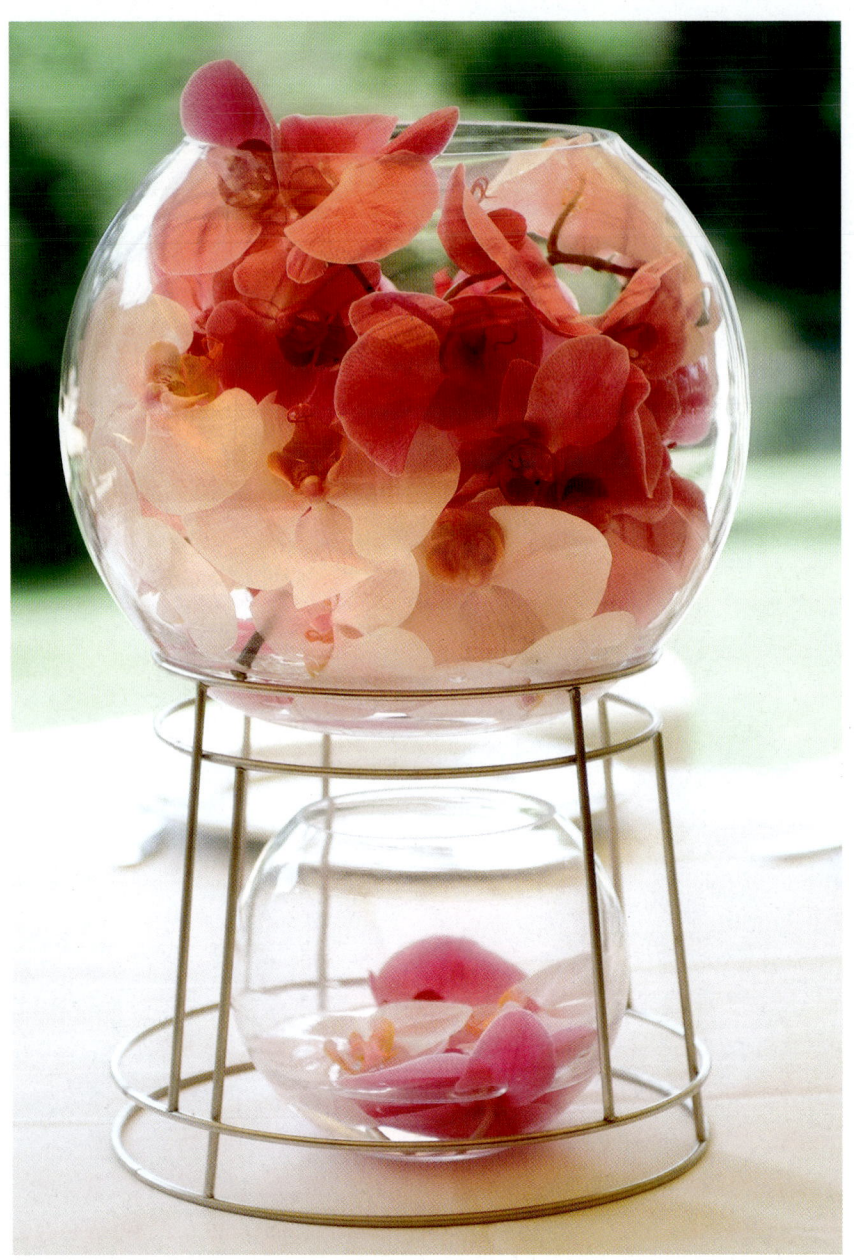

FIG. 28   ISO 200 f/4 at 1/300th

The pinks and the greens are in perfect contrast in this picture. Julie and I shoot for the other suppliers at a wedding as well as the bride and groom. It is very good for a long-term marketing strategy to be continually helpful to the rest of the industry.

over, take their order, and show an acknowledged friendship toward you. Your guests will not be presented with a bill at any time and once the meeting has closed and they have left you can settle up at your leisure. The cost of this elegant meeting room should be no more than £30 and it will ensure you have the ideal opportunity to close the sale.

The object of the meeting is to build rapport with the couple and, assuming they meet your criteria, to book their wedding. There are a couple of extra qualifying factors that I determine at the meeting before I let the sale close. Are the clients 'Warm Fuzzies'? and do they like having their photograph taken? Warm Fuzzies are people who are fun, light-hearted, easy to get on with, and easy to please. 'Cold Pricklies' on the other hand are difficult

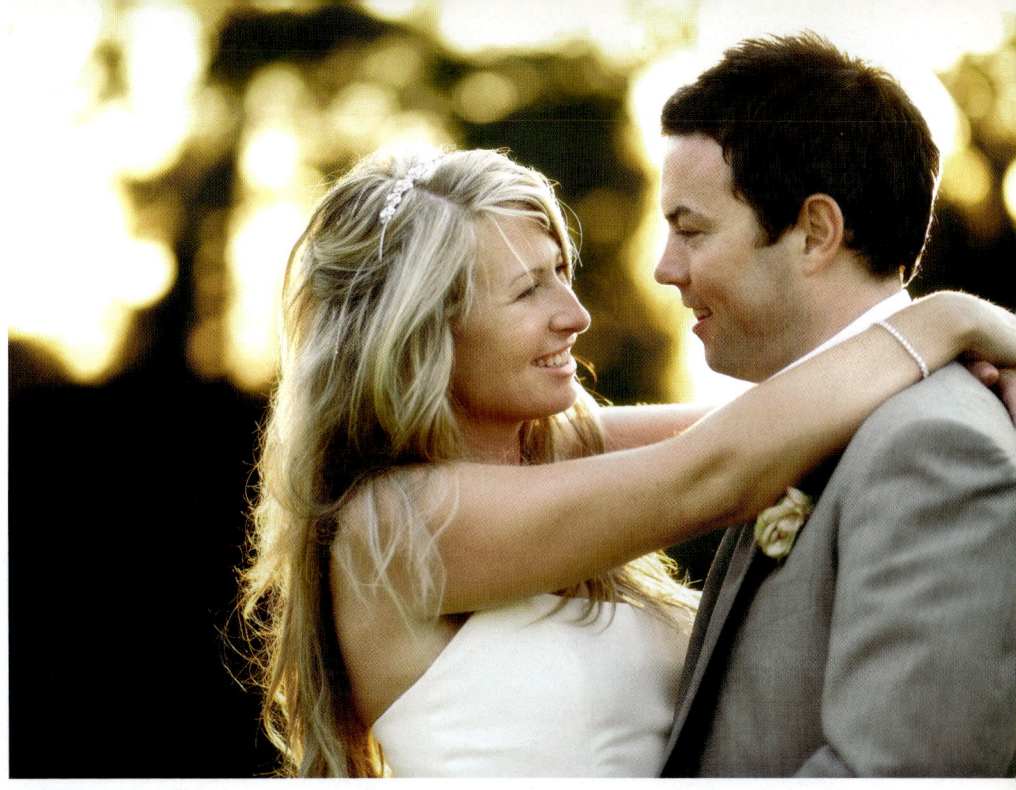

FIG. 29   ISO 400 f/3.2 at 160th

Late evening sunlight after dinner is a great time for a few relaxed pictures.

to please, stern, calculating and are always hard work. A Cold Prickly fiancé will often study the prints in an album so closely that he fails to see the photograph. The term 'pixel peeper' was invented for this kind of client. We only shoot the weddings of Warm Fuzzies. I suggest you do too. If clients hate having their photograph taken or hate themselves in photographs, imagine how hard it is going to be for you on the wedding day itself. Faced with this knowledge I would ask the question 'Why are you considering investing so much money on wedding photography if you don't like pictures of yourselves?' The answer may be 'We want you to capture all of our friends and our families in your own style and to cover the events at our wedding as they happen.' This is the kind of answer that I would like to hear and one that will let me proceed.

The close is the next logical step if you have had a few laughs and get on with each other. This is done with a simple line like 'Julie and I would love to photograph your wedding, I know we will have a great time, and if you feel the same way please read through this contract, sign it, and send it back to us with the deposit.' The response might well be, 'I can write you a check now...' If the client wants to take the contract home, that's fine too. You have done your bit, now let them come to the right decisions together. You must put a time limit to their decision making process by saying, 'I'll hold your date for 2 weeks to give you the time you need to make a decision. Do please look at other photographers' work if you feel you need to. In the meantime if you have any further questions please don't hesitate to email or phone us.' Thank them for their time and say your goodbyes.

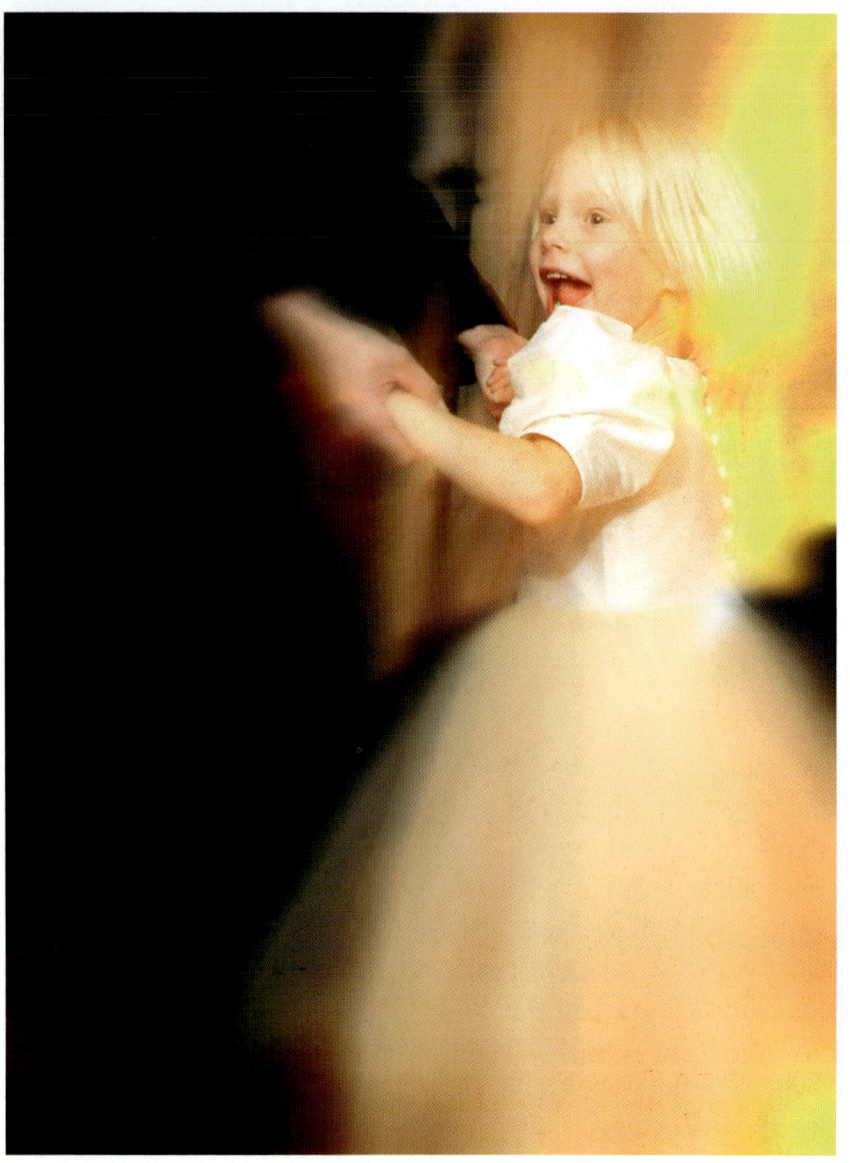

FIG. 30   ISO 800 f/4 at 1/6th

I dragged the shutter for this picture of a flower girl dancing with the best man. A splash of flash froze the action just where I needed it.

opposite

FIG. 31   ISO 400 f/5.6 at 11 seconds

This is Highclere castle at late dusk lit by the glow from red fireworks. The moon is just above the building. I chose a long exposure of 11 seconds and used a tripod for stability.

The final follow-up

Should you need to follow up an enquiry meeting, treat it as a courtesy call to let the couple know you are making their date available again. If they have yet to book a photographer probe a little deeper. If they have booked a competitor, politely find out who it is, compliment them on their choice, and ask why they didn't choose you. This feedback is invaluable in the evolution of your products and services. Finally, wish them a happy wedding and if you do baby photography have a fun moment of introducing this product line to them should they need it in the future.

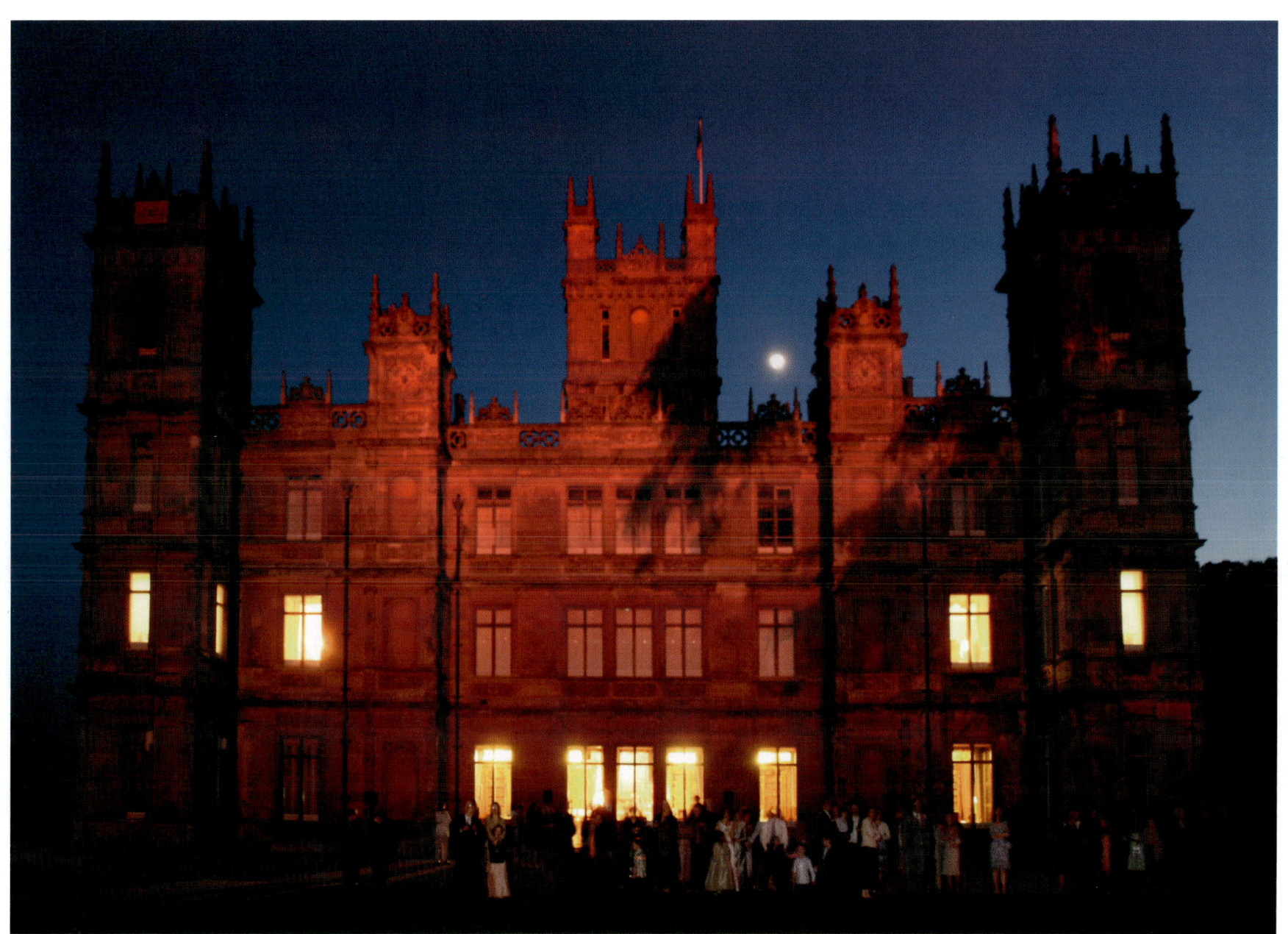

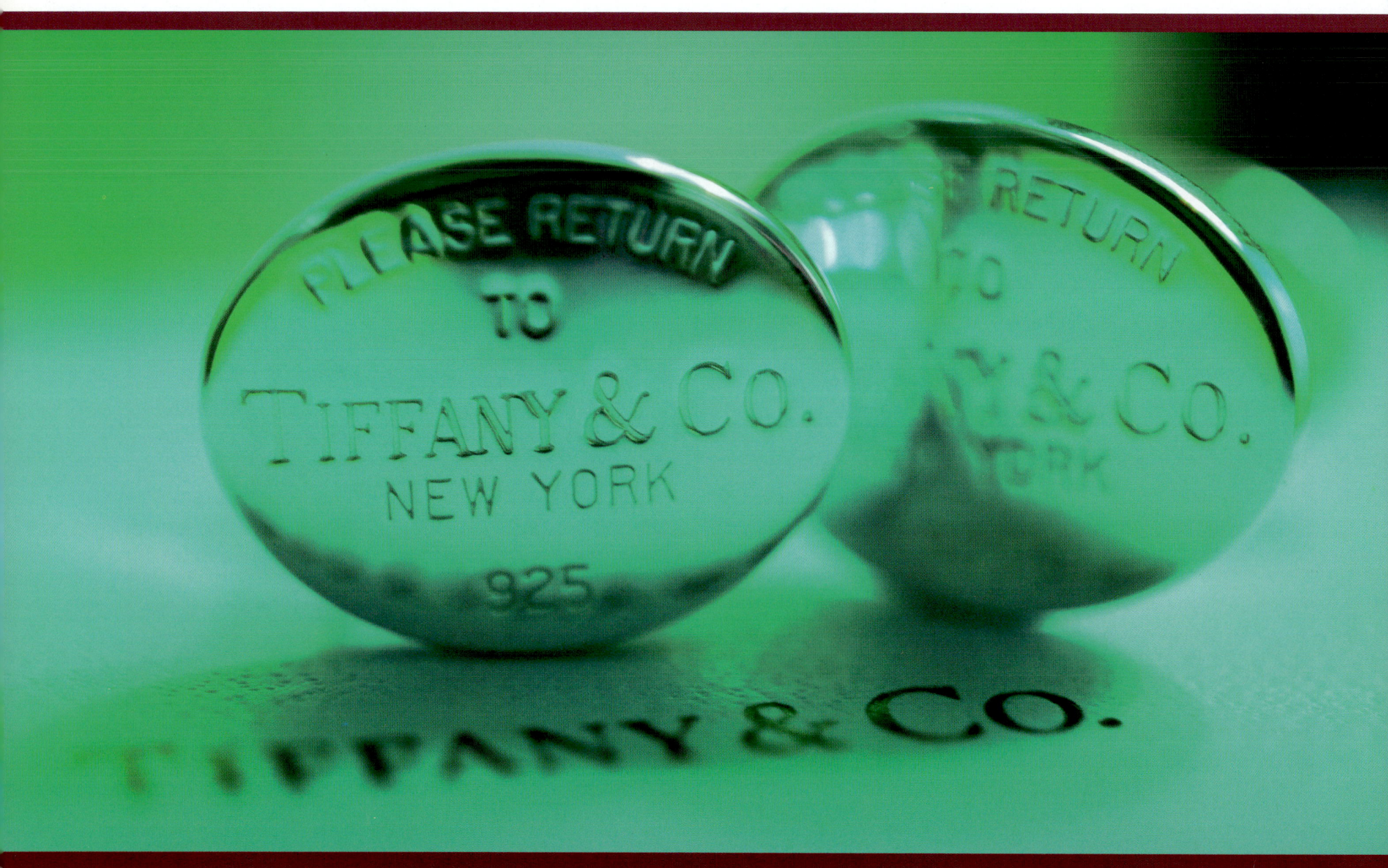

11
Financial Mastery – Your Route to Healthy Profits

opposite

TIP HEALTH WARNING! - Getting to grips with bookkeeping, spreadsheets, profit and loss forecasting, tax returns, VAT, salaries and general accounting is one of the least liked elements of running a successful photography business. However, ignoring or playing down these matters could SERIOUSLY DAMAGE THE FINANCIAL HEALTH OF YOUR BUSINESS! So please persist. It has to be done and once you understand what's needed, you will find chasing the profit both creative and rewarding.

could get everything else right – the photography, the service, the presentation, even the marketing – but without financial plans, analysis, controls, and strategies, you could still be struggling to make ends meet.

So first off, do yourself a favor and get decent bookkeeping software package from day one. Choose a system that's easy to use, delivers powerful reporting, and can be upgraded as your company grows. Before making the purchase, you should also

opposite

FIG. 1   ISO 400 f/4 at 1/5th

Occasionally, brand names are important to the couple and it becomes important to capture the detail.

In this chapter I reveal how we did it – how the financial side of Lovegrove Weddings climbed from deep in the red to very healthy profits in just a few seasons. The fact is that you

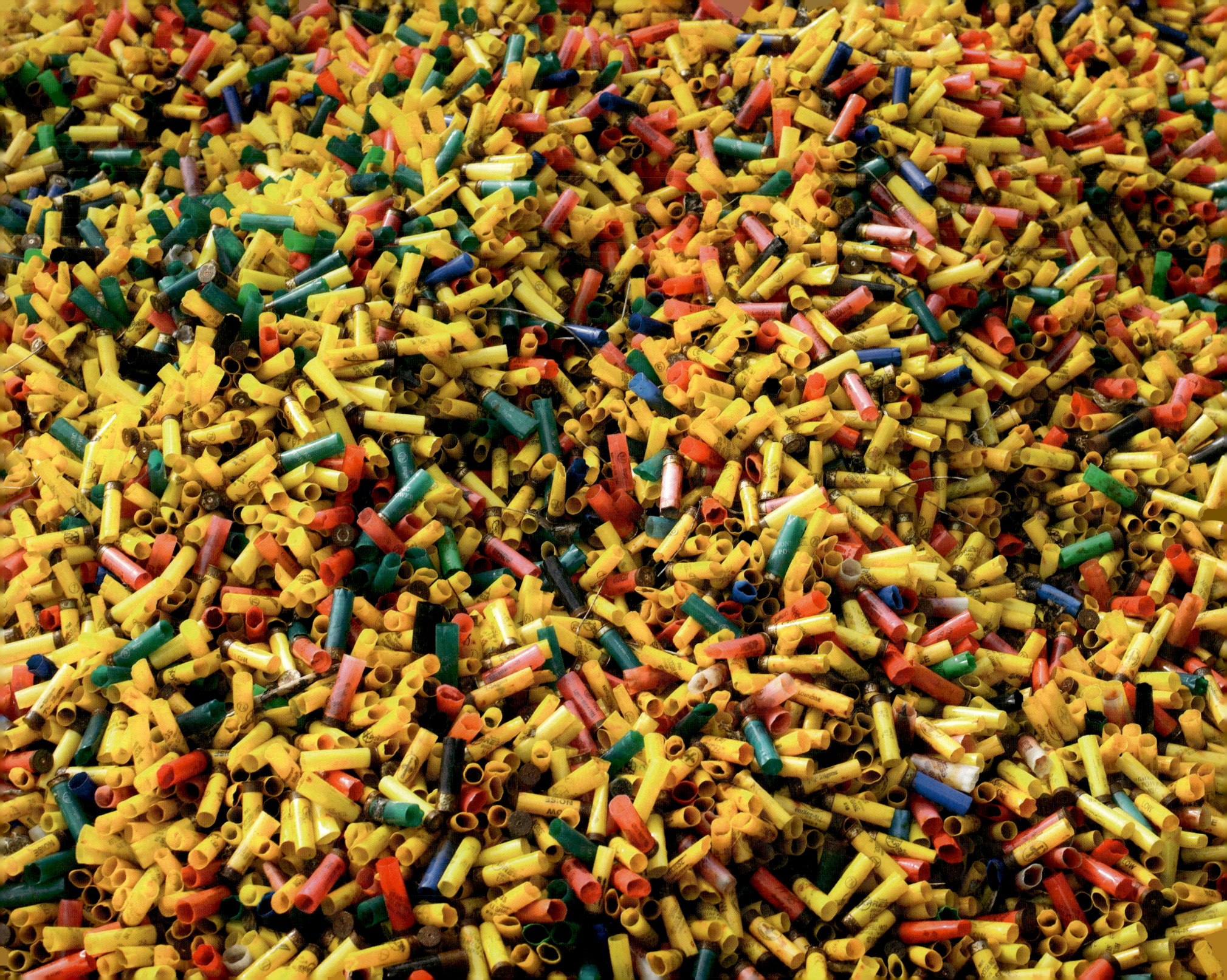

FIG. 2   ISO 100 at f/8 at 1/90th

I saw this pile of used twelve-bore shotgun cartridges at a morning shoot with the guys and I just had to get a picture. Keep your eyes open for details; this picture made the album.

make sure that the person putting together your end-of-year accounts is familiar with the software you have chosen.

> **TIP** ACCOUNTING PACKAGES – Here are a couple to consider:
>
> 'QuickBooks' works well for businesses with up to £5M turnover and 20 staff. It also 'holds your hand' while you get started.
>
> 'Sage' is 'the accountant's friend' and also works well, but for the inexperienced is less user-friendly.

When drawing up your financial plan, set out your costs and income in both an individual job basis and a season-to-season basis. You can scale up the individual job figures to build a picture of the season and you can call upon the fixed cost data for the season to create the individual job figures. Juggling figures until a financial plan is achieved is a very necessary part of the business. This financial mastery doesn't come naturally to most photographer s so don't skip this chapter because it looks scary. It's like a lot of difficult-looking things; once you get into them, you'll wonder why you were ever worried.

Let's look at the figures for a typical wedding.

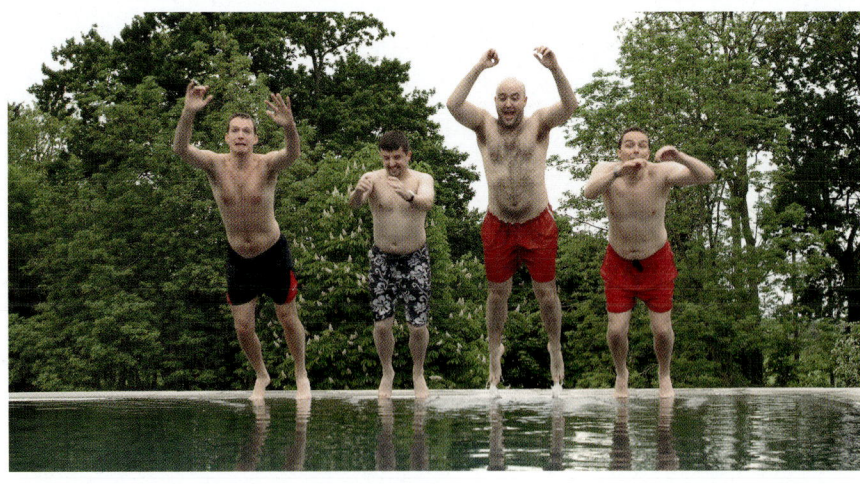

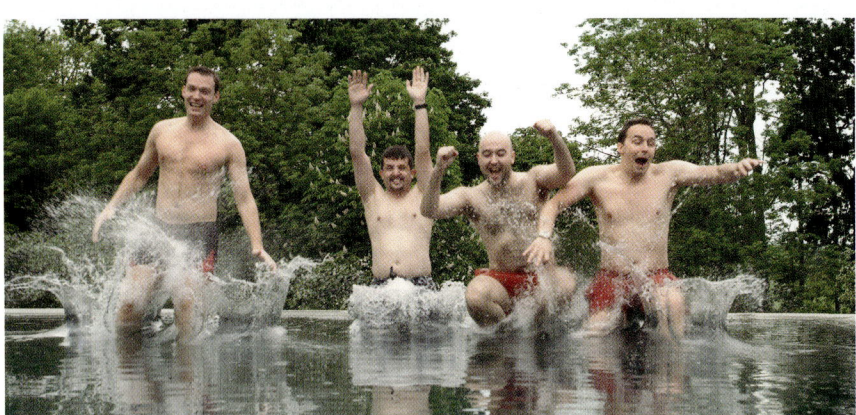

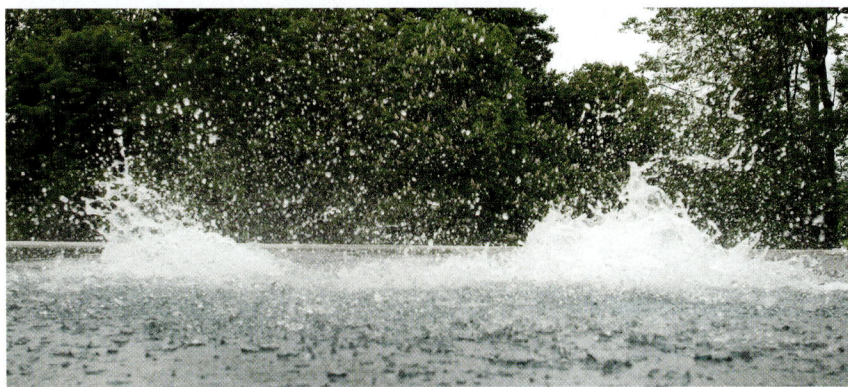

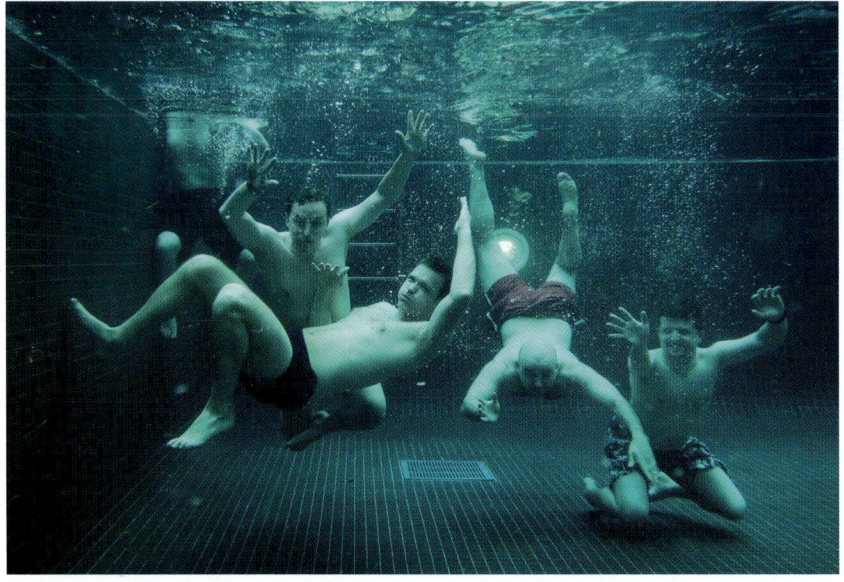

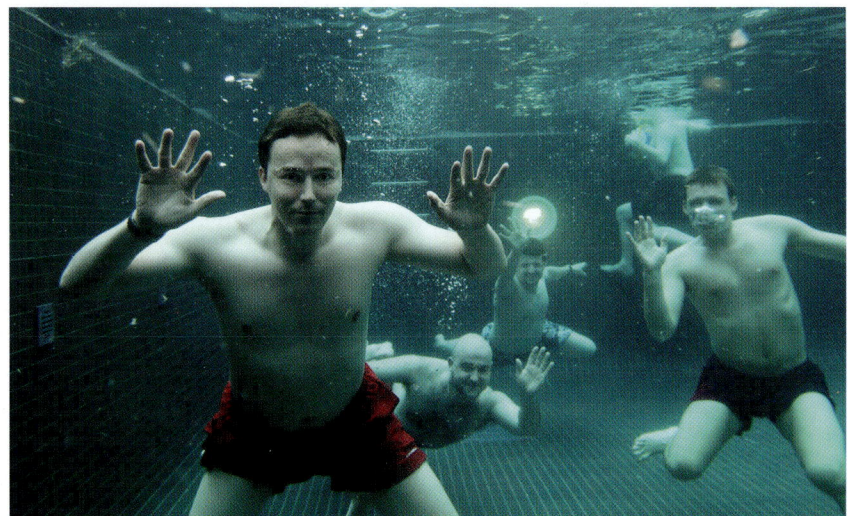

opposite

FIGS 3–7   ISO 200 f/4 at 1/500th and ISO 200 f/4 at 1/180th

It's great fun to set up a sequence like this. I shot the underwater pictures through a small window in the side of the pool.

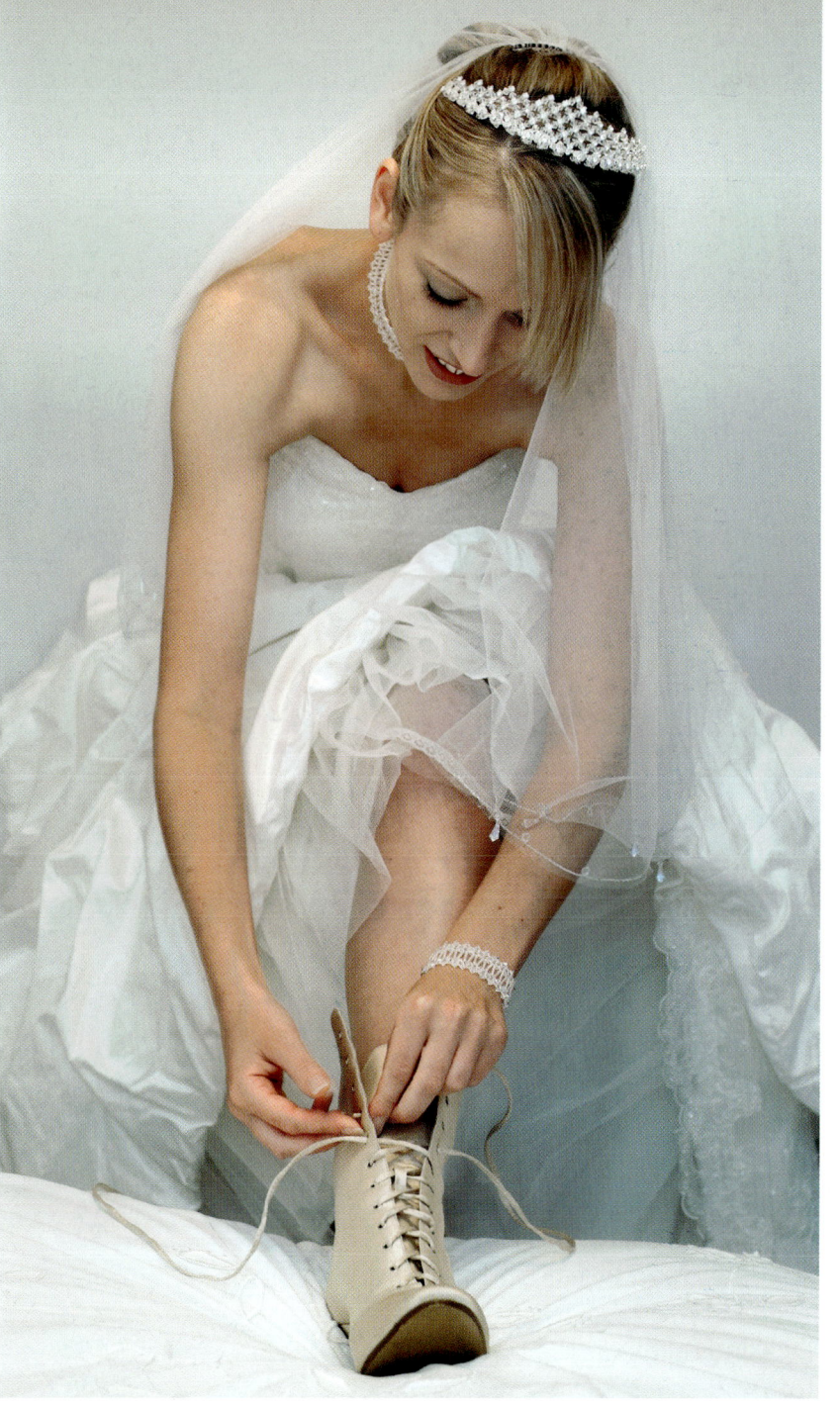

FIG. 8   ISO 400 f 4 at 1/90th

This bride had a novel pair of boots for her wedding day. This picture of Julie's captures the spirit in which they are worn.

Direct expenses:

Cost of acquisition, advertising, etc.	£250
Hospitality at enquiry and planning meetings	£20
Suit dry cleaning	£20
Travel expenses, 60 miles @ £0.40	£24
Photographic consumables, batteries, etc.	£5
Album	£300
Prints	£100
Total direct expenses per wedding	£719

Indirect expenses:

These are often calculated as a percentage of the annual charges. For instance, if you photograph 40 weddings a year

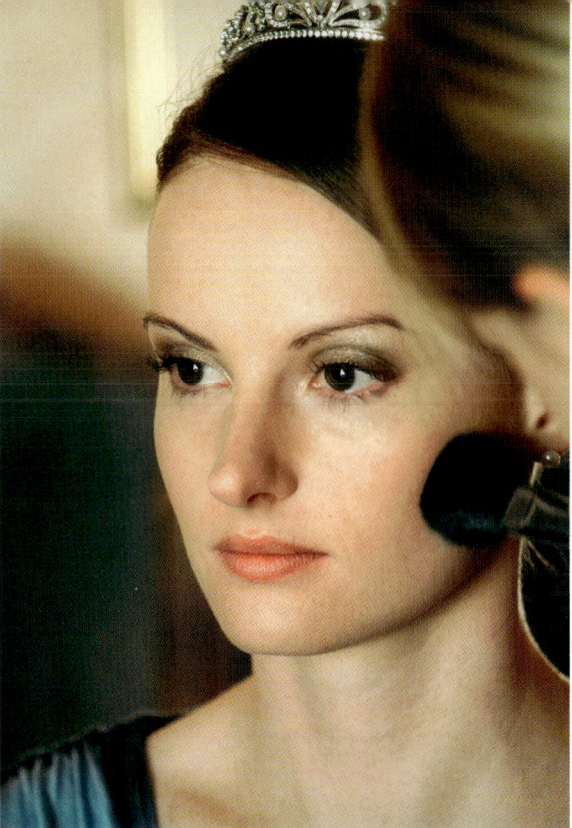

Fig. 9   ISO 800 f/4 at 1/90th

Simple close-up details of the make-up session are always worth capturing. Wait until the end to capture the finishing touches and radiant beauty.

and no portraits the annual charges can be divided by 40 for each item below.

Business premises rent, rates, etc.	£100
Electricity, gas, water, etc.	£50
Accounting services	£20
Insurance	£25
Memberships	£3
Camera equipment depreciation	£80
Computer and business equipment depreciation	£50
Telephone and broadband	£10
Interest on loans	£25
Total indirect expenses	£363
Total expenses	£1082

Income @ £2000 less VAT	£1650
Expenses	£1082
Profit/pre tax income per wedding	£568
Annual profit (40 weddings)	£22,720

Be as accurate as you can when setting out these figures. Even a slight optimism can result in an error of more than 10% and that might just mean the difference between being able to pay the mortgage or not.

Using the above figures, each wedding has a profit of £568 for an income of £1650 (£2000 less the vat). That shows a profit margin of nearly 35%. This is typical of a healthy business.

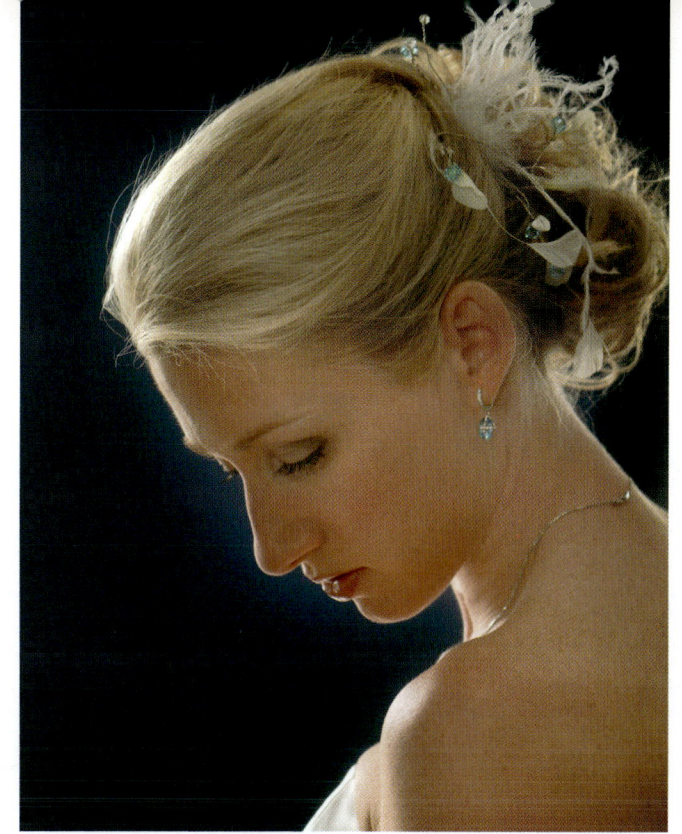

Fig. 10   ISO 200 f/4 at 1/60th

Julie shot into sunlight to capture this beautiful profile shot of a bride.

BUSINESS MULTIPLIERS {very important stuff}

Price increase

Let's look at the effect of increasing prices by 10% on the previous model. The income from each wedding will now be £1826 (£2200 less the vat), minus expenses at £1082 leaving a profit of £744. This has taken the profit margin up to 40% from 35%. If you still shoot 40 weddings, you will make a profit of £29,760. This is an increase of £7040 or a whopping 30% on the pre-increase figures. You could choose to shoot less weddings of course, because now you only need to shoot 33 weddings instead of 40 to get the same profit of £22,720.

(Complicated math is required to compute this result, involving redistribution of fixed costs over less weddings etc.)

Cutting costs

Reducing expenditure is the most effective way to increase profit without having to add value to your product. Every pound or dollar you save goes straight to the bottom line as profit. Working on our original 35% profit margin, a saving of £100 has the same effect on profit as an increase of sales of £286. Fixed expenditure is the most obvious to challenge first as it doesn't affect product quality. When you are convinced your power, communications, vehicle running costs, and the like are

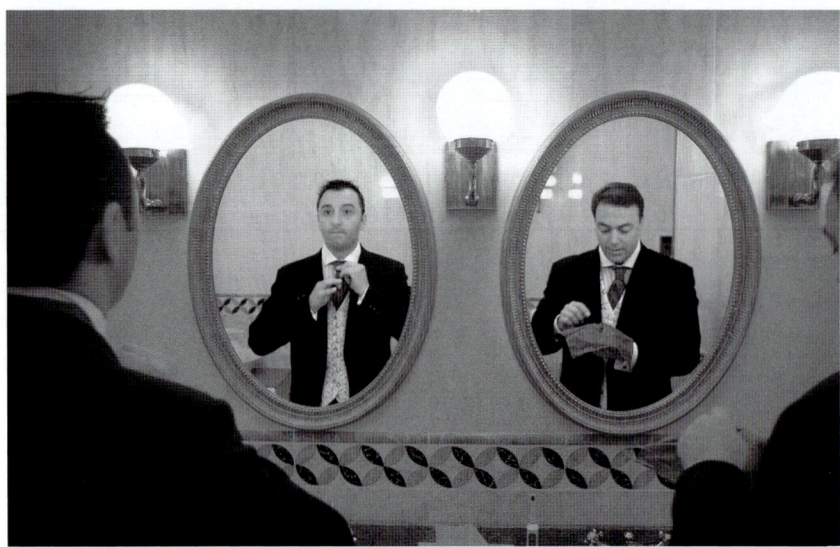

FIG. 11   ISO 800 f/2.8 at 1/100th

Two mirrors, a groom, a best man, and a photographer make up this shot. I was careful not to see my reflection in the mirrors.

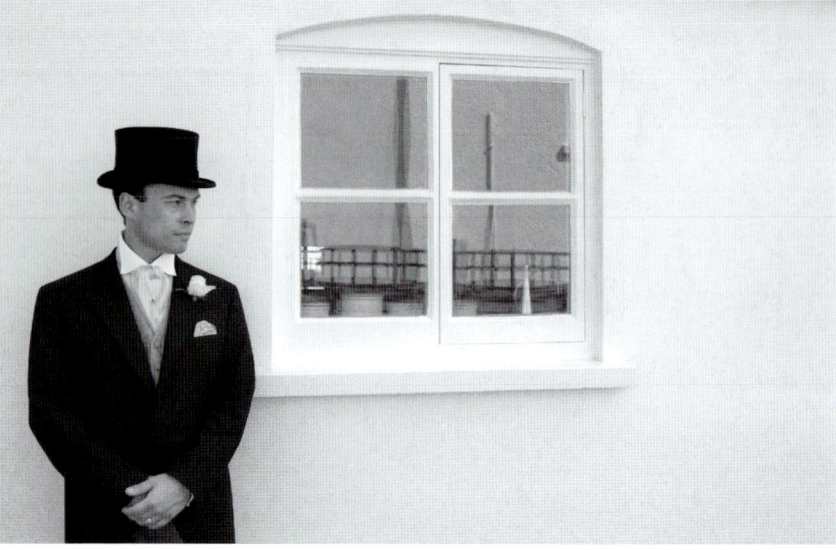

FIG. 12   ISO 400 f/4 at 1/2000th

Simple elegance and contrast make this picture of the groom at his home before the wedding leap off the page.

as low as they can be, turn your attention to your direct costs. Warning! Don't squeeze your suppliers too hard because you need them as part of your team.

The process of juggling figures should continue until you have a workable solution. If you have to increase your fees you will also have to increase the value in your product. You can do this by including pictures at a higher resolution perhaps or extending the coverage you provide on the wedding day. Be creative and get it right from the start.

Creating a pricing policy

When Julie and I made a step change in our pricing structure in 1999, we found that the leads generated by referral couldn't afford our newly hiked prices. It was hard to justify the price increase to these new leads and as a result we were literally starting from scratch. Because of this experience we have only made one other step change in our pricing strategy since. A big change in price band will result in losing venues, referrals, and the recommendation of associates – florists, dress designers,

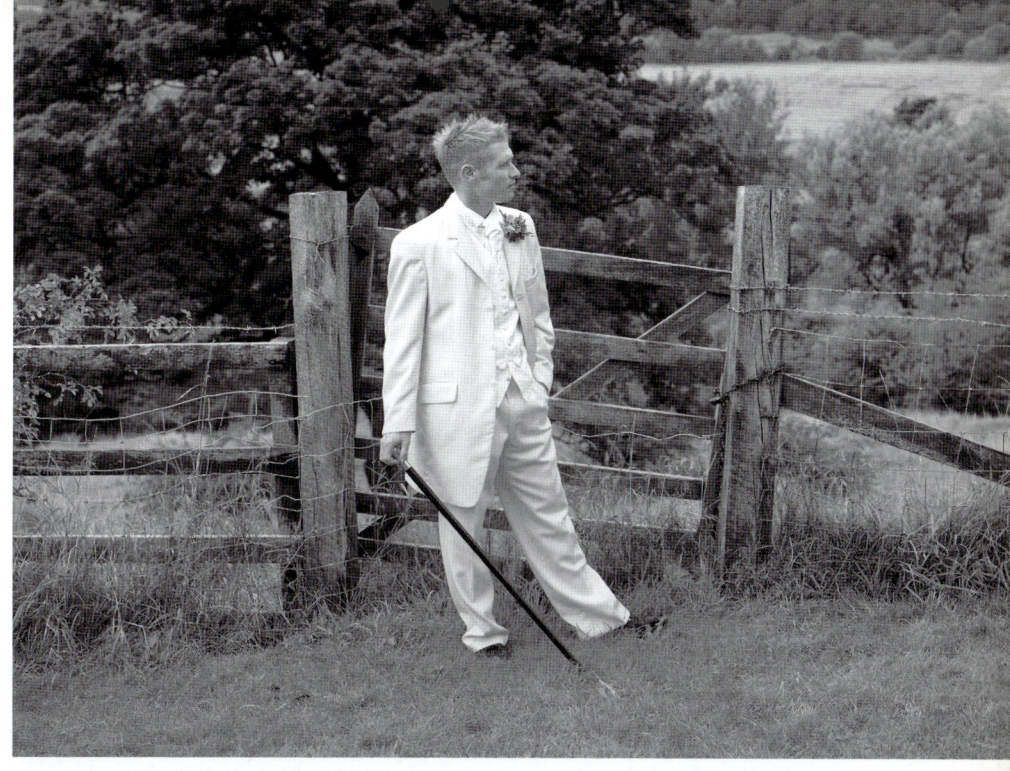

FIG. 13   ISO 400 f/7 at 1/400th

I placed this groom against a dark background and included a rustic gate in the composition. The cane was a great accessory to the groom's pose.

wedding planners, and so on. You will have to court the attention of new suppliers at the next level up and this is where the competition really starts. It is not uncommon to have 12 photographers or more actively seeking to photograph weddings at a single top venue at the same time. The venue managers and in-house coordinators are only going to recommend the best photographers or, as I have found in some cases, the ones who literally buy their way in.

The alternative to a step change price increase is to use an *evolving* strategy with a far more stealthy approach. Confectionary manufacturers are masters of this. The chocolate bar gets just a bit smaller while the price stays the same, then it gets smaller

again six months later, again without a price increase, then it goes back to just above its original size and becomes the 'new bigger bar' and incorporates the all important price increase of up to 20%. The important lesson here is you cannot increase price without adding value. The two go hand in hand.

So here's an example of a stealthy evolutionary price increase strategy to give maximum growth while retaining the best referral opportunities until the brand value really kicks in during seasons 4 and 5. This relies on the photographer gaining experience and shooting more pictures that sell each year as a result. It also relies on an investment of effort in brand building and other marketing activities.

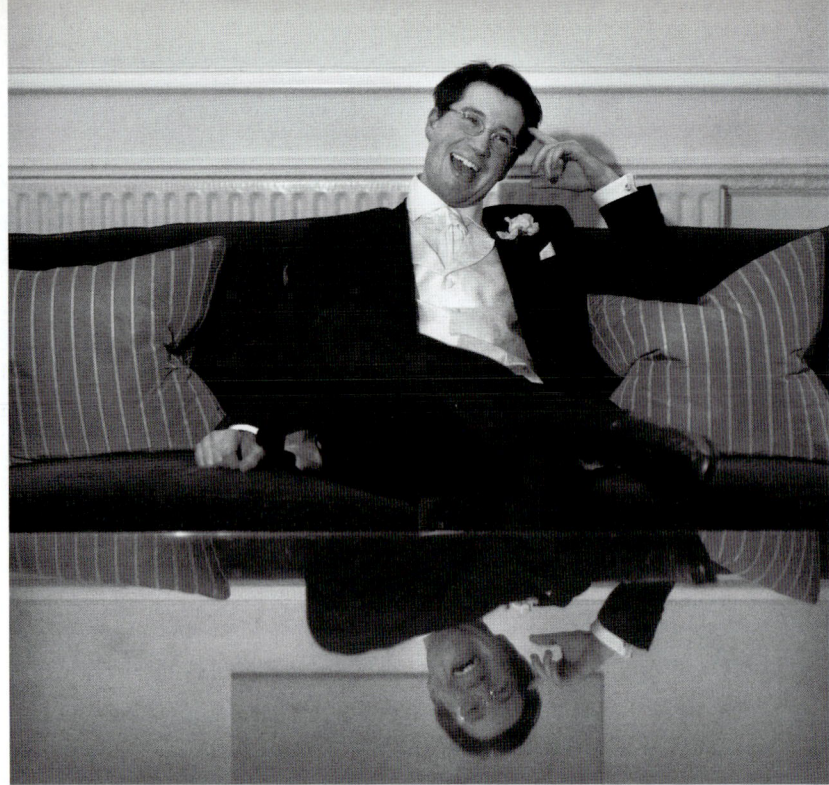

FIG. 14   ISO 400 f/4 at 1/30th

I love using reflections from glass-topped tables in my portraits. I created a moment of fun and captured it with off-camera flash.

Season 1: £2000 to include an album and the first 75 pictures, extras at £20 each.
Assuming an average sale of 100 prints, the total sale value is £2500.

Season 2: £2250 to include an album and the first 75 pictures, extras at £22 each.
Assuming an average sale of 140 prints, the total sale value is £3680 – a 47% increase on Season 1.

Season 3: £2500 to include an album and the first 50 pictures, extras at £25 each.
Assuming an average sale of 150 prints, the total sale value is £5000 – a 36% increase on Season 2 and a 100% increase on Season 1.

Season 4: £3950 to include a luxury album and the first 100 pictures, extras at £30 each.
Assuming an average sale of 160 prints, the total sale value is £5750 – a 15% increase on Season 3 and a 130% increase on Season 1.

Season 5: £5000 to include a luxury album, the first 75 pictures and a CD of the album, images at high resolution, extras at £35 each.
Assuming an average sale of 180 prints, the total sale value is £8765 – a 52% increase on Season 4 and a 250% increase on Season 1.

If you are going through growth, change, or are at the foot of the learning curve, it is a good idea to set your ideal targets in

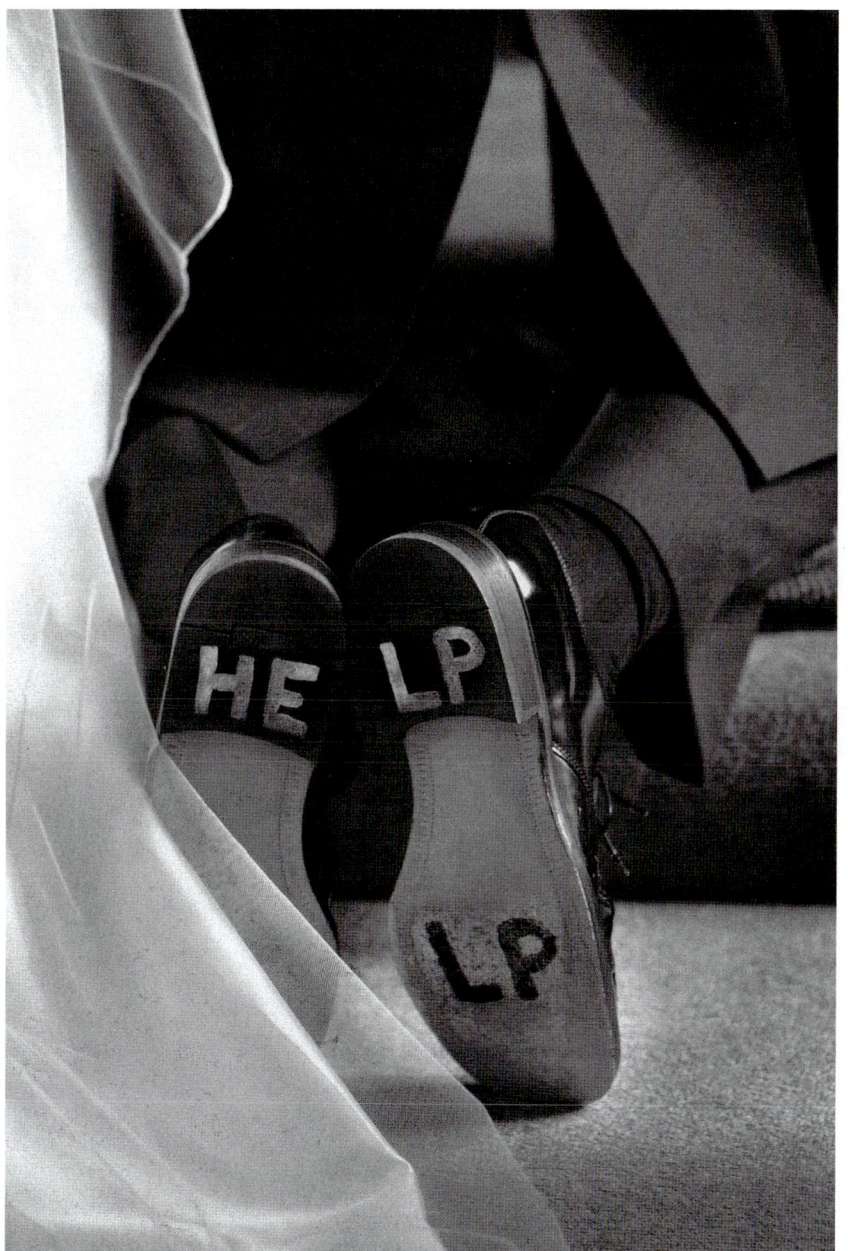

FIG. 15   ISO 1600 f/2.8 at 1/60th

I was in on the plot to decorate the groom's shoes; so when the time came I was poised to capture this classic shot. I expected to see this sort of prank on a regular basis but it has only happened once in my first 300 weddings. This kind of picture has a wide commercial appeal.

this way. Plan for your career progression. Plan a pricing policy for the next four or five seasons. The numbers will be different to those shown above but have an idea of where you are going, otherwise you may never get there. TIP: Don't spend 15 years getting to the top, do it in 3 or 5 at the most.

SETTING YOUR PRICE: HOW MUCH CAN YOU CHARGE?

Sometimes it's hard to quantify value. Customer service, brand position, risk reversal, trust, rapport, and fun factor are all foggy areas that go into the equation of perceived value. Add to these the subjective quality of photography, albums, and presentation and you can see how hard it is to set a price. I have

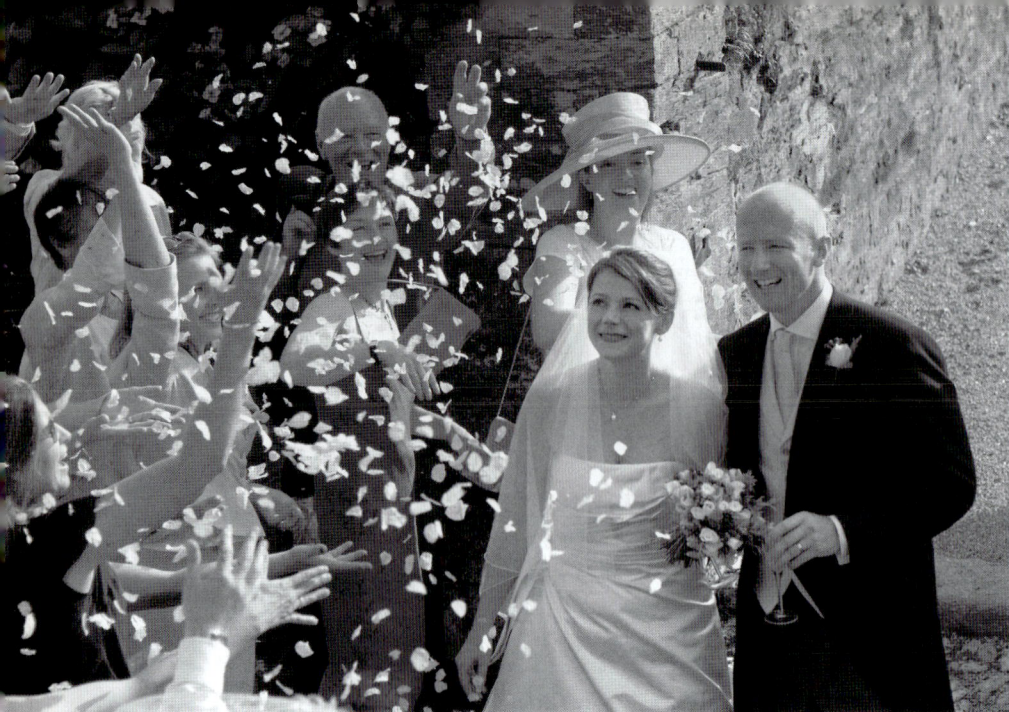

Fig. 16   ISO 400 f/4 at 1/1500th

Shooting into the light at moments like this highlights the petals. I held the camera above my head to get a top shot perspective.

often heard photographers asking, 'How can the Lovegroves justify such high prices? I use the same albums, the same lab, the same cameras and consider myself to be just as good a photographer....' Perhaps those photographers fail to see the value of a brand, the value in our customer experience and the fine detail touches we put into our product. Examples of product value reflecting price can be found all around us. Two car manufacturers might use similar amounts of materials to make their products, have similar manufacturing tolerances, similar R&D costs, yet their products could sell for vastly different prices. These differences can often be justified by such things as 'feel good factor,' pride of ownership, reliability, value retention, brand position, after sales service, and so on. Let's look at the factors that affect value more closely.

PRODUCT QUALITY

The quality of your photography, post production, printing, and album preparation are the most obvious things that come to mind when discussing product quality. There are however many other factors to consider. What coverage do you offer on the wedding day? What level of support and advice do you deliver before the wedding? How professional is your website? Are your letters and correspondence nicely printed, personally signed, and delivered in handmade envelopes? Do you wear sharp suits on the wedding day? Is your car cool and always clean? What image are your clients buying into? These are all questions that you need to ask to assess a price point for your work. There are hidden factors too. Do you offer a written guarantee? Do you

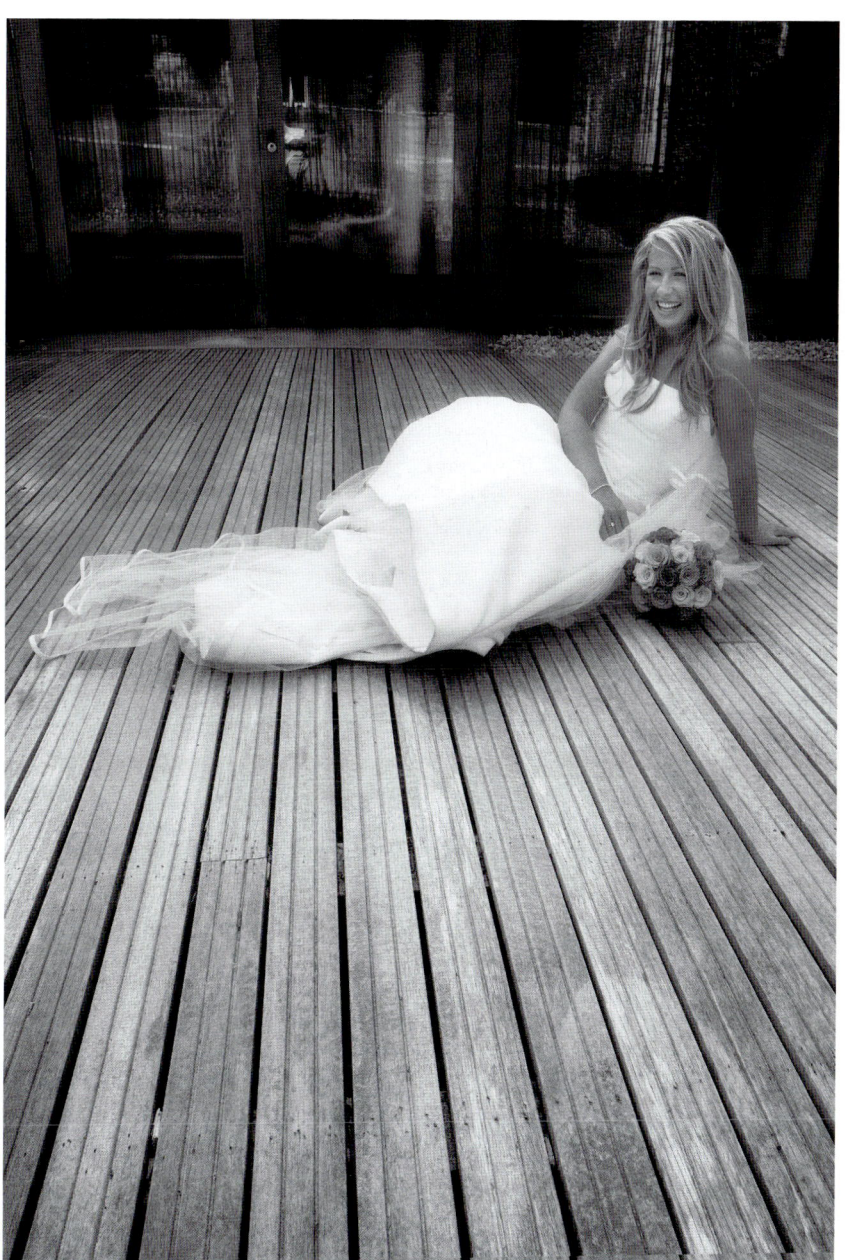

Fig. 17   ISO 400 f/14 at 1/160th

This decking provides great lead-in lines to the bride. She is sitting on the piece of veil fabric that Julie keeps in her camera bag for just this kind of thing.

have a full backup camera kit including lenses? Do you have a contingency plan in case you are ill or break a leg? Remember you are only as good as your weakest link. Keep everything in balance and it becomes easier to set a high price point.

MARKET AND COMPETITION

The other most obvious factors that affect how much you can charge are the marketplace and your competition.

Get to know the marketplace you are trading in. How much are your ideal clients prepared to pay for the right wedding photographers? How many potential clients are getting married in this price band each year? Ask the key venues how many

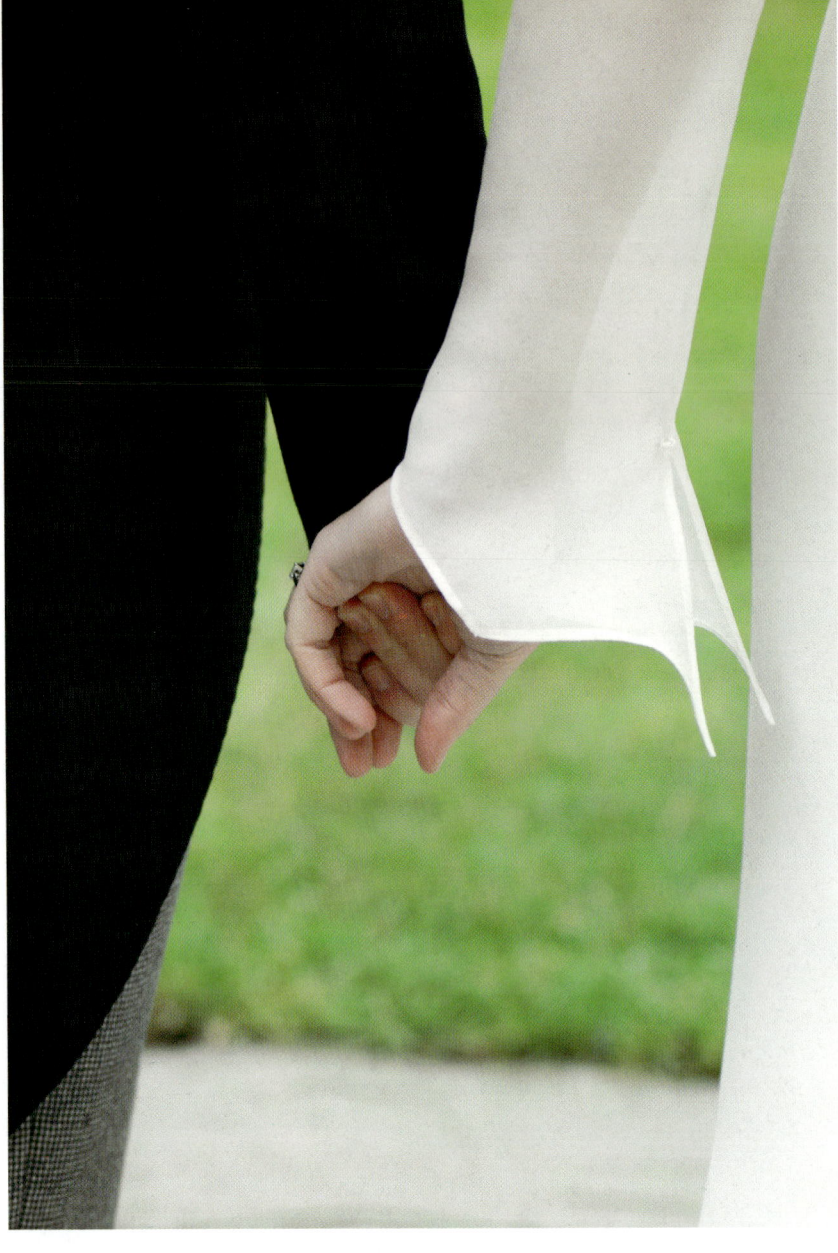

FIG. 18   ISO 800 f/4 1/90th

We always take shots like this if the opportunity allows. This picture has since been used by a greetings card company.

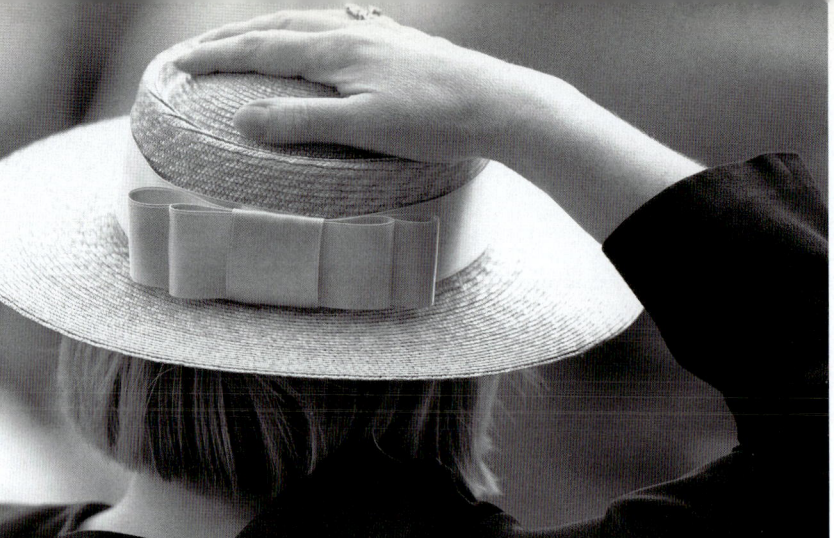

FIG. 19   ISO 800 f/4 at 1/850th

When the wind blows pictures like this happen. This is a great picture to help set the scene and compliment the main story in a wedding album.

weddings they have got booked. Find out what photographers are shooting the weddings. These photographers are your competition. When a new venue comes on the scene, get in there. A new emerging market is easy pickings for a new emerging photographer fizzing with enthusiasm.

Know everything there is to know about your competition. What do they do that you could do better? What are your unique selling points? If they are not charging enough for the quality and service they offer, and they are holding you back as a consequence, tell them. Work together on improving the service and quality our profession provides.

Once you have assessed your position in the marketplace and how much added value you offer, you should be able to put a

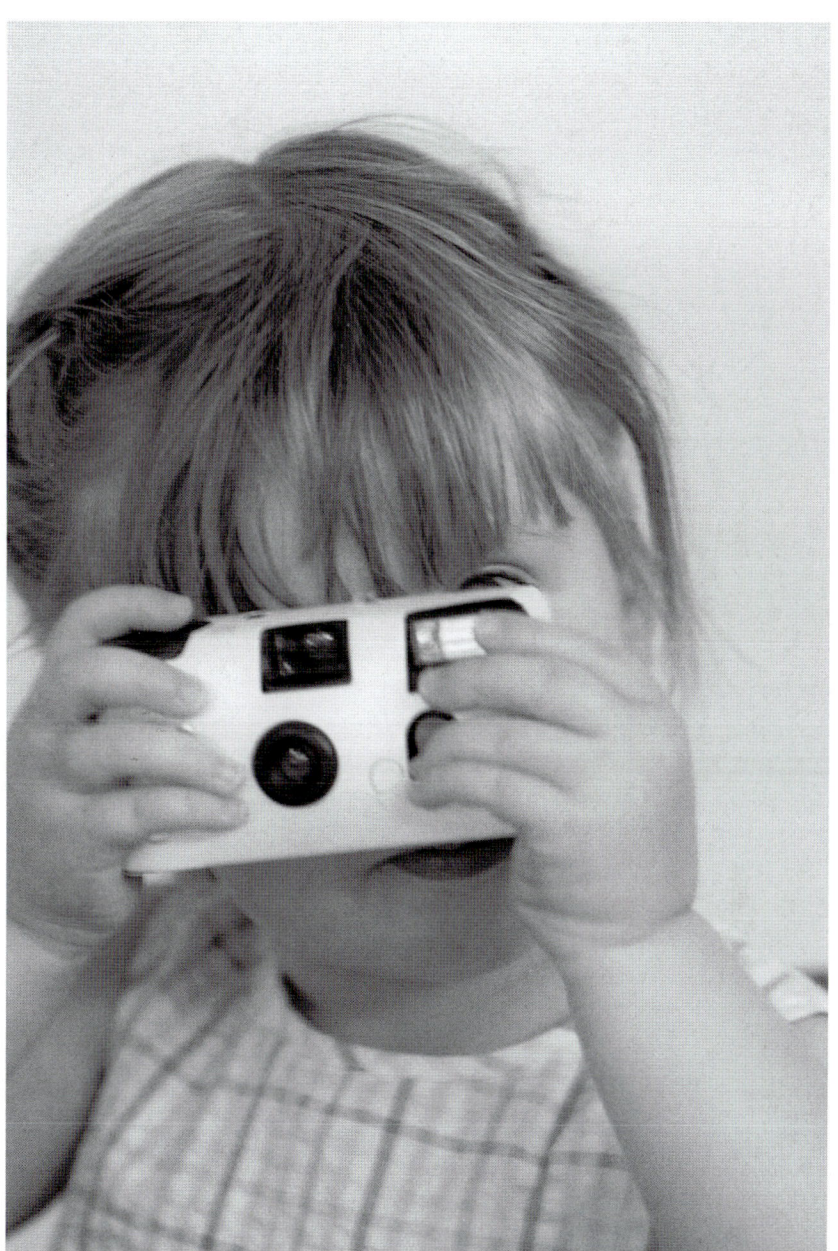

Fig. 20 ISO 1000 f/2.8 at 12/50th

This is the next generation of wedding photographer in the making.

price on your work. So with your product and price set, you can get on raising capital to fund your business.

RAISING CAPITAL

Plan your finance needs carefully. Start by putting together a business plan that has a focus on financial forecasting. Get the plan together in a basic form and then question everything. Microsoft Excel is a good tool to use for this purpose. Don't be too optimistic: realistic forecasting of your profit and loss is vital if you want to attract funding from a bank manager or venture capitalist. Write the plan with the end reader in mind. A bank manager will be looking for security while an investor will be looking for growth.

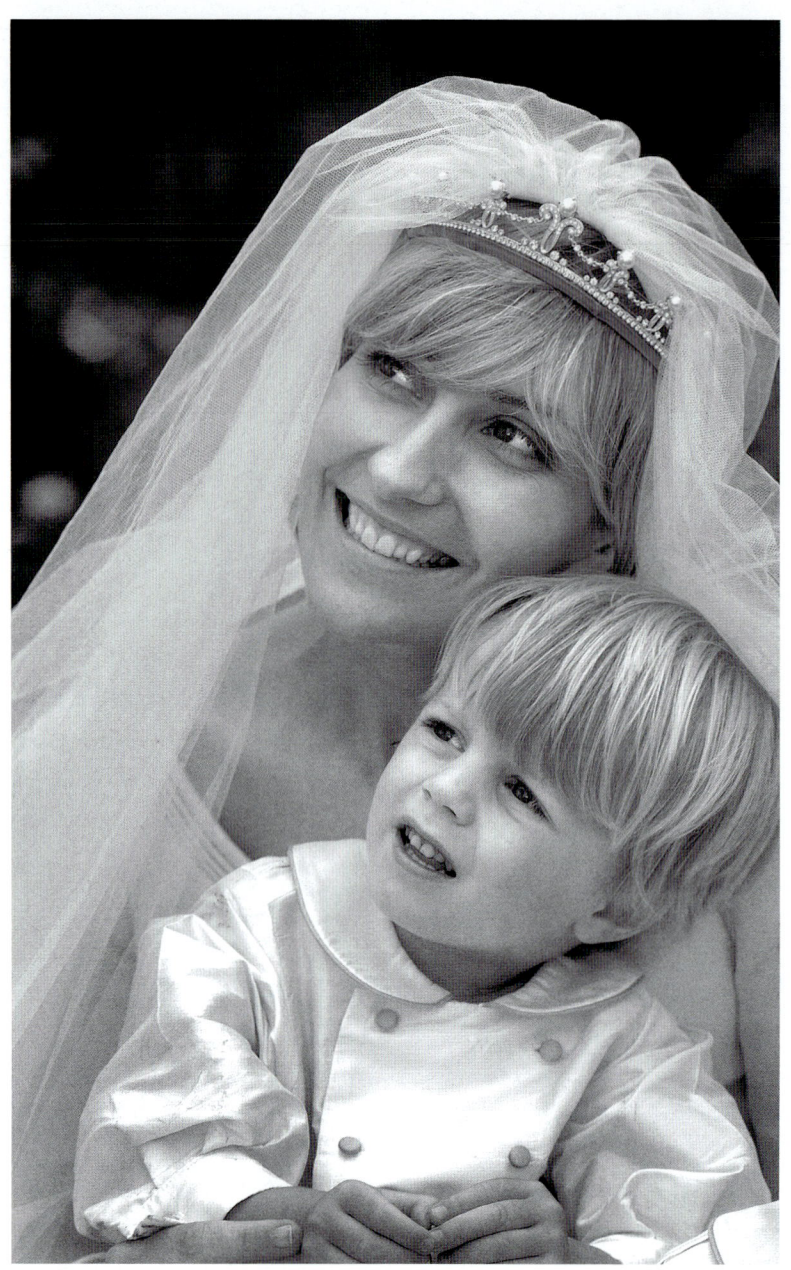

Fig. 21   ISO 400 f/4 at 1/1200th

A beautiful bride and a pageboy attired for a traditional English wedding.

Your borrowing options will often be determined by your business plan. Use the figures you have worked out for a typical wedding and map them out on a timeline. Work two complete seasons ahead. For the moment you will have to guess how many weddings to enter for each month in turn. The number you enter will be the target for your marketing so do keep it achievable. Next enter your direct and indirect costs. Finally, enter your income each month bearing in mind that each job may have a split payment of deposit, fees, and extra sales. These payments will need to be shown in the corresponding months they are to be made.

Julie once asked, 'How overdrawn are we going to get before you go back to the BBC with cap in hand?' At that time we had a £40,000 overdraft and we were in a still worsening position.

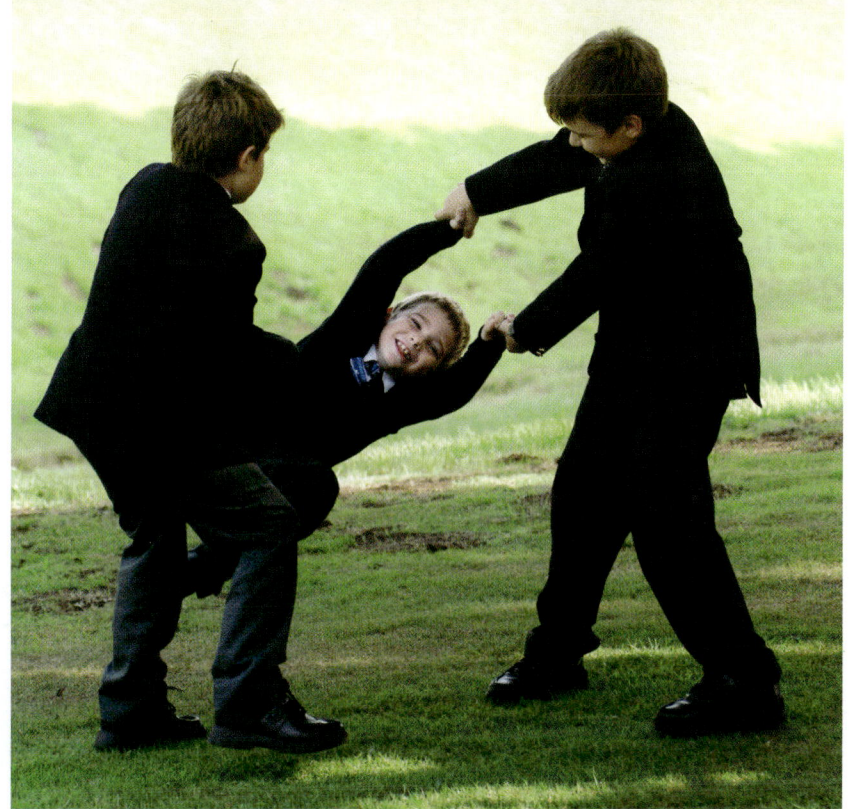

FIG. 22 ISO 400 f/4 at 1/500th

Boys will be boys. This kind of shot celebrates all that is good about boyhood.

Julie and I wrote our first full business plan in 2000. The plan showed an increasing deficit for several more months caused by our training costs, product development, and marketing. All these costs had to be dealt with before a steady income stream developed. We were investing in Jorgensen albums and had to put together some great show products, we were advertising heavily in the main wedding magazines, and we were on a well-structured training program. Apart from these direct costs we had a mortgage, equipment depreciation, and a family to feed. Getting the cycle of income to exceed costs takes time in the wedding photography industry. There is often a whole year delay from the time you invest in marketing and product design to the time the weddings take place and the income starts to flow.

This long delay between sowing the seed and reaping the rewards is risky and not great for cash flow either. Even when we had a pair of great show albums and some effective marketing we still found the delay in the resulting income difficult to deal with. Julie and I thought long and hard and after much deliberation and consultation with other photographers we came up with a pretty good solution. We increased our deposit from £200 to £500. This was all that was needed to turn the business around. Imagine having 20 weddings in the diary for the next season having taken £200 deposits from them all. You will have just £4000 in the bank. With the deposit level at £500 that figure is a whopping £10,000. The difference is enough to fund a continuing marketing and product development program. With a continuous stream of income close to the investment

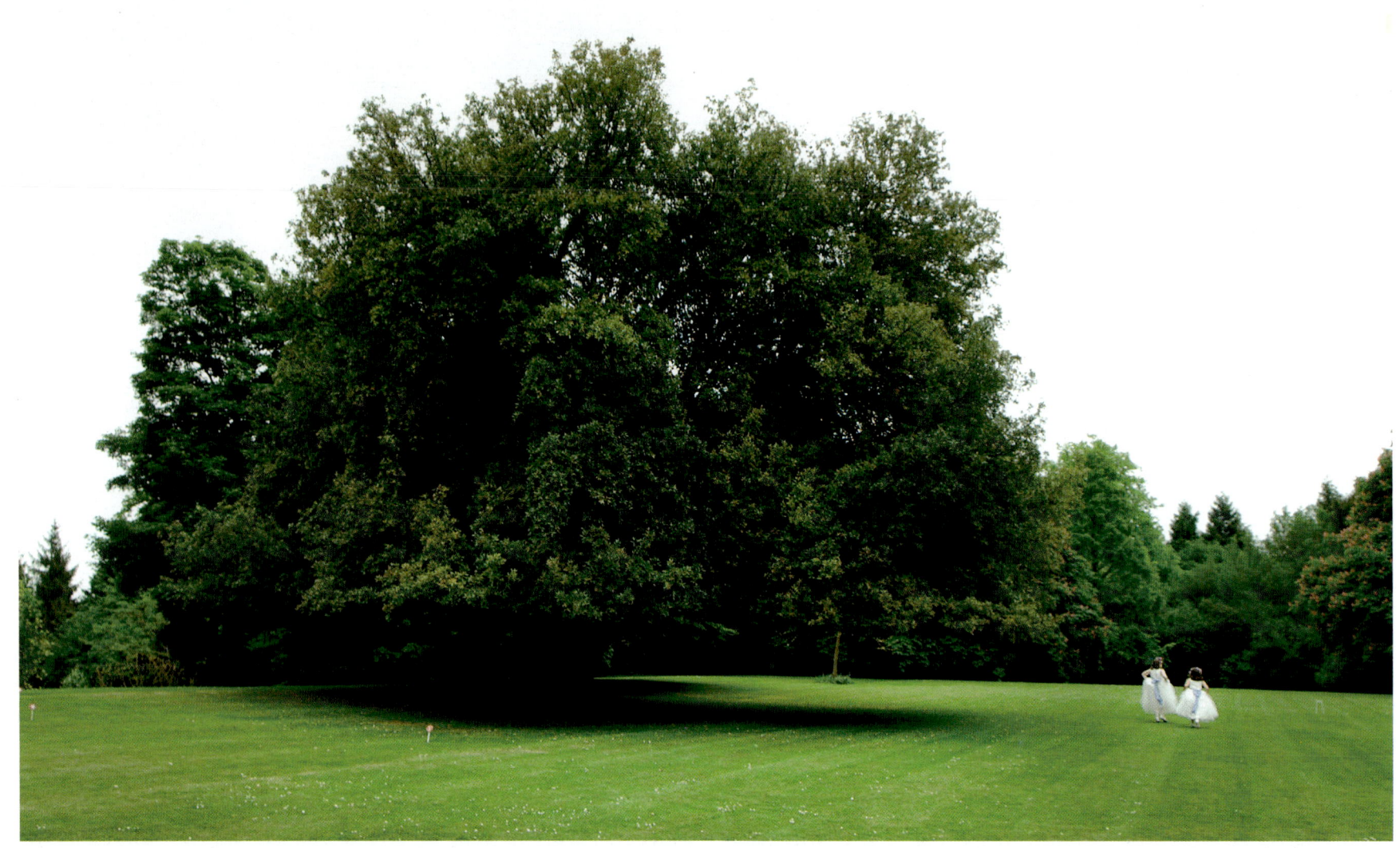

FIG. 23   ISO 800 f/4 at 1/1800th

I took this frame with a wide lens to show the scale and relative size of the girls and the tree. This running away shot captures the fun and freedom the girls are having and triggers childhood memories for the bride.

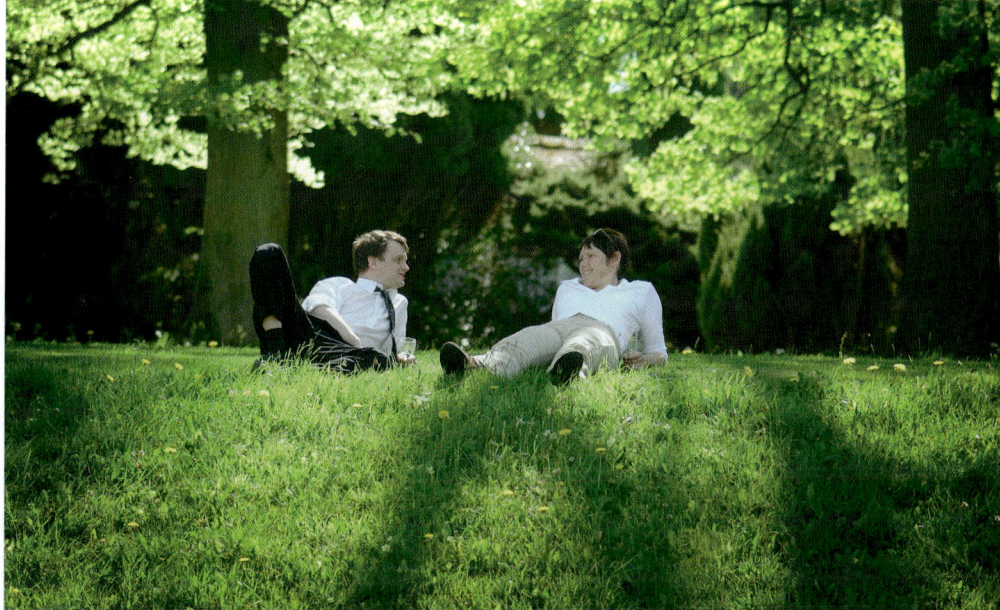

FIG. 24   ISO 320 f/3.4 at 1/1000th

Even the adults take time out to relax away from the main party. This picture sums up the lazy days of summer.

point, the business plan showed far less risk and the bank lent us the start-up capital we needed.

Other forms of borrowing require plenty of research to keep costs and risks at a minimum. Personal credit cards, personal unsecured loans, and loans secured against a property are worth investigating but expose you to high risk. A bank manager shouldn't lend you money based on a flawed business plan, but without their expert eye on your proposals you run the risk of setting yourself up to fail.

Well done for getting this far. Most photographers would have skipped this chapter. Now you have the edge over them! Read on for a slice of wisdom.

THE PERIL OF DISCOUNTING

Never discount. That's it! Top advice you should take seriously. Offer extra product if you have to, but never cut the fee. Here's why: if you have a profit margin of 35% and you offer your clients a 10% discount, you need to shoot 40% more weddings just to make the same profit. Let me put it another way, every £100 sale gives you £35 profit. If you discount by 10% your profit margin goes down to 25%. So to make the same £35 profit, you would need to sell £140 worth of product. Discounting is financial madness. Don't do it.

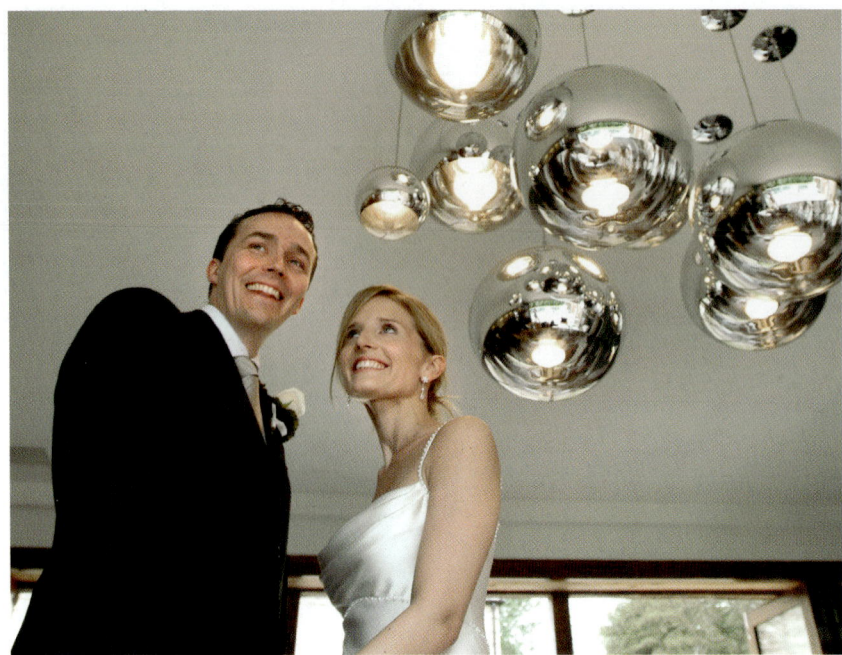

FIG. 25   ISO 200 f/4 at 1/60th

I wanted to include the funky light fittings at the Babington House spa. I shot from a low viewpoint to get the right look while Julie engaged the couple.

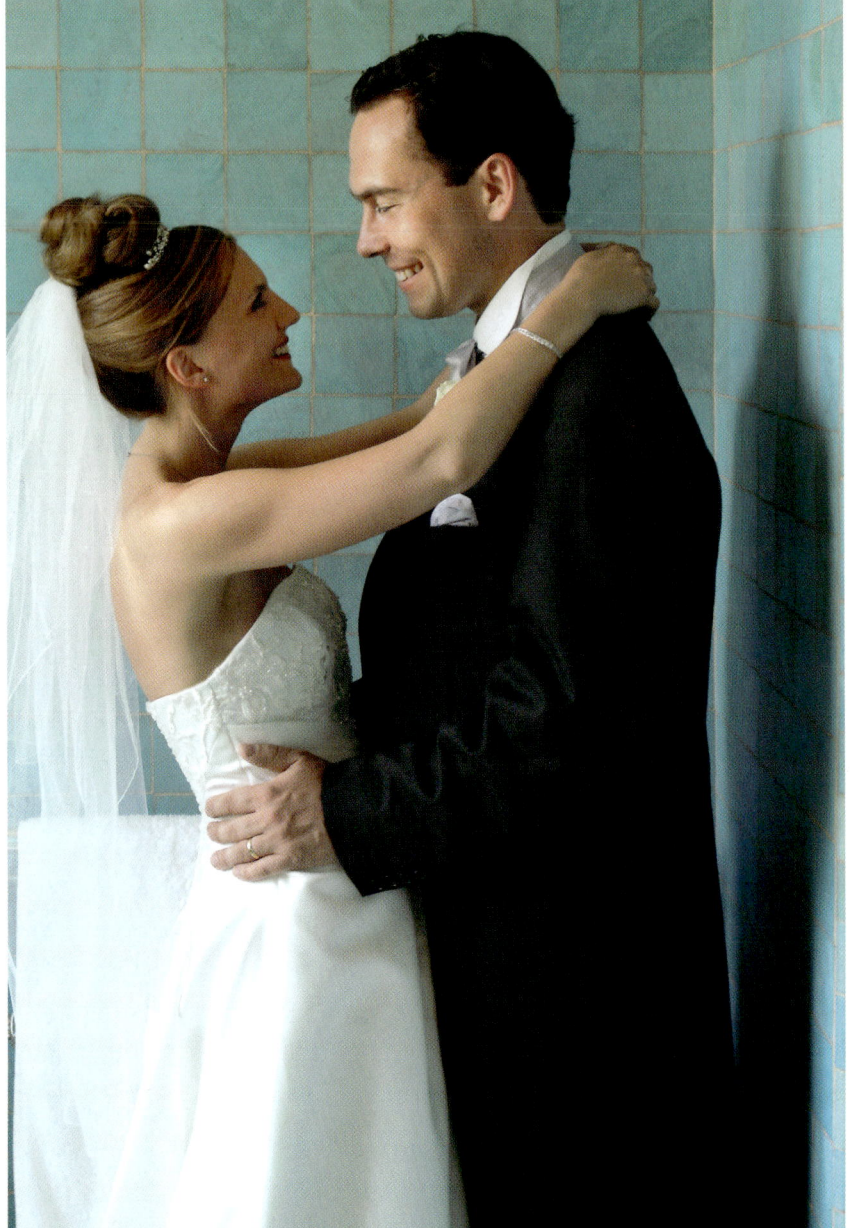

FIG. 26   ISO 400 f/4 at 1/45th

I love the turquoise tiles in this art deco bathroom at Eltham Palace in London. The couple were lit with the natural daylight in the room.

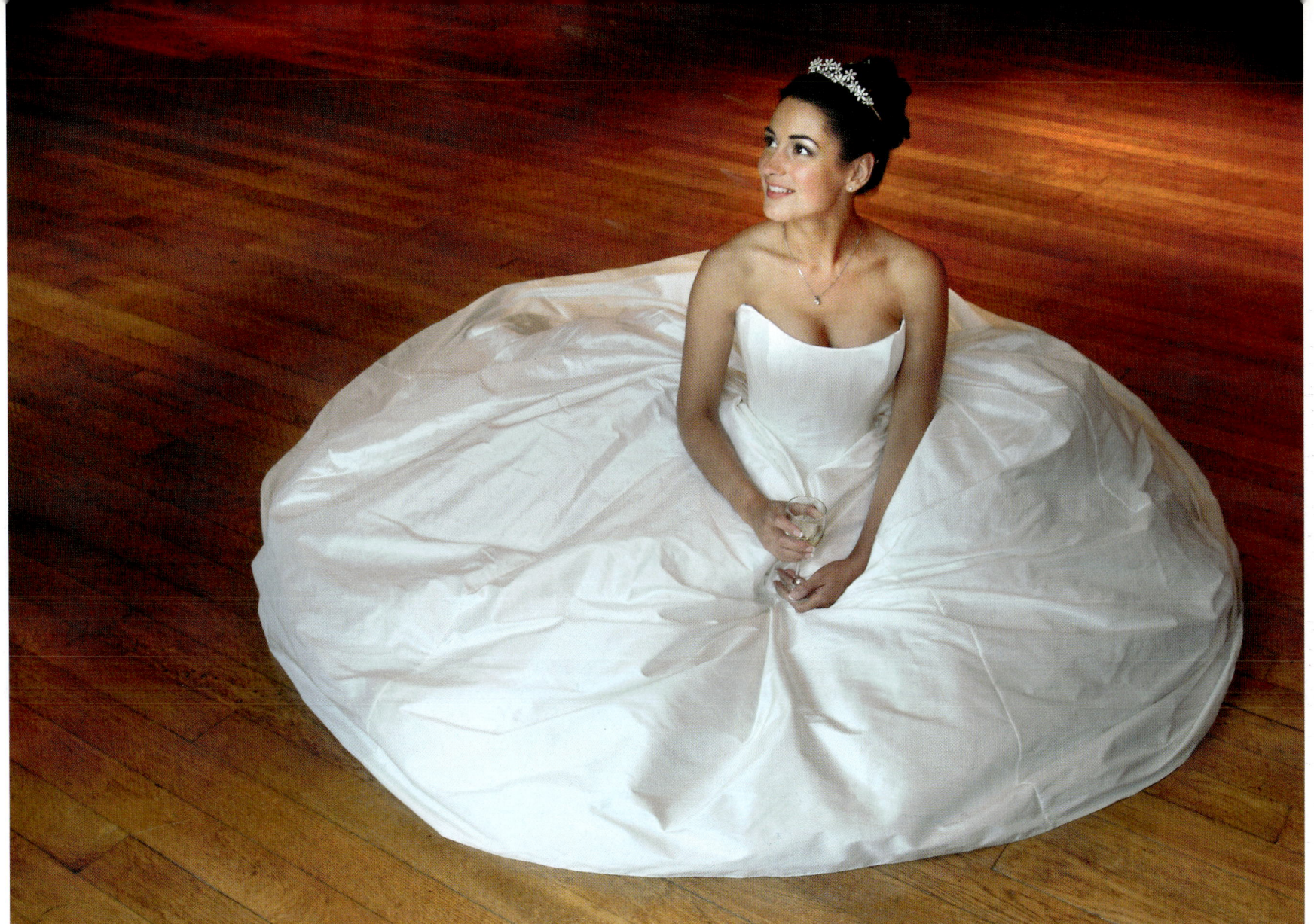

FIG. 27   ISO 800 f/4 at 1/45th

This picture took a bit of setting up. First of all I placed the bride on the ground facing the window. Julie then arranged the dress while I switched on the tungsten room lights and then I took the picture. The bride had asked for this shot and it's not one we have done since.

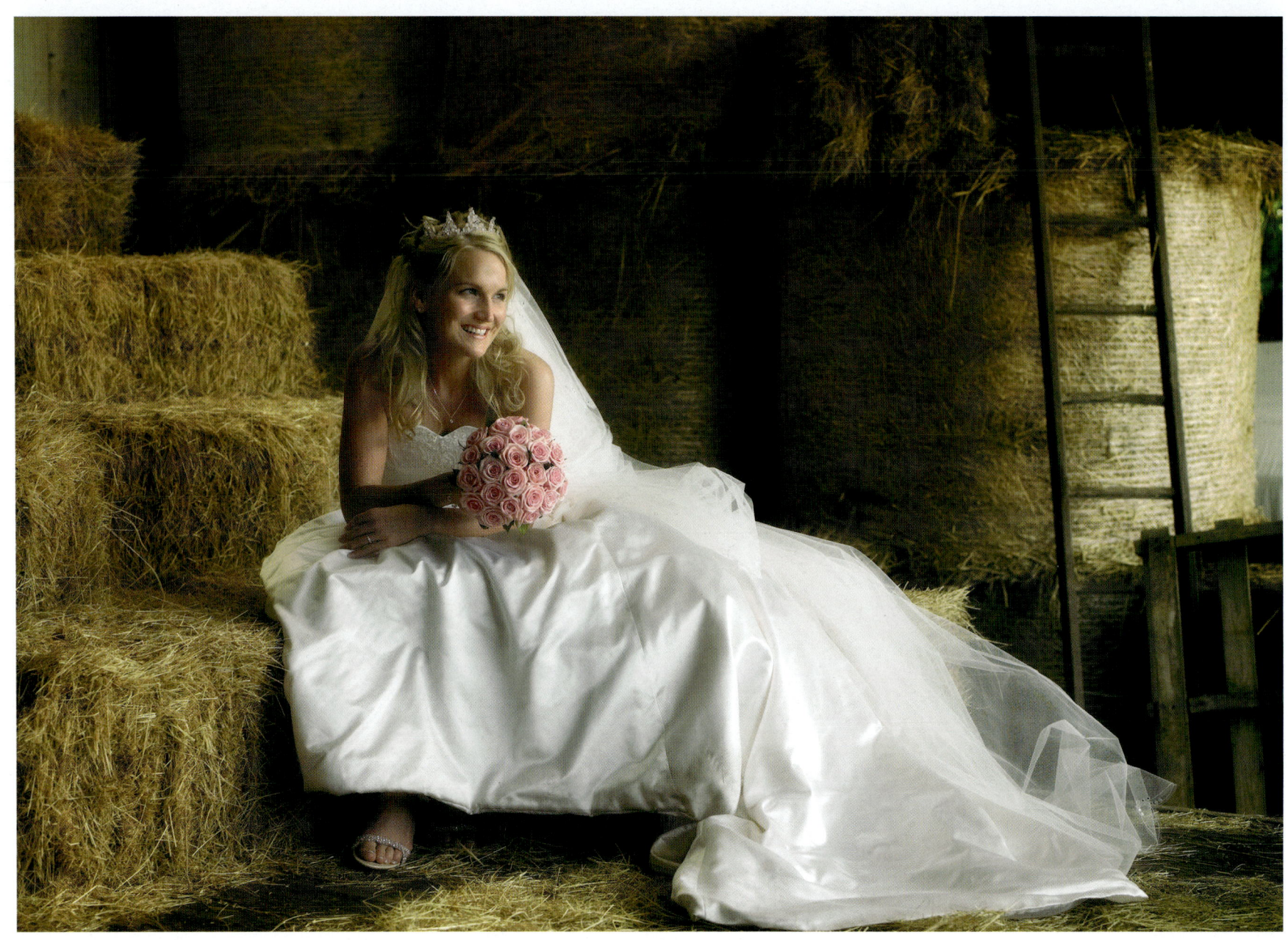

FIG. 28   ISO 400 f/5.6 at 1/300th

FIG. 29   ISO 400 f/4.8 at 1/350th

We passed this hay barn en route from the ceremony to the reception. I just had to get this picture. I shot into the unlit side of the bride's face and the groom created the reaction.

I have always explored different viewpoints and the best pictures I make are rarely taken from eye height. Here the bride and groom are practicing their first dance while their guests finish dinner.

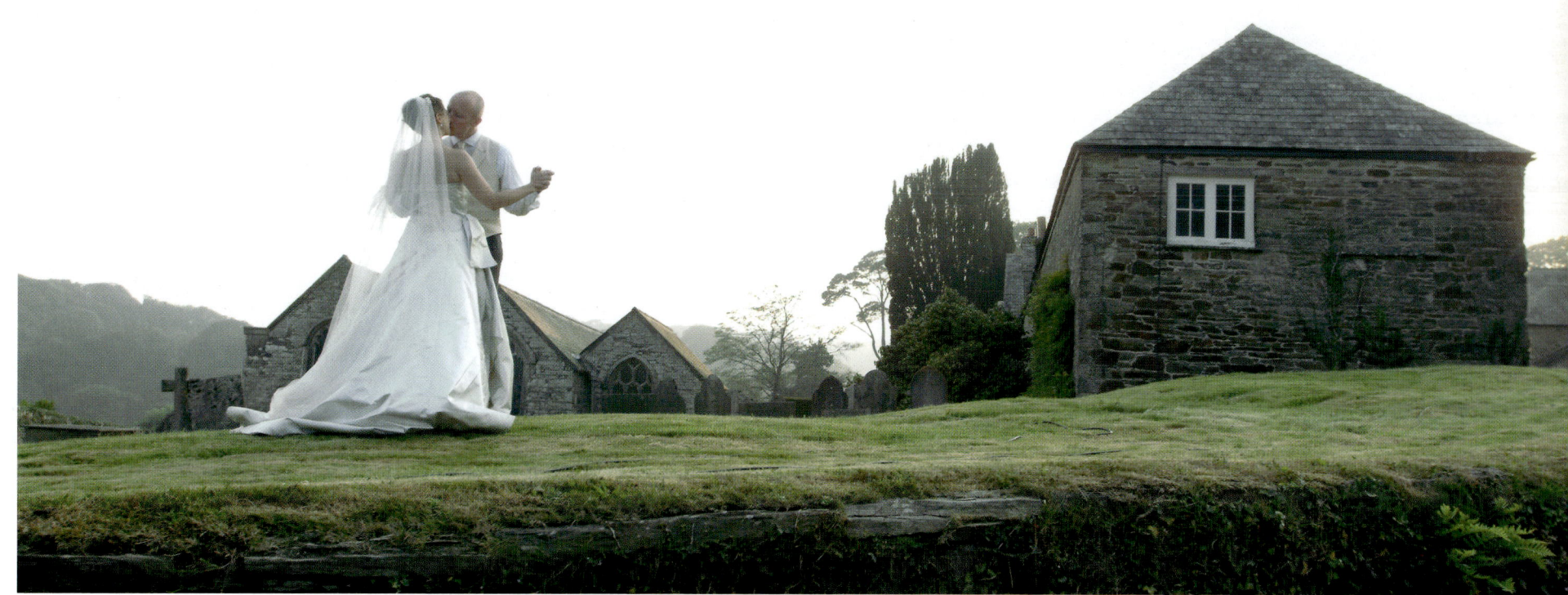

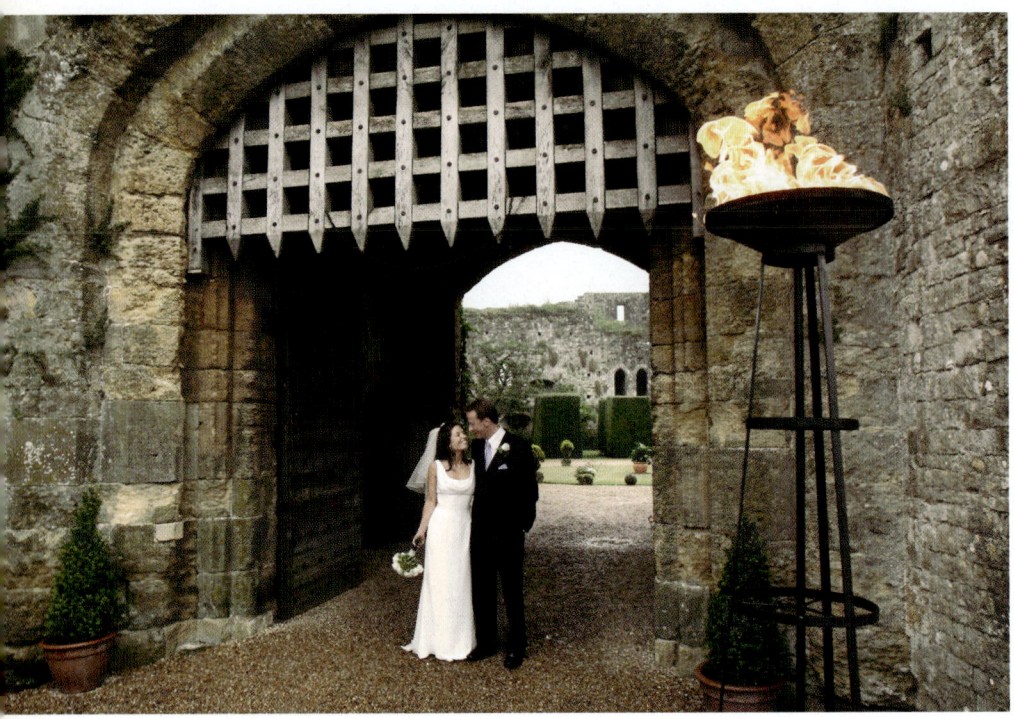

FIG. 30   ISO 800 f/4 at 1/500th

I like fire, and where I can get it in the pictures I will. The portcullis makes a dramatic backdrop.

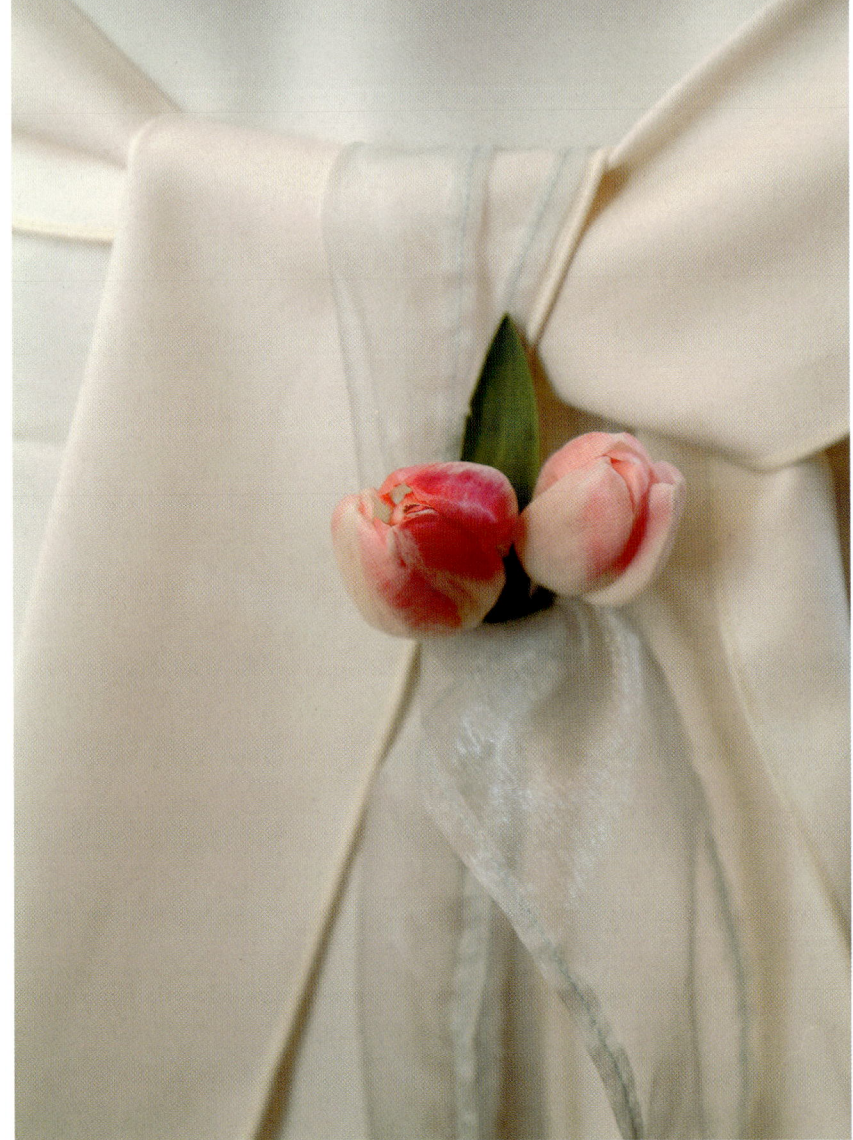

FIG. 31   ISO 200 f/4 at 1/25th

Julie took this simple picture of tulips on the back of a ceremony chair. We often move furniture around to get the best light before resetting it after.

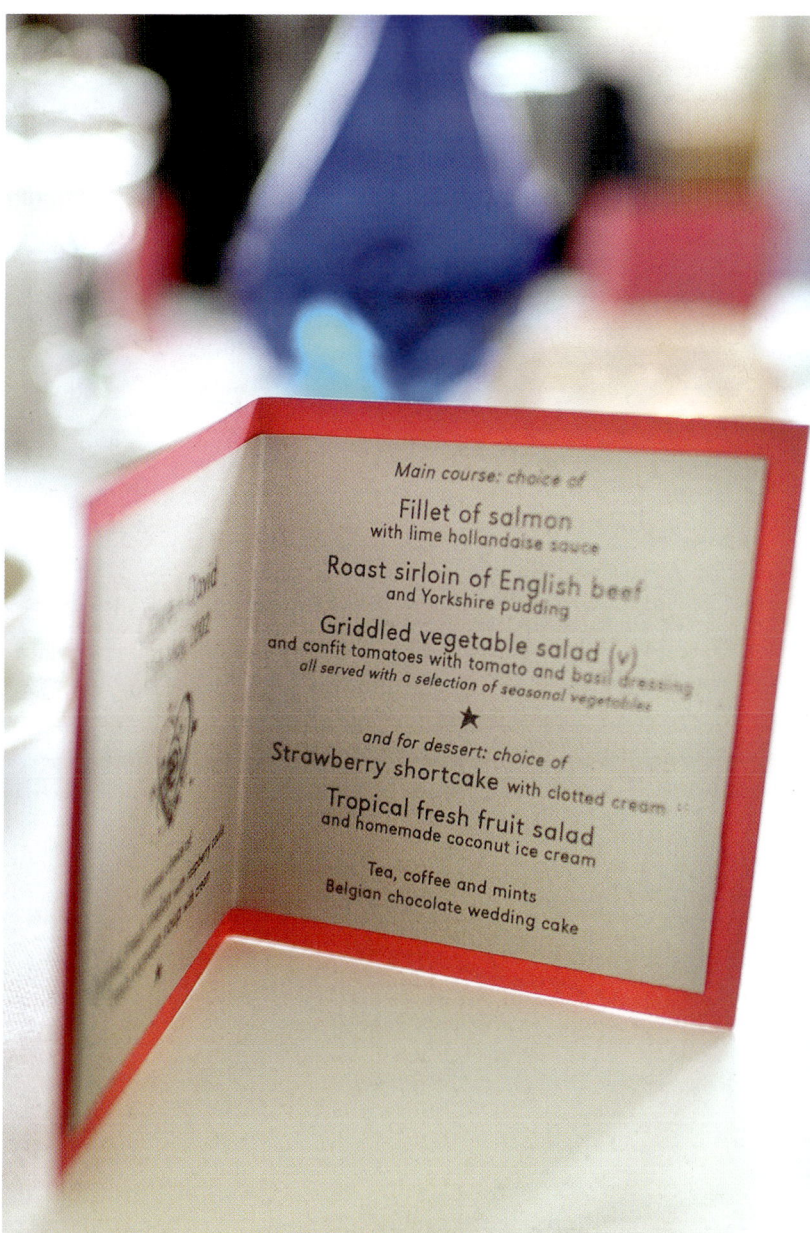

FIG. 32   ISO 800 f2.8 at 1/250th

Menus are great details that add another dimension to the album. We like to capture on camera all the senses of the day, and taste is an important one of them.

FIG. 33   ISO 800 f/4 at 1/25th

The craft of the chocolatier is best captured in closeup.

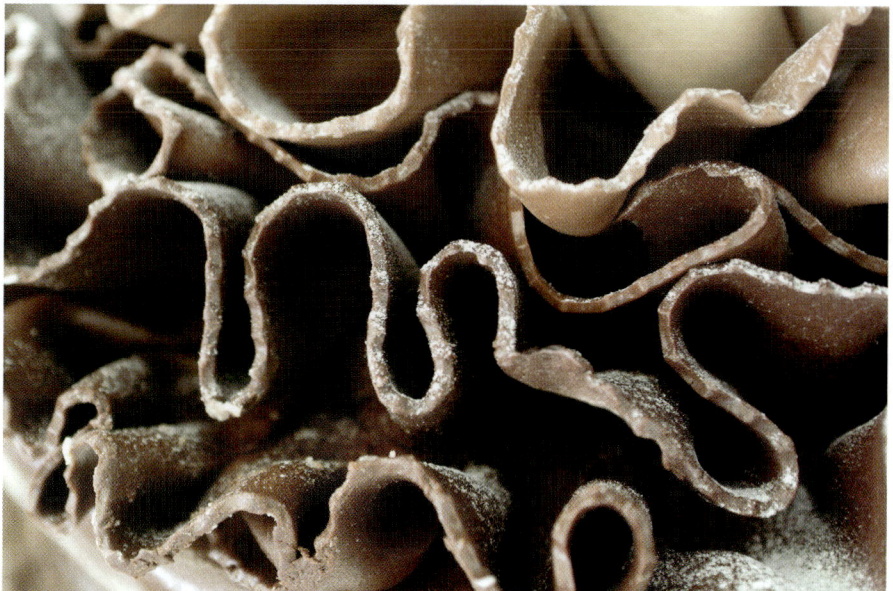

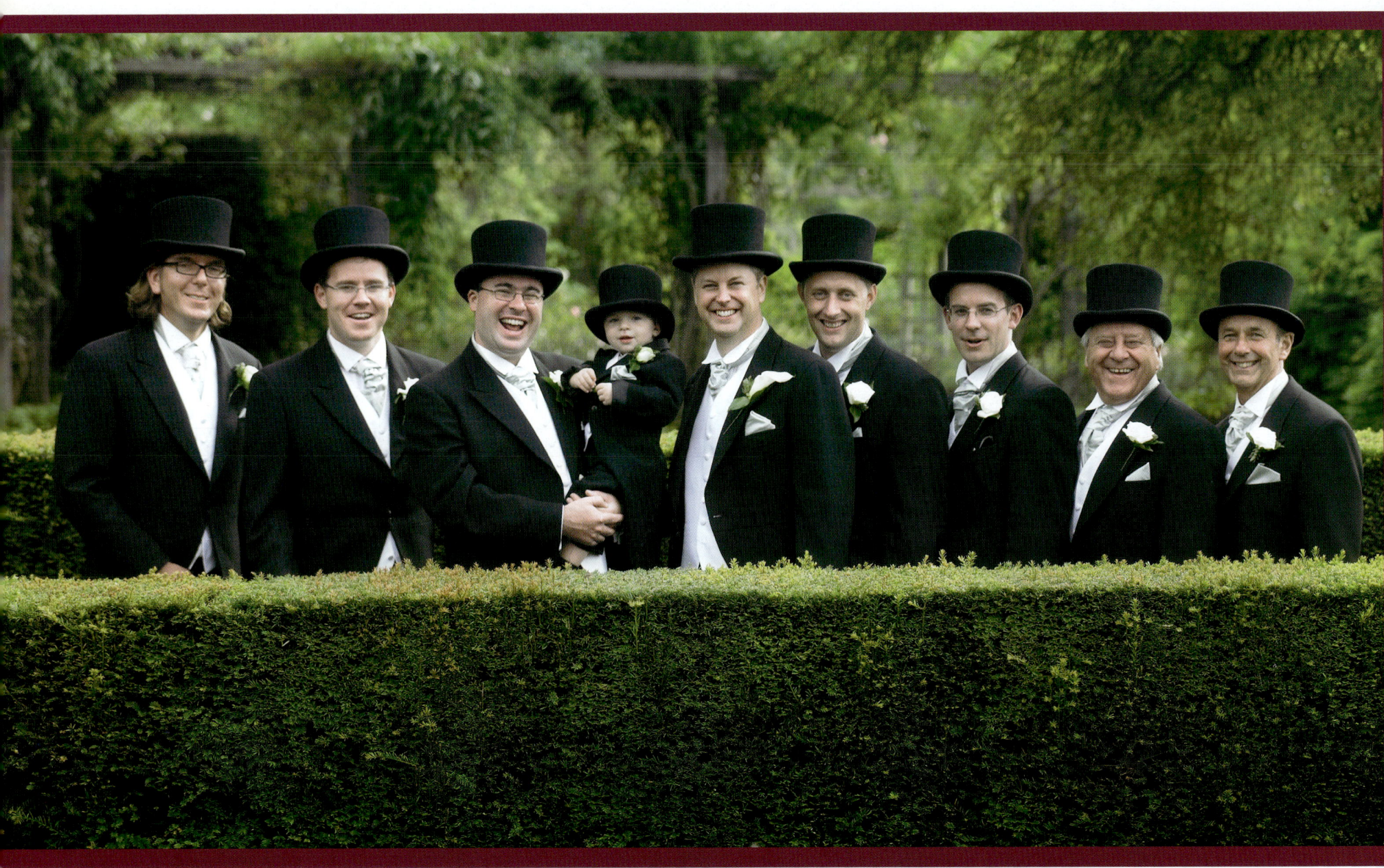

12
Products

A wedding photographer's product base consists of abstract and immediate elements including service, creativity, experience, professionalism, and a range of items for sale. Some of these elements affect the value of your service now but are long forgotten in years to come. The product line I want to discuss is made up of the tangible items that the clients take away with them to show their friends, family, children, and eventually grandchildren. The most obvious product for a wedding photographer to provide is an album of prints. Ever since the dawn of photography albums of prints have been a core product for collections of pictures. This is changing and the change is fast. In 2007, it is quite normal for photographers to deliver their images to the client in electronic format. Some photographers resist the changes but ultimately the clients have their way. When planning your product line

remember that wedding photography is a retail industry. The rules of retail business rarely change. There are two opposing arguments that regularly come into play. 'Give the customers what they want' and 'Give the customers what they need.' You could say these two arguments form the basis of world politics too. There is always a balance between morality and desire. In 2005, McDonald's restaurant chain was under pressure to provide healthier meals, not by its customers, but by its critics. McDonald's customers wanted burgers, but in some cases they needed salads. Careful repositioning of the brand took place to

opposite

FIG. 1   ISO 200 f/4.8 at 1/160th

I like to shoot extreme panoramic format pictures. This group of men work so well behind the hedge. It can really be cropped top and bottom to suit the product or frame it is going in.

I find it amazing just how good a well-taken image can look at just a few hundred pixels wide on a screen of an iPod or on a website. All the information is there to provide the laughs, set the scene, and give the picture value.

promote a healthier lifestyle. Salads and healthy meal options were introduced as a result. McDonald's were careful not to alienate their loyal customer base and continued to offer a super size meal option too.

How does this relate to wedding photography? Well, I suggest you aim to give your customers what they want and build your product line around their desire. You may choose to have additional products you feel compelled to offer to meet your responsibilities as you see them. We live in a time where immediate benefits are perceived as far more important than long-term benefits. Wedding albums with acid-free pages and fine prints produced on archival papers are what customers need to preserve their images for the enjoyment of their children and grandchildren in the years to come. However, the next generation of couples to get married are more likely to want digital files instead of prints. They will probably share their pictures using email, and by sending picture texts from their mobile phone. They may produce slideshows on DVD or make picture books using Apple's iPhoto or other online book design software. Today's public are happy to view their pictures on iPods and other low resolution personal electronic devices. The same revolution happened in the music industry with the rise of the MP3 format. For the most part, Hi-Fi has been replaced with reasonable quality sound from small, compact, inexpensive equipment. Convenience, portability, and instant access are the key to providing creative content to the new generation.

My only concern is about the long-term risk of losing valuable pictures as formats and systems change. I expect what goes around will come around and in years to come the album of fine prints may rule supreme again.

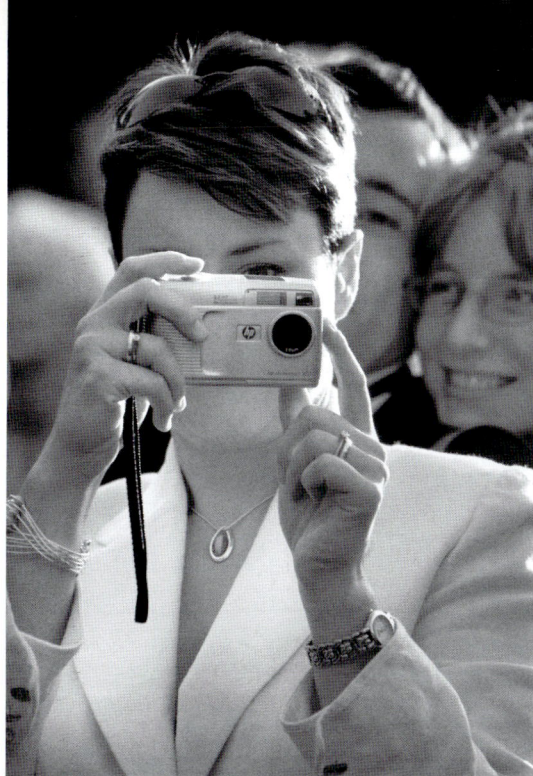

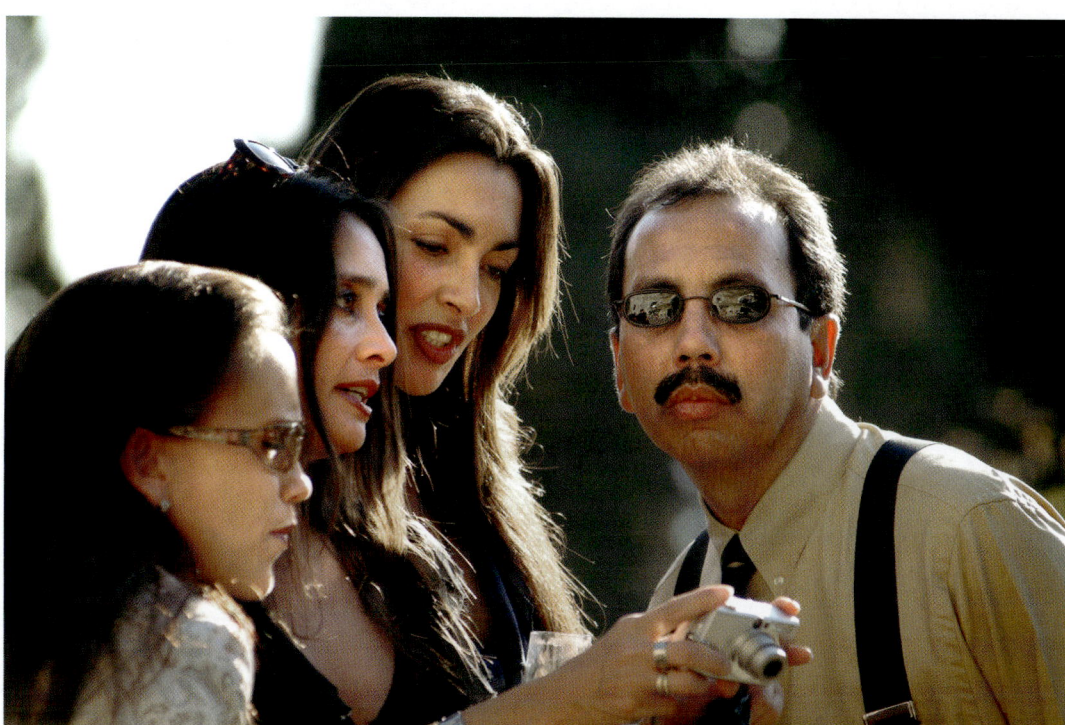

Julie and I have chosen a portfolio of products that reflect these challenging times. We provide picture-only options supplying edited files on disk at high, medium, and low resolutions. We also offer Jorgensen album packages and have an à la carte menu for other products. The principal idea behind our pricing structure is that the client is buying the image not the bit of paper it is printed on or the disk it is stored on.

Don't kid yourself that if you provide prints in an album you can force your clients to buy reprints. It is far too easy with today's compact cameras for a customer to photograph every one of your prints in the main wedding album and have the pictures printed at a shop in the high street or via ftp over the Internet. The solution to the problem of substandard copies is to provide high quality files on disk of all the images in the album together with advice on how and where to get great prints made. The solution to the loss of revenue through copyright abuse is to charge enough for your images in the first place.

Providing albums of prints has its own problems. There are a lot of costs and time associated with album production. Some photographers spend as much as a week designing, printing, and constructing a wedding album. Time is a valuable resource and ultimately your production capability may be the restricting factor in your wedding business. Being a photographer one day a week doesn't seem like a challenge but making 50 wedding albums

following pages

FIGS 4–11

Here are a few examples of some album spreads

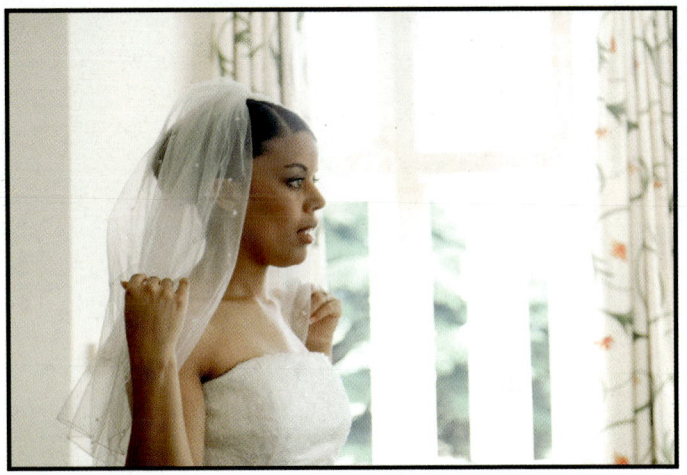
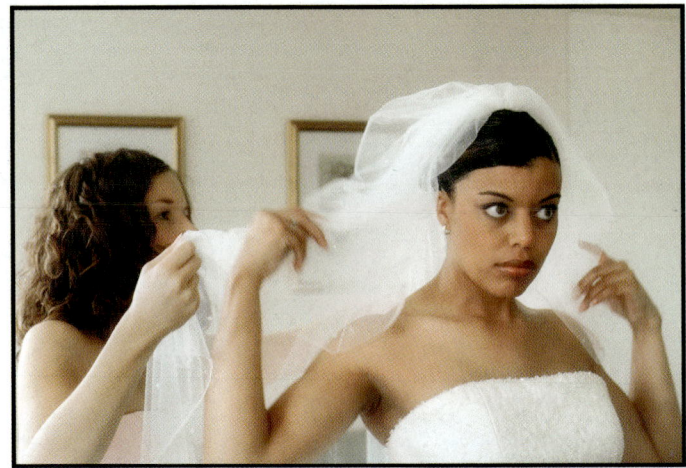
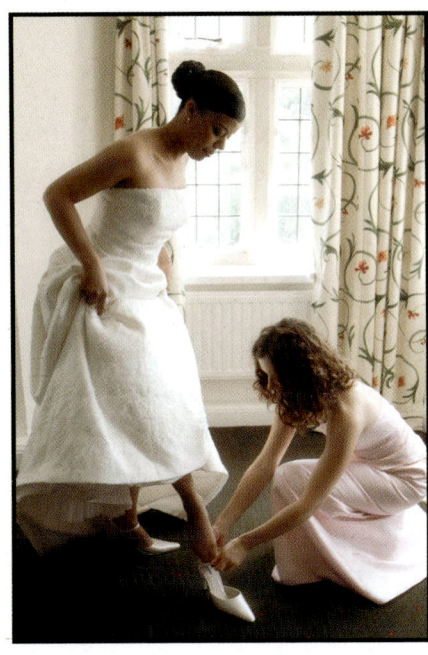
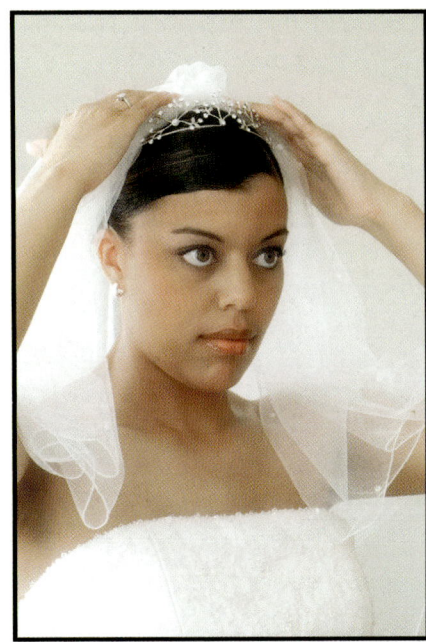
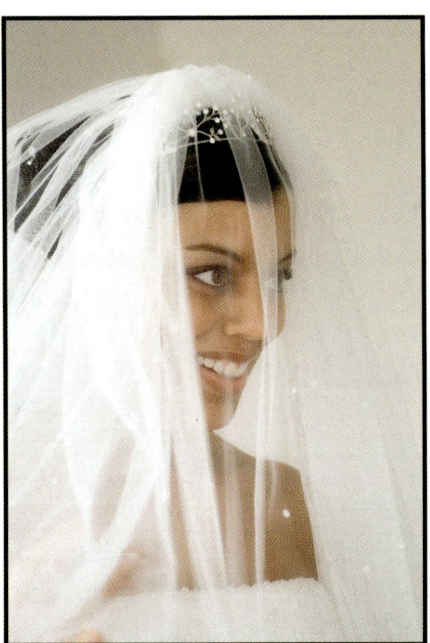

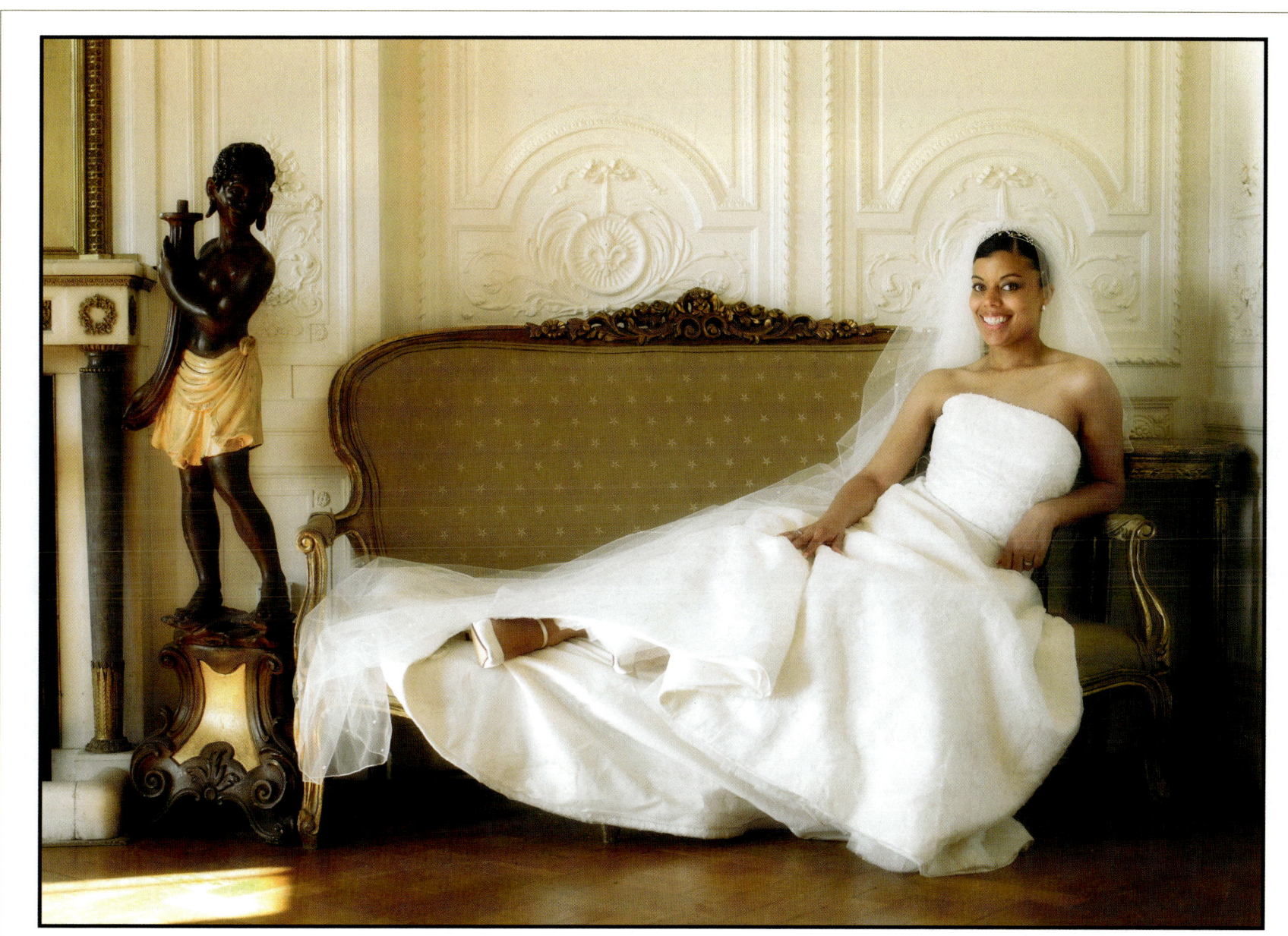

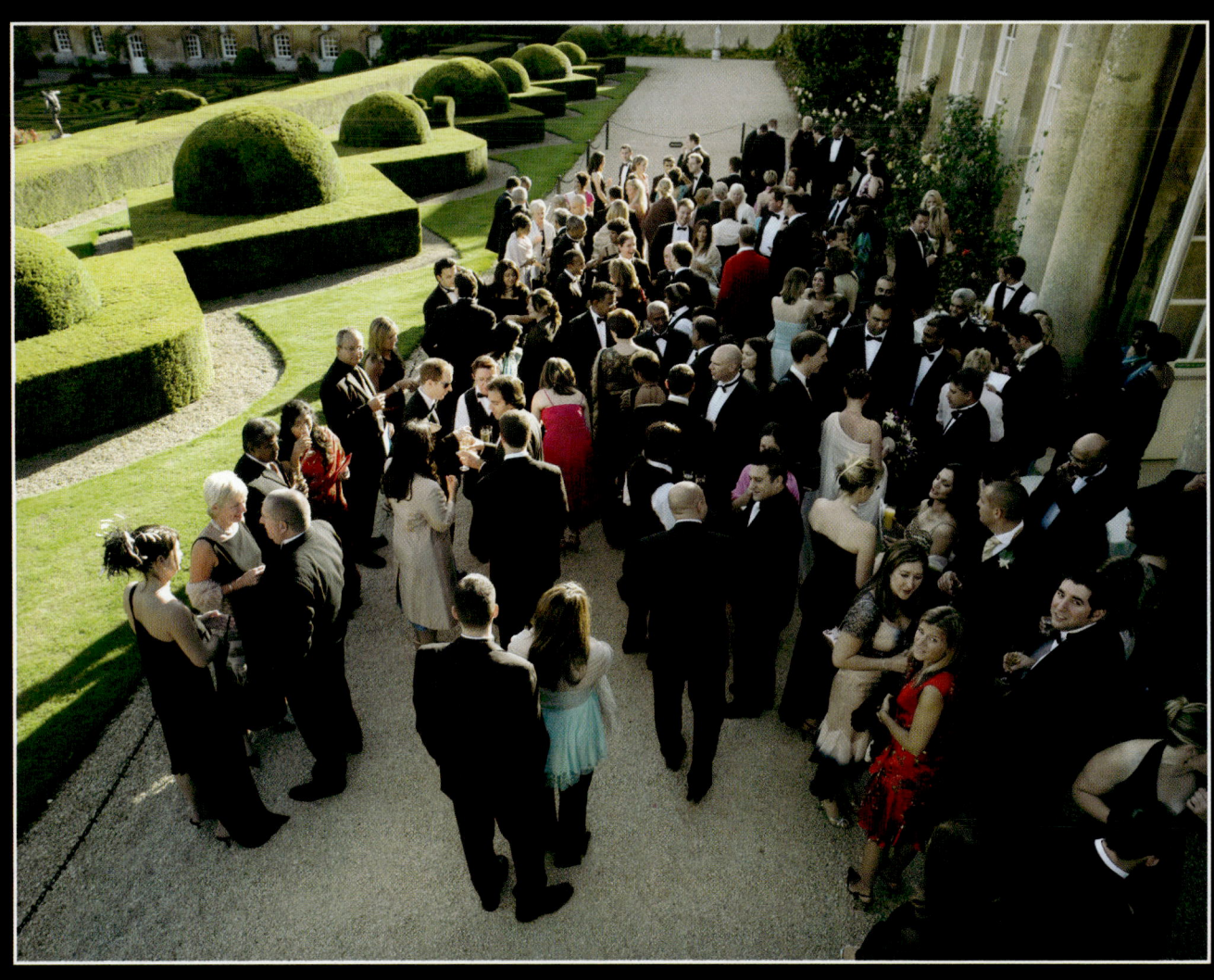

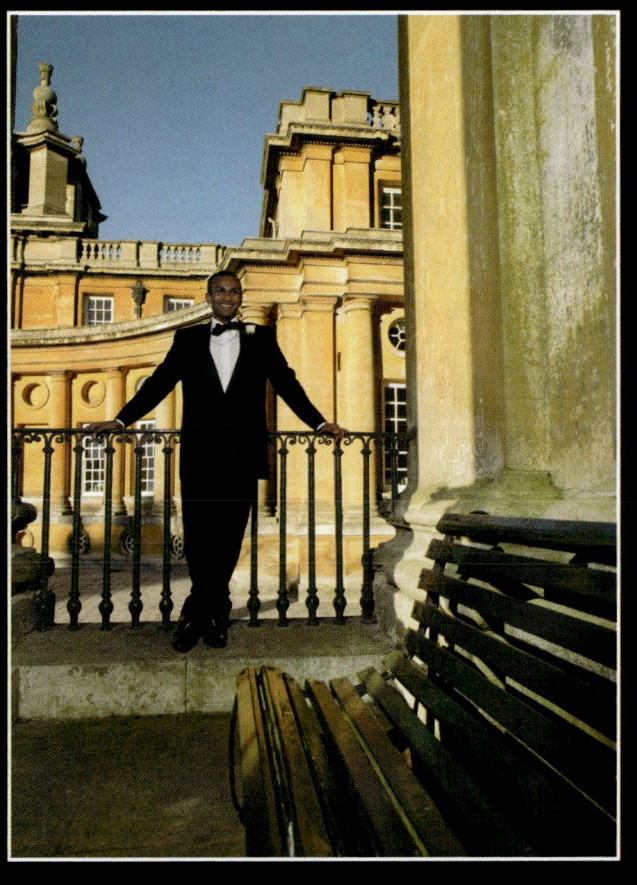
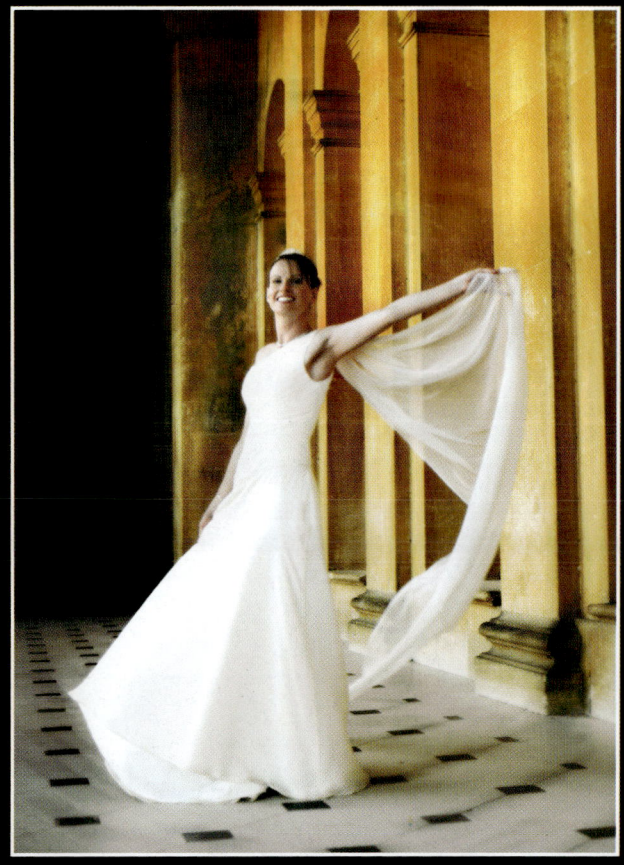

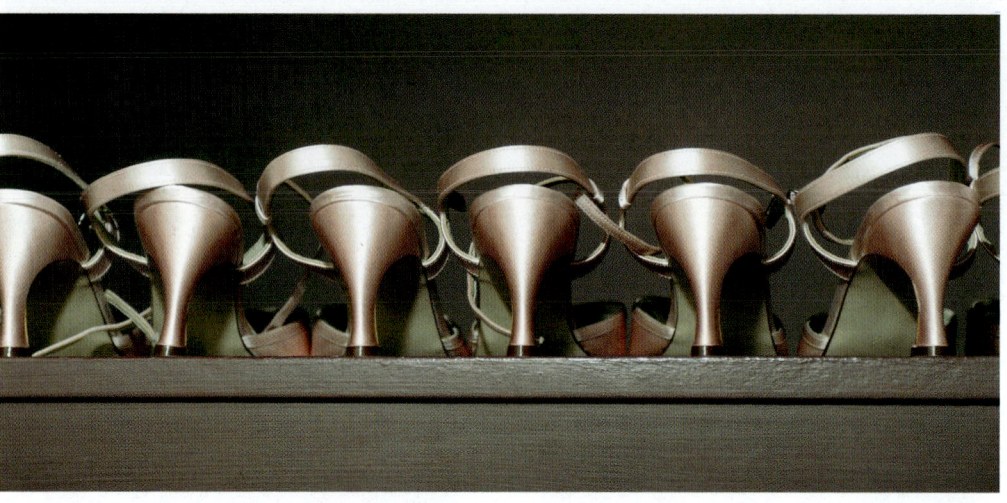

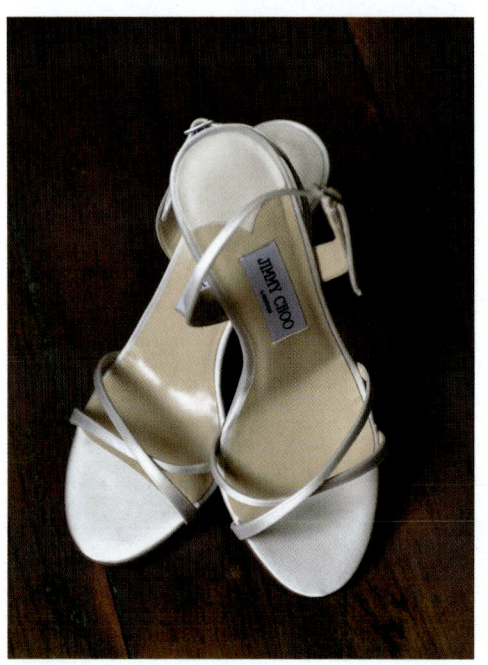

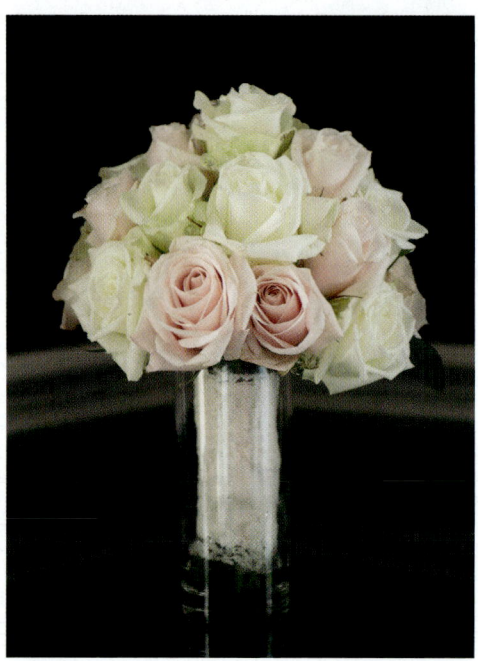

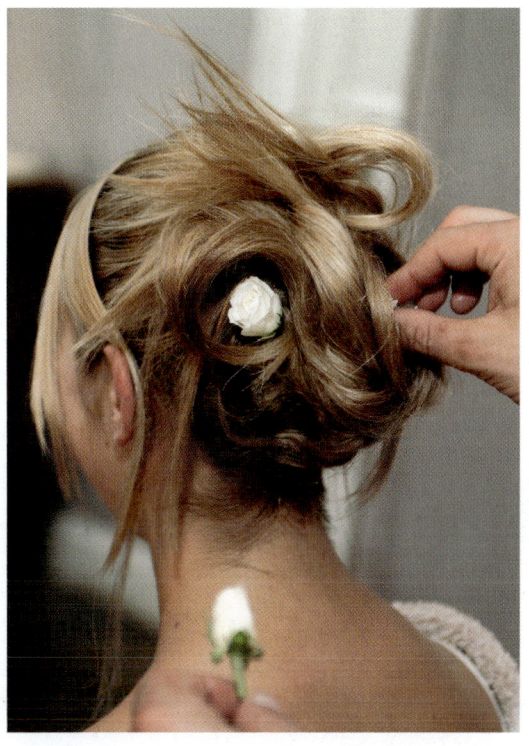

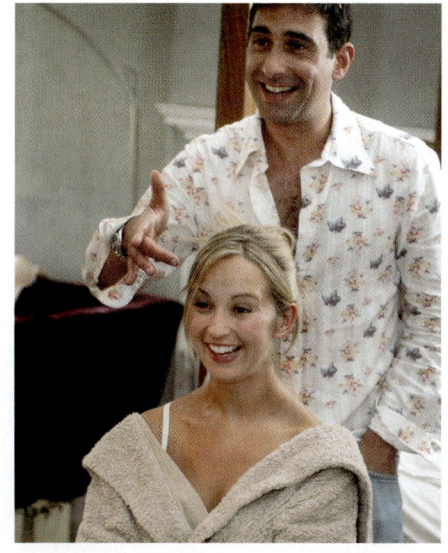

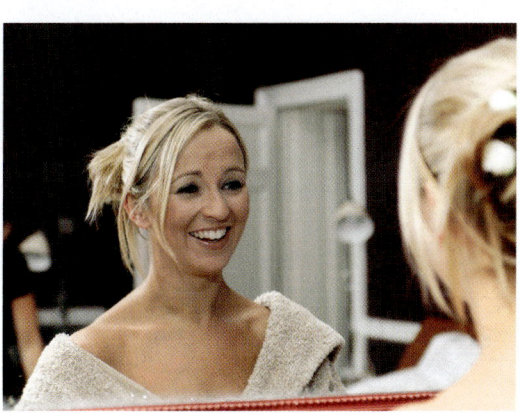

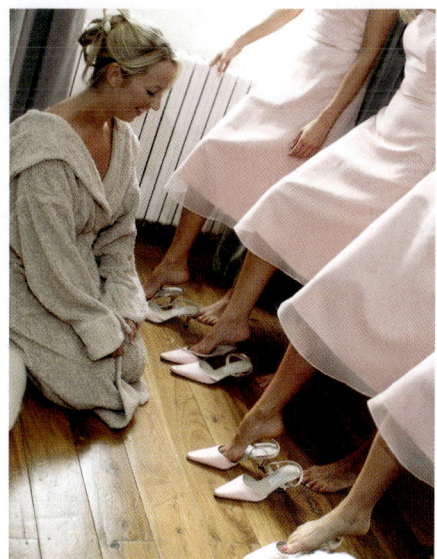

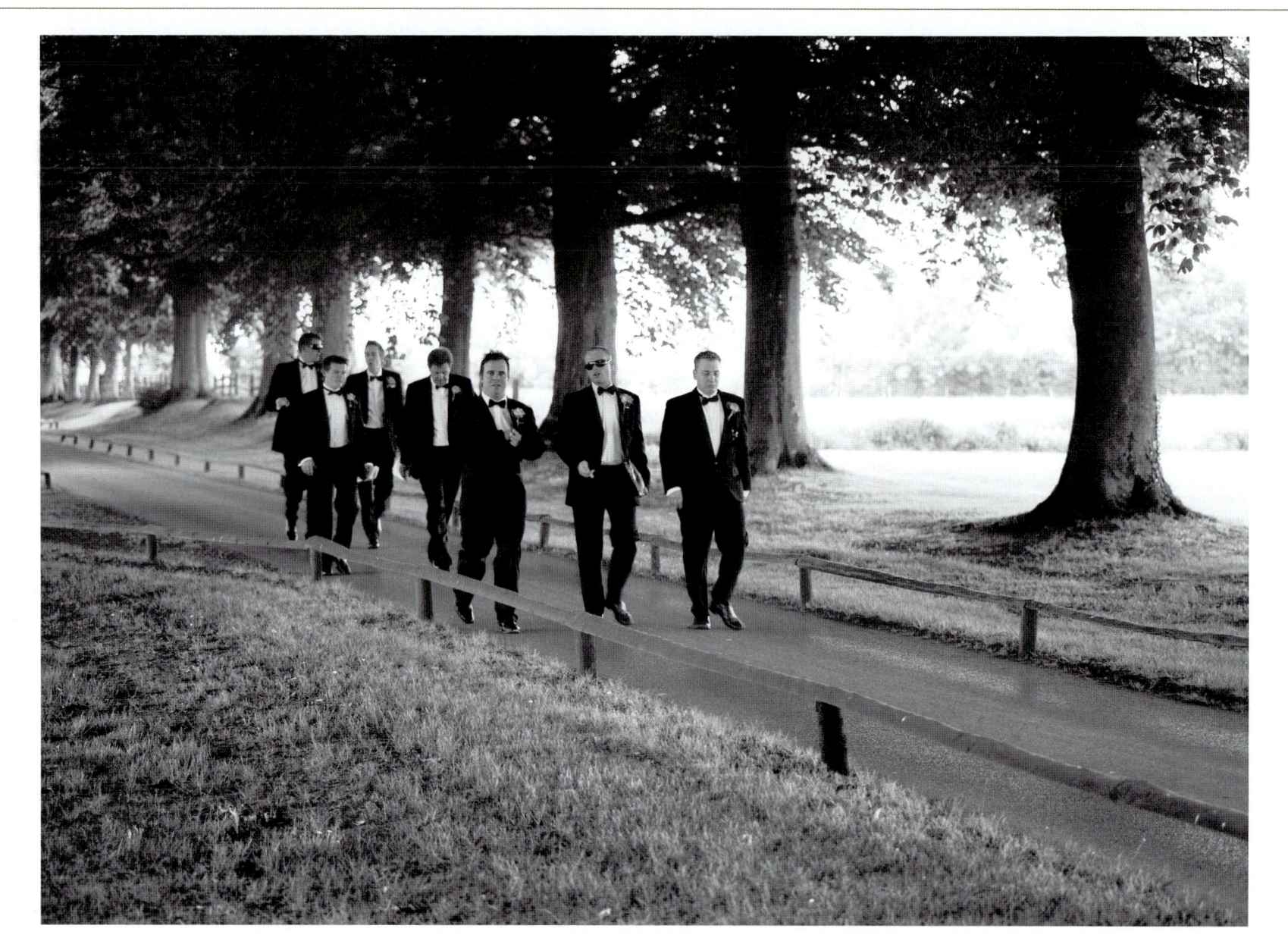

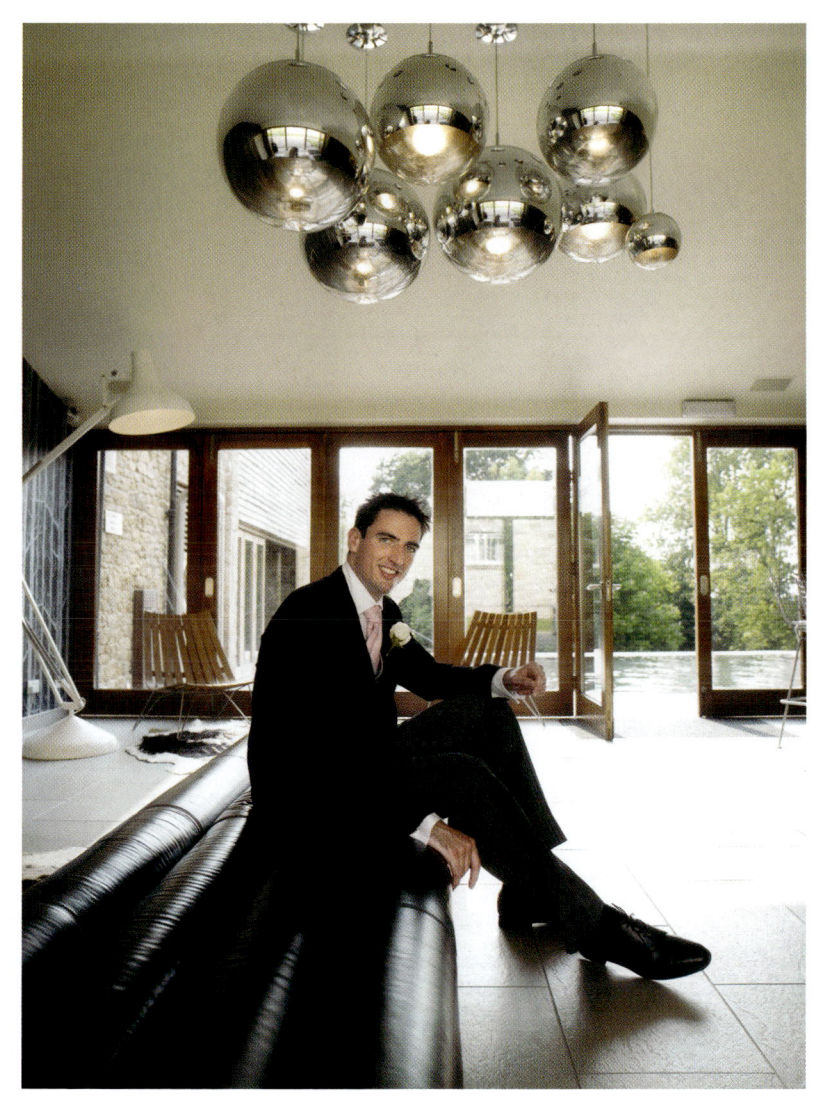
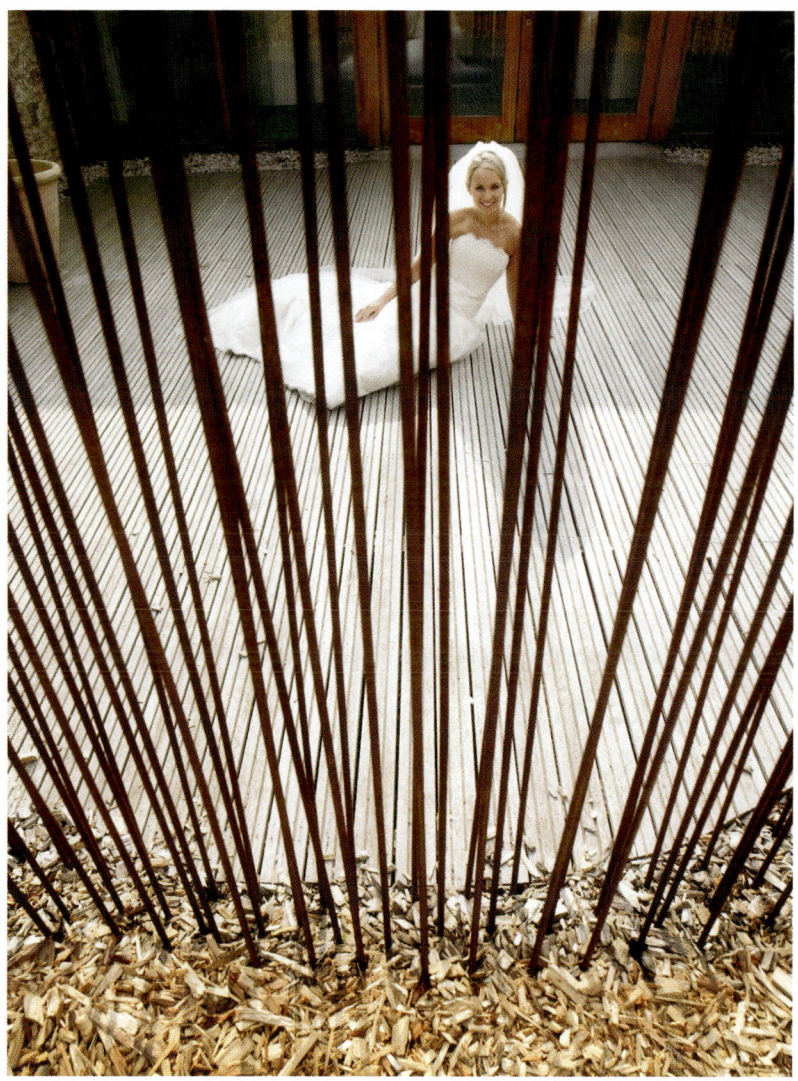

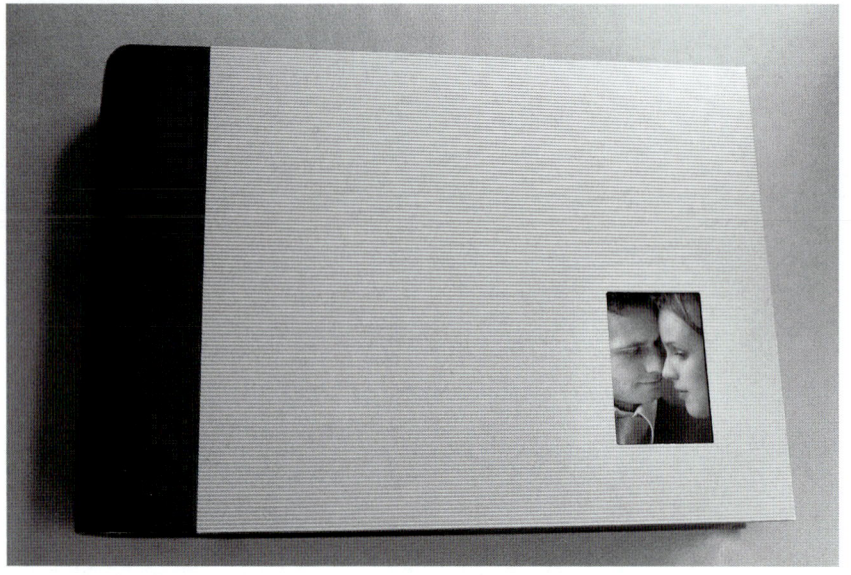

FIG. 12

This is the cover from an early Jorgensen show album of ours. Pictures inserted in the cover are rarely asked for nowadays.

opposite

FIGS 13 & 14   ISO 400 f9.5 at 1/350th and ISO 400 f/4.8 at 1/180th

Where repeating patterns occur I like to shoot square on for maximum impact.

in a year might seem too much like hard work. Never undersell the wedding album. Use the finest materials to maximize the perceived value of your albums and you can charge enough money for each book to hire in-production help if you so wish.

Make your albums unique, give them a style, and keep them well beyond the capabilities of even your most creative clients. Stick to your design rules and produce albums that are self-supporting, complete bodies of work that have a continuity of style from cover to cover. In the example page layouts shown in this chapter, all taken from matted albums, we have used several design principles. We make all the 'window bars' the same size on every page of an album. The people in the images face into the spread rather than out of the album; the outside edges of each image on a page align to form a neat rectangle; and ideally each page has at least one plane of symmetry.

We have found that over the past few years there has become a bigger demand for color images and now our albums have far less black and white prints as a result. When we supply our images on disk we always include a color option of all the images, even the ones that we think work better in black and white. The fashion of mixing color and monochrome images in the same album may well be on its way out too. A good indicator of changing styles is the editorial section of mainstream wedding magazines. In the UK magazines, there are no longer any black and white, spot color, toned, or tilted pictures. Keep an eye on the imagery that is inspiring your potential customers in order to spot new trends in picture style. Include them in your work if you want to stay current or avoid them if you want your picture style to stay timeless or classic.

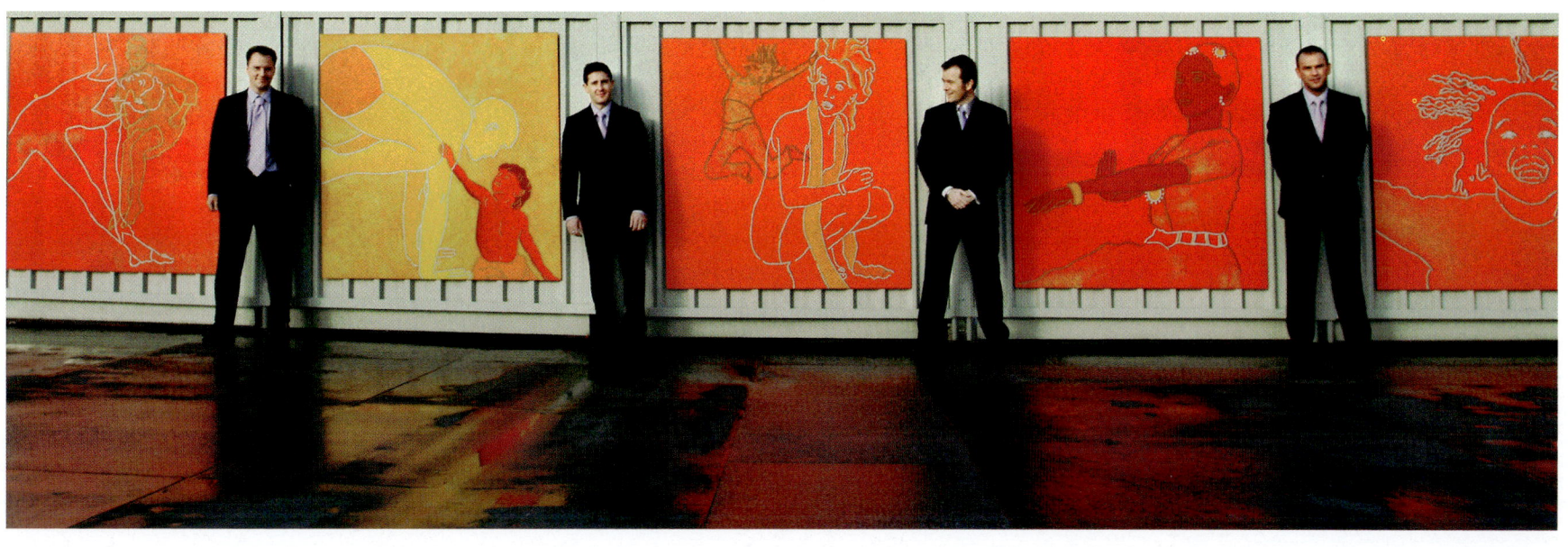

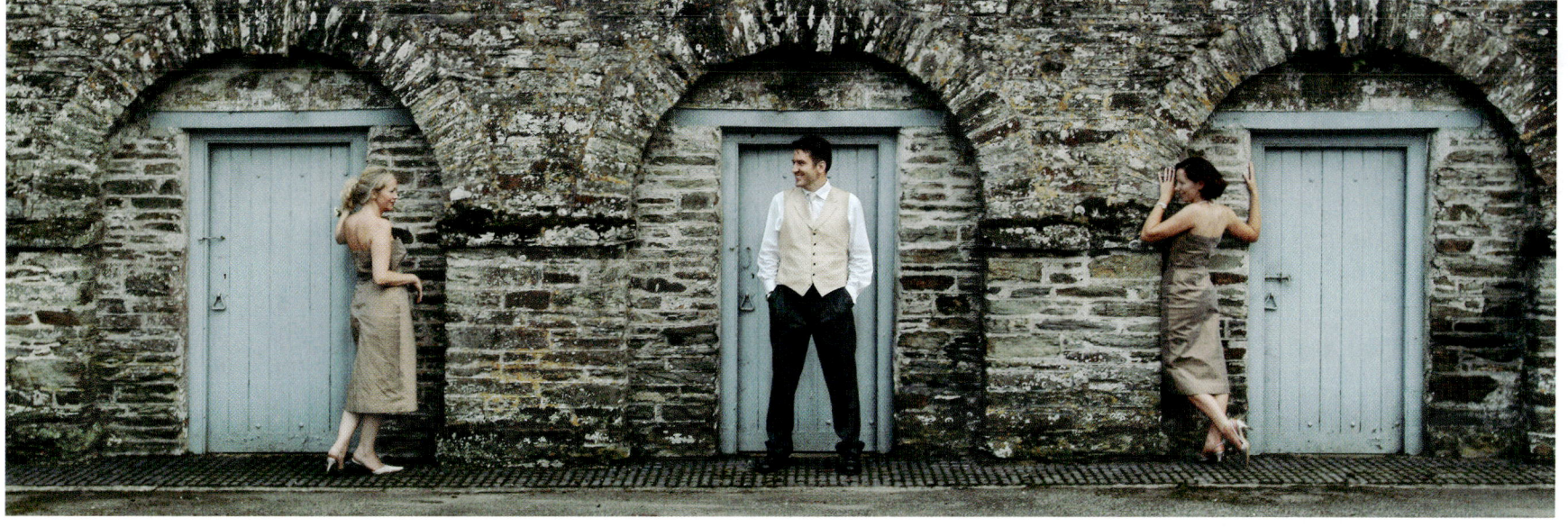

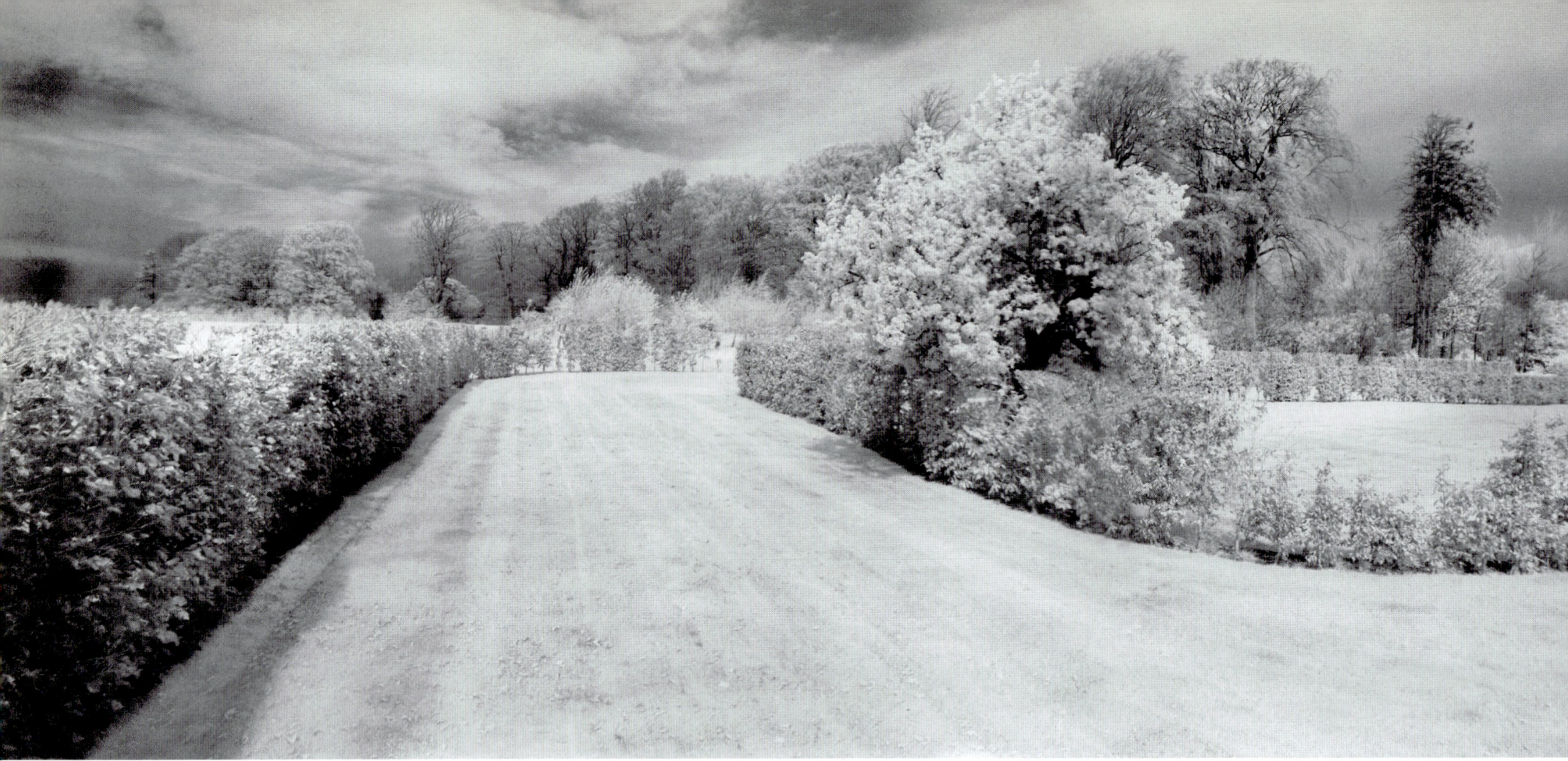

FIG. 15   ISO 200 at f/5.6 for 2 seconds per exposure for three frames. Stitched using Panorama Maker software.

I shot true infrared for a while on one of my Fujifilm S2 cameras fitted with a Hoya 77 mm R72 filter I had made by special order. The pictures looked great but not for the album. They were just too different from the normal pictures and upset the style. This picture of Weddeburn Castle in Scotland is 4 feet wide on the wall above the bride and groom's bed.

WEDDING MUSIC FOR SHOW REELS AND VIEWING SESSIONS

I often get asked what music we use in the viewing or salesroom when we are presenting our clients with their pictures for the very first time. My ans wer is we choose music that fits with the style of the client. There are classic tracks that always go down well and others that are best avoided. I chose to list a few of the tracks to avoid as it makes a more interesting read.

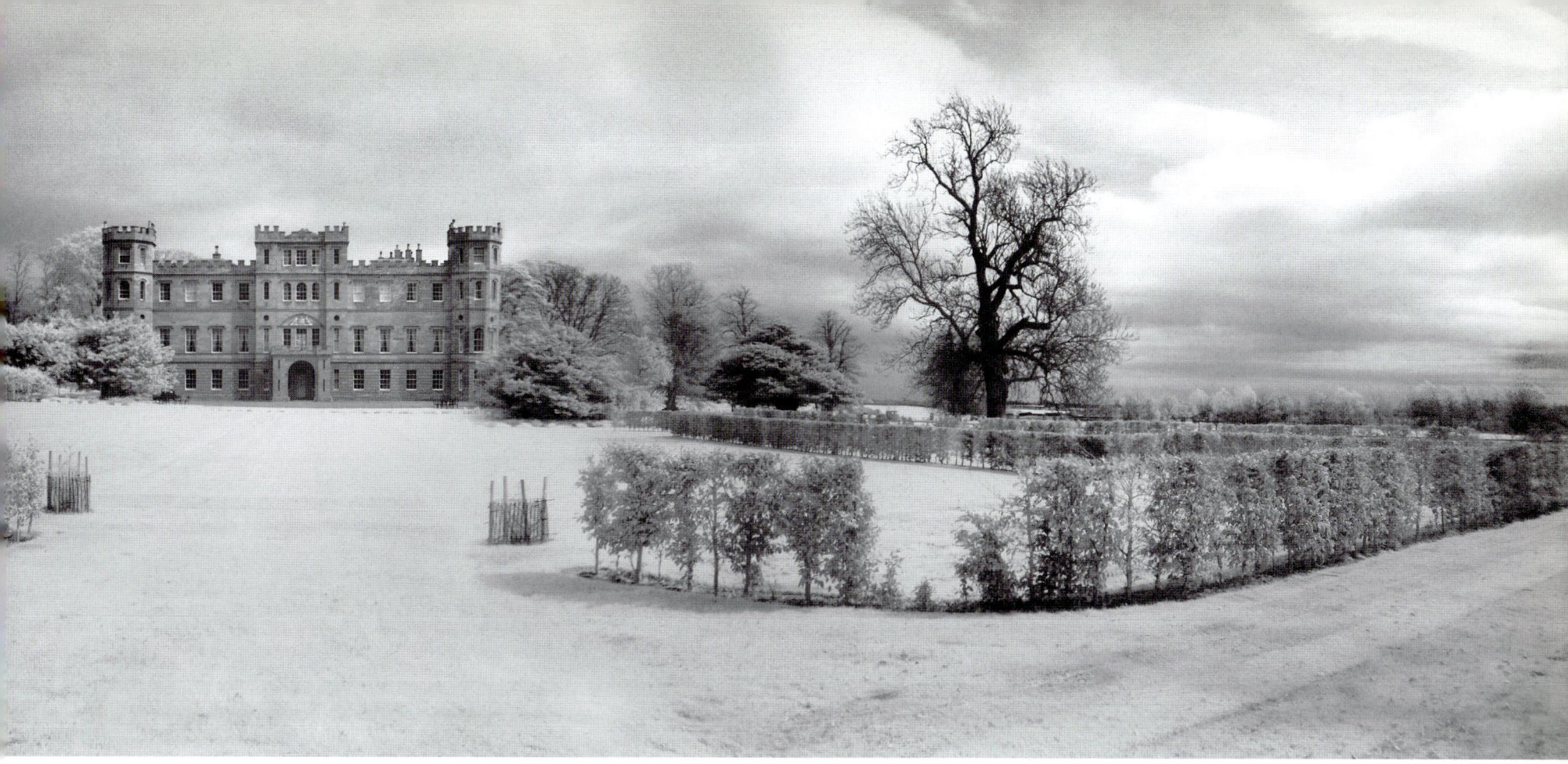

Music you should NOT use in the Viewing Room!

Track name	Artist
If You Leave Me Now	Chicago
Don't Leave Me This Way	Harold Melvin
Leave Right Now	Will Young
Haitian Divorce	Steely Dan
If Leaving Me Is Easy	Phil Collins
Every Time We Say Goodbye	Ella Fitzgerald

Track name	Artist
I'm Not In Love	10cc
All Cried Out	Alison Moyet
Can't Get Used To Losing You	Andy Williams
Dancing With Myself	Billy Idol
You're So Vain	Carly Simon
I'll Never Fall In Love Again	Carpenters
The Road To Hell	Chris Rea
I Never Loved You Anyway	The Corrs

Track name	Artist	Track name	Artist
She's Gone	Daryl Hall & John Oates	Won't get fooled again	the who
Runaway	Del Shannon	All By Myself	Jamie O' Neal
Don't Leave Home	Dido	Lyin' Eyes	The Eagles
Desperado	The Eagles	Never Ever	All Saints
Evil Woman	ELO	All Cried Out	Alison Moyet
Now That The Magic Has Gone	Joe Cocker	All That She Wants	Ace Of Base
Breaking Us In Two	Joe Jackson	Sexed Up	Robbie Williams
She's Out Of My Life	Michael Jackson	You Can't Always Get What You Want	The Rolling Stones
If Leaving Me Is Easy	Phil Collins		
I Want To Break Free	Queen	Everyday I Love You Less And Less	Kaiser Chiefs
Everybody Hurts	R.E.M.		
You've Lost That Loving Feeling	Righteous Brothers	Since U Been Gone	Kelly Clarkson
Take The Money And Run	Steve Miller Band	Seasons in the Sun	Terry Jacks
The Sun Ain't Gonna Shine Anymore	The Walker Brothers	Behind These Hazel Eyes	Kelly Clarkson

Index